808.82 OUR
Our drama

P9-BYB-787

Thank you for returning
your books on time.

Abington Free Library
1030 Old York Road
Abington, PA 19001

Our Dramatic Heritage

VOLUME 6

Purchased with funds contributed by

the Drama Club of

Upper Dublin High School

in memory of

BARBARA WENGERT

2001

Our Dramatic Heritage

VOLUME 6: *Expressing the Inexpressible*

Edited by Philip G. Hill

ABINGTON FREE LIBRARY
1030 OLD YORK ROAD
ABINGTON, PA 19001

Fairleigh Dickinson

Rutherford ● Madison ● Teaneck
Fairleigh Dickinson University Press
London and Toronto: Associated University Presses

JUL 1 1 2001

© 1992 by Associated University Presses, Inc.

All rights reserved.

Associated University Presses
440 Forsgate Drive
Cranbury, NJ 08512

Associated University Presses
25 Sicilian Avenue
London WC1A 2QH, England

Associated University Presses
P.O. Box 39, Clarkson Pstl. Stn.
Mississauga, Ontario
L5J 3X9 Canada

The paper used in this publication meets the requirements
of the American National Standard for Permanence of Pape
for Printed Library Materials Z39.48-1984.

Library of Congress Cataloging-in-Publication Data
(Revised for vol. 6)

Our dramatic heritage.

   Contents: v. 1. Classical drama and the
early Renaissance—v. 2. The Golden Age—
[etc.]—v. 6. Expressing the inexpressible.
   1. European drama.   I. Hill, Philip G.
(Philip George), 1934–   .
PN6111.087   1983   808.82   81-65294
ISBN 0-8386-3106-1 (v. 1)
ISBN 0-8386-3107-X (v. 2)
ISBN 0-8386-3421-4 (v. 6)

ABINGTON FREE LIBRARY
1030 OLD YORK ROAD
ABINGTON, PA. 19001

PRINTED IN THE UNITED STATES OF AMERICA

JUL 1 1 2001

Contents

Acknowledgments

Caution: Professionals and amateurs are hereby warned that these plays and translations, being fully protected under the copyright laws of the United States of America, the British Commonwealth, including the Dominion of Canada, and all other countries that are signatories to the Universal Copyright Convention and the International Copyright Union, are subject to royalty. All rights, including professional, amateur, motion picture, recitation, lecturing, public reading, radio broadcasting, and television, are strictly reserved. All inquiries for rights must be addressed to the copyright owners.

Acknowledgment is made to copyright holders and publishers for permission to reprint the following:

King Ubu by Alfred Jarry. Translated by Michael Benedikt and George E. Wellwarth. Copyright © 1964 by Michael Benedikt and George E. Wellwarth. Reprinted by permission of Georges Borchardt, Inc.

The Bug in Her Ear by Georges Feydeau. Translated by Sharon Parsell. Copyright © 1984 by Sharon Parsell. Reprinted by permission of Sharon Parsell.

Six Characters in Search of an Author by Luigi Pirandello. Translated by Stanley Vincent Longman. Reprinted with permission of the Pirandello family and of Stanley Vincent Longman, translator. Copyright © 1985 by Stanley Vincent Longman. Inquiries on production rights for this translation should be addressed to Mr. Longman, Department of Drama, University of Georgia, Athens, Ga. 30602.

Orphée by Jean Cocteau. Translated by Carl Wildman. Reprinted from Jean Cocteau, *The Infernal Machine and Other Plays*. Copyright © 1962 by Charles Wildman. Reprinted by permission of New Directions Publishing Corporation as to the United States of America, its dependencies, Canada, and the Philippines, and by permission of Dr. Jan van Loewen, Ltd., as to the rest of the world.

Red Magic by Michel de Ghelderode. Translated by George Hauger. Reprinted from *Ghelderode: Seven Plays* by Michel de Ghelderode, translated by George Hauger. Copyright © Editions Gallimard 1950, 1952, 1955, 1957. Copyright © 1964 Hill and Wang, Inc. Reprinted by permission of Hill and Wang (a division of Farrar, Straus & Giroux, Inc.) as to the United States of America, the Philippines, and Canada, and by permission of Editions Gallimard; as to the rest of the world.

Blood Wedding by Federico Garcia Lorca. Translated by James Graham-Luján and Richard L. O'Connell. Reprinted from Federico Garcia Lorca, *Three Tragedies*. Copyright © 1947, 1955 by New Directions Publishing Corporation. Reprinted by permission of New Directions.

Ondine by Jean Giraudoux. Adapted into English by Maurice Valency. Copyright © 1951, 1953, 1954 by Maurice Valency and reprinted by permission of Random House, Inc., as to the United States, its dependencies, the Philippines, Canada, and elsewhere, except the British Commonwealth (excluding Canada). Copyright © 1954, 1956 (Acting Edition) by Maurice Valency and reprinted by permission of International Creative Management as to the United Kingdom and the English-speaking countries other than the United States and Canada.

Thieves' Carnival by Jean Anouilh. Translated by Lucienne Hill. Reprinted from *Seven Plays* by Jean Anouilh, translated by Lucienne Hill. Copyright © 1952 by Jean Anouilh and Lucienne Hill. Copyright © 1967 by Hill and Wang, Inc. Reprinted by permission of Hill and Wang (a division of Farrar, Straus & Giroux, Inc.) as to the United States, the Philippines, and Canada, and by permission of Dr. Jan van Loewen, Ltd., as to the rest of the world. Caution: *Thieves' Carnival* is the sole property of the author and is fully protected by the copyright. It may not be acted either by professionals or by amateurs without written consent. Public reading and radio or television broadcasts are likewise forbidden. All inquiries concerning rights except stock and amateur rights should be addressed to the author's agent, Dr. Jan van Loewen, Ltd., International Copyright Agency, 21 Kingly Street, London W1R 5LB. All inquiries concerning stock and amateur rights should be addressed to Samuel French, Inc., 45 West Twenty-fifth Street, New York, N.Y. 10010.

Introduction

Volume 5 of *Our Dramatic Heritage* included the late nineteenth- and early twentieth-century plays that exhibited their authors reacting to realism by invoking poetry and by objectifying inner truth through expressionism. The plays came largely from northern Europe and the Germanic languages. Volume 6 covers the same time period but draws its plays from Latin Europe, centering upon a twentieth-century interest in transcending cognitive reason altogether and relying upon the unconscious creativity of the artist to communicate directly with the unconsciousness of his or her audience without necessarily engaging the consciousness of either.

Throughout the years since realism first triumphed in European drama, many theatrical artists have attempted to transcend what they perceived as the flat, prosaic staidness of realism in order to free the theater for more expressive forms. Repeatedly, as each such movement has peaked and begun to recede, realism has reasserted its fascination and reestablished itself as the modern theatrical norm. The ultimate reaction to realism has been its total collapse into nonsense, nihilism, and the absurd; this approach to theater reached its fullest expression only after World War II had made meaninglessness a daily horror, but, although postwar absurdism lies beyond the scope of this volume, its roots are to be found in the 1890s and in the experimental theater of the 1920s and 1930s. This volume explores the dramatic literature of that exciting period.

It would be pleasant to issue other volumes that would trace European drama from World War II to the present day, but at this writing the copyright restrictions surrounding many of these modern plays are too severe to permit appropriate anthologizing. World War II thus provides a suitable stopping place for tracing a performing tradition through two-and-one-half millennia. Copyright holders, translators, editors and others have been cooperative and helpful almost without exception in developing this collection from an idea to a reality. The quality of their work speaks loudly and clearly throughout the present volumes, capturing the richness and variety of this performing tradition as fully as now seems possible short of actual theatrical production. It is to the prospect of just such exciting new productions that these volumes are finally dedicated.

Our Dramatic Heritage
VOLUME 6

The Blind

Maurice Maeterlinck

During the last years of the nineteenth century, many of the artists who were dissatisfied with realism and naturalism formed a group centered in Paris, which became known as the Symbolists. Although it is perilous to think of an artistic movement as an organized and planned effort, when in fact most artists express what they find in themselves and only incidentally join together with like-minded artists in what is sometimes discernible as a "movement," the Symbolists were an unusually closely knit group. The artists involved worked, and for the most part lived, in Paris; they knew each other and acknowledged common goals and leaders; and they issued, from time to time, manifestos attempting to define their artistic views. There was nearly as much dissent from as agreement with these manifestos, indicating that unanimity of artistic aim was still far from achieved even in so small a group. Maurice Maeterlinck was the best playwright among them, the man who deserves most of the credit for creating a Symbolist theater, and the winner of the Nobel Prize for Literature in 1911.

In general, Symbolists adhered to the "art for art's sake" notions then widely admired, believing that perfection of form was essential to the creation of a great work of art. On the other hand, they rejected the naturalistic idea that the content for art was to be found in the external details of everyday life. The true meanings of life were indeed perceivable by common people, they thought, but only by the mysterious and instinctive processes that were beyond scientific demonstration but in tune with the fundamental rhythms of nature. Thus, an artist who sought to express such truths must abandon the world of surface reality and seek, through symbols, to "express the inexpressible." Because language was inadequate to express such truths, the symbols required for doing so must spring spontaneously from the finely tuned sensitivity of the artist and could never be explained by some simple mathematical equivalency to more ordered phenomena. With an almost religious air of mystery, the Symbolists turned first of all to music as the art form most abstract and most attuned to the unconscious, and then sought equivalent processes in the other arts. Poetry, for example, became suggestive and indirect in its imagery, finally abandoning metrical form altogether in its attempt at communion with the artist's "inner dream." The plays of Ibsen, then being produced at the Théâtre Libre, demonstrated the effectiveness of symbol on the stage, but in a realistic context that the Symbolists considered all wrong. They sought an atmosphere of mystery in which might be created a "theatre of the soul." It was into these circles that an aspiring young Belgian writer was introduced in 1885.

Maurice Maeterlinck was christened Mauritius Polyderus Maria Bernardus

Maeterlinck upon his birth in Ghent on August 29, 1862. His father was a well-to-do property owner with neither understanding nor sympathy for artistic endeavors; his mother was not culturally inclined either, but was sensitive and understanding enough to encourage her son's literary ambitions. He was educated at the Jesuit Collège de Sainte Barbe, where the fear of God and the temptations of the flesh were so vigorously taught that Maeterlinck later came to reject organized religion altogether. He attended the University of Ghent where, to please his father, he took a degree in law in 1885. Ostensibly to study French law, Maeterlinck persuaded his father to finance a six-month sojourn in Paris, the center of the artistic and literary world. Upon his dutiful return to Ghent, he practiced law until 1889, but every spare moment was devoted to writing; he was completely caught up in Symbolist literature.

Maeterlinck wrote several poems and a short story, then published his first play, *The Princess Maleine,* in 1889. It received glowing critical praise, and Maeterlinck gave up the practice of law altogether. He rented an apartment in Brussels, but commuted frequently to Paris, where the Théâtre d'Art, under the direction of Paul Fort, was experimenting with avant-garde productions. It was there that *The Intruder* was produced on May 20, 1891, and *The Blind* later that same year. These one-act plays beautifully illustrated Maeterlinck's idea of what a Symbolist theater should be, and they were received with great enthusiasm by the intelligentsia of Paris. In 1893, Maeterlinck's first major full-length play, *Pelléas and Mélisande,* was directed in Paris by Lugné-Poë, and in 1895 its success was repeated in London. In the meantime, Maeterlinck had concluded that human actors were not sufficiently passive and remote to capture the otherworldly quality he sought in his dramas, and in 1894 he wrote three plays for marionettes, two of which, *Interior* and *The Death of Tintagiles,* still have some appeal.

In 1895, Maeterlinck met the actress Georgette Leblanc. Although they never married, they lived together until 1918, and Maeterlinck began to write plays tailored to her talents. He also lost interest in Symbolist theories and created plays with more conventional story lines that aimed at more box office appeal. The result was a decrease in artistic merit, and the balance of Maeterlinck's plays are without enduring interest. His one great success was *The Blue Bird* (1909), which, under the direction of Stanislavski, was a hit at the Moscow Art Theatre and was later produced throughout the world. Appealing to children and adults, it captured some of the fairy-tale atmosphere of the earlier Symbolist plays but with a cloying optimism quite opposite to their dark vision. Maeterlinck married Renée Dahon in 1919. He continued to write essays and poetry, dabbled in parapsychology and extrasensory perception, and moved about Europe and America to avoid the two world wars. He died of a heart attack in Nice on May 6, 1949.

The Blind very well illustrates the Symbolist principles as Maeterlinck applied them to the theater. First produced on December 11, 1891, at the Théâtre d'Art, it scored an immediate success with most reviewers and with its coterie audiences. Its impact depends entirely upon the mood created, with nuance and indirection the chief means of achieving this mood. Maeterlinck's Symbolist theater has been termed *static* theater, or *theater of silence,* for very little happens by way of plot and the moments of silence are often of greater significance than the words spoken. The symbols that Maeterlinck has selected for use in the play are certainly neither unusual nor obscure (blindness, cold, a dog, an island), but their overall pattern implies a great deal more than is actually stated and the ultimate success of the play in performance depends upon an audience responding to the totality of those stimuli at an emotional more than an intellectual level. The visual elements of production are especially significant in any appreciation of the play; the reader must keep in mind, for example, the dominating presence of the priest's corpse throughout the play, a presence that could not be missed in the theater, but that easily slips into the subconscious in reading.

The stark image at the opening of the play, with twelve blind people unaware of the corpse of their leader propped against a tree in their midst, is virtually a statement of the entire play's impact at the outset. The action of the play is to explore this bizarre relationship, and layer upon layer of symbolic significance crowds into the mind as the action progresses. In a Platonic sense, human beings are all blind, aware only of the shadows on the cave wall rather than of the reality that is the true meaning of life. Even among the blind, some are born blind and some become so; some even retain the marginal ability to distinguish light from darkness. They rely on the Priest to lead them through the world, but his help is now gone for good. Perhaps Maeterlinck is suggesting that the Church is now useless as a guide for living; perhaps the priest represents Christ, who has died to save his people but whose disciples must now carry the load by themselves. Any conclusions are deliberately left vague.

As the play progresses, the original image is expanded and enriched. Maeterlinck's short simple sentences would be banal in a realistic context, but here they operate in a rhythmical manner to enhance poetically the mood of fear and apprehension. All of the senses of the spectator are engaged through the imagery of the language as well as through the tangible imagery of the theater, so that the blind people seem quite natural when they speak of feeling moonlight and hearing the stars. By the end of the play, the audience is ready for the mysterious presence of whom even the baby is aware. Whether this presence is Death (somewhat delayed, since the priest has been dead for hours) or something even more mysterious and threatening is characteristically left unexplained; it is the terrible reality of the spiritual world that human beings can never fully penetrate in this life, but that poets and dreamers can make faintly discernible through their special gift. The creation of this mood is the essence of Maeterlinck's art; its rational explication remains, in Maeterlinck's opinion, impossible. Neither character development, plot, nor theme in its usual sense, was of interest to the Symbolists. True art was to be experienced rather than analyzed, and more abstract elements such as music or the phonics of language were of greater significance in creating a theatrical experience than were the traditional ones.

In its purest form (never very pure, at that), Symbolism lasted only about ten years. In Maeterlinck's case, other interests took him elsewhere and his later theatrical achievements are not in a class with his early Symbolist plays. The great significance of the Symbolist movement lay in the departure that it represented from the realistic and naturalistic norms just then coming to dominate the mainstream theater, and in its influence that can be traced in much of the twentieth-century European drama. His Nobel Prize notwithstanding, Maeterlinck is not regarded today by most critics as one of the great playwrights, but his Symbolist plays are still staged with some frequency and his influence has been acknowledged by a great many of the better playwrights who have come after him.

The Blind
(Les Aveugles)

Translated by Richard Hovey

Characters

The Priest
Three Men Who Were Born Blind
A Very Old Blind Man
Fifth Blind Man, who is also deaf
Sixth Blind Man, who can distinguish light and darkness
Three Old Blind Women in Prayer
A Very Old Blind Woman
A Young Blind Girl
A Blind Madwoman
An Infant, child of the Madwoman
A Dog

An ancient Norland forest, with an eternal look, under a sky of deep stars.
In the centre, and in the deep of the night, a very old priest is sitting, wrapped in a great black cloak. The chest and the head, gently upturned and deathly motionless, rest against the trunk of a giant hollow oak. The face is fearsome pale and of an immovable waxen lividness, in which the purple lips fall slightly apart. The dumb, fixed eyes no longer look out from the visible side of Eternity and seem to bleed with immemorial sorrows and with tears. The hair, of a solemn whiteness, falls in stringy locks, stiff and few, over a face more illuminated and more weary than all that surrounds it in the watchful stillness of that melancholy wood. The hands, pitifully thin, are clasped rigidly over the thighs.
On the right, six old men, all blind, are sitting on stones, stumps and dead leaves.

On the left, separated from them by an uprooted tree and fragments of rock, six women, also blind, are sitting opposite the old men. Three among them pray and mourn without ceasing, in a muffled voice. Another is old in the extreme. The fifth, in an attitude of mute insanity, holds on her knees a little sleeping child. The sixth is strangely young, and her whole body is drenched with her beautiful hair. They, as well as the old men, are all clad in the same ample and sombre garments. Most of them are waiting, with their elbows on their knees and their faces in their hands; and all seem to have lost the habit of ineffectual gesture and no longer turn their heads at the stifled and uneasy noises of the Island. Tall funereal trees,—yews, weeping-willows, cypresses,—cover them with their faithful shadows. A cluster of long, sickly asphodels is in bloom, not far from the priest, in the night. It is unusually oppressive, despite the moonlight that here and there struggles to pierce for an instant the glooms of the foliage.

FIRST BLIND MAN. [*Who was born blind.*]
He hasn't come back yet?

SECOND BLIND MAN. [*Who also was born blind.*] You have awakened me.

FIRST BLIND MAN. I was sleeping, too.

THIRD BLIND MAN. [*Also born blind.*] I was sleeping, too.

FIRST BLIND MAN. He hasn't come yet?

SECOND BLIND MAN. I hear nothing coming.

16

THIRD BLIND MAN. It is time to go back to the Asylum.

FIRST BLIND MAN. We ought to find out where we are.

SECOND BLIND MAN. It has grown cold since he left.

FIRST BLIND MAN. We ought to find out where we are!

THE VERY OLD BLIND MAN. Does any one know where we are?

THE VERY OLD BLIND WOMAN. We were walking a very long while; we must be a long way from the Asylum.

FIRST BLIND MAN. Oh! The women are opposite us.

THE VERY OLD BLIND WOMAN. We are sitting opposite you.

FIRST BLIND MAN. Wait, I am coming over where you are. [*He rises and gropes in the dark.*]—Where are you?— Speak! Let me hear where you are!

THE VERY OLD BLIND WOMAN. Here; we are sitting on stones.

FIRST BLIND MAN. [*Advances and stumbles against the fallen tree and the rocks.*] There is something between us.

SECOND BLIND MAN. We had better keep our places.

THIRD BLIND MAN. Where are you sitting?—Will you come over by us?

THE VERY OLD BLIND WOMAN. We dare not rise!

THIRD BLIND MAN. Why did he separate us?

FIRST BLIND MAN. I hear praying on the women's side.

SECOND BLIND MAN. Yes; the three old women are praying.

FIRST BLIND MAN. This is no time for prayer!

SECOND BLIND MAN. You will pray soon enough, in the dormitory!

The three old women continue their prayers.

THIRD BLIND MAN. I should like to know who it is I am sitting by.

SECOND BLIND MAN. I think I am next to you. [*They feel about them.*]

THIRD BLIND MAN. We can't reach each other.

FIRST BLIND MAN. Nevertheless, we are not far apart. [*He feels about him and strikes with his staff the* FIFTH BLIND MAN, *who utters a muffled groan.*] The one who cannot hear is beside us.

SECOND BLIND MAN. I don't hear everybody; we were six just now.

FIRST BLIND MAN. I am going to count. Let us question the women, too; we must know what to depend upon. I hear the three old women praying all the time; are they together?

THE VERY OLD BLIND WOMAN. They are sitting beside me, on a rock.

FIRST BLIND MAN. I am sitting on dead leaves.

THIRD BLIND MAN. And the beautiful blind girl, where is she?

THE VERY OLD BLIND WOMAN. She is near them that pray.

SECOND BLIND MAN. Where is the mad woman, and her child?

THE YOUNG BLIND GIRL. He sleeps; do not awaken him!

FIRST BLIND MAN. Oh! How far away you are from us! I thought you were opposite me!

THIRD BLIND MAN. We know—nearly— all we need to know. Let us chat a little, while we wait for the priest to come back.

THE VERY OLD BLIND WOMAN. He told us to wait for him in silence.

THIRD BLIND MAN. We are not in a church.

THE VERY OLD BLIND WOMAN. You do not know where we are.

THIRD BLIND MAN. I am afraid when I am not speaking.

SECOND BLIND MAN. Do you know where the priest went?

THIRD BLIND MAN. I think he leaves us for too long a time.

FIRST BLIND MAN. He is getting too old. It looks as though he himself has no longer seen for some time. He will not admit it, for fear another should come to take his place among us; but I suspect he hardly sees at all any more. We must have another guide; he no longer listens to us, and we are getting too numerous. He and the three nuns are the only people in the house who can see; and they are all older than we are!—I am sure he has misled us and that he is looking for the road. Where has he gone?—He has no right to leave us here. . . .

THE VERY OLD BLIND MAN. He has gone a long way: I think he said so to the women.

FIRST BLIND MAN. He no longer speaks except to the women?—Do we no longer exist?—We shall have to complain of him in the end.

THE VERY OLD BLIND MAN. To whom will you complain?

FIRST BLIND MAN. I don't know yet; we shall see, we shall see.—But where has he gone, I say?—I am asking the women.

THE VERY OLD BLIND WOMAN. He was weary with walking such a long time. I think he sat down a moment among us. He has been very sad and very feeble for several days. He is afraid since the physician died. He is alone. He hardly speaks any more. I don't know what has happened. He insisted on going out to-day. He said he wished to see the Island, a last time, in the sunshine, before winter came. The winter will be very long and cold, it seems, and the ice comes already from the North. He was very uneasy, too: they say the storms of the last few days have swollen the river and all the dikes are shaken. He said also that the sea frightened him; it is troubled without cause, it seems, and the coast of the Island is no longer high enough. He wished to see; but he did not tell us what he saw.—At present, I think he has gone to get some bread and water for the mad woman. He said he would have to go a long way, perhaps. We must wait.

THE YOUNG BLIND GIRL. He took my hands when he left; and his hands shook as if he were afraid. Then he kissed me. . . .

FIRST BLIND MAN. Oh! Oh!

THE YOUNG BLIND GIRL. I asked him

what had happened. He told me he did not know what was going to happen. He told me the reign of old men was going to end, perhaps. . . .

FIRST BLIND MAN. What did he mean by saying that?

THE YOUNG BLIND GIRL. I did not understand him. He told me he was going over by the great lighthouse.

FIRST BLIND MAN. Is there a lighthouse here?

THE YOUNG BLIND GIRL. Yes, at the north of the Island. I believe we are not far from it. He said he saw the light of the beacon even here, through the leaves. He has never seemed more sorrowful than to-day, and I believe he has been weeping for several days. I do not know why, but I wept also without seeing him. I did not hear him go away. I did not question him any further. I was aware that he smiled very gravely; I was aware that he closed his eyes and wished to be silent. . . .

FIRST BLIND MAN. He said nothing to us of all that!

THE YOUNG BLIND GIRL. You do not listen when he speaks!

THE VERY OLD BLIND WOMAN. You all murmur when he speaks!

SECOND BLIND MAN. He merely said "Good-night" to us when he went away.

THIRD BLIND MAN. It must be very late.

FIRST BLIND MAN. He said "Good-night" two or three times when he went away, as if he were going to sleep. I was aware that he was looking at me when he said "Good-night; good-night."—The voice has a different sound when you look at any one fixedly.

FIFTH BLIND MAN. Pity the blind!

FIRST BLIND MAN. Who is that, talking nonsense?

SECOND BLIND MAN. I think it is he who is deaf.

FIRST BLIND MAN. Be quiet!—This is no time for begging!

THIRD BLIND MAN. Where did he go to

get his bread and water?

THE VERY OLD BLIND WOMAN. He went toward the sea.

THIRD BLIND MAN. Nobody goes toward the sea like that at his age!

SECOND BLIND MAN. Are we near the sea?

THE OLD BLIND WOMAN. Yes; keep still a moment; you will hear it.

Murmur of a sea, near by and very calm, against the cliffs.

SECOND BLIND MAN. I hear only the three old women praying.

THE VERY OLD BLIND WOMAN. Listen well; you will hear it across their prayers.

SECOND BLIND MAN. Yes; I hear something not far from us.

THE VERY OLD BLIND MAN. It was asleep; one would say that it awaked.

FIRST BLIND MAN. He was wrong to bring us here; I do not like to hear that noise.

THE VERY OLD BLIND MAN. You know quite well the Island is not large. It can be heard whenever one goes outside the Asylum close.

SECOND BLIND MAN. I never listened to it.

THIRD BLIND MAN. It seems close beside us to-day; I do not like to hear it so near.

SECOND BLIND MAN. No more do I; besides, we didn't ask to go out from the Asylum.

THIRD BLIND MAN. We have never come so far as this; it was needless to bring us so far.

THE VERY OLD BLIND WOMAN. The weather was very fine this morning; he wanted to have us enjoy the last sunny days, before shutting us up all winter in the Asylum.

FIRST BLIND MAN. But I prefer to stay in the Asylum.

THE VERY OLD BLIND WOMAN. He said also that we ought to know something of the little Island we live on. He himself had never been all over it; there is a mountain that no one has climbed, valleys one fears to go down into, and caves into which no one has ever yet penetrated. Finally he said we must not always wait for the sun under the vaulted roof of the dormitory; he wished to lead us as far as the seashore. He has gone there alone.

THE VERY OLD BLIND MAN. He is right. We must think of living.

FIRST BLIND MAN. But there is nothing to see outside!

SECOND BLIND MAN. Are we in the sun, now?

THIRD BLIND MAN. Is the sun still shining?

SIXTH BLIND MAN. I think not: it seems very late.

SECOND BLIND MAN. What time is it?

THE OTHERS. I do not know.—Nobody knows.

SECOND BLIND MAN. Is it light still? [*To the* SIXTH BLIND MAN.]—Where are you?—How is it, you who can see a little, how is it?

SIXTH BLIND MAN. I think it is very dark; when there is sunlight, I see a blue line under my eyelids. I did see one, a long while ago; but now, I no longer perceive anything.

FIRST BLIND MAN. For my part, I know it is late when I am hungry: and I am hungry.

THIRD BLIND MAN. Look up at the sky; perhaps you will see something there!

All lift their heads skyward, with the exception of the three who were born blind, who continue to look upon the ground.

SIXTH BLIND MAN. I do not know whether we are under the sky.

FIRST BLIND MAN. The voice echoes as if we were in a cavern.

THE VERY OLD BLIND MAN. I think, rather, that it echoes so because it is evening.

THE YOUNG BLIND GIRL. It seems to me that I feel the moonlight on my hands.

THE VERY OLD BLIND WOMAN. I believe there are stars; I hear them.

THE YOUNG BLIND GIRL. So do I.

FIRST BLIND MAN. I hear no noise.

SECOND BLIND MAN. I hear only the noise of our breathing.

THE VERY OLD BLIND MAN. I believe the women are right.

FIRST BLIND MAN. I never heard the stars.

THE TWO OTHERS WHO WERE BORN BLIND. Nor we, either.

A flight of night birds alights suddenly in the foliage.

SECOND BLIND MAN. Listen! listen!—what is up there above us?—Do you hear?

THE VERY OLD BLIND MAN. Something has passed between us and the sky!

SIXTH BLIND MAN. There is something stirring over our heads; but we cannot reach there!

FIRST BLIND MAN. I do not recognize that noise.—I should like to go back to the Asylum.

SECOND BLIND MAN. We ought to know where we are!

SIXTH BLIND MAN. I have tried to get up; there is nothing but thorns about me; I dare not stretch out my hands.

THIRD BLIND MAN. We ought to know where we are!

THE VERY OLD BLIND MAN. We cannot know!

SIXTH BLIND MAN. We must be very far from the house. I no longer understand any of the noises.

THIRD BLIND MAN. For a long time I have smelled the odor of dead leaves—

SIXTH BLIND MAN. Is there any of us who has seen the Island in the past, and can tell us where we are?

THE VERY OLD BLIND WOMAN. We were all blind when we came here.

FIRST BLIND MAN. We have never seen.

SECOND BLIND MAN. Let us not alarm ourselves needlessly. He will come back soon; let us wait a little longer. But in the future, we will not go out any more with him.

THE VERY OLD BLIND MAN. We cannot go out alone.

FIRST BLIND MAN. We will not go out at all. I had rather not go out.

SECOND BLIND MAN. We had no desire to go out. Nobody asked him to.

THE VERY OLD BLIND WOMAN. It was a feast-day in the Island; we always go out on the great holidays.

THIRD BLIND MAN. He tapped me on the shoulder while I was still asleep, saying: "Rise, rise; it is time, the sun is shining!"—Is it? I had not perceived it. I never saw the sun.

THE VERY OLD BLIND MAN. *I* have seen the sun, when I was very young.

THE VERY OLD BLIND WOMAN. So have I; a very long time ago; when I was a child; but I hardly remember it any longer.

THIRD BLIND MAN. Why does he want us to go out every time the sun shines? Who can tell the difference? I never know whether I take a walk at noon or at midnight.

SIXTH BLIND MAN. I had rather go out at noon; I guess vaguely then at a great white light, and my eyes make great efforts to open.

THIRD BLIND MAN. I prefer to stay in the refectory, near the seacoal fire; there was a big fire this morning. . . .

SECOND BLIND MAN. He could take us into the sun in the courtyard. There the walls are a shelter; you cannot go out when the gate is shut,—I always shut it.—Why are you touching my left elbow?

FIRST BLIND MAN. I have not touched you. I can't reach you.

SECOND BLIND MAN. I tell you somebody touched my elbow!

FIRST BLIND MAN. It was not any of us.

SECOND BLIND MAN. I should like to go away.

THE VERY OLD BLIND WOMAN. My God! My God! Tell us where we are!

FIRST BLIND MAN. We cannot wait for eternity.

A clock, very far away, strikes twelve slowly.

THE VERY OLD BLIND WOMAN. Oh, how far we are from the asylum!

THE VERY OLD BLIND MAN. It is midnight.

SECOND BLIND MAN. It is noon.—Does any one know?—Speak!

SIXTH BLIND MAN. I do not know, but I think we are in the dark.

FIRST BLIND MAN. I don't know any longer where I am; we slept too long—

SECOND BLIND MAN. I am hungry.

THE OTHERS. We are hungry and thirsty.

SECOND BLIND MAN. Have we been here long?

THE VERY OLD BLIND WOMAN. It seems as if I had been here centuries!

SIXTH BLIND MAN. I begin to understand where we are. . . .

THIRD BLIND MAN. We ought to go toward the side where it struck midnight. . . .

All at once the night birds scream exultingly in the darkness.

FIRST BLIND MAN. Do you hear?—Do you hear?

SECOND BLIND MAN. We are not alone here!

THIRD BLIND MAN. I suspected something a long while ago: we are overheard.—Has he come back?

FIRST BLIND MAN. I don't know what it is: it is above us.

SECOND BLIND MAN. Did the others hear nothing?—You are always silent!

THE VERY OLD BLIND MAN. We are listening still.

THE YOUNG BLIND GIRL. I hear wings about me!

THE VERY OLD BLIND WOMAN. My God! My God! Tell us where we are!

SIXTH BLIND MAN. I begin to understand where we are. . . . The Asylum is on the other side of the great river; we crossed the old bridge. He led us to the north of the Island. We are not far from the river, and perhaps we shall hear it if we listen a moment. . . . We must go as far as the water's edge, if he does not come back. . . . There, night and day, great ships pass, and the sailors will perceive us on the banks. It is possible that we are in the wood that surrounds the lighthouse; but I do not know the way out. . . . Will any one follow me?

FIRST BLIND MAN. Let us remain seated!—Let us wait, let us wait. We do not know in what direction the great river is, and there are marshes all about the Asylum. Let us wait, let us wait. . . . He will return . . . he must return!

SIXTH BLIND MAN. Does any one know by what route we came here? He explained it to us as he walked.

FIRST BLIND MAN. I paid no attention to him.

SIXTH BLIND MAN. Did any one listen to him?

THIRD BLIND MAN. We must listen to him in the future.

SIXTH BLIND MAN. Were any of us born on the Island?

THE VERY OLD BLIND MAN. You know very well we came from elsewhere.

THE VERY OLD BLIND WOMAN. We came from the other side of the sea.

FIRST BLIND MAN. I thought I should die on the voyage.

SECOND BLIND MAN. So did I; we came together.

THIRD BLIND MAN. We are all three from the same parish.

FIRST BLIND MAN. They say you can see it from here, on a clear day,—toward the north. It has no steeple.

THIRD BLIND MAN. We came by accident.

THE VERY OLD BLIND WOMAN. I come from another direction. . . .

SECOND BLIND MAN. From where?

THE VERY OLD BLIND WOMAN. I dare no longer dream of it. . . . I hardly remember any longer when I speak of it. . . . It was too long ago. . . . It was colder there than here. . . .

THE YOUNG BLIND GIRL. I come from very far. . . .

FIRST BLIND MAN. Well, from where?

THE YOUNG BLIND GIRL. I could not tell you. How would you have me explain!—It is too far from here; it is beyond the sea. I come from a great country. . . . I could only make you understand by signs: and we no longer see. . . . I have wandered too long. . . . But I have seen the sunlight and the water and the fire, mountains, faces, and strange flowers. . . . There are none such on this Island; it is too gloomy and too cold. . . . I have never recognized their perfume since I saw them last. . . . And I have seen my parents and my sisters. . . . I was too young then to know where I was. . . . I still played by the seashore. . . . But oh, how I remember having seen! . . . One day I saw the snow on a mountain-top . . . I began to distinguish the unhappy. . . .

FIRST BLIND MAN. What do you mean?

THE YOUNG BLIND GIRL. I distinguish them yet at times by their voices. . . . I have memories which are clearer when I do not think upon them. . . .

FIRST BLIND MAN. I have no memories.

A flight of large migratory birds pass clamorously, above the trees.

THE VERY OLD BLIND MAN. Something is passing again across the sky!

SECOND BLIND MAN. Why did you come here?

THE VERY OLD BLIND MAN. Of whom do you ask that?

SECOND BLIND MAN. Of our young sister.

THE YOUNG BLIND GIRL. I was told he could cure me. He told me I would see some day; then I could leave the Island. . . .

FIRST BLIND MAN. We all want to leave the Island!

SECOND BLIND MAN. We shall stay here always.

THIRD BLIND MAN. He is too old; he will not have time to cure us.

THE YOUNG BLIND GIRL. My lids are shut, but I feel that my eyes are alive. . . .

FIRST BLIND MAN. Mine are open.

SECOND BLIND MAN. I sleep with my eyes open.

THIRD BLIND MAN. Let us not talk of our eyes!

SECOND BLIND MAN. It is not long since you came, is it?

THE VERY OLD BLIND MAN. One evening at prayers I heard a voice on the women's side that I did not recognize; and I knew by your voice that you were very young. . . . I would have liked to see you, to hear you. . . .

FIRST BLIND MAN. I didn't perceive anything.

SECOND BLIND MAN. He gave us no warning.

SIXTH BLIND MAN. They say you are beautiful as a woman who comes from very far.

THE YOUNG BLIND GIRL. I have never seen myself.

THE VERY OLD BLIND MAN. We have never seen each other. We ask and we reply; we live together, we are always together, but we know not what we are! . . . In vain we touch each other with both hands; the eyes learn more than the hands. . . .

SIXTH BLIND MAN. I see your shadows sometimes, when you are in the sun.

THE VERY OLD BLIND MAN. We have never seen the house in which we live; in vain we feel the walls and the windows; we do not know where we live! . . .

THE VERY OLD BLIND WOMAN. They say it is an old château, very gloomy and very wretched, where no light is ever seen except in the tower where the priest has his room.

FIRST BLIND MAN. There is no need of light for those who do not see.

SIXTH BLIND MAN. When I tend the flock, in the neighborhood of the Asylum, the sheep return of themselves when they see at nightfall that light in the tower. . . . They have never misled me.

THE VERY OLD BLIND MAN. Years and years we have been together, and we have never seen each other! You would say we were forever alone! . . . To love, one must see.

THE VERY OLD BLIND WOMAN. I dream sometimes that I see. . . .

THE VERY OLD BLIND MAN. I see only in my dreams. . . .

FIRST BLIND MAN. I do not dream, usually, except at midnight.

SECOND BLIND MAN. Of what can one dream where the hands are motionless?

A flurry of wind shakes the forest, and the leaves fall, thick and gloomily.

FIFTH BLIND MAN. Who touched my hands?

FIRST BLIND MAN. Something is falling about us!

THE VERY OLD BLIND MAN. That comes from above; I don't know what it is. . . .

FIFTH BLIND MAN. Who touched my hands?—I was asleep; let me sleep!

THE VERY OLD BLIND MAN. Nobody touched your hands.

FIFTH BLIND MAN. Who took my hands? Answer loudly; I am a little hard of hearing. . . .

THE VERY OLD BLIND MAN. We do not know ourselves.

FIFTH BLIND MAN. Has some one come to give us warning?

FIRST BLIND MAN. It is useless to reply; he hears nothing.

THIRD BLIND MAN. It must be admitted, the deaf are very unfortunate.

THE VERY OLD BLIND MAN. I am weary of staying seated.

SIXTH BLIND MAN. I am weary of staying here.

SECOND BLIND MAN. It seems to me we are so far from one another. . . . Let us try to get a little nearer together,—it is beginning to get cold. . . .

THIRD BLIND MAN. I dare not rise! We had better stay where we are.

THE VERY OLD BLIND MAN. We do not know what there may be among us.

SIXTH BLIND MAN. I think both my hands are in blood; I would like to stand up.

THIRD BLIND MAN. You are leaning toward me,—I hear you.

The BLIND MADWOMAN *rubs her eyes violently, groaning and turning obstinately toward the motionless priest.*

FIRST BLIND MAN. I hear still another noise. . . .

THE VERY OLD BLIND WOMAN. I think it is our unfortunate sister rubbing her eyes.

SECOND BLIND MAN. She is never doing anything else; I hear her every night.

THIRD BLIND MAN. She is mad; she never speaks.

THE VERY OLD BLIND WOMAN. She has never spoken since she had her child . . . She seems always to be afraid. . . .

THE VERY OLD BLIND MAN. You are not afraid here, then?

FIRST BLIND MAN. Who?

THE VERY OLD BLIND MAN. All the rest of us.

THE VERY OLD BLIND WOMAN. Yes, yes; we are afraid.

THE YOUNG BLIND GIRL. We have been afraid for a long time.

FIRST BLIND MAN. Why did you ask that?

THE VERY OLD BLIND MAN. I do not know why I asked it. . . . There is something here I do not understand. . . . It seems to me I hear weeping all at once among us. . . .

FIRST BLIND MAN. There is no need to fear; I think it is the madwoman.

THE VERY OLD BLIND MAN. There is something else beside. . . . I am sure there is something else beside. . . . It is not that alone that makes me afraid.

THE VERY OLD BLIND WOMAN. She always weeps when she is going to give suck to her child.

FIRST BLIND MAN. She is the only one that weeps so.

THE VERY OLD BLIND WOMAN. They say she sees still at times.

FIRST BLIND MAN. You do not hear the others weep.

THE VERY OLD BLIND MAN. To weep, one must see.

THE YOUNG BLIND GIRL. I smell an odor of flowers about us.

FIRST BLIND MAN. I smell only the smell of the earth.

THE YOUNG BLIND GIRL. There are flowers,—there are flowers about us.

SECOND BLIND MAN. I smell only the smell of the earth.

THE VERY OLD BLIND WOMAN. I caught the perfume of flowers in the wind. . . .

THIRD BLIND MAN. I smell only the smell of the earth.

THE VERY OLD BLIND MAN. I believe the women are right.

SIXTH BLIND MAN. Where are they?—I will go pluck them.

THE YOUNG BLIND GIRL. At your right. Rise!

The SIXTH BLIND MAN *rises slowly and advances groping, and stumbling against the bushes and trees, toward the asphodels, which he breaks and crushes on his way.*

THE YOUNG BLIND GIRL. I hear you breaking the green stalks. Stop! Stop!

FIRST BLIND MAN. Don't worry yourselves about flowers, but think of getting home.

SIXTH BLIND MAN. I no longer dare return on my steps.

THE YOUNG BLIND GIRL. You need not return.—Wait.—[*She rises.*] Oh, how cold the earth is! It is going to freeze.—[*She advances without hesitation toward the strange, pale asphodels; but she is stopped, in the neighborhood of the flowers, by the uprooted tree and the fragments of rock.*] They are here.—I cannot reach them; they are on your side.

SIXTH BLIND MAN. I believe I am plucking them.

He plucks the scattered flowers, gropingly, and offers them to her; the night birds fly away.

THE YOUNG BLIND GIRL. It seems to me I saw these flowers in the old days. . . . I no longer know their name. . . . Alas, how sickly they are, and how soft the stems are! I hardly recognize them. . . . I think it is the flower of the dead.

She twines the asphodels in her hair.

THE VERY OLD BLIND MAN. I hear the noise of your hair.

THE YOUNG BLIND GIRL. It is the flowers.

THE VERY OLD BLIND MAN. We shall not see you. . . .

THE YOUNG BLIND GIRL. I shall not see myself, any more. . . . I am cold.

At this moment the wind rises in the forest, and the sea roars suddenly and with violence against cliffs very near.

FIRST BLIND MAN. It thunders!

SECOND BLIND MAN. I think there is a storm rising.

THE VERY OLD BLIND WOMAN. I think it is the sea.

THIRD BLIND MAN. The sea?—Is it the sea?—But it is hardly two steps from us!—It is at our feet! I hear it all about me!—It must be something else!

THE YOUNG BLIND GIRL. I hear the noise of breakers at my feet.

FIRST BLIND MAN. I think it is the wind in the dead leaves.

THE VERY OLD BLIND MAN. I think the women are right.

THIRD BLIND MAN. It will come here!

FIRST BLIND MAN. What direction does the wind come from?

SECOND BLIND MAN. It comes from the sea.

THE VERY OLD BLIND MAN. It always comes from the sea. The sea surrounds us on all sides. It cannot come from anywhere else. . . .

FIRST BLIND MAN. Let us not keep on thinking of the sea!

SECOND BLIND MAN. We must think of it. It will reach us soon.

FIRST BLIND MAN. You do not know if it be the sea.

SECOND BLIND MAN. I hear its surges as if I could dip both hands in them. We cannot stay here! It is perhaps all about us.

THE VERY OLD BLIND MAN. Where would you go?

SECOND BLIND MAN. No matter where! No matter where! I will not hear this noise of waters any longer! Let us go! Let us go!

THIRD BLIND MAN. I think I hear something else.—Listen!

A sound of footfalls is heard, hurried and far away, in the dead leaves.

FIRST BLIND MAN. There is something coming this way.

SECOND BLIND MAN. He is coming! He is coming! He is coming back!

THIRD BLIND MAN. He is coming with little quick steps, like a little child.

SECOND BLIND MAN. Let us make no complaints to him to-day.

THE VERY OLD BLIND WOMAN. I believe that is not the step of a man!

A great dog enters in the forest, and passes in front of the blind folk.—Silence.

FIRST BLIND MAN. Who's there?—Who are you?—Have pity on us, we have been waiting so long! . . . [*The dog stops, and coming to the blind man, puts his fore paws on his knees.*] Oh, oh, what have you put on my knees? What is it? . . . Is it an animal?—I believe it is a dog. . . . Oh, oh, it is the dog, it is the Asylum dog! Come here, sir, come here! He comes to save us! Come here! come here, sir!

THE OTHERS. Come here, sir! Come here!

FIRST BLIND MAN. He has come to save us! He has followed our tracks all the way! He is licking my hands as if he had just found me after centuries! He howls for joy! He is going to die for joy! Listen, listen!

THE OTHERS. Come here! Come here!

THE VERY OLD BLIND MAN. Perhaps he is running ahead of somebody. . . .

FIRST BLIND MAN. No, no, he is alone.—I hear nothing coming.—We need no other guide; there is none better. He will lead us wherever we want to go; he will obey us. . . .

THE VERY OLD BLIND WOMAN. I dare not follow him. . . .

THE YOUNG BLIND GIRL. Nor I.

FIRST BLIND MAN. Why not? His sight is better than ours.

SECOND BLIND MAN. Don't listen to the women!

THIRD BLIND MAN. I believe there is a change in the sky. I breathe freely.

The air is pure now. . . .

THE VERY OLD BLIND WOMAN. It is the sea wind passing about us.

SIXTH BLIND MAN. It seems to me it is getting lighter; I believe the sun is rising. . . .

THE VERY OLD BLIND WOMAN. I believe it is getting colder. . . .

FIRST BLIND MAN. We are going to find our way again. He is dragging me! . . . He is dragging me. He is drunk with joy!—I can no longer hold him back! . . . Follow me, follow me. We are going back to the house! . . .

He rises, dragged by the dog, who leads him to the motionless priest, and stops.

THE OTHERS. Where are you? Where are you?—Where are you going?—Take care!

FIRST BLIND MAN. Wait, wait! Do not follow me yet; I will come back. . . . He is stopping.—What is the matter with him?—Oh, oh, I touched something very cold!

SECOND BLIND MAN. What are you saying?—We can hardly hear your voice any longer.

FIRST BLIND MAN. I have touched—I believe I am touching a face!

THIRD BLIND MAN. What are you saying?—We hardly understand you any longer. What is the matter with you?—Where are you?—Are you already so far away?

FIRST BLIND MAN. Oh, oh, oh!—I do not know yet what it is.—There is a dead man in the midst of us.

THE OTHERS. A dead man in the midst of us?—Where are you? Where are you?

FIRST BLIND MAN. There is a dead man among us, I tell you! Oh, oh, I touched a dead man's face!—You are sitting beside a dead man! One of us must have died suddenly. Why don't you speak, so that I may know who are still alive? Where are you?—Answer! Answer, all of you!

The blind folk reply in turn, with the exception of the MADWOMAN *and the* DEAF

MAN. *The* THREE OLD WOMEN *have ceased their prayers.*

FIRST BLIND MAN. I no longer distinguish your voices. . . . You all speak alike! . . . Your voices are all trembling.

THIRD BLIND MAN. There are two that have not answered. . . . Where are they?

He touches with his stick the FIFTH BLIND MAN.

FIFTH BLIND MAN. Oh! Oh! I was alseep; let me sleep!

SIXTH BLIND MAN. It is not he.—Is it the madwoman?

THE VERY OLD BLIND WOMAN. She is sitting beside me; I can hear that she is alive. . . .

FIRST BLIND MAN. I believe . . . I believe it is the priest!—He is standing up! Come, come, come!

SECOND BLIND MAN. He is standing up?

THIRD BLIND MAN. Then he is not dead!

THE VERY OLD BLIND MAN. Where is he?

SIXTH BLIND MAN. Let us go see!

They all rise, with the exception of the MADWOMAN *and the* FIFTH BLIND MAN, *and advance, groping, toward the dead.*

SECOND BLIND MAN. Is he here?—Is it he?

THIRD BLIND MAN. Yes, yes, I recognize him.

FIRST BLIND MAN. My God! My God! What will become of us?

THE VERY OLD BLIND WOMAN. Father! Father!—Is it you? Father, what has happened?—What is the matter?—Answer us!—We are all about you. Oh! Oh! Oh!

THE VERY OLD BLIND MAN. Bring some water; perhaps he still lives.

SECOND BLIND MAN. Let us try. . . . He might perhaps be able to take us back to the Asylum. . . .

THIRD BLIND MAN. It is useless; I no longer hear his heart.—He is cold.

FIRST BLIND MAN. He died without speaking a word.

THIRD BLIND MAN. He ought to have forewarned us.

SECOND BLIND MAN. Oh! How old he was! . . . This is the first time I ever touched his face. . . .

THIRD BLIND MAN. [*Feeling the corpse.*] He is taller than we.

SECOND BLIND MAN. His eyes are wide open. He died with his hands clasped.

FIRST BLIND MAN. It was unreasonable to die so. . . .

SECOND BLIND MAN. He is not standing up, he is sitting on a stone.

THE VERY OLD BLIND WOMAN. My God! My God! I did not dream of such a thing! . . . Such a thing! . . . He has been sick such a long time. . . . He must have suffered to-day. . . . Oh, oh, oh!—He never complained; he only pressed our hands. . . . One does not always understand. . . . One never understands! . . . Let us go pray about him; go down on your knees. . . .

The women kneel, moaning.

FIRST BLIND MAN. I dare not go down on my knees.

SECOND BLIND MAN. You cannot tell what you might kneel on here.

THIRD BLIND MAN. Was he ill? . . . He did not tell us. . . .

SECOND BLIND MAN. I heard him muttering in a low voice as he went away. I think he was speaking to our young sister. What did he say?

FIRST BLIND MAN. She will not answer.

SECOND BLIND MAN. Will you no longer answer us?—Where are you, I say?—Speak.

THE VERY OLD BLIND WOMAN. You made him suffer too much; you have made him die. . . . You would not go on; you would sit down on the stones of the road to eat; you have grumbled all day . . . I heard him sigh . . . He lost heart. . . .

FIRST BLIND MAN. Was he ill? Did you know it?

THE VERY OLD BLIND MAN. We knew nothing. . . . We never saw him. . . . When did we ever know anything behind our poor dead eyes? . . . He never complained. Now it is too late . . . I have seen three die . . . but never in this way! . . . Now it is our turn.

FIRST BLIND MAN. It was not I that made him suffer.—I said nothing.

SECOND BLIND MAN. No more did I. We followed him without saying anything.

THIRD BLIND MAN. He died, going after water for the madwoman.

FIRST BLIND MAN. What are we going to do now? Where shall we go?

THIRD BLIND MAN. Where is the dog?

FIRST BLIND MAN. Here; he will not go away from the dead man.

THIRD BLIND MAN. Drag him away! Take him off, take him off!

FIRST BLIND MAN. He will not leave the dead man.

SECOND BLIND MAN. We cannot wait beside a dead man. We cannot die here in the dark.

THIRD BLIND MAN. Let us remain together; let us not scatter; let us hold one another by the hand; let us all sit on this stone. . . . Where are the others? . . . Come here, come, come!

THE VERY OLD BLIND MAN. Where are you?

THIRD BLIND MAN. Here; I am here. Are we all together?—Come nearer me.—Where are your hands?—It is very cold.

THE YOUNG BLIND GIRL. Oh, how cold your hands are!

THIRD BLIND MAN. What are you doing?

THE YOUNG BLIND GIRL. I was putting my hands on my eyes; I thought I was going to see all at once. . . .

FIRST BLIND MAN. Who is weeping so?

THE VERY OLD BLIND WOMAN. It is the madwoman sobbing.

FIRST BLIND MAN. And yet she does not know the truth.

THE VERY OLD BLIND MAN. I think we are going to die here.

THE VERY OLD BLIND WOMAN. Perhaps some one will come. . . .

THE VERY OLD BLIND MAN. Who else would come? . . .

THE VERY OLD BLIND WOMAN. I do not know.

FIRST BLIND MAN. I think the nuns will come out from the Asylum. . . .

THE VERY OLD BLIND WOMAN. They do not go out after dark.

THE YOUNG BLIND GIRL. They never go out.

SECOND BLIND MAN. I think the men at the great lighthouse will perceive us. . . .

THE VERY OLD BLIND MAN. They never come down from their tower.

THIRD BLIND MAN. They will see us, perhaps. . . .

THE VERY OLD BLIND WOMAN. They look always out to sea.

THIRD BLIND MAN. It is cold.

THE VERY OLD BLIND MAN. Listen to the dead leaves. I believe it is freezing.

THE YOUNG BLIND GIRL. Oh! How hard the earth is!

THIRD BLIND MAN. I hear on my left a sound I do not understand.

THE VERY OLD BLIND MAN. It is the sea moaning against the rocks.

THIRD BLIND MAN. I thought it was the women.

THE VERY OLD BLIND WOMAN. I hear the ice breaking under the surf.

FIRST BLIND MAN. Who is shivering so? It shakes everybody on the stone.

SECOND BLIND MAN. I can no longer open my hands.

THE VERY OLD BLIND MAN. I hear again a sound I do not understand.

FIRST BLIND MAN. Who is shivering so among us? It shakes the stone.

THE VERY OLD BLIND MAN. I think it is a woman.

THE VERY OLD BLIND WOMAN. I think the madwoman is shivering the hardest.

THIRD BLIND MAN. We do not hear her child.

THE VERY OLD BLIND WOMAN. I think he is still nursing.

THE VERY OLD BLIND MAN. He is the only one who can see where we are!

FIRST BLIND MAN. I hear the north wind.

SIXTH BLIND MAN. I think there are no

more stars; it is going to snow.

SECOND BLIND MAN. Then we are lost!

THIRD BLIND MAN. If any one sleeps, he must be aroused.

THE VERY OLD BLIND MAN. Nevertheless, I am sleepy.

A sudden gust sweeps the dead leaves around in a whirlwind.

THE YOUNG BLIND GIRL. Do you hear the dead leaves?—I believe some one is coming toward us.

SECOND BLIND MAN. It is the wind; listen!

THIRD BLIND MAN. No one will ever come.

THE VERY OLD BLIND MAN. The great cold will come. . . .

THE YOUNG BLIND GIRL. I hear walking far off.

FIRST BLIND MAN. I hear only the dead leaves.

THE YOUNG BLIND GIRL. I hear walking far away from us.

SECOND BLIND MAN. I hear only the north wind.

THE YOUNG BLIND GIRL. I tell you some one is coming toward us.

THE VERY OLD BLIND WOMAN. I hear a sound of very slow footsteps.

THE VERY OLD BLIND MAN. I believe the women are right.

It begins to snow in great flakes.

FIRST BLIND MAN. Oh, oh! What is it falling so cold upon my hands?

SIXTH BLIND MAN. It is snowing.

FIRST BLIND MAN. Let us press close to one another.

THE YOUNG BLIND GIRL. No, but listen! The sound of footsteps!

THE VERY OLD BLIND WOMAN. For God's sake, keep still an insant.

THE YOUNG BLIND GIRL. They come nearer! They come nearer! Listen!

Here the child of the BLIND MADWOMAN *begins suddenly to wail in the darkness.*

THE VERY OLD BLIND MAN. The child is crying.

THE YOUNG BLIND GIRL. He sees! He sees! He must see something if he cries. [*She seizes the child in her arms*

and advances in the direction from which the sound of footsteps seems to come. The other women follow her anxiously and surround her.] I am going to meet him.

THE VERY OLD BLIND MAN. Take care.

THE YOUNG BLIND GIRL. Oh, how he cries!—What is the matter with him?—Don't cry.—Don't be afraid; there is nothing to frighten you, we are here; we are all about you.—What do you see?—Don't be afraid at all.—Don't cry so!—What do you see?—Tell me, what do you see?

THE VERY OLD BLIND WOMAN. The sound of footsteps draws nearer and nearer: listen, listen!

THE VERY OLD BLIND MAN. I hear the rustling of a gown against the dead leaves.

SIXTH BLIND MAN. Is it a woman?

THE VERY OLD BLIND MAN. Is it a noise of footsteps?

FIRST BLIND MAN. Can it be perhaps the sea in the dead leaves?

THE YOUNG BLIND GIRL. No, no! They are footsteps, they are footsteps, they are footsteps!

THE VERY OLD BLIND WOMAN. We shall know soon. Listen to the dead leaves.

THE YOUNG BLIND GIRL. I hear them, I hear them almost beside us; listen, listen!—What do you see? What do you see?

THE VERY OLD BLIND WOMAN. Which way is he looking?

THE YOUNG BLIND GIRL. He keeps following the sound of the steps.—Look, look! When I turn him away, he turns back to see. . . . He sees, he sees, he sees!—He must see something strange!

THE VERY OLD BLIND WOMAN. [*Stepping forward.*] Lift him above us, so that he may see better.

THE YOUNG BLIND GIRL. Stand back, stand back. [*She raises the child above the group of blind folk.*]—The footsteps have stopped amongst us.

THE VERY OLD BLIND WOMAN. They are

here! They are in the midst of us! . . .

THE YOUNG BLIND GIRL. Who are you?

Silence.

THE VERY OLD BLIND WOMAN. Have pity on us!

Silence.—The child weeps more desperately.

King Ubu

Alfred Jarry

It would be convenient for students of dramatic literature if the twentieth century had begun in 1900, as the calendar suggests. For many, however, the nineteenth century did not end until the last of the great naturalistic playwrights ceased writing, somewhere in the 1890s or early in the 1900s. For some, the nineteenth century has never ended. But for most people interested in avant-garde drama, the twentieth century began on December 11, 1896, when Alfred Jarry's *King Ubu* was produced in Paris. The riots in the theater were unlike any seen since the production of Victor Hugo's *Hernani* in 1830. It was clear even to those in the audience who, like William Butler Yeats, did not understand much French, that an event of revolutionary importance was taking place.

Alfred Henri Jarry's life was as strange as his play. He was born on September 8, 1873, in Laval in northwestern France. His mother left her husband and took the six-year-old boy and his older sister to live with their maternal grandparents on the northern seacoast, and it was there that Jarry received most of his schooling. He entered the *lycée* in Rennes in 1888, where he joined two of his schoolmates, the Morin brothers, in writing a skit satirizing their physics teacher, Professor Hébert. This skit was expanded and performed in a number of versions during the three years that Jarry remained in Rennes; as a marionette play it was produced in the attic of the Morin home, and later in the Jarry home, to the fiendish delight of the students involved. Professor Hébert, known in those skits as Père Heb or Hébé, was evidently an older man of less than electric presence in the classroom, and the boys delighted in tormenting him with pranks in school and satire outside it. Père Hébé was the direct ancestor of Father Ubu.

Jarry moved to Paris in 1891 to continue his schooling, but the Bohemian life of the city soon shifted his interests elsewhere. Regarded even then as eccentric in his behavior, he became something of a court jester to the Symbolists and to other avant-gardists whose artistic work was the rage of Paris. He began to write, and occasionally to publish, taking an interest in poetry and criticism as well as in drama. Some early Ubu material appeared in 1893, and *King Ubu* was published in its present form in June of 1896. At the same time, Jarry became an administrative assistant to Lugné-Poë, director of the Théatre de l'Oeuvre, and persuaded him to produce *King Ubu* late in that same year. The violent reaction surrounding the two scheduled performances merely whetted Jarry's appetite for notoriety, and, following the example of such luminaries as Oscar Wilde, he began to make his life into his art. Adopting the boorish behavior of Ubu as his public pose, always treading the fine line between comicality and outright offensiveness, Jarry lived in a half-world of drugs and alcohol, startling his peers and scandalizing respectable society with his outlandish dress and Bohemian life-style, and continuing to publish original and challenging works. Two further plays about Ubu, *Ubu Cuckolded* (not published until 1944) and *Ubu Enchained* (1900) failed to attract the attention enjoyed by *King Ubu*, and Jarry's novels, poems, and theoretical writings never earned him enough money to support his alcoholism. Perhaps the most interesting of these latter works was an essay-novel on "pataphysics," Jarry's invented science which pervades most of his work and which helps to interpret Ubu. "Pataphysics," Jarry explained, "is the science of the realm beyond metaphysics. . . . It will study the laws which govern exceptions and will explain the universe supplementary to this one. . . . Pataphysics is the science of imaginary solutions." Jarry died on November 1, 1907, of meningeal tuberculosis, complicated by acute alcoholism and malnutrition.

The excitement surrounding the opening night of *King Ubu* can be traced in the first place to its scatalogical language. The first word spoken from the stage was "merdre," which Jarry created by inserting an extra letter in "merde" (shit). Such language had never before been heard on the French stage, and fifteen minutes of shouting and uproar followed it. The performance was repeatedly interrupted each time this and other offensive words occurred, and Jarry took great, if perverse, pleasure in the pandemonium he had created. On the surface, *King Ubu* can be seen as little more than the sophomoric and obscene nonsense of the schoolboys who created its earliest version; its plot is an obvious parody of *Macbeth*, with elements of *Hamlet* and *King Lear* thrown in, not unlike what might be created by any college fraternity on Skit Night. As Jarry's fertile imagination worked over this material, however, its patent nonsense began to express his inner consciousness in a manner not unlike that of the Symbolists with whom he associated daily. Indeed, many critics include Jarry among the Symbolist writers, although he in fact broke altogether new ground. The absurdity of Ubu's behavior began to express the absurdity of the human dilemma just as the science of pataphysics begins to make a kind of perverse sense, and audience members found themselves facing psychological and ontological truths that were discomforting and even frightening. As one first-night critic noted, "In spite of the idiotic action and mediocre structure, a new type has emerged, created by an extravagant and brutal imagination, more a child's than a man's. Père Ubu exists. . . . He will become a popular legend of base instincts, rapacious and violent." The monster who seemed almost beyond human comprehension in 1896, has reappeared again and again in real life in the twentieth century, and a great deal of important twentieth-century playwriting has been devoted to an attempt to express this absurdity.

A careful reading of *King Ubu* does not dispel the perception that it is nonsense, but one must bear in mind that some nonsense is inspired nonsense, which can communicate with a spectator through his subconscious even while lulling his reason with foolery. It is the character of Ubu himself which, more than any other single factor, elevates *King Ubu* to dramatic art of a significant order, for Ubu is the living embodiment of all that is crass, offensive, and boorish in human nature. Even Falstaff, who must be counted as an ancestor of Ubu's, is more a lovable rogue than an offensive pig; it was a major departure from theatrical tradition to portray frankly on the stage all of the most unlovely characteristics of human nature, and yet to do so in an exuberant spirit that left the spectator wavering between outrage and laughter. The traditional standards of good taste are abandoned utterly ("Screw good taste," Jarry is quoted as saying), and the baser aspects of Ubu's nature are frankly paraded both to arouse raucous laughter and to characterize him full

Unpleasant though many of these qualities may be, they are undeniably human; Ubu lives precisely because he embodies the qualities that the spectator knows are present in himself and that "good taste" has traditionally prevented acknowledging, sometimes even to one's self. Changing social mores in the twentieth century have permitted more open examination of these darker sides of human nature, and new levels of bestiality by national leaders have verified what these darker traits are capable of when unfortunately linked with power. The perceptive opening night critic who noted that "Ubu exists," was, in fact, foreshadowing the history of the twentieth century.

What is less evident from a reading of the script is Jarry's commitment to a new stagecraft for producing his new play. As an active associate in Lugné-Poë's company, Jarry was able to involve himself intimately in the production, and what he wrought was as radical a departure from traditional stagecraft as was the script from traditional playwriting. Ubu was to wear a mask (though ultimately the actor playing the role would not do so), and horses were suggested by hanging a cardboard horse's head around an actor's neck. A single set was used, consisting chiefly of a painted backdrop in a childlike style that jumbled together indoors and outdoors, apple trees and painted furniture, snow falling and a skeleton. (This drop was painted by Jarry himself, as well as Bonnard, Vuillard, Toulouse-Lautrec, and Sérusier.) An actor in evening dress tripped across the stage on the points of his toes between scenes to hang a signboard announcing the location of the next scene. The vocal style, especially of Ubu, was to be flat, staccato and conventionalized, and the costumes outlandish. In short, the marionette theater that had long fascinated Jarry was to be used as a point of departure for human production. Perhaps the most vivid image remaining in the minds of most of the spectators at the opening performance was that of Ubu leaping about the stage waving a toilet brush in place of a scepter.

Powerful though the shock of this first production of *King Ubu* was in 1896, its impact was limited to those activists of the Paris avant-garde who could crowd into two performances. Although Jarry and his creation were notorious in Paris for a decade thereafter, further attempts at production of *King Ubu* and Jarry's other plays came to little. The Paris art world was in search of new titillations and new wonders, and Jarry's eccentricities quickly palled. After World War I, however, the artists such as Cocteau and Artaud who were to lead the significant movements of the 1920s, paid glowing tribute to Jarry as their pioneer, and the absurdists whose post–World War II drama became one of the major theatrical achievements of the century acknowledged a vast and profound debt to Jarry. Indeed, in 1949, Ionesco and a group of other artists founded the College of Pataphysics with the tongue-in-cheek purpose of furthering Jarry's science and the serious function of publishing Jarry's work and that of others writing in his mode. Twentieth-century drama, which had begun on December 11, 1896, was finally paying appropriate tribute to its founder.

King Ubu
(Ubu Roi)

Translated by Michael Benedikt and George E. Wellwarth

Characters and Costumes

Father Ubu: Casual gray suit, a cane always stuffed in his right-hand pocket, bowler hat. A crown over his hat at the beginning of Act II, Scene 2. Bareheaded at the beginning of Act II, Scene 6. Act III, Scene 2, crown and white hood, flaring to a royal cape. Act III, Scene 4, cloak, cap pulled down over his ears; same outfit, but with bare head in Scene 7. Scene 8, hood, helmet, a sword stuck in his belt, a hook, chisels, a knife, a cane still in his right-hand pocket. A bottle bounces at his side. Act IV, Scene 5, cloak and cap but without above weapons or stick. In the sailing scene a small suitcase is in Father Ubu's hand.

Mother Ubu: Concierge's clothes or a toiletries saleswoman's ensemble. Pink bonnet or a hat with flowers and feathers and a veil. An apron in the feasting scene. Royal cloak at the opening of Act II, Scene 6.

Captain Bordure: Hungarian musician's costume, very close-fitting, red. Big mantle, large sword, crenelated boots, feathery hat.

King Wenceslas: Royal mantle and the crown Ubu wears after murdering him.

Queen Rosemonde: The mantle and crown Mother Ubu later wears.

Boleslas, Ladislas (sons of King Wenceslas and Queen Rosemonde): Gray Polish costumes, heavily frogged; short pants.

Bougrelas (the youngest son): Dressed as a child in a little skirt and bonnet.

General Lascy: Polish costume, with an admiral's hat with white plumes, and a sword.

Stanislas Leczinsky: Polish costume. White beard.

John Sobieski, Nicholas Rensky: Polish costume.

The Czar, Emperor Alexis: Black clothing, enormous yellow sword, dagger, numerous military decorations, big boots. Huge frill at the throat. Hat in the form of a black cone.

The Palotins (Giron, Pile, Cotice): Long beards, fur-trimmed greatcoats, shitr-colored; or red or green if necessary; tights beneath.

Crowd: Polish costume.

Michael Federovitch: Same. Fur hat.

Nobles: Polish costume, with cloaks edged with fur or embroidery.

Advisers, Financiers: Swathed in black, with astrologers' hats, eyeglasses, pointed noses.

Phynancial Flunkies: The Palotins.

Peasants: Polish costume.

The Polish Army: In gray, with frogging and fur trimmings: three men with rifles.

The Russian Army: Two horsemen: uniform like that of the Poles, but green, with fur headgear. They carry cardboard horses' heads.

A *Russian Footsoldier:* In green, with headgear.
Mother Ubu's Guards: Polish costume, with halberds.
A Captain: General Lascy.
The Bear: Bordure in bearskin.
The Phynancial Horse: Large wooden rocking horse on casters, or else cardboard horse's head, as required.
The Crew: Two men in sailor suits, in blue, collars turned down, and so on.
The Captain of the Ship: In a French naval officer's uniform.
Jailer
Messenger: [*Jarry did not include suggestions for the costuming of these two characters in these notes, which were published from manuscript by the Collège de 'Pataphysique in 1951.*]

COMPOSITION OF THE ORCHESTRA

Oboes
Pipes
Blutwurst
Large Bass
Flageolets   Transverse Flutes
Flute
Little Bassoon   Big Bassoon
Triple Bassoon   Little Black Cornets
Shrill White Cornets
Horns   Sackbuts   Trombones
Green Hunting Horns   Reeds
Bagpipes
Bombardons   Timbals
Drum   Bass Drum
Grand Organs

Act 1

Scene 1

FATHER UBU *and* MOTHER UBU *onstage.*
FATHER UBU. Shitr!
MOTHER UBU. Well, that's a fine way to talk, Father Ubu. What a pigheaded ass you are!

FATHER UBU. I don't know what keeps me from bouncing your head off the wall, Mother Ubu!
MOTHER UBU. It's not *my* head you ought to be cracking, Father Ubu.
FATHER UBU. By my green candle, I don't know what you're talking about.
MOTHER UBU. What's this, Father Ubu, you mean to tell me you're satisfied with the way things are?
FATHER UBU. By my green candle, shitr, madam, certainly I'm satisfied with the way things are. After all, aren't I Captain of the Dragoons, confidential adviser to King Wenceslas, decorated with the order of the Red Eagle of Poland, and ex-King of Aragon—what more do you want?
MOTHER UBU. What's this! After having been King of Aragon you're satisfied with leading fifty-odd flunkies armed with cabbage-cutters to parades? When you could just as well have the crown of Poland replace the crown of Aragon on your big fat nut?
FATHER UBU. Ah! Mother Ubu I don't know what you're talking about.
MOTHER UBU. You're so stupid!
FATHER UBU. By my green candle, King Wenceslas is still very much alive; and even if he does die he's still got hordes of children, hasn't he?
MOTHER UBU. What's stopping you from chopping up his whole family and putting yourself in their place?
FATHER UBU. Ah! Mother Ubu, you're doing me an injustice, and I'll stick you in your stewpot in a minute.
MOTHER UBU. Ha! Poor wretch, if I were stuck in the pot who'd sew up the seat of your pants?
FATHER UBU. Oh, really! And what of it? Don't I have an ass like everyone else?
MOTHER UBU. If I were you, I'd want to install that ass on a throne. You could get any amount of money, eat sausages all the time, and roll around the streets in a carriage.
FATHER UBU. If I were king I'd have

them build me a big helmet just like the one I had in Aragon which those Spanish swine had the nerve to steal from me.

MOTHER UBU. You could also get yourself an umbrella and a big cape which would reach to your heels.

FATHER UBU. Ah! That does it! I succumb to temptation. That crock of shitr, that shitr of crock, if I ever run into him in a dark alley, I'll give him a bad fifteen minutes.

MOTHER UBU. Ah! Fine, Father Ubu, at last you're acting like a real man.

FATHER UBU. Oh, no! Me, the Captain of the Dragoons, slaughter the King of Poland! Better far to die!

MOTHER UBU. [*Aside.*] Oh, shitr! [*Aloud.*] So, then, you want to stay as poor as a churchmouse, Father Ubu?

FATHER UBU. Zounds, by my green candle, I'd rather be as poor as a starving, good rat than as rich as a wicked, fat cat.

MOTHER UBU. And the helmet? And the umbrella? And the big cape?

FATHER UBU. And what about them, Mother Ubu?

He leaves, slamming the door.

MOTHER UBU. [*Alone.*] Crap, shitr, it's hard to get him started, but, crap, shitr, I think I've stirred him up. With the help of God and of myself, perhaps in eight days I'll be Queen of Poland.

Scene 2

A room in FATHER UBU's *house, with a splendidly laid table.* FATHER UBU *and* MOTHER UBU *onstage.*

MOTHER UBU. So! Our guests are very late.

FATHER UBU. Yes, by my green candle, I'm dying of hunger. Mother Ubu, you're really ugly today. Is it because company's coming?

MOTHER UBU. [*Shrugging her shoulders.*] Shitr!

FATHER UBU. [*Grabbing a roast chicken.*] Gad, I'm hungry; I'm going to have a

piece of this bird. It's a chicken, I think. Not bad at all.

MOTHER UBU. What are you doing, you swine? What will be left for our guests?

FATHER UBU. There will be plenty left for them. I won't touch another thing. Mother Ubu, go to the window and see if our guests are coming.

MOTHER UBU. [*Going.*] I don't see anything.

Meanwhile, FATHER UBU *takes a piece of veal.*

Ah, here come Captain Bordure and his boys. What are you eating now, Father Ubu?

FATHER UBU. Nothing, a little veal.

MOTHER UBU. Oh! The veal! The veal! The ox! He's eaten the veal! Help, help!

FATHER UBU. By my green candle, I'll scratch your eyes out.

The door opens.

Scene 3

Enter CAPTAIN BORDURE *and his followers.*

MOTHER UBU. Good day, gentlemen; we've been anxiously awaiting you. Sit down.

CAPTAIN BORDURE. Good day, madam. Where's Father Ubu?

FATHER UBU. Here I am, here I am! Good lord, by my green candle, I'm fat enough, aren't I?

CAPTAIN BORDURE. Good day, Father Ubu. Sit down, boys.

They all sit.

FATHER UBU. Oof, a little more, and I'd have bust my chair.

CAPTAIN BORDURE. Well, Mother Ubu! What have you got that's good today?

MOTHER UBU. Here's the menu.

FATHER UBU. Oh! That interests me.

MOTHER UBU. Polish soup, roast ram, veal, chicken, chopped dog's liver, turkey's ass, charlotte russe . . .

FATHER UBU. Hey, that's plenty, I should think. You mean there's more?

MOTHER UBU. [*Continuing.*] Frozen pudding, salad, fruits, dessert, boiled beef, Jerusalem artichokes, cauliflower à la shitr.

FATHER UBU. Hey! Do you think I'm the Emperor of China, to give all that away?

MOTHER UBU. Don't listen to him, he's feeble-minded.

FATHER UBU. Ah! I'll sharpen my teeth on your shanks.

MOTHER UBU. Try this instead, Father Ubu. Here's the Polish soup.

FATHER UBU. Crap, is that lousy!

CAPTAIN BORDURE. Hmm—it isn't very good, at that.

MOTHER UBU. What do you want, you bunch of crooks!

FATHER UBU. [Striking his forehead.] Wait, I've got an idea. I'll be right back.

He leaves.

MOTHER UBU. Let's try the veal now, gentlemen.

CAPTAIN BORDURE. It's very good—I'm through.

MOTHER UBU. To the turkey's ass, next.

CAPTAIN BORDURE. Delicious, delicious! Long live Mother Ubu!

ALL. Long live Mother Ubu!

FATHER UBU. [Returning.] And you will soon be shouting long live Father Ubu. [He has a toilet brush in his hand, and he throws it on the festive board.]

MOTHER UBU. Miserable creature, what are you up to now?

FATHER UBU. Try a little.

Several try it, and fall, poisoned.

Mother Ubu, pass me the roast ram chops, so that I can serve them.

MOTHER UBU. Here they are.

FATHER UBU. Everyone out! Captain Bordure, I want to talk to you.

THE OTHERS. But we haven't eaten yet.

FATHER UBU. What's that, you haven't eaten yet? Out, out, everyone out! Stay here, Bordure.

Nobody moves.

You haven't gone yet? By my green candle, I'll give you your ram chops. [He begins to throw them.]

ALL. Oh! Ouch! Help! Woe! Help! Misery! I'm dead!

FATHER UBU. Shitr, shitr, shitr! Outside! I want my way!

ALL. Everyone for himself! Miserable Father Ubu! Traitor! Meanie!

FATHER UBU. Ah! They've gone. I can breathe again—but I've had a rotten dinner. Come on, Bordure.

They go out with MOTHER UBU.

Scene 4

FATHER UBU, MOTHER UBU, and CAPTAIN BORDURE onstage.

FATHER UBU. Well, now, Captain, have you had a good dinner?

CAPTAIN BORDURE. Very good, sir, except for the shitr.

FATHER UBU. Oh, come now, the shitr wasn't bad at all.

MOTHER UBU. Chacun à son goût.

FATHER UBU. Captain Bordure, I've decided to make you Duke of Lithuania.

CAPTAIN BORDURE. Why, I thought you were miserably poor, Father Ubu.

FATHER UBU. If you choose, I'll be King of Poland in a few days.

CAPTAIN BORDURE. You're going to kill Wenceslas?

FATHER UBU. He's not so stupid, the idiot; he's guessed it.

CAPTAIN BORDURE. If it's a question of killing Wenceslas, I'm for it. I'm his mortal enemy, and I can answer for my men.

FATHER UBU. [Throwing his arms around him.] Oh! Oh! How I love you, Bordure.

CAPTAIN BORDURE. Ugh, you stink, Father Ubu. Don't you ever wash?

FATHER UBU. Rarely.

MOTHER UBU. Never!

FATHER UBU. I'll stamp on your toes.

MOTHER UBU. Big shitr!

FATHER UBU. All right, Bordure, that's all for now; but, by my green candle, I swear on Mother Ubu to make you Duke of Lithuania.

MOTHER UBU. But. . . .

FATHER UBU. Be quiet, my sweet

child. . . .
They go out.

Scene 5

FATHER UBU, MOTHER UBU, *and a messenger onstage.*

FATHER UBU. Sir, what do you want? Beat it, you're boring me.

THE MESSENGER. Sir, the king summons you.

He leaves.

FATHER UBU. Oh, shitr! Great Jumping Jupiter, by my green candle, I've been discovered; they'll cut my head off, alas! Alas!

MOTHER UBU. What a spineless clod! And just when time's getting short.

FATHER UBU. Oh, I've got an idea: I'll say that it was Mother Ubu and Bordure.

MOTHER UBU. You fat Ubu, if you do that. . . .

FATHER UBU. I'm off right now.

He leaves.

MOTHER UBU. [*Running after him.*] Oh, Father Ubu, Father Ubu, I'll give you some sausage!

She leaves.

FATHER UBU. [*From the wings.*] Oh, shitr! You're a prize sausage yourself.

Scene 6

The palace. Onstage are KING WENCESLAS, *surrounded by his officers;* CAPTAIN BORDURE; *the king's sons,* BOLESLAS, LADISLAS, *and* BOUGRELAS; *and* FATHER UBU

FATHER UBU. [*Entering.*] Oh! You know, it wasn't me, it was Mother Ubu and Bordure.

KING WENCESLAS. What's the matter with you, Father Ubu?

CAPTAIN BORDURE. He's drunk.

KING WENCESLAS. So was I, this morning.

FATHER UBU. Yes, I'm potted, because I've drunk too much French wine.

KING WENCESLAS. Father Ubu, I desire

to recompense your numerous services as Captain of the Dragoons, and I'm going to make you Count of Sandomir today.

FATHER UBU. Oh, Mr. Wenceslas, I don't know how to thank you.

KING WENCESLAS. Don't thank me, Father Ubu, and don't forget to appear tomorrow morning at the big parade.

FATHER UBU. I'll be there, but be good enough to accept this toy whistle. [*He presents the king with a toy whistle.*]

KING WENCESLAS. What can I do with a toy whistle at my age? I'll give it to Bougrelas.

BOUGRELAS. What an idiot Father Ubu is!

FATHER UBU. And now I'll scram. [*He falls as he turns around.*] Oh! Ouch! Help! By my green candle, I've split my gut and bruised my butt!

KING WENCESLAS. [*Helping him up.*] Did you hurt yourself, Father Ubu?

FATHER UBU. Yes, I certainly did, and I'll probably die soon. What will become of Mother Ubu?

KING WENCESLAS. We shall provide for her upkeep.

FATHER UBU. Your kindness is unparalleled. [*He leaves.*] But you'll be slaughtered just the same, King Wenceslas.

Scene 7

FATHER UBU's *house. On stage are* GIRON, PILE, COTICE, FATHER UBU, MOTHER UBU, CONSPIRATORS, SOLDIERS, *and* CAPTAIN BORDURE.

FATHER UBU. Well, my good friends, it's about time we discussed the plan of the conspiracy. Let each one give his advice. First of all, I'll give mine, if you'll permit me.

CAPTAIN BORDURE. Speak, Father Ubu.

FATHER UBU. Very well, my friends, I'm in favor of simply poisoning the king by slipping a little arsenic in his lunch. At the first nibble he'll drop dead, and then I'll be king.

ALL. How base!

FATHER UBU. What's that? You don't like my suggestion? Let Bordure give his.

CAPTAIN BORDURE. I'm of the opinion that we should give him one good stroke of the sword and slice him in two, lengthwise.

ALL. Hooray! How noble and valiant.

FATHER UBU. And what if he kicks you? I remember now that he always puts on iron shoes, which hurt a great deal, for parades. If I had any sense I'd go off and denounce you for dragging me into this dirty mess, and I think he'd give me plenty of money.

MOTHER UBU. Oh! The traitor, the coward, the villain, and sneak.

ALL. Down with Father Ubu!

FATHER UBU. Gentlemen, keep calm, or I'll get mad. In any case, I agree to stick out my neck for you. Bordure, I put you in charge of slicing the king in half.

CAPTAIN BORDURE. Wouldn't it be better to throw ourselves on the king all together, screaming and yelling? That way we might win the troops to our side.

FATHER UBU. All right, then. I'll attempt to tread on his toes; he'll protest, and then I'll say, SHITR, and at this signal you'll all throw yourselves on him.

MOTHER UBU. Yes, and as soon as he's dead you'll take his scepter and crown.

CAPTAIN BORDURE. And I'll pursue the royal family with my men.

FATHER UBU. Yes, and be extra sure that you catch young Bougrelas. [*They go out. Running after them and bringing them back.*] Gentlemen, we have forgotten an indispensable ceremony: we must swear to fight bravely.

CAPTAIN BORDURE. How are we going to do that? We don't have a priest.

FATHER UBU. Mother Ubu will take his place.

ALL: Very well, so be it.

FATHER UBU. Then you really swear to

kill the king?

ALL. Yes, we swear it. Long live Father Ubu!

Act 2

Scene 1

The palace. Onstage are KING WENCESLAS, QUEEN ROSEMONDE, BOLESLAS, LADISLAS, *and* BOUGRELAS.

KING WENCESLAS. Mr. Bougrelas, you were very impertinent this morning with Mr. Ubu, knight of my orders and Count of Sandomir. That's why I'm forbidding you to appear at my parade.

QUEEN ROSEMONDE. But, Wenceslas, you need your whole family around you to protect you.

KING WENCESLAS. Madam, I never retract my commands. You weary me with your chatter.

BOUGRELAS. It shall be as you desire, my father.

QUEEN ROSEMONDE. Sire, have you definitely decided to attend this parade?

KING WENCESLAS. Why shouldn't I, madam?

QUEEN ROSEMONDE. For the last time, didn't I tell you that I dreamed that I saw you being knocked down by a mob of his men and thrown into the Vistula, and an eagle just like the one in the arms of Poland placing the crown on his head?

KING WENCESLAS. On whose?

QUEEN ROSEMONDE. Oh Father Ubu's.

KING WENCELAS. What nonsense! Count de Ubu is a very fine gentleman who would let himself be torn apart by horses in my service.

QUEEN ROSEMONDE *and* BOUGRELAS. What a delusion!

KING WENCESLAS. Be quiet, you little ape. And as for you, madam, just to show you how little I fear Mr. Ubu,

I'll go to the parade just as I am, without sword or armor.

QUEEN ROSEMONDE. Fatal imprudence! I shall never see you alive again.

KING WENCESLAS. Come along, Ladislas, come along, Boleslas.

They go out. QUEEN ROSEMONDE *and* BOUGRELAS *go to the window.*

QUEEN ROSEMONDE *and* BOUGRELAS. May God and holy Saint Nicholas protect you!

QUEEN ROSEMONDE. Bougrelas, come to the chapel with me to pray for your father and your brothers.

Scene 2

The parade grounds. Onstage are the Polish army, KING WENCESLAS, BOLESLAS, LADISLAS, FATHER UBU, CAPTAIN BORDURE *and his men,* GIRON, PILE, *and* COTICE.

KING WENCESLAS. Noble Father Ubu, accompany me with your companions while I inspect the troops.

FATHER UBU. [*To his men.*] On your toes, boys. [*To the king.*] Coming, sir, coming.

UBU'*s men surround the king.*

KING WENCESLAS. Ah! Here is the Dantzick Horseguard Regiment. Aren't they magnificent!

FATHER UBU. You really think so? They look rotten to me. Look at this one. [*To the soldier.*] When did you last shave, varlet?

KING WENCESLAS. But this soldier is absolutely impeccable. What's the matter with you, Father Ubu?

FATHER UBU. Take that! [*He stamps on his foot.*]

KING WENCESLAS. Wretch!

FATHER UBU. Shitr! Come on, men!

CAPTAIN BORDURE. Hooray! Charge!

They all hit the king; a Palotin explodes.

KING WENCESLAS. Oh! Help! Holy Mother, I'm dead.

BOLESLAS. [*To* LADISLAS.] What's going on? Let's draw.

FATHER UBU. Ah, I've got the crown! To the others, now.

CAPTAIN BORDURE. After the traitors!

The princes flee, pursued by all.

Scene 3

QUEEN ROSEMOND *and* BOUGRELAS *onstage.*

QUEEN ROSEMONDE. At last I can begin to relax.

BOUGRELAS. You've no reason to be afraid.

A frightful din is heard from outside.

Oh! What's this I see? My two brothers pursued by Father Ubu and his men.

QUEEN ROSEMONDE. Oh, my God! Holy Mother, they're losing, they're losing ground!

BOUGRELAS. The whole army is following Father Ubu. I don't see the king. Horror! Help!

QUEEN ROSEMONDE. There's Boleslas, dead! He's been shot.

BOUGRELAS. Hey! Defend yourself! hooray, Ladislas!

QUEEN ROSEMONDE. Oh! He's surrounded.

BOUGRELAS. He's finished. Bordure's just sliced him in half like a sausage.

QUEEN ROSEMONDE. Alas! Those madmen have broken into the palace; they're coming up the stairs.

The din grows louder.

QUEEN ROSEMONDE *and* BOUGRELAS. [*On their knees.*] Oh, God, defend us!

BOUGRELAS. Oh! That Father Ubu! The swine, the wretch, if I could get my hands on him. . . .

Scene 4

The same. The door is smashed down. FATHER UBU *and his rabble break through.*

FATHER UBU. So, Bougrelas, what's that you want to do to me?

BOUGRELAS. Great God! I'll defend my mother to the death! The first man to make a move dies.

FATHER UBU. Oh! Bordure, I'm scared. Let me out of here.

A SOLDIER. [*Advancing.*] Give yourself

up, Bougrelas!

BOUGRELAS. Here, scum, take that! [*He splits his skull.*]

QUEEN ROSEMONDE. Hold your ground, Bougrelas; hold your ground!

SEVERAL. [*Advancing.*] Bougrelas, we promise to let you go.

BOUGRELAS. Good-for-nothings, sots, turncoats! [*He swings his sword and kills them all.*]

FATHER UBU. I'll win out in the end!

BOUGRELAS. Mother, escape by the secret staircase.

QUEEN ROSEMONDE. And what about you, my son? What about you?

BOUGRELAS. I'll follow you.

FATHER UBU. Try to catch the queen. Oh, there she goes. As for you, you little. . . . [*He approaches* BOUGRELAS.]

BOUGRELAS. Great God! Here is my vengeance! [*With a terrible blow of his sword he rips open* FATHER UBU's *paunch-protector.*] Mother, I'm coming!

He disappears down the secret staircase.

Scene 5

A cave in the mountains. Young BOUGRELAS *enters, followed by* QUEEN ROSEMONDE.

BOUGRELAS. We'll be safe here.

QUEEN ROSEMONDE. Yes, I think so. Bougrelas, help me! [*She falls to the snow.*]

BOUGRELAS. What's the matter, Mother?

QUEEN ROSEMONDE. Believe me, I'm very sick, Bougrelas. I don't have more than two hours to live.

BOUGRELAS. What do you mean? Has the cold got you?

QUEEN ROSEMONDE. How can I bear up against so many blows? The king massacred, our family destroyed, and you, the representative of the most noble race that has ever worn a sword, forced to flee into the mountains like a common brigand.

BOUGRELAS. And by whom, O Lord, by whom? A vulgar fellow like Father Ubu, an adventurer coming from no one knows where, a vile blaggard, a shameless vagabond! And when I think that my father decorated him and made him a count and that the next day this low-bred dog had the nerve to raise his hand against him.

QUEEN ROSEMONDE. Oh, Bougrelas! When I remember how happy we were before this Father Ubu came! But now, alas! All is changed!

BOUGRELAS. What can we do? Let us wait in hope and never renounce our rights.

QUEEN ROSEMONDE. May your wish be granted, my dear child, but as for me, I shall never see that happy day.

BOUGRELAS. What's the matter with you? Ah, she pales, she falls. Help me! But I'm in a desert! Oh, my God! Her heart is stilled forever. She is dead? Can it be? Another victim for Father Ubu! [*He hides his face in his hands, and weeps.*] Oh, my God! How sad it is to have such a terrible vengeance to fulfill! And I'm only fourteen years old! [*He falls down in the throes of a most extravagant despair. Meanwhile, the souls of* WENCESLAS, BOLESLAS, LADISLAS, *and of* QUEEN ROSEMONDE *enter the cave. Their ancestors, accompanying them, fill up the cave. The oldest goes to* BOUGRELAS *and gently awakes him.*] Ah! What's this I see? My whole family, all my ancestors . . . how can this be?

THE SHADE. Know, Bougrelas, that during my life I was the Lord Mathias of Königsberg, the first king and founder of our house. I entrust our vengeance to your hands. [*He gives him a large sword.*] And may this sword which I have given you never rest until it has brought about the death of the usurper.

All vanish, and BOUGRELAS *remains alone, in an attitude of ecstasy.*

Scene 6

The palace. Onstage are FATHER UBU, MOTHER UBU *and* CAPTAIN BORDURE.

FATHER UBU. No! Never! I don't want to! Do you want me to ruin myself for these buffroons?

CAPTAIN BORDURE. But after all, Father Ubu, don't you see that the people are waiting for the gifts to celebrate your joyous coronation?

MOTHER UBU. If you don't give out meat and gold, you'll be overthrown in two hours.

FATHER UBU. Meat, yes! Gold, no! Slaughter the three oldest horses—that'll be good enough for those apes.

MOTHER UBU. Ape, yourself! How did I ever get stuck with an animal like you?

FATHER UBU. Once and for all, I'm trying to get rich; I'm not going to let go of a cent.

MOTHER UBU. But we've got the whole Polish treasury at our disposal.

CAPTAIN BORDURE. Yes, I happen to know that there's an enormous treasure in the royal chapel; we'll distribute it.

FATHER UBU. Just you dare, you wretch!

CAPTAIN BORDURE. But, Father Ubu, if you don't distribute money to the people, they'll refuse to pay the taxes.

FATHER UBU. Is that a fact?

MOTHER UBU. Yes, of course!

FATHER UBU. Oh, well, in that case I agree to everything. Withdraw three millions, roast a hundred and fifty cattle and sheep—especially since I'll have some myself!

They go out.

Scene 7

The palace courtyard is full of people, including FATHER UBU *crowned,* MOTHER UBU, CAPTAIN BORDURE, *and flunkies carrying meat.*

PEOPLE. There's the king! Long live the king! Hooray!

FATHER UBU. [*Throwing gold.*] Here, that's for you. It doesn't make me very happy to give you any money;

it's Mother Ubu who wanted me to. At least promise me you'll really pay the taxes.

ALL. Yes! Yes!

CAPTAIN BORDURE. Look how they're fighting over that gold, Mother Ubu. What a battle!

MOTHER UBU. It's really awful. Ugh! There's one just had his skull split open.

FATHER UBU. What a beautiful sight! Bring on more gold.

CAPTAIN BORDURE. How about making them race for it?

FATHER UBU. Good idea! [*To the people.*] My friends, take a look at this chest of gold. It contains three hundred thousand Polish coins, of the purest gold, guaranteed genuine. Let those who wish to compete for it assemble at the end of the courtyard. The race will begin when I wave my handkerchief, and the first one to get here wins the chest. As for those who don't win, they will share this other chest as a consolation prize.

ALL. Yes! Long live Father Ubu! What a king! We never had anything like this in the days of Wenceslas.

FATHER UBU. [*To* MOTHER UBU, *with joy.*] Listen to them!

All the people line up at the end of the courtyard.

One, two, three! Ready!

ALL. Yes! Yes!

FATHER UBU. Set! Go!

They start, falling all over one another. Cries and tumult.

CAPTAIN BORDURE. They're coming! They're coming!

FATHER UBU. Look! The leader's losing ground.

MOTHER UBU. No, he's going ahead again.

CAPTAIN BORDURE. He's losing, he's losing! He's lost! The other one won.

ALL. Long live Michael Federovitch! Long live Michael Federovitch!

MICHAEL FEDEROVITCH. Sire, I don't know how to thank your Majesty. . . .

FATHER UBU. Think nothing of it, my

dear friend. Take your money home with you, Michael; and you others, share the rest—each take a piece until they're all gone.

ALL. Long live Michael Federovitch! Long live Father Ubu!

FATHER UBU. And you, my friends, come and eat! I open the gates of the palace to you—may you do honor to my table!

PEOPLE. Let's go in, let's go in! Long live Father Ubu! He's the noblest monarch of them all!

They go into the palace. The noise of the orgy is audible throughout the night. The curtain falls.

Act 3

Scene 1

The palace. Onstage are FATHER UBU, *and* MOTHER UBU.

FATHER UBU. By my green candle, here I am king of this country, I've already got a fine case of indigestion, and they're going to bring me my big helmet.

MOTHER UBU. What's it made out of, Father Ubu? Even if we are sitting on the throne, we have to watch the pennies.

FATHER UBU. Madam my wife, it's made out of sheepskin with a clasp and with laces made out of dogskin.

MOTHER UBU. That's very extraordinary, but it's even more extraordinary that we're here on the throne.

FATHER UBU. How right you are, Mother Ubu.

MOTHER UBU. We owe quite a debt to the Duke of Lithuania.

FATHER UBU. Who's that?

MOTHER UBU. Why, Captain Bordure.

FATHER UBU. If you please, Mother Ubu, don't speak to me about that buffroon. Now that I don't need him

any more, he can go whistle for his dukedom.

MOTHER UBU. You're making a big mistake, Father Ubu; he's going to turn against you.

FATHER UBU. Well, now, the poor little fellow has my deepest sympathy, but I'm not going to worry about him any more than about Bougrelas.

MOTHER UBU. Ha! You think you've seen the last of Bougrelas, do you?

FATHER UBU. By my financial sword, of course I have! What do you think that fourteen-year-old midget is going to do to me?

MOTHER UBU. Father Ubu, pay attention to what I'm going to say to you. Believe me, you ought to be nice to Bougrelas to get him on your side.

FATHER UBU. Do you think I'm made of money? Well, I'm not! You've already made me waste twenty-two millions.

MOTHER UBU. Have it your own way, Father Ubu; he'll roast you alive.

FATHER UBU. Fine! You'll be in the pot with me.

MOTHER UBU. For the last time, listen to me: I'm sure that young Bougrelas will triumph, because he has right on his side.

FATHER UBU. Oh, crap! Doesn't the wrong always get you more than the right? Ah, you do me an injustice, Mother Ubu, I'll chop you into little pieces.

MOTHER UBU *runs away, pursued by* FATHER UBU.

Scene 2

The Great Hall of the palace, with FATHER UBU, MOTHER UBU, OFFICERS *and* SOLDIERS; GIRON, PILE, COTICE, NOBLES IN CHAINS, FINANCIERS, MAGISTRATES, *and* CLERKS.

FATHER UBU. Bring forward the Nobles' money box and the Nobles' hook and the Nobles' knife and the Nobles' book! And then bring forward the Nobles.

NOBLES *are brutally pushed forward.*

MOTHER UBU. For goodness' sakes, control yourself, Father Ubu.

MOTHER UBU. I have the honor to announce to you that in order to enrich the kingdom I shall annihilate all the Nobles and grab their property.

NOBLES. How awful! To the rescue, people and soldiers!

FATHER UBU. Bring forward the first Noble and hand me the Nobles' hook. Those who are condemned to death, I will drop down the trap door. They will fall into the Pig-Pinching Cellars and the Money Vault, where they will be disembrained. [*To the* NOBLE.] Who are you, buffroon?

THE NOBLE. Count of Vitebsk.

FATHER UBU. What's your income?

THE NOBLE. Three million rixthalers.

FATHER UBU. Condemned! [*He seizes him with the hook and drops him down the trap door.*]

MOTHER UBU. What vile savagery!

FATHER UBU. Second Noble, who are you?

The NOBLE *doesn't reply.*
Answer, buffroon!

THE NOBLE. Grand Duke of Posen.

FATHER UBU. Excellent! Excellent! I'll not trouble you any longer. Down the trap. Third Noble, who are you? You're an ugly one.

THE NOBLE. Duke of Courland, and of the cities of Riga, Reval, and the Mitau.

FATHER UBU. Very good! Very good! Anything else?

THE NOBLE. That's all.

FATHER UBU. Well, down the trap, then. Fourth Noble, who are you?

THE NOBLE. The Prince of Podolia.

FATHER UBU. What's your income?

THE NOBLE. I'm bankrupt.

FATHER UBU. For that nasty word, into the trap with you. Fifth Noble, who are you?

THE NOBLE. Margrave of Thorn, Palatin of Polack.

FATHER UBU. That doesn't sound like very much. Nothing else?

THE NOBLE. It was enough for me.

FATHER UBU. Half a loaf is better than no loaf at all. Down the trap. What's the matter with you, Mother Ubu?

MOTHER UBU. You're too ferocious, Father Ubu.

FATHER UBU. Please! I'm working! And now I'm going to have MY list of MY property read to me. Clerk, read MY list of MY property.

THE CLERK. County of Sandomir.

FATHER URU. Start with the big ones.

THE CLERK. Princedom of Podolia, Grand Duchy of Posen, Duchy of Courland, County of Sandomir, County of Vitebsk, Palatinate of Polack, Margraviate of Thorn.

FATHER UBU. Well, go on.

THE CLERK. That's all.

FATHER UBU. What do you mean, that's all! Oh, very well, then, bring the Nobles forward. Since I'm not finished enriching myself yet, I'm going to execute all the Nobles and seize all their estates at once. Let's go; stick the Nobles in the trap.

The NOBLES *are pushed into the trap.*
Hurry it up, let's go, I want to make some laws now.

SEVERAL. This ought to be a good one.

FATHER UBU. First I'm going to reform the laws, and then we'll proceed to matters of finance.

MAGISTRATES. We're opposed to any change.

FATHER UBU. Shitr! To begin with, Magistrates will not be paid any more.

MAGISTRATES. What are we supposed to live on? We're poor.

FATHER UBU. You shall have the fines which you will impose and the property of those you condemn to death.

A MAGISTRATE. Horrors!

A SECOND. Infamy!

A THIRD. Scandal!

A FOURTH. Indignity!

ALL. We refuse to act as judges under such conditions.

FATHER UBU. Down the trap with the Magistrates!

They struggle in vain.

MOTHER UBU. What are you doing, Father Ubu? Who will dispense justice now?

FATHER UBU. Why, me! You'll see how smoothly it'll go.

MOTHER UBU. I can just imagine.

FATHER UBU. That's enough out of you, buffrooness. And now, gentlemen, we will proceed to matters of finance.

FINANCIERS. No changes are needed.

FATHER UBU. I intend to change everything. First of all, I'll keep half the taxes for myself.

FINANCIERS. That's too much.

FATHER UBU. Gentlemen, we will establish a tax of 10 percent on property, another on commerce and industry, a third on marriages and a fourth on deaths—fifteen francs each.

FIRST FINANCIER. But that's idiotic, Father Ubu.

SECOND FINANCIER. It's absurd.

THIRD FINANCIER. It's impossible.

FATHER UBU. You're trying to confuse me! Down the trap with the Financiers!

The FINANCIERS *are pushed in.*

MOTHER UBU. But, Father Ubu, what kind of king are you? You're murdering everybody!

FATHER UBU. Oh, shitr!

MOTHER UBU. No more justice, no more finances!

FATHER UBU. Have no fear, my sweet child; I myself will go from village to village, collecting the taxes.

Scene 3

A peasant house in the outskirts of Warsaw. Several peasants are assembled.

A PEASANT. [*Entering.*] Have you heard the news? The king and dukes are all dead, and young Bougrelas has fled to the mountains with his mother. What's more, Father Ubu has seized the throne.

ANOTHER. That's nothing. I've just come from Cracow where I saw the bodies of more than three hundred nobles and five hundred magistrates, and I

hear that the taxes are going to be doubled and that Father Ubu is coming to collect them himself.

ALL. Great heavens! What will become of us? Father Ubu is a horrible beast, and they say his family is abominable.

A PEASANT. Listen! Isn't somebody knocking at the door?

A VOICE. [*Outside.*] Hornsbuggers! Open up, by my shitr, by Saint John, Saint Peter, and Saint Nicholas! Open up, by my financial sword, by my financial horns, I'm coming to collect the taxes!

The door is smashed in, and FATHER UBU *enters followed by hordes of tax collectors.*

Scene 4

FATHER UBU. Which one of you is the oldest?

A peasant steps forward.

What's your name?

THE PEASANT. Stanislas Leczinski.

FATHER UBU. Fine, hornsbuggers! Listen to me, since if you don't these gentlemen here will cut your ears off. Well, are you listening?

STANISLAS. But your Excellency hasn't said anything yet.

FATHER UBU. What do you mean? I've been speaking for an hour. Do you think I've come here to preach in the desert?

STANISLAS. Far be it from my thoughts.

FATHER UBU. I've come to tell you, to order you, and to intimate to you that you are to produce forthwith and exhibit promptly your finance, unless you wish to be slaughtered. Let's go, gentleman, my financial swine, vehiculize hither the phynancial vehicle.

The vehicle is brought in.

STANISLAS. Sire, we are down on the register for a hundred and fifty-two rixthalers which we paid six weeks ago come Saint Matthew's Day.

FATHER UBU. That's very possible, but I've changed the government and run an advertisement in the paper that says you have to pay all present taxes twice and all those which I will levy later on three times. With this system, I'll make my fortune quickly; then I'll kill everyone and run away.

PEASANTS. Mr. Ubu, please have pity on us; we are poor, simple citizens.

FATHER UBU. Nuts! Pay up.

PEASANTS. We can't, we've already paid.

FATHER UBU. Pay up! Or I'll stick you in my pocket with torturing and be-heading of the neck and head! Hornsbuggers, I'm the king, aren't I?

ALL. Ah! So that's the way it is! To arms! Long live Bougrelas, by the grace of God King of Poland and Lithuania!

FATHER UBU. Forward, gentlemen of Finance, do your duty.

A struggle ensues; the house is destroyed, and old STANISLAS *flees across the plain alone.* FATHER UBU *stays to collect the money.*

Scene 5

A dungeon in the Fortress of Thorn, in which are CAPTAIN BORDURE *in chains and* FATHER UBU.

FATHER UBU. So, Citizen, that's the way it is: you wanted me to pay you what I owed you; then you rebelled because I refused; you conspired and here you are retired. Horns of finance, I've done so well you must admire it yourself.

CAPTAIN BORDURE. Take care, Father Ubu. During the five days that you've been king, you've committed enough murders to damn all the saints in Paradise. The blood of the king and of the nobles cries for vengeance, and their cries will be heard.

FATHER UBU. Ah, my fine friend, that's quite a tongue you've got there. I have no doubt that if you escaped, it would cause all sorts of complications, but I don't think that the dungeons of Thorn have ever let even one of the honest fellows go who have been entrusted to them.

Therefore I bid you a very good night and I invite you to sleep soundly, although I must say the rats dance a very pretty saraband down here.

He leaves. The jailers come and bolt all the doors.

Scene 6

The Palace at Moscow. Onstage are the EMPEROR ALEXIS *and his court, and* CAPTAIN BORDURE.

ALEXIS. Infamous adventurer, aren't you the one who helped kill our cousin Wenceslas?

CAPTAIN BORDURE. Sire, forgive me, I was carried away despite myself by Father Ubu.

ALEXIS. Oh, what a big liar! Well, what can I do for you?

CAPTAIN BORDURE. Father Ubu imprisoned me on charges of conspiracy; I succeeded in escaping and I have ridden five days and five nights across the steppes to come and beg your gracious forgiveness.

ALEXIS. What have you got for me as proof of your loyalty?

CAPTAIN BORDURE. My honor as a knight, and a detailed map of the town of Thorn. [*Kneels and presents his sword to* ALEXIS.]

ALEXIS. I accept your sword, but by Saint George, burn the map. I don't want to owe my victory to an act of treachery.

CAPTAIN BORDURE. One of the sons of Wenceslas, young Bougrelas, is still alive. I would do anything to restore him.

ALEXIS. What was your rank in the Polish Army?

CAPTAIN BORDURE. I commanded the fifth regiment of the Dragoons of Vilna and a company of mercenaries in the service of Father Ubu.

ALEXIS. Fine, I appoint you second in command of the tenth regiment of Cossacks, and woe to you if you betray me. If you fight well, you'll be rewarded.

CAPTAIN BORDURE. I don't lack courage, sire.

ALEXIS. Fine, remove yourself from my sight.

He leaves.

Scene 7

UBU'S *Council Chamber, with* FATHER UBU, MOTHER UBU, AND PHYNANCIAL ADVISERS.

FATHER UBU. Gentlemen, the meeting has begun, and see that you keep your ears open and your mouths shut. First of all, we'll turn to the subject of finance; then we'll speak about a little scheme I've thought up to bring good weather and prevent rain.

AN ADVISER. Very good, Mr. Ubu.

MOTHER UBU. What a stupid fool!

FATHER UBU. Take care, madam of my shitr, I'm not going to stand for your idiocies much longer. I'd like you to know, gentlemen, that the finances are proceeding satisfactorily. The streets are mobbed every morning by a crowd of the local low-life, and my men do wonders with them. In every direction you can see only burning houses, and people bent under the weight of our finances.

THE ADVISER. And are the new taxes going well, Mr. Ubu?

MOTHER UBU. Not at all. The tax on marriages has brought in only eleven cents so far, although Father Ubu chases people everywhere to convince them to marry.

FATHER UBU. By my financial sword, hornsbuggers, Madam financieress, I've got ears to speak with and you've a mouth to listen to me with.

Shouts of laughter.

You're mixing me up and it's your fault that I'm making a fool of myself! But, horn of Ubu! . . .

A messenger enters.

Well, what do you have to say for yourself? Get out of here, you little monkey, before I pocket you with beheading and twisting of the legs.

MOTHER UBU. There he goes, but he's left a letter.

FATHER UBU. Read it. I don't feel like it, or come to think of it perhaps I can't read. Hurry up, buffrooness, it must be from Bordure.

MOTHER UBU. He says that the Czar has received him very well, that he's going to invade your lands to restore Bougrelas, and that you're going to be killed.

FATHER UBU. Oh! Oh! I'm scared! I'm scared. I bet I'm going to die. Oh, poor little man that I am! What will become of me, great God? This wicked man is going to kill me. Saint Anthony and all the saints, protect me, and I'll give you some phynance and burn some candles for you. Lord, what will become of me? [*He cries and sobs.*]

MOTHER UBU. There's only one safe course to follow, Father Ubu.

FATHER UBU. What's that, my love?

MOTHER UBU. War!!!

ALL. Great heavens! What a noble idea!

FATHER UBU. Yes, and I'll be the one to get hurt, as usual.

FIRST ADVISER. Hurry, hurry, let's organize the army.

SECOND. And requisition the provisions.

THIRD. And set up the artillery and the fortresses.

FOURTH. And get up the money for the troops.

FATHER UBU. That's enough of that, now, you, or I'll kill you on the spot. I'm not going to spend any money. That's a good one, isn't it! I used to be paid to wage war, and now it's being waged at my expense. Wait—by my green candle, let's wage war, since you're so excited about it, but let's not spend a penny.

Scene 8

The camp outside Warsaw.

SOLDIERS AND PALOTINS. Long live Poland! Long live Father Ubu!

FATHER UBU. Ah, Mother Ubu, give me my breastplate and my little stick. I'll soon be so heavy that I won't be able to move even if I'm being chased.

MOTHER UBU. Pooh, what a coward!

FATHER UBU. Ah! Here's the sword of shitr running away first thing and there's the financial hook which won't stay put!!! [*Drops both.*] I'll never be ready, and the Russians are coming to kill me.

A SOLDIER. Lord Ubu, here's your ear-pick, which you've dropped.

FATHER UBU. I'll kill you with my shitr hook and my gizzard-saw.

MOTHER UBU. How handsome he is with his helmet and his breastplate! He looks just like an armed pumpkin.

FATHER UBU. Now I'll get my horse. Gentlemen, bring forth the phynancial horse.

MOTHER UBU. Father Ubu, your horse can't carry you—it's had nothing to eat for five days and it's about to die.

FATHER UBU. That's a good one! I have to pay twelve cents a day for this sway-backed nag and it can't even carry me. You're making fun of me, horn of Ubu, or else perhaps you're stealing from me?

MOTHER UBU *blushes and lowers her eyes.* Now bring me another beast, because I'm not going to go on foot, hornsbuggers!

An enormous horse is brought out. I'm going to get on. Oops, better sit down before I fall off.

The horse starts to leave. Stop this beast. Great God, I'm going to fall off and be killed!!!

MOTHER UBU. He's an absolute idiot. There he is up again; no, he's down again.

FATHER UBU. Horn of Physics, I'm half dead. But never mind, I'm going to the war and I'll kill everyone. Woe to him who doesn't keep up with me! I'll put him in my pocket with twisting of the nose and teeth and

extraction of the tongue.

MOTHER UBU. Good luck, Mr. Ubu!

FATHER UBU. I forgot to tell you that I'm making you the regent. But I'm keeping the financial book, so you'd better not try and rob me. I'll leave you the Palotin Giron to help you. Farewell, Mother Ubu.

MOTHER UBU. Farewell, Father Ubu. Kill the Czar thoroughly.

FATHER UBU. Of course. Twisting of the nose and teeth, extraction of the tongue and insertion of the ear-pick.

The army marches away to the sound of fanfares.

MOTHER UBU. [*Alone.*] Now that that big fat booby has gone, let's look to our own affairs, kill Bougrelas, and grab the treasure.

Act 4

Scene 1

The Royal Crypt in the Cathedral at Warsaw.

MOTHER UBU. Where on earth is that treasure? None of these slabs sounds hollow. I've counted thirteen slabs beyond the tomb of Ladislas the Great along the length of the wall, and I've found nothing. Someone seems to have deceived me. What's this? The stone sounds hollow here. To work, Mother Ubu. Courage, we'll have it pried up in a minute. It's stuck fast. The end of this financial hook will do the trick. There! There's the gold in the middle of the royal bones. Into the sack with it. Oh! What's that noise? Can there be someone alive in these ancient vaults? No, it's nothing; let's hurry up. Let's take everything. This money will look better in the light of day than in the middle of these graves. Back with the stone. What's that! There's that noise

again! There's something not quite
right about this place. I'll get the rest
of this gold some other time—I'll
come back tomorrow.

A VOICE. [*Coming from the tomb of*
JOHN SIGISMUND.] Never, Mother
Ubu!

MOTHER UBU *runs away terrified, through
the secret door, carrying the stolen gold.*

Scene 2

The Main Square in Warsaw, with
BOUGRELAS *and his men,* PEOPLE *and*
SOLDIERS.

BOUGRELAS. Forward, my friends! Long
live Wenceslas and Poland! That old
blaggard Father Ubu is gone; only
that old witch Mother Ubu and her
Palotin are left. I'm going to march
at your head and restore my father's
house to the throne.

ALL. Long live Bougrelas!

BOUGRELAS. And we'll abolish all taxes
imposed by that horrible Father Ubu.

ALL. Hooray! Forward! To the palace,
and death to the Ubus!

BOUGRELAS. Look! There's Mother Ubu
coming out on the porch with her
guards!

MOTHER UBU. What can I do for you,
gentlemen? Ah! It's Bougrelas.

The crowd throws stones.

FIRST GUARD. They've broken all the
windows.

SECOND GUARD. Saint George, I'm done
for.

THIRD GUARD. Hornsass, I'm dying.

BOUGRELAS. Throw some more stones,
my friends.

PALOTIN GIRON. Ho! So that's the way it
is! [*He draws his sword and leaps into the
crowd, performing horrible slaughter.*]

BOUGRELAS. Have at you! Defend yourself, you cowardly pisspot!

They fight.

GIRON. I die!

BOUGRELAS. Victory, my friends! Now
for Mother Ubu!

Trumpets are heard.

Ah! The Nobles are arriving. Run

and catch the old hag.

ALL. She'll do until we can strangle the
old bandit himself!

MOTHER UBU *runs away pursued by all the
Poles. Rifle shots and a hail of stones.*

Scene 3

The Polish Army marching in the Ukraine.

FATHER UBU. Hornass, godslegs, cows-
heads! We're about to perish,
because we're dying of thirst and
we're tired. Sir Soldier, be so good as
to carry our financial helmet, and
you, Sir Lancer, take charge of the
shitr-pick and the physic-stick to un-
encumber our person, because, let
me repeat, we are tired.

The soldiers obey.

PILE. Ho, my Lord! It's surprising that
there are no Russians to be seen.

FATHER UBU. It's regrettable that the
state of our finances does not permit
us to have a vehicle commensurate to
our grandeur; for, for fear of demol-
ishing our steed, we have gone all the
way on foot, leading our horse by the
bridle. When we get back to Poland,
we shall devise, by means of our
physical science and with the aid of
the wisdom of our advisers, a way of
transporting our entire army by
wind.

COTICE. Here comes Nicholas Rensky,
in a great hurry.

FATHER UBU. What's the matter with
him?

RENSKY. All is lost. Sir, the Poles have
revolted, Giron has been killed, and
Mother Ubu has fled to the mountains.

FATHER UBU. Bird of night, beast of
misery, owl's underwear! Where did
you hear this nonsense? What won't
you be saying next! Who's responsible for this? Bougrelas, I'll bet.
Where'd you just come from?

RENSKY. From Warsaw, noble Lord.

FATHER UBU. Child of my shitr, if I
believed you I would retreat with the
whole army. But, Sir Child, you've

got feathers in your head instead of brains and you've been dreaming nonsense. Run off to the outposts, my child; the Russians can't be far, and we'll soon be flourishing our arms, shitr, phynancial, and physical.

GENERAL LASCY. Father Ubu, can't you see the Russians down there on the plain?

FATHER UBU. It's true, the Russians! A fine mess this is. If only there were still a way to run out, but there isn't; we're up here on a hill and we'll be exposed to attack on all sides.

THE ARMY. The Russians! The enemy!

FATHER UBU. Let's go, gentlemen, into our battle positions. We will remain on top of the hill and under no circumstances commit the idiocy of descending. I'll keep myself in the middle like a living fortress, and all you others will gravitate around me. I advise you to load your guns with as many bullets as they will hold, because eight bullets can kill eight Russians and that will be eight Russians the less. We will station the infantry at the foot of the hill to receive the Russians and kill them a little, the cavalry in back of them so that they can throw themselves into the confusion, and the artillery around this windmill here so that they can fire into the whole mess. As for us, we will take up our position inside the windmill and fire through the window with the phynancial pistol, and bar the door with the physical stick, and if anyone still tries to get in let him beware of the shitr-hook!!!

OFFICERS. Your orders, Lord Ubu, shall be executed.

FATHER UBU. Fine, we'll win, then. What time is it?

GENERAL LASCY. It's eleven o'clock in the morning.

FATHER UBU. In that case, let's have lunch, because the Russians won't attack before midday. Tell the soldiers, my lord General, to take a crap and strike up the Financial Song.

LASCY *withdraws.*

SOLDIERS *and* PALOTINS. Long live Father Ubu, our great Financier! Ting, ting, ting; ting, ting, ting; ting, ta-ting!

FATHER UBU. Oh, how noble, I adore gallantry!

A Russian cannon ball breaks one of the arms of the windmill.

Aaaaah! I'm frightened. Lord God, I'm dead! No, no, I'm not.

Scene 4

A CAPTAIN. [*Entering.*] Lord Ubu, the Russians are attacking.

FATHER UBU. All right, all right, what do you want me to do about it? I didn't tell them to attack. Nevertheless, gentlemen of Finance, let us prepare ourselves for battle.

GENERAL LASCY. Another cannon ball!

FATHER UBU. Ah! That's enough of that! It's raining lead and steel around here, and it might put a dent in our precious person. Down we go.

They all run away. The battle has just begun. They disappear in the clouds of smoke at the foot of the hill.

A RUSSIAN. [*Thrusting.*] For God and the Czar!

RENSKY. Ah! I'm dead.

FATHER UBU. Forward! As for you, sir, I'll get you because you've hurt me, do you hear? You drunken sot, with your popless little popgun.

THE RUSSIAN. Ah! I'll show you! [*He fires.*]

FATHER UBU. Ah! Oh! I'm wounded, I'm shot full of holes, I'm perforated, I'm done for, I'm buried. And now I've got you! [*He tears him to pieces.*] Just try that again.

GENERAL LASCY. Forward, charge, across the trench! Victory is ours!

FATHER UBU. Do you really think so? So far my brow has felt more lumps than laurels.

RUSSIAN KNIGHTS. Hooray! Make way for the Czar!

Enter the CZAR, *accompanied by* CAPTAIN BORDURE *in disguise.*

A POLE: Great God! Every man for himself, there's the Czar!

ANOTHER. Oh, my God, he's crossed the trench.

ANOTHER. Bing! Bang! Four more chopped up by that big ox of a lieutenant.

CAPTAIN BORDURE. So! The rest of you won't surrender, eh? All right, your time has come, John Sobiesky! [*He chops him up.*] Now for the others! [*He massacres Poles.*]

FATHER UBU. Forward, my friends! Capture that rat! Make mince-meat of the Muscovites! Victory is ours! Long live the Red Eagle!

ALL. Charge! Horray! Godslegs! Capture the big ox.

CAPTAIN BORDURE. By Saint George, they've got me.

FATHER UBU. Ah! it's you, Bordure! How are you, my friend? I, and all the company, are very happy to welcome you again. I'm going to broil you over a slow fire. Gentlemen of the Finances, light the fire. Oh! Ah! Oh! I'm dead. I must have been hit with a cannon ball at least. Oh! My God, forgive my sins. Yes, it's definitely a cannon ball.

CAPTAIN BORDURE. It was a pistol with a blank cartridge.

FATHER UBU. Oh, you're making fun of me! All right, into the pocket you go! [*He flings himself upon him and tears him to pieces.*]

GENERAL LASCY. Father Ubu, we're advancing on all fronts.

FATHER UBU. I can see that. But I can't go on any more, because everyone's been stepping on my toes. I absolutely have to sit down. Oh, where's my bottle?

GENERAL LASCY. Go get the Czar's bottle, Father Ubu!

FATHER UBU. Ah! Just what I had in mind. Let's go. Sword of Shitr, do your duty, and you, financial hook, don't lag behind! As for you, physical stick, see that you work just as hard and share with the little bit of wood the honor of massacring, scooping out, and imposing upon the Muscovite Emperor. Forward, my Phynancial Horse! [*He throws himself on the* CZAR.]

A RUSSIAN OFFICER. Look out, Your Majesty!

FATHER UBU. Take that! Oh! Ow! Ah! Goodness me. Ah! Oh, sir, excuse me, leave me alone. I didn't do it on purpose! [*He runs away, pursued by the* CZAR.] Holy Mother, that madman is coming after me! Great God, what shall I do? Ah, I've got that trench ahead of me again. I've got him behind me and the trench in front of me! Courage! I'm going to close my eyes! [*He jumps the trench. The* CZAR *falls in.*]

THE CZAR. God, I've fallen in!

THE POLES. Hooray! The Czar has fallen in!

FATHER UBU. I'm afraid to turn around. Ah! He fell in. That's fine; they've jumped on him. Let's go, you Poles; swing away; he's a tough one, that swine! As for me, I can't look. But our prediction has been completely fulfilled: the physical stick has performed wonders, and without doubt I would have been about to have killed him completely, had not an inexplicable fear come to combat and annul in us the fruits of our courage. But we suddenly had to turn tail, and we owe our salvation only to our skill in the saddle as well as to the sturdy hocks of our Phynancial Horse, whose rapidity is only equaled by its solidity and whose levitation makes its reputation, as well as the depth of the trench which located itself so appropriately under the enemy of us, the presently-before-you Master of Phynances. That was very nice, but nobody was listening. Oops, there they go again!

The Russian dragoons charge and rescue the CZAR.

GENERAL LASCY. It looks like it's turning into a rout.

FATHER UBU. Now's the time to make tracks. Now then, gentlemen of Poland, forward! Or rather, backward!

POLES. Every man for himself!

FATHER UBU. Come on! Let's go! What a big crowd, what a stampede, what a mob! How am I ever going to get out of this mess? [*He is jostled.*] You there, watch your step, or you will sample the boiling rage of the Master of Phynances. Ha! There he goes. Now let's get out of here fast, while Lascy's looking the other way.

He runs off; the CZAR *and the Russian Army go by, chasing Poles.*

Scene 5

A cave in Lithuania. It is snowing. Huddled inside are FATHER UBU, PILE, *and* COTICE.

FATHER UBU. Oh, what a bitch of a day! It's cold enough to make the rocks crack open, and the person of the Master of Phynances finds itself severely damaged.

PILE. Ho! Mr. Ubu, have you recovered from your fright and from your flight?

FATHER UBU. Well, I'm not frightened any more, but, believe me, I'm still running.

COTICE. [*Aside.*] What a turd!

FATHER UBU. Well, Sire Cotice, how's your ear feeling?

COTICE. As well as can be expected, sir, considering how bad it is. I can't get the bullet out, and consequently the lead is making me tilt.

FATHER UBU. Well, serves you right! You're always looking for a fight. As for me, I've always demonstrated the greatest valor, and without in any way exposing myself I massacred four enemies with my own hand, not counting, of course, those who were already dead and whom we dispatched.

COTICE. Do you know what happened to little Rensky, Pile?

PILE. A bullet in his head.

FATHER UBU. As the poppy and the dandelion are scythed in the flower of their age by the pitiless scythe of the pitiless scyther who scythes pitilessly their pitiful parts—just so little Rensky has played the poppy's part: he fought well, but there were just too many Russians around.

PILE *and* COTICE. Hey! Sir Ubu!

AN ECHO. Grrrrr!

PILE. What's that? On guard!

FATHER UBU. Oh, no! Not the Russians again! I've had enough of them. And, anyway, it's very simple: if they catch me I'll just put them all in my pocket.

Scene 6

The same. Enter a bear.

COTICE. Ho! Master of Phynances!

FATHER UBU. Oh! What a sweet little doggie! Isn't he cute?

PILE. Watch out! What a huge bear! Hand me my gun!

FATHER UBU. A bear! What a horrible beast! Oh, poor me, I'm going to be eaten alive. May God protect me! He's coming this way. No, he's got Cotice. I can breathe again!

The bear jumps on COTICE. PILE *attacks him with his sword.* UBU *takes refuge on a high rock.*

COTICE. Save me, Pile! Save me! Help, Sir Ubu!

FATHER UBU. Fat chance! Get out of it yourself, my friend; right now I'm going to recite my Pater Noster. Everyone will be eaten in his turn.

PILE. I've got him, I'm holding him.

COTICE. Hold him tight, my friend, he's starting to let me go.

FATHER UBU. Sanctificetur nomen tuum.

COTICE. Cowardly lout!

PILE. Oh! It's biting me! O Lord, save us, I'm dead.

FATHER UBU. Fiat voluntas tua!

COTICE. I've wounded it!

PILE. Hooray! It's bleeding now.

ABINGTON FREE LIBRARY, 1030 OLD YORK ROAD, ABINGTON PA 19001

While the Palotins shout, the bear bellows with pain and UBU *continues to mumble.*

COTICE. Hang on, while I find my exploding brass knuckles.

FATHER UBU. Panem nostrum quotidianum da nobis hodie.

PILE. Haven't you got it yet? I can't hold on any longer.

FATHER UBU. Sicut et nos dimittimus debitoribus nostris.

COTICE. Ah! I've got it.

A resounding explosion; the bear falls dead.

PILE *and* COTICE. Victory!

FATHER UBU. Sed libera nos a malo. Amen. Is he really dead? Can I come down now?

PILE. [*With disgust.*] Just as you like.

FATHER UBU. [*Coming down.*] You may be assured that if you are still alive and if you tread once more the Lithuanian snow, you owe it to the lofty virtue of the Master of Phynances, who has struggled, broken his back, and shouted himself hoarse reciting paternosters for your safety, and who has wielded the spiritual sword of prayer with just as much courage as you have wielded with dexterity the temporal one of the here-attendant Palotin Cotice's exploding brass knuckles. We have even pushed our devotion further, for we did not hesitate to climb to the top of a very high rock so that our prayers had less far to travel to reach heaven.

PILE. Disgusting pig!

FATHER UBU. Oh, you beast! Thanks to me, you've got something to eat. What a belly he has, gentlemen! The Greeks would have been more comfortable in there than in their wooden horse, and we very barely escaped, my dear friends, being able to satisfy ourselves of his interior capacity with our own eyes.

PILE. I'm dying of hunger. What can we eat?

COTICE. The bear!

FATHER UBU. My poor friends, are you going to eat it completely raw? We don't have anything to make a fire with.

PILE. What about our flintstones?

FATHER UBU. Ah, that's true. And it seems to me that not far from here there is a little wood where dry branches may be found. Sire Cotice, go and fetch some.

COTICE *runs off across the snow.*

PILE. And now, sir Ubu, you can go and carve up the bear.

FATHER UBU. Oh, no. It may not be completely dead yet. Since it has already half-eaten you, and chewed upon all your members, you're obviously the man to take care of that. I'll go and light the fire while we're waiting for him to bring the wood.

PILE *starts to carve up the bear.*

Oh! Watch out! It just moved.

PILE. But Sir Ubu, it's stone cold already.

FATHER UBU. That's a pity. It would have been much better to have had him hot. We're running the risk of giving the Master of Phynances an attack of indigestion.

PILE. [*Aside.*] Disgusting fellow! [*Aloud.*] Give me a hand, Mr. Ubu; I can't do everything myself.

FATHER UBU. No, I'm sorry I can't help you. I'm really excessively fatigued.

COTICE. [*Re-entering.*] What a lot of snow, my friends; anyone would think this was Castile or the North Pole. Night is beginning to fall. In an hour it'll be dark. Let's make haste while we can still see.

FATHER UBU. Did you hear that, Pile? Get a move on. In fact, get a move on, both of you! Skewer the beast, cook the beast, I'm hungry!

PILE. Well, that does it! You'll work or you'll get nothing, do you hear me, you big hog?

FATHER UBU. Oh! It's all the same to me; I'd just as soon eat it raw; you're the ones whose stomachs it won't agree with. Anyway, I'm sleepy.

COTICE. What can we expect from him, Pile? Let's cook dinner ourselves. We just won't give him any, that's all. Or

ABINGTON FREE LIBRARY, 1030 OLD YORK ROAD, ABINGTON, PA. 1900]

at most we'll throw him a few bones.

PILE. Good enough. Ah, the fire's catching.

FATHER UBU. Oh, that's very nice. It's getting warm now. But I see Russians everywhere. My God, what a retreat! Ah! [*He falls asleep.*]

COTICE. I wonder if Rensky was telling the truth about Mother Ubu being dethroned. It wouldn't surprise me at all.

PILE. Let's finish cooking supper.

COTICE. Now, we've got more important problems. I think it would be a good idea to inquire into the truth of the news.

PILE. You're right. Should we desert Father Ubu or stay with him?

COTICE. Let's sleep on it; we'll decide tomorrow.

PILE. No—let's sneak off under cover of darkness.

COTICE. Let's go, then.

They go.

Scene 7

FATHER UBU. [*Talking in his sleep.*] Ah, Sir Russian Dragoon, watch out, don't shoot in this direction; there's someone here. Oh, there's Bordure; he looks mean, like a bear. And there's Bougrelas coming at me! The bear, the bear! He's right below me; he looks fierce. My God! No, I'm sorry I can't help you! Go away, Bougrelas! Don't you hear me, you clown? There's Rensky now, and the Czar. Oh, they're going to beat me up. And Mother Ubu. Where did you get all that gold? You've stolen my gold, you miserable witch; you've been ransacking my tomb in Warsaw Cathedral, under the moon. I've been dead a long time; Bougrelas has killed me and I've been buried in Warsaw next to Ladislas the Great, and also at Cracow next to John Sigismund, and also at Thorn in the dungeon with Bordure. There it is again. Get out of here, you nasty bear! You look like Bordure. Do you hear, you devilish beast? Now, he can't hear me, the Salopins have cut his ears off. Disembrain them, devitalize them, cut off their ears, confiscate their money and drink yourself to death, that's the life of a Salopin, that's happiness for the Master of Phynances. [*He falls silent and sleeps.*]

Act 5

Scene 1

It is night. FATHER UBU *is asleep. Enter* MOTHER UBU, *without seeing him. The stage is in total darkness.*

MOTHER UBU. Shelter at last. I'm alone here, which is fine, but what an awful journey: crossing all Poland in four days! And even before that, everything happened to me at once! As soon as that fat fool left, I went to the crypt to grab what I could. And right after that, I was almost stoned to death by that Bougrelas and his madmen. I lost the Palotin Giron, my knight, who was so stricken by my beauty that he swooned whenever he saw me, and even, I've been told, when he didn't see me, which is the height of passion. He would have let himself be cut in two for my sake, the poor boy. The proof is that he was cut in four, by Bougrelas. Snip, snap, snop! I thought I'd die. Right after that, I took to flight, pursued by the maddened mob. I flee the palace, reach the Vistula, and find all the bridges guarded. I swim across the river, hoping to escape my persecutors. Nobles come from every direction and chase me. I die a thousand deaths, surrounded by a ring of Poles, screaming for my blood. Finally I wriggle out of their clutches, and after four days of running across the snow of my former kingdom, I reach my refuge here. I haven't had a thing to eat or drink for four days. Bougrelas was right behind me. . . . And here I am, safe at last. Oh, I'm nearly dead of cold and exhaustion. But I'd really like to know what's become of my big buffroon—I mean my honored spouse. Have I fleeced him! Have I taken his rixthalers! Have I pulled the wool over his eyes! And his starving phynancial horse: he's not going to see any oats very soon, either, the poor devil. Oh, what a joke! But alas! My treasure is lost! It's in Warsaw, and let anybody who wants it, go and get it.

FATHER UBU. [*Starting to wake up.*] Capture Mother Ubu! Cut off her ears!

MOTHER UBU. Oh, my God! Where am I? I'm losing my mind. Good Lord, no!

> God be praised
> I think I can see
> Mr. Ubu
> Sleeping near me.

Let's show a little sweetness. Well, my fat fellow, did you have a good sleep?

FATHER UBU. A very bad one! That was a tough bear! A fight of hunger against toughness, but hunger has completely eaten and devoured the toughness, as you will see when it gets light in here. Do you hear, my noble Palotins?

MOTHER UBU. What's he babbling about? He seems even stupider than when we left. What's the matter with him?

FATHER UBU. Cotice, Pile, answer me, by my bag of shitr! Where are you? Oh, I'm afraid. Somebody did speak. Who spoke? Not the bear, I suppose. Shitr! Where are my matches? Ah! I lost them in the battle.

MOTHER UBU. [*Aside.*] Let's take advantage of the situation and the darkness and pretend to be a ghost. We'll make him promise to forgive us our little pilfering.

FATHER UBU. By Saint Anthony, somebody is speaking! Godslegs! I'll be damned!

MOTHER UBU. [*Deepening her voice.*] Yes, Mr. Ubu, somebody is indeed speaking, and the trumpet of the archangel which will call the dead from dust and ashes on Judgment Day would not speak otherwise! Listen to my stern voice. It is that of Saint Gabriel who cannot help but give good advice.

FATHER UBU. To be sure!

MOTHER UBU. Don't interrupt me or I'll fall silent, and that will settle your hash!

FATHER UBU. Oh, buggers! I'll be quiet, I won't say another word. Please go on, Madam Apparition!

MOTHER UBU. We were saying, Mr. Ubu, that you are a big fat fellow.

FATHER UBU. Very fat, that's true.

MOTHER UBU. Shut up, Goddammit!

FATHER UBU. Oh my! Angels aren't supposed to curse!

MOTHER UBU. [*Aside.*] Shitr! [*Continuing.*] You are married, Mr. Ubu?

FATHER UBU. Absolutely. To the Queen of Witches.

MOTHER UBU. What you mean to say is that she is a charming woman.

FATHER UBU. A perfect horror. She has claws all over her; you don't know where to grab her.

MOTHER UBU. You should grab her with sweetness, Sir Ubu, and if you grab her thus you will see that Venus herself couldn't be as nice.

FATHER UBU. Who did you say has lice?

MOTHER UBU. You're not listening, Mr. Ubu. Try and keep your ears open now. [*Aside.*] We'd better get a move on; it's getting light in here. Mr. Ubu, your wife is adorable and delicious; she doesn't have a single fault.

FATHER UBU. Ah, you're wrong there: there isn't a single fault that she doesn't have.

MOTHER UBU. That's enough now. Your wife is not unfaithful to you!

FATHER UBU. I'd like to see someone who could stand making her unfaithful. She's an absolute harpy!

MOTHER UBU. She doesn't drink!

FATHER UBU. Only since I've taken the key to the cellar away from her. Before that, she was drunk by seven in the morning and perfumed herself with brandy. Now that she perfumes herself with heliotrope, she doesn't smell so bad any more. Not that I care about that. But now I'm the only one that can get drunk!

MOTHER UBU. Stupid idiot! Your wife doesn't steal your gold.

FATHER UBU. No, that's peculiar.

MOTHER UBU. She doesn't pinch a cent!

FATHER UBU. As witness our noble and unfortunate Phynancial Horse, who, not having been fed for three months, has had to undergo the entire campaign being dragged by the bridle across the Ukraine. He died on the job, poor beast!

MOTHER UBU. That's all a bunch of lies—you've got a model wife, and you're a monster.

FATHER UBU. That's all a bunch of truth. My wife's a slut, and you're a sausage.

MOTHER UBU. Take care, Father Ubu!

FATHER UBU. Oh, that's right, I forgot whom I was talking to. I take it all back.

MOTHER UBU. You killed Wenceslas.

FATHER UBU. That wasn't my fault, actually. Mother Ubu wanted it.

MOTHER UBU. You had Boleslas and Ladislas killed.

FATHER UBU. Too bad for them. They wanted to do me in.

MOTHER UBU. You didn't keep your promise to Bordure, and moreover, you killed him.

FATHER UBU. I'd rather I ruled Lithuania than he. For the moment, neither of us is doing it. Certainly you can see that I'm not.

MOTHER UBU. There's only one way you can make up for all your sins.

FATHER UBU. What's that? I'm all ready to become a holy man; I'd like to be a bishop and have my name on the calendar.

MOTHER UBU. You must forgive Mother Ubu for having sidetracked some of the funds.

FATHER UBU. What do you think of this: I'll pardon her when she's given everything back, when she's been soundly thrashed, and when she's revived my phynancial horse.

MOTHER UBU. He's got that horse on the brain. Ah, I'm lost, day is breaking!

FATHER UBU. Well, I'm happy to know at last for sure that my dear wife steals from me. Now I have it on the highest authority. Omnis a Deo scientia, which is to say: omnis, all; a Deo, knowledge; scientia, comes from God. That explains this marvel. But Madam Apparition is so silent now! What can I offer her to revive her? What she said was very entertaining. But, look, it's daybreak! Ah! Good Lord, by my Phynancial Horse, it's Mother Ubu!

MOTHER UBU. [*Brazenly.*] That's not true, and I'm going to excommunicate you.

FATHER UBU. Ah, you old slut!

MOTHER UBU. Such impiety!

FATHER UBU. That's too much! I can see very well that it's you, you half-witted hag! What the devil are you doing here?

MOTHER UBU. Giron is dead and the Poles chased me.

FATHER UBU. And the Russians chased me. So two great souls meet again.

MOTHER UBU. Say rather that a great soul has met an ass!

FATHER UBU. Fine, and now its going to meet this little monster.

He throws the bear at her.

MOTHER UBU. [*Falling down crushed beneath the weight of the bear.*] Oh, great God! How horrible! I'm dying! I'm suffocating! It's chewing on me! It's swallowing me! I'm being digested!

FATHER UBU. He's dead, you gargoyle! Oh, wait, perhaps he's not Lord, he's not dead, save us. [*Climbing back on his rock.*] Pater noster qui es. . . .

MOTHER UBU. [*Disentangling herself.*] Where did he go?

FATHER UBU. Oh, Lord, there she is again. Stupid creature, there's no way of getting rid of her. Is that bear dead?

MOTHER UBU. Of course, you stupid ass, he's stone cold. How did he get here?

FATHER UBU. [*Bewildered.*] I don't know. Oh, yes, I do know. He wanted to eat Pile and Cotice, and I killed him with one swipe of a Pater Noster.

MOTHER UBU. Pile, Cotice, Pater Noster? What's that all about? He's out of his mind, my finance!

FATHER UBU. It happened exactly the way I said. And you're an idiot, you stinkpot!

MOTHER UBU. Describe your campaign to me, Father Ubu.

FATHER UBU. Holy Mother, no! It would take too long. All I know is that despite my incontestable valor, everybody beat me up.

MOTHER UBU. What, even the Poles?

FATHER UBU. They were shouting: Long live Wenceslas and Bougrelas! I thought they were going to chop me up. Oh, those madmen! And then they killed Rensky!

MOTHER UBU. I don't care about that! Did you know that Bougrelas killed Palotin Giron?

FATHER UBU. I don't care about that! And then they killed poor Lascy!

MOTHER UBU. I don't care about that!

FATHER UBU. Oh, well, in that case, come over here, you old slut! Get down on your knees before your master. [*He grabs her and throws her on her knees.*] You're about to suffer the extreme penalty.

MOTHER UBU. Ho, ho, Mr. Ubu!

FATHER UBU. Oh! Oh! Oh! Are you all through now? I'm just about to begin: twisting of the nose, tearing out of the hair, penetration of the little bit of wood into the ears, extraction of the brain by the heels, laceration of the posterior, partial or perhaps even total suppression of the spinal marrow (assuming that would make her character less spiny), not forgetting the puncturing of the swimming bladder and finally the grand re-enacted decollation of John the Baptist, the whole taken from the very Holy Scriptures, from the Old as well as the New Testament, as edited, corrected and perfected by the here-attendant Master of Phynances! How does that suit you, you sausage? [*He begins to tear her to pieces.*]

MOTHER UBU. Mercy, Mr. Ubu!

A loud noise at the entrance to the cave.

Scene 2

The same, and BOUGRELAS *who rushes into the cave with his soldiers.*

BOUGRELAS. Forward, my friends. Long live Poland!

FATHER UBU. Oh! Oh! Wait a moment, Mr. Pole. Wait until I've finished with madam my other half!

BOUGRELAS. [*Hitting him.*] Take that, coward, tramp, braggart, laggard, Mussulman!

FATHER UBU. [*Countering.*] Take that! Polack, drunkard, bastard, hussar, tartar, pisspot, inkblot, sneak, freak, anarchist!

MOTHER UBU. [*Hitting out also.*] Take that, prig, pig, rake, fake, snake, mistake, mercenary!

The soldiers throw themselves on the UBUS, *who defend themselves as best they can.*

FATHER UBU. Gods! What a battle!

MOTHER UBU. Watch out for our feet, Gentlemen of Poland.

FATHER UBU. By my green candle, when will this endlessness be ended? Another one! Ah, if only I had my Phynancial Horse here!

BOUGRELAS. Hit them, keep hitting them!

VOICES FROM WITHOUT. Long live Father Ubu, our Great Financier!

FATHER UBU. Ah! There they are. Hooray! There are the Father Ubuists. Forward, come on, you're desperately needed, Gentlemen of Finance.

Enter the PALOTINS, *who throw themselves into the fight.*

COTICE. All out, you Poles!

PILE. Ho! We meet again, my Financial sir. Forward, push as hard as you can, get to the exit; once outside, we'll run away.

FATHER UBU. Oh! He's my best man. Look the way he hits them!

BOUGRELAS. Good God! I'm wounded!

STANISLAS LECZINSKI. It's nothing, Sire.

BOUGRELAS. No, I'm just a little stunned.

JOHN SOBIESKI. Fight, keep fighting, they're getting to the door, the knaves.

COTICE. We're getting there; follow me everybody. By conseyquence of the whiche, the sky becomes visible.

PILE. Courage, Sire Ubu!

FATHER UBU. Oh! I just crapped in my pants. Forward, hornsbuggers! Killem, bleedem, skinnem, massacrem, by Ubu's horn! Ah! It's quieting down.

COTICE. There are only two of them guarding the exit!

FATHER UBU. [*Knocking them down with the bear.*] And one, and two! Oof! Here I am outside! Let's run now! Follow, you others, and don't stop for anything!

Scene 3

The scene represents the Province of Livonia covered with snow. The UBUS *and their followers are in flight.*

FATHER UBU. Ah! I think they've stopped trying to catch us.

MOTHER UBU. Yes, Bougrelas has gone to get himself crowned.

FATHER UBU. I don't envy him that crown, either.

MOTHER UBU. You're quite right, Father Ubu.

They disappear into the distance.

Scene 4

The bridge of a close-hauled schooner on the Baltic. FATHER UBU *and his entire gang are on the bridge.*

THE CAPTAIN. What a lovely breeze!

FATHER UBU. We are indeed sailing with a rapidity which borders on the miraculous. We must be making at least a million knots an hour, and these knots have been tied so well that once tied they cannot be untied. It's true that we have the wind behind us.

PILE. What a pathetic imbecile!

A squall arises, the ship rolls, the sea foams.

FATHER UBU. Oh! Ah! My God, we're going to be capsized. The ship is leaning over too far, it'll fall!

THE CAPTAIN. Everyone to leeward, furl the foresail!

FATHER UBU. Oh, no, don't put everybody on the same side! That's imprudent. What if the wind changed direction—everybody would sink to the bottom of the sea and the fishes would eat us.

THE CAPTAIN. Don't rush, line up and close ranks!

FATHER UBU. Yes, yes, rush! I'm in a hurry! Rush, do you hear! It's your fault that we aren't getting there, brute of a captain. We should have been there already. I'm going to take charge of this myself. Get ready to tack about. Drop anchor, tack with the wind, tack against the wind. Run up the sails, run down the sails, tiller up, tiller down, tiller to the side. You see, everything's going fine. Come broadside to the waves now and everything will be perfect.

All are convulsed with laughter; the wind rises.

THE CAPTAIN. Haul over the jibsail, reef over the topsail!

FATHER UBU. That's not bad, it's even good! Swab out the steward and jump in the crow's-nest.

Several choke with laughter. A wave is shipped.

Oh, what a deluge! All this is the result of the maneuvers which we just ordered.

MOTHER UBU *and* PILE. What a wonderful thing navigation is!

A second wave is shipped.

PILE. [*Drenched.*] But watch out for Satan, his pomps and pumps.

FATHER UBU. Sir boy, get us something to drink.

They all sit down to drink.

MOTHER UBU. What a pleasure it will be to see our sweet France again, our old friends and our castle of Mondragon!

FATHER UBU. We'll be there soon. At the moment we've passed below the castle of Elsinore.

PILE. I feel cheerful at the thought of seeing my dear Spain again.

COTICE. Yes, and we'll amaze our countrymen with the stories of our wonderful adventures.

FATHER UBU. Oh, certainly! And I'm going to get myself appointed Minister of Finances in Paris.

MOTHER UBU. Oh, that's right! Oops, what a bump that was!

COTICE. That's nothing, we're just doubling the point of Elsinore.

PILE. And now our noble ship plows at full speed through the somber waves of the North Sea.

FATHER UBU. A fierce and inhospitable sea which bathes the shores of the land called Germany, so named because the inhabitants of this land are all cousins-german.

MOTHER UBU. That's what I call true learning. They say that this country is very beautiful.

FATHER UBU. Ah! Gentlemen! Beautiful as it may be, it cannot compare with Poland. For if there were no Poland, there would be no Poles!

The Bug in Her Ear

Georges Feydeau

Even while Jarry was startling the avant-garde of Paris with *King Ubu*, Georges Feydeau was becoming wealthy by providing the vast Parisian theater-going public with farcical entertainment that suited their tastes. Indeed, Feydeau was so successful and popular that he was dismissed by serious scholars as a mere craftsman (not unlike the critical reception accorded Molière over two centuries earlier), and for more than a quarter century after his death his works lay largely forgotten. After World War II, however, there began a serious revival of Feydeau's work in France and a widespread recognition that Feydeau had been the best French farceur since Molière. Gradaually his plays are being translated and performed in other languages, and it finally appears that the popularity Feydeau enjoyed in his own day is being converted into the international recognition that is his due.

Georges Léon Jules Marie Feydeau was born in Paris on December 8, 1862, the son of a well-to-do stockbroker and sometime writer. The elder Feydeau's realistic novel *Fanny,* had attracted significant attention in 1858, but eventually its author had devoted himself to making money rather than to writing. The boy was introduced to the theater at a very early age, and wrote his first play when only six or seven years old; he was to claim in later years that playwriting was for him a means of avoiding the soberer responsibilities of schoolwork. Before his eighteenth birthday Feydeau saw the first professional performance of a monologue he had written, and his first professionally produced one-act play, *Gibier de Potence,* appeared when he was twenty-three. There followed a string of minimally successful full-length comedies, but, taking the published criticism of these works to heart, Feydeau retired from the stage for a year or two to study the works of Labiche and the other successful comic playwrights of the preceding generation. He reemerged in 1892 with *Monsieur Chasse* and *Champignol malgré lui,* which ran for hundreds of performances each and established Feydeau as the major farceur of the era.

For the next sixteen years, Feydeau was the undisputed master of light comedy on the Parisian stage. The chief plays of this period (of the thirty-nine in his lifetime) include *Le Dindon* (1898), *La Dame de Chez Maxim* (1899), and *Occupe-toi d'Amélie* (1908). Toward the end of his life, Feydeau turned to comedies of a somewhat more bitter twist, perhaps as a result of an unhappy private life that included the breakup of his marriage. These plays were never as successful as the madcap farces of his earlier period, although Feydeau remained an important and active force in the French theater until his death on June 5, 1921. He was elected to the Académie Française, an honor never accorded to Molière.

La puce à l'oreille, literally "the flea in her ear," appeared on March 2, 1907. The title derives from a French idiom approximately equivalent to the American expression, "to put a bug in one's ear," meaning to drop a hint. The play ranks among Feydeau's very best, and serves as an excellent example of the kind of precision work at which Feydeau was a master. One need not look for literary merit in *The Bug in Her Ear,* however. Feydeau's language is far from poetry, his characterizations nothing more than skin deep, and thematic content nonexistent. But in the intricate details of structuring a plot, and in the mastery of all the physical elements of the theater in order to create organized chaos and irrepressible laughter, Feydeau had no peer. Drawing upon the well-made play formula pioneered by Eugene Scribe, Feydeau created farcical plots as finely crafted as a well-oiled machine; every event in *The Bug in Her Ear* grows logically out of what has gone before it, and none can be omitted or transposed without doing violence to the mathematical precision with which the entire structure has been created. Gradually, as each occurrence leads to the next, events of the play become less and less probable in terms of ordinary reality, and yet the implacable logic with which they have been assembled moves the audience to the brink of absurdity—and, in some cases, right over the brink. It is the special province of good farce to create so total a suspension of disbelief as to render believable the wildly improbable, and Feydeau was the unchallenged master of this technique. Given the character types (and they are little more than types) that are assembled in *The Bug in Her Ear,* and given the jealous wife's decision to test her husband's fidelity in a manner shamelessly acknowledged to be straight out of the theater, one can only find each succeeding event of the plot reasonably related to what has gone before it. Yet the narrowly controlled chaos that climaxes each act is completely absurd.

Feydeau was a master at combining the visual elements of theater for maximum farcical impact. Thus, doors open and close all over the set, characters dash in and out narrowly missing the confrontation that would unravel the confusion, and mechanical contrivances and improbable coincidences control the fortunes of the characters. It is impossible to know how many makers of silent movies were Feydeau fans, but clearly, many of the techniques so scrupulously developed by Feydeau were the same ones that the silent motion pictures were to popularize for the world. Feydeau carefully worked out each detail of movement and business as he constructed his play scripts, to such an extent that directors are generally agreed that no Feydeau stage direction may safely be overlooked. He even went so far in the third act of *Occupe-toi d'Amélie* as to place a musical staff over a key bit of dialogue in order to instruct the actor as to the exact inflectional pattern in which the line should be spoken. This attention to production detail is most unusual among playwrights and would be resented in some plays by directors who value interpretational freedom, but in Feydeau's case it reveals meticulous attention to crafting a production out of all the theatrical elements available, putting the emphasis on the craftsmanship function of playwriting rather than on the literary one.

Feydeau's characters are reminiscent of the *commedia dell'arte,* at least in the sense that they are types more than they are unique, three-dimensional human beings. Much in the manner of Ben Jonson, Feydeau unerringly finds the one quality in each character to exaggerate wildly out of proportion, for maximum comic effect and also for exposing human folly. Feydeau shares with most great farceurs a capacity for functioning perilously close to the borderline of outright cruelty in character delineation, finding high humor in such otherwise painful problems as a cleft palate, impotency, and physical punishment. His characters rarely feel much sense of true love, warm sentiment, or even of old-fashioned virtue, but rather are deliciously and devotedly wicked. Such characters demand the utmost sincerity in acting, with almost fanatical devotion to the objectives that motivate them but with little of the Stanislavskian attention to inner purpose and feeling that less mechanically demanding acting entails. Feydeau has described his formula for successful playwriting as arranging for two characters who shouldn't meet to do so; this formula points up the importance of character development to farce, for the characters (each with his own peculiarity) are created first and then set in motion to create their plot. In another context, however, Feydeau insisted that there were only two important roles in his plays, he who kicks and he who gets kicked, with the latter being the starring role. This, too, reveals something about the simplicity that lies behind the apparent complexity of his plots.

It is more than incidental that language problems and difficulties of communication lie behind much of *The Bug in Her Ear* as well as many other Feydeau plays. At the most obvious level, Camille has a cleft palate, Homenides is Spanish and speaks with a thick accent, and Kruger is German and speaks no other language at all (in the original, he is an Englishman named Rugby who speaks only English). At a more important level, the difficulties between Chandebise and his wife are fundamentally those of communication: they have been happily married for some years, but they are still unable to exchange the simple ideas that would clear up all misunderstandings in the first act. The absurdity of even attempting to communicate in a world going mad has already been noted in connection with Jarry's *King Ubu,* and Feydeau was responding to the same perceptions in creating a farcical world in which insanity is normative and genuine communication completely out of the question. Feydeau, of course, had no thematic considerations in mind in creating his plays, but simply responded to the world as he saw it while attempting to entertain his public. Still, these two playwrights, Feydeau and Jarry, ushered in the twentieth century in the French theater with opposite and yet complementary concepts of absurdity as the only rational response to an irrational world. Their views were to mature through the work of other twentieth-century French playwrights into one of the dominating modes in post–World War II European drama.

In the meantime, *The Bug in Her Ear* remains, as do many of Feydeau's better works, simply an outstandingly effective theater piece. Utterly without pretensions to philosophical depth or literary accomplishment, and demanding the utmost skill and concentration in production, *The Bug in Her Ear* is as effectively crafted a farce as may be found anywhere. The structural skill exhibited by a playwright like Feydeau sometimes looks disarmingly simple. In fact, it is among the most demanding of theatrical arts.

The Bug in Her Ear
(La puce à l'oreille)

Translated by Sharon Parsell

Characters

Victor-Emmanuel
   Chandebise   } Played by the same actor
Poche
Camille Chandebise, Victor-Emmanuel's
  nephew and secretary
Roberta Chandebise, Victor-Emmanuel's
  wife
Roman Tournel, in love with Roberta
Dr. Finache
Carlos Homenides de Histangua
Lucy Homenides, his wife
Edward, the Chandebises' butler
Antoinette, his wife
Arthur Ferraillon, hotel keeper
Olivia Ferraillon, his wife
Bernard, hotel employee
Eugenia, hotel employee
Kruger, hotel guest

*The play takes place in June. Acts 1 and 3
are in Paris; act 2 is in Montretout. The
CHANDEBISE's drawing room. English de-
cor. A decorated flat on the left; a divided
flat on the right. At the rear is a large,
curved bay in whose center is a double
door with glass panes and exterior locks.
To the right and left of the bay there are
doors which have exterior locks. On the
left, downstage, a window. On the right,
downstage, there is a mahogany door; it
can be locked from the inside. In the
middle ground on the divided flat there is
a high fireplace with all its fittings. On
either side of the fireplace there are fabric
panels trimmed with gold-headed nails.
The short curtains at the window and the
bay have the same fabric and trim as these
panels. The furniture is mostly mahogany
and English in style. At the rear there is a
tall, narrow chest of drawers on the wall
between the bay and the door on the
right. Balancing it on the left of the bay is
a pedestal table. On the left between the
window and the rear there is a small table
with three drawers. In the window recess
there is a backless bench. Downstage from
the bench is an English portable writing
desk whose legs form an "X." At the
beginning of the scene the desk is closed.
Centerstage, on the left, and behind the
bench, there is a small couch whose back is
trimmed in mahogany. The back of the
couch is placed on a diagonal to the
audience. Balancing it across stage is a
fancy table and four chairs. Stage right, a
large table sits perpendicular to the audience; it has a chair at each end. There
is a mirror over the fireplace, English
engravings are on the walls, and knick-
knacks fill the room. In the exterior hall,
in front of the bay doors there is a bench,
and a wall telephone is above it. The
audience cannot see the door leading to
the main staircase which is supposedly on
the left parallel to the panel that separates
the door on the left from the bay.*

Act 1

As the curtain rises CAMILLE *is leaning against the tall chest with his back to the bay; he is reading a file which he has taken from one of the open drawers. Mild weather. The door on the left opens slowly and* ANTOINETTE's *head inquisitively leans into the room. She sees* CAMILLE, *leans into the room on tiptoes, grabs his head with both her hands, and gives him a quick kiss.*

CAMILLE. [*Surprised, regaining his balance, in a grumpy voice, not pronouncing any of his consonants.*] Watch out!

ANTOINETTE. Don't worry! The bosses have gone out.

CAMILLE. All right!

ANTOINETTE. Quick! A little peck! [CAMILLE *shrugs his shoulders like a grumpy child.*] Come on! [CAMILLE *looks at her for a moment, deciding between laughter and anger; then rousing himself brusquely, he greedily gives her a big kiss. At that moment* EDWARD *and* FINACHE *enter from the other door.*]

EDWARD. [*From the vestibule.*] Please, come in, doctor.

ANTOINETTE *and* CAMILLE. Oh! [*They separate.* CAMILLE *scurries like a rabbit through the door on the right.* ANTOINETTE *quickly crosses left and stands stupidly as if waiting for orders.*]

EDWARD. [*First to* ANTOINETTE *while* FINACHE *comes downstage a little to the right.*] All right, what are you doing here?

ANTOINETTE. [*Nonplussed.*] What? Me? I'm waiting for orders, orders for dinner.

EDWARD. What orders? Don't you know that the master and the missus have gone out? Back to the stove! A cook doesn't belong in the salon.

ANTOINETTE. But. . . .

EDWARD. Go on! Out! [ANTOINETTE, *grumbling, exits left.*]

FINACHE. [*Seated at the left of the table.*] You certainly know how to handle your wife.

EDWARD. You have to treat women like that. If you don't lead them, they'll lead you. None of that for me!

FINACHE. Bravo!

EDWARD. You see, sir, that little woman is a poodle about fidelity but a tiger about jealousy. She's always sneaking around the apartment trying to spy on me. She thinks she's on to something . . . the upstairs maid and me.

FINACHE. [*With irony which* EDWARD *misses.*] So, she's on to you, is she?

EDWARD. Now really! Me involved with the upstairs maid?

FINACHE. [*Rising.*] Well, what does it matter as long as your master isn't here?

EDWARD. [*Jovially, his hands tucked into the bib of his apron.*] What difference does that make? I have the time to keep you company.

FINACHE. [*Somewhat nonplussed.*] What? Certainly! How kind of you; but I wouldn't want to keep you from your work.

EDWARD. [*The same.*] I have nothing to do now, anyway.

FINACHE. [*Bowing ironically.*] Well, then, can you tell me when M. Chandebise will be home?

EDWARD. Not for another quarter of an hour.

FINACHE. Damn it! [*Taking his hat from the table putting it on as he goes upstage.*] In that case I'm going to entrust you with a message for him.

EDWARD. Oh, sir, you are too kind!

FINACHE. It's nothing, it's nothing. Our lives aren't purely for the benefit of others. I have a patient to see near here. God, I'll have to finish that one off quickly!

EDWARD. [*Misunderstanding, scandalised.*] Sir!

FINACHE. [*Catching his thought.*] No, no heavens, no! It's not what you think! After all, I make my living curing people. I meant that I would cut short my call and be back in a quarter of an hour.

EDWARD. [*Bowing.*] It would be bad

manners to detain you any longer.

FINACHE. [*With affected contrition.*] You will excuse me, then. [FINACHE *starts to go out.* EDWARD *crosses to above the table, and* FINACHE *comes downstage.*] Now, if M. Chandebise should come before I get back [*Taking a file from his pocket.*], give him this. Tell him that I have examined his client and found him in perfect health. He can insure him in all confidence.

EDWARD. [*Indifferently and distracted.*] Ah!

FINACHE. [*Mocking.*] Is that all right with you?

EDWARD. [*Absent mindedly.*] Oh!

FINACHE. Obviously, I couldn't care less, but it is a matter of some importance to M. Chandebise, who is the Paris director of the Boston Life Company.

EDWARD. [*Familiarly.*] Oh, yes, with the boss! [FINACHE *bows acquiescently.*] And with me too!

FINACHE. There you go! The boss, if you will permit me. Tell him that his grandee—what's his name—Don Carlos Homenides de Histangua, is in first class shape.

EDWARD. Oh! Histangua! Yes, yes, I know. His wife is waiting for madam in the other room.

FINACHE. What a small world we live in! I examined the husband this morning; and the wife is in the other room.

EDWARD. They had dinner here the day before yesterday.

FINANCHE. My goodness!

EDWARD. [*Sitting at the right of the table as if he were at home.* FINACHE *is standing on the other side.*] Tell me something, Doctor, while I still have you. . . .

FINACHE. I'll say one thing for you, you're not shy.

EDWARD. [*Naturally and good-naturedly.*] Why should I be? I want to ask you about something my lady and I discussed this morning.

FINACHE. [*Precisely.*] Mme. Chandebise?

EDWARD. No, not her, my wife.

FINACHE. Oh, your wife!

EDWARD. Yes, my lady! "Your wife" doesn't sound respectful enough.

FINACHE. [*Bowing ironically.*] Please, forgive me.

EDWARD. [*Picking up his train of thought.*] What do you call. . . . Please sit down.

FINACHE. [*Obeying ironically.*] Certainly.

EDWARD. [*Facing* FINACHE, *sitting on the chair so that only the back two legs are on the floor.*]What do you call those things on either side of your stomach? [*To clarify, he taps lighly on each side of his stomach.*]

FINACHE. [*Facing* EDWARD.] Oh, that would be your ovaries.

EDWARD. I have those too?

FINACHE. [*Trying to remain serious.*] Very well, we shall take them out.

EDWARD. [*Standing up and going downstage.*] Oh, no! I want to keep them.

FINACHE. [*Who has also stood up.*] See here, old man, I certainly won't take them from you.

EDWARD. [*Crosses* FINACHE *at the rear of the stage.*] Well, you might!

LUCY. [*Entering through the door on the left to* EDWARD.] Tell me, my friend. . . . [*Seeing* FINACHE.] Oh, excuse me, sir. [*To* EDWARD.] Are you sure that Mme. Chandebise will be back soon?

EDWARD. Indeed, madam! Madam told me that if madam. . . . What was your name again?

LUCY. [*Coming to his aid.*] Homenides de Histangua.

EDWARD. [*Seconding her.*] Yes, that was it! "Comes to call. . . ."

FINACHE. Whew! "Comes to call. . . ."

EDWARD. [*To* FINACHE *with a forced dignity.*] Exactly! [*To* LUCY.] "Don't let her leave before I see her."

LUCY. That's what her note said; and I must say I was shocked by it. But, I can only wait a little longer.

EDWARD. Indeed, madam. [LUCY *goes upstage as if to go into the other room but she stops to listen to* EDWARD.] Now, as I was saying. . . .

FINACHE. [*Ironically.*] As you were saying.

EDWARD. [*Bowing.*] Dr. Finache [*They exchange bows.*], the Chief Physician of the Boston Life Company, told me that he examined madam's husband this morning.

LUCY. Well!

FINACHE. [*Crossing to her.*] It's true, madam; I had the honor of examining Senor de Histangua this morning.

LUCY. What? My husband being examined! What a funny idea!

FINACHE. All insurance companies have these little quirks. I salute you, madam, your husband is in excellent health. What a man!

LUCY. [*With a low sigh, falling into a chair on the left which faces the couch.*] You don't have to tell me that.

FINACH. It's very flattering.

LUCY. Yes . . . and very tiring!

FINACHE. Life is not easy.

EDWARD. [*With a sigh.*] Mme. Plucheux dreams of the same thing!

LUCY. Who is Mme. Plucheux?

EDWARD. My spouse! She's always putting me to shame. She should have a husband like yours.

FINACHE. Well then, maybe something could be arranged with madam's authorization and the consent of Senor de Histangua.

EDWARD. Goodness no!

LUCY. [*Gaily as she stands up.*] And a "no" from me to that!

FINACHE. [*Laughing.*] Forgive me, madam; Edward, the rogue, made me say such silly things. [*Crossing the stage to get his hat.*] I'd better hurry if I want to get back in a quarter of an hour. [*Bowing.*] Madam, it was a pleasure.

LUCY. [*Bowing.*] And no hard feelings, Doctor.

FINACHE. I certainly hope not. [*He goes downstage with* EDWARD.]

EDWARD. [*With the* DOCTOR.] Back to what we were discussing, Doctor. When I lean over like this, my ovaries. . . .

FINACHE. Ah, I see! Take a good laxative, that will ease the pain. [*They exit.*]

LUCY. [*Watching them exit.*] What a character! [*Looking at her watch.*] It's after one o'clock. Did Roberta summon me to cool my heels until she got home? [*She sits on the left, picks up a magazine, and flips through it distractedly.*]

CAMILLE. [*Entering from the right and going to the chest to replace the file that he had taken earlier, as he see* LUCY.] Oh! Excuse me, madam. [CAMILLE *has a cleft palate. He pronounces no consonants, only vowels.*]

LUCY. [*Lifting her head and nodding slightly.*] What?

CAMILLE. No doubt you are waiting for the Director of the Boston Life Company.

LUCY. [*Somewhat nonplussed.*] What?

CAMILLE. [*Trying to speak more clearly.*] I said, "No doubt you are waiting for the Director of the Boston Life Company."

LUCY. [*With a nervous smile.*] Excuse me, I didn't understand what you said.

CAMILLE. [*Slowly but still garbled.*] I asked if you were here to see the Dir. . . .

LUCY. [*Cutting off his words and as if to excuse herself for not understanding.*] No, no! I'm not speaking German.

CAMILLE. [*The same.*] But neither am I!

LUCY. Perhaps you should speak to the butler; this is not my house. I'm waiting for my friend Mme. Chandebise.

CAMILLE. [*Same.*] Oh, oh, excuse me! [*Bowing backwards to the chest.*] I thought you were here to see the Director of the Boston Life Company.

LUCY. Of course, of course.

CAMILLE. [*Puts the file in the drawer and exits stage right.*] Please excuse me.

LUCY. [*Astonished after he exits.*] What was that—Swahili? [*As she speaks, she crosses to the right.*]

EDWARD. [*Entering from the bay.*] I came to see how you were getting along.

LUCY. [*Quickly to* EDWARD.] Oh! My friend, tell me who was that man? . . .

EDWARD. [*Taken by surprise.*] What man?

LUCY. The one who talks like this. [*She imitates* CAMILLE.] A, ou, e, a, i, ou, a . . . or something like that.

EDWARD. [*Laughing.*] Oh, you mean M. Camille!

LUCY. Is he a foreigner?

EDWARD. No, of course not. He's M. Chandebise's nephew, his brother's son. He is hard to understand; you see, madam, he can only pronounce vowels.

LUCY. Goodness!

EDWARD. It's hard when you first hear him, but after awhile it becomes easier. I'm just now getting the hang of it.

LUCY. Has he given you lessons?

EDWARD. No, not that way; your ear gradually gets used to his speech.

LUCY. [*Sitting to the left of the table.*] I see.

EDWARD. M. Chandebise has hired him as his secretary. You see, it's been hard for him to find a job because of his speech defect.

LUCY. Heavens! A man who only has vowels to offer!

EDWARD. You're right, it's not enough. I know that you have to have both vowels and consonants to write, but writing isn't the only thing in life. [*Going upstage, above the table.*] It's too bad, isn't it. Such an intelligent, well-bred boy! Can you believe it, he's never had a mistress!

LUCY. Good heavens!

EDWARD. [*Naively.*] At least that I know of.

LUCY. [*Standing.*] Well, he certainly has it easy here.

EDWARD. [*Sighing.*] Ah, yes! [*Seeing* ROBERTA *enter from the bay.*] Ah! Here she is now!

LUCY. [*Going to her.*] At last!

ROBERTA. [*Entering in a rush.*] Oh, my dear friend, I am so upset. [*To* EDWARD *as she crosses to the table where she puts her purse.*] Leave us alone, Edward.

EDWARD. Yes, madam. [*To* LUCY.] May I leave, madam?

LUCY. Of course! [*He exits.*]

ROBERTA. [*Putting her hat on the table to the right of the rear door.*] I made you wait.

LUCY. [*Facetiously.*] Really?

ROBERTA. I was on a wild goose chase. I'll explain it all to you. [*Quickly, she crosses to* LUCY.] Lucy, I asked you to come on a very serious matter: my husband is cheating on me!

LUCY. What? Victor-Emmanuel?

ROBERTA. Yes, Victor-Emmanuel.

LUCY. What a shock that must have been.

ROBERTA. The rat! Wait 'til I get my hands on him!

LUCY. Can you do that? Do you have proof?

ROBERTA. Not yet! The coward! Oh, but I will get it.

LUCY. How?

ROBERTA. I don't know; that's why you're here . . . to help me. [*She sits on the couch.*]

LUCY. [*Standing near her.*] Me?

ROBERTA. You! Don't say no, Lucy. You were my best friend at school. Even though we've been apart for ten years, there are some things that you don't forget. I left you as Lucy Vicard and found you as Lucy Homenides de Histangua. Your name may have gotten longer, but your heart is still the same. You are still my best friend in the world.

LUCY. That's for sure!

ROBERTA. You're the only one I can turn to in this matter.

LUCY. [*Without conviction as she sits by* ROBERTA *on the couch.*] How kind you are to say that.

ROBERTA. [*Without transition.*] Tell me; what am I to do?

LUCY. [*Bewildered.*] About what?

ROBERTA. Getting the goods on my husband.

LUCY. How should I know? Is that why you asked me to come?

ROBERTA. Of course.

LUCY. You'll get the best of him. First off, who told you that your husband was straying? He's certainly been a faithful husband until now.

ROBERTA. Has he?

LUCY. As long as you don't have proof.

ROBERTA. I am not mistaken about this.

LUCY. Very well, perhaps your husband is like that.

ROBERTA. I'm not a child who believes everything she's told. What would you say if suddenly your husband, who had been an excellent hus-band—in—uh—every way possible, stopped being a husband? Pouf. . . . from one day to the next!

LUCY. [*Delicately.*] I would say, "Oh!"

ROBERTA. Indeed, you would say, "Oh!" That's what they tell you before it happens. I found his continual atten-tion, our eternal spring a little boring and monotonous. I said to myself, "Oh, for a cloud, a quarrel, a worry, anything." I had about decided to take a lover, simply to add a little spice to my life.

LUCY. You, a lover?

ROBERTA. Yes, heavens! We all have those moments! I had just about overcome my inhibitions! Remember your dinner partner from the other evening, Roman Tournel? Not to name names of course. You saw how he was courting me. It was all very amusing, and I know that I have him in the palm of my hand.

LUCY. Oh!

ROBERTA. It would be so easy, as he said; after all, he is my husband's best friend. [*Standing up.*] Oh, but now, I can't think of taking a lover, now that my husband is cheating on me.

LUCY. [*Standing and crossing to the right.*] May I tell you something?

ROBERTA. Certainly.

LUCY. Down deep you're crazy about your husband.

ROBERTA. Do you think so?

LUCY. Does that bother you?

ROBERTA. Certainly. It irritates me. I was about to cheat on him, but he's already cheating on me! That's too much!

LUCY. [*As she is getting her coat.*] It is a delicate situation!

ROBERTA. You do see my point?

LUCY. [*As she puts her coat on the table on the right.*] Yes, of course. But what you have told me is not proof.

ROBERTA. [*Going upstage to the table.*] What? I have proved nothing to you? When a husband who has been like a constant torrent for years suddenly goes . . . pouf . . . dry. Nothing!

LUCY. [*Seated to the left of the table.*] Well, yes! That Spanish river, the Man-zanares, is like that. Just because he's run dry doesn't mean he's changed his bed.

ROBERTA. Oh!

LUCY. You've been to the casino when people have made a run on the bank. Then you meet them later, and they don't have a cent to their name.

ROBERTA. [*Passionately and considering* LUCY's *words.*] But if only he had that last cent. He's always broken the bank before. [*She goes upstage to the table where her hat is.*]

LUCY. You see, that doesn't prove that he's totally cleaned out; it only proves that he's a little short at the moment. That's all.

ROBERTA. [*Listening as she leans against the table at the rear, with her arms crossed.*] Yes and no. [*Coming down-stage to the table, she rummages in her purse from which she pulls a pair of suspenders. She brandishes them under* LUCY's *nose.*] And what about these?

LUCY. What about them?

ROBERTA. [*Peremptorily.*] Suspenders!

LUCY. So it would appear.

ROBERTA. Do you know whose they are?

LUCY. Your husband's, I presume.

ROBRTA. [*Quickly.*] You see, you're be-ginning to believe me.

LUCY. No, of course not! Since we are in your house I assumed that they be-longed to your husband and not some other man.

ROBERTA. [*Putting the suspenders back in her purse. She puts the purse on the table at the rear and comes downstage to cen-*

ter.] Perfect! Now can you explain why these suspenders arrived in this morning's mail?

LUCY. In the mail?

ROBERTA. Yes, in a package addressed to him. I opened it by mistake as I was inspecting his mail.

LUCY. And why were you inspecting his mail?

ROBERTA. [*Naturally.*] To find out what was in it.

LUCY. [*Bowing ironically.*] That *is* a reason.

ROBERTA. You see!

LUCY. What do you mean "by mistake"?

ROBERTA. Anything that's not addressed to me, for goodness' sake.

LUCY. Oh.

ROBERTA. So, if he received his suspenders in the morning mail, he must have left them somewhere.

LUCY. [*Rising and crossing left.*] You're right!

ROBERTA. Can you guess where that "somewhere" is?

LUCY. [*Feigning fear.*] I'm afraid to ask!

ROBERTA. The Kozy Kitty Hotel, my dear!

LUCY. What's that?

ROBERTA. Certainly not a family inn.

LUCY. [*Shaking her head.*] The Kozy Kitty Hotel.

ROBERTA. [*Going upstage to the table to get the box. She comes downstage with it.*] Here, you can see for yourself. Look, it's a printed label and below the name is my husband's address, "M. Chandebise, 95 Boulevard Malesherbes."

LUCY. [*Reading the label.*] The Kozy Kitty Hotel.

ROBERTA. And in Montretout! You know its reputation. I won't bore you with the details now. [*She puts the box on the table on the right.*] There's no mistake about it; all my facts are in order. I was there!

LUCY. Oh!

ROBERTA. Good Lord yes, just to allay my doubts, to make sure that my husband wasn't a little . . . a little. . . .

LUCY. [*Coming to her aid.*] Manzanares?

ROBERTA. Yes, I couldn't have said it better! What to do about this, I asked myself, because it has put a bug in my ear. [*She goes to get the box and carries it back where she found it.*]

LUCY. That's for sure!

ROBERTA. If you could have seen the hotel! My dear, it looked like a candy box.

LUCY. What do you mean, "If I could have seen. . . ."

ROBERTA. Well, I saw it with my own eyes.

LUCY. What?

ROBERTA. That's why I was late.

LUCY. Oh.

ROBERTA. You see, I decided that the only way to clear the whole matter up was to talk to the innkeeper. Don't think for a minute that you can get anything out of an innkeeper. They keep insisting that they know nothing.

LUCY. That's the A.B.C.'s of their trade.

ROBERTA. That's true enough. You can't imagine what he said to me. "Madam, if I told you the names of my guests, you would be the first one never to come here." Yes, to me! It was quite impossible to pull anything out of him. He was as helpful as a dead fish.

LUCY. [*With a pout.*] You're making him out better than he is.

ROBERTA. I knew then that you and I would have to get to the bottom of this matter. Men stick together so. We'll have to outsmart them. You are more clever than I, and you have the facts before you. What are we to do?

LUCY. You've caught me unaware.

ROBERTA. Oh, think of something!

LUCY. What if you asked your husband for an explanation?

ROBERTA. How can you suggest that? He'd only answer me with a lie. No one can lie like a man . . . unless it's a woman.

LUCY. It all comes to the same thing since we are the only two beings in creation. Wait! Maybe there is a way; it's a trick I often used in the theatre.

ROBERTA. What is it?

LUCY. It's not very original, but it sometimes works with men. You take a piece of writing paper, well-perfumed, address it to your husband—a sizzling letter, mind you—as if it were from another woman, and invite him to a rendez-vous.

ROBERTA. A rendez-vous?

LUCY. To which you go yourself. If he comes, you've got him.

ROBERTA. Yes, yes! You're right, it's not very original. Sometimes, though, it's the tried and true methods that get the best results. [*She looks for the writing desk, brings it to the couch and opens it there.*] We are going to write to Victor-Emmanuel now.

LUCY. [*In an off-handed manner.*] Let's write to Victor-Emmanuel.

ROBERTA. [*Seated on the couch, starting to write, then stopping.*] But, he'll recognize my handwriting.

LUCY. [*Feigned seriousness.*] Yes, if you've written to him before, he certainly will.

ROBERTA. [*Standing up.*] Wait, yours! He doesn't know it! You are going to write him! [*As she says this, she grabs* LUCY *and pushes her onto the couch.*]

LUCY. [*Resisting.*] No, no, I can't! It's too delicate!

ROBERTA. Very well, then, I appeal to your delicacy. [*Severely.*] You are my best friend in the world, aren't you?

LUCY. [*Weakly.*] Oh, you're going to lead me straight to hell!

ROBERTA. You'll meet my husband there.

LUCY. What good will that do me? [*Resigned, sitting on the couch, in front of the desk.*] All right, give me some writing paper.

ROBERTA. [*Above the desk, taking a packet of paper from the desk.*] Here you are!

LUCY. Not that kind; he'd recognize that in a flash.

ROBERTA. Oh, how stupid of me! You're right! [*Going to the table between the* window and the door on the left.] Wait, I have something that is much better; the paper I bought for my sister's children. [*She waves three or four sheets of lacy paper with flowers painted on it.*]

LUCY. That? He'll think a cook is stuck on him, and he won't come.

ROBERTA. [*Nodding her head.*] You're right.

LUCY. Don't you have any alluring paper?

ROBERTA. [*Taking a box of paper from the table.*] Good Lord! Here's the paper I bought for the country, but it's not very alluring.

LUCY. No, it isn't, but we'll perfume it heavily.

ROBERTA. I have the perfect thing for that: a bottle of Passion Flower that I pushed aside because I couldn't stand the scent. Wait. [*As she is talking, she goes to push the button which is on the right of the window. At this moment* CAMILE, *coming from the room on the right, looks inquisitively into the room. He has a file in his hand.*]

CAMILLE. I beg your pardon!

ROBERTA. [*Standing near the little table on the left.*] What do you want, Camille?

CAMILLE. [*As before.*] Don't mind me. I only wanted to see if Victor-Emmanuel had come home.

ROBERTA. [*In the most natural conversational tone.*] No, not yet. Why?

CAMILLE. Because I have some papers for him to sign and I need to ask him some questions about this new contract. I don't understand it, and I wanted. . . .

ROBERTA. I'm sure he won't be much longer.

CAMILLE. Then, I'll wait. What else can I do? He's certainly not here.

ROBERTA. Indeed, indeed! [*To* LUCY *who has been listening open-mouthed to the conversation. Her eyes go from one speaker to the other. Finally, she looks at* ROBERTA *with admiration.*] Why are you looking at me like that?

LUCY. [*Disconcerted.*] What? No reason, no reason!

CAMILLE. [*Jovially.*] You see, my dear cousin did finally come in. She didn't make you wait too long, did she?

LUCY. [*Somewhat nonplussed by this speech, trying to appear to understand.*] Indeed, sir, yes, we met earlier, and we even chatted for a moment.

ROBERTA. [*Maliciously.*] No, no that's not what he said. He said that I had finally come in and you didn't have to wait too long.

CAMILLE. [*Approving.*] Yes, that's it!

LUCY. [*Embarrassed and trying to appear friendly.*] Oh, yes, yes, perfect!

ROBERTA. [*Making the introductions.*] M. Camille Chandebise, our cousin, Mme. Carlos Homenides de Histangua. [*Camille bows as Roberta comes downstage on the left.*]

LUCY. [*Standing up.*] Pleased to meet you. Please excuse me for not understanding you earlier; I'm a little hard of hearing.

CAMILLE. [*Jovially.*] Oh, how kind of you to say that, madam, but in fact, I am hard to understand because I have a speech defect.

LUCY. [*Smiling stupidly.*] Yes, of course. [*Appealing to ROBERTA for help.*]

ROBERTA. [*Trying to be serious.*] He said he has a speech defect.

LUCY. [*Playing shocked.*] Can it be so? Well, maybe it is true, now that you've pointed it out to me.

CAMILLE. [*Forcing a smile and a bow.*] Oh, you're too generous!

ANTOINETTE. [*Entering from the bay and coming downstage.*] Madam rang?

ROBERTA. [*As LUCY is sitting back down on the couch.*] Not for you, for Adele. I rang twice.

ANTOINETTE. Adele is in her room, so I came.

ROBERTA. Well, it doesn't matter. Go to my room and bring me that bottle of Passion Flower perfume in the right drawer of my dressing table.

ANTOINETTE. Yes, madam.

ROBERTA. You'll recognize it by the purple label.

ANTOINETTE. Yes, madam. [*As she begins to leave, she sees that she is to CAMILLE's left. Facetiously—in mock embarrassment—she walks around in a semi-circle, making sure that their eyes meet. With her back to the audience she pinches CAMILLE's left buttock with her left hand. She exits with a holier-than-thou air.*]

CAMILLE. [*Jumping because of the pain.*] Oh!

ROBERTA *and* LUCY. [*Startled.*] What was that?

CAMILLE. [*As ANTOINETTE leaves.*] Nothing, nothing at all, just a sharp pain in my hip that made me jump.

ROBERTA. It must be rheumatism.

CAMILLE. [*Rubbing his hip as he backs out of the room bowing and scraping.*] Evidently, it must be my rheumatism.

ROBERTA. Evidently!

CAMILLE. I'll go back to my work, ladies. [*Continuing to bow his way out.*]

LUCY. [*Bowing slightly.*] Sir!

CAMILLE. [*Finally at the door.*] Ladies! [*He exits. The two women watch him leave, and when he is out of sight, they break out laughing.*]

LUCY. How you can understand a word he says is beyond me.

ROBERTA. [*Maliciously.*] Is that why you were looking at me so strangely?

LUCY. Of course.

ROBERTA. What do you expect? It's the continued exposure. It was sweet of you to pretend that you had not noticed his speech defect.

LUCY. I didn't want to be impolite.

ANTOINETTE. [*Entering left with the bottle of perfume.*] Is this the one, Madam?

ROBERTA. [*Taking the bottle.*] Yes, it is, thank you. [*She sits in one of the chairs facing the couch where LUCY is still seated. ANTOINETTE exits.*] Let's see how much of the letter we can get done before my husband gets home.

LUCY. You're right. [*Starting to write.*] Let's see, how are we going to bait the trap?

ROBERTA. Hmm!

LUCY. First of all, when did our mysterious lady fall madly in love with your husband?

ROBERTA. Hmmm?

LUCY. Have you been to the theatre lately?

ROBERTA. Last Wednesday with M. Tournel.

LUCY. M. Tournel?

ROBERTA. The one who is courting me.

LUCY. Ah! That makes it even better! You'll see. [*Writing.*] "Sir, I saw you the other night at the theatre. . . .

ROBERTA. [*With a pout.*] Don't you think that's a little formal for a love letter?

LUCY. Too formal?

ROBERTA. It sounds like a process server had written it. I don't know, maybe we should just start it, "I am the one who couldn't take my eyes off you the other night at the theatre," and forget about the "Dear Sir." Think about it!

LUCY. But of course! You've really got a knack for this!

ROBERTA. [*Modestly.*] Oh goodness, it seems to me that's how it should be done.

LUCY. Well, then, we're in agreement about how to do it. [*She puts the first sheet of paper back into the desk and pulls out a clean sheet.*] "I am the one who couldn't take my eyes off you the other night. . . ."

ROBERTA. [*Dictating.*] "At the theatre." There, it's warm, it's direct!

LUCY. It lives! [*Continuing.*] "You were in a box with your wife and another man. . . ."

ROBERTA. M. Tournel.

LUCY. [*As she is writing.*] Yes, but our mysterious lady wouldn't know that. "The people with me told me your name. . . ."

ROBERTA. [*Repeating as if she were taking dictation.*] "Told me your name. . . ."

LUCY. [*Repeating as she writes.*] "Name. That's how I know who you are."

ROBERTA. Isn't this easy?

LUCY. [*Writing.*] "Since that evening you have been in my dreams constantly."

ROBERTA. Don't you think that's a little thick?

LUCY. Of course, of course! But it's what

we need! We all know love is blind; we're the ones that can see. But does that matter?

ROBERTA. If you're sure, keep on going.

LUCY. [*Writing.*] "I'm about to do something crazy. Do you want to do it with me? I'll be waiting for you this afternoon at five o'clock at the Kozy Kitty Hotel."

ROBERTA. The same hotel? Won't he be suspicious?

LUCY. Of course not; it will excite him. [*Writing.*] In parenthesis: "Montretout, Seine. Ask for M. Chandebise's room."

ROBERTA. [*Dictating.*] "I'm counting on you."

LUCY. [*Nodding in approval as she writes.*] "I'm counting on you!" Perfect! You've got what it takes!

ROBERTA. You've still got to be trained.

LUCY. [*Writing.*] "A woman who loves you." Now for the perfume.

ROBERTA. [*Who has opened the perfume while LUCY has been writing.*] Here you are. [*She hands over the perfume.*]

LUCY. This will really be good! [*She puts the perfume on her fingers and then pinches the paper.*]

ROBERTA. [*Watching her and exclaiming as the ink runs from the perfume.*] Oh!

LUCY. [*Same reaction.*] Goodness! [*She stands up to better observe.*]

ROBERTA. We've ruined it!

LUCY. We have.

ROBERTA. We'll have to start over.

LUCY. Wait! Maybe we can use this. [*Sitting back down and writing.*] "P.S. As I wrote you, I couldn't hold back my tears. Think of them as tears of joy and not of despair." Here goes nothing! Long live Passion Flower!

ROBERTA. He'll think that many tears are strange for a woman alone.

LUCY. Let it be! He won't notice a thing. And now for the address. [*Writing on the envelope.*] "M. Victor-Emmanuel Chandebise, 95 Boulevard des Malesherbes. Personal." [*Standing up and sealing the envelope.*] Now we need someone to make sure that he gets this.

ROBERTA. [*Who has closed the desk and taken it back to its original place.*] Who can we get? Of course! You!

LUCY. [*Giving a start.*] Me? Oh no!

ROBERTA. Oh yes! Think! I can't trust a servant with this—we'd risk being found out. I can't do it either because someone might recognize me. Then we'd really be in the soup. It has to be you. No one knows you here.

LUCY. You're giving me all the dirty work!

ROBERTA. You are my best friend, aren't you?

LUCY. Yes, but don't abuse the privilege. [*An exterior doorbell rings.*]

ROBERTA. There's the bell; my husband must be home. [*Going left upstage and pointing out the door on the left.*] Quick! Through here! That door on the right will lead you into the vestibule.

LUCY. [*Going upstage, center, to reach the door.*] Good! I'll see you soon.

ROBERTA. Soon. [LUCY *exits as* ROBERTA *goes to hide the perfume in the little table on the left. At this moment the bay door opens and the audience sees* CHANDEBISE *speaking to* EDWARD *and followed by* TOURNEL.]

CHANDEBISE. [*With his hat still on.*] And the Doctor said he would be back?

EDWARD. Yes, sir.

CHANDEBISE. Very well. [*To* TOURNEL *who is holding his hat.*] Come in, old man. [*He motions for him to precede him.* TOURNEL *comes downstage to the right of the table on the right.*] Just a moment, I have some papers to sign.

ROBERTA. [*Whom they haven't noticed.*] Even Camille waits on you as if you were the Messiah.

CHANDEBISE. [*At the left of the table on the right and somewhat above it.*] Well, there you are.

TOURNEL. [*From his position.*] Oh, good day, my dear.

ROBERTA. Good day, M. Tournel. [*To her husband.*] Yes, I'm here.

CHANDEBISE. I met Tournel in the lobby, so we came up together.

ROBERTA. [*Indifferently.*] Oh.

TOURNEL [*Taking some papers from his briefcase and putting them on the table.*] Yes, I brought a list of prospective clients.

CHANDEBISE. Wonderful! You must give it to me at once. [*As he speaks he adjusts his pants as if his suspenders are too tight.*]

ROBERTA. [*Who picks up on this gesture.*] What's wrong with your pants; are your suspenders too tight?

CHANDEBISE. Yes.

ROBERTA. Are those the ones I bought you?

CHANDEBISE. What? Oh yes, yes.

ROBERTA. They didn't bother you before.

CHANDEBISE. They're too tight.

ROBERTA. [*Starting towards him.*] Let me loosen them for you.

CHANDEBISE. [*Pulling back instinctively.*] No, no, don't bother. I'll loosen them myself.

ROBERTA. [*Primly.*] As you will.

CHANDEBISE. [*To* TOURNEL.] Will you excuse me for a moment?

TOURNEL. Of course, go on. [CHANDEBISE *opens the door to the room on the right.*]

CAMILLE. [*From offstage.*] Ah!

CHANDEBISE. [*Irritated by* CAMILLE'*s greeting.*] Very well, I'll be there in a moment. [*He exits, closing the door behind him.*]

TOURNEL. [*He rushes to* ROBERTA, *who is standing to the left rear, as soon as* CHANDEBISE *exits.*] Oh, Roberta, Roberta! How I dreamed of you.

ROBERTA. [*Dampening his enthusiasm.*] No, my friend! No thanks! I can't think of such things when my husband is cheating on me.

TOURNEL. [*Confused.*] What?

ROBERTA. It's fine as long as I don't have anything more serious to think about.

TOURNEL. But Roberta, Roberta! You told me! You led me to hope!

ROBERTA. That's possible. But that was before the suspenders! Now there are the suspenders! Goodbye! [*She exits to the left.*]

TOURNEL. [*Confused momentarily.*] What a minx! What? Suspenders? What was that all about? Suspenders? [*As he speaks he goes to the left of the table on the right.*]

CAMILLE. [*On the right side of the bay door, jovially.*] M. Tournel! My cousin wants you.

TOURNEL. [*Ill-tempered.*] What?

CAMILLE. [*Trying to articulate but failing.*] My cousin wants you.

TOURNEL. [*Same spirit.*] I can't understand a word you're saying. When you decide to speak more clearly. . . .

CAMILLE. Just a moment! [*He takes a note pad from his coat pocket, a pencil from his shirt pocket and begins to write out his message, syllable by syllable.*]

CAMILLE. My cousin wants to see you. [*As he finishes, he tears off the sheet and hands it to* TOURNEL.]

TOURNEL. [*Reading.*] "My cousin wants to see you." Why didn't you say so? [*Grumbling, he gathers up his papers, puts them in his briefcase, and goes upstage and exits stage right. He forgets his briefcase.*]

CAMILLE. [*Once* TOURNEL *has exited.*] The cad! [*Coming downstage, center stage.*] I was nice enough to come get him, and he treated me like dirt! [*At this moment the bay door opens.* EDWARD *ushers* FINACHE *into the room.*]

EDWARD. Yes, Doctor, he's in now.

FINACHE. Ah, good!

EDWARD. [*Exiting.*] I'll tell him you're here. [CAMILLE *continues to complain but doesn't hear them enter.*]

CAMILLE. It's too much! I told him politely, "Tournel, my cousin wants to see you." He made me repeat the message, then I had to spell it out for him. And he had the nerve to say, "Why didn't you say so?" That's the last time I'll put myself out for a porcupine like him!

FINACHE. [*Watching* CAMILLE.] Well, have you taken to reciting monologs?

CAMILLE. [*Startled.*] What? Oh, it's you, Doctor. I was just complainting about someone who had given me a hard time.

FINACHE. [*Not understanding.*] Oh, good, don't bother. [*Changing his tone.*] Tell me, you rascal, what's new? Any wild parties?

CAMILLE. [*Quickly going to him and in a low voice.*] Shhh! Quiet!

FINACHE. You're right! Here you are the chaste Camille and have your reputation to think of.

CAMILLE. [*Uncomfortable.*] Please! . . .

FINACHE. Unfortunately, even you will have to be defrocked at some time or another. It happens to us all. I can't believe how you've pulled the wool over their eyes.

CAMILLE. [*Forcing a laugh.*] Yes, yes!

FINACHE. Did you take my advice?

CAMILLE. Which?

FINACHE. About the Kozy Kitty Hotel?

CAMILLE. [*Frightened.*] Shhh! Quiet!

FINACHE. But that's our secret! Did you go?

CAMILLE. [*Hesitates, looks right, then left, finally in a whisper.*] Yes.

FINACHE. How did you like it?

CAMILLE. [*Rolling his eyes heavenward.*] Oh!

FINACHE. Not bad, eh? As I told you, when I need—uh—stimulation I go there, too. But your secret is safe with me. Go on, tell your cousin I'm here.

CAMILLE. [*Enchanted by this conversation.*] It was heaven.

FINACHE. Before I forget about it, I have that contraption for you.

CAMILLE. [*Coming downstage.*] What contraption?

FINACHE. [*Pulling a small box from his pocket.*] The one that I promised you—it will enable you to speak like everyone else.

CAMILLE. Ah! Yes! Do you have it there?

FINACHE. Indeed! Before I give it to you let me explain why it will help your speech. The roof of your mouth did not have the time to form before you were born. So, sounds, instead of hitting this natural barrier which should throw them out of your mouth, rattle around in your head.

CAMILLE. So, that's it!

FINACHE. It is that barrier that I am giving you. Look how pretty and nicely packaged it is!

CAMILLE. Oh!

FINACHE. [*Opening the box.*] A silver plate, my boy, just like in fairy tales.

CAMILLE. [*Clasping his hands in admiration.*] Will I really be able to talk?

FINACHE. What?

CAMILLE. Will I. . . . Wait a minute. [*He starts to put the palate in his mouth.*]

FINACHE. [*Stopping him with an upraised palm.*] No, no, not like that! You'll have to soak it in a boric acid solution first; you don't know who's had their hands on it.

CAMILLE. You're right. I said [*Trying to articulate as best he can.*], will I really be able to speak?

FINACHE. [*Who has understood.*] Will you be able to speak? I'll say! If you have the talent, you can even try out for the Comédie-Française.

CAMILLE. [*Radiant.*] Ah!!! I'll put it to soak immediately. [*He goes upstage.*]

CHANDEBISE. [*From off stage.*]! CAMILLE!

FINACHE. Someone's calling you.

CAMILLE. Tell him that I'll be right back. [*He disappears at the rear.*]

CHANDEBISE. [*Entering right.*] Camille!

FINACHE. [*Going to him.*] He'll be back in a moment; he had something to take care of. Ah, how are you? [*They shake hands.*]

CHANDEBISE. Ah, hello, Finache. I'm fine, how are you? It's always good to see you. Let's see, I had something to talk to you about.

FINACHE. I was by earlier; did Edward tell you?

CHANDEBISE. Oh, yes, Histangua's certificate. He looks to be in top shape!

FINACHE. First class! Here's the report. [*He takes the file from his pocket and hands it to* CHANDEBISE.]

CHANDEBISE. [*Taking it.*] Thank you.

FINACHE. [*Sitting to the left of the table.*] What's on your mind?

CHANDEBISE. [*Sitting across from him to the right of the table.*] I want to ask you about a very delicate matter. Something quite extraordinary has happened to me.

FINACHE. What can it be?

CHANDEBISE. Let's see, how can I explain this to you? As you know, my wife is a tasty little morsel.

FINACHE. I can't help but agree with you on that.

CHANDEBISE. Good! You know, too, that no one is a better husband than I.

FINACHE. Ah?

CHANDEBISE. [*Somewhat irritated.*] What do you mean, "Ah"!

FINACHE. I don't know, old man.

CHANDEBISE. Very well, let me continue. You would not be shocked to learn that my wife is both a lover and a wife. That is, I've never looked at anyone else. I am a first rate husband.

FINACHE. Ah?

CHANDEBISE. What do you mean, "Ah"?

FINACHE. I'm very happy for you, that's all. I don't understand why this preamble?

CHANDEBISE. [*Rising, then sitting on the edge of the table closest to the rear.*] You'll see in a moment. Have you seen the new play "Anything to Declare"?

FINACHE. Eh?

CHANDEBISE. I asked if you had seen "Anything to Declare"?

FINACHE. Good God!

CHANDEBISE. Well, have you or haven't you?

FINACHE. [*Leering.*] Let me explain; I wasn't alone in my box, so. . . .

CHANDEBISE. [*Laughing.*] Oh, of course! You don't remember it all that well.

FINACHE. [*Laughing.*] In a word!

CHANDEBISE. No matter! You probably saw enough of it to catch the drift of the plot. A well-bred young man and his wife are on their honeymoon. He is giving his bride her first lesson in the principles of married love, when, in the middle of the lesson, a customs official bursts into their compartment and demands, "Anything to declare?" The young man is brutally distracted from the task at hand.

FINACHE. Oh yes, now I remember—vaguely.

CHANDEBISE. Vaguely? Very well, old man! I can see that the customs man didn't pass by your box. [*He stands and goes center stage.*]

FINACHE. [*Laughing, slyly.*] No, he didn't.

CHANDEBISE. [*Going, as he speaks, to the chair on the left side of the stage. He takes it, turns it to him, and sits astride it.*] In brief, every time the young man returns to his lessons, he sees the customs man and hears, "Anything to declare?" He is obsessed and cannot carry out his mission at all.

FINACHE. How dreadful!

CHANDEBISE. [*With conviction.*] Isn't it? [*Standing.*] Well, my friend, that's exactly what's happened to me.

FINACHE. Eh?

CHANDEBISE. Exactly! One fine day about a month ago [*He takes the chair back to its original place.*] I was, as is my habit, very amorous. I indicated this to Mme. Chandebise who welcomed the suggestion. Then suddenly, I really don't know what happened. . . .

FINACHE. [*Slyly.*] The customs man came in?

CHANDEBISE. [*Distracted.*] Yes! [*Quickly.*] Eh? Uh, of course not! But in any case, it's as if I have been stricken with a sickness, some disorder. I feel like I've become a child, a little boy again. [*Using a childish voice, he measures out his steps to the rhythm of the words.*]

FINACHE. Damn! How terrible!

CHANDEBISE. [*Turning his eyes downward, then with a pout.*] That's for sure. [*Changing his tone.*] My God, I've never been so upset in my life. It's such a shock after my glorious past. I keep telling myself that things will soon revert to their normal course.

FINACHE. That's life!

CHANDEBISE. But when will they revert to normal? I keep telling myself to have courage and my powers will return. Is it normal to think about such matters when I should be concentrating on the matter at hand? Naturally, nothing happens, and I am seized by anxiety anew.

FINACHE. Poor fellow!

CHANDEBISE. Poor fellow, indeed! In any case, it's all over. I am obsessed by that. I no longer ask myself—I don't dare say to myself, "Tonight." I say to myself, "Tonight, I won't." . . . And bingo, nothing happens.

FINACHE. [*Joking.*] Perhaps, you could. . . .

CHANDEBISE. What? See here, Finache, this is not a joking matter.

FINACHE. [*Getting up.*] Ah, well, why not? You thought I would find your story tragic, but it happens every day. You are simply a victim of autosuggestion. So it is up to you to change the situation. Try positive thinking! Knowledge is power!

CHANDEBISE. What? What?

FINACHE. Instead of saying "Can I?," An attitude that hinders you, say "I CAN!" That's all there is to it. Never doubt yourself. And don't ever mix up your self-respect in this. So much of this problem has to do with self-respect. Never mix self-respect and love—they simply don't go together. You should have told your wife this, not me. You should have approached her with gentleness and openness instead of closing her out. Perhaps she might have laughed, you could have laughed together. Then the two of you would have been able to put aside this uneasiness that has turned your lives upside down.

CHANDEBISE. [*Thoughtfully.*] Maybe you are right.

FINACHE. In addition, I suggest you take up a sport. Let me examine you. You're working too hard, spending too much time in the office. [*He puts his knee in the small of* CHANDEBISE's *back and his hands on* CHANDEBISE's *shoulders.*] See, you have a tendency to stoop. That's why I prescribed those American suspenders. Have you tried them yet?

CHANDEBISE. [*Lifting his vest to show the suspenders.*] Yes! And to force myself to wear them, I gave all my old ones to Camile. I must say these are really ugly.

FINACHE. Peuh! You're the only one that will see them.

CHANDEBISE. That's what you think. Just a moment ago, my wife was poking her nose into them.

FINACHE. What does it matter?

CHANDEBISE. [*Going right.*] Why add this ridicule to the other?

FINACHE. [*Following him.*] Watch out! You're putting vanity where it has no place. [*Changing his tone.*] Go on, take off your coat so that I can examine you. [*As* CHANDEBISE *takes off his coat, the rear door opens and* LUCY, *following* EDWARD, *enters.*]

LUCY. [*To* EDWARD.] Tell madam that I'm here.

CHANDEBISE. [*Quickly putting his coat on backwards.*] Oh!

EDWARD. Yes, madam. [*He exits.*]

CHANDEBISE. [*To* FINACHE.] Just a moment! [*To* LUCY.] Ah, dear lady.

LUCY. How are you?

CHANDEBISE. Well, tell me, how are you? Have you come to see my wife?

LUCY. In a manner of speaking. I'm returning after running an errand. I saw her a few minutes ago. And this gentleman as well.

FINACHE. [*Bowing.*] My pleasure.

CHANDEBISE. In that case, I don't need to introduce you. You didn't notice some nervousness, did you?

LUCY. [*Indicating* FINACHE.] In the Doctor?

CHANDEBISE. No, in my wife. I don't know what has gotten into her this morning: I've had to handle her with kid gloves.

LUCY. She didn't act that way with me.

CHANDEBISE. Lucky for you.

ROBERTA. [*Appearing in the left door.*] Ah, there you are.

LUCY. [*Going to her.*] Hello again.

ROBERTA. [*In a whisper.*] Well?

LUCY. [*In a whisper.*] It's done.

ROBERTA. Good!

EDWARD. [*Carrying the letter on a tray.*] The messenger just delivered a personal letter for you, sir.

CHANDEBISE. [*Shocked.*] For me? Heavens! [*To the two women.*] You will excuse me? [*He takes out his lorgnon and puts it on the tip of his nose, opens the letter, skims it, and unable to contain his surprise, exclaims.*] My word!

ROBERTA. [*Quickly.*] What is it?

CHANDEBISE. Nothing!

ROBERTA. [*Treacherously.*] Some problem?

CHANDEBISE. Oh! No, no. It's . . . it has to do with insurance.

ROBERTA. [*Drily.*] Oh! [*To* LUCY, *whispering angrily.*] Let's go! It's all too clear now. [*They exit left.*]

CHANDEBISE. [*To* FINACHE *as he goes left.*] As you can see, old man, women are quite unpredictable.

FINACHE. What?

TOURNEL. [*Entering stage right with a file under his arm.*] Have you forgotten all about me?

CHANDEBISE. Ah, there you are. Come in; I have something to share.

TOURNEL. [*Coming downstage after putting the file on the table.*] What's up? [*To* FINACHE.] Hello, Doctor.

FINACHE. Hello, Tournel.

CHANDEBISE. Boys, hold on to your hats! [*Playing it for effect.*] I've made a conquest!

FINACHE *and* TOURNEL. What?

TOURNEL. You?

FINACHE. You?

CHANDEBISE. Quite a shock, isn't it? See, I'm inventing nothing. [*Holding onto each word as he reads.*] "I am the one who couldn't take my eyes off you the other night at the theatre."

TOURNEL. You?

FINACHE. [*Preening.*] Why not me? How

wonderful! She couldn't take her eyes off me.

TOURNEL. What luck!

CHANDEBISE. [*Shaking his hand.*] Thank you.

TOURNEL. [*Taking the letter from him and continuing to read.*] "You were in a box with your wife and another man. . . ."

CHANDEBISE. Another man! Why that's you! "And another man." That is, "X," a newcomer, a speck of dust.

TOURNEL. So what?

CHANDEBISE. Aha! It's my turn now. [*Taking the letter.*] "The people with me told me your name. That's how I know who you are."

TOURNEL. [*Bantering.*] What a woman!

CHANDEBISE. Since that evening you have been in my dreams. . . ."

TOURNEL *and* FINACHE. [*Not quite understanding.*] No!

CHANDEBISE. [*Delighted.*] She's dreaming about me! [*Challenging* TOURNEL.] Did you hear that, Tournel?

TOURNEL. Does it say that?

CHANDEBISE. [*Holding the letter up as proof.*] Indeed it does, old man. See for yourself.

FINACHE. [*Examining the evidence.*] Yes, it does say that.

TOURNEL. [*Still not convinced.*] God! That's strange! [*To* FINACHE.] Don't you think so?

FINACHE. [*Not knowing how to answer.*] Peuh: There's nothing strange about dreams.

TOURNEL. Obviously. [*Mocking.*] I suppose it depends on what you've been eating.

CHANDEBISE. Well, what do you think?

TOURNEL. It's too funny!

CHANDEBISE. [*Continuing to read.*] "I'm about to do something crazy. Do you want to do it with me?" Poor dear, she's really fallen hard for me. [*To* FINACHE.] Hasn't she, Finache?

FINACHE. Why not?

CHANDEBISE. We shall see. Remember what I told you earlier?

FINACHE. [*Casually.*] Peuh! [*He sits to the right of the table.*]

CHANDEBISE. [*Reading.*] "I'll be waiting for you this afternoon at five o'clock at the Kozy Kitten Hotel."

FINACHE. [*Startled.*] The Kozy Kitten Hotel?

CHANDEBISE. [*Going to the left of the table.*] Yes, in Montretout.

FINACHE. Bravo! How practical! She really knows what she's doing!

CHANDEBISE. Why that hotel?

FINACHE. A dream, old man. That's where I have my fun.

CHANDEBISE. You see, that's what comes from living such a clean life. I don't know the place.

FINACHE. Ah well, I'm sure that Tournel! . . .

TOURNEL. [*Going above the table.*] No, I only know the name.

CHANDEBISE. [*Brusquely.*] Oh, gentlemen!

FINACHE *and* TOURNEL. What?

CHANDEBISE. She was crying.

TOURNEL *and* FINACHE. No!

CHANDEBISE. How romantic! She was crying! Listen! "P.S. As I wrote you, I couldn't hold back my tears. Think of them as tears of joy and not of despair." Poor dear! You can't say she isn't. Look how her tears cover the letter. [*He shoves the letter under* TOURNEL's *nose.* TOURNEL *is standing, his arms resting on the table.*]

TOURNEL. [*Sniffing the letter.*] Well, men!

FINACHE *and* CHANDEBISE. What?

TOURNEL. What makes her tears smell so strong? [*He goes center stage.*]

FINACHE. Oh, tears have their secrets, their mysteries. We must respect their essence.

CHANDEBISE. [*Rising.*] Go on, make fun of me. Aha! You see, Tournel, I can also make a conquest. While we were watching the play and not suspecting a thing, a woman was devouring us with her eyes.

TOURNEL. Amazing, isn't it?

CHANDEBISE. [*To* TOURNEL.] Did you catch her staring at us?

TOURNEL. No, I thought I saw someone,

but I assumed that she was interested in me.

CHANDEBISE. You're right! [*Brusquely.*] How could I be so stupid! Obviously, obviously. . . .

TOURNEL *and* FINACHE. What? [FINACHE *rises.*]

CHANDEBISE. It's not me she's attracted to; it's you!

TOURNEL. Me?

CHANDEBISE. But of course. She's mistaken me for you. Since my name was on the reservations, she probably assumed that I was you.

TOURNEL. [*Conceitedly.*] Are you sure?

CHANDEBISE. My God, yes!

TOURNEL. [*Same tone.*] Yes, maybe you're right.

CHANDEBISE. Look at me! Do you think that I could inspire passion? As for you, why it's quite natural; that's your function in life. [*To* FINACHE.] That's his function. You have the knack of turning women's heads. Look how handsome you are.

TOURNEL. [*Flattered, protesting because of propriety.*] No, no, you're too generous.

CHANDEBISE. It's no mystery that you are a lady-killer.

FINACHE. And even so, you don't realize your powers.

TOURNEL. No, I'm blessed with charm, that's all.

CHANDEBISE. Charm, that's all! You Romeo, you're too modest! Haven't women committed suicide because of you?

TOURNEL. [*Modestly.*] Oh, once. . . .

CHANDEBISE. And? . . .

TOURNEL. Well, she survived it.

CHANDEBISE. That doesn't change the fact that she tried it.

TOURNEL. Well, it's debatable. She got food poisoning from eating mussels.

CHANDEBISE *and* FINACHE. Mussels?

TOURNEL. I had just left her. She let it be known that she did it out of grief for me. However, she always said that if she wanted to die, she would not choose mussels since it was too

risky for her health.

CHANDEBISE. [*Somewhat categorically.*] There's no mistake about it: the letter was addressed to me, but it was meant for you.

TOURNEL. [*Hesitantly to* FINACHE.] What do you think?

FINACHE. [*Opening out his arms, indicating that he does not want to get involved.*] Oh. . . .

CHANDEBISE. Yes, yes! Although it's not addressed to you, you are the one who should go.

TOURNEL. [*Without conviction.*] Oh, no!

CHANDEBISE. Besides, I am not free this evening. We are having a dinner for our director from America.

TOURNEL. Really, I shouldn't. . . .

CHANDEBISE. Listen to yourself, you're dying to go!

TOURNEL. Do you think so?

CHANDEBISE. Look at your nose; see how it's twitching.

TOURNEL. [*Touching the tip of his nose.*] Hmm, my nose! It is twitching. Very well, I accept.

CHANDEBISE. [*Giving him a light tap on the shoulder.*] Go, Romeo, go! [*He comes downstage a bit.*]

TOURNEL. Well, this is turning out nicely! [*To* FINACHE.] I was planning on a little adventure, but that seems to be temporarily stalled.

CHANDEBISE. [*Going upstage and standing between them.*] Oh? With whom?

TOURNEL. [*Startled by* CHANDEBISE.] With . . . no, I can't tell you right now.

CHANDEBISE. [*To* FINACHE *as he mimicks* TOURNEL.] He can't tell me! [*To* TOURNEL.] Go, Romeo, go!

TOURNEL. Your mysterious lady will be an interesting distraction.

CHANDEBISE. [*In a jovial tone.*] Take her with my compliments.

TOURNEL. [*Imitating him.*] My, how kind you are! [*Without transition.*] Give me the letter.

CHANDEBISE. Oh no! Why should I? You don't need it. All you have to do is go to the hotel and ask for the room in my name. You see, it's not very often that I get letters like this. I want my grandchildren—should I have any—to find it among my papers; then they will be able to say, "Grandfather was quite a man!" At least my descendants will know that I was able to excite passion. Let's go, Finache! Examine me.

TOURNEL. [*Falling into step behind him.*] What about these papers? [*He comes downstage to the table and holds up the file.*]

CHANDEBISE. Two minutes, and I'm yours! Come on, Finache, let's go in here where we won't be disturbed. [*They exit stage right.*]

TOURNEL. [*Holding the file, muttering.*] Two minutes, two minutes. Then it will be something else. [*Smiling to himself after a moment.*] The Kozy Kitten Hotel! Who is this woman who is taken with me?

ROBERTA. [*Entering with her hat in her hand.*] My husband isn't here?

TOURNEL. He's with the Doctor. Shall I call him for you?

ROBERTA. No, no. Don't disturb them. When you see him, tell him that Madame de Histangua and I have gone out. I'll be in late because I'm planning to have dinner with a friend.

TOURNEL. He's not going to be in early either.

ROBERTA. [*Quickly, almost cutting him off.*] Oh? What do you mean?

TOURNEL. [*Not hearing her suspicion.*] What? Why he told me that he has a dinner meeting with his director from America.

ROBERTA. He told you that. That's news to me. Besides, it's not true, their dinner is tomorrow. I saw the invitation myself. Well!

TOURNEL. Oh, maybe he's gotten his dates mixed up. Let me ask him. [*He starts to go fetch* CHANDEBISE.]

ROBERTA. [*Stopping him.*] Never mind! He never makes mistakes like that. Don't waste your time. It's perfectly

clear that he's using this as an alibi for coming in late tonight. I know his game.

TOURNEL. [*Trying to make amends.*] Please believe me. He was quite sure about the date with me. Surely, he doesn't have a reason to lie to me.

ROBERTA. I see your little game. Now that you know that you don't have a chance with me because my husband is cheating on me, you're trying to convince me that he is the most faithful of husbands.

TOURNEL. Please take my word for it, I'm not lying to you.

ROBERTA. We shall see about that. Good-bye! [*She goes upstage to the left.*]

TOURNEL. [*Wanting to stop her.*] Roberta.

ROBERTA. Oh, Heavens! [*She shuts the door in his face as she exits.*]

TOURNEL. [*Instinctively jumping back in shock.*] Damn it! Answer me!

CAMILLE. [*Entering from the rear with a small, colored glass full of water and a packet of boric acid.*] Ah, M. Tournel! Are you in a better mood now?

TOURNEL. [*In the same tone as* ROBERTA.] You, damn it! [*As he speaks, he exits right.*]

CAMILLE. [*Slightly nonplussed.*] What a jerk! [*He goes to the table where he puts his glass of water to add the boric acid.*] What a lot of trouble to find this boric acid. [*He dumps the acid into the glass, takes the class in one hand and the palate in the other. He carefully inspects the palate.*] There! Soak, my palate, soak. [*He lets the palate fall into the water, and puts the glass on the mantle piece.*]

EDWARD. [*Entering.*] Senor Homenides de Histangua.

HOMENIDES. [*Entering briskly.*] Amigo!

CAMILLE. Ah, Senor de Histangua.

HOMENIDES. Senor Chandebise, he is here?

CAMILLE. Yes, yes, my cousin will be right with you. He's with his doctor at the moment.

HOMENIDES. Bueno, bueno! [CHANDEBISE *and* FINACHE *enter from the right.*]

CAMILLE. Here they are now!

FINACHE. [*Going upstage as if to leave*]. In short, just do as I told you.

CHANDEBISE. Very well, I understand.

HOMENIDES. Amigo! How is it with you?

CHANDEBISE. Ah, dear friend, how are you?

HOMENIDES. Bueno! And ze Doctor, he is good? Your health, it goes well?

FINACHE. As always! And you? Excuse me, I must be on my way.

HOMENIDES. De nada.

FINACHE. I'm off! So long!

HOMENIDES, CAMILLE, *and* CHANDEBISE. So long!

FINACHE. [*Stopping in the door as he exits.*] Happy hunting at the Kozy Kitten Hotel!

CAMILLE. [*From above the table, turning on his heels.*] That idiot! [*He exits right.*]

FINACHE. So long! [*He exits.*]

HOMENIDES. [*As soon as* FINACHE *exits.*] My wife, she is here?

CHANDEBISE. Indeed, she's with my wife.

HOMENIDES. Si, si! I comprende. She told me she would take my front.

CHANDEBISE. [*Confused, looking shocked.*] She would take your front?

HOMENIDES. Si! She come?

CHANDEBISE. Oh, you mean, she would get here before you.

HOMENIDES. Si, is what I say.

CHANDEBISE. Of course; shall I tell her you're here?

HOMENIDES. No! I will see her soon enough. Ah, Chandebise! Bueno! Thees morning I was at you company. There I saw you Doctor.

CHANDEBISE. Yes, he has given me your report.

HOMENIDES. Si! He makes me ourinate!

CHANDEBISE. What?

HOMENIDES. Ourinate, piss, piss!

CHANDEBISE. [*Catching on.*] Of course!

HOMENIDES. Porqué?

CHANDEBISE. What?

HOMENIDES. Why he makes me ourinate?

CHANDEBISE. To see if you are a good risk to insure.

HOMENIDES. For me? Iss not for me, the insurance, iss for my wife.

CHANDEBISE. [*Startled.*] What? But you didn't tell me that.

HOMENIDES. I say to you, I want insurance. You not ask me iss for me or iss for my wife.

CHANDEBISE. [*Jovially.*] Oh well, we can easily clear up this little matter. Madam Homenides will just have to stop by the office.

HOMENIDES. You do the same to her as me?

CHANDEBISE. Of course.

HOMENIDES. [*Very cold, very correct.*] I no permit it!

CHANDEBISE. But. . . .

HOMENIDES. [*Raising his voice by degrees.*] I no permit it, I tell you! I no permit it! [*He passes in front of* CHANDEBISE.]

CHANDEBISE. No need to get excited: we simply have these rules.

HOMENIDES. [*Turning about quickly so that he is facing* CHANDEBISE, *violently.*] Rules! I break! I piss for her!

CHANDEBISE. [*Equally energetically.*] No, that's impossible!

HOMENIDES. Bueno! No insurance! Iss all!

CHANDEBISE. Now, you can't be that jealous.

HOMENIDES. Iss not yaloussie, is inferior to ze dignity.

CHANDEBISE. Oh, don't be so old fashioned.

HOMENIDES. Yalousse? Iss not possible!!

CHANDEBISE. [*Trying to be friendly.*] You're that sure of your wife? Well, I must say that doesn't shock me.

HOMENIDES. Iss not her! She know she make eyes at an hombre, I keel her! Iss simple, no?

CHANDEBISE. Oh!

HONENIDES. [*Taking a revolver from his pocket.*] See, is my gonne.

CHANDEBISE. [*Instinctively putting his hand out to protect himself and scurrying behind* HOMENIDES.] Watch it, watch it! Don't wave that thing around!

HOMENIDES. [*Shrugging.*] No dancher!

CHANDEBISE. [*Not reassured.*] Be careful, in any case.

HOMENIDES. [*Through clenched teeth.*] Before, I fight duel with a senor. Caramba! He take a bullet in ze back, ze back, I tell you.

CHANDEBISE. [*Bewildered.*] You shot him in the back?

HOMENIDES. [*Brutally.*] No, I shoot at her.

CHANDEBISE. Oh, I see now what you mean. [*He makes a gesture with his hands of a couple embracing.*]

HOMENIDES. Verdad?

CHANDEBISE. [*Trying to calm him down.*] Uh, yes.

HOMENIDES. [*Calmer.*] She know. I tell her our wedding noche.

CHANDEBISE. [*Aside.*] What a charming fellow!

HOMENIDES. [*Putting the revolver back in his pocket and going left.*] She know I mean business!

TOURNEL. [*Entering stage right.*] Ah, there you are, old man.

CHANDEBISE. Just a moment.

TOURNEL. No, right now! I have other things to do.

CHANDEBISE. In a moment. Get those files ready for me so that I can see them at once.

TOURNEL. [*Ill-humored.*] All right. [*He exits, closing the door behind himself.*]

HOMENIDES. Who iss thes hombre?

CHANDEBISE. Tournel?

HOMENIDES. Tournel?

CHANDEBISE. A friend as well as a business associate.

HOMENIDES. Oh!

CHANDEBISE. [*Not realizing that* TOURNEL *has left.*] A charming fellow! Tournel! What, he's not here! His only fault is that he has the morals of an alleycat.

HOMENIDES. [*Indulgently.*] Pfiff!

CHANDEBISE. He's in a hurry to leave because he's got a woman waiting for him.

HOMENIDES. [*Laughing.*] Oh, ho!

CHANDEBISE. [*Somewhat conceitedly.*] When I say, "waiting for him," she could be expecting me. [*Taking the letter from the handkerchief pocket of his coat.*] Because her letter, overflowing with passion, was addressed to me.

HOMENIDES. [*Interested.*] Iss so? [*With curiosity.*] Thes senora, who iss?

CHANDEBISE. I have no idea; the letter was not signed. [*He pushes the letter back into his pocket.*]

HOMENIDES. [*Seriously.*] Some unknown lady, no doubt.

CHANDEBISE. I'm beginning to think that. She must be a woman of the world . . . someone's bored wife.

HOMENIDES. You can tell?

CHANDEBISE. [*Not understanding.*] What did you say?

HOMENIDES. [*Raising his voice.*] You can tell?

CHANDEBISE. [*Repeating mechanically.*] You can tell? Oh, now I see! From her style, of course. Professionals are less sentimental and more obvious. See for yourself. [*He hands the letter to* HOMENIDES.]

HOMENIDES. [*Laughing as he takes the letter.*] Iss a cuckold in here, no?

CHANDEBISE. You find that funny?

HOMENIDES. [*Jubilantly.*] Si, iss funny!

CHANDEBISE. Naughty boy!

HOMENIDES. [*Skimming the letter, then gasping.*] No!

CHANDEBISE. [*Confused.*] What?

HOMENIDES. [*Shouting as he crosses the stage in long strides.*] Caramba! Hija de la perra que te pario!

CHANDEBISE. What is it?

HOMENIDES. Iss ze handwriting of my wife!

CHANDEBISE. What did you say?

HOMENIDES. [*Lunging towards* CHANDEBISE *and pushing him against the table.*] You feelthy peeg!

CHANDEBISE. [*Trying to get away.*] Uh, uh!

HOMENIDES. [*Holding* CHANDEBISE *by the throat with one hand and looking for his revolver with the other.*] My boulédogue, where iss my boulédogue?

CHANDEBISE. [*Looking around the room for a dog.*] He has a dog?

HOMENIDES. [*Taking the gun from his pocket.*] Ah, here it iss!

CHANDEBISE. [*Seeing the revolver pointed at him.*] Now, see here!

HOMENIDES. [*Cocking the gun, still holding* CHANDEBISE *against the table—his knee in* CHANDEBISE's *stomach.*] Iss ze handwriting of my wife!

CHANDEBISE. [*Finally getting away, going right, above the table.*] No, no, it can't possibly be your wife—they all write like that these days.

HOMENIDES. [*Going left.*] No, I know iss her handwriting.

CHANDEBISE. And what of it? It is not I who am going but Tournel.

HOMENIDES. Tournel! Zat hombre who wass joust here? Bueno! I keel him.

CHANDEBISE. [*Quickly going to the right rear door.*] Let's get him in here and tell him what's going on. We'll have this cleared up in no time.

HOMENIDES. [*Who has managed to block the door.*] No, you no can do. It muss go on. I want ze proof. I will keel him.

CHANDEBISE. [*Trying to calm him down.*] Hold on, Histangua. [*From off stage they hear the voices of* ROBERTA *and* LUCY.]

HOMENIDES. [*Threatening* CHANDEBISE *with the gun as he pushes him towards the door on the right.*] Iss my wife's voice. Go on!

CHANDEBISE. Histangua—my friend!

HOMENIDES. Si, I am you friend, but I will keel you like a dogue.

CHANDEBISE. [*Not knowing what to do or say, exiting through the door.*] No, no! [HOMENIDES *locks the door and mops his forehead.*]

LUCY. [*Entering, followed by* ROBERTA.] Ah, here you are, my dear.

HOMENIDES. [*Trying to appear calm.*] Si, Si, I am here.

ROBERTA. [*Going to* HOMENIDES.] Hello, Senor de Histangua.

HOMENIDES. Buenas dias, senora. Esta ben? And you husband?

ROBERTA. He's fine, thank you.

HOMENIDES. And you children?

ROBERTA. But, we don't have any.

HOMENIDES. Oh, iss too bad! Bueno! Maybe some other time.

ROBERTA. [*Laughing.*] Perhaps!

LUCY. [*Suspecting something.*] Is there something the matter with you?

HOMENIDES. [*Containing his anger.*] No, nada!

LUCY. [*Not convinced.*] Do you need me? I'm going out with Roberta.

HOMENIDES. No, go!

LUCY. In that case, goodbye!

ROBERTA. Goodbye, Senor.

HOMENIDES. [*Furious.*] Hasta la vista, senora!

LUCY. [*Not wanting to leave him angry.*] Que tienes, querido mío? Que te pasa por que me pones una cara así?

HOMENIDES. [*Nervous but trying to contain himself.*] Te aseguro que no tengo nada.

LUCY. Oh! Jesus! Que carácter tan insoportables tienes!

They exit.

HOMENIDES. [*As soon as the women exit.*] Oh, you hussy, you! [*He goes right as one hears knocking from the locked door. He dashes to the door.*] Alto, alto, or I keel you! [*The noise stops. He goes upstage toward the rear door just as* TOURNEL *enters through it.*]

TOURNEL. [*To* HOMENIDES.] Where's M. Chandebise?

HOMENIDES. [*Aside, baring his teeth.*] Aha, ze dog, Tournel. [*Aloud, with a fake smile covering his murderous urges.*] So, senor, he no here.

TOURNEL. [*Not perceiving* HOMENIDES's *state of mind.*] Would you be kind enough to tell him—if you see him— that I left the papers on his desk. All he has to do is note the names.

HOMENIDES. [*Facing* TOURNEL.] Si, senor, si.

TOURNEL. I simply can't wait for him any longer.

HOMENIDES. [*His nerves showing through his affected joviality.*] So, zat's it! Go, go.

TOURNEL. [*Shocked.*] What?

HOMENIDES. [*Carried away.*] Go or I. . . .

[*He makes a gesture as if to strangle* TOURNEL.]

TOURNEL. Or you'll what?

HOMENIDES. [*Getting control of himself.*] Nada, senor, nada. [*Jovially.*] Go on, go.

TOURNEL. [*Going upstage.*] What a strange man! Goodbye, sir! [*He exits through the rear door.*]

HOMENIDES. Ah, is stuffy! [*He sees the glass of water with* CAMILLE's *palate in it and goes to it.*] Aha! [*He gulps the contents of the glass.*] Ah, bueno! [*Suddenly the taste registers on him.*] Pouah! What is in ze water, is salty! [*With disgust he puts the glass on the table and goes upstage left.*]

CAMILLE. [*Entering through the right rear door and going to the table.*] Ah, Senor de Histangua, are you alone?

HOMENIDES. [*Lunging towards him.*] Oh, you! [*Calming down.*] Joust in time, I leave.

CAMILLE. Oh.

HOMENIDES. When I leave [*Pointing towards the locked door.*] you open zat door. You master, he is behind it. Go! [*He puts on his coat.*]

CAMILLE. [*Bewildered.*] What, my master?

HOMENIDES. [*Angrily, having reached the rear in giant steps.*] Si! Como podria imaginarme que mi mujer tuviese un amante! [*He exits like a cyclone.*]

CAMILLE. [*Half bewildered, half mocking.*] Que mi mujer tuviese un amante! [*Laughing.*] You can't understand a thing the man says! [*Going towards the door.*] My master, what master! [*He opens the door and is shocked when he sees* CHANDEBISE.] You!

CHANDEBISE. [*Still gripped by fear, not daring to venture into the room.*] Is he gone?

CAMILLE. Who?

CHANDEBISE. [*Still in the threshold.*] Ho . . . Homenides?

CAMILLE. Yes.

CHANDEBISE. And Mme. Homenides?

CAMILLE. With Roberta.

CHANDEBISE. Well now, what of Tournel?

CAMILLE. He just left

CHANDEBISE. [*Entering the room.*] He's gone! Dash it! There's not a moment to lose! Who can I send to warn them? Of course, Edward!

CAMILLE. What are you talking about?

CHANDEBISE. That place, that place! For God's sake, over there! [*Putting his coat on backwards.*] We're sitting on a volcano, a terrible tragedy! Perhaps even a double murder.

CAMILLE. [*Shocked.*] What's going on?

CHANDEBISE. Hurry up. Perhaps we can get to Tournel's house before the banquet. My hat, where's my hat?

CAMILLE. My God! What's going on?

CHANDEBISE. [*Quickly.*] There's no time to explain. If Tournel comes back while I am gone, tell him under no circumstances is he to go to his rendez-vous. It's a matter of life or death.

CAMILLE. [*Shocked.*] Life or death!

CHANDEBISE. Do you understand—life or death?

CAMILLE. [*Overwhelmed.*] Indeed, I do.

CHANDEBISE. What a mess. My God, what a mess! [*He exits right.*]

CAMILLE. [*Going left.*] What's gotten into everybody today? There must be something in the air.

TOURNEL. [*Entering abruptly from the rear.*] I forgot my briefcase.

CAMILLE. Tournel!

TOURNEL. [*Finding his briefcase on the table.*] Ah, here it is!

CAMILLE. [*Running towards him, unintelligible.*] I beg you, don't go. It's a matter of life or death.

TOURNEL. What?

CAMILLE. [*Trying to hold him back.*] To the rendez-vous, the rendez-vous! Don't go! It's life or death!

TOURNEL. [*Turning around and trying to shake* CAMILLE *from his back.*] Bug off! I can't understand a word you're saying.

CAMILLE. [*Gathering himself up and running after* TOURNEL.] Tournel!!

TOURNEL. Hang it! Goodbye! [*He exits through the rear door.*]

CAMILLE. [*Running to the mantlepiece where he had left his palate.*] My palate, where's my palate? [*Seeing it on the table.*] Ah, there it is! [*He crosses quickly, puts the palate in his mouth and goes upstage.*] Tournel! Tournel!

CHANDEBISE. [*With his hat on, running towards the sound.*] Who are you calling like that?

CAMILLE. [*Poised between the hall and the salon, now clearly intelligible.*] Why Tournel! I have never seen such a lout. I told him your message, and he wouldn't even listen to me.

CHANDEBISE. [*Shocked, falling into a chair.*] My God! He can talk!

CAMILLE. [*Running out of the room, as the curtain falls.*] Tournel! Wait! Tournel!

Act 2

At the Kozy Kitty Hotel, second floor lobby. Everything is gaudy and suggestive. The stage is divided into two parts. On the left, taking up about three-fifths of the stage, is the lobby. At the rear is a staircase coming up into the lobby and leading up to the upper floors. Downstage on the left there is a table against the wall. There are coat hooks above it with a livery jacket and a hunting cap on one of the hooks. Further up left is the door to Kruger's room. Above this is the hallway leading to the other rooms. One of these doors is visible to the audience. Between the hall and the door is the electric buzzer board. To the right of the hall, there is a partition which separates the hall from the two contiguous rooms. This partition ends in a piece of curved molding on the audience side. The back side of the partition gives access by a door to a room. Upstage there is a door which leads to an interior room; therefore, this room is not visible. There is a bench against the partition.

In the room on the right there is a canopied bed located on a raised, carpeted platform without corners. There is a little white lacquered table against the partition. There is a chair next to the bed. There is another chair on the wall between the window and the door to the bathroom. On each side of the bed there is a buzzer button, the centers of which look like targets. These buttons activate the turntable on which the bed is placed. The panel and the bed are all that is turned. The panel behind the bed forms the diameter of the turntable. When the turntable is activated, an identical panel and bed appear from the other side. The heads of both beds must face the window. The feet face the door to the lobby.

In this act, the roles of CHANDEBISE and POCHE are played by the same actor; therefore he will have to make quick changes. It is suggested that POCHE wear CHANDEBISE's costume under his own and that the costume be fastened for quick changes. POCHE is wearing blue-green livery pants, a copper-colored vest, a pink cotton shirt, and felt bedroom slippers which cover CHANDEBISE's shoes. An apron and a loud tie complete POCHE's costume. As the act opens, EUGENIA is preparing the room on the right.

FERRAILLON. [*Entering from the hallway on the left.*] Eugenia, Eugenia! [*Reaching the door to the room on the right.*] Eugenia!

EUGENIA. [*No reaction, continuing her dusting.*] Sir?

FERRAILLON. [*In the doorway.*] What are you doing?

EUGENIA. Why, I'm doing the room.

FERRAILLON. [*Entering the room.*] You call that done?

EUGENIA. But, sir!

FERRAILLON. How can you call this room done? Look at this bed! If I didn't know better, I'd swear there were still people in it.

EUGENIA. [*Wounded.*] Oh, damn!

FERRAILLON. Come on, don't take it so hard; have some pride. You're acting like this place is not legit.

EUGENIA. [*Ironically.*] Oh!

FERRAILLON. Remember, this is a first

class hotel where only married people come. [*He goes upstage.*]

EUGENIA. Yes, but not to each other.

FERRAILLON. [*Quickly coming back.*] What business is that of yours? And who told you that you can judge my clientel, young lady? Now, make up that bed again. Be quick about it! [*He tears the covers off the bed and goes into the hall.*]

EUGENIA. [*Aside.*] What a slave driver!

OLIVIA. [*Entering from the rear with a load of sheets. She is an overblown, gaudy woman in her late fifties.*] What's the matter, dear? [*She puts the sheets on the table on the left.*]

FERRAILLON. That girl won't do a lick of work. I wish I had had her in my regiment, then we'd see how she would put out.

OLIVIA. [*Severely.*] Now, Arthur.

FERRAILLON. On the drillfield, on the drillfield. I was only joking! Besides, I've seen too much of that in my time.

OLIVIA. I certainly hope so!

FERRAILLON. [*Seeing* BERNARD *entering from below.* BERNARD *looks like a whipped dog.* FERRAILLON *grabs him by the collar.*] Ah, there you are! Where have you been? In that dive again?

BERNARD. Me?

FERRAILLON. It's five o'clock. Why aren't you in bed where you should be? Do you want to work or not?

BERNARD. [*Timidly.*] Yes.

FERRAILLON. Then, go to bed. [BERNARD *goes upstage and stops at the sound of* FERRAILLON's *voice.*] It's true, isn't it? You're a good-for-nothing old man lucky enough to have rheumatism. And I'm stupid enough to give you a job. Why, I ask myself? Because I'm too kind-hearted and because I won't see my uncle live in poverty. And you thank me by spending all your time in some dive.

BERNARD. Listen. . . .

FERRAILLON. No! Dives. Those places should be closed for the sake of public morality. [*To* BERNARD.] And what

if we had needed the sick old man while you were out? Who would have taken your place? Not me, that's for sure! What would have happened if some one had gotten caught?

BERNARD. I can only guess. . . .

FERRAILLON. Good! Now, get to work. Go on, to your room. [BERNARD, *cowed, lowers his head and heads for the interior room.*] That's family for you! He expects me to do everything but he gives nothing in return.

KRUGER. [*Lurching out of the room on the left and falling onto* FERRAILLON's *back.*] Hat jemand telefoniert?

FERRAILLON. [*Shocked and turning around.*] What?

KRUGER: Hat jemand telefoniert?

FERRAILLON *and* OLIVIA *look at each other in bewilderment.*

KRUGER. [*Seeing that they didn't understand him, sweetly to* OLIVIA.] Bitte, hat jemand telefoniert?

OLIVIA. No, nobody, sir.

KRUGER. [*Grumbling.*] Vielen Dank. [*He goes back into his room, furious.* FERRAILLON *and* OLIVIA *look at each other bewildered.*]

FERRAILLON. [*After a moment.*] What did he say?

OLIVIA. I think he asked if anyone had come.

FERRAILLON. How strange that he insists on talking to you in German.

OLIVIA. He doesn't speak our language.

FERRAILLON. That's no reason for me to understand his. [*Imitating him.*] "Telefoniert." He should be happy that he's given us a few laughs.

OLIVIA. Poor man! It's the third time that's he's come and the third time that his lady friend has stood him up.

FERAILLON. It's always like that with women—"Telefoniert?" That would surely make them run the other way.

OLIVIA. [*Approving.*] Humph! [*Picking up the sheets.*] Back to work. I'll take these sheets to the linen closet.

FERRAILLON. Don't bother. [*Calling.*] Eugenia! [*After finishing the bed, she has gone into the bathroom from which she now exits.*]

EUGENIA. Sir?

FERRAILLON. Have you finished the room?

EUGENIA. [*With her duster and bucket.*] As you wished, sir.

FERRAILLON. [*Above the door.*] I know, I know! A room's finished when you want it to be.

EUGENIA. [*Heading towards the hallway on the left.*] Ready to be undone again as soon as it's done.

FERRAILLON. Spare me your moralizing. Here, take this stack of sheets to the linen closet.

EUGENIA. Me?

FERRAILLON. Well, you don't expect me to do it, do you?

EUGENIA. [*Putting her duster and bucket in the hallway, with a sigh of resignation.*] All right! [*Aside.*] This is a job for a dunce. [*She goes upstage towards the staircase. She stops when she hears* OLIVIA's *voice.*]

OLIVIA. While I'm thinking about it [*Pointing to the room on the right.*], don't rent this room; it's reserved.

FERRAILLON. [*Lighting a cigar.*] Oh? By whom?

OLIVIA. M. Chandebise. [*To* EUGENIA.] You remember him.

EUGENIA. Oh yes, the one who talked like this. [*She imitates* CAMILLE's *speech defect.*)

OLIVIA. Exactly.

FERRAILLON. [*Seated on the bench.*] Oh, he's coming today?

OLIVIA. Yes, here's the telegram he sent. [*Catching sight of* EUGENIA *who is eavesdropping.*] That's good, Eugenia.

EUGENIA. [*Misinterpreting.*] Why thank you, madam.

OLIVIA. No, no, I meant that's all for now. I don't need you any more.

EUGENIA. Yes, madam. [*Aside as she goes off.*] That shocked me too. [*She goes upstage towards the staircase.*]

OLIVIA. No, take the stairs in the hall. That way you won't risk seeing any of our guests with that pile of sheets.

EUGENIA. Yes, madam. [*She exits left.*]

OLIVIA. [*To* FERRAILLON.] Here's the telegram: "Reserve for about five o'clock the same room as before. Chandebise." That means the one over there. [*She points to the room on the right.*]

FERRAILLON. [*Getting up.*] Fine! I'll give it the host's once over. [*He enters the room, followed by* OLIVIA.] All is in order now.

OLIVIA. What about the bathroom? It's important that everything in the bathroom be in tip top shape. [*She goes into the bathroom.*]

FERRAILLON. Now, let's see if that old fool is at his post. [*He presses the button on the left side of the bed. The turntable turns around to reveal* BERNARD *in the bed from the other side.*]

BERNARD. [*On his back, reciting a familiar refrain.*] Oh, my aching back. Ohhh! [*He has on a night shirt and night cap.*]

FERRAILLON. [*Stopping him.*] Good! Don't wear yourself out; it's only me.

BERNARD. [*Sitting up in bed.*] Oh, it's you. You see, how you're always tricking me. Well, here I am in my office.

FERRAILLON. Well, old man, what am I paying for? Back into the drawer with you. [*He pushes the button, and the bed revolves to reveal the first bed.*] It's working. [OLIVIA *comes out of the bathroom and falls into step with* FERRAILLON.] Where's Poche?

OLIVIA. [*Following her husbnad.*] In the cellar bringing up some wood.

FERRAILLON. [*Extreme left of stage.*] In the cellar? Are you crazy? How many times have I told you that his only fault is staying drunk? And you've sent him to the cellar!

OLIVIA. But the wine is under lock and key. Surely, there's no danger.

FERRAILLON. It's just that I know him so well, the lout. Many's the time he's told me that he's stopping drinking. I knew him in the regiment where he was my orderly for three years. I've heard his promises to repent: he would go from Monday to Saturday without a drop. But on Sundays, whew, he'd get stewed again.

OLIVIA. [*Philosophically.*] Oh well, maybe that kept him going.

FERRAILLON. He never forgot that day. I never threw him into the brig, but I gave him a beating or two. That kept him on his toes until Saturday. But as soon as Sunday rolled around, he was back to his old habits. Now don't think that he wasn't a good soldier— honest, hard-working, and devoted. How I used to knock him around and rough him up! What fun it was to give him a swift kick in the seat of his pants! After all, the king wasn't his cousin.

OLIVIA. [*Kittenish, putting her head on* FERRAILLON's *shoulder and batting her eyes up at him.*] Oh, what a fighter you are.

FERRAILLON. [*Modestly.*] Yes, I used to enjoy it, but now it tires me out, you see. Just the same, he's the kind of servant that I like. He's not like the servants of today whom you have to sweet talk all the time. So two weeks ago when I found out that he was out of work, I didn't hesitate to hire him.

OLIVIA. [*Going right.*] You did a good deed. [*At this moment* POCHE, *with a load of wood on his back, appears on the stairs coming up from the cellar. He is in his work clothes with ill-combed hair. On first glance he appears to be* CHANDEBISE's *double, but on closer examination, it is obvious that he is a coarser, less-refined man of an inferior social class. He has a telegram in his hand.*]

FERRAILLON. Speak of the Devil, here he is! What is it, Poche?

POCHE. [*Saluting, in his best military voice.*] A telegram, sir!

FERRAILLON. [*Imitating his tone as he goes to him.*] "A telegram, sir!" [*He takes the telegram from* POCHE *and goes to* OLIVIA.] Thank you. [*Looking at* POCHE *who has gone downstage left and is looking at him stupidly.*] My God, he's ugly! [*To* POCHE *who has assumed military bearing.*] Stop gaping at me like a

fool! [*He opens the telegram as he is talking.*] More from Chandebise! [*At this moment* EUGENIA *appears from upstairs and enters the lobby as* FERRAILLON *is reading the telegram.*] "Reserve good room for me."

OLIVIA. [*Ironically.*] Haven't we done that already?

FERRAILLON. "Admit whoever comes in my name." [*To* EUGENIA *who has reached the lobby and to* POCHE.] Did you two hear that? If someone asks for M. Chandebise's room, show them to that one. [*Indicating the room on the right.*]

EUGENIA. Yes, sir.

POCHE. [*Saluting.*] Yes, sir!

FERRAILLON. And now, back to work! [EUGENIA *exits through the hallway.* POCHE *remains contemplating his master.*] Well? Didn't you hear me, you cossack? [*Taking* POCHE *by the arm and turning him around.*] Go on, out! [*He kicks him in the seat of the pants.* POCHE *starts up the stairs as he looks at his master with an almost radiant smile.*] Look how happy he is! I told you that he was devoted to me, the animal. [*Loudly.*] Off with you! [*In his hurry to obey,* POCHE *almost misses one of the steps.*]

OLIVIA. [*After* POCHE's *exit.*] He's a good sort.

KRUGER. [*Coming from his room, going to* FERRAILLON *who has started up the stairs and has his back turned to the audience.*] Hat jemand telefoniert?

FERRAILLON. [*Startled and quickly turning around.*] Huh?

KRUGER. Haben Sie nicht verstanden; ich frage ob eine Dame telefoniert hat?

FERRAILLON. No, nobody, damn it!

KRUGER. Danke. [*He pops back into his room.*]

OLIVIA. [*After* KRUGER *exits.*] Ah, a man in love!

FERRAILLON. He keeps popping out of that room like a cork.

OLIVIA. You're right, he has unnerved you.

FINACHE. [*Coming up the staircase.*] Hello, Colonel!

FERRAILLON *and* OLIVIA. Ah, Doctor!

FINACHE. Hello, Madam Ferraillon. Do you have a room for me?

OLIVIA. We always have a room for you, Doctor.

FINACHE. Has anyone asked for me?

FERRAILLON. Not yet, Doctor.

FINACHE. Ah, so much the better.

FERRAILLON. Have you been successful lately?

FINACHE. Successful enough! I have a little something going.

OLIVIA. Well, you haven't been here in over a month.

FINACHE. I've been flitting around, here and there.

FERRAILLON. It's bad not to be faithful.

FINACHE. But it's the same one, I'm seeing only one woman now.

FERRAILLON. I wasn't talking about women, I was talking about us.

FINACHE. I see.

FERRAILLON. If everyone were faithful in love, we'd have to close up.

FINACHE. Well put. [*Changing his tone.*] What's going on? There is no one greeting guests downstairs. I didn't see the boy in the office.

OLIVIA. Poche?

FINACHE. Poche? No, I meant Gabriel, that handsome boy.

FERRAILLON. That's right! Obviously you don't know that we had to let him go.

FINACHE. Why? He was such a handsome addition to the surroundings.

FERRAILLON. There you have it, he was too handsome.

OLIVIA. He was beginning to flirt with the customers.

FINACHE. You don't say!

FERRAILLON. You see, it was quite impossible. Who would want to bring his mistress here if he risked seeing her carried off by the help. We are, after all, a respectable establishment.

FINACHE. [*Sitting on the bench, in approval.*] To be sure. . . .

FERRAILLON. In this business, you need discipline. I know that from being in the army, as you well know.

FINACHE. Then you really were a colonel?

OLIVIA. Was he a colonel!

FERRAILLON. I was a sergeant-major in the twenty-ninth regiment, that's why everybody calls me Colonel.

FINACHE. Well, you're colonel to the civilians.

FERRAILLON. [*Genially.*] That's true. What's a promotion or two in private life? [*To* OLIVIA.] My dear, will you see if number ten is ready for the Doctor?

OLIVIA. Yes, dear. [*She starts up the stairs.*]

FINACHE. [*Pointing to the room on the right.*] Isn't number five free?

FERRAILLON. Alas, no!

FINACHE. [*Disappointed.*] Oh!

FERRAILLON. But number ten is just like it.

FINACHE. Bah! On to number ten, then.

OLIVIA. [*On the stairs.*] I'll have it ready in a moment.

FERRAILLON. That's fine, dear. [*She exits.*]

FINACHE. [*After* OLIVIA *has left.*] What a wonderful woman Madam Ferraillon is.

FERRAILLON. Yes and so serious.

FINACHE. You know, I feel as if I've seen her somewhere before.

FERRAILLON. [*Shaking his head.*] Did you ever hear of a courtesan called La Belle Castana? They nicknamed her Dimples.

FINACHE. [*Searching his memory.*] Castana? Let me think.

FERRAILLON. She was the Duke of Gennevilliers' mistress.

FINACHE. Oh yes, she was the one that they served up completely nude at a banquet on a silver platter.

FERRAILLON. There, you've got it! [*Satisfied.*] That's my wife. I married Dimples.

FINACHE. [*Taken aback.*] My compliments!

FERRAILLON. She fell for me when I was

a sergeant in the twenty-ninth regiment. [*As a justification.*] I was a handsome fellow . . . the uniform, you know. She was always a pushover for a uniform.

FINACHE. Dimples! [*He laughs.*]

FERRAILLON. That's right. I'll tell you something else—she wanted to keep me.

FINACHE. No!

FERRAILLON. Indeed! I would have none of that. On the other hand, she had some money put aside, a nice body, and a reputation. So, I proposed to her and here we are!

FINACHE. [*Sitting on the bench.*] My compliments.

FERRAILLON. However, I did make some conditions; after all, I do have principles. I told her after the wedding, no more affairs, no more lovers. Because—I don't know if you're like me—but I feel once a woman is married, she doesn't need lovers.

FINACHE. [*Dead serious.*] You're absolutely right.

FERRAILLON. After all, we must be respectable. Then we opened this hotel. [*He goes left.*]

FINACHE. [*Rising.*] How wise you are.

FERRAILLON. So, we live modestly as good citizens saving up for our old age. That's why I've been thinking about what you told me the last time you were here. You remember—life insurance.

FINACHE. So, you've decided on it?

FERRAILLON. Yes, after all, I am forty-five and my wife is [*He coughs.*] about fifty-two.

FINACHE. [*Coolly.*] Well, that's not too much of a difference. They say that there should be seven or eight years between spouses.

FERRAILLON. [*Not convinced.*] It would be better if the wife were younger.

FINACHE. That's not always the case. Sometimes the husband is younger.

FERRAILLON. Evidently, evidently. [*Changing his tone.*] If I wanted to insure her, in case of her death, the poor dear. . . .

FINACHE. Her? Damn it! Fifty-two! It would be a lot cheaper to insure you.

FERRAILLON. Me? If you insist. Provided that when she dies. . . .

FINACHE. No, no! In the case of your death. . . .

FERRAILLON. My death? That's not at all what I had in mind.

FINACHE. Then we'll work out a combination policy. Come by our office.

FERRAILLON. When?

FINACHE. Every morning from ten to eleven at the offices of the Boston Life Company, 95 Boulevard Malesherbes.

FERRAILLON. [*Writing on his cuff.*] "Boulevard Malesherbes." Good! Who should I ask for?

FINACHE. The director of the company; I'll tell him to expect you.

FERRAILLON. Wonderful! Thank you for your troubles!

FINACHE. You're entirely welcome.

OLIVIA. [*From above.*] Doctor, do you want to see your room?

FINACHE. [*Bounding towards the staircase.*] I certainly do want to see it! Indeed, I do. . . . [*To* FERRAILLON *from the stairs.*] If anyone asks for me, tell me at once. [*He exits.*]

FERRAILLON. [*With a little bow as* FINACHE *exits.*] Isn't love grand?

KRUGER. [*Popping out of his room again.*] Hat jemand telefoniert?

FERRAILLON. Not again!

KRUGER. Schweinhund, hat jemand telefoniert?

FERRAILLON. [*Smiling as he mutters under his breath.*] What a bore!

KRUGER. [*Cupping his ear.*] Wie, bitte?

FERRAILLON. [*As above.*] What a bore!

KRUGER. [*Not understanding.*] Borscht?

FERRAILLON. [*Most pleasant.*] Yes, you Kraut. Don't look at me with such big eyes. Thank goodness, you can't understand what I'm saying, but you are a bore.

KRUGER. Ah, Borscht! Vielen Dank.

FERRAILLON. At your service. [KRUGER *starts back into his room when* ROBERTA *appears on the staircase. She is heavily veiled.*]

KRUGER. [*Astonished at her appearance.*] Gott im Himmel!

FERRAILLON. May I help you, madam?

ROBERTA. Yes, M. Chandebise's room.

FERRAILLON. [*Opening the door to the room on the right.*] This way, madam. [KRUGER *continues to stare at* ROBERTA *since he cannot make out her features. He investigates her from all angles as he sings a little nonsense tune.*]

KRUGER. [*Continuing to dance around* ROBERTA *who is shocked by his behavior.*] "Ach du lieber Augustin, Augustin, Augustin, Ach du lieber Augustin, Alles ist weg." [*Satisfying himself that* ROBERTA *is not his girlfriend.*] Nein. Sie ist nicht die Dame. [*He goes back into his room, hands in his pocket, whistling his little tune.*]

ROBERTA. [*Recovering her composure.*] What on earth's the matter with him?

FERRAILLON. Pay no attention to him, madam; he's just a crazy foreigner.

ROBERTA. [*Coming downstage left.*] Well, he doesn't lack gall! [*To* FERRAILLON.] Has anyone checked into this room? [*She lifts her veil a bit.*]

FERRAILLON. [*Coming downstage too.*] No one, madam. Am I mistaken, weren't you here this morning?

ROBERTA. Eh?

FERRAILLON. Yes, yes, I understand. Madam flatters me. I felt sure that my discretion would incline madam to use my services. But I didn't expect you so soon.

ROBERTA. [*Shocked.*] Sir! I can't permit you to suppose. . . .

FERRAILLON. [*Bowing.*] Pardon me, madam. [*Going to the door of the room.*] If madam would permit me. . . .

ROBERTA. [*Goes to the door of the room. She gives* FERRAILLON *a haughty look.*] Shh! [*She goes to the right side of the room.*]

FERRAILLON. [*Entering the room after her.*] Here's the room, madam. You can see how comfortable it is. The bed. . . .

ROBERTA. [*Haughtily cutting off his words.*]

Thank you, I can see for myserlf.

FERRAILLON. [*Taken aback.*] Ah! [*Aside as he passes to the bathroom.*] What a shrew! [*Aloud.*] Here's the bathroom—hot and cold running water, bath and shower.

ROBERTA. [*Annoyed.*] Very well, I don't intend to live here.

FERRAILLON. Yes, madam. [*Going to the bed.*] Let me show you the special feature of the bed—in case of emergency. See these buttons on each side. . . .

ROBERTA. [*Going right.*] Please, that's enough. No more explanations. Leave me now.

FERRAILLON. [*Taken aback.*] But, madam.

ROBERTA. I said, leave.

FERRAILLON. As you wish. [*He goes to the door.*] Madam, I am at your service.

ROBERTA. [*Nervously.*] Goodbye, sir; goodbye.

FERRAILLON. [*As he closes the door behind him.*] What a sour puss!

ROBERTA. What a rude man!

FERRAILLON. [*Catching sight of* POCHE *who has appeared on the stairs with an empty wood carrier.*] Ah, Poche!

POCHE. [*Looking tenderly and saluting.*] Sir?

FERRAILLON. Have you brought all the wood up?

POCHE. One more load, sir.

FERRAILLON. Good! Hop to it. And would you please put on your coat instead of leaving it hanging there, where it doesn't belong? [*As he talks,* FERRAILLON *indicates the livery coat and the cap hanging on the coat hook above the console.*] You should be in uniform when our guests arrive.

POCHE. Yes, sir! [*He starts out as the bell rings.*]

FERRAILLON. Wait. Someone buzzed. [*He consults the buzzer board.*] It's the German. Go see what he wants.

POCHE. Yes, sir! [*He puts the wood carrier against the staircase and heads towards the room on the left without taking his eyes off* FERRAILLON. *He knocks on* KRUGER's *door.*]

KRUGER. [*From inside.*] Herein! [POCHE *enters* KRUGER'*s room.* ROBERTA, *who has been inspecting her room, opening the window, etc., goes into the bathroom.*]

TOURNEL. [*Entering from below.*] Excuse me! M. Chandebise's room?

FERRAILLON. This way, sir. If I'm not mistaken, you're not M. Chandebise?

TOURNEL. That's right; I'm here in his place.

FERRAILLON. [*Nodding his head.*] His telegram instructed me to allow whoever came in his name to use the room. The lady is already here, sir.

TOURNEL. Ah! What's she like?

FERRAILLON. [*Looking at him in disbelief.*] If you're asking for my opinion, sir, I think you'll find her pleasing enough.

TOURNEL. You see, we haven't met.

FERRAILLON. Oh?

TOURNEL. I just wanted to be prepared in case she was an old hag.

FERRAILLON. Let me reassure you; although she's somewhat ill-humored, she's quite pretty.

TOURNEL. [*Trying to appear disinterested.*] What does her character matter? That's not what brings me here.

FERRAILLON. [*Somewhat disapproving.*] Indeed not! This way please. [*He leads* TOURNEL *into the room. He closes the open window.* TOURNEL *puts his hat on the little table that is against the partition.*]

POCHE. [*Coming from* KRUGER'*s room, speaking rapidly.*] At once, sir. [*Aside.*] He asked for a "telefoniert." What on earth can that be? [*After a pause.*] I'll bring him some vermouth. [*He goes to the stairs, picks up the carrier, and goes downstairs.*]

FERRAILLON. No one here? Let me check the bath. [*He knocks on the door to the bath.*]

ROBERTA. [*From the bath.*] What is it?

FERRAILLON. [*With his cheek against the door.*] Your gentleman is here.

ROBERTA. Just a moment.

FERRAILLON. [*Respectfully circling around* TOURNEL *to reach the door.*] Madam is there, sir.

TOURNEY. Uh, very well.

FERRAILLON. [*From the doorway.*] That's what you think.

TOURNEL. [*Closing the door on* FERRAILLON *who then goes upstairs.*] Thank you! [*Glancing around him.*] Hmm, not bad, the room looks comfortable enough. [*Catching sight of the electric buttons on the bed.*] Well, if we got bored, we can always play darts. [*He mimics throwing a dart towards the right button.*] But that isn't all! Let's see, everything is presented in a most original manner. Ah, how amusing! [*He sits on the bed and then pulls the bed curtains around him so that he is completely hidden.*]

ROBERTA. [*Popping out of the bathroom. She still has her hat on.*] Ah, there. . . . [*Seeing no one.*] Well, where is he?

TOURNEL. [*From inside the bed.*] Yoohoo!

ROBERTA. [*Aside.*] "Yoohoo." Just a moment.

TOURNEL. Yoohoo! [ROBERTA *goes to the bed, pulls the curtain with her right hand, and slaps* TOURNEL *with the back of her left hand.*]

ROBERTA. There!

TOURNEL. Oh! [*He jumps out of the bed.*]

ROBERTA. [*Falling back.*] It's not him.

TOURNEL. Roberta, ah, Roberta!

ROBERTA [*Shocked.*] M. Tournel!

TOURNEL. If only I had known! [*Holding his cheek.*] What a pleasant surprise!

ROBERTA. What are you doing here?

TOURNEL. [*With style.*] What does that matter? [*Quickly, trying to explain.*] Ah, a love affair. There was a woman who fell in love with me . . . at the theater . . . the thunderbolt . . . she wrote me and out of the goodness of my soul, I. . . .

ROBERTA. No, no, not that!

TOURNEL. [*Confusing her protest with a foul mood.*] But this woman . . . I'm not interested . . . I don't know her or love her. Only you! My dream has come true! You are here, with me. You are completely mine! You see, our prayers are answered! [*He tries to* bring her into this arms.]

ROBERTA. [*Pulling away.*] Leave me alone!

TOURNEL. No!

ROBERTA. That letter was not addressed to you but to my husband.

TOURNEL. No, no, it can't be! He's ugly. We are here together. Perhaps the person made a mistake.

ROBERTA. [*Cutting his words short.*] No, that's not it at all. I wrote that letter to my husband.

TOURNEL. [*Shocked.*] You?

ROBERTA. Indeed, I did!

TOURNEL. You wrote a love letter to your husband?

ROBERTA. I wanted to find out if he was cheating on me. If he would come to this rendez-vous.

TOURNEL. [*Triumphantly.*] Aha! You see! You spurned my attentions because you thought your husband was being unfaithful to you. You see, he didn't come but delegated me to come in his place to lend some reality to this affair.

ROBERTA. [*Convinced by his argument.*] You're right!

TOURNEL. Do you know what he said when he read your letter? "What does this woman want? She must know that I would never cheat on my wife."

ROBERTA. He said that?

TOURNEL. Yes!

ROBERTA. Oh how happy that makes me. [*She falls into* TOURNEL's *arms and kisses him on both cheeks.*]

TOURNEL. Ah, Roberta, my Roberta! [*He has his right arm around his waist as he uses his left arm to make dramatic gestures.*] See, you should never have doubted him. [*He kisses her greedily.*] Smack! Smack! Now you see! Smack! Smack! You have nothing to reproach him about! Smack! Smack! You don't have any reason to trick him. [*More kisses.*] Smack! Smack! Poor, dear man.

ROBERTA. You're right. [*She kisses him.*] I was wrong. How silly of me to sus-

pect him! [*More kisses.*] Oh, dear husband, how naughty of me! Please forgive me. [*Kisses.*]

TOURNEL. [*Lyrically.*] No, no! No need! Come to me, that is enough.

ROBERTA. [*Lyrically.*] Yes, that will be my punishment.

TOURNEL. [*Overcome.*] Oh, Roberta, I love, I love, I love you, I love you! Roberta, my Roberta.

ROBERTA. Oh no! What I heard, I thought, was my husband saying "yoohoo."

TOURNEL. [*Carried away.*] What difference who said it. We'll do it for him.

ROBERTA. What?

TOURNEL. [*Exalted, pulling her to him.*] Yoohoo! Roberta, my Roberta.

ROBERTA [*Struggling.*] Tournel! Tournel! What do you mean? Let me get hold of my emotions. [*She pulls away.*]

TOURNEL. [*Pressing his case.*] No, no! Let's take advantage of the situation while it's still hot.

ROBERTA. [*Struggling against him.*] Tournel, now see here!

TOURNEL. [*Without hearing her.*] At these moments emotions are at their most intense. [*Dragging her to the bed.*] Come to me; come to me.

ROBERTA. [*Shocked.*] What? What are you doing? Where are you taking me?

TOURNEL. [*One foot on the bed platform, dragging* ROBERTA *behind him.*] Why, here! Where happiness awaits us.

ROBERTA. What? There! You're crazy! [*She shoves him, and he falls, sitting, onto the bed. She goes left.*] What do you take me for?

TOURNEL. [*Bewildered.*] Didn't you lead me to believe that I had your consent?

ROBERTA. [*Quickly and haughtily.*] To be your lover! [*Going right with dignity.*] But not to sleep with you! What do you take me for, a prostitute?

TOURNEL. [*On the edge of the bed, pleading.*] But what, then?

ROBERTA. [*With all her dignity.*] Why, to flirt, to be carried away with emotion, to speak to you with my eyes, to walk hand in hand. I'm giving you the best part of me.

TOURNEL. [*Raising his head towards* ROBERTA.] What's that?

ROBERTA. Why, my mind, my heart.

TOURNEL. Oh pfutt!

ROBERTA. [*Haughtily.*] And what were you thinking of?

TOURNEL. [*Getting up passionately.*] What every man thinks of when he sets out to take a lover. [*Striding towards* ROBERTA.] Everything has conspired to bring us together, even your husband. Why, he's the one who sent me here! Yes, indeed, madam, your husband sent me here.

ROBERTA. My husband!

TOURNEL. Yes, madam, your husband! Why resist us, we have you outnumbered! [*He tries to embrace her.*]

ROBERTA. [*Pulling away.*] Tournel, see here, calm down!

TOURNEL. [*Following her.*] Do you think I'm going to be happy with a mere flirtation, speaking with our eyes, half of your person? And the least useful, at that, under the circumstances.

ROBERTA. [*Taking refuge behind the little table, against the wall.*] Tournel, see here!

TOURNEL. What do you expect me to do with your mind and your heart?

ROBERTA. Oh!

TOURNEL. [*Theatrically, going right.*] Yes, you're offering me a rosy picture, the prospect of emptiness, of desires never satisfied. And what do I get for my devotion? Running your errands, walking your dog when he needs to go. [*Crossing to* ROBERTA *who is cowering in the corner.*] No, no, no!

ROBERTA. [*Terrified.*] Tournel!

TOURNEL. [*In front of her face.*] Nooo! [*Menacing.*] And since you are ignorant of the fundamental rules of love affairs, I will teach them to you.

ROBERTA. [*Terrorized and pleading.*] Tournel, please.

TOURNEL. Don't think for a minute that I'm going to let you make me look like a fool. Not when I have you within my grasp will I leave this room like a dumb school boy.

ROBERTA. Tournel, please!

TOURNEL. No! You are mine! You belong to me! And I want you! [*He grabs her by the waist and starts to drag her to the bed.*]

ROBERTA. [*Defending herself as she can.*] Tournel, let's talk about this.

TOURNEL. No! [ROBERTA *manages to push him down; she jumps on the bed, and she puts her finger on the button on the right.*] One more step and I'll ring.

TOURNEL. Ring as you want, I'll just answer that we're not to be disturbed. [*He goes to the door.* ROBERTA *pushes the button. The bed turns with* ROBERTA *on it, and the other bed with* BERNARD *in it appears.*]

ROBERTA. [*From the other side of the partition.*] Help, Heavens, help!

TOURNEL. [*His back is turned to the bed and he has not seen what has happened. He assumes her cries are consent.*] Ah, you can call for help! That's fine with me! [*Aside, triumphantly.*] She's mine! [*He jumps madly onto the bed where he expects to see* ROBERTA *and embraces* BERNARD.] Oh Roberta, Roberta! [*Jumping back when he sees* BERNARD.] What? [*He is completely bewildered by this turn of events and does not know how to react.*]

BERNARD. [*His usual refrain.*] Oh, my back, my aching back!

TOURNEL. [*Regaining control.*] What's this?

BERNARD. My aching back!

TOURNEL. What are you doing here? Where did you come from? How did you get in here?

BERNARD. [*Sitting up bewildered.*] Huh?

TOURNEL. And Roberta? Where is she? [*Opening the hall door and calling.*] Roberta! Roberta! [*Aside.*] No one! [*He leaves the door open as he crosses to the bathroom.*] Roberta! Roberta! [*He enters the bathroom.*]

ROBERTA. [*Coming from the hidden room*

where the turntable took her.] What happened? Where am I? Oh, good Lord! Tournel! Tournel! [*Aside.*] Oh, enough of this hotel. I'm getting out of here. [*She runs towards the stairs. As soon as she has disappeared,* KRUGER *pops out of his room.*]

KRUGER. Bitte! [*Finding no one to talk to him, he crosses to the stairway and starts down it, calling.*] Bitte! Bitte!

ROBERTA. [*Fleeing up the stairs.*] Oh no, my husband! My husband's coming up the stairs! [*She runs into* KRUGER'S *room.*]

KRUGER. [*Startled but willing to make the best of the situation.*] Ach! Liebchen, oh, la la!

He dashes across the stage, enters his room, and closes the door behind him.

POCHE. [*From the stairwell coming downstage.*] Damn! I couldn't find the vermouth. Not surprising since I gave it to Bernard yesterday. [*Heading for the invisible room.*] Bernard!

BERNARD. [*Reading his paper in bed, glasses on his nose.*] In here!

POCHE. [*Going to the door of the room.*] Oh, there you are. Tell me, what did you do with the vermouth?

BERNARD. It's in the other room, on the dresser.

POCHE. Ah, good! [*He heads back for the invisible room.*]

TOURNEL. [*Coming out of the bathroom and entering the lobby. He takes his hat from the table.*] No one! Where is she? [*He goes towards the staircase. At that moment* KRUGER *and* ROBERTA *burst out of Kruger's room. She's trying to get away, and he's trying to catch her.*]

KRUGER. Ach! Liebchen! Liebchen! Geh'nicht! Bleib! Bleib!

ROBERTA. [*Almost at the same time.*] Let go of me! You, you randy old goat!

TOURNEL. [*Coming back.*] Ah, there you are! [*At that moment,* ROBERTA *pushes* KRUGER *away and steps back to slap him.* TOURNEL *manages to get between them and receives the slap.*]

TOURNEL. [*Rubbing his cheek.*] Oh!

KRUGER. Ach, vielen Dank!

TOURNEL. [*Quickly acknowledging* KRUGER *as he pushes* ROBERTA *towards the room.*] Not at all! [*Muttering,* KRUGER *enters his room.* ROBERTA *followed by* TOURNEL *enters the other room.*]

TOURNEL. [*Closing the door behind them.*] Ah, Roberta! Roberta!

ROBERTA. Please, don't be so emotional. My husband. . . .

TOURNEL. Yes!

ROBERTA. My husband is here!

TOURNEL. [*Mechanically.*] What? Chandebise?

ROBERTA. Yes, Victor-Emmanuel in a servant's uniform. How can that be? I don't know. To catch us, that's for sure.

TOURNEL. [*Shocked.*] That's not possible.

BERNARD. [*Out of habit.*] Oh, my back . . . my aching. . . .

ROBERTA. Oh!

TOURNEL . [*Startled.*] What?

ROBERTA. [*Pointing to* BERNARD.] What's he doing there?

TOURNEL. Oh, him? I haven't the foggiest idea. He just appeared out of the blue complaining about his back. [*To* BERNARD.] What are you doing here?

BERNARD. But you sent for me.

TOURNEL. I did?

ROBERTA. [*Going to the bed.*] Get him out of here at once.

TOURNEL. Absolutely! [*To* BERNARD.] Go, go! Get out of here.

BERNARD. If it wouldn't be too much trouble, press that button, and I'll go back where I came from.

TOURNEL. Right! I won't waste a minute's time. [*He pushes the button on the left.*]

ROBERTA. [*As the bed is turning.*] That's too much! Having spectators!

TOURNEL. But, my dear, let me reassure you, it's not my fault. [*As they are talking, the bed completes its turn, and* POCHE, *seated in the bed with a bottle of vermouth in his hand, appears.*]

POCHE. [*About to take a drink.*] What? What's going on?

ROBERTA. [*Jumping right.*] My God!

TOURNEL. [*Jumping left.*] Chandebise!!

ROBERTA. My husband! I'm lost!

TOURNEL. [*Going quickly to the bed and grabbing hold of* POCHE.] Hey, hey, don't believe everything you see!

ROBERTA. Please, please, don't condemn us without a hearing.

POCHE. [*Bewildered.*] Huh?

TOURNEL. [*Passionately.*] We appear guilty but I swear to you that we are not guilty.

ROBERTA. Yes, he's telling the truth. Neither one of us dreamed we'd meet the other one here.

TOURNEL. All this because of that letter.

ROBERTA. Yes, the letter. It's all my fault. I had it written because. . . .

TOURNEL. That's it, that's it! She's telling the truth.

ROBERTA. [*Kneeling on the platform.*] Oh, I beg you, forgive me. I thought you were playing around on me.

POCHE. Me?

ROBERTA. Tell me that you believe me, that you don't doubt me.

POCHE. But yes, yes! [*Utterly confused.*] What's the matter with them?

ROBERTA. [*Startled as* POCHE *begins to laugh idiotically.*] I beg you, Victor-Emmanuel, don't laugh like that; it upsets me.

POCHE. [*Cutting off his laughter.*] My laugh?

ROBERTA. Now I see, you don't believe me.

TOURNEL. [*Coming up to the platform.*] We're telling the truth.

ROBERTA. Oh, goodness! How to convince you!

POCHE. [*Abruptly, standing up and starting to leave.*] Listen, excuse me, but I have to take this vermouth to number four.

ROBERTA. [*Following him to the door, grabbing his arm, and making him turn towards her.*] Victor-Emmanuel, what's wrong with you?

POCHE. [*Shocked.*] Me?

TOURNEL. [*Who has also followed* POCHE, *turning him from the other side.*] How can you talk about vermouth at a time like this?

POCHE. Number four is waiting for it. Here, you take it.

ROBERTA. Enough, enough of this comedy. Beat me, slap me! [*She falls at his feet.*] But I love you more than you'll ever know.

TOURNEL. [*Also falling at* POCHE's *feet.*] Beat me too!

POCHE. [*His glance moving from one to the other.*] Well . . . I say . . . now, madam, please!

ROBERTA. [*Sadly.*] You've never called me madam before.

POCHE. Me?

ROBERTA. [*Grabbing his hands.*] Oh, tell me that. . . .

TOURNEL. [*Same action from the other side.*] Yes, tell her.

POCHE. [*Bewildered by the sight of them on their knees.*] Oh, I want to. Let me reassure you, madam. [*He kneels to be on their level.*]

TOURNEL. Please don't be so formal. Call her Roberta.

POCHE. Well, Roberta, let me assure you.

ROBERTA. Oh, tell me that you believe me.

POCHE. [*Not wanting to contradict her.*] Yes, yes, I believe you!

TOURNEL. Oh, happy day!

ROBERTA. [*With elan.*] Then kiss me, kiss me!

POCHE. [*Not believing his ears.*] What? Me?

ROBERTA. Kiss me, or I'll know that you think the worst.

POCHE. Oh, all right. [*All three are kneeling.* POCHE *wipes his mouth with the back of his hand, puts both arms around her—without letting go of the bottle—and kisses her on both cheeks.*]

ROBERTA. [*Radiantly.*] Ah!

TOURNEL. [*Exhorting them.*] That's it, that's it!

ROBERTA. [*Kissing* POCHE's *hands.*] Ah, thank you, thank you.

POCHE. [*Licking his lips.*] What soft skin!

TOURNEL. [*Standing up, lyrically.*] And me too, kiss me!

POCHE. [*As he and* ROBERTA *also stand.*] Huh? You too?

TOURNEL. Yes, to prove that you don't doubt me.

POCHE. All right. [*He starts to kiss* TOURNEL.] Whew, he's a big sucker! [*He steps on the platform to kiss* TOURNEL.]

TOURNEL. [*His conscience lightened.*] Ah, that's good!

POCHE. Yeah, especially the lady.

ROBERTA. "The lady!"

POCHE. [*Trying to head for the door.*] And now I have to take this vermouth to number four.

ROBERTA. Still?

TOURNEL. [*Blocking his passage and holding him in place.*] What? Are you still playing your joke on us?

ROBERTA. [*Pulling him towards her.*] Are you my husband or not?

POCHE. Me? No, I'm bell boy here.

TOURNEL. [*Falling back in shock.*] What?

ROBERTA. [*Same action.*] My God, Victor-Emmanuel has lost his mind!

POCHE. No, no, that's not it at all. My name is Poche, and if you don't believe me, ask Bernard. [*He goes back to the bed.*]

ROBERTA. [*Following him.*] Bernard?

TOURNEL. [*Following too.*] Who's Bernard?

POCHE. Why the sick old man. Wait a minute. [*He pushes the button on the left, and the turntable turns* BERNARD *in his bed into the room.*]

BERNARD. Oh, my back, my aching. . . .

POCHE. [*Sitting on the foot of the bed.*] No, not now. Tell them who I am.

BERNARD. [*Sitting up.*] Who you are? Don't you know?

POCHE. Sure I do, but madam doesn't.

ROBERTA. [*Coming closer.*] Yes, who is he?

BERNARD. Why, he's Poche!

TOURNEL *and* ROBERTA. [*Astonished.*] Poche!

BERNARD. The bellboy.

POCHE. See, didn't I tell you?

ROBERTA. [*Still confused.*] What, can it be true?

FERRAILLON. [*From the top of the stairs as he is entering the lobby.*] Poche!

TOURNEL. A dead ringer! Now wait a minute. That's not possible. He's trying to trick us.

FERRAILLON. Poche, Poche!

POCHE. Sir! Excuse me, the boss is calling.

ROBERTA. [*Just as he leaves the room, she grabs him by the arm, spins him around, and heads out of the room.*] The boss? Well, we'll see about that. [TOURNEL *does the same.*]

TOURNEL. Don't move! [*He follows* ROBERTA *out of the room.*]

ROBERTA. [*To* FERRAILLON.] Sir, sir!

FERRAILLON. Madam?

ROBERTA. Would you please tell us who this man is. [*She points to* POCHE *who is coming out of the room.*]

TOURNEL. Yes!

FERRAILLON. Poche!

POCHE. [*To* ROBERTA *and* TOURNEL.] See?

ROBERTA *and* TOURNEL. [*Looking at each other in shock.*] Poche!

FERRAILLON. [*Going up to* POCHE.] Poche! Come here! And a bottle in your hand! [*Seizing him by the right arm and pulling him along. With each step, he kicks him, turning him round and round. Finally he returns him to his original place.*] You animal! You cur! You good for nothing drunk! [*With each kick* POCHE—*still held by* FERRAILLON—*makes a little jump and cries, "Oh!"*]

TOURNEL *and* ROBERTA, *who are holding onto each other for support, gasp, "Oh!" each time* POCHE *is kicked.*]

POCHE. There, what did I tell you?

FERRAILLON. [*Grabbing the bottle from* POCHE.] You're up to your old tricks.

TOURNEL *and* ROBERTA. What?

POCHE. But, Boss, it's for number four.

FERRAILLON. I'll take it to him myself. [*Starts kicking* POCHE *again.*]

POCHE. But, Boss.

FERRAILLON. [*Guiding him to the stairs.*] Now get out of here and be quick about it!

POCHE. Yes, Boss. [*As he is going down the stairs.*] See, what did I tell you?

FERRAILLON. Please, sir and madam, forgive me. Our bellboy is a stinking lush. [*He leaves through the hallway on the left.* TOURNEL *and* ROBERTA *are left standing with their mouths open, completely bewildered.*]

ROBERTA. [*After a moment, shaking her head.*] The bellboy! He's the bellboy!

TOURNEL. [*Leaning against the console.*] Roberta!

ROBERTA. What?

TOURNEL. We kissed the bellboy.

ROBERTA. I was just about to say the same thing.

TOURNEL. I don't understand; I'm absolutely astounded! A dead ringer! It's not possible!

ROBERTA. We have to trust our eyes. The way the owner treated him convinced me that it could not be my husband. Such kicks! Oh no, Victor-Emmanuel would never had stood still for such kicks in his. . . .

TOURNEL. [*Coldly.*] Back!

ROBERTA. Yes!

TOURNEL. That's true.

ROBERTA. [*Falling onto the bench.*] Oh, my dear! What a scene! My throat's dry. Water, please, get me some water.

TOURNEL. [*Mechanically patting his pockets.*] Water? Water?

ROBERTA. Not in your pockets!

TOURNAL. Oh, yes, yes, water!

ROBERTA. [*Standing up.*] In the room.

TOURNEL. [*Hurrying into the room.*] Yes, yes, water! [*To* BERNARD.] Where's the water?

BERNARD. [*Looking up from his paper.*] Why, in the bathroom.

TOURNEL. Thank you! [*He enters the bathroom.*]

ROBERTA. [*Entering the room, in passing to* BERNARD.] Can you believe it? He's the bellboy?

BERNARD. Life's like that. [*She crosses to the window which she opens for a breath of fresh air.* BERNARD *goes back to reading the paper.* POCHE *has returned from below with a fresh load of wood. As he enters one of the logs falls off.*]

POCHE. [*To* EUGENIA, *who is coming down the stairs.*] Hey, Eugenia, put that log back on my back.

EUGENIA. Gladly. [*She picks up the log and arranges it on the pile.* POCHE's *back is to the audience and he is starting up the stairs.*]

ROBERTA. [*Closing the window.*] Ah, there! Tournel, where are you, what are you doing? [*Going into the bathroom.*] Oh yes, my glass of water.

CAMILLE. [*Gaily, dashing up the stairs, holding* ANTOINETTE's *hand. They boldly enter the lobby.* CAMILLE's *speech is clear because of the palate.*] Come on baby, my sweet. It's time to pay up; your big bad Camille is going to love you to death. Our room awaits us.

POCHE. [*Entering from above comes between them.*] May I help you, sir?

CAMILLE. Yes, I wanted. . . . [*Startled when he sees* POCHE.] Victor-Emmanuel! [*He turns and dashes into the room up right.*]

ANTOINETTE. [*Same reaction.*] Sir! [*She runs into* KRUGER's *room.*]

POCHE. [*As he goes upstage.*] Why is everybody calling me Victor-Emmanuel today? [*He goes upstairs as* EUGENIA *exits left. At this moment,* ROBERTA, *followed by* TOURNEL, *comes out of the bathroom.*]

TOURNEL. [*To* ROBERTA.] There, are you feeling better now?

ROBERTA. Yes, no, I don't know. What an afternoon. I feel weak, as if I were going to faint.

TOURNEL. [*Dashing to her.*] No, no, don't do that!

ROBERTA. I can't help it. I'm not doing it for pleasure, you know.

TOURNEL. Of course not! Here, lie down for a moment and compose yourself. [*He gently leads her to the bed.*]

ROBERTA. [*Allowing herself to be led.*] Oh, how can I refuse you. [*She falls back on the bed and gives a cry when she falls on* BERNARD's *body.*]

ROBERTA *and* BERNARD. Oh! [*She jumps up and goes right.*]

TOURNEL. What's the matter? [*To* BERNARD.] Oh, it's you. Why are you still here?

BERNARD. [*Sitting up.*] Well, you called me.

ROBERTA. [*Nervously, approaching the bed.*] No, that's not true. [*Shaking* TOURNEL.] Please make him leave. Let's not waste time discussing it.

TOURNEL. [*To* ROBERTA.] Of course! [*To* BERNARD.] Go, back where you came from. [*He presses the button on the left.*]

ROBERTA. [*Mounting the platform without realizing that it is a turntable. Furiously.*] It's not nice to invade people's rooms. [*Gasping as the turntable starts to turn.*] Oh!

TOURNEL. [*Grabbing her off the turntable.*] Hey!

CAMILLE. [*Appearing on the other bed.*] Oh, no! [*Recognizing* ROBERTA *and* TOURNEL.] Ah, ha!

TOURNEL *and* ROBERTA. [*Turning at his voice and jumping back.*] Camille! [*They run madly out into the lobby.*]

CAMILLE. [*Aloud.*] I beg your pardon! The bed turned!

ROBERTA. [*Stopping in her tracks.*] It can't be Camille, I can understand him.

TOURNEL. [*Running to* ROBERTA.] You're right, it can't be him.

CAMILLE. [*Getting off the bed.*] The bed turned.

ROBERTA. [*Extreme left, changing her flight and running to the stairs.*] I've had enough of this; let's get out of here.

TOURNEL. [*Same action.*] At once! [*They exit.*]

CAMILLE. Tournel and Roberta here! What can that mean? If they recognized me, I've had it! [*He enters the lobby after closing the door behind him.*] Oh, well. And now for Antoinette. What can she be doing? [*Entering* KRUGER's *room boldly.*] Antoinette! [*Surprised.*] Oh! [*A lot of noise comes from* KRUGER's *room—angry voices, knocked over furniture, broken glass.*]

ROBERTA. [*Reappearing, followed by* TOURNEL.] Edward! My God! Edward's here too!

TOURNEL. [*Running behind* ROBERTA.] Your butler! How embarrassing! My God, what a mess! [*They dash into the*

hallway on the left. Noise continues to come from KRUGER's *room. Suddenly the door opens and* CAMILLE *is thrown into the lobby with* KRUGER *hot on his heels.*]

KRUGER. Raus! Raus!

CAMILLE. [*Regaining control.*] But sir!

KRUGER. [*Back to the audience, facing* CAMILLE.] Ach! Zum Teufel! [*He hits him full in the mouth.*]

CAMILLE. Oh! [*Another punch in the mouth which dislodges the palate.* CAMILLE's *speech defect now returns as the palate shoots out of his mouth.*] Oh, my palate; I've lost it! [*He wants to scoop it up.*]

KRUGER. [*Seizng him bodily and pushing him into the room up right.*] Raus! Raus, mit Dir!

CAMILLE. [*As he is carried away.*] My palate! I want my palate!

KRUGER. [*Tossing him into the room.*] Hier! Nimm das! [*Crossing the stage, returning to his room.*] Was für ein Dummkopf! [*Entering his room.*] Also, liebchen! [*The door closes.* EDWARD *enters from the staircase.*]

EDWARD. [*As he comes downstage.*] Isn't there anyone here? [*He spies* CAMILLE's *palate, looks at it, and then nudges it with his foot.*] Hmm, why it's silver! [*Picking it up.*] And it's wet.

EUGENIA. [*Coming from the hallway on the left, stopping as she puts her foot on the first step of the staircase.*] May I help you?

EDWARD. Ah, miss! [EUGENIA *goes to him.*] First of all, some one must have lost this. For the life of me I can't figure out what it's for. [*He hands her the palate.*]

EUGENIA. [*Examining it.*] It must be an old fashioned piece of jewelry. [*She holds it up to her chest as if it were a brooch.* CAMILLE *comes out of his room, searching with his eyes plastered to the floor, for his palate.*]

CAMILLE. I must find my palate. [*He almost bumps into* EDWARD, *then raises his head, recognizes* EDWARD, *pivots around, and trying to make himself as small as possible, dashes from the lobby.*] God! Edward! [*He disappears back into his room.*]

EUGENIA. [*Who along with* EDWARD *has not observed* CAMILLE's *action.*] One of our guests must have lost it. I'll leave it at the desk.

EDWARD. Very good! Now, tell me, has a woman asked for M. Chandebise's room?

EUGENIA. Why, yes.

EDWARD. Is she still here?

EUGENIA. Sir! That's none of my business!

EDWARD. Please, I must see her. Her husband is on his way here with murder on his mind.

EUGENIA. [*Shocked.*] Oh, goodness!

EDWARD. I must warn her at once.

EUGENIA. Well, in that case! I saw her go into that room. [*She points to* KRUGER's *room.*]

EDWARD. [*Going to the door of* KRUGER's *room.*] Very good! [*He knocks.*]

KRUGER. Herein!

EDWARD. [*Entering the room.*] Excuse me, sir!

ANTOINETTE *and* KRUGER. Oh!

EDWARD. My wife! [*More sounds of an upheaval.*]

EUGENIA. [*Returning after she has started upstairs.*] What's going on? [*AN-TOINETTE bursts out of the room. Her hair is messed up, she is carrying her hat and clutching her blouse to her bare chest.*]

ANTOINETTE. [*Wildly, dashing towards the stairs.*] Oh, help, Edward's here, help! [*The fight continues for a moment, then* EDWARD *bursts out of the room in hot pursuit of his wife.*]

EDWARD. Stop her! Stop her!

KRUGER. [*Grabbing him by the left arm as* EDWARD *tries to catch* ANTOINETTE, KRUGER *spins him around and pushes him against the wall.*] Dummkopf!

EDWARD. [*As his body hits the wall.*] Oh!

EUGENIA. [*In reaction.*] Ah!

KRUGER. Zum Tod mit Dir! [*Continuing to push him into the wall.*] Da!

EDWARD. [*Painfully.*] Oh!

KRUGER. Und Da!

EDWARD. But she's my wife.

KRUGER. Noch einmal!

EDWARD. Oh! Let me go.

KRUGER. [*Letting go of him and returning to his room.*] Raus!

EDWARD. What luck! She cheats on me, and I'm the one who gets beat up.

EUGENIA. You should have told me you were the husband.

EDWARD. How was I to know that I was the husband? [EUGENIA *shrugs, heads toward the stairs; at this moment* POCHE *is coming down stairs with his wood hook in his hand.*] Oh no, how could she do that to me, the tart? Just a moment, just a moment. [*He dashes to the staircase where he sees* POCHE *and* EUGENIA *chatting.*] Ah, sir!

POCHE. [*Taken aback.*] What?

EDWARD. Sir! You have a hook in your hand.

POCHE. Well, yes, I do. And why not?

EDWARD. Sir, sir, she's cheating on me!

POCHE. [*Jovially.*] So?

EDWARD. [*Pointing to* KRUGER's *room.*] Sir, with a German!

POCHE. Oh, yes, "telefoniert!"

EDWARD. He didn't tell me his name. Sir, if you have no need of me at the moment, will you permit me to chase after the wench and teach her a lesson?

POCHE. Why, of course.

EDWARD. Thank you, sir. Just wait till I catch up with her! [*He exits.*]

POCHE. [*Coming downstage.*] There's something funny in the air today; this place is a mad house.

LUCY's *voice.* [*From below.*] Watch where you're going! [*A bell rings.*]

EUGENIA. [*Looking at the board.*] That's your ring. Go see what they want.

POCHE. [*Entering the hallway.*] All right, all right. [*He exits.*]

LUCY. [*Entering from below, looking around.*] Wasn't that Edward, the Chandebise's butler?

EUGENIA. May I help you?

LUCY. Ah, miss, that man that almost knocked me over on the stairs, isn't he the Chandebise's butler?

EUGENIA. It's possible, madam, because

he asked for M. Chandebise's room. That's all I know. The rest was very confusing. He came to warn a lady whose husband had discovered all and when he saw the lady, wow! She was his wife! It was a real puzzle.

LUCY. Surely, you're making it all up.

EUGENIA. I'm only telling you what I saw.

LUCY. Well then, please show me M. Chandebise's room.

EUGENIA. [*Indicating the room on the right.*] It's that one.

LUCY. Thank you; I'm going in.

EUGENIA. As you will, madam, my orders are to show whoever comes to the room. [*She goes towards the stairs, then exits left.*]

LUCY. Thank you. [*She knocks on the door.*]

CAMILLE. [*Coming out of his room, looking for his palate.*] I must find my palate. [*He almost bumps into* LUCY.]

LUCY. [*Facing the door as she knocks.*] What, no answer? [*She knocks again.*]

CAMILLE. [*Turns toward her, recognizes her, and dashes downstairs.*] Madam de Histangua! I've seen enough! What a hotel!

LUCY. [*Opening the door and entering the room.*] No one? How can that be? Roberta told me, "I'll catch my husband between five and five-ten. Get there at five-thirty, and it will all be over." Didn't she wait for me? Let's see! [*She goes to the bathroom, which she inspects.*]

CAMILLE. [*Reappearing in a frenzy and dashing into the room up right.*] Victor-Emmanuel's still here!

LUCY. [*Entering the lobby and going downstage.*] How strange! Well, too bad, I must be on my way. [*She turns, goes upstage to the stairs in order to leave.*]

CHANDEBISE. [*Entering from below, dressed in his business suit from Act 1.*] Did some one call me? [*Seeing* LUCY.] Was it you?

LUCY. M. Chandebise!

CHANDEBISE. [*Taking her eagerly by the hand and pulling her to stage front.*] At last, I've found you!

LUCY. [*Shocked.*] What's going on?

CHANDEBISE. Did you see Edward?

LUCY. What?

CHANDEBISE. [*In a hurry.*] I sent him to you; I couldn't come myself. Uh, uh, a banquet kept me from coming. Then I realized that it was tomorrow. So, I dashed over to tell you myself.

LUCY. To tell me what?

CHANDEBISE. [*Changing his tone.*] Oh, you unhappy child; what folly! To fall in love with me, of all people.

LUCY. [*Stepping back.*] What?

CHANDEBISE. [*Authoritatively.*] I know everything! Why didn't you sign your letter?

LUCY. [*Becoming more confused.*] What letter?

CHANDEBISE. The one which invited me here.

LUCY. [*Understanding.*] Oh! You don't think that I. . . .

CHANDEBISE. Without realizing what I was doing, I showed it to your husband.

LUCY. [*Falling back.*] What?

CHANDEBISE. He recognized your writing.

LUCY. What are you saying?

CHANDEBISE. And he threatened to kill you.

LUCY. [*Stridently.*] Caramba! Where is he?

CHANDEBISE. Hot on our trail.

LUCY. On our trail? And we're standing here? Come on, we've got to get out of here.

CHANDEBISE. [*Following her down the stairs.*] Ah, the follies of love! [*They exit in a frenzy.* OLIVIA *enters from the hallway on the left.*]

OLIVIA. Eugenia! Eugenia! Now, where is that girl? [*She is facing the right side of the stairs, blocking the stairs from below.*]

CHANDEBISE. [*Flying up the stairs, followed by* LUCY.] He's here! Your husband's here. Save yourself!

LUCY. My husband! I'm done for!

OLIVIA. What's going on?

CHANDEBISE. [*Bumping into* OLIVIA, *spinning her around, which pushes her into* Lucy.] Get out of my way!

OLIVIA. Eh?

LUCY. [*Same action.*] Get away from me! [LUCY *runs into the room on the right and into the bathroom.* CHANDEBISE *runs into* KRUGER'S *room.*]

OLIVIA. Madam!

ROBERTA. [*Entering from the hallway, followed by* TOURNEL. *Her face is veiled.*] Let's get out of here. I won't be happy until we've left this awful place. [*Bumping into* OLIVIA.] Get out of my way. [*She pushes her away from the stairs.*]

OLIVIA. Oh!

TOURNEL. [*Same action.*] Yes, let's leave. Move over! [*They exit down the stairs.*]

OLIVIA. [*Confused.*] What was that all about?

VOICE OF HISTANGUA. [*From below.*] Where aire zey? I keel zem, I estrangle zem. [*Gasp from* ROBERTA *and* TOURNEL.]

OLIVIA. [*Going to the right of the stairs.*] What's going on now?

ROBERTA. [*Reappearing in a frenzy.*] Senor de Histangua! [*Bumping into* OLIVIA.] Out of my way!! [*She twirls her around.*]

OLIVIA. Oh!

TOURNEL. [*Same action.*] It's that crazy Spaniard! What? You're still here? [*He spins* OLIVIA *around. He runs into the hallway on the left.*]

OLIVIA. [*Out of breath.*] Oh, my goodness, my goodness!

HOMENIDES. [*Like a wild man, brandishing his gun.*] Tournel et una senora in disguise. Iss my wife! Oh, ze misérable! [*He follows the others.*]

OLIVIA. Where are you going, sir?

HOMENIDES. [*Twirling her around.*] I keel zem both! Get out off my way. [*He dashes into the hallway.*]

OLIVIA. Kill them? Oh, my God! Help, help!

FERRAILLON. [*Entering from above, followed by* EUGENIA.] What's going on? What's all this racket?

OLIVIA. [*Out of breath.*] Oh, Arthur! That wild man is threatening to kill everyone.

FERRAILLON. [*Startled.*] Who?

OLIVIA. [*Swooning into* EUGENIA'S *arms.*] Oh, oh, oh!

EUGENIA. Sir! Sir!

FERRAILLON. [*Going to support* OLIVIA *from the other side.*] Here, let's get her over there. [*He indicates the room off the hallway that is visible to the public. He follows the two women into the room.*] Get her some smelling salts.

EUGENIA. Yes, sir.

FERRAILLON. [*Going to* KRUGER'S *door.*] What? Another ruckus in the German's room? What now? [*Suddenly the door opens and* KRUGER *and* CHANDEBISE, *locked in combat, are revealed.* CHANDEBISE *is holding onto the door frame as* KRUGER *is trying to pull him off.*]

KRUGER. Lass mich allein! Lass mich allein!

CHANDEBISE. [*Resisting* KRUGER.] Let go of me; let go of me!

FERRAILLON. [*Coming between them.*] What's going on here? [KRUGER *shoves* CHANDEBISE, *who falls into* FERRAILLON. *The force of the fall throws* FERRAILLON *onto the bench.* CHANDEBISE *then falls onto the bench too.* KRUGER, *grumbling, returns to his room.*]

FERRAILLON. [*Taken aback when he sees* CHANDEBISE.] Poche!

CHANDEBISE. [*Rising and standing in front of* FERRAILLON.] What did you say?

FERRAILLON. [*Grabbing him by the left arm and giving him a swift kick after each curse.*] You skunk!

CHANDEBISE. [*Giving a jump each time he is kicked.*] What's going on?

FERRAILLON. You loafer!

CHANDEBISE. But!

FERRAILLON. You pig!

CHANDEBISE. [*Breaking away.*] What are you calling me?

FERRAILLON. [*Menacingly.*] What?

CHANDEBISE. [*Pulling away.*] I am M. Chandebise, Director of the Boston Life Company.

FERRAILLON. [*Raising his hand to strike* CHANDEBISE.] He's drunk as a skunk again.

CHANDEBISE. Sir, I shall make a complaint.

FERRAILLON. [*Grabbing* CHANDEBISE *and starting to kick him again.*] Complain, will you?

CHANDEBISE. [*Giving a little jump with each kick.*] Oh!

FERRAILLON. Take this for Chandebise.

CHANDEBISE. Oh!

FERRAILLON. And this, and this, and this! [*At each kick* CHANDEBISE *says, "Oh!"*]

CHANDEBISE. How dare you!

FRRAILLON. [*Grabbing* CHANDEBISE's *coat.*] What's this? [*He tries to pull* CHANDEBISE's *coat off.*]

CHANDEBISE. [*Trying to defend himself.*] What are you doing?

FERRAILLON. Are you trying to play a joke on me? [*He rips off* CHANDEBISE's *jacket.*]

CHANDEBISE. Now, see here!

FERRAILLON. [*Pulling off* CHANDEBISE's *hat.*] Take that thing off! [*He puts the coat and hat on a free hook.*]

CHANDEBISE. [*Floored by this behavior.*] He's crazy!

FERRAILLON. [*Taking* POCHE's *cap and livery jacket from their hook.*] Here! Put on your uniform! [*He boxes* CHANDEBISE *about the ears.*]

CHANDEBISE. No.

FERRAILLON. Now be quick about it!

CHANDEBISE. Indeed I won't!

FERRAILLON. [*Forcing him into the jacket.*] You don't want to, eh? Now hurry up!!

CHANDEBISE. [*Becoming submissive.*] Yes sir, yes sir!

FERRAILLON. [*Pointing him to the stairs.*] Now get out of here! Go to your room! Hurry it up!

CHANDEBISE. [*Stumbling towards the stairs.*] Yes, sir! He's a madman.

FERRAILLON. [*Starting to chase after him.*] What did you say? Do you want me to teach you another lesson?

CHANDEBISE. [*Dashing up the stairs.*] No, no!

FERRAILLON. [*From the first step.*] All right! Now scram!

CHANDEBISE. [*Without taking his eyes off* FERRAILLON *as he goes upstairs.*] He's crazy!

FERRAILLON. [*Bounding up the stairs behind him.*] I'll give you what for! [CHANDEBISE *scrambles on up the stairs.*]

FERRAILLON. [*Returning to the lobby.*] That's what drink will do to a man. Stone drunk again! Why are the best servants always drunk? [*He comes down stage.*]

EUGENIA. [*Bursting out of* OLIVIA's *room, she leaves the door open. The audience can hear Olivia's moaning.*] Sir! Sir!

FERRAILLON. What is it now?

EUGENIA. Madam is having an attack!

FERRAILLON. More trouble! [*Turning to* EUGENIA.] Listen, go up to number ten and ask Dr. Finache if he can spare a moment for my wife.

EUGENIA. I'm on my way, sir. [*She exits quickly up the stairs.*]

FERRAILLON. Ah, a moment's peace! What a day! [*He enter's* OLIVIA's *room from which the audience can hear low moans.*] What is it, my sweet? What's wrong? [*The door closes.* POCHE *enters from the left, carrying some letters in his hand. As he reaches center stage, he unties his apron.*]

POCHE. I'll take these letters to the post office. [*He puts the apron on its hook then realizes that his cap and coat are missing.*] What's this? Who pinched my things? Well at least they left me a hat and a coat. [*He tries on* CHANDEBISE's *hat.*] Hmm, not a bad fit. One coat's as good as another. I'll put this one back when mine turns up. [*He pulls the coat on over his uniform vest. He starts to leave as he hears a buzz.*] What do they want now? [*He exits left.*]

EUGENIA. [*Entering, followed by* FINACHE.] Over there, sir!

FINACHE [*Pulling on his coat as he enters the lobby.*] Don't get the idea that I come here to make house calls.

What's wrong with her?

EUGENIA. Oh, nothing much, just a little spell.

FINACHE. A spell?

EUGENIA. Yes, a spell, a fright, a uh, uh, you know.

FINACHE. A spell? A fright? Talk so that I can understand you.

EUGENIA. She's had a nervous collapse.

FINACHE. You disturbed me for that? Well, just take a siphon bottle and spray her with it. That will calm her down.

EUGENIA. Since you're here, why don't you have a look at her.

FINACHE. Well, if you insist.

EUGENIA. Oh, thank you sir! This way, please! [*The door to* OLIVIA's *room opens, and the audience hears her low moans. The door closes behind them.* CHANDEBISE, *in* POCHE's *coat and cap, appears at the top of the stair case.*]

CHANDEBISE. Is . . . is that madman gone? [*Coming down the stairs as he speaks.*] If that's the way he welcomes his guests, I can't imagine coming here a second time. What an idiot! [*Going to the clothes tree where* FER- RAILLON *hung his clothes.*] My coat? My hat? Where are they? [*He gets down on his knees to look for them. At that moment* ROBERTA *and* TOURNEL *appear at the top of the stairs.*]

ROBERTA. We've lost him! Quick, a taxi!

TOURNEL. There's the bellboy.

ROBERTA. Oh yes, the bellboy.

CHANDEBISE. [*Still looking for his clothes.*] Maybe they're here.

ROBERTA. [*Calling to* CHANDEBISE *who has his back to her.*] Poche, call us a taxi.

CHANDEBISE. What?

TOURNEL. A taxi!

CHANDEBISE. [*Startled.*] My wife!

TOURNEL. Eh?

ROBERTA. [*Startled.*] My husband!! [*She flees down the stairs.*]

CHANDEBISE. Tournel, how dare you!

TOURNEL. It was him!

CHANDEBISE. [*Menacing* TOURNEL.] What are you doing here with my wife? [*He grabs* TOURNEL *by the throat.*]

TOURNEL. [*Half-strangled.*] Have you already forgotten?

CHANDEBISE. What?

TOURNEL. What we just explained to you.

CHANDEBISE. [*He pushes* TOURNEL *onto the bench.*] What did you explain to me? [*Pulling him up.*] Answer me, do you hear, answer me.

TOURNEL. Well, uh, well, ah.

FERRAILLON. [*Entering like a whirlwind.*] What's going on now? [*He grabs* CHANDEBISE *by the right arm and pushes him left.* TOURNEL *takes his opportunity to escape.*] Poche, not again!

CHANDEBISE. The madman!

FERRAILLON. [*Starting to kick* CHANDEBISE *as before.*] You swine.

CHANDEBISE. [*Jumping into the air.*] Oh!

FERRAILLON. Animal!

CHANDEBISE. Oh!

FERRAILLON. You wretch!

CHANDEBISE. Now see here!

FERRAILLON. Haven't you had enough yet?

CHANDEBISE. [*Pulling away.*] Help, help! A madman is attacking me.

FERRAILLON. [*Chasing him up the stairs.*] I'll give you what for, you filthy drunk! Get to your stinking hole. I'll lock you up myself and not let you out until you're sober. Now get up there! [*They disappear up the stairs. As they disappear,* KRUGER *comes out of his room.*]

KRUGER. Zum Teufel! Was für eine schweinerei! Ich will alles rein machen. Ich mach es wieder in Ordnung! [*He exits down the stairs.*]

CAMILLE. [*Peeking out of his room and entering the lobby.*] I'd better get out of here while the coast is clear.

LUCY. [*Coming out of the bathroom, crossing to the door, and listening at it.*] I don't hear anything.

CAMILLE. [*Looking around the floor.*] I don't see my palate. [*He circles around the lobby and ends up face to face with* LUCY.]

LUCY. [*In the lobby.*] I hope he's gone.

CAMILLE. Madam de Histangua! [*Turning on his heels to escape.*]

LUCY. Camille! [*Grabbing hold of him.*] Camille, don't leave me. Don't abandon me! My husband is after me . . . with a gun. He intends to kill everybody.

CAMILLE. My God!

LUCY. Please, don't leave me!

CAMILLE. No, no!

HOMENIDES. [*From above.*] Where aire zey? Les missérables?

LUCY. My husband!

CAMILLE. Let's get out of here! [*They dash to the stairs where they bump into* KRUGER *who is coming back up the stairs.* CAMILLE *dashes into the room on the right while* LUCY *disappears into* KRUGER's *room.*]

KRUGER. [*Perplexed by this turn of events but overjoyed to see a pretty woman running into his room.*] Oh! Was für eine Frau! [*He quickly enters his room.*]

HOMENIDES. [*Dashing into the lobby from the stairs.*] Where aire zey? I keel zem! Where aire zey? Where iss ze room off Senor Chandebise? Iss nobody here in zis hotel? [*He exits down the stairs.*]

POCHE. [*Entering from left.*] What's that awful noise?

LUCY. [*Trying to escape from* KRUGER *who is holding her tight.*] Let go of me, you fool. [*She whirls around and slaps him.*]

KRUGER. Donnerwetter! [*He goes back into his room.*]

POCHE. [*Laughing.*] How touching!

LUCY. [*Running to him.*] Oh, M. Chandebise!

POCHE. What?

LUCY. Heaven has sent you! Save me! Hide me!

POCHE. What's wrong with you, lady?

LUCY. [*Clutching* POCHE's *vest.*] My husband is after me! He wants to kill me!

POCHE. What did you say?

LUCY. Help me, help me!

POCHE. [*Guiding her by the right arm.*] Come, the exit's this way.

HOMENIDES. [*From below.*] Oh! Caramba! I haff you now!

LUCY. [*Reappearing in a flash, followed by* POCHE.] There he is! [*Going to the door to* CAMILLE's *room. All this time he has been standing guard against the door so that it cannot be opened.*] Let me in, let me in!

CAMILLE. [*Pushing even harder against the door.*] I will not!

POCHE. Hurry up! [*Confused, she heads towards* KRUGER's *room.*] No, not there, that's the German's room.

LUCH. Where, then?

POCHE. There, Bernard's room. [HOMENIDES, *who has kept up his stream of invective, bursts into the lobby like a madman.*]

HOMENIDES. No eusse! I see you now! You no can hide!

EUGENIA. [*Coming out of* OLIVIA's *room.*] May I help you, sir?

HOMENIDES. Senor Chandebise and ze lady wizh imm?

EUGENIA. [*Pointing to* CAMILLE's *room.*] There, sir, that room. [*She exits left.*]

HOMENIDES. [*At the door.*] Opin up, opin up! I keel you!

CAMILLE. Not on your life!

HOMENIDES. [*Forcing the door.*] Opin up, I tell you! Uno, dos, tres! [*On the third shove, the door flies open.* CAMILLE *falls to the floor from the force,* HOMENIDES *pulls him up and grabs him by the throat.*] My wife, whaire iss she? I keel her!

CAMILLE. [*On the extreme right, terrified, and not aware of what he is saying.*] But I don't have her. I give you my word. See for yourself. [*He turns his pockets inside out as a way of proof.*]

HOMENIDES. [*Not listening, going left.*] Whain I find her I keel her jouzte like zat fly over zair. [*He points the gun towards the button on the bed and shoots. The bed revolves and reappears with* LUCY *and* POCHE *on it.*]

LUCY. My husband! [*She escapes, followed by* POCHE.]

HOMENIDES. My wife! [*He chases after them, shooting off his gun.* LUCY *and* POCHE *escape.* HOMENIDES *is restrained by the hotel guests who are brought into*

the lobby by the gunshots. Their attempts
to restrain him are in vain. He is brought
under control as the curtain falls.]

Act 3

*Same set as Act 1. Note: The double doors at
the rear are to be opened from one side
only except in the special cases indicated.
As the curtain rises, the stage is empty; the
doors are closed.* ANTOINETTE *enters
quickly through one of the center doors
which she closes behind her. She is still in
the process of putting her cook's uniform
back on. Her apron and cap are still in
her hand.*

ANTOINETTE. Heavens! Edward's on his
way here! There's no time! [*She finally gets her uniform straightened.*]
That really took a lot out of me!
Wow!

EDWARD'S VOICE. [*From the left.*] Antoinette, Antoinette!

ANTOINETTE. Oh! [*She runs to lock the
rear door.*]

EDWARD'S VOICE. [*Coming closer.*] Antoinette!

ANTOINETTE. [*As she is putting on her cap
and apron.*] Oh, God!

EDWARD'S VOICE. [*From behind the double
doors.*] Antoinette! [*He shakes the
doors.*] Open up, you wench! Damn,
she's locked herself in there! [*His
voice trails off left.*] Just you wait!

ANTOINETTE. Quick! [*She unlocks the door
and tiptoes into the room down right.*]

EDWARD. [*Still in his street clothes entering
from the left.*] Where is she? Antoinette? Antoinette?

ANTOINETTE. [*Entering right, very calm.*]
What are you shouting about?

EDWARD. So there you are. Why did you
lock yourself in?

ANTOINETTE. [*Feigning ignorance.*] What?

EDWARD. I said, "Why did you lock
yourself in?"

ANTOINETTE. [*In total control.*] What? I

wasn't locked in.

EDWARD. [*Angered by her control.*] We'll
see about that! [*He strides to the door,
tries the lock, and is amazed to discover
that the door opens.*] Well!

ANTOINETTE. [*Leaning against the table,
with her arms crossed, her eyes on the
ceiling and with great irony.*] Have you
forgotten how to unlock the door?

EDWARD. Well, it does stick sometimes.
Never mind, it's not important. Why
don't you tell me what you were
doing at the Kozy Kitten Hotel this
afternoon?

ANTOINETTE. [*Feigning ignorance.*]
Where?

EDWARD. The Kozy Kitty Hotel.

ANTOINETTE. The Kozy Kitty Hotel?

EDWARD. Don't "Kozy Kitty" me. Don't
try to put one over on me. I saw you
there not half an hour ago.

ANTOINETTE. [*In great shock.*] What? You
saw me there?

EDWARD. Yes, you!

ANTOINETTE. [*Calmly.*] I haven't budged
all afternoon.

EDWARD. [*Unable to hide his cynicism.*]
What do you mean?

ANTOINETTE. I'm telling you the truth.

EDWARD. You haven't budged all afternoon? Well! Certainly, I expected you
to come up with a clever explanation,
but to claim that you weren't at the
hotel—no, I can't take that.

ANTOINETTE. Well, I can't tell you what
isn't so.

EDWARD. But I saw you with my own
eyes.

ANTOINETTE. [*In total control.*] What does
that prove.?

EDWARD. What?

ANTOINETTE. Whether you saw me or
not. I wasn't there.

EDWARD. You've got your nerve! I saw
you there, half undressed, in the
arms of a German.

ANTOINETTE. Me?

EDWARD. [*Face to face with her.*] Yes, you!
The fool almost beat me up.

ANTOINETTE. A German? Me? But how
can that be? I don't know a word of

German.

EDWARD. [*With a forced laugh.*] That's a reason? Knowing the language isn't necessary for certain things. All you need is a look. You weren't in the German's arms?

ANTOINETTE. I didn't budge all afternoon.

EDWARD. I'll be damned! [*Going left, through his teeth.*] She's lying with the best of them. [*Going back to her.*] So, you didn't budge from here? We'll see about that. [*Going to the rear.*]

ANTOINETTE. [*Uneasy, moving towards him.*] What are you going to do?

EDWARD. [*Turning towards her.*] Ask the doorman.

ANTOINETTE. The doorman!

EDWARD. He'll tell me if you went out. [*He starts upstage. The discussion becomes more and more heated. She grabs him, he brushes her hand away, and she grabs him with her other hand. They say their next two speeches at almost the same time.*]

ANTOINETTE. Edward, don't be silly. Don't bring the doorman into this stupid argument. Do you want him to make fun of you?

EDWARD. Aha! I've got you now! You didn't expect that, did you? You thought you could put one over on me, didn't you?

ANTOINETTE. We'll see, Edward.

EDWARD. [*Pushing her away.*] Indeed we will.

ANTOINETTE. [*Throwing her hands up in frustration.*] Do as you will. [*She goes to the table, leans against it with her arms crossed, face to the audience.*]

EDWARD. [*He dashes into the hall, leaving both doors open behind him and grabs the telephone, rings it, and picks up the receiver.*] Ah, it's you M. Ploumard! Good! Tell me, now don't be shocked by my questions, I simply have to know. What time did my wife go out this afternoon? [*A silence, AN-TOINETTE's face registers anguish.*] What? She didn't go out? [ANTOI-NETTE's *face relaxes and she gives a sigh of relief.*] Are you sure she didn't go out this afternoon? What, the two of you ate soup together? [*A small smile comes to* ANTOINETTE's *face, her eyes are mocking.*] What? Since no one was up stairs, she came down to eat with you. [*Not believing his ears.*] Well, we'll see about that.

ANTOINETTE. [*Still leaning against the table, facing the audience, with her arms crossed. She raises five fingers to the audience, as she inclines her head towards the phone.*] That cost me five francs.

EDWARD. [*Nonplussed.*] I just don't understand. . . . It can't be so. Well, thank you, excuse me for bothering you. [*He peevishly hangs up the phone, comes back into the room in an angry mood. He closes the door behind him.*]

ANTOINETTE. [*Mockingly.*] Well?

EDWARD. [*Brutally.*] Leave me alone. [*He goes left.*] Are you implying that I'm crazy or blind to the truth?

ANTOINETTE. [*Starting towards the left rear door.*] Men do stupid things when they're jealous.

EDWARD. All right! Go on, get back to the kitchen. [*The doorbell rings.*] We'll talk about this later.

ANTOINETTE. As you will. [*She shrugs her shoulders as she exits. The doorbell rings again.*]

EDWARD. [*Still in his bad humour.*] All right, all right! [*Aside.*] Either she's an expert liar or I need glasses. [*The bell rings again.*] I'm coming! [*He exits. The audience hears the sound of the front door being opened and the sounds of* ROBERTA's *and* EDWARD's *voices.* ROBERTA *enters, followed by* TOURNEL. *She goes to the couch.* TOURNEL *remains to the left of the center door.*]

ROBERTA. Didn't you hear the bell?

EDWARD. [*Preoccupied as he answers the questions.*] Yes, madam, I was just. . . .

ROBERTA. My husband? Has my husband come in yet?

EDWARD. Eh? No, madam.

ROBERTA. Very well, leave us.

EDWARD. Yes, madam. [*As he exits, his mutterings are directed towards* AN-

TOINETTE.] The hussy!

TOURNEL. [*Catching the word.*] What did you say?

EDWARD. What? Oh, I wasn't talking about you, sir.

TOURNEL. I hope not! [EDWARD *exits.* TOURNEL *presses his advantage.*] Now, my dear, now that you are home, I. . . .

ROBERTA. [*Near the couch, as she is taking off her hat and gloves, turning towards* TOURNEL.] You're not going to leave me, are you? [*She puts her hat and gloves on a nearby piece of furniture.*]

TOURNEL. [*Crestfallen.*] What?

ROBERTA. [*Nervous, not able to stay in one place.*] I don't know what kind of mood my husband will be in when he comes home. You saw how he looked ready to strangle you when we ran into him that second time at the hotel. Don't you see, if the madness comes over him again. . . .

TOURNEL. [*As calm as she is nervous.*] Perhaps it would be better if I were here.

ROBERTA. I don't want to be alone when he comes in.

TOURNEL. [*Resigned.*] Very well. [*He comes downstage.*]

ROBERTA. You don't appear enthusiastic about this.

TOURNEL. [*Without enthusiasm.*] Well, you see. . . .

ROBERTA. You're all like that: audacious in business but reluctant in responsibility.

TOURNEL. First of all, what responsibility? Nothing happened.

ROBERTA. [*Going to him.*] It wasn't your fault that nothing happened. Anyway, my husband doesn't know that nothing happened. Surely when he saw us there, he suspected something. His anger was proof of that.

TOURNEL. Obviously, by God. I don't understand why it took so long for him to get angry.

ROBERTA. You're right!

TOURNEL. When he burst in the first time, sitting on that bed with a bottle in his hand. . . .

ROBERTA. Yes.

TOURNEL. He didn't appear too shocked to see us there. He even looked pleased with it, you might say.

ROBERTA. Did he ever! He even hugged us.

TOURNEL. Absolutely! Then when we saw him later in that uniform, he lunged towards us and appeared indignant. Usually in these adventures, you make up your mind at once and don't take the time to reflect on it.

ROBERTA. That's just what I thought. I don't understand it at all. [*The doorbell rings.*] Oh dear, there's the bell; maybe it's him.

TOURNEL. [*Nervous.*] Now? [*Sound of the door being opened.*]

LUCY'S VOICE. Is madam back? [*Sound of the door being closed.*]

EDWARD'S VOICE. Yes, madam, she is.

ROBERTA. Oh, no! Lucy's here! [*She goes upstage to the rear door which she opens.*] Ah! Do come in.

LUCY. [*Entering and going to the table.*] Oh, Roberta, Roberta! What drama! What tragedy!

ROBERTA. [*Lifting her eyes heavenward.*] You don't have to tell me!

LUCY. My legs are like jelly. [*She demonstrates.*]

ROBERTA *and* TOURNEL. [*In sympathy.*] Oh!

LUCY. [*Falling into the chair to the left of the table.*] I'm afraid to go home. [*Without transition and in the same tone.*] Oh, hello, M. Tournel. Please excuse me.

TOURNEL. Don't worry, we have plenty of time.

LUCY. [*Without hearing him and returning to her problems.*] I'll go live somewhere else . . . under a bridge. I'm too scared to find myself face to face with that wild man, my husband. Oh, no!

ROBERTA. Yes, let's talk about your husband. What a madman! When he saw Tournel and me at the Kozy Kitty Hotel. . . . I don't know what came over him . . . he chased after us brandishing a gun. He looked like he wanted to kill us.

TOURNEL. He certainly did! Can you tell us why?

LUCY. [*Standing up.*] What! You were part of his fox hunt too?

TOURNEL. Indeed! What a volcano! What a quick temper he has!

LUCY. [*Leaning against the table on the right.*] At least he didn't catch me. Happily I found your husband and he helped me escape. Without his help, I would have been caught, and no telling what would have happened.

ROBERTA. My husband did what?

LUCY. Helped me. But then he scared me too.

ROBERTA. Oh?

LUCY. I don't know if it was the excitement or what but all of a sudden he went out of his mind.

ROBERTA. So you noticed it too?

LUCY. Yes, I noticed it. I had seen him ten minutes earlier and he had told me about my husband's mood and begged me to get out of there. Then snap! Following that, a wild chase, a dash down the stairs. When we reached the street, he looked at me strangely and asked, "Who is that wild Indian? Do you know him?" I was stunned because he was referring to my husband, so then I said to him, "Of course you know him, he's my husband, and you know him almost as well as you know me." Then he said to me, "But I don't know you! Who are you?" [*Trembling slightly.*] My goodness, my goodness! I said to myself, "He's lost his mind." I stared at him closely to see if he was teasing me. . . . Oh, goodness. . . . Then he let out a stream of incomprehensible words.

ROBERTA. [*To* TOURNEL.] You see, you see—just like he was with us.

TOURNEL. Like with us.

LUCY. How was I to know that he would be the bellboy . . . that he would bring up the wood . . . that someone would have stolen his uniform, all sorts of stupid things?

ROBERTA. It's crazy!

TOURNEL. Crazy.

LUCY. And suddenly, what should come into his mind? He wanted to drag me into a bar—me!

ROBERTA *and* TOURNEL. Oh!

LUCY. You should have seen me! I jumped back and said, "Now see here, M. Chandebise." And he said to me, "I'm Poche, Poche."

ROBERTA. [*To* TOURNEL.] You see, "Poche, Poche."

TOURNEL. [*Sitting down into the chair to the right of the little table on the left.*] Yes, that was his stock answer to us.

LUCY. Oh, was I frightened! I humored your husband until we got to the bar, then I fled as quickly as I could. You know, I think I'm still on the run. [*She falls into the chair to the left of the table.*]

ROBERTA. I'm so confused. I don't know whether your husband has lost his mind or whether it was all a practical joke. It's so confusing.

TOURNEL. [*Brusquely aloud and in a serious tone.*] What difference does it make?

THE TWO WOMEN. What?

TOURNEL. [*In a comforting voice.*] What a day!

ROBERTA. That's all? I thought you would. . . .

TOURNEL. No!

ROBERTA. What a mess!

TOURNEL. Indeed.

LUCY. Between a husband who wants to shoot your brains out. . . .

ROBERTA. And one who is losing his.

TOURNEL. Enough of this!

ALL THREE. Weren't we lucky! [*The bell rings. Instinctively* LUCY *and* TOURNEL *stand and go to* ROBERTA *who is center stage.*]

LUCY. [*In a low voice.*] There's the bell.

ROBERTA *and* TOURNEL. Yes.

TOURNEL. Maybe it's Chandebise.

ROBERTA. I don't think so; he has his key.

TOURNEL. Which he sometimes forgets.

ROBERTA. That's true.

TOURNEL. [*Back to the audience, facing the two women.*] I remember one time last winter, it was snowing. . . .

ROBERTA. [*Cutting him off.*] No, my dear, no stories now. It's not the time.

TOURNEL. All right. [*He returns to his chair.*]

ROBERTA. Oh, goodness!

LUCY. Haven't they answered the door yet?

ROBERTA. I don't know. However, if someone rings. . . .

TOURNEL. Someone must be there.

ROBERTA. Obviously.

TOURNEL. Well, that's what I thought. [*Sounds of the front door opening and closing.*]

EDWARD. [*Entering in a fright.*] Madam, madam!

ROBERTA. Well, what is it?

EDWARD. Madam!

ROBERTA. What?

EDWARD. It's M. Chandebise!

TOURNEL *and* LUCY. And?

ROBERTA. Well?

EDWARD. Well, I don't know what's come over him. I opened the door and he came in like this [*He imitates* POCHE's *walk.*] and he said to me, "Is this M. Chandebise's house?"

ALL. What?

EDWARD. Yes, madam! At first I thought he was joking, so to play along I laughed, "Ha, ha, of course this is M. Chandebise's house, ha, ha." But he didn't join in. He didn't budge and he said to me, "Tell him that I've come about the uniform."

ALL. No!

EDWARD. Yes!

ROBERTA. Oh no, this farce is starting up again! [*To* EDWARD *energetically.*] Where is he now?

EDWARD. Waiting in the hall.

TOURNEL *and* LUCY. Eh!

ROBERTA. [*Surprised.*] What? He's waiting?

TOURNEL *and* LUCY. In the hall?

ROBERTA. We'll see about this! [*She goes*

upstage followed by the others. She pushes open the double doors. TOURNEL *and* ROBERTA *are on the left,* EDWARD *and* LUCY *on the right.* POCHE *is sitting on the edge of his seat, hat on his head, waiting patiently. At the sight of these people who are more serious looking than he, he smiles.*]

ALL. [*Recoiling in surprise.*] Oh!

ROBERTA. Well, what are you doing there?

POCHE. Excuse me?

ROBERTA. Why are you sitting in the hall like a delivery boy?

POCHE. [*Barely tipping his hat.*] Madam?

EVERYONE. "Madam?"

ROBERTA. "Madam!" All right, come in. [*She comes downstage.*]

POCHE. [*On the threshold of the room.*] I was waiting for M. Chandebise.

TOURNEL *and* LUCY. What?

ROBERTA. What did you say?

EDWARD. "Madam!" Did you hear him call her "madam"?

POCHE. [*Tapping* EDWARD's *stomach with his hat.*] Hey, I know you from the Kozy Kitty Hotel.

EDWARD. Yes, sir.

POCHE. Your wife is playing around on you.

EDWARD. [*Vexed.*] Oh, sir!

ROBERTA. What did he say?

POCHE. [*Turning towards* ROBERTA *when he hears her voice.*] And madam too. You're the one I kissed. [*Going towards her.*] Hello!

ROBERTA. [*Pulling* TOURNEL *in front of her to protect her.*] Oh my God, Tournel! Tournel, what's wrong with him?

TOURNEL. Come, my friend.

POCHE. [*Indicating* TOURNEL.] And you're the gigolo! So, how's it going?

TOURNEL. [*Pulling him away.*] Now see here, Victor-Emmanuel!

POCHE. [*Center stage.*] No! It's Poche! Poche!

LUCY. There! It's Poche! [*Going right.*]

POCHE. [*Recognizing* LUCY, *going to her.*] You're the one I saved from the wild Indian. Boy, we had quite a time, didn't we?

LUCY. [*Somewhat shocked.*] Ah, yes, yes. [*Feeling cornered, she inches down the length of the table until she can escape to join the others.*]

POCHE. [*Overcome with laughter.*] He! He! You all live together! He! That's a laugh!

ALL. [*They are all huddled together against this madman.*] Oh!

EDWARD. Yes, sir.

POCHE. Now don't forget to tell M. Chandebise. . . .

LUCY. [*To* ROBERTA.] Did you hear him?

EDWARD. [*To* POCHE.] Yes, sir. [*He exits, closing the door behind him.*]

TOURNEL. Why is he acting like such a fool?

ROBERTA. It certainly can't be because of a practical joke.

POCHE. [*Approaching the little group to give his explanations.*] It's because I left my uniform hanging, you see. . . .

LUCY *and* TOURNEL. [*Not wanting to contradict him.*] Of course.

ROBERTA. [*Leaving the group to confront* POCHE.] See here! We've had enough of this.

POCHE. [*Nonplussed, his mouth falls open.*] Ah!

ROBERTA. [*In a firm voice.*] If you're sick, just tell us, and we'll take care of you. If on the other hand, it's just a whim that's entered your mind, I'm here to tell you that it's not funny.

POCHE. Oh.

ROBERTA. Let me explain things to you. It's as simple as A plus B. There's nothing between M. Tournel and me. Lucy will be happy to confirm that for me.

LUCY. Absolutely.

ROBERTA. Now, that should be enough! If you want to persist in this madness, M. Tournel will be happy to set things straight. [*As she is talking, she grabs hold of* TOURNEL'S *sleeve. He has been talking to* LUCY. ROBERTA *shoves him towards* POCHE.]

TOURNEL. [*As he is shoved.*] Me?

POCHE. [*As* TOURNEL *bumps into his stomach, the force sends him reeling*

backwards to the left.] Oh?

ROBERTA. Absolutely! Whether you believe us or not, at least stop acting like such an idiot.

POCHE. Me?

ROBERTA. Yes, you. A little while ago you believed us, you held us in your arms. Then, not ten minutes later, you almost choked M. Tournel.

POCHE. I almost choked you?

TOURNEL. Yes.

ROBERTA. What does it matter? Do you believe us or not?

POCHE. But. . . .

ROBERTA. Well, then, give me a good kiss and it will be over once and for all.

POCHE. I'd rather give you ten than one!

ALL. All in good time! [POCHE *wipes his mouth with the back of his hand and gets ready to kiss* ROBERTA.]

ROBERTA. [*Pushing* POCHE *away as he starts to kiss her cheek.*] Oh!

TOURNEL. [*Stopping* POCHE'S *fall.*] Oh!

ALL. What?

ROBERTA. [*Indignantly.*] You've been drinking.

POCHE. Eh?

ROBERTA. You smell like a brewery!

POCHE. Me?

ROBERTA. [*Grabbing his chin and pushing him under* TOURNEL'S *nose.*]: See for yourself, my dear.

TOURNEL. [*Reeling from the smell.*] Good God!

ROBERTA. There.

TOURNEL. Whew! Like a wine cellar.

ROBERTA. [*Reproachful and indignant.*] You're drinking. You're drinking now.

ALL. Oh!

POCHE. What? Drinking? You can't call two or three pints to build up my blood drinking. You'd do the same.

ROBERTA. You see, he's drunk, completely drunk.

ALL. [*Scandalized.*] Oh!

POCHE. [*Following* ROBERTA.] Let me tell you something. . . . I'm not at all. . . . And another thing, little lady!

ROBERTA. [*Shooing him away.*] Get out of here, go sleep it off!

POCHE. What?

TOURNEL. Oh, Victor-Emmanuel!

POCHE. [*In* TOURNEL's *face.*] Poche, I said, Poche. [*On each "P," his spittle flies into* TOURNEL's *face.*]

TOURNEL. [*Overcome by the fumes, pushing him away.*] All right, Poche, if you insist.

LUCY. [*Stepping back to avoid* POCHE.] Oh!

POCHE. [*Getting his balance.*] Yes, I insist! [*Aside.*] It's the truth. [*Grumbling.*] If this keeps up, I'm going to get really mad.

ROBERTA. It's shameful.

EDWARD. [*Running into the room.*] The doctor's here, madam.

ALL. Ah!

FINACHE. [*Entering and to* ROBERTA.] What's wrong? Edward said he was just about to call me. [*Acknowledging* POCHE.] Hello, Chandebise.

POCHE. [*Looking around to see who is being addressed.*] Where is this Chandebise?

FINACHE. [*Thinking it is a joke.*] He! He! Very funny! [*To* ROBERTA.] What's going on here?

ROBERTA. [*Indicating* POCHE.] He's dead drunk.

FINACHE. [*Caught by surprise.*] What? Him?

EDWARD. [*Same action.*] What? The master?

TOURNEL *and* LUCY. Yes!

ROBERTA. Smell his breath.

FINACHE. [*Going to* POCHE.] It can't be so! You, drunk?

POCHE. [*Shrugging his shoulders to gain sympathy.*] Me? Phew. . . .

FINACHE. [*Getting a blast of* POCHE's *breath, falling back.*] Oh!

POCHE. It's a lie.

FINACHE. [*To* ROBERTA, *alluding to* POCHE.] No doubt about it.

ROBERTA. There, you see.

EDWARD. [*Scandalized.*] Oh, sir!

POCHE. What?

FINACHE. What did you do to drink yourself into such a state?

POCHE. What? You too? [*Going to* FINACHE.] Now listen here, my good man.

FINACHE. My good man?

POCHE. Have you finished with me? I'm no drunker than you.

FINAHCE. [*Trying to calm him.*] Now, calm down.

POCHE. [*Addressing himself in succession to each person. They nervously answer "yes" to his demands.*] Here's the truth! Everyone's been after me since I got here. What do you want from me? I'm here to see M. Chandebise, and I will see M. Chandebise. That's all there is to it. [*He puts his hat on, walks up and down the stage in a rage. All the characters are in a line, on a diagonal, starting from the back of the couch.*]

FINACHE. [*Not believing his ears.*] Oh!

ROBERTA. [*To* FINACHE.] What did I tell you?

LUCY. He has moments of sanity and then . . . nothing.

TOURNEL. He's been like this since this afternoon.

FINACHE. Oh, he has it bad. [*They look at* POCHE, *shaking their heads.*]

POCHE. [*Perceiving that they are staring at him.*] What now? Why are you looking at me like that? I'm a good fellow, I just don't like to be made a fool of.

FINACHE. Yes, my friend.

ALL. Yes, yes.

POCHE. But. . . . [*He continues to pace as he grumbles.*]

ROBERTA. [*To* FINACHE.] Can you believe it?

TOURNEL. Can you? [POCHE, *in a foul mood, sits in the chair to the left of the table on the right.*]

LUCY *and* EDWARD. Oh!

FINACHE. [*Whispering, without his eyes leaving* POCHE.] I can't get over it. Has he recognized any of you?

ROBERTA. None of us, isn't that so, Edward?

EDWARD. No one.

FINACHE. These hallucinations, this amnesia, this loss of identity, I've only seen in confirmed alcoholics.

ALL. No!

FINACHE. He'll soon have the D.T.'s.

ALL. [*Looking at* POCHE *with sympathy.*] Oh.

POCHE *angrily slams his hat down on the table.*

ALL. [*Startled.*] Oh!

ROBERTA. But that doesn't make sense. He never takes more than a small drink after his meals.

TOURNEL. And sometimes he doesn't even finish that.

EDWARD. That's right! Most of the time, I finish it off so that it won't be wasted.

LUCY. You see, not even a drink at every meal.

FINACHE. The amount doesn't matter because alcoholism is not a matter of the amount but of the person's temperament.

TOURNEL. There you have it.

ALL. What?

FINACHE. His temperament.

TOURNEL. Indeed! [*To* FINACHE, *satisfied with his superior knowledge.*] They don't understand. [*His back to the audience.*] It's the tendency that one has—more or less—to become a . . . an idiot.

FINACHE. [*Agreeing at first with* TOURNEL's *explanation.*] What? That's not it at all.

TOURNEL. [*Shocked.*] I thought. . . .

FINACHE. By temperament, I mean the ability that an individual has to withstand the effects of something. For example, one man could drink a quart of alcohol a day and feel no effects while his neighbor might drink a glass a day and become alcoholic.

POCHE. [*Watching them from a distance.*] Humph, I bet they're making fun of me.

FINACHE. Naturally, those are the ones who are the most troublesome because they are not lying. One drink after meals! What difference could that make? Nothing until the crisis happens, and there you have the result. [*They are all plastered against one another, knees slightly bent, and their eyes riveted on* POCHE *with compassion.*]

ALL. Oh!

POCHE. [*After a moment.*] Tell me, you bunch of onions, what's so funny?

ALL. What?

POCHE. [*Putting on his hat and getting up.*] You heard what I said. This had better stop or we're in trouble.

FINACHE. [*Going to him.*] What, dear friend, what then?

POCHE. I'm not an idiot, you'll see.

FINACHE. [*Trying to calm him.*] There, there. [*To the others.*] Irritability, don't you see. It's another symptom.

POCHE. [*Coming to him.*] What?

FINACHE. Nothing, my friend, nothing. Give me your hand.

POCHE. [*Shocked.*] My hand?

FINACHE. [*Demonstrating by holding his hand out in front of him, with the fingers spread.*] Come on, let me have it.

POCHE. [*Obeying.*] Why? [*His hand is trembling badly.*]

ROBERTA. Oh! Look how his hand's shaking.

ALL. Oh!

FINACHE. [*Taking hold of* POCHE's *forearm.*] There, you see. The tremor of an alcoholic. It's one of the most characteristic symptoms.

POCHE. [*Jumping anger.*] Ah ha! Ah ha! Ah ha!

ALL. [*Jumping in fear.*] Ah!

POCHE. [*Prancing in a rage between* FINACHE *and* ROBERTA.] That's enough, enough, I say.

ALL. [*Quickly moving out of his way.*] Oh, good heavens!

FINACHE. [*Trying to restore calm.*] Now, now, old man.

POCHE. [*To* ROBERTA.] You want to make me angry, don't you? [*To* FINACHE.] You want to make me angry too, don't you?

ALL. No, no!

ROBERTA. Please, calm down, my dear.

POCHE. [*Turning towards* ROBERTA.] Ah, you! Go to hell!

ROBERTA. [*Shocked.*] What? What did he say?

FINACHE. [*Pushing her upstage as he is talking. The others follow.*] Nothing,

nothing. Don't pay attention to him. When he's like this, he's not in his right mind. Leave us alone. Don't irritate him.

ROBERTA. [*From the rear.*] It's too much! He really is an alcoholic. Telling me. . . . What did he tell me?

FINACHE. [*Herding them all towards the door on the left.*] Now, now, he's too excited. Let Edward and me try to get him to bed.

ROBERTA. [*About to exit.*] Ah, yes, try to get him to bed, because. . . .

FINACHE. Yes, yes! Go on, Tournel! [*To* LUCY.] Madam, please accept my apologies.

LUCY. Of course, Doctor. Oh, it's so sad, at his age.

TOURNEL. Yes, I remember some years ago seeing a twelve year old alcoholic. It was in the summer. . . .

ROBERTA. No, no! You can tell us that another time. [*They exit.* EDWARD *is in front of the center door.*]

FINACHE. [*Going to* POCHE *who is still pacing up and down.*] Well, let's see, old friend.

POCHE. That was smart of you to get them to leave; things were about to get bad.

FINACHE. I agree with you totally.

POCHE. Those people . . . are they a little cracked?

FINACHE. [*Playing along.*] A little cracked?

POCHE. [*To* EDWARD, *who had joined them.*] That's what I said, a little cracked.

EDWARD. [*Following* FINACHE's *example.*] A little cracked?

POCHE. You should have given me a sign, slipped it to me real low. "They're crackers." [*To* FINACHE, *who has profited from* POCHE's *conversation to take his pulse.*] What are you doing to my hand?

FINACHE. [*Holding his watch in his right hand to time* POCHE's *pulse.*] Why nothing! It's just a gesture of friendship.

POCHE. [*With insouciance.*] Ah! [*Pulling*

his hand away.] I wasn't fooled by them. [*Laughing.*] Nuts are always like that.

FINACHE. [*Putting his watch back in his pocket.*] That's strange. You have almost no pulse.

POCHE. What?

FINACHE. I said, "You have almost no pulse." [*To* EDWARD.] He has almost no pulse.

POCHE. [*Jovially.*] That comes from clean living! [*Laughing at his own joke.*]

FINACHE. [*Humoring him.*] Very funny! [*Whispering to* EDWARD *as he taps him on the arm.*] Laugh! Laugh!

EDWARD. Me? If you insist. [*Without conviction.*] Ha, ha, ha!

POCHE. [*Indicating* EDWARD.] That made the flunky laugh.

FINACHE. Yes, it did. [*Becoming serious.*] There! Now that we've had a good laugh, let's get serious.

POCHE. What?

FINACHE. Now wait, I'm your friend. [*In a serious voice.*] You do know who I am, don't you?

POCHE. No.

FINACHE. [*Taken aback.*] Ah, I see. Well now, I am your doctor, your good doctor. I am the one who takes care of your aches, your sniffles, your diets. You know, the good doctor.

POCHE. Yes, yes, I know; I'm not stupid. You're a doctor.

FINACHE. There!

POCHE. [*Aside.*] What's gotten into him?

FINACHE. [*Profoundly.*] Now, I think. . . . As I am looking at you that you must be worn out.

POCHE. Me?

FINACHE. Yes, yes, you're worn out. [*To* EDWARD.] He's tired.

EDWARD. Yes, he's tired.

POCHE. Tired? By God, why shouldn't I be? Up at five, sweeping out the lobby, waxing the floors, bringing up the wood. . . .

FINACHE. Obviously.

EDWARD. Obviously.

FINACHE *and* EDWARD. [*Exchanging a knowing glance.*] Oh!

FINACHE. Well, in that case, why don't
you change clothes and go to bed?

POCHE. Me? No!

FINACHE. All right, at least get out of
that uncomfortable coat. Edward,
why don't you go get M. Chandebise's most comfortable dressing
gown?

POCHE. But what about my uniform?

FINACHE. Yes, of course, while we're
waiting for it. [*Motioning* EDWARD.]
Edward!

EDWARD. At once, sir. [*He goes into the
room on the right.*]

FINACHE. [FINACHE *tries to force* POCHE
*into the bedroom by pushing him as hard
as he can. There is a to and fro motion as*
FINACHE *forces his weight against the
unbudging* POCHE.] There, see how
comfortable that bed looks.

POCHE. Hey, quit rocking me like that!

FINACHE. You're going to stretch
out. . . .

POCHE. You're making me seasick.

FINACHE. And have a nice sleepy-bye.

POCHE. [*Turning around.*] Me? But what
about M. Chandebise?

FINACHE. M. Chandebise? [*Aside, raising
his arms heavenward.*] My God! [*To*
POCHE.] Well, if he tells you anything,
let me know about it.

POCHE. [*Satisfied.*] Ah! Good!

EDWARD. [*Bringing in the dressing gown.*]
Here's the dressing gown.

FINACHE. There! Let's get that jacket
off.

POCHE. [*Allowing them to take off his
jacket.*] Well, all right. Go on and do
whatever you want with me.

FINACHE. That's a good boy! [EDWARD
hands him the dressing gown.] My,
doesn't that look nice on you!

POCHE. [*Knotting the cord around his
waist.*] I look like one of those fancy
coachmen that you see driving
around town.

FINACHE. [EDWARD *puts the jacket on the
chair to the right of the table.*] There!
Now don't you feel better?

POCHE. You're right, this is more comfortable than my uniform.

FINACHE. Of course it is! And now, a
little bird tells me that you are getting a little thirsty.

POCHE. [*Jovially.*] What a naughty little
fellow!

FINACHE. [*Laughing.*] Isn't he? So, I'm
going to give you something to
drink. It may not taste very good, but
you must drink it down at once.

POCHE. Some strong stuff?

FINACHE. Of course!

POCHE. [*Going right.*] Go, go. My thirst is
killing me.

FINACHE. Wonderful! [*Whispering to* ED-
WARD *who has returned after disposing of
the jacket.*] Do you have some spirits
of ammonia in the house?

EDWARD. Yes, sir.

POCHE. [*Not hearing what the others are
saying.*] What a windfall! What a
windfall! [*He sits to the left of the table.*]

FINACHE. Good! We're going to give
him ten drops in a glass of water.

EDWARD. Very well, sir.

FINACHE. And then when he's sobered
up, I want you to take him. . . . Wait,
I'll write a prescription for him.

EDWARD. Yes, sir.

FINACHE. [*Going right.*] Where's some
writing paper?

EDWARD. [*Pointing to the writing table
which is in front of the window.*] In that
writing desk.

FINACHE. [*Going to the writing desk.*] Ah,
thank you! Now, take him and put
him to bed.

EDWARD. Yes, sir. [*Quite affectionate to*
POCHE.] Come on, sir. Won't you
come with me? Why don't you take
my arm?

POCHE. [*Touched, stands and lets himself be
led away.*] You're a good-hearted fellow.

EDWARD. [*As he is leading* POCHE *to the
room on the right.*] Oh, sir! You're so
kind.

POCHE. Yes, yes. It really hurts me that
your wife's playing around on you.

EDWARD. What?

POCHE. Dammit yes! You're the one
who told me.

EDWARD. Oh, that's not at all true; she was having soup with the doorman.

POCHE. [*As he exits.*] Oh well! If that's all she had! [*As soon as he exits, the actor must change from* POCHE'*s costume into* CHANDEBISE'*s costume, including the uniform vest, so that the robe will cover* CHANDEBISE'*s costume since he will not have time to change after his next exit.*]

FINACHE. [*Taking the writing desk to the couch and opening it. He is facing the audience.*] Whew, what a smell! The paper must be perfumed. [*He passes the purple paper under his nose. It is the sheet that* LUCY *wrote her first draft on. The audience is able to see the handwriting on the paper.*] Isn't this interesting! [*He replaces the paper in the desk, walks around the couch, sits down on the couch with his back to the audience and begins to write; the front door is heard to open and close.*] Someone's coming; it must be Camille. [*Camille enters from the hall. He is out of breath.*]

CAMILLE. [*Without his palate.*] Oh, Doctor, you won't believe what happened to me at that hotel of yours.

FINACHE. [*Seated, not understanding a word of what* CAMILLE *has said.*] What? What? Don't talk so fast.

CAMILLE. If you only knew what happened!

FINACHE. Put your palate in, damnit! I went to a lot of trouble to get it for you, now use it!

CAMILLE. I've lost it!

FINACHE. What?

CAMILLE. A German gave me a punch in the chops. [*He mimics* KRUGER'*s punching him in the mouth.*]

FINACHE. [*Barely understanding what is being told to him.*] A German gave you a punch in the chops?

CAMILLE. And that's not all that happened. I thought that I was living a nightmare there today. You won't believe whom I saw in that hotel. Tournel . . . and Roberta . . . and Chandebise—with a load of wood on his back. Why, I ask, a load of wood? And Mme. Homenides . . . and her husband who chased after me with a gun. Bang! Bang! I tell you, it's been quite a day. What a tragedy, my God, what a tragedy. [*He falls into a chair to the left of the table on the right.*]

ANTOINETTE. [*Entering left.*] Madam wants to know how her husband is.

FINACHE. Her husband? Better. Tell her, "better." [*Getting up.*] Or better yet, I'll tell her myself.

CAMILLE. What's wrong with him?

FINACHE. Nothing, he's just under the weather.

CAMILLE. [*Shaking his head.*] My goodness.

EDWARD. [*Entering from the room on the right.*] He's sleeping.

FINACHE. Wonderful!

EDWARD. [*Picking* POCHE'*s hat up from the table.*] Good evening, sir.

CAMILLE. Good evening, Edward.

FINACHE. [*From the rear, near* ANTOINETTE.] Very well, Edward. Will you prepare the spirits of ammonia while I speak to madam?

EDWARD. Certainly, sir. [EDWARD *exits by the rear door. He leaves both sides open.* FINACHE *and* ANTOINETTE *exit left.*]

CAMILLE. My God! It's a complete mystery to me. I don't understand a thing that happened to me. [*Getting up and coming downstage.*] I'm like a leaf buffeted by the wind. [*A knock is heard from the bedroom.*] Come in! I'm losing my mind.

POCHE. [*Still in his dressing gown.*] Excuse me. . . .

CAMILLE. [*Startled.*] Victor-Emmanuel!

POCHE. [*Trying to joke by adopting a serious tone.*] Here's another one that I saw at the Kozy Kitty Hotel today.

CAMILLE. [*Aside, believing that he is being reprimanded.*] Damn!

POCHE. I can't believe it.

CAMILLE. [*Aside.*] He recognized me! [*Going to* POCHE, *looking him square in the face.*] I was about to tell you! I had a good reason for being there, an excellent reason. I heard that someone. . . .

POCHE. [*Listening in shock—his mouth*

agape—as he tries to understand
CAMILLE, *trying tactfully to figure out why* CAMILLE *is not speaking clearly.*]
What's he got in there?

CAMILLE. [*Taken aback.*] What?

POCHE. Spit it out, boy!

CAMILLE. [*Vexed.*] But I don't have anything in my mouth. I said there was someone . . . eh . . . there who asked about our policies.

POCHE. [*Cutting him short.*] Cut it out, you're boring me.

CAMILLE. [*Taken aback.*] Oh!

POCHE. I'm not interested. It's just that I was about to die of thirst in there. I guess they've forgotten to bring me my drink.

CAMILLE. Who? [*It comes out "Oooh."*]

POCHE. [*Not understanding.*] Oooh?

CAMILLE. [*Trying to articulate better and louder.*] Who?

POUCHE. Oh, "who," I thought you said, "Oooh." The doctor.

CAMILLE. He must have forgotten; I'll go get it.

POCHE. Ah, thank you. I'm dry as a bone.

CAMILLE. In that case, I'll hurry.

POCHE. Thank you. [*He goes back into the bedroom. The actor must immediately be ready to make his next entrance as* CHANDEBISE.*]

CAMILLE. [*In front of the table.*] Whew! I was sure that he would really chew me out. He's not as narrow-minded as I thought. Thank goodness! [*The front door opens and closes. Through the open double doors the audience sees* CHANDEBISE *arriving. He is putting his keys into his pocket.*]

CAMILLE. [*Turning to see* CHANDEBISE *entering from the hallway.*] Oh!

CHANDEBISE. [*Startled by* CAMILLE's *outcry.*] What is it?

CAMILLE. [*Confused, pointing first to* CHANDEBISE, *then to the bedroom door.*] On, my goodness, there and there.

CHANDEBISE. [*To the left of the table.*] What is it?

CAMILLE. [*At a loss, bumping into the furniture.*] My goodness! I'm crazy. I'm going crazy!

CHANDEBISE. [*Taking a step towards him.*] What's wrong, Camille?

CAMILLE. Don't come near me! I've gone crazy! [*He exits through the right rear door.*]

CHANDEBISE. [*Confused by this welcome.*] He's delirious. There must be something in the air today. Oh, that hotel! What a nightmare, what a nightmare. [*Seeing his jacket on the chair to the right of the table.*] Ah, my jacket! How did it get here? I can't wait to get out of this uniform. [*As he is talking, he takes off the uniform and puts on his jacket.*] To think that I had to come home in that uniform. The doorman almost made me use the servants' entrance.

CAMILLE. [*Crossing the vestibule from right to left, grabbing hold of* EDWARD *who is coming from the other direction. He's like a madman.*] Edward, I'm crazy, crazy I tell you. [*He lets go of* EDWARD, *continues to shout, "I'm crazy" and exits left.* EDWARD *is taken aback.*]

CHANDEBISE. It's still going on.

EDWARD. [*Entering.*] What's wrong with M. Camille? What's wrong with him?

CHANDEBISE. I was just asking myself that, Edward.

EDWARD. Oh, sir, you recognized me!

CHANDEBISE. Of course, I recognize you. Is this some kind of a joke? Why shouldn't I recognize you?

EDWARD. [*Quickly.*] Eh? I don't know, sir, I don't know. [CAMILLE, *followed by* FINACHE, ROBERTA, TOURNEL, *and* LUCY *enters from the left.*]

CAMILLE. There's two of him, I tell you two. There and there.

ALL. What?

CAMILLE. [*Dashing away through the rear door.*] I'm going crazy! Oh, Heavens!

ALL. What's wrong with him?

ROBERTA. [*Going to* CHANDEBISE.] We're here, dear. We want to know. . . .

CHANDEBISE. You! Here! And Tournel with you! [TOURNEL *is to the right of the sofa.*]

ROBERTA *and* TOURNEL. What?

CHANDEBISE. [*Grabbing* TOURNEL *by the*

collar and pulling him to the right.]
What were you doing there? What
were you doing with my wife in that
love nest?

ALL. Oh!

ROBERTA. Not again.

TOURNEL. [*Still in* CHANDEBISE's *grasp.*]
but we've explained it to you a hundred times already.

CHANDEBISE. [*Still pushing* TOURNEL *by
the lapels.*] Explained what? Go on, go
on! You think you can get away with
this? Get out! [*Everyone follows the
movement at a distance. They end up to
the left of the table.*]

ROBERTA. Darling!

CHANDEBISE. [*Turning towards them.*] Get
out!

LUCY. M. Chandebise!

CHANDEBISE. Oh, madam, please forgive me. [*To the others.*] Get out! Get
out of my sight. [*He paces, exasperated.*]

FINACHE. [*Encouraging them to leave by the
left.*] Go on, go on! Don't irritate him.
He's in full crisis. You can come back
when he's calmer.

ROBERTA. [*Letting herself be carried
away.*] Ah, his crisis, his crisis! It's too
much for me. [*She and* LUCY *exit.*]

FINACHE. Well now, well now! [*To* TOUR-
NEL.] Tournel, please.

TOURNEL. [*Following the women.*] He's not
lucid; he can't string two ideas together. [EDWARD *exits by the double
doors and closes them behind him.*]

FINACHE. [*Going to* CHANDEBISE *as soon as
everyone has left.*] Now, dear friend,
what is it?

CHANDEBISE. [*In front of the table on the
right.*] Please forgive me, Finache. I
had to vent my anger.

FINACHE. That's all right. It was a release. It should make you feel better.

CHANDEBISE. [*Still nervous.*] Yes, I'm
calmer now.

FINACHE. Of course. You're getting better already. You're starting to
recognize people, to know who you
are.

CHANDEBISE. [*In shock.*] What?

FINACHE. You're getting better and better.

CHANDEBISE. What? Recognizing people, knowing who I am? What are
you saying?

FINACHE. What?

CHANDEBISE. Is this a joke? Don't I
always recognize people and know
who I am?

FINACHE. I didn't mean that, I. . . .

CHANDEBISE. I can get carried away, but
I never lose control. You know that.

FINACHE. [*Quickly, not to contradict him.*]
Of course I know that!

CHANDEBISE. [*Satisfied.*] There.

FINACHE. Yes, yes. But all the same, if I
were you, I'd have stayed in bed.

CHANDEBISE. [*Taken aback.*] What?

FINACHE. Why did you put your jacket
on?

CHANDEBISE. That's a funny one! Because I was tired of parading around
as a porter.

FINACHE. [*Raising his eyes heavenward.*] A
porter! Oh!

CHANDEBISE. Maybe you think it's fun
to see yourself as a flunky.

FINACHE. [*Aside.*] Ay, ay, ay!

CHANDEBISE. [*Coming downstage from the
left of the table.*] Can you believe it, old
man, me in a unform!

FINACHE. [*Aside.*] He's obsessed!

CHANDBISE. I saw everything at that
hotel of yours, the Kozy Kitty Hotel.

FINACHE. So, you were there?

CHANDEBISE. Of course!

FINACHE. You didn't have to go there.

CHANDEBISE. [*Parrying his words.*] Indeed, I was there. What a madhouse!
A fight here, a fight there! A madman for an owner! He made me put
on this uniform, then locked me up
in a room. I had to escape over the
roofs, almost broke my neck. And
Homenides! Ho-me-ni-des! I've had
it, I tell you, I've had it!

FINACHE. [*Aside.*] It's worse than I
thought; my God, much worse.

CHANDEBISE. I can't get it all out of my
head. [*He goes right.*]

EDWARD. [*Entering with a glass of water*

and the spirits of ammonia on a tray.]
Here you are.

CHANDEBISE. [*Turning to* EDWARD.] What
is it, Edward?

EDWARD. [*Going to* FINACHE.] Nothing,
sir. The doctor asked me. . . .

FINACHE. [*To* CHANDEBISE.] Yes, yes, I
did.

CHANDEBISE. Ah! [*He goes up right.*]

FINACHE. [*To* EDWARD, *who has handed
him the tray.*] Thank you. [*He takes the
ammonia and begins to pour it into the
glass.*]

EDWARD. [*In a whisper to the doctor.*] Is
this what you wanted? [*Half asphyxi-
ated by the ammonia, he turns his head
away.*]

FINACHE. [*Counting the drops, with his
head turned away from the glass.*] Two
. . . Three . . . What?

EDWARD. Is he any better?

FINACHE. Oh! No! Oh! No!

EDWARD. No?

FINACHE. Oh! No! . . . six . . . seven.

EDWARD. Oh!

FINACHE. He's delirious! Delirious!
Eight . . . nine . . . ten.

CHANDEBISE. [*Coming downstage to the left
of the table.*] Is there something
wrong, Doctor?

FINACHE. No, of course, not. [*Going to
CHANDEBISE, holding the glass at arm's
length to avoid the fumes and twirling it
to mix the solution.*] Here, drink this.

CHANDEBISE. What?

FINACHE. Yes! It will calm you down
after all the excitement you've had.

CHANDEBISE. Ah, thank you, You're
right, that fit of anger a little while
ago made me thirsty. [*He takes the
glass.*]

FINACHE. That's for certain. [*He covers
the top of the glass as he hands it to
CHANDEBISE.*] Drink it down at once;
it's quite strong.

CHANDEBISE. [*Not paying attention.*] Oh!
[*He gulps it into his mouth, he drops the
glass on the table, shoves everyone out of
his way, and dashes to the window.*]

FINACHE. [*Right behind him.*] Remember,
I warned you how strong it was.

Swallow it, swallow it!

CHANDEBISE. [*Throwing open the the window and spitting out what is in his
mouth.*] Ah! . . . Bah!

EDWARD *and* FINACHE. [*Disappointed.*]
Oh.

CHANDEBISE. [*Furious.*] What is this, a
joke? It's not at all funny.

FINACHE. See here, Chandebise. . . .

CHANDEBISE. Leave me alone! You jerk!
[*He goes to the right rear.*]

FINACHE. [*Following him.*] Where are you
going?

CHANDEBISE. To wash out my mouth! If
you think that tasted good. . . . [*He
exits.*]

FINACHE [*Overwhelmed, examining the
empty glass.*] Oh, he spit it all out! It
was all for nothing.

FERRAILLON'S VOICE. M. Chandebise,
please.

EDWARD'S VOICE. This way, sir.

FINACHE. [*Looking into the hallway.*] Ah,
Ferraillon, what a surprise!

FERRAILLON'S VOICE. Doctor!

FINACHE. Do come in. [*He goes left.*]

FERRAILLON. [*Entering, followed by* ED-
WARD.] Excuse me.

FINACHE. [*Sitting on the couch.*] Have you
come about the insurance?

FERRAILLON. Oh no, sir, there's no time
for that today; I'll come in some
morning for that. I'm here to return
something that belongs to M. Camille
Chandebise. We found it at the hotel.
[*He takes the palate out of his pocket.*]

EDWARD. [*Quite near* FERRAILLON.] Oh, I
recognize that—I'm the one who
found it.

FERRAILLON. [*Saluting* EDWARD.] Sir!

EDWARD. [*Presenting himself.*] Edward,
butler to M. Chandebise.

FERRAILLON. [*Coldly.*] Pleased to meet
you.

FINACHE. [*Catching a glimpse of what* FER-
RAILLON *is holding.*] Let me see that.
[FERRAILLON *hands it to* FINACHE.] Yes,
it's Camille's palate. How did he lose
his palate in town? And how did you
know it was his?

FERRAILLON. By the name and address

engraved on it.

FINACHE. Of course! "Camille Chandebise, 95 Boulevard Malesherbes." What a good idea.

FERRAILLON. And useful if he should forget his calling cards. [*He mimics presenting a calling card.*]

FINACHE. He'll be pleased to have it back; I'll see that he gets it.

ANTOINETTE. [*Dashing in from the rear.*] Sir, sir! There's something the matter with M. Camille! I just found him in the bathroom—completely nude—taking a shower.

FINACHE. What's the matter now?

FERRAILLON. A shower at this hour?

FINACHE. It's madness! [*To* FERRAILLON.] Well, there's the man you wanted to see! He's taking a shower. Why, I don't know. [*To* ANTOINETTE.] Where's the bathroom?

ANTOINETTE. [*Indicating the right side of the hallway.*] This way, sir.

FINACHE. [*Exiting followed by* ANTOINETTE.] What's gotten into everyone this evening? What's going on?

FERRAILLON. [*Near the left rear door.* EDWARD *is on the right. As he is talking to* EDWARD, *he comes downstage towards the table on the right.*] Taking a shower at this time of night! What a silly idea! [*His eye falls on the livery jacket and cap which* CHANDEBISE *discarded.*] I can't believe my eyes. That's Poch's uniform. [*He picks it up.*] And his cap! Not bad, is it? What's it doing here? [*To* EDWARD *who has joined him.*] Has my porter been here?

EDWARD. Your porter? Why would he come here?

FERRAILLON. That's what I'd like to know.

CHANDEBISE. [*Entering from the right and coming down left.*] What a terrible taste.

FERRAILLON. [*Startled by the sight of* CHANDEBISE.] What! Poche! Poche! here! [*He lunges forward to grab hold of* CHANDEBISE.]

CHANDEBISE. [*Shocked.*] What's that mad-

man doing here? [*He tries to avoid* FERRAILLON's *grasp. Separated by the table, they engage in a see-saw motion—* CHANDEBISE *trying to avoid* FERRAILLON; FERRAILLON *grabbing for* CHANDEBISE.]

FERRAILLON. You animal, what are you doing here? [*Grabbing* CHANDEBISE.]

CHANDEBISE. Oh, la la!

FERRAILLON. [*Spinning* CHANDEBISE *around.*] Parading my uniform around town!

CHANDEBISE. Oh, la la!

EDWARD. [*Trying to separate them.*] Sir, what are you doing?

FERRAILLON. [*To* EDWARD *as he continues to struggle with* CHANDEBISE.] Leave me alone; scram.

CHANDEBISE. [*Finally breaking loose.*] Oh, la la! Don't let go of him! [*He runs from the room.*]

FERRAILLON. [*Struggling against* EDWARD.] Let go of me! [*He breaks loose; the force of the movement sends* EDWARD *spinning.*]

EDWARD. [*Trying to restrain* FERRAILLON.] See here, that's my boss. M. Chandebise. [*The hall door slams.*]

FERRAILLON. [*Pushing* EDWARD *away.*] Your boss? He's my servant! I should know him! [*He runs out of the room with the uniform in his hands.*]

EDWARD. [*On his heels.*] No, no, no!

CHANDEBISE. [*Poking his head around the corner of the left rear door, nervously.*] Has he gone? [*Entering and going left.*] I tricked him by slamming the front door and making him think that I had run out of the house. He's hot on my trail! [*Sighing.*] Hah, he's gone! [*A confusion of voices is heard in the entryway.*]

EDWARD'S VOICE. Sir, please let me announce you.

HOMENIDES' VOICE. I go in, I tell you, I go in.

CHANDEBISE. What now? [HOMENIDES *enters by forcefully pushing open the door.*]

HOMENIDES. [*With a pistol case under his arm.* EDWARD, *having given up trying to stop Homenides, disappears.*] You!

CHANDEBISE. [*Cornered.*] Homenides! [*He tries to escape.*]

HOMENIDES. [*Striding to him, commandingly.*] Don't move!

CHANDEBISE. [*Begging for mercy.*] My friend.

HOMENIDES. [*With a withering look.*] We no more friends! [*He puts his pistol case on a chair facing the couch.*] You get away from me once, but no more! I find you! Ze police when zey arrest me, zey take away me pistolé end zey make me promise not to yuse ze pistolés again. [*With a sigh of regret.*] I promise zem!

CHANDEBISE. [*Reassured.*] Good thinking!

HOMENIDES. So, zey geef me back ze pistolés! Here I haf ze dueling pistolés.

CHANDEBISE. [*Taken aback.*] What?

HOMENIDES. [*Reassuring him.*] Not to worry! No want to shoot you. Zey are here—for how you say—to make a moment of truth.

CHANDEBISE. [*Somewhat reassured.*] Oh, I see.

HOMENIDES. I no want to murder you.

CHANDEBISE. [*Still more reassured.*]. My sentiments exactly.

HOMENIDES. Here are ze pistolés, one iss loaded, ze other iss not.

CHANDEBISE. [*Very concerned.*] I would prefer the first.

HOMENIDES. [*Making a sound that makes* CHANDEBISE *jump back.*] Ayii! [*Calming down, taking a piece of chalk out of his pistol case.*] I draw a circle around your heart. [*He draws the circle on* CHANDEBISE'S *chest.*]

CHANDEBISE. Hey, watch that! [*He tries to erase the circle.*]

HOMENIDES. [*Drawing a circle over his heart.*] See, I do ze same.

CHANDEBISE. [*Aside.*] He should have been a tailor.

HOMENIDES. [*After returning the chalk to the case and taking out the guns.*] We each take ze pistolé end point it at ze heart of ze othair. End zen, bang,

bang! Ze one who gets ze bullet, iss muerto.

CHANDEBISE. And then what?

HOMENIDES. [*Shouting again, completely startling* CHANDEBISE.*] Ayii! [*Becoming calm and courteous.*] Iss a douel like in my country.

CHANDEBISE. [*Somewhat disquieted.*] I see.

HOMENIDES. [*Presenting the choice of pistols by presenting their grips to* CHANDEBISE.] Take a pistolé, I tell you.

CHANDEBISE. [*Circling around* HOMENIDES.] No thank you; I never take a thing between meals.

HOMENIDES. [*Fiercely.*] Take it or I keel you.

CHANDEBISE. [*Aware now that it is not a joke.*] You're serious! Oh, my God! Help! Help! [*He runs like a rabbit through the rear door.*]

HOMENIDES. [*In pursuit.*] Chandebise!

CHANDEBISE'S VOICE. [*From the left.*] Help! Help!

HOMENIDES' VOICE. You come back, you come back!

CHANDEBISE'S VOICE. Help! Help! [*He reappears from the left, dashes across the stage, and runs into the room on the right. As soon as he enters a loud shout is heard. He then runs back into the room.*] What, me? I'm sleeping in my own bed. The house is haunted! The house is haunted!

HOMENIDES' VOICE. Whaire iss he, ze dogue?

CHANDEBISE. [*Recognizing* HOMENIDES' *voice.*] Oh! [*He dashes through the rear door and locks it behind him. Someone backstage must shout out "Help!" so that the audience hears* CHANDEBISE'S *voice from backstage. The actor, meanwhile, has put the dressing gown back on so that he can reappear as* POCHE.]

HOMENIDES. [*Running onstage, then upstage to the door through which* CHANDEBISE *has disappeared.*] You come back, you come back! [*He rattles the door knob in vain.*]

CHANDEBISE'S VOICE. [*Sounding from the right.*] Help! Help!

HOMENIDES. [*Dashing to the right rear door*

which is also locked.] Open, I tell you, open it.

CHANDEBISE'S VOICE. [*Crossing from right to left.*] Help! Help!

HOMENIDES. [*Dashing to the door on the left which is also locked.*] Open up, you dogue, open up! [*He rattles the door.*]

POCHE. [*Entering from the room on the right in his dressing gown and slippers, still sleepy.*] It's impossible to sleep around here.

HOMENIDES. [*Confronting* POCHE *with the pistols in his hand.*] Zaire you are, you dogue! Take ze pistolé!

POCHE. [*Startled.*] My God! It's the wild Indian!

HOMENIDES. [*Going right.*] You want I keel you?

POCHE. [*Dashing to the center doors.*] What did you say? My God! [*He discovers that the door is locked.*]

HOMENIDES. [*On his track.*] Ah ha! I hafe you now! You not get away zis time!

POCHE. [*Running to each of the other doors and finding that they are locked.*] Oh la la! [*He finally reaches the window which is still open and jumps through it.*] Ah!

HOMENIDES. [*Running to the window to stop* POCHE.] Ah, ze dogue! He will keel himself. [*Looking out the window.*] No, he iss all right! Now, I keel him! [*He goes right.*] Yes, I keel him. [*He holds his throat as if he were choking.*] Ay! I am thirsty! [*He sees the half empty glass of ammonia and water.*] Ah! [*He picks it up and drinks avidly. As soon as the liquid hits his mouth, he wants to spit it out. He runs to the window and spits out the liquid.*] Pouah! [*He shakes his fists to the sky.*] Ay! Zey hafe no taste here! [*He finds himself by the writing desk which* FINACHE *left open.*] Ay, what a smell! Ze perfume, ze letter, my wife! [*Taking out the first draft of* LUCY'S *letter.*] Ay! Iss her handwriting! [*Reading.*] "Sir, I saw you the other night at the theatre." Iss ze same as ze one in my pocket. [*Taking the other out of his pocket to compare them.*] Porqué? Porqué here? In ze desk of Mme. Chandebise? Zis I must know!

[*Dashing to the left rear door and pounding on it.*] Open! Open!

TOURNEL. [*Opening the door.*] What is it?

HOMENIDES. [*Grabbing him by the lapels.*] Tournel, you tell me.

TOURNEL. Damn, the cowboy!

HOMENIDES. Zis letter. . . .

TOURNEL. Let go of me!

ROBERTA. [*Entering left.*] What is it now?

HOMENIDES. [*Pushing* TOURNEL *away and going to* ROBERTA.] Now, you? Why I find zis letter in you desk?

ROBERTA. [*Startled to see the letter.*] Sir, what are you doing in my desk?

HOMENIDES. Iss not important! [*Trying to contain his rage.*] Porqué? Porqué, ze handwriting of my wife?

ROBERTA. [*Trembling.*] Uh!

HOMENIDES. She come to you house to make up love letters?

ROBERTA. Of course, in my house. You're quite mistaken about her. You have her innocence in your hands.

HOMENIDES. Eh? Como?

ROBERTA. What do you mean "como?" Surely, you don't think she'd use my paper to invite my husband to a rendezvous? There's nothing between them. . . .

TOURNEL. [*Finishing* ROBERTA's *thought.*] Nothing at all.

HOMENIDES. [*Confused.*] Qué, qué?

ROBERTA. Ah, qué, que! Here's your wife, ask her yourself.

HOMENIDES. [*Running to* LUCY.] Ah, you tell me. . . .

LUCY. [*Trying to escape.*] My husband!

HOMENIDES. [*Catching her by the wrist and dragging her downstage.*] No, you stay! You tell me, one word can make me happy. Zis letter, zis letter!

LUCY. [*Shocked to see the letter in her husband's hands.*] What?

HOMENIDES. I find it. Poruqé? Porqué?

LUCY. [*Looking to* ROBERTA.] It's a secret.

ROBERTA. Go on Lucy, solve the riddle for him before it drives him crazy.

HOMENIDES. Si!

LUCY. [*To* ROBERTA.] Shall I?

ROBERTA. [*Indifferently.*] Go on, do it!

LUCY. As you will. [*To her husband.*]

What an Othello you'd have made!
Haven't you figured it out? [*To*
ROBERTA.] What a dodo! [*To* HOME-
NIDES.] Roberta creia tener motivo de
dudar de la fiedelidad de su marido.

HOMENIDES. Cómo?

LUCY. Entonces para probarlo decidió
darte una cita galant . . . a la cual
también asistiría.

HOMENIDES. [*Impatiently.*] Pero, la carta!
La carta!

LUCY. [*Becoming angry.*] Eh! La carta!
Espera, hombre! [*Calming down and
emphasizing her words.*] Si ella hubiese
escrito la carta a su marido, éste
hubiera reconocido su letra.

HOMENIDES. [*A glimmer of hope as he
begins to understand.*] Después! Después!

LUCY. Entonces ella me ha encargado
de escribir en su lugar.

HOMENIDES. [*Not believing his ears.*] No!
Es verdad? [*To* ROBERTA.] Es verdad?

ROBERTA. [*Startled to be addressed in a
language that she does not understand.*]
What?

HOMENIDES. Is verdad what she tell me?

ROBERTA. It's all verdad. [*Aside.*] What
do I have to lose?

HOMENIDES. Ah, senora, senora!
Cuando pienso que me he metido
tantas ideas en la cabeza?

ROBERTA. [*With a comic bow.*] You're welcome!

HOMENIDES. [*To* LUCY.] Ah! Qué estúpido! Estúpido soy! [*To* TOURNEL *as
he beats himself on the chest in mock
contrition.*] Ah! No soy más que un
bruto! Un bruto! Un bruto!

TOURNEL. [*Mimicking* HOMENIDES.] Yes,
we almost died trying to tell you.

HOMENIDES. [*Not listening to him, turning
to* LUCY.] Ah! Querida! Perdóname
mis estupideces!

LUCY. Te perdono, pero no vuelvas a
hacerlo.

HOMENIDES. [*Bringing her to the couch.*]
Ah! Querida mia! Ah! Yo te quiero!
[*They sit hand in hand.*]

ROBERTA. [*To* TOURNEL.] How quickly
they understand each other in Span-

ish! [*At this moment the left rear door
opens.* FINACHE, CAMILLE *and* CHAN-
DEBISE *enter quickly as* EDWARD *ushers
them into the room.*]

FINACHE. Now, now, be reasonable;
don't lose your heads!

CAMILLE. [*In his bathrobe and without his
palate.*] I told you that I saw him in
two places at once—there and there.
[*He indicates the drawing room and the
bedroom.*]

CHANDEBISE. [*On the right.*] And I, I
found myself face to face with myself
in my own bed.

FINACHE. [*Skeptically.*] Oh!

HOMENIDES. [*From the couch.*] Qué? Qué?

CHANDEBISE. [*At the sight of* HOMENIDES,
he turns on his heels to flee.] Homenides! What's he doing here?

HOMENIDES. [*Stopping him.*] Come! Iss
nothing to fear. Iss over. I know how
write ze letter. Ze lady from ze theatre is not my wife, iss you wife.

CHANDEBISE. [*To* ROBERTA.] You?

ROBERTA. [*From the left of the table.*] For
the fortieth time, yes.

CHANDEBISE. Forty times?

TOURNEL. [*From the right of the table.*]
Absolutely! And each time, you embraced us, and that was that. [*He goes
to join* ROBERTA *near the table between the two rear doors.*]

CHANDEBISE. What did he say?

HOMENIDES. End to zink I make you
jump out ze window.

CHANDEBISE. What?

EVERYONE. Out the window?

HOMENIDES. Was ze anger in me.

CHANDEBISE. What? You made me jump
out the window?

HOMENIDES. Si! I make you do it! You
come from zaire. [*He indicates the door
to the bedroom.*] End hop! Zrough ze
window!

CHANDEBISE [*Striding to the right.*] That's
it, that's it! We're all suffering from
the same hallucination. You saw me
jump out the window and I saw myself in my own bed.

CAMILLE. And I saw you there and
there.

CHANDEBISE. [*Still on the right.*] Absolutely! The proof is that I know I didn't jump out that window.

HOMENIDES. What you say?

FINACHE. [*Holding his head in his hands.*] Oh la la! It's too much for me, too much.

TOURNEL. It's magic, magic.

FERRAILLON. [*Entering with* POCHE's *dressing gown under his arm.*] Ladies and gentlemen, pardon me. . . .

CHANDEBISE. The madman! [*He dashes under the table on the right.*]

FINACHE *and* CAMILLE.
  Ferraillon!
ROBERTA. The man from } [*All together.*]
  the Kozy Kitty Hotel!
TOURNEL. The hotel man!

FERRAILLON. A moment ago as I was passing by in the street, my porter jumped out of that window and almost fell on top of me.

ALL. What?

TOURNEL, CAMILLE, *and* HOMENIDES. It was the porter.

FERRAILLON. And he was running away in this robe.

ROBERTA. [*Coming to the left of the table.*] Why, that's my husband's dressing gown! [*Looking around for* CHANDEBISE.] Isn't it, dear? Where is he? [*Calling.*] Victor-Emmanuel! Victor-Emmanuel! [*She goes upstage and opens the right door and calls through it.*]

ALL. Victor-Emmanuel! [EDWARD *goes to look through the left door while* TOURNEL *looks through the right door.*]

FERRAILLON. [*Noticing* CHANDEBISE *on his knees under the table.*] Ah ha!

EVERYONE. What?

FERRAILLON. Poche! You're still here! [*He tries to drag* CHANDEBISE *out from under the table.*]

EVERYONE. What, Poche?

CHANDEBISE. [*As* FERRAILLON *pulls him out from under the table.*] Ah! Oh! Ah! Oh!

FERRAILLON. [*Punching him.*] You wretch! Animal! You scum!

EVERYONE. Oh!

ROBERTA. [*Coming between them.*] Please

sir, that's my husband!

FERRAILLON. [*Taken aback.*] What?

CHANDEBISE. This man is obsessed! Every time he sees me, he thinks I'm a punching bag!

FERRAILLON. He's your husband?

ROBERTA. Absolutely! M. Chandebise.

FERRAILLON. No, it can't be true! He's the exact portrait of Poche, my porter.

EVERYONE. Poche!

FERRAILLON. Yes, the same one who just jumped out the window.

EVERYONE. [*Taken aback.*] Oh!

CHANDEBISE. Now I see! The man I took to be me in my bed was Poche!

EVERYONE. Poche!

ROBERTA. He's the one we saw at the hotel with a bottle in his hand!

TOURNEL. He's the one who embraced us!

EVERYONE. It was Poche!

LUCY. He was the one who tried to drag me into that dive!

CAMILLE. And who had a load of wood on his back.

EVERYONE. It was Poche!

CHANDEBISE. Poche, Poche! Always Poche! Damnit! I'm sorry he got away so quick. I would have liked to meet my twin!

FERRAILLON. You're always welcome at the Kozy Kitty Hotel.

CHANDEBISE. Me? At the Kozy Kitty Hotel? No, no! I've seen enough of it.

ROBERTA. [*Contrived.*] Enough of the beautiful eyes of your unknown admirer?

CHANDEBISE. I'd be careful if I were you. Imagine, setting a trap for me.

ROBERTA. Forgive me, it was wrong of me to do it. After all, I wasn't sure of your fidelity.

CHANDEBISE. What? Good God? Whatever for?

ROBERTA. Because, because. . . . [*She whispers in his ear.*]

CHANDEBISE. No! Is that all?

ROBERTA. Yes, because of that!

CHANDEBISE. Oh, well!

ROBERTA. What did you expect? I know

it's stupid; but it did put a bug in my ear.

CHANDEBISE. Damn bug, get out of there! Or better yet, I'll kill it tonight.

ROBERTA. [*Ironically.*] You?

CHANDEBISE. [*Sheepishly.*] Well, I'll try.

CAMILLE. [*Stepping out and with his back to the crowd. As he starts to address them, the curtain falls.*] If you only knew what happened. . . .

EVERYONE. [*From the heart.*] No, no! To-morrow! Tomorrow!

Six Characters in Search of an Author

Luigi Pirandello

At virtually the same time that many writers in northern Europe were rejecting the outer reality of naturalism in order to explore inner reality through expressionism, a playwright in the south was questioning whether any reality exists at all. Luigi Pirandello turned to playwriting rather late in his life, but the vicissitudes of his early years had left scars upon him in such a way that he was extraordinarily well equipped for expressing the insights of the post-World War I years in Europe. These insights, magnified by the added agonies of World War II, have proved to be the dominating ones of midtwentieth-century European playwriting, and the post–World War II playwrights have been almost unanimous in paying tribute to Pirandello for his pioneering efforts.

Luigi Pirandello was born in Agrigento, Sicily, on June 28, 1867. His father had been a street fighter for Garibaldi, and was later the prosperous owner of sulfur mines; he openly fought the Mafia, but raised his family in the firmly authoritarian tradition of the closed Sicilian society. When the family moved to Palermo, Luigi attended the secondary school there, publishing his first poetry as early as 1883. He went on to study philosophy and law at the University of Palermo and then at the University of Rome, finally earning a doctorate in philology at Bonn University in Germany in 1891. Returning to Rome, Pirandello worked as a freelance writer and published his first novel in 1893. In 1894, he dutifully married Antonietta Portulano in accordance with an arrangement worked out between his father and the bride's father, a Sicilian business associate. Both families being wealthy, Pirandello was able to settle comfortably in Rome and continue his writing; his novels attracted moderate attention in Italy, and Pirandello supplemented his author's royalties by teaching Italian literature at a college for young girls in Rome. He became the father of two boys and a girl.

In 1904, a flood destroyed the Sicilian sulfur mines, and Pirandello's father's money, as well as that of his father-in-law, was suddenly no longer available. This blow, coupled with the difficult birth of their youngest child, unhinged Antonietta's sanity, and in the ensuing years she became increasingly paranoid. Unable to afford a private sanitorium and unwilling to commit her to a a public institution, Pirandello and his children lived with their insane mother until 1919. The constant struggle with her psychosis colored all of Pirandello's later writing; he notes that a mad woman "led my hands as I wrote." Convinced among other things that

Pirandello was unfaithful to her, she even accused him of having an affair with their daughter; the daughter's suicide attempt is one further illustration of the severe strain under which the family labored. The financial burden was also severe, and it was financial success with a play that eventually turned Pirandello to virtually full-time playwriting.

Pirandello had written plays as a student and published one as early as 1896, but he had no success at finding producers and concluded in rather surly fashion that the theater was a debased art form in which he did not care to work. Even when two of his early plays were produced in Rome in 1910 *(Sicilian Limes* and *The Vise),* he took no serious interest. In 1916, however, a friend introduced him to a producer who was in need of new scripts and who persuaded Pirandello, a respected novelist, to write one for his company. *Think, Giacomino!* was successful enough to earn Pirandello a good deal of money, and he turned virtually his full attention to the theater for the rest of his life. At the age of fifty, Pirandello embarked on what proved to be his primary calling. In the next eight years he wrote twenty-eight plays; he wrote nearly forty in his lifetime. Of these, the best known outside Italy, besides *Six Characters in Search of an Author,* are *Right You Are, if You Think You Are* (1917), *Henry IV* (1922), and *Tonight We Improvise* (1930).

When he was in his twenties, Pirandello had participated in a socialist uprising in Sicily, but by middle age he had become cynically convinced that all government was equally useless. When Mussolini rose to power in Italy, Pirandello became an open, avowed, and supportive Fascist, although it is still not clear how much of his support arose from personal conviction and how much from the fact that Mussolini, who needed the political respectability that the support of a world-renowned author could give him, reciprocated in 1925 by providing financial support to the Teatro d'Arte, which Pirandello founded. During the ensuing years, the company toured Europe, the United States, and South America. Eventually it closed for lack of continuing financial support, but Pirandello's support of Mussolini's regime was international gossip. His plays ceased to please audiences as much as they had during the early 1920s, but he nevertheless was awarded the Nobel Prize for Literature in 1934. He died of pneumonia on December 10, 1936.

Six Characters in Search of an Author is certainly Pirandello's most celebrated play, and many critics regard it as his best. Its first performance, on May 10, 1921, in Rome, was an international sensation, with critics, audience, and actors fighting on the stage and an organized effort required to rescue Pirandello from the melee. Within a year or two it had been performed, somewhat less violently but with marked success, in all the major Western capitals, and Bernard Shaw termed it "the most original dramatic production of any people in any age." Not only was it original in the philosophical questions it raised, but it was also brilliantly original in the extraordinary structural technique of presenting characters (as distinct from either actors or real people) who sought to create their own story on the stage. Pirandello reports that the characters took shape in his imagination as characters for a novel, but that he found himself unable to shape their story into a satisfactory plot. It was then that the central idea for the play suddenly came to him. Pirandello published several revisions of the play, most notably in 1925 after directing it himself; it is upon this revised, definitive version that the accompanying new translation is based.

First appearances to the contrary notwithstanding, *Six Characters in Search of an Author* is not a play within a play. The story of a man, his wife, and her four children (three by another man) is in fact never fully told within the play; it has no satisfactory ending (as Pirandello himself had perceived in attempting to shape it into a plot) and serves primarily to develop the six characters and the relationships among them. Rather, *Six Characters in Search of an Author* is exactly what its title states, the story of six characters, never fully realized by their creator and anxiously seeking some means of fulfilling their destiny. This search for a stage upon which to complete their story exists at a literal level, for fictional theatrical characters, once created, still need to be portrayed on a stage in order fully to exist; in another sense, theatrical characters may be said to live forever as imaginative creations, and thus to achieve the immortality for which ordinary human beings strive but never achieve. At the same time, Pirandello contrasts these characters' search for a stage with the desire of any actors to find a stage upon which to perform, and shows that what the actors do in such circumstances is inevitably false because acting is by its nature imitation—art—and not life. Furthermore, he contrasts both the characters and the actors with life itself, in which human beings are constantly seeking a "stage" upon which to act out their destiny, with consequent confusion for all concerned as to where reality stops and artifice begins. It was a master stroke of theatrical crafts-manship on Pirandello's part to find so ideal a metaphor for those aspects of the human condition that he wished to probe.

That the play opens on a bare stage is not a very original idea, for a great many plays have used the theater itself to call attention to its own theatricality. In fact, showing a bare stage with the actors drifting in for rehearsal is really a twisted form of realism itself, as it asks an audience (within the usual limits of suspension of disbelief) to believe that the environment in which it finds itself is real and the people on stage really engaged in what they seem to be doing. But the entrance of the characters lifts the play into the realm of fantasy, for the notion of portraying characters (as distinct from either real people or actors) is virtually unprecedented in dramatic literature. The nature of theater and the nature of life are brilliantly compared as the play progresses; the story of the characters attempting to realize themselves upon the stage shifts focus alternately between life and imitation of life, between reality and mask, so that the essence of each is held up to scrutiny.

Beneath this inventive plot structure lies an inter-connecting series of ideas as challenging as the form itself. Pirandello noted that he had the "misfortune" to be among the "philosophical writers," those who use the theatrical medium to explore ideas and to seek meaning in life. For Pirandello, this was a despairing search, for he found no dependable truth. Truth as Pirandello saw it was an ever-shifting chimera, and what is truth for one person is frequently not truth for another. Not only is there no consistent truth, but attempts to communicate about an individual's perception of truth are also doomed to failure, since communication itself is generally impossible. The agony of the six characters is created by their inability to settle upon a firm truth that accounts for their circumstances, but this agony is increased by their inability to communicate satisfactorily with each other or with outsiders about their circumstances. Finally, as Pirandello sees it, sanity itself is suspect; with neither dependable truth nor the ability to communicate about it, it is impossible to judge whether the distorted perceptions of another are truth or insanity. The distinction between truth and illusion, as old as Plato but as new as the expressionists then at work in Germany, was investigated by Pirandello in a fashion that was peculiarly relevant to a war-torn Europe that seemed to have lost both truth and sanity. Twentieth-century despair, so brilliantly explored by generations of artists throughout the century, was brought to its first full expression by Piran-dello.

Pirandello thought of himself as a comedian, and his plays are indeed cast in a comic mode. As a director of his own works, Pirandello imposed a fast pace, comic timing, and an improvisational sense inherited from the *commedia dell'arte,* all of which bespoke a wry sense of the inherent comicality of the situations created in the plays. On the other hand, there is great anguish in his plays as well, frequently erupting into obvious suffering and misery, that is a far cry from traditional comedy. Here as elsewhere, Pirandello pioneered in what was to become a singularly twentieth-century mode of combining comedy and tragedy, with the anguished laugh and the caustic groan never very far apart. The perception that laughter may be the only appropriate response to the absurdity of the universe is perhaps the dominant thematic note in twentieth-century European drama, and in a very real sense it may be said to have begun with Pirandello.

Pirandello was often not as popular in Italy as he was abroad, and unquestionably some of his plays have not endured very well the test of time. At his best, however, he remains challenging and effective: *Six Characters in Search of an Author* is as exciting in the theater today as it was when rioting greeted its initial performance. Its neat juxtaposition of the theater itself with the theatricality of life, its elusive but compelling comparisons among real life, acting, and fictional characters, remain challenging and innovative theater even after more than half a century. The philosophical insights of Pirandello have become those of much of mankind, as the absurdity that he perceived has indeed been acted out on the stage of life. Sanity and insanity, laughter and anguish, appearance and reality have dissolved into one another in the twentieth century as Pirandello perceived. His is a frightening world, but one that grips the theater-goer's consciousness.

Six Characters in Search of an Author (Sei personaggi in cerca d'autore)

Translated by Stanley Vincent Longman

Characters in the Play-in-the-Making
The Father
The Mother
The Stepdaughter
The Son
The Boy (non-speaking role)
The Little Girl (also non-speaking)
Madame Pace (evoked later in the play)

The Actors in the Company
The Director
The Leading Lady
The Leading Man
The Second Lady
The Ingenue
The Juvenile Lead
Other actors and actresses
The Stage Manager
The Prompter
The Properties Man
A Stage Hand
Sam, Another Stage Hand
George, Light Board Operator (voice off)
The Doorman
Walk-ons and other stage hands

The stage of a theatre; daytime.
Note: The play has no acts or scenes in the usual sense. The performance will be interrupted twice, however: the first time, without the curtain falling, when the stage is vacated as the DIRECTOR *and the* CHARACTERS *retire to plan the play and the* ACTORS *take a break, and the second*

time when the STAGE HAND *mistakenly drops the curtain.*

Act 1

When the audience enters the theatre, they confront an empty stage just as it would appear during the day. There are no wings or scenery; it is indeed dark and almost empty. It gives the impression that no one had expected an audience at all: nothing is playing tonight. There are two small stairways on the left and right, leading from the auditorium onto the stage. On the left side, on the forestage, there is a little table and an armchair with the back to the audience as the director's own chair. There are two other small tables, one bigger than the other, and surrounded by several chairs set on the forestage for use as needed in the rehearsal coming up. Other chairs are scattered over the stage for the actors, and a piano stands almost hidden in the background.

When the lights go out in the house, the STAGE HAND *enters wearing a pair of coveralls with a tool belt. He takes down a set of boards which he arranges for making a flat, placing triangular plyboard*

129

pieces at the corners. He then kneels, takes a hammer from his belt, and begins to nail the plates in place. After a few blows of the hammer, the STAGE MANAGER *enters from the door to the dressing rooms.*

STAGE MANAGER. Hey! What do you think you're doing?

STAGE HAND. What's it look like? I'm nailing a flat together.

STAGE MANAGER. At this hour?

He looks at his watch.

It's already ten-thirty. Any minute now the director will be here to start rehearsal.

STAGE HAND. Well, I've got to have time to do my work, too, you know.

STAGE MANAGER. You'll get your chance, but not now.

STAGE HAND. Yeah? When?

STAGE MANAGER. When rehearsal's over. Come on. Get this stuff out of here and let me set up for the second act of *The Rules of the Game.*

The STAGE HAND *picks up the boards, muttering and fuming, and carries them off. Meanwhile, bit by bit, the* ACTORS *and* ACTRESSES *begin arriving on the stage, sometimes singly, sometimes in groups. In all there are some ten or twelve of them, enough for Pirandello's play,* The Rules of the Game, *called for today's rehearsal. They greet one another and the* STAGE MANAGER. *Some go off to the dressing rooms, while others, including the* PROMPTER, *carrying the script rolled up under his arm, remain on stage to await the* DIRECTOR'S *arrival. Seated and standing about, they engage in improvised conversation. Here someone lights a cigarette, there someone is complaining about the role he was assigned, while another reads aloud from a trade paper. The actors should be dressed in light, gay colors. They engage in lively, animated discussion. After a bit, one actor might sit at the piano to bang out a dance tune, and the younger actors might take up the beat and break into a dance.*

STAGE MANAGER. [*Clapping his hands to recall the actors to duty.*] All right, all right, cut it out, everyone! The Di-

rector's here!

The music, dancing, and chatter stop suddenly. Everyone turns to look out into the house. The DIRECTOR *enters through the door at the back of the house. He wears a Homburg hat, carries a cane, and holds a large cigar clamped in his teeth. He moves down the center aisle and climbs one of the little stairways onto the stage, greeting the actors as he comes. The* PROMPTER *hands him the morning mail, including a newspaper and a manuscript in a mailer.*

DIRECTOR. No letters?

PROMPTER. None. This is all the mail there is.

DIRECTOR. [*Handing the* PROMPTER *the manuscript.*] Take it to the office. [*He looks about and then turns to the* STAGE MANAGER.] I can hardly see in this place. How about a little light, all right?

STAGE MANAGER. Sure. Hey, George! Are you on the board? Ah, bring up the rehearsal light, say B 4, 5 and 6.

A stark, white light comes up on stage.

Okay! That looks good!

Meanwhile, the PROMPTER *takes his place, turns on his lamp, and spreads out his script in front of himself.*

DIRECTOR. [*Clapping his hands.*] All right, everyone, let's get started. [*He turns to the* STAGE MANAGER.] We're missing someone, aren't we?

STAGE MANAGER. The Leading Lady isn't here yet.

DIRECTOR. Again?

He looks at his watch.

We're already ten minutes late. Look, you'll have to impose a fine on her. Throw the book at her. That's the only way she'll learn to be prompt for rehearsals.

LEADING LADY. [*From the rear of the house, even before the* DIRECTOR *has finished speaking.*] No, no! Take it easy! I'm here. I'm here.

She is dressed entirely in white, with a grand, arrogant hat. She carries an elegant little dog under her arm. She runs down the aisle and up onto the stage.

DIRECTOR. You seem determined to make us wait for you.

LEADING LADY. Forgive me. I tried and tried but I just couldn't get a cab. You haven't started yet, I see, and I don't enter first anyway. I don't see what all the fuss is about. Say, Mike. . . .

She calls the STAGE MANAGER *over and hands him the little dog.*

Be a dear and put her in one of the dressing rooms.

DIRECTOR. [*Muttering under his breath.*] If it isn't one bitch, it's another!

He claps his hands again, and turns to the STAGE MANAGER.

All right, all right! *The Rules of the Game,* Second Act.

He settles himself in his armchair.

Quiet, everyone! Now, who's on stage?

The ACTORS *disperse, leaving the forestage empty and taking up positions to the sides. Three, however, remain on stage ready to begin the scene. The* LEADING LADY *also remains, not having paid attention to the* DIRECTOR's *question. She sits elaborately at one of the little tables.*

DIRECTOR. I take it you've decided you're in this scene after all?

LEADING LADY. I? Why, no!

DIRECTOR. Well, then, clear off, for God's sake!

The LEADING LADY *rises with dignity and joins the other actors.*

DIRECTOR. [*To the* PROMPTER.] All right, from the top! Let's go!

PROMPTER. [*Reading from the script.*] "The house of Leone Gala. It is a strange room serving both as a dining room and as a study."

DIRECTOR. [*Turning to the* STAGE MANAGER.] Let's pull the flats for the red room.

STAGE MANAGER. [*Making a note.*] Okay. The red room.

PROMPTER. "The table is set and the desk is covered with papers and books. There are bookshelves and a glass-encased china cabinet exhibiting elegant dinner wear. There is a door

upstage leading to Leone's bedroom. Stage left is the exit to the kitchen, and the main entrance to the house stands on stage right."

DIRECTOR. [*Standing and walking about to indicate these locations.*] All right, listen everybody. Over there, the main entrance, and here, the way into the kitchen.

He turns to the actor playing the part of "Socrates."

You will enter and exit this way.

To the STAGE MANAGER.

Put up the ornamental doorway here to the back and put up curtains.

He returns to his chair.

STAGE MANAGER. Very well.

PROMPTER. "Scene One: Leone Gala, Guido Venanzi, and Filippo called 'Socrates'. . . ."

To the DIRECTOR.

Do you want me to read the stage directions as well?

DIRECTOR. Sure! I've told you so a hundred times!

PROMPTER. "At rise, Leone Gala, wearing a chef's hat and an apron, is intent on scrambling an egg in a bowl with a wooden spoon. Filippo is beating another egg, also attired as a chef. Guido Venanzi sits nearby listening."

LEADING MAN. Say, do I really have to wear one of those silly chef's hats?

DIRECTOR. Of course you do. That's what it says, doesn't it?

He points at the script.

LEADING MAN. I'm sorry, but that's ridiculous.

DIRECTOR. [*He jumps to his feet in a rage.*] Ridiculous, you say, huh? Do you think it's my fault that France hasn't sent us any good plays lately and that we're reduced to putting on Pirandello's plays that no one understands? Huh? And do you know why no one understands them? Because he perversely contrived them to annoy every critic, actor, and audience member! That's why!

The ACTORS *laugh. Then he turns on the*

LEADING MAN.

Yes, you'll wear a chef's hat! And you'll beat that egg, too! But do you suppose that you are simply beating an egg? No! Think again! You are also symbolizing the shell of that egg you're beating!

The ACTORS *laugh again and begin to exchange ironic remarks.*

Quiet! Listen when I'm talking to you! [*He turns again to the* LEADING MAN.] That's right, the shell of that egg. In other words, you represent the empty form of reason without the substance of instinct, which is blind! You are reason and your wife is instinct. Neither of you is complete. See, the "rules of the game" put each in his own role so you become your own puppet: you manipulate yourself. You got that?

LEADING MAN. No I don't.

DIRECTOR. Neither do I! But let's get on with it. It's all a crock anyway. [*Confidentially.*] Listen, assume a position at least one quarter open. If you don't, the obscure dialogue will be falling in the cracks.

He claps his hands again.

Okay, here we go!

PROMPTER. Excuse me. There is a draft in here. Do you mind if I move my table?

DIRECTOR. Sure, sure, go ahead.

The DOORMAN *of the theatre has entered the theatre wearing a beret. He has come down the central aisle and he is approaching the stage to tell the* DIRECTOR *about the arrival of the* SIX CHARACTERS *who have also entered the auditorium following the* DOORMAN *at a distance, looking about themselves in bewilderment and anguish.*

Whoever stages this play must take pains to insure that the characters can never be confused with the actors. Their arrangement on stage indicated in the stage directions will help. Beyond that, they might be lit by different colored spots. An effective solution would be to use special masks for the characters, masks built of

material that does not soften with perspiration and yet remains lightweight and modeled to leave the eyes, nostrils, and mouth open. This will permit the characters to convey subtler qualities of the play. They should not at all events appear as ghosts or phantoms, but rather as concrete reality, immutable creations of the imagination and as such much more real and consistent than the ever-changing personalities of the actors. Masks will aid in giving the impression of a person created by art and fixed each one in its appropriate basic expression: remorse for the FATHER, *revenge for the* STEPDAUGHTER, *disdain for the* SON, *pain for the* MOTHER *with fixed wax tears within the dark circles under her eyes and down her cheeks, like the faces of the statues of the grieving Virgin Mary. The cut and material of their clothing should also be distinct, without the least extravagance, with rigid pleats and almost statuesque fullness giving somewhat the impression that the material could not be bought in any store nor the clothing made in any tailor's shop.*

The FATHER *is in his fifties. His hair is thinning, his skin tawny, and his mustache thick and curly above a mouth still young and fresh, often bent into an uncertain, slightly vain smile. He is pale, especially in his broad forehead. His eyes are blue, oval, lucid, and keen. He wears light trousers and a dark jacket. He alternates between speaking gently and smoothly and speaking harshly and bitterly.*

The MOTHER *appears weighed down by a great burden of shame and humiliation. She wears a heavy mourning veil, and a humble black dress. When the veil is lifted, her face is not twisted in suffering but seems waxen. She keeps her eyes lowered almost always.*

The STEPDAUGHTER *is eighteen. She is insolent and impudent, but beautiful. She, too, is in mourning, but with a flashy elegance. She shows an open contempt for the timid, afflicted, bewildered behavior of her dreary little fourteen-year-old brother (also dressed in black.) At the same time she exhibits an alert tenderness for the small sister, a four-year-old girl dressed in white with a black silk sash at her waist.*

The SON *is twenty-two years old. He is tall, and he stands rigid, seemingly out of disdain for the* FATHER *and gloomy indifference to the* MOTHER. *He wears a violet overcoat with a green scarf thrown around his neck.*

DOORMAN. [*His beret in his hands, he addresses the* DIRECTOR.] Excuse me, please, sir.

DIRECTOR. What the hell is it now?

DOORMAN. Here are some people asking for you.

The DIRECTOR *and the* ACTORS *turn in amazement to look out into the house.*

DIRECTOR. Can't you see we're rehearsing here? You know very well that no one comes in here during rehearsal.

He squints, looking out into the house.

Who are you people? What do you want?

FATHER. [*He comes to the bottom of one of the stairs.*] We're looking for a playwright.

DIRECTOR. A playwright? What playwright?

FATHER. Any playwright, sir.

DIRECTOR. There's no playwright here. We're not rehearsing a new play.

STEPDAUGHTER. [*Running up the steps onto the stage.*] Well, then, so much the better. *We'll* be your new play.

AN ACTOR. [*Voice rising above the comments and laughter of the others.*] Oh, listen to her!

FATHER. [*Following her onto the stage.*] Yes, yes, of course, if there is no playwright here. . . . [*Turning to the* DIRECTOR.] except that she, you understand, does not want. . . .

He is referring to the MOTHER *who has come up the first steps with the two children. The* SON *meanwhile remains below in irritable detachment.*

DIRECTOR. Are you people playing games with us?

FATHER. Games! Good heavens, no! We're bringing you a drama of pain and suffering.

STEPDAUGHTER. We could make your fortune!

DIRECTOR. Do us a favor and get out of here. We don't have time for madmen.

FATHER. Oh, sir, you know very well that life is full of infinite absurdities that plainly need not appear lifelike just because they *are* life.

DIRECTOR. What the devil are you talking about?

FATHER. You called us madmen. Well, I'm talking about madness. What is it but madness to attempt to re-create life's absurdities by making them plausible on stage? Forgive me, but isn't that the very basis of your art?

This causes the actors to grumble.

DIRECTOR. So, you think our art is the work of madmen?

FATHER. Well, isn't it? Making something that's not true seem true? You do it not out of necessity, but for amusement. Isn't it your art to give life on stage to imaginary characters?

DIRECTOR. [*Abruptly, giving voice to the seething anger of his actors.*] I'll have you know, dear sir, that acting is a noble profession! It may be that today's playwrights give us nothing but inane plays filled with puppets instead of human beings, but we can still take pride in having given life here, on these very boards, to immortal works.

FATHER. [*Riding over the actors' applause.*] Exactly! There you said it: giving life. And those living beings are more alive now than those who breathe and wear street clothes! They may be less real, but they are more true. Exactly! We're in perfect agreement.

The actors look at each other in amazement.

DIRECTOR. What? But you were just saying. . . .

FATHER. No, no, excuse me, sir, but you declared that you had no time for madmen. Surely no one would know better than you yourself that human fantasy, that rare madness, is the very instrument that produces great art.

DIRECTOR. All right, all right! So what?

FATHER. Nothing, sir. It's just that madness gives life in so many ways, and in so many forms: tree or rock, water or butterfly . . . or woman. Yes, even characters are born this way.

DIRECTOR. And you, with these other people, were born a character?

FATHER. Exactly. Alive, just as you see us.

The DIRECTOR *and the actors stare for a moment, then begin to burst into laughter, one after another.*

Don't laugh! You must not laugh, because we carry within us a drama of suffering. You can surely tell that just by looking at this woman veiled in black.

Saying this, he extends his hand to the MOTHER *to help her climb the last steps onto the stage and to escort her with solemnity to a portion of the stage now illuminated with a strange light. The* BOY *and the* LITTLE GIRL *follow closely. The* SON *also moves up, but takes a position apart and well behind the others. The* STEPDAUGHTER *stands before them leaning against the proscenium. The actors are at first astounded. Then they come to admire this movement, and they break out in applause as if for a spectacle played for them.*

DIRECTOR. [*At first he too is amazed, but then he turns contemptuous. He turns to the* ACTORS.] Come on, stop that! Be quiet!

Then to the CHARACTERS

And you! On your way! Get out of here!

He turns to the STAGE MANAGER.

Get them out of here, for God's sake.

STAGE MANAGER. Okay, let's go. Let's go.

He comes forward but stops as if suddenly frightened by something.

FATHER. [*To the* DIRECTOR.] No, no, don't you see? We. . . .

DIRECTOR. [*Shouting.*] Damn it, we've got work to do here!

AN ACTOR. Nobody can make fun of us this way!

FATHER. I'm amazed at your disbelief!

Aren't you people used to seeing a playwright's characters spring to life right here in front of you, on this stage? Or perhaps the problem is that there is no script there [*Pointing to the prompter's table.*] that contains us? Is that it?

STEPDAUGHTER. [*Walking up to the* DIRECTOR, *smiling coquettishly.*] Believe me, we are really six most interesting characters, sir. Interesting, but lost.

FATHER. [*Pushing her aside.*] Yes, lost. That's right. Lost in the sense that the playwright who created us decided that he would not, or could not, put us into a full work. And that was a crime, sir, because whoever is born this way as a living character, can laugh at death. He cannot die! The man will die, yes, the playwright, the writer, the character's creator, but not the character. He will never die. And he need not have extraordinary gifts or prodigious accomplishments to go on living as he does. Who was Sancho Panza? Who was Falstaff? They go on living because they found a rich context and an imagination that together nurtured them into eternity.

DIRECTOR. All right, all right! But what do you want here?

FATHER. We want to live!

DIRECTOR. Into eternity?

FATHER. No, sir. Just for a moment, in you.

AN ACTOR. Oh, come now!

LEADING LADY. They want to live in us!

A YOUNG ACTOR. [*Pointing at the* STEPDAUGHTER.] I'm game if she wants to pick me!

FATHER. Listen, everyone: we'll have to improvise the play, you understand, but if you sir [*meaning the* DIRECTOR] and your actors are willing, we can bring it off between us very quickly.

DIRECTOR. What do you mean, "bring it off," "improvise"? I'll have you know we perform dramas and comedies: *plays.* We don't play games.

FATHER. Very well. That is why we've

come to you. This *is* a play.

DIRECTOR. Oh? And where's the script?

FATHER. It's in us.

The ACTORS *laugh.*

The play is in us. *We* are the play. And we cannot wait to perform it, because its passion drives us to it.

STEPDAUGHTER. [*Tauntingly and impudently.*] *My* passion, if you want to know, sir, *my* passion . . . for him!

She points at the FATHER, *and makes to embrace him, but then breaks into harsh laughter.*

FATHER. Stay put for now. And please, don't laugh like that!

STEPDAUGHTER. No? Well then, maybe you people will permit me, even if I am in mourning, to show you how I can dance and sing.

She slides into a rendition of a French night club song, complete with seductive dance. As she dances, the actors, especially the young ones, move toward her, some holding their hands out as if to seize her, but she deftly avoids them. When she finishes, the actors burst into applause. She becomes diffident and distant when the DIRECTOR *tries to talk with her.*

ACTORS *and* ACTRESSES. [*Laughing and clapping.*] Brava! Brava! Well done! Beautiful!

DIRECTOR. Quiet! Shut up, all of you! Where do you think you are, in a nightclub? [*He takes the* FATHER *aside.*] Tell me, is she crazy?

FATHER. Crazy? No, not crazy! It's something much worse!

STEPDAUGHTER. [*Running to the* DIRECTOR.] Worse! Oh, yes, sir! Much worse! Listen: put this play on stage quickly, because then you'll see me . . . at a certain point, when this adorable child here. . . . [*She takes the* LITTLE GIRL *by the hand and brings her to the* DIRECTOR.] Isn't she darling? [*She takes her up in her arms and kisses her.*] Dearest little one! [*She puts her back on the ground, and then adds almost reluctantly.*] Well, God will take this little darling from her Mother. And this imbecile. . . . [*She pulls the* BOY

forward by his sleeve] this imbecile will do the stupidest thing, just like the idiot he is. . . . [*She pushes him back to the* MOTHER.] Anyway, then you will see me take flight! Yes! I'll run away. And it can't come too soon, I tell you, it can't be too soon! Because after what happened between me and him. . . . [*She points to the* FATHER, *winking lasciviously.*] I can't stand to be in this company or to witness the torture that Mother suffers because of that jerk, that scarecrow. [*Pointing at the* SON.] Look at him! Just look! Indifferent, cold, detached, because, you see, he is the legitimate son! And so he is full of contempt for me, for that one [*The* BOY.] and the darling little creature, because we're bastards. You understand? We're bastards!

She goes to the MOTHER *and embraces her.*

And this poor Mother, who is Mother of us all, *he* refuses to recognize her as his. He treats her from beginning to end as the Mother only of us bastards—that's how vile he is!

She says all this rapidly in great excitement, her voice rising through to the last "bastards," and then dropping to spit out quietly but intensely the last five words.

MOTHER. [*In great anguish, to the* DIRECTOR.] Sir, in the name of these two little children, I beg you. . . . [*She loses her resolve.*] Oh, my God. . . .

FATHER. [*Running to help her while all the* ACTORS *remain astounded and uncertain.*] Oh, please, a chair, bring a chair for this poor widow!

ACTORS. [*Running to help.*] Is it true? Is she really fainting?

DIRECTOR. A chair! Quick!

One of the ACTORS *brings a chair. The others crowd around solicitously. Once she is seated and the faint has passed she tries to prevent the* FATHER *from lifting her veil to reveal her face.*

FATHER. Look at her, sir. Look. . . .

MOTHER. Don't! Please stop!

FATHER. Let them see you!

He lifts the veil.

MOTHER. [*Putting her hands to her face,*

desperately.] Oh sir, I beg you to stop this man from carrying out his plan. It means nothing but horror to me!

DIRECTOR. I can't understand any longer what's happening here. What is this all about? [*Turning to the* FATHER.] She is your wife?

FATHER. Yes, my wife.

DIRECTOR. But how can she be a widow if you are still alive?

At this, the ACTORS *relieve their tension in loud laughter.*

FATHER. Don't laugh! You must not laugh! You must not, because, you see, this is her tragedy. There was another man in her life, a man who should also be here.

MOTHER. No! No!

STEPDAUGHTER. Luckily for him, he's dead. Two months ago. That's why we're in mourning, you see.

FATHER. But his death has nothing to do with his not being here. He is not here because . . . now, listen closely, please . . . because her drama does not concern the love of two men, for whom she had no feeling beyond a certain gratitude (for him, not for me!). No, the drama comes not of her being a woman, but rather of her being a mother. It turns upon these four children she bore by her two men.

MOTHER. *My* two men? You dare call them mine, as if I had them, wanted them? No! Listen, sir, it was him . . . he forced that other one on me, forced me to go away with the other man.

STEPDAUGHTER. That's not true!

MOTHER. What do you mean, not true?

STEPDAUGHTER. Just that! It's not true!

MOTHER. What could you know about it?

STEPDAUGHTER. It's not true!

She turns to the DIRECTOR.
    Don't believe her. You know why she says that? Because of him. [*She points to the* SON.] She tortures herself for not having cared for him. She wants him to understand that she aban-

doned him at the age of two only because he [*Pointing at the* FATHER] forced her to do so.

MOTHER. He did! He forced me, as God is my witness! Ask him! Ask him if it isn't true. She knows nothing about it.

STEPDAUGHTER. I know that so long as my Father was alive, you were content and at peace. Deny it, if you can!

MOTHER. I don't deny it, no. . . .

STEPDAUGHTER. He always loved and cared for you.

She abruptly turns on the BOY.
    Isn't that right? Eh? Say so! Why don't you say something, you fool?

MOTHER. Leave the poor boy alone! Why do you want to make me into an ingrate? I do not offend his memory. I only said that it was not my fault, not my pleasure, that took me away from that house and my son! It was not my fault!

FATHER. It's true. I did it.

Pause.

LEADING MAN. [*To his companions.*] Say, this is quite a show!

LEADING LADY. And we're the audience this time.

JUVENILE LEAD. For once, yeah!

DIRECTOR. [*He now has become deeply interested.*] Let's listen! Quiet!

And so saying, he descends the stairs into the auditorium and stands there as a spectator to gain an impression of the scene.

SON. [*Still standing apart from the others. He speaks coldly, quietly, and ironically.*] Yes, we're about to hear a little philosophy! He is going to tell you all about the "demon of experiment."

FATHER. You are a cynical idiot.

He turns out to the auditorium to address the DIRECTOR.
    He makes fun of me because of that phrase that gave me comfort.

SON. Words! Words!

FATHER. Yes, words! As if they have not given comfort to us all. Which of us has not faced an inexplicable fact, a consuming evil, and sought a word to give us some peace?

STEPDAUGHTER. A consuming remorse, for example. That above all else!

FATHER. Remorse? No, words have never been enough to relieve my remorse.

STEPDAUGHTER. Oh, yes! There was also that little bit of money. Money! Yes, gentlemen, there were those one hundred *lire* he meant to leave as payment.

The ACTORS *recoil in horror.*

SON. [*With contempt aimed at her.*] Oh, this is vile!

STEPDAUGHTER. Vile is it? The money was there tucked inside a pale blue envelope and lying on the little mahogany table in the back room of Madame Pace's shop. You understand me, sir? She was one of those *"madames"* who sell *"robes et manteaux"* in their elegant shops, and hire us poor girls from good families to work in the *"atelier"* in back.

SON. You seem to think you've bought the right to act the tyrant with those hundred *lire* that he was about to pay, but which finally, don't forget, there was no reason to pay.

STEPDAUGHTER. But it was a close thing, a very close thing.

Laughter.

MOTHER. Shame. Shame, Daughter.

STEPDAUGHTER. Shame? This is my revenge. I am trembling, sir, trembling in anticipation of living that scene! The room, and over there the showcase of coats, and there the studio couch, and there the screen, and, yes, there the little mahogany table with the pale blue envelope containing the hundred *lire*. I see it! I could pick it up! But, you gentlemen, you must turn your backs because I'm almost naked. I'm not blushing any more, though, because it's time for him to blush. [*She points at the* FATHER.] But at that moment, I tell you, he was pale, very pale. [*To the* DIRECTOR.] Believe me, sir!

DIRECTOR. I can't make head or tail of all this.

FATHER. I can see why, with everything so jumbled. Impose a little order and let me talk. You needn't pay attention to the disgrace she wants to heap on me so vigorously. Some explanation is called for.

STEPDAUGHTER. Oh, no! We'll hear no stories! This is not a place for storytelling.

FATHER. I'm not telling stories. I want to explain to him.

STEPDAUGHTER. Oh, sure! In your own way!

At this point, the DIRECTOR *climbs back onto the stage to restore order.*

FATHER. But all our troubles may come from just that, our words! Words! Every one of us carries a whole world within. How can we ever understand each other if I put all the meaning and feeling of what's within me into my words while whoever listens gives them the meaning and feeling of what's within him? We think we understand one another, but never do! Look: all the pity I felt for this woman [*He gestures toward the* MOTHER.] she took as ferocious cruelty instead.

MOTHER. But you threw me out!

FATHER. There, you hear her? Threw you out? Do you really think that I threw you out?

MOTHER. You know how to talk, I don't. . . . Believe me, sir, after he married me . . . who knows why? . . . I was such a poor, humble woman. . . .

FATHER. That's the reason there. I married you for your humility. That is what I loved in you, thinking. . . .

The MOTHER *protests and the* FATHER *throws up his hands in dismay at the impossibility of making her understand. He turns back to the* DIRECTOR.

You see? She protests. Oh, it is beyond belief, this deafness of hers, this mental deafness! She has a heart, yes, compassion for her children, but she is deaf in the mind, deaf to the point of distraction, I tell you.

STEPDAUGHTER. Oh, yes. Now let him tell you how lucky we've been because of his intelligence!

FATHER. Oh, if we only knew what evil would come of the good we intend!

The LEADING LADY *has been watching the* LEADING MAN *and the* STEPDAUGHTER *flirting and has become annoyed. She steps up to the* DIRECTOR.

LEADING LADY. Are we going to rehearse or not?

DIRECTOR. Of course, but let me listen a moment.

JUVENILE LEAD. This is something new!

INGENUE. Just fascinating!

LEADING LADY. Oh yes, for anyone who's fascinated!

She darts a glance at the LEADING MAN.

DIRECTOR. [*Speaking to the* FATHER.] But you must explain very clearly, please. *He sits.*

FATHER. Very well. You see, sir, there was a poor man living with us. I supported him and he served as my secretary. My wife and he got along very well. They understood one another. There was nothing wrong in it, no shadow of evil, you understand: it was completely innocent. Neither of them would ever be capable of a base or disloyal thought.

STEPDAUGHTER. So he thought it for them! And then carried it out as well!

FATHER. That's not so! I never intended anything except the best for them and for myself as well, I confess it. Sir, it came to such a point that I could not say a word to either of them without their sharing a glance of recognition. They would try to catch each other's eye in order to decide how to respond to what I was saying without irritating me. That in itself was enough, as she surely knew, to keep me in a state of constant rage and intolerable exasperation.

DIRECTOR. Why didn't you simply throw the man out?

FATHER. I did! I threw him out, sir. But

then this woman began wandering about the house like a lost soul, like a pet who'd lost her master.

MOTHER. That's not it! No!

FATHER. [*Abruptly, turning to her as if to anticipate what she means.*] Ah, the son, right?

MOTHER. He had already torn my son from my breast, sir.

FATHER. But not out of cruelty. It was to help him grow up healthy and strong, in touch with the earth.

STEPDAUGHTER. And just look at him now!

FATHER. Is it my fault that he grew up like that? I gave him to a peasant woman to nurse, out in the country, because my wife did not seem strong enough. I married her for that weakness and humility, the very same reason. You may call it a whim, but what's to be done? I've always aspired to a solid moral sanity.

The STEPDAUGHTER *bursts into raucous laughter.*

Make her stop! I can't bear it!

DIRECTOR. Shut up! Let me hear him, for God's sake!

At once she cuts off her laughter, and moves off to the side, where she returns to her earlier detached, distant attitude. Meanwhile, the DIRECTOR *descends into the auditorium to gain a sense of the scene.*

FATHER. I could no longer live with this woman. [*He refers to the* MOTHER.] But, believe me it was not so much because it had become so tiresome and tedious, although it had. It was because of the agonizing pain I felt for her.

MOTHER. So he sent me away!

FATHER. Yes, yes, I sent her away. And well provided for, too. I sent her to that man to be free of me.

MOTHER. He wanted to rid himself of me!

FATHER. Yes, that, too. I admit it. And only great harm came of it! Still, I meant well and I did it more for her sake than mine, I swear it!

He puts his hand up in a gesture of swear-

ing. Then he turns to her again.
Tell me, did I ever lose sight of you?
Did I? Never! Not until that day he
suddenly took you to live in another
town. I knew nothing of it, and yet
he did it because of me, because he
foolishly feared the interest I took,
an interest I assure you that was
pure, without ulterior motive. I felt a
great tenderness watching that little
family grow. She can testify to that.
[*He points to the* STEPDAUGHTER.]

STEPDAUGHTER. Oh, indeed! When I
was little, with curls hanging down to
my shoulders and a skirt so short my
panties showed, I would spot him
standing across from the entrance to
my school as soon as I came out in
the afternoon. He came to watch me
develop. . . .

FATHER. This is treachery! It's detestable!

STEPDAUGHTER. Really? Why?

FATHER. Detestable! [*He turns abruptly
and excitedly to the* DIRECTOR *to explain.*] After she left my house, sir, it
suddenly seemed empty. She had
been my nightmare, but she did fill
the house. Alone, I was like a
trapped fly banging about between
the screen and the window pane.
That one there [*He points to the* SON]
was brought up in the country . . .
and somehow when he returned he
no longer seemed mine. Lacking the
mother, he grew up completely
apart, without anything to do with
me, emotionally or intellectually.
After that, and I know this will seem
strange to you, sir, my curiosity was
aroused. Gradually I was attracted to
this little family. I wanted to see the
result of my doing. Thoughts of her
began to fill that emptiness I felt. I
needed to know that she was in
peace, that she was well provided for
and that she really was well rid of the
complex torments of my spirit. And
to find out, I would go and watch
that girl coming out of school.

STEPDAUGHTER. Oh, yes! He would follow me through the streets. He
would smile at me, and when I
reached home, he would wave at me,
like this! I looked at him askance. I
was annoyed. I didn't know who he
was. I told Mama about him and she
knew at once who he was.

The MOTHER *nods.*
She did not send me back to that
school for several days. Then when I
did go back, there he was again waiting at the exit. He was standing there
looking silly, holding a paper bag. He
came up to me and caressed me.
Then he reached into the bag and
brought out a big, beautiful straw hat
with a garland of little May roses. A
gift for me!

DIRECTOR. But, my friends, all this is
merely exposition, a story.

SON. [*Disdainfully.*] Yes. Literature! Literature!

FATHER. What do you mean, literature?
This is life, sir! Passion!

DIRECTOR. Maybe so, but still it's un-
stageable.

FATHER. You're right, but then all this
happened long ago and I'm not asking you to stage it. In fact, you can
see that she is no longer that little girl
with curls down to her shoulders.

STEPDAUGHTER. . . . and lace panties
showing below my skirt.

FATHER. The plot begins now, sir . . .
new, complex. . . .

STEPDAUGHTER. [*She steps forward with a
proud and sultry air.*] As soon as my
Father died. . . .

FATHER. [*Interrupting to keep her from
talking.*] . . . there was such poverty,
you see. They came back here without my knowing it. She [*Meaning the
MOTHER*] stupidly kept me in the
dark. She scarcely knows how to
write, but she could have had her
daughter or even that little boy write
to me about their desperate need.

MOTHER. How was I to know he felt this
way?

FATHER. That was exactly your failing:
you never sensed any of my feelings.

MOTHER. After all those years away, after all that had happened. . . .

FATHER. Was it my fault that one fine day the fellow took you off to another town? [*He turns back to the* DIRECTOR.] I tell you, they were here one day and gone the next. He had found some job elsewhere. I couldn't find any trace of them. And so, naturally, little by little my interest in them declined over the years. The plot picks up, sir, when they return to town. It captures interest at once by its unexpectedness and violence. You see, I had allowed the demands of the flesh to draw me out of my house, that flesh so miserably demanding. . . . It *is* misery for a lonely man trying to avoid degrading ties, a man not yet old enough to do without women and no longer young enough to go out openly in search of one. What am I saying? Misery? It's a horror! What woman would give herself to him in love? None! You'll say I should do without, right? Ah, sir, we can all put on a good face and appear dignified when we're in company . . . but in our heart of hearts we all know things so secret they could never be confessed. One gives in to temptation; one gives in so as to rise above it afterward. Yes, then we hurriedly regain that former dignity and bury that shame out of sight. And so it is with everyone! It is just that most haven't the courage to say so.

STEPDAUGHTER. Yet they all have the courage to do it! All of them!

FATHER. Yes, all of them! But only in secret! The real courage is in confessing it. Anyone who does is regarded as a cynic. Yet, he's not, sir. He's like all the others, but better than the others, because he's not afraid to expose that blush of shame that our human bestiality provokes, that shame that closes our eyes to its every remnant, its every memory. And what about the woman? She looks at you, invitingly, provocatively. Seize her! And as soon as she feels herself taken, she closes her eyes at once. It is a sign of her surrender. It is also a way of saying to you, "Blind yourself. I am already blind."

STEPDAUGHTER. Suppose she doesn't close them any more? Suppose she no longer feels the need to hide her own shame, and so sees his clearly and impassively, while he goes on blinding himself without love. Oh, how disgusting he is with all the intellectual contortions he uses to expose the beast and at the same time save it, excuse it. . . . I don't want to hear it! When he tries to simplify life, throwing out all that separates humanity from the beasts, all that is chaste, all the pure feeling, idealism, duty, modesty, and even shame, he only transforms his remorse into a contemptuous and nauseous vision. All his philosophy is an excuse for lechery and all his anguish, crocodile tears.

DIRECTOR. Come, let's get down to the facts, my friends. This is merely discussion.

FATHER. You're right, sir! But a fact is like a sack: it cannot stand up when it's empty. To make it stand up, you must fill it with all the reasons and all the feelings that caused it. How could I have known that she [*He points to the* MOTHER] would return to town after the man's death and in utter poverty go looking for work in the shop of that . . . that Madame Pace?

STEPDAUGHTER. An elegant dressmaker, if you people want to know. She serves the best ladies, up front, but she has a fine operation going, because these same fine ladies serve her, too . . . without quite knowing it, if you catch my meaning.

MOTHER. Believe me, sir, it never occurred to me that the hag hired me because she had her eye on my daughter.

STEPDAUGHTER. Poor Mama! Do you

know what the old witch did? As soon as I brought in the work my Mother had done, she would claim Mother had spoiled it and threaten to deduct the cost of the material from her pay. Then, I would end up paying, while poor, dear Mama thought she was making sacrifices for us by spending her nights sewing all those dresses for Madame Pace.

The ACTORS *murmur in disgust.*

DIRECTOR. [*Abruptly.*] And it was there, was it, that one day you encountered. . . .

STEPDAUGHTER. [*Pointing at the* FATHER.] . . . him, him! Yes! An old client. Oh, what a scene we have for you! A stunner!

FATHER. Including the moment when she, the Mother, suddenly appeared.

STEPDAUGHTER. Almost in time!

FATHER. [*Shouting.*] No! In time! Because luckily I recognized her in time! And I took them all home. Now imagine, if you can, our situation, hers and mine: she and I in the same house, and I unable to look anyone in the face.

STEPDAUGHTER. Very funny! After that, how could I present myself as a modest, well-brought-up young lady in accord with his damnable aspirations to a life of "solid moral sanity"?

FATHER. For me, the drama lies in that, sir: that each of us thinks of himself as a single person, and yet it is not true. There are many persons, not one, all fulfilling the possibilities that lie there. So for some people you are this person, for others that, and they are all different. Meanwhile, you delude yourself into thinking that you are "one for all," always the same "one" in every act you do. You realize this fully whenever you're caught in a disgraceful act that abruptly holds you up for all to see, as if you were hanging naked from a hook. You know you are not summed up in that one act and you protest the atrocious injustice of being judged and held in

pillory for it. Now surely you see the treachery of this girl. She surprised me in a place and in an act where she should never have known me, a part of me that should not exist for her. And she tries to impose on me an identity that simply should not exist for her, a reality based on a fleeting, shameful moment in my life! That is the pain I feel most, sir, and you'll see that it gives the drama intense meaning. But then each of us has his own story. His, for example. . . . [*He points to the* SON.]

SON. Leave me out of this! I have nothing to do with it.

FATHER. What do you mean, you have nothing to do with it?

SON. I have nothing to do with it, and I want nothing to do with it. You know very well that I was not made to be thrown into the midst of you people.

STEPDAUGHTER. Vulgar people that we are! He is so fine! But you surely have noticed how he lowers his eyes when I shoot him a look of contempt. That's because he knows the harm he's done me.

SON. [*Scarcely looking at her.*] I?

STEPDAUGHTER. You! You! I was on the streets because of you!

The ACTORS *express shock.*

Did you not deny me any sense of welcome in your house? We were treated as intruders invading the realm of your "legitimacy." Sir, I'd like you to witness some of our close scenes, his and mine. He claims I lorded it over everyone. But see? It was precisely that behavior of his that justified my "vile act" as he called it: entering his house with my Mother, who is also his Mother, as if we owned it.

SON. [*Stepping forward slowly.*] They can have their fun ganging up on me, if they like. But think what it's like for a son, living quietly at home, to see an impudent young woman arrive, her nose in the air, asking for the Father, speaking with him about God knows what, and then to see her return even more haughtily, bringing that little girl with her, and finally to see her treating the Father in a strange, ambiguous, clipped manner, asking for money in a way that implied somehow that he owed it to her. . . .

FATHER. I did owe it to her, and to your Mother!

SON. What did I know about that? Whenever had I seen her? Whenever had I heard about her? Yet, one day she appears here along with her [*Pointing to the* STEPDAUGHTER.], and that boy and that little girl. They tell me, "See, she's your Mother, too!" I get some idea from her manner [*Again indicating the* STEPDAUGHTER.] why they settled in our house. . . . Sir, I cannot and will not express my reactions, my feelings. I don't care to think about them myself, so you cannot expect me to contribute any action here. Believe me, sir, I am an unrealized character dramatically. I am ill-at-ease in their company. Leave me alone.

FATHER. Wait a minute! After all, just because you are so. . . .

SON. What do you know about what I am? When did you ever bother your head about me?

FATHER. I admit it, yes. But this is an important complication, your pulling away just when your Mother came into the house, your cruel aloofness! Think what it must have been like for her, seeing you for the first time, now grown up, not knowing you and yet knowing you are her son. . . .

He points to the MOTHER, *and addresses the* DIRECTOR.

Look at her. She's weeping!

STEPDAUGHTER. [*In a rage, stamping her foot.*] So stupid of her!

FATHER. [*Suddenly, now pointing to the* STEPDAUGHTER.] And she can't stand it, you can tell.

He turns back to the SON.

He says he has nothing to do with this, and yet the plot almost turns

upon him. Look at that little boy always standing pressed against his Mother in bewilderment and humiliation. . . . It's all his [*the* SON's] fault! Perhaps the boy's situation is the most painful of all . . . he feels extraneous; he feels mortified at being taken into the house, as if for charity. . . . He is very like his Father! Humble, taciturn. . . .

DIRECTOR. Oh well, he'll never do. We'll cut him: you have no idea what a nuisance children are on stage.

FATHER. Oh, well, he is gone early, and the little girl even before him, you see.

DIRECTOR. Very good. Yes! I tell you this really interests me; it interests me a great deal. I can tell there's the stuff of a good play here.

STEPDAUGHTER. With a character like me, how could it fail?

FATHER. [*Putting her aside, anxious for the* DIRECTOR's *decision.*] Shut up, you!

DIRECTOR. [*Continuing without noticing the interruption.*] Yes, it has a novelty, it's new. . . .

FATHER. Yes, indeed, it's new. . . .

DIRECTOR. It takes a lot of nerve, I must say, for you to come here and throw it at me this way!

FATHER. You understand, sir, born as we are for the stage. . . .

DIRECTOR. You aren't amateur actors, are you?

FATHER. No. I said born for the stage because. . . .

DIRECTOR. Come now, you must have acted before!

FATHER. No, sir, except to the extent we all play roles, the ones that others assign to us in life. And then when passion rises to the surface, I naturally become a little theatrical. . . .

DIRECTOR. Never mind, never mind. You understand, my dear sir, that without a playwright. . . . Look, I could recommend one to you. . . .

FATHER. No, no. Listen: you do it!

DIRECTOR. Me? What do you mean?

FATHER. Yes, you. Why not?

DIRECTOR. Because I've never written a play, that's why not.

FATHER. But please, couldn't you do it now? It's nothing: everyone does it. Look, we are all here, alive in front of you. That makes it easy.

DIRECTOR. It'll take more than that.

FATHER. What do you mean, more than that? Just watch us live our drama. . . .

DIRECTOR. Sure, but we need someone to write it out.

FATHER. No. Just write it out when you have it all here in front of you, in action, scene by scene. You'll only have to sketch it out on paper, and you can develop it later while you rehearse.

DIRECTOR. [*Climbing back onto the stage.*] Hmm . . . it's tempting, I must admit . . . it's tempting. Yes, we could give it a try, do a little rehearsing, see what happens. . . .

FATHER. Oh. yes. You'll see such scenes played out! I can give you some in-dications right away, you see!

DIRECTOR. I'm tempted . . . yes. Let's give it a try. . . . Come with me to my office.

He turns to the ACTORS.

Take a break, people, but don't go too far away. Be back here in fifteen, twenty minutes. [*Back to the* FATHER.] Come along. Let's try it. Perhaps something really extraordinary will come up. . . .

FATHER. I know it will! But shouldn't the others come with us?

He indicates the other CHARACTERS.

DIRECTOR. Yes, come on.

He moves off, but then returns to talk to the ACTORS.

Listen, now, be sure to be back here within a quarter of an hour.

The DIRECTOR *and the six* CHARACTERS *cross over the stage and disappear. The* ACTORS *remain, as if amazed, looking at one another.*

LEADING MAN. Is he serious? What's he doing?

JUVENILE LEAD. This is just nuts.

ANOTHER ACTOR. Does he expect us to stand out here improvising?

JUVENILE LEAD. The Commedia lives again!

LEADING LADY. If he thinks he can use me for such games. . . .

INGENUE. I won't stand for it.

ANOTHER ACTOR. I'd like to know who they are.

STILL ANOTHER. What do you think? They're either crazy or they're all charlatans.

JUVENILE LEAD. And he drops every-thing for them.

INGENUE. What arrogance! He fancies himself a playwright!

LEADING MAN. It's unheard of! Ladies and gentlemen, if the theatre has fallen to this. . . .

ANOTHER ACTOR. I think it's fun.

STILL ANOTHER. Ah, well, let's wait and see what comes of it.

And so conversing among themselves, the ACTORS *disperse, leaving by the back door on stage or into the dressing rooms. The curtain remains open. The play is inter-rupted for a quarter of an hour.*

Act 2

After the bells announce that the play is about to begin again, the ACTORS, *the* STAGE MANAGER, *the* STAGE HAND, *the* PROMPTER, *the* PROPS MAN *begin to filter onto stage from the back door, the dressing rooms, and even the auditorium. The* DIRECTOR *and the* SIX CHARACTERS *also appear out of his office. The lights fade in the house, and come back up on stage.*

DIRECTOR. All right, let's go, people. Is everyone here? Now, listen. Let's get started. Sam!

STAGE HAND. Right here!

DIRECTOR. We'll need to set up a small room, see? A three-fold with a door in the central flat will do. Chop, chop!

The STAGE HAND *runs off to tend to this while the* DIRECTOR *consults with the* STAGE MANAGER, *the* PROPS MAN, *the* PROMPTER, *and the* ACTORS *about the scene they are about to put together, which indeed consists of the three-fold flat with wallpaper of pink and gold stripes. The* DIRECTOR *turns first to the* PROPS MAN. Look in storage and see if you can't find a studio couch.

PROPS MAN. Okay. There's that green one.

STEPDAUGHTER. No, no, not green! It was yellow, with a flower pattern, velvet, very large and comfortable.

PROPS MAN. We don't have anything like that.

DIRECTOR. Oh, well, it doesn't matter. Bring out what there is.

STEPDAUGHTER. What do you mean, it doesn't matter? The famous sofa of Madame Pace!

DIRECTOR. Just for rehearsal purposes. Please, stay out of this. [*He turns to the* STAGE MANAGER.] See if there isn't a glass display case, rather low and long, all right?

STEPDAUGHTER. And the little table. The little mahogany table for the pale blue envelope.

STAGE MANAGER. There's that little gilded one.

DIRECTOR. All right. Get that one.

FATHER. A mirror.

STEPDAUGHTER. And a screen. We need a screen, I tell you. Otherwise I can't do the scene.

STAGE MANAGER. Yes, ma'am. We've dozens of screens, don't worry.

DIRECTOR. [*To the* STEPDAUGHTER.] We need some kind of clothes rack, right?

STEPDAUGHTER. Oh, yes! For lots of clothes.

DIRECTOR. [*Back to the* STAGE MANAGER.] See what you can find: a rack, clothes, hangers, the works.

STAGE MANAGER. Yes, sir. I'll take care of it.

He runs off to tend to these things. Meanwhile the DIRECTOR *talks to the* PROMPTER, *and then to the* CHARACTERS *and* ACTORS, *and he oversees the placement of pieces as they arrive on stage.*

DIRECTOR. Take your places. Here's a scenario of the play as we've sketched it out. [*He hands the* PROMPTER *a sheet of paper.*] I have to ask you to do something special for us.

PROMPTER. You want me to take it all down in shorthand?

DIRECTOR. Could you? You know shorthand?

PROMPTER. I may not know prompting, but shorthand, ah. . . .

DIRECTOR. Better and better! Go get some paper out of my office, a pile of it—as much as you can find there. Follow the scene moment by moment and try to get down all the lines, at least the most important ones!

The PROMPTER *runs off, and returns shortly with a fine pile of paper. Then the* DIRECTOR *turns to the* ACTORS.
Move out, people. Here, take places over here on stage left and watch this closely.

LEADING LADY. Look here, excuse me, but we. . . .

DIRECTOR. Don't worry. You won't have to improvise.

LEADING MAN. Well, what do we do?

DIRECTOR. Nothing! Look and listen and learn. Everyone will have his part all written out later. First off let's have a run-through and they [*Pointing to the* CHARACTERS.] are going to do it.

FATHER. [*Standing amazed in the midst of the confusion on stage.*] We? Excuse me, but what do you mean, "run-through"?

DIRECTOR. It's a rehearsal . . . for them! [*Pointing to the* ACTORS.]

FATHER. But if we already are the characters. . . .

DIRECTOR. Fine, fine! But the "characters" don't act here, sir. Actors do that. The characters belong in the script . . . [*He points at the* PROMPTER'*s papers.*] there, when there *is* a script.

FATHER. Exactly! Since there isn't one

and since you people are lucky enough to have the characters themselves in front of you. . . .

DIRECTOR. Oh, fine! It seems you people want to do everything! Even perform the piece for the audience.

FATHER. Sure. I mean, here we are.

DIRECTOR. What a fine show that'll be!

LEADING MAN. And what are the rest of us supposed to do, huh?

DIRECTOR. So now you people think you know how to act, is that it? Ha!

The ACTORS *break into laughter.*

There! You see? They're laughing at you! [*He laughs himself, and then recollects himself.*] Ah, yes, that reminds me: we need to cast the play. Seems easy enough. The parts fall right into place. You, madam [*The* SECOND LADY.] will play the Mother. [*He turns to the* FATHER.] We'll need a name for her, you know.

FATHER. It's Amalia.

DIRECTOR. But that *is* her name. We don't want to use her real name.

FATHER. Why not? I mean, she is Amalia. But, look here, if this lady must be [*He indicates the* SECOND LADY.] . . . I would see this woman [*Now he points to the* MOTHER.] as Amalia. But do as you think best. [*He becomes bewildered.*] I don't know what to say . . . I'm beginning to seem, I don't know, false somehow, even the sound of my voice, my very words. . . .

DIRECTOR. Don't worry about it; don't worry. We'll work out the right tone. And as for the name, if you want it to be "Amalia," why "Amalia" it'll be! Now let's cast the other parts: you [*The* JUVENILE LEAD.] be the Son, you [*The* LEADING LADY.] ma'am, you be the Stepdaughter.

STEPDAUGHTER. What? What? That lady? She's to be me? [*She breaks into laughter.*]

DIRECTOR. What is there to laugh about, eh?

LEADING LADY. No one dares laugh at me! No one! Either I get respect or I'm leaving, you understand?

STEPDAUGHTER. Oh, oh, please, excuse me. I'm not laughing at you.

DIRECTOR. You should feel honored to be played by. . . .

LEADING LADY. . . . by "that lady!"

STEPDAUGHTER. But I said I was not laughing at her. Believe me.

FATHER. Yes, that's it, sir! Our particular manner. . . .

DIRECTOR. What about your particular manner? Do you think it comes from within you? Do you think it's yours? No! Not at all!

FATHER. What? Our own manner isn't ours?

DIRECTOR. Of course not! Your manner is our material. We'll take it and give it body and shape and full expression through voice and gesture. That's the work of these actors, who, I would have you know, have given expression to far more elevated material than yours. And if yours is going to hold the stage, it will be thanks to my actors.

FATHER. I don't want to contradict you, sir. But you must believe me that it is insufferable for us, we who are just as you see us, with these bodies, with these faces. . . .

DIRECTOR. As for the faces, make-up will take care of them.

FATHER. Fine. But there's the voice . . . the gestures. . . .

DIRECTOR. Oh, come on! On stage, you cannot be yourself. You can't! This is the actor who will play you. Understand?

FATHER. I understand, yes, sir. But now I think I also understand why our playwright, who saw us alive as you see us, did not want to create us for the stage. I wish no offense to your actors, God forbid, but when I think of myself being played by, I don't know by whom. . . .

LEADING MAN. [*Rising haughtily and approaching him, followed by a group of laughing young* ACTRESSES.] By me, if you don't mind.

FATHER. I am deeply honored, sir. [*He bows slightly.*] But look, it seems to me, no matter how much he tries, with the best will and with all his art, to assimilate me within him, no matter how. . . . [*He becomes confused.*]

LEADING MAN. Come to the point!

The ACTRESSES *laugh.*

FATHER. What I'm trying to say is that his portrayal, even using make-up to look like me. . . . I mean, with his build. . . .

All the ACTORS *are now laughing.*

I tell you, it could scarcely be a portrayal of me as I really am. Instead—the face aside—it'll be him interpreting me as I seem to him, as he feels I feel, but not how I myself feel within myself. I think whoever may come to judge us must take that into account.

DIRECTOR. My God, he's already thinking about the critics! Let the critics say whatever they like! Why am I standing around listening to this? Let's get on with this show if we can!

He moves aside and looks around the stage.

Come, come! Is the scenery set?

To the ACTORS *and* CHARACTERS.

Get up. Move aside. Let me have a look.

He comes down off the stage.

Let's not waste any more time.

To the STEPDAUGHTER.

How do you like it?

STEPDAUGHTER. Really, I don't recognize it at all.

DIRECTOR. Here we go again. Look, no one is pretending to duplicate that back room you know so well at Madame Pace's shop. [*To the* FATHER.] You said a little room with flowered wallpaper, right?

FATHER. Yes, sir. White.

DIRECTOR. Well, this isn't white. It's striped, but so what? As for the furniture, that seems to be roughly correct, too. Bring that little table out here!

The STAGE HANDS *do so. Meanwhile he turns to the* PROPS MAN.

You need to provide an envelope, preferably pale blue, and give it to the gentleman. [*He indicates the* FATHER.]

PROPS MAN. A business envelope?

FATHER. No! Did you ever see a pale blue business envelope?

PROPS MAN. Oh. Of course not. I'll be right back. [*He exits.*]

DIRECTOR. All right, let's go! The first scene is the young lady's.

The LEADING LADY *steps forward.*

No, not you! You wait a bit. I'm referring to the young lady. [*He indicates the* STEPDAUGHTER.] As for you, you just watch. . . .

STEPDAUGHTER. . . . how I live it!

LEADING LADY. I'll live it, too, don't you worry. Just you wait!

DIRECTOR. [*His hands to his head.*] Please, ladies! That's enough! Now, this first scene involves the young lady and Madame Pace. Oh. . . .

He is suddenly confused. He climbs back onto stage.

What about her?

FATHER. She's not with us, sir.

DIRECTOR. Now what do we do?

FATHER. But she's alive, too, just as we are.

DIRECTOR. Fine! But where is she?

FATHER. Here, permit me. [*He turns to some* ACTRESSES.] If you ladies would be so good as to loan me your hats for a moment. . . .

ACTRESSES. Our hats? What? What is he saying? Why? Wait a minute!

DIRECTOR. What do you want with their hats?

The ACTORS *laugh.*

FATHER. Just to put them on this clothes rack for a moment. Would any of you be so good as to take off your coat?

ACTORS *and* ACTRESSES. [*As before.*] Now he wants a coat? What next? He must be nuts. What's the point? Just the coat, that's all?

FATHER. I want to hang it here for just a moment. I'll give it right back. Will any of you do me that favor?

ACTRESSES. [*Some do take off their hats,*

and one her coat, while they continue to laugh and giggle. They come forward and hang them here and there on the rack.] Well, why not? Here you are! This fellow is really funny, you know that? Must we put them on display?

FATHER. Exactly, madam, on display.

DIRECTOR. Do you mind telling us what this is all about?

FATHER. You see, perhaps we can cause her to appear by dressing the stage a bit and spreading these several articles of her business about the set. This may persuade her to come into our midst. . . .

He looks pointedly toward the door in the middle of the central flat of the three-fold. Look! Look!

The door opens and MADAME PACE *steps into the new stage setting. She is indeed a great hag, wearing a carrot-colored wig, a bright pink rose stuck into it at a jaunty Spanish angle. She wears an awkwardly elegant dress of gaudy red silk. In one hand she carries a feathered fan and in the other her cigarette and holder. The instant she appears the* ACTORS *and the* DIRECTOR *flee to the edges of the stage with cries of surprise. Some even clamber down the steps and make to run up the aisle. The* STEPDAUGHTER, *however, crosses directly to* MADAME PACE, *whom she faces humbly as if she were her servant.*

STEPDAUGHTER. Here she is. This is her!

FATHER. [*Beaming.*] What did I tell you? This is Madame Pace.

DIRECTOR. What kind of trick is this?

LEADING MAN. Really, what is all this?

JUVENILE LEAD. Where did she come from?

INGENUE. They've been holding her in reserve; that's my guess.

LEADING LADY. Hmmph! What disgusting hocus-pocus!

FATHER. [*Riding over these protests.*] Please, please! Why do you belittle this moment as untrue? Is your mundane, ordinary reality somehow better than this reality? Here is a prodigy this very stage set has brought to life. This scenery and these props have attracted, evoked and formed her! And who has a greater right to live here on this stage than she? No one, because she is truer than any of you, than anyone at all! Which one of you will play the part of Madame Pace? Well, here is the real Madame Pace! Surely you recognize that the actress is less true than Madame Pace in person. Look there: my stepdaughter knew her at once and went right up to her. Just watch this! Just watch this scene!

Hesitantly, the DIRECTOR *and the* ACTORS *turn to the stage. Already the* STEPDAUGHTER *and* MADAME PACE *have launched into their scene, speaking together very quietly and normally, against all stage practice, and so naturally, when the* ACTORS *turn their attention to them and see* MADAME PACE *put her hand under the* STEPDAUGHTER's *chin and lift her head to force her to look her in the face, they have to strain to make out the words. Finally, however, they give up in irritation.*

DIRECTOR. Well?

LEADING MAN. What is she saying?

LEADING LADY. We can't hear a word!

JUVENILE LEAD. Speak up, can't you? Louder!

STEPDAUGHTER. [*She tears herself away from* MADAME PACE, *who remains behind, her face contorted into a bizarre smile. The* STEPDAUGHTER *walks into the midst of the* ACTORS.] Louder? Well, how loud do you want it? These are not things you talk about at the top of your lungs, you know. Oh yes, *I* could say them out loud, to put *him* to shame [*Pointing at the* FATHER.] That is my revenge! But for the madame, it means something else. It means jail!

DIRECTOR. Oh, fine, fine! So this is it? Listen, my dear, here you can't go on like that! You've got to be heard! We can't even hear you standing right on stage. Think what it'll be like when there's an audience out there. You've got to *play* the scene. You can talk aloud between yourselves, you know, because we wouldn't actually be listening. Just pretend you're alone together in the back room of the shop where no one can hear you.

The STEPDAUGHTER *politely shakes her head, smiling maliciously.*

What do you mean, no?

STEPDAUGHTER. [*Mysteriously, sotto voce.*] There is someone who *will* hear if she speaks aloud.

DIRECTOR. I suppose you have someone else to spring on us!

The ACTORS *make to clear the stage again.*

FATHER. No, no! She's talking about me. I should be over there behind the doorway, ready to come in. Madame knows it. Here, let me take my place now.

He starts to go behind the three-fold, but the DIRECTOR *stops him.*

DIRECTOR. Wait a minute. We've got to respect the conditions of the theatre, see? Before you go back there. . . .

STEPDAUGHTER. Oh, let him go! I am dying to live this scene, I tell you. If he is ready, I am even more so! Let's do it!

DIRECTOR. [*Shouting.*] No! Wait! First you need to play that scene with that woman. We've got to get that scene down first. Can't you see that?

STEPDAUGHTER. Oh, for God's sake, she's only telling me what you already know: that my Mother's work is badly done again and the material is ruined, and that I'll have to cooperate if I want her to continue to help us in our poverty.

MADAME PACE. [*She has a crazy, self-conscious accent.*] Heah, heah, sah. Ah haf no desiah to seek pwofit or to take advantage.

DIRECTOR. [*Astounded.*] What? Is that the way she speaks?

The ACTORS *chuckle among themselves, and then burst into raucous laughter.*

STEPDAUGHTER. [*Also laughing.*] Yes, sir. She has her very own way of speaking. It's a mixture of everything. I admit, it is funny.

MADAME PACE. Ah, eet seem to me bad mahnners to laugh at me thees way. Ah speak the only way Ah know how, mistah.

DIRECTOR. Oh my, oh my! On the contrary, please, do talk like that. It produces just the right effect! I can't think of a better way to provide a bit of comic relief from the crudeness of the basic situation here. Please, go right ahead and speak that way. It's great!

STEPDAUGHTER. Great! Sure it is! To hear someone make certain propositions in such a language very nearly makes a joke of it. You can't help laughing as soon as you're told that "a sarteen ole genelmens" would like "to amooze himsowf" with you, isn't that right, madame?

MADAME PACE. Ole? Oh, ya, hee's ole, deerie, but awl the betteh fo you, caws eef you don lahk heem, at leas he breeng you weesdum.

MOTHER. [*She bursts forward to the astonishment and consternation of the* ACTORS *who had not been watching her. Now they try to restrain her, but not before she has yanked the wig from* MADAME PACE's *head and thrown it to the ground.*] You witch! You witch! Murderer! Oh, my daughter!

STEPDAUGHTER. [*Running to stop her.*] No, no, Mama, no! Please!

FATHER. [*Also running to her, simultaneously.*] Hey, hey! Behave yourself! Here, sit down. Take this chair.

MOTHER. Take her out of here!

STEPDAUGHTER. [*To the* DIRECTOR, *who also ran to the* MOTHER.] We can't do it with her here. We can't.

FATHER. We can't all be together, don't you see? She wasn't here when we met. Being together spoils it. It anticipates it all.

DIRECTOR. It doesn't matter. For the time being we're only trying to sketch it all in. Everything is useful to me.

Later I'll sort out the confusing elements and put it all to rights.

He goes to the MOTHER *and conducts her back to her chair.*

Come, come, ma'am. Be good and take your place here.

STEPDAUGHTER. [*Meanwhile she has returned to the scene, where she addresses* MADAME PACE.] Come on, then, madame.

MADAME PACE. [*Offended.*] Oh no, thenk you vary mooch. Ah do no theeng with your mahther present.

STEPDAUGHTER. Oh, the hell with it! Show in the "ole genelmens" so he can "amoose hisowf" with me!

Turning imperviously to face the crowd.

We've finally got to play this scene. Let's go! The scene!

She turns back to MADAME PACE.

You! You can go!

MADAME PACE. Oh, Ah'm gohne, Ah'm gohne, Ah moost soorly am gohne. . . .

She snatches up her wig from the ground and glares angrily at the guffawing AC- TORS, *and storms out the door in the center of the three-fold.*

STEPDAUGHTER. [*To the* FATHER.] And now, you enter! Don't bother to go behind the set. You needn't actually come through that door. Suppose you've already come in. Here: I am standing here, modestly, with my head hanging. . . . Now, do it! Speak! Say it! "Good afternoon, Miss. . . ."

DIRECTOR. [*He has already descended the steps off the stage.*] Oh, listen to her! Really, are you directing this thing or am I?

To the FATHER, *who is standing aside bewildered.*

Do what she asks. Yes, go upstage of her as if you had just entered.

[*The* FATHER *does so in a state of confusion. He appears pale but infused with the reality of his created life. He smiles from his position against the three-fold as if somewhat disoriented in the drama about to fall on him. The* ACTORS *rivet their attention on the scene as it unfolds. The* DIRECTOR *turns to the* PROMPTER.]

And you, make sure you get this down!

The Scene

FATHER. [*Coming forward with a new voice.*] Good afternoon, Miss.

STEPDAUGHTER. [*With a slight shudder.*] Good afternoon.

FATHER. [*He studies her, peering below her hat that nearly hides her face. He discovers that she is very young, and he exclaims to himself under his breath partly out of compassion for her and partly for fear that he was about to compromise himself.*] Ah! . . . but . . . this isn't the first time, is it? Not the first time you've come here?

STEPDAUGHTER. No sir.

FATHER. You've been here before?

She nods her head.

More than once?

He waits a moment for her response. Again he studies her face below the hat. He smiles.

Well, then, come on . . . there's no need to by shy, now. . . . Allow me to remove this hat.

STEPDAUGHTER. [*Abruptly so as to prevent him from doing so.*] No, sir. I'll take it off myself!

She does so and again shudders. To one side as a group apart, the MOTHER, *the* SON, *and the two* CHILDREN *watch the scene. The* MOTHER *is on edge, following every movement and every word those two perform with expressions varying among pain, disdain, anxiety and horror. From time to time she might hide her face or utter a groan.*

MOTHER. Oh, God!

FATHER. [*He pauses a moment with the sound of that groan, but then takes up the scene again in the same tone as before.*] Here. Give it to me. I'll put it up for you.

He takes the hat from her hands.

On such a beautiful little head as yours I should like to see a finer, a worthier hat. Would you help me select one from among these in madame's collection?

INGENUE. Hey, look out! Those are our hats, you know!

DIRECTOR. Quiet, for God's sake! Don't try being funny now! This is the scene!

To the STEPDAUGHTER.

Pick up where you left off, Miss.

STEPDAUGHTER. [*Still in the scene.*] No, thank you, sir.

FATHER. Come now, don't say no. Take one as a favor to me. I'd be offended otherwise. Look, there are some beauties here. It'll please the madame. That's why she put them on display here.

STEPDAUGHTER. No, sir. Really, I couldn't wear one of those.

FATHER. You mean you're worried about what they'll say when you get home wearing a new hat? Is that it? Well, forget it. You know what you can tell them? Eh?

STEPDAUGHTER. That's not the reason, sir. I couldn't wear one because I am . . . as you see . . . I'm surprised you didn't notice.

She shows him her black clothing.

FATHER. In mourning? Oh, I see! Yes. Please forgive me. I am truly sorry.

STEPDAUGHTER. [*Summoning up her courage and trying to overcome her disdain and nausea.*] Please, sir, it's all right. Not another word about it. I should thank you, rather than you taking pity on me. Forget what I told you, please. You see, I myself. . . .

She forces herself to smile and approach him.

I really must not think about being dressed this way.

DIRECTOR. [*To the* PROMPTER *and coming up onto the stage.*] Hold it. Don't write that down. Omit that last line.

Turning to the STEPDAUGHTER *and the* FATHER.

It's going very well.

Then to the FATHER *alone.*

Then, you embrace her just as we

discussed it before!

To the ACTORS.

It's a lovely scene, this little hat scene, don't you think?

STEPDAUGHTER. But the best is yet to come. Can't we go on?

DIRECTOR. One moment. [*To the* ACTORS *again.*] Now this, naturally, has to be played with a light touch. . . .

LEADING MAN. Yes, yes, a sort of nonchalance, don't you think?

LEADING LADY. Why, we'll do it marvelously! Here, let's give it a try, what do you say?

LEADING MAN. I was thinking, you know. . . . Here, I'll just go behind the flat to make my entrance.

He disappears behind the three fold.

DIRECTOR. [*To the* LEADING LADY.] All right then, look: the scene between you and Madame Pace is just now over, right? I'll get that dialogue down later. So now, you stand in the room alone and . . . but, where are you going?

LEADING LADY. Just a minute. I'm going to get my hat. . . .

She takes her hat from the clothes rack and puts it on.

DIRECTOR. Wonderful! Now, you stand just here, your head bent forward. Yes, yes, that's it!

STEPDAUGHTER. [*Amused.*] But, she's not even dressed in black!

LEADING LADY. I *will* be dressed in black, and much more smartly than you.

DIRECTOR. Be quiet, please! Stand aside and watch this. You might learn something.

He claps his hands.

All right, all right! From the top! Let's go!

He descends into the house to gain distance on the scene. The LEADING MAN *enters with the raffish, jaunty air of an aging gallant. These two* ACTORS *perform the scene in a manner totally different from the* CHARACTERS, *but in no way as a parody. Indeed, the scene seems cleaner, neater in its effects. Naturally, as the*

STEPDAUGHTER *and the* FATHER *listen to and watch the scene, they cannot recognize themselves at all, and they give expression to their surprise, astonishment, and chagrin in various ways: by smiling, making gestures, or even protesting aloud, as we shall see. From time to time we are also aware of the* PROMPTER *feeding the* ACTORS *their lines.*

LEADING MAN. "Good afternoon, Miss. . . ."

FATHER. No! Not like that!

The STEPDAUGHTER *bursts into laughter.*

DIRECTOR. Shut up, both of you! And, once and for all, will you please stifle that laughter of yours? How do you expect us to work?

STEPDAUGHTER. [*Coming forward to the edge of the stage.*] Forgive me, but I can't help it. The lady is standing there where she should be, but perfectly still. I tell you, if anyone came in and said "Good afternoon" the way he just did, I would burst into laughter as I just did.

FATHER. [*Also coming forward.*] Oh, yes, you see, the tone . . . that certain air. . . .

DIRECTOR. What are you talking about? What air, what tone? Please, stand aside and let me see the scene.

LEADING MAN. [*Now he also steps forward.*] Now, look here, if I'm supposed to play an older man who goes to one of those houses. . . .

DIRECTOR. I know, I know. Don't mind them, just go on, please! It's going very well.

He waits until the ACTORS *take their positions.*

All right, then. . . .

LEADING MAN. "Good afternoon, Miss."

LEADING LADY. "Good afternoon. . . ."

LEADING MAN. [*He makes the same gesture as the* FATHER *had done, lifting her chin to peer at her face under the hat brim, but giving distinct expression first to the compassion and then fear he had observed in the* FATHER.] "Ah . . . but . . . this isn't the first time, I hope. Not the first time you've come here?"

FATHER. [*He can't help correcting him.*] Not "I hope." "Is it?" "Is it?"

DIRECTOR. Say it as a question: "Is it?"

LEADING ACTOR. I heard him [*meaning the* PROMPTER] say "I hope."

DIRECTOR. Fine, fine! What's the difference? "I hope" or "Is it?" Go right on. But, look here, make it maybe just a little lighter. Here, let me show you what I mean. . . .

He runs up onto stage, goes behind the flat, and does the role from the entrance.

"Good afternoon, Miss."

LEADING LADY. "Good afternoon."

DIRECTOR. "Ah! . . . but . . . this isn't. . . ."

He turns to the LEADING MAN *asking him to notice the way in which he looks at the* LEADING LADY *under the brim of her hat.* You see . . . first surprise . . . then a sense of fear, compassion.

He picks up the role again.

". . . this isn't the first time, is it? Not the first time you've come here. . . ."

Again, he turns to the LEADING MAN.

Do I make myself clear? [*Then, to the* LEADING LADY.] Then, you say, "No, sir." [*Back to the* LEADING MAN.] What shall I say? As the French say, *souplesse*: a certain suppleness, eh?

He looks intently at the LEADING MAN *until he nods. Then, he leaves the stage again and the* ACTORS *take up their positions.*

LEADING LADY. "No, sir."

LEADING MAN. "You've been here before?"

DIRECTOR. No. Wait. First let her nod in response, right? "You've been here before?"

The LEADING LADY *raises her face somewhat, showing her eyes clenched shut in disgust.*

Now down!

The LEADING LADY *nods twice.*

STEPDAUGHTER. [*Scarcely able to restrain herself.*] Oh, God!

She slaps her hand over her mouth to stifle her laugh.

DIRECTOR. What is it?

STEPDAUGHTER. Nothing!

DIRECTOR. [*To the* LEADING MAN.] Your

line. Go on.

LEADING MAN. "More than once? Well, then, come on . . . there's no need to be shy, now. . . . Allow me to remove this hat."

The LEADING MAN *says this in such a way and with such a gesture, that the* STEPDAUGHTER *cannot restrain herself any longer. The laugh comes out between her fingers, and finally she gives up and gives vent to an open, raucous laugh.*

LEADING LADY. I have no intention of playing the clown for that woman, I tell you.

LEADING MAN. Neither do I. Let's forget it.

DIRECTOR. [*At the top of his voice.*] Stop that! Shut up!

STEPDAUGHTER. Oh . . . yes . . . forgive me. . . . Do forgive me!

DIRECTOR. You're an ill-bred brat, do you know that? What gall!

FATHER. Yes, sir, I know, yes, but forgive her. . . .

DIRECTOR. [*Jumping back onto the stage.*] What do you mean "forgive her?" She's insufferable.

FATHER. Yes, but believe me, all this seems so strange, so. . . .

DIRECTOR. Strange? What are you talking about? What's strange? Why?

FATHER. Understand, sir, I admire your actors. I do. Why, this gentleman and that lady, they certainly do know. . . . But, well, to put it bluntly, they are not us.

DIRECTOR. Of course not! What do you expect? They're actors!

FATHER. Exactly. Actors. And they do our roles well, both of them, but believe me, from our point of view, they are doing some other scene entirely. They are trying to do the same scene, but it just is not. It's not!

DIRECTOR. What do you mean, it's not the same? How's it different?

FATHER. Well . . . it's become theirs, you see. It's not ours any more.

DIRECTOR. Of course it's theirs! I told you that before.

FATHER. I understand, I know. . . .

DIRECTOR. Well then, stop going on and on about it. [*To the* ACTORS.] We'll simply have to rehearse by ourselves. Rehearsing with the playwright around can drive you crazy. They're never satisfied! [*He turns back to the* STEPDAUGHTER *and the* FATHER.] Come on, let's pick up the scene again with them, and let's see if you can keep from laughing.

STEPDAUGHTER. Oh, I won't laugh! I won't! Because this is the moment I've been waiting for. You can be sure I won't laugh.

DIRECTOR. All right, then: when you say "Forget what I told you . . . I really must not think about being dressed this way. . . ." [*To the* FATHER.] You must answer at once, "Yes, I see, I see," and then you ask. . . .

STEPDAUGHTER. What? What is this?

DIRECTOR. . . . why she is in mourning.

STEPDAUGHTER. But that's not right, sir! That's not what happened. When I said, "I really must not think about being dressed this way," do you know what he said? Do you? He said, "Well, in that case, let's just take off that little dress!" And within minutes, I stood naked before him.

DIRECTOR. Oh, great! Just great! That ought to bring down the house!

STEPDAUGHTER. But it's true! That's what happened!

DIRECTOR. Suppose it did! So what? For crying out loud, think about it a minute! We're in the theatre here. We can show what's true, sure, but only up to a certain point.

STEPDAUGHTER. Suppose you tell me what you'd rather do instead.

DIRECTOR. You'll see. Just give me a chance, all right?

STEPDAUGHTER. No! I won't stand for it. You want to take my disgust, all the cruel reasons that I am what I am, and create some sort of sentimental pastiche. I can see it now: he asks me why I am in mourning, and I reply, my eyes swimming in tears, that only two months ago my Daddy died, isn't that it? Oh, no, my dear sir. He has got to say what he really said: "Well, in that case, let's just take off that little dress!" And I, still mourning in my heart after just two months, I went there, behind that screen, and with these fingers, these fingers that still quiver with shame, I unbuttoned that dress, and then unhooked my bra. . . .

DIRECTOR. Come on, now! What are you telling me?

STEPDAUGHTER. [*Shouting.*] The truth! I'm telling you the truth!

DIRECTOR. All right. I know, I know. I don't deny it's the truth. And believe me, I understand your agony, your shame, and your horror. But please, you have to understand that this won't work on stage.

STEPDAUGHTER. Won't work? Well, in that case, thank you very much, I'm leaving!

DIRECTOR. But, don't you see? . . .

STEPDAUGHTER. I'm leaving! What *will* work on stage you two have already settled, back there in your office. I know that now! He wants to go right to the playing of his spiritual torment, but I want to play *my* drama. *My* drama, you understand!?

DIRECTOR. Oh, so that's it? You've finally said it: *your* drama! Well, it's not just yours, you know. It belongs to all of you. It's his [*indicating the* FATHER.] and hers [*the* MOTHER.]. We can't let one character come forward elbowing the others aside and take over the whole stage. The characters have to maintain a balance within the play's framework. Everything has to be playable. Sure, I know everyone has a life within that he or she wants to bring out. But the difficulty is that we have to measure it out and give each feeling, each emotion its right proportion. Selecting the right details, we can suggest the rest of the character's life within. Oh, it would be nice if each character could have a little monologue, or maybe a little

conference with the audience, in which everything boiling within could come spewing forth! Ah, beautiful! But, my dear, you mustn't get yourself all worked up. Really! It'd be in your best interests, because you'll create a bad impression if you give vent to all this rending fury, all this shame and disgust. After all, you yourself said this wasn't the first time. There had been others before him at Madame Pace's.

STEPDAUGHTER. [*She lowers her head. After a pause, she speaks quietly.*] That's true. But for me, all those others *were* him.

DIRECTOR. They were him? What do you mean?

STEPDAUGHTER. When someone falls into disgrace, the person responsible for the first miserable step is responsible for all those that come after. And for me, that person was him, *him*! Even before I was born, it was him. Look at him! You can see it's true!

DIRECTOR. Well and good! And do you suppose that he shrugs off the weight of that remorse? You know he does not. Give him a chance to play that.

STEPDAUGHTER. How? Tell me that! How can he "play" his "noble" remorse, all his "moral" torment, if you save him the horror of finding himself, one fine day, in the arms of a woman whose mourning dress he'd blithely asked her to take off? In the arms of that little girl he used to watch coming out of school every afternoon?

The MOTHER, *hearing these things, is overcome by a surge of uncontrollable anguish. Her suppressed groans finally give way in a plaintive cry. Everyone is moved. There is a long pause.*
Today you have us all to yourselves, just as we are, unknown to any audience. Tomorrow you may give whatever shape you like to our play. But do you want to see the real drama? Discover how it really was?

DIRECTOR. I couldn't ask for anything more. It'll give us that much more to choose from when we do the play.

STEPDAUGHTER. All right. Have the Mother enter.

MOTHER. [*She breaks out of her sobs and cries out.*] No, no! Don't let her do it! Don't let her!

DIRECTOR. But it is just so that we can see it, ma'am!

MOTHER. I can't do it. I just can't!

DIRECTOR. But why not, if it has all happened already?

MOTHER. No, it's happening now! It happens always! My suffering is not over, sir! I am present and alive every moment of my suffering, and it renews itself constantly. Have you ever heard a word from those two little ones? They can't talk, sir! They are tied to me in order to keep that suffering alive. But for themselves, they don't exist any more! And that other one [*Pointing to the STEP-DAUGHTER.*], she has fled, run away from me, and gotten lost. Yes, lost! If I see her now, here, it is only to keep the anguish alive, the anguish that I've endured even for her.

FATHER. The eternal moment. It is just as I explained to you, sir. She [*Speaking of the STEPDAUGHTER.*] is here in order to fix me once and for all in pillory, for that one fleeting, shameful moment of my life. She cannot give it up, and you, sir, you cannot save me from it.

DIRECTOR. I know. I didn't say I wouldn't play the scene. Why, it will form the nucleus of the first act, right up to the moment when she [*The MOTHER.*] enters and surprises you. . . .

FATHER. Yes, yes! Because that is my sentence, my condemnation. The suffering we've all endured culminates in that last scream of hers.

STEPDAUGHTER. It still echoes in my ears! It has driven me crazy. You can play me however you please, sir! It doesn't matter. I can even remain dressed, so long as my arms, yes just

my arms, remain naked. Because, see, standing like this. . . .

She embraces the FATHER, her head against his chest.

with my head like so and my arm up around his neck, I could see the pulse in the vein, here. That pulsing vein aroused in me such disgust, I forced myself to squint . . . like so, watching that vein while I lay my head on his chest, just like this! Cry out, Mama! Cry out just as you did then!

MOTHER. [*Rushing to separate them.*] No! No, my daughter! Don't!

She pulls them apart, and turns on the FATHER.

You brute! This is my daughter! Don't you see that this is my daughter!?

DIRECTOR. [*He steps back to the edge of the stage the moment the scream is heard and the ACTORS react in fear.*] Wonderful! Wonderful! And right at that moment, curtain! Curtain!

FATHER. [*Running to him.*] Exactly! Yes! Because that is just as it was, sir!

DIRECTOR. Yes. Right at this moment, down comes the curtain. Curtain!

Abruptly the curtain falls, leaving the FATHER and the DIRECTOR out in front of it.

What a damned fool! I call for the curtain, meaning that the act should end at this point, and he really brings it down!

He goes to the curtain and holds it open for the FATHER, saying:

But it's good! Very good! What an effect! This is just how it should end. Yes, I'll guarantee the first act, anyway.

He disappears with the FATHER.

Act 3

When the curtain re-opens, we see that the stage hands have struck the setting for

MADAME PACE's *back room and have set up a little garden fountain. The* ACTORS *are seated in a row on one side of the stage, the* CHARACTERS *on the other. The* DIRECTOR *is standing in the middle of the stage, his fist to this jaw as he ponders his plan of action.*

DIRECTOR. All right, let's take on the Second Act. Now, look, leave all this to me, as we agreed before. Everything is going to be fine.

STEPDAUGHTER. It opens when we enter his house [*She points to the* FATHER.] against the wishes of that one over there [*Referring to the* SON.]

DIRECTOR. Fine, fine, fine. Please, leave this to me!

STEPDAUGHTER. So long as you make his displeasure show.

MOTHER. For all the good it's done us. . . .

STEPDAUGHTER. What does that matter, so long as it adds to *his* remorse?

DIRECTOR. Look, I know all that! It stands out right at the beginning, I assure you. Now, let me work.

MOTHER. I want you to know that I tried every way I could think of. . . .

STEPDAUGHTER. . . . to placate me, to let me know that he didn't mean to be aloof. [*She turns to the* DIRECTOR.] Do as she says, because it's true! I'll enjoy it, you see, because the more she begs him, and tries to work her way into his heart, the more aloof he becomes. He's so distant, he is nearly absent!

DIRECTOR. Are we going to get on with the Second Act or not?

STEPDAUGHTER. I won't say another word. But listen, putting everything in the garden won't work no matter how much you want it to.

DIRECTOR. Why not?

STEPDAUGHTER. Because he [*The* SON.] always stays closed up in his room, all to himself. What's more, that whole episode with the boy, bewildered and lost as he was, took place in the house, as I told you.

DIRECTOR. Sure! But, you know we can't put signs out on an easel or change the set three or four times an act!

LEADING MAN. It used to be done. . . .

DIRECTOR. Yes, back in the days when audiences were like this little girl here.

LEADING LADY. Yes, and illusions were easier to create.

FATHER. Illusion! Please, don't use that word! It is too cruel!

DIRECTOR. What the devil do you mean by that?

FATHER. Yes, it's cruel! Surely you understand that!

DIRECTOR. Well, what are we supposed to say? We're simply talking about the illusion that we're about to create here on this stage, for the audience. . . .

LEADING MAN. . . . with our performance. . . .

DIRECTOR. . . . the illusion of a reality!

FATHER. I understand that, sir. But you do not seem to understand us. Forgive me, but, you see, what for you actors is simply a sort of game. . . .

LEADING LADY. What do you mean, game! We're not children! We're serious actors!

FATHER. I never said otherwise. I use the word "game" to refer to the artistic creation of just that illusion of reality you were talking about.

DIRECTOR. All right, then!

FATHER. Well, then, surely you can see that for us there is no reality outside of this illusion.

DIRECTOR. [*Stunned, looking around at his* ACTORS, *all of them equally baffled.*] What are you talking about?

FATHER. [*Eyeing them all with a faint smile.*] Of course! It has to be that way! What for you is an illusion to be shaped, to be played with, is for us our only reality.

He pauses, and approaches the DIRECTOR. And that is true not for just us, you know. Think about it!

He fixes the DIRECTOR *in the eye.* Can you tell me who you are?

DIRECTOR. [*Uneasy, half-smiling.*] What? Who am I? I am myself!

FATHER. And suppose I told you that

you're wrong, and that you are really me?

DIRECTOR. I'd tell you you're crazy!

The ACTORS *laugh.*

FATHER. And they're right to laugh, because now we're playing a game, a game that lets you tell me, just for the sake of the play, that that gentleman there [*The* LEADING MAN.], who is "him," must now be "me," who meanwhile am "myself," standing before you. There, you see I've trapped you.

The ACTORS *laugh again.*

DIRECTOR. But we've been through all that! Do we have to go over it again?

FATHER. No, no. That's not what I really wanted to say. Instead, I want you to step outside this game [*Glancing at the* LEADING LADY.] . . . this *art form* you practice here with these actors . . . and again I ask you, quite seriously, who are you?

DIRECTOR. [*He turns to the* ACTORS, *half amused, half irritated.*] Well, that takes nerve! He passes himself off as a character and has the gall to ask me who I am!

FATHER. A character, sir, can always ask a man who he is, because a character is a "somebody," with a life of his own and his own particular traits that make him who he is. But a man—not necessarily you, but a man in the general sense, you understand—cannot be anything but a "nobody."

DIRECTOR. Well, fine! But you are asking me, the Director. I am the Director!

FATHER. [*Quietly and humbly.*] Just to know if you really see yourself. Think how different you are from the way you once saw yourself, with all the illusions you carried then, just a few short years ago. Think how real they seemed, all those things within yourself and about yourself, things you took for reality. Now try to recall those illusions that mattered so much to you, that inspired such fervent belief in you. It's difficult,

isn't it? They're gone! Tell me, doesn't it make the ground quiver beneath your feet—I don't mean the boards of this stage, but the very earth! And consider, everything that now seems so important, all your present reality, will be tomorrow's illusion?

DIRECTOR. [*Confused by the speciousness of the argument.*] So? What are you trying to tell them?

FATHER. Oh, nothing. I'd just like you to recognize that while we [*Meaning the* CHARACTERS.] have no reality aside from this "illusion," your concrete and vivid reality of today is destined to be tomorrow's illusion.

DIRECTOR. [*Almost laughing in his face.*] Oh, wonderful! And now I suppose you're going to tell us that this play of yours is more real than I!

FATHER. [*With absolute seriousness.*] Of course!

DIRECTOR. Oh, really?

FATHER. I thought you understood that from the beginning.

DIRECTOR. More real than I?

FATHER. Certainly, if your reality changes from day to day. . . .

DIRECTOR. Why, of course it does! It changes all the time, just as it does for everyone.

FATHER. Not for us! Don't you see? That's the difference. Ours doesn't change, it can't change, it can't be other than it is, because it is fixed, set once and for all just as it is. It's awful! This immutable reality! It should make you shudder just to stand near us this way.

DIRECTOR. [*Rising up abruptly, suddenly struck by an idea.*] But I'd like to know when a character has ever jumped out of his part to make speeches, expound and explain himself the way you do. Can you tell me that? I've never heard the like!

FATHER. You've never seen it because authors usually hide the creative process. Whenever characters are alive, truly alive, before their author, he can do nothing but follow their words, their gestures, their acts as dictated to him. He has to let them be what they will be; if he doesn't, he'll be the worse for it. Any time a character is born, he acquires an independence even from his author, such that he can be imagined in situations the author never thought of, or can take on a significance the author never dreamt of.

DIRECTOR. Of course. I know that.

FATHER. Well then, why should you be surprised at us? Think what it must be like for a character to suffer the disgrace of being born alive to a playwright who then decided to deny him his life. Wouldn't you expect him to do just what we're doing with you? After all, believe me, we spent hours with him, trying to persuade him, push him, convince him. Sometimes I would talk to him, sometimes she would [the STEPDAUGHTER] and sometimes that poor Mother. . . .

STEPDAUGHTER. It's true. How many times I went to tempt him in the melancholy of his study at the hour of dusk when he'd have fallen into his overstuffed armchair too tired to rise and turn on the light. And so the shadows filtered into the room and we with them. Yes! We came to tempt him. . . .

She moves as if she were there in that study, yet annoyed by the presence of the ACTORS.

If only you would all go away and leave us alone! Mama there with that son, I with the little girl, and that boy over there, always by himself, and then I with him [*The* FATHER] and finally I alone, all by myself . . . in those shadows. . . .

She leaps up suddenly as if she had thrown herself into her vision, shining in the shadows.

Oh, my life! What scenes! What scenes we offered him! I, especially, because I tempted him more than any of the others!

FATHER. Oh, yes, and it could very well have been your fault that he denied us! That's right: you were pushy, insistent, and always out of control.

STEPDAUGHTER. Nonsense! That's how he wanted me to be!

She goes to the DIRECTOR *as if to speak in confidence.*

You know, I think it was his contempt for the decadence of the modern theatre, pandering as it does to public taste. . . .

DIRECTOR. Oh, good God! Do get to the point, people! We've got to get down to cases!

STEPDAUGHTER. Well, it seems to me you'll have enough "cases" on your hands without adding our entrance into his house. [*Indicating the* FATHER.] You yourself said that we can't put signs out on an easel or change the set every five minutes.

DIRECTOR. Exactly! We've got to group the scenes together into a single, close-knit action, not the way you'd have it, with the little boy coming home from school and moving among the shadows from room to room, hiding behind the doors, pondering over some scheme that . . . what did you say it did?

STEPDAUGHTER. Consumed him, consumed him completely.

DIRECTOR. All right, if you say so. And you say his eyes grew wider and wider, right?

STEPDAUGHTER. Yes, sir, just as you see him now.

DIRECTOR. Fine! And then, simultaneously, you want us also to see the little girl playing innocently in the garden. One in the house and the other in the garden. How is that supposed to be?

STEPDAUGHTER. Oh, yes, out in the sun! Happy! That was my only reward, to see her happiness, her joy out in the garden. There we were taken from the misery, the squalor of that horrible little room where we all slept together, and me with her. Just think of it, how awful to lay my contaminated body next to hers and have her hold me with those little, loving, innocent arms. Whenever she'd see me in the garden, she would run to me and take my hand. She wanted to show me, not the big flowers, but the "wee witto fwowers." She would rejoice in those.

So saying, she breaks into tears remembering the moments they shared in the garden. Her emotion affects everyone. The DIRECTOR *approaches her and speaks almost paternally.*

DIRECTOR. We'll create the garden, don't worry. We'll put all the scenes together in the garden.

He calls off-stage.

Hey, Sam, fly in that batten with the cypress trees right here in front of the fountain.

Two cypress trees fly in and settle on stage in front of the fountain, where a stage hand goes to work to nail their braces in place.

There, that should serve to give us an idea of the place. All right, Sam, now fly in the cyclorama.

SAM. [*Off-stage.*] What's that?

DIRECTOR. Give us a little sky. Fly in the blue backdrop just upstage of the fountain.

A stark white backdrop flies in.

No! Not the white one! I said sky! Oh, never mind. Let it be, I'll take care of it. Hey, George, are you on the board? Cut the lights, and give me some atmosphere, a little blue from the third electric, those scoops aimed on the backdrop. . . . Yes, that's it! Wonderful!

Indeed, he has created a mysterious, moonlit scene, which causes even the ACTORS *to speak softly and move gently. The* DIRECTOR *turns to the* STEPDAUGHTER.

There, how's that? Now, the boy doesn't have to hide behind doors, he can hide behind the trees here in the garden. But you know, it's not going to be easy to easy to find a little girl to act that scene with you and the

"wee witto fwowers."

He turns to the BOY.

Come here, you! Let's set the stage a bit.

The BOY *does not move.*

Come on!

He pulls him forward, trying to get him to hold his head upright, without success.

I tell you, these children can be a nuisance! Say, what's the matter with him? Why can't he at least say something?

He takes the BOY *and conducts him behind the cutout of a cypress tree.*

Come here! Let me see. Hide yourself just here, like that. Now, try to stick your head out just a little, to watch the goings-on. . . .

Turning to the STEPDAUGHTER.

Now, suppose the little girl were to surprise him out here spying that way. Wouldn't that cause him to say at least a word or two?

STEPDAUGHTER. Don't expect him to say anything so long as that one is here. [*Pointing at the* SON.] You'll have to send him away.

SON. [*Moving toward the little stairs off the stage.*] I'd be delighted. I couldn't ask for anything better.

DIRECTOR. No! Wait a minute! Where are you going?

The MOTHER *rises, overcome with anguish at the thought that he might be really leaving. Instinctively, she holds out her arms as if to detain him, but she does not move from her place. Meanwhile, the* SON *has arrived at the lip of the stage, where the* DIRECTOR *holds him back.*

SON. I have nothing to do with all this. Let me go. Please! Let me go!

DIRECTOR. What do you mean, nothing to do with this?

STEPDAUGHTER. [*Calmly and ironically.*] Go ahead. Let him go!

FATHER. He has to play that terrible scene in the garden with his Mother.

SON. I'm not playing any scene! I told you that from the beginning! Let me go!

STEPDAUGHTER. [*She runs to the* DIREC-

TOR, *who holds the* SON.] Please. Let him go.

She has the DIRECTOR *take his hand away and then turns to the* SON.

All right! Go on! Get out!

The SON *turns and steps out toward the stairs, but remains in place as if held there by some occult force. Then, with everyone's eyes following him, he moves slowly along the edge of the stage toward the other stairway. When he gets there, however, he is again held back. The* STEP-DAUGHTER, *who has watched him defiantly, now bursts into laughter.*

You see? He can't! He can't! He has to remain here, as if chained to this very stage. As for me, once what has to happen happens, I will run away. Yes, I will, because I hate him, because I cannot stand the sight of him. But so long as I am still here in his company, he can't leave. He'll have to remain with this fine Father of his and that Mother there without any of her other children. . . .

She turns to the MOTHER.

Come on, Mama! Come. . . .

She turns back to the DIRECTOR.

You see that? She stood up to hold him back. . . . Come, come, Mama. . . . Think, sir, what courage it takes to show your actors what she feels so deeply. See? She's ready to live her scene!

And in fact, the MOTHER *has approached the* SON *as soon as the* STEPDAUGHTER *finishes. She opens her arms to show she is ready.*

SON. But not me! I'm not ready! If I can't leave, all right, I'll stay, but I'm not playing any scene. Nothing!

FATHER. [*To the* DIRECTOR, *almost shivering.*] You can force him, sir. Force him!

SON. Nobody can force me!

FATHER. I can force you!

STEPDAUGHTER. Wait! First, the little girl has to go to the fountain.

She runs to the LITTLE GIRL *and crouches beside her, taking her face in her hands.*

My little darling! You're frightened, aren't you? Your beautiful big eyes are wondering where we are now. This is a stage, dearest, a stage. What's a stage? Don't you see, it's a place where they play at being serious. They make plays. And now they're making our play. Seriously, you understand? And you're in it, too. . . .

She takes her in her arms.

Oh, little darling, little darling, how awful the play is for you! How awful the things that have been thought up for you! The garden, the little fountain. . . . But they're all fake, you know! That's the trouble, dearest: it's all fake! Ah, maybe that's all the better for you: maybe you'd like a fake fountain better than a real one. All the better to play in, right? But I'm sorry, it's all a game for other people, not for us. For us it's real. It's a real, beautiful, large, green fountain reflecting all the surrounding bamboo in the shadows, their images broken by the little ducks swimming on the water. And you want to grab one of those little ducks. . . .

With a cry that throws fear into everyone.

No, Rosetta! No! No! Mama's not paying attention to you because of that scoundrel, her son there! As for me, I'm pre-occupied with a thousand devils in my head. . . . And that other one. . . .

She turns in her usual manner to the BOY.

What are you doing there like a beggar on the street? It'll be your fault, too, if that little girl drowns! You, you just stand there, as if to remind me that it was all my fault for bringing you all into this house!

She seizes his arm to force his hand out of his pocket.

What have you got there? What are you hiding? Let me see your hand!

She pulls the hand out revealing, to everybody's horror, that he is holding a gun. She looks at it for a moment as if with satisfaction, and then she says soberly.

Ah! Where did you get this thing?

Then, because the BOY *stands there in wide-eyed bewilderment, saying nothing.*
You little fool! I tell you, if I were you, I wouldn't kill myself; I'd kill one of those two, or both of them, the Father and the Son!

She throws him back behind the cypress tree. Then she goes back to the LITTLE GIRL *and places her in the fountain, laying her down inside so that she is completely hidden from view. Then she crouches down laying her head in her arms resting on the edge of the fountain.*

DIRECTOR. Beautiful!

He turns to SON.
And then, at that moment. . . .

SON. What do you mean, at that moment? It's not true! There never was a scene between her and me! Never! [*Indicating the* MOTHER.] Let her tell you how it was.

Meanwhile, the SECOND LADY *and the* JUVENILE LEAD *have detached themselves from the others. The one begins to study the* MOTHER *attentively, while the other follows every move of the* SON, *in order later to play the roles.*

MOTHER. It's true, sir! I went into his room. . . .

SON. You hear! In my room! Not in the garden!

DIRECTOR. It doesn't matter! I told you, we've got to combine scenes into a single act.

SON. [*Noticing the* JUVENILE LEAD.] What do you want?

JUVENILE LEAD. Nothing. I'm just observing you.

SON. [*To the* SECOND LADY.] And you! You, too! Studying your part?

DIRECTOR. Of course! Of course! You ought to be grateful for their attention.

SON. Oh, yes, thanks very much! Haven't you caught on to the fact that you can never do this play? We simply aren't in you, and so all your actors can do is to study us and ape us. How can anyone find life in a mirror that throws back fixed, frozen images of our expressions, grotesque grimaces we could never recognize?

FATHER. He's right! He's absolutely right! Tell them!

DIRECTOR. [*To the* JUVENILE LEAD *and the* SECOND LADY.] All right, move away from him.

SON. It doesn't matter. I'm out of all this.

DIRECTOR. Do be quiet, please! Let me hear your Mother. [*To her.*] Well, then, you say you entered his room?

MOTHER. Yes. I went into his room. I couldn't stand it any more. I had to unburden my heart of all that anguish that oppressed me. But as soon as he saw me enter. . . .

SON. . . . there was no scene, I tell you. I left. I ran out of that room so as not to make a scene. I never make scenes, you understand? Never!

MOTHER. That's true! He's right.

DIRECTOR. But, *now,* now we have to make that scene. We need that scene between her and him. It's indispensable!

MOTHER. I'm ready for it. If only you could find the way for me to talk with him, just for a moment, long enough to tell him all that is in my heart.

FATHER. [*He approaches the* SON *and speaks violently.*] Do it! Do it for your Mother! She's your Mother, for God's sake!

SON. I'm not doing anything!

FATHER. [*Grabbing him by the collar and shaking him.*] Damn it, you will obey! You will do it! Can't you hear her calling out for you? Do you have ice water running in your veins?

SON. [*Also seizing the* FATHER.] No! No! Will you stop once and for all?

General excitement. The MOTHER *is frightened. She tries to intervene.*

MOTHER. Please! Please, don't!

FATHER. [*Still holding fast.*] You will obey, do you hear me? You will!

SON. [*He struggles with the* FATHER *and finally throws him down at the head of one of the stairways. Everyone is horrified.*] What is this madness of yours?

Why must you parade your shame, our shame in front of everyone? I'll have nothing to do with it, I tell you, nothing! And that goes for our playwright, too. Obviously, he wanted nothing more to do with us and put us aside.

DIRECTOR. But, after all, you did come here!

SON. He did, not I! [*Referring to the* FATHER.]

DIRECTOR. But you are here as well.

SON. He is the one who wanted to come here. He dragged us along and then threw himself into concocting a plot with you back there in the office, throwing into it the shameful things that happened, which would be bad enough, but also things that never happened at all.

DIRECTOR. Well, at least tell me what *did* happen. Give me the real story! You came out of your room without saying anything, right?

SON. [*Trying to contain himself.*] Yes! I wanted to avoid a scene.

DIRECTOR. Yes, yes, go on! What did you do?

SON. [*Moving into the midst of the stage, everyone's attention riveted on him.*] Nothing. . . . As I was crossing the garden. . . . [*He stops. He is grim and distracted.*]

DIRECTOR. [*Fascinated by his reticence.*] Yes? Crossing the garden?

SON. [*Frustrated and anxious, he hides his face in his hands.*] Why are you forcing me to say it? It's horrible!

The MOTHER *is trembling. She utters a suppressed groan as she looks toward the fountain. The* DIRECTOR *notices her, then turns again to the* SON *with growing apprehension.*

DIRECTOR. The little girl?

SON. [*Looking straight forward into the auditorium.*] There, in the fountain. . . .

FATHER. [*Still on the ground, looking piteously toward the* MOTHER.] And, then she followed him, see?

DIRECTOR. [*To the* SON, *anxiously.*] And

then what did you do?

SON. I realized what had happened. I ran toward the fountain to rescue her . . . but all of a sudden, I stopped. There, behind the trees, I saw something that froze me in my tracks. The boy . . . the boy stood there stock still, with a look of madness in his eyes, staring at his little drowned sister in the fountain.

The STEPDAUGHTER *still resting against the fountain, begins to sob desperately like an echo to the* SON's *narrative. There is a pause.*

I started toward him, but then. . . .

From behind the cypress tree, where the BOY *is hidden, comes the resounding report of the revolver. The* MOTHER *cries out. General pandemonium erupts. Everyone runs to find out what happened.*

MOTHER. My son! My son! Help! Help me!

The DIRECTOR *tries to force his way into the crowd. Meanwhile the body of the* BOY *is carried off behind the backdrop.*

DIRECTOR. Is he wounded? Is he really wounded?

With the exception of the DIRECTOR *and the* FATHER, *who remains on the floor, everyone rushes off behind the backdrop. Their hushed and anguished voices can be heard. Then, one by one, the* ACTORS *return to the stage.*

THE LEADING LADY. [*Coming on from the right, weeping.*] He's dead! That poor boy is dead! What is happening?

THE LEADING MAN. [*Re-entering from the left, laughing.*] What do you mean, dead? It's all pretense! Pretense! Don't believe it!

ACTORS ON THE RIGHT. What do you mean, pretense? It's reality. It's true! He's dead!

ACTORS ON THE LEFT. No! It's pretense, pretense!

FATHER. [*Jumping to his feet.*] Pretense?! This is reality, I tell you, reality!

And he, too, disappears behind the backdrop.

DIRECTOR. Reality? Pretense? Ah, go to hell, the whole lot of you. Hey, George! Give us some light down here, okay? Light! Light!

Suddenly, the stage and the theatre house are flooded in a blazing white light. The DIRECTOR *heaves a sigh as if he had been liberated from a nightmare. Everyone stares about himself with suspicion and fear in the eyes.*

Nothing like this has ever happened to me! I've lost a whole day's work! [*He looks at his watch.*] Go on. Get out of here, all of you. Go! It's too late to get back into rehearsal. We'll pick up again this evening.

Quickly, the ACTORS *empty the stage.*

Hey, George! Cut the lights!

He has scarcely said that when the whole theatre is plunged into pitch blackness.

Oh, for God's sake! Give me a little something so I can see my way out of here.

As if by mistake, a greenish light comes up behind the backdrop projecting against the drop the oversized images of the CHARAC-TERS *without the* BOY *or the* LITTLE GIRL. *Seeing them, the* DIRECTOR *rushes from the stage in terror. After a moment, the* STEPDAUGHTER's *shadow abruptly shrinks and leaves the tableau as she steps forward away from the source of light and exits. Slowly the* MOTHER's *shadow turns to the* SON, *her arms outstretched toward him. The* STEP-DAUGHTER *re-enters, now in front of the drop. She runs to one of the little stairways. Part way down, she stops and looks back at the frozen silhouette. She lets out a strident laugh, runs down the stairs and up the aisle, where she stops one more time to laugh at the three gigantic characters who seem fixed in an eternal tableau. She disappears out the back of the house. Again, from the foyer, we hear her laughter. After another moment, the light fades on the tableau. Then, the lights gradually come up on stage. It now looks much as it did at the outset of the play.*)

Orphée

Jean Cocteau

Clement Eugène Jean Maurice Cocteau was certainly the most active member of the French avant-garde during the first half of the twentieth century, a man whose aesthetic creed, "Surprise me" (adopted from Diaghilev), was indeed the basis of his life and a key to any understanding of his work. Cocteau was active in virtually every area of art, and thus did not make the sustained contribution to the theater that he might otherwise have made, but the work that he did was the major link between Jarry's pioneering efforts and the fully developed theater of the absurd in the middle part of the century. Cocteau was born at Maisons-Laffitte, a suburb of Paris, on July 5, 1889, the son of well-to-do middle-class parents. Following the death of his father, Jean and his brother and sister were raised by their mother in Paris, and Jean attended the Lycée Condorcet. As early as 1909, Cocteau published a volume of poems that attracted some attention, and he was soon caught up in the swirl of Parisian artistic life. Although physically unsuited for combat, he bluffed his way into a series of adventures on the fighting front during World War I, but before the war had ended he became involved in writing some dialogue for Diaghilev's 1917 ballet, *Parade*, an event of extraordinary notoriety that influenced the avant-garde theater into the 1920s.

It is not practical to trace here Cocteau's extensive involvement with avant-garde artists and works during the ensuing decades. He maintained an acquaintanceship with virtually every artist of note in Paris, and was himself active in music, painting, dance, poetry, and criticism as well as in the theater. His major plays include *The Marriage on the Eiffel Tower* (1921), *The Infernal Machine* (a modern version of the Oedipus legend, 1934), *Intimate Relations* (1938), and *The Eagle Has Two Heads* (1946). In his later years, Cocteau became interested in motion pictures, and adapted several of his plays into successful films. He was elected to the Académie Française in 1955, and died of a heart attack at his country home at Milly-la-Forêt on October 11, 1963.

Orphée has been Cocteau's most successful work for the theatre; since its original production at the Théâtre des Arts in Paris on June 15, 1926 (when it enjoyed a two-week run), it has been widely produced throughout the world, especially at colleges and in avant-garde theaters. The play well illustrates Cocteau's goals in art, "magic, scandal, spectacle"; although it is no longer scandalous in its content, its form, more than half a century after that original production, is still sufficiently unusual to excite attention for its own sake; the play's use of magic and spectacle is the most notable feature that has attracted the continuing attention of producers and directors. Written during the heyday of surrealism, *Orphée* can best be under-stood as a theatrical manifestation of the surrealistic impulse evident in the painting of such artists as Dali, although Cocteau was in disagreement with certain of the surrealists at the time he wrote it. Surrealism attempts to objectify in a painting or on the stage the creative, subconscious mind, freely associating in order to bring into consciousness what, according to Freudian theory, would ordinarily be buried in the mind. The surrealists believed that the creative artist was peculiarly equipped by his talent and sensitivity to express such impulses, and a Daliesque landscape thus displayed wild distortions of reality that laid bare the artist's subconscious attitudes toward that reality. Similarly, *Orphée*, although loosely built around the ancient myth of Orpheus and Eurydice, is in fact a stream of theatrical images evoked in the playwright's imagination by his reaction to this myth. It celebrates the mystery of artistic creation itself, satirizing and at the same time examining the artist's place in society and what adjustments the artist might reasonably make to that society.

Hence, the play is not to be seen as a logically concatenated series of events in the usual sense of a plot. Such plot as exists is a rather vapid retelling of the Orpheus legend, just as the characters are inconsistent and hollow when measured by traditional standards. Rather, the play moves swiftly through a series of events strung loosely around this legend, with each event constituting a theatrical surprise (a chair is removed from under an actor, and he remains suspended in midair) and yet a kind of surrealistic logic—Eurydice immediately perceives (correctly) that Heurtebise is an emissary from the hereafter. A technique of this sort is very difficult to maintain for any extended period of time; Cocteau is metaphorically correct in maintaining in his prologue that "we are playing at a great height, and without a safety-net." Throughout the relatively short playing time of *Orphée*, he has achieved a remarkable level of sustained surprise that rivets the attention of the playgoer and releases his own subconscious responses in a most successful fashion. One may note that Cocteau is more clever than he is philosophically complex, without thereby denigrating his considerable theatrical achievement in *Orphée*.

One of Cocteau's chief contributions to twentieth-century dramatic theory is his enunciation of the concept of "poetry of the theatre." Whereas the classical theater had regularly made use of poetic language as the normative form of theatrical dialogue, it was Cocteau's perception that this was merely poetry *in* the theater—a result that might be achieved any time that a poet's words were spoken aloud. Poetry *of* the theatre, on the other hand, was the evocation of meaning and mood by the poetic juxtaposition of all theatrical elements, so that scenery, costumes, dialogue, movement, and the rest might each contribute meaningfully to a theatrical "poem" of genuine artistic merit. The great classical dramas had always done this, Cocteau maintained, but the modern theater had thrown out such poetic use of theatrical elements along with romanticism's poetic language. Realism, which might thus aspire to poetry of the theater despite its prose language, had degenerated into the prosaic and the dull. Obviously other nineteenth- and twentieth-century play-wrights before Cocteau had achieved what Cocteau meant by poetry of the theatre, but none had described what they were doing so succinctly. Certainly Cocteau's felicitous phrase describes aptly what he was doing in *Orphée*, for scenery, proper-ties, and stage illusions combine with prose dialogue to create a theatrical impact far greater than the sum of its parts. Just as the reader of poetry must open himself to the imagistic and emotional flow of the poem in order fully to appreciate it, so the viewer of *Orphée* must be attuned to its emotional impact rather than to analyzing its plot and characters in traditional terms.

As with many avant-gardists, Cocteau liked to shock his audience as one form of "surprise." Thus, the first letters of the words tapped out by the horse form, in French, the same word that had shocked all Paris when Jarry used it (though slightly distorted) in *King Ubu*. The French sentence, "Madame Eurydice reviendra des enfers," may be translated literally as "Madame Eurydice will return from hell," but certainly much of the theatrical impact is lost in such a translation. Cocteau's own lifestyle created some scandal in 1920s Paris as well, thus adding a measure of piquancy to the idea of attending one of his plays. His homosexual preferences were openly flaunted, and during this period he was smoking some ten pipes of opium per day (a habit he later overcame after taking a cure at a sanitorium).

Cocteau frequently returned to themes and ideas that especially appealed to him. The Orpheus legend fascinated him throughout his creative life, perhaps because he saw in it the prototype of the creative artist and the problem of the artist's adjustment to society. He reworked the story in several different forms, most notably in a 1950 film that was an adaptation of the present play but that enlarged upon certain of the characters and themes. Heurtebise is another instance of a recurring entity, in this case a character who often appeared as a guardian angel for the inspiration-struck poet. Cocteau insisted that the character's strange name (literally, "break-wind") came to him in a burst of inspiration while riding on an elevator. He found it on the manufacturer's name plate, although when he later returned to the same elevator, the plate read "Otis." This sort of apparent preciosity has led some critics to suggest that the jack-of-all-trades is, in this case, master of none, that Cocteau's cleverness is in fact shallow. Performance experience strongly suggests, however, that audiences do indeed respond to the subconscious appeal of Cocteau's juxtaposed images, that Cocteau's cleverness at least in this case works out effectively in a stage production that is genuinely impressive.

If Cocteau's play is not a masterpiece, it is very nearly one. Through several decades when one avant-garde was continually replacing another, Cocteau remained among the foremost experimentalists, restlessly seeking new dramatic forms that would finally "express the inexpressible" as the earlier symbolists had sought to do. Always a figure of controversy himself, Cocteau lived to see the absurdity of post–World War II Europe expressed in even greater controversy in the theater of the absurd. Cocteau formed the most important experimental link between the inspired nonsense of Jarry and the fully developed philosophy and aesthetic of the midcentury absurdists.

Orphée
A Tragedy in One Act and an Interval

Translated by Carl Wildman

Characters
Orphée (Orpheus), a poet
Eurydice, his wife
Heurtebise, a glazier
The Horse
Death
Azrael, experienced assistant to Death
Raphael, novice assistant to Death
Commissioner of Police
The Scrivener
Voice of the Postman

Notes on Costume (by Cocteau):

The costumes in fashion at the time of the performance should be adopted. ORPHÉE and EURYDICE are in very inconspicuous country clothes.

HEURTEBISE wears pale blue workman's overalls with a dark muffler round his neck and white bathing-shoes. He is bronzed and hatless. He never leaves off his glazier's apparatus (window-panes).

The COMMISSIONER OF POLICE and the SCRIVENER wear black frock-coats, panamas, goatees, and buttoned boots.

DEATH is a very beautiful young woman in a bright pink evening dress and fur cloak. Her hair, frock, cloak, shoes, gestures, and gait are in the latest fashion. She has large blue eyes painted on a domino. Her nurse's tunic should also be of great elegance.

Her assistants wear the uniform, linen masks, and rubber gloves of operating surgeons.

Notes on Scenery (by Cocteau):

Thrace. A room in Orphée's villa. It is a strange room rather like the room of a conjuror. In spite of the April-blue sky and the clear light, one suspects that it is surrounded by mysterious forces. Even familiar objects have a suspicious air.

First of all, in a box in the form of a niche, well in the center, there lives a white horse, whose legs are very much like those of a man. On the right of the horse is another little niche in which an empty pedestal stands framed by laurel. On the extreme right a door which opens on to the garden; when the door is open, the leaf hides the pedestal. On the left of the horse an earthenware wash-basin. On the extreme left a French window, pushed half outwards—it looks on to the terrace which surrounds the villa.

In the foreground in the right wall is a very large mirror; in the background a bookcase. In the middle of the left wall a door opening into Eurydice's room. A sloping ceiling closes in the room like a box.

The room is furnished with two tables and three white chairs. On the right a writing-table and one of the chairs.

On the left of the stage, the second table which is covered with a cloth reaching to the floor, and thereon fruits, plates, a decanter, and glasses, like the cardboard objects of jugglers. One chair stands squarely behind this table, and one near by on the right.

A chair cannot be added or taken away, nor the openings distributed otherwise, for this is a *practical* set, in which the smallest detail plays its part like the apparatus in an acrobatic number.

Apart from the sky-blue and the pad of dark red velvet that borders the top of the little door of the box dissimulating the middle of the horse's body—there is no color.

The scenery should recall the sham aeroplanes and ships of certain photographers.

After all, there is that same harmony, made of harsh simplicity, between the setting, characters, and events as between model and painted canvas in the plain *camaïeu* style of card portraits.

Notes on Producing (by Cocteau):

The mirror allows people to enter and leave the stage by an opening into the wings at the height of the frame. The opening is hidden by a glistening panel.

The bookcase should have one real pigeon-hole in which a real book is slipped. At the top of the bookcase should be a slot from which a piece of paper can be taken.

The pedestal holds an actor kneeling on a cushion so tnat his head appears in the niche.

The horse is the front of a horse; a horse's head with very curved neck, on a man in tights. The door of the box hides the upper part of the legs and the breast.

A black curtain on a rod can close the niche.

The wash-basin is a sham.

When HEURTEBISE pretends he is working, he first frees the view of the window by carrying up to the wall on the left the table which is laid. Then, at the order ("Get up on this chair") he takes the chair which was behind the table and puts it in the frame of the French window. He puts his left foot on it and his right foot on a stool hidden behind the door. He lifts his hands up to the panes. A stage-hand holds him by an unseen belt from which a ring projects under his glazier's apparatus. When ORPHÉE removes the chair, he flies. This very simple arrangement, discovered by Pitoëff, is extraordinarily effective.

The glazier's apparatus of HEURTEBISE supports panes of various kinds. His head stands out against some mica. The panes behind him are of a glistening material which sends out gleams at all angles.

In the wings, near the audience, an electric machine with a deep roar. (A vacuum cleaner can be used.)

When DEATH goes into Eurydice's room, she removes her bandage. A stage-hand gives her the dove which she takes by the legs so that its wings beat. She reappears. RAPHAEL cuts the thread. She disappears behind the scenery to the right of the window, where the dove is taken from her hands; she recoils on the terrace with a gesture as if having freed the dove into the air. (Note: "It is not necessary to say that there is no symbol in the play. Nothing but simple language, *acted poetry*. This dove is a commonplace.")

After the remark of HEURTEBISE: "I will bring him back, I promise you," the light lowers and becomes milky. Once this new aquarium light is fixed, DEATH enters. Her arm appears through the mirror first and the left arms of the assistants become the assistants themselves.

On leaving, DEATH hurries, freezes a

moment, her hand extended in front of the mirror. Her assistants do the same.

When the curtain for the interval falls, wait a while to see if the spectators applaud before ringing up again, so that this card-trick in the abstract does not have the appearance of a false maneuver.

The disappearance of EURYDICE. In a theater without a trap, the light is lowered on a dimmer. EURYDICE rises with a gesture of horror and slips slowly behind the table. When darkness is complete, the end of some black material is passed to ORPHÉE who stands by the door of the bedroom. He stretches the material to the table and EURYDICE escapes behind it. The material is pulled sharply into the wings and the lights are thrown on full. The whole maneuver takes place in the winking of an eye. Even in a theater furnished with a trap, EURYDICE should disappear slowly and the light be lowered with her.

Three Musicians suffice for the arrival of the Bacchantes. One man: drums and cymbals. Another: jazz-set. A third: kettle-drums. The rhythms should torture like the tom-tom of savages.

After the third "Ladies!" of ORPHÉE, the drums make a terrible noise. Windows are heard breaking, something heavy falls, and a chair goes over. A small lamp, hidden on the left in the footlights, comes on. It is the lighting given to the crimes in the Musée Grévin. On the ground near the cloth the head is seen against the white background of the overturned chair. The chair is knocked over and the head put into place during the blackout which blinds the spectators. The actor lies in the wings and speaks from the bedroom.

While the police are knocking on the door and the angel is picking up the head, putting it on the pedestal, and opening the door, full light is given and the actor substitutes his head for the mask. While the COMMISSIONER and the SCRIVENER are going out, the actor withdraws and replaces the mask.

Prologue

The actor who plays the part of ORPHÉE *appears before the curtain.*

Ladies and gentlemen, this prologue is not by the author and I expect he would be surprised to hear it. The tragedy in which we are going to act develops on very delicate lines. I will ask you, therefore, if you are not satisfied with our work, to wait till the end before you express your feelings. Here is the reason for my request: we are playing at a great height, and without a safety-net. The slightest untimely noise and the lives of my comrades and my own may be imperiled.

Scene 1

ORPHÉE *behind the table on the right, consulting a spiritualist alphabet.* EURYDICE *seated left, near the table which is laid.*

EURYDICE. Can I move?

ORPHÉE. One moment.

EURYDICE. He's stopped tapping.

ORPHÉE. Sometimes he leaves a long interval between the first letter and the others.

EURYDICE. They can be guessed!

ORPHÉE. Please, please!

EURYDICE. You must admit, it's always the same word.

ORPHÉE. H, H. . . . Carry on, horse. Go on, quick, after the letter H . . . I'm listening to you.

EURYDICE. What patience! You have no mind, but your horse has—you think.

ORPHÉE. I'm listening. Now, horse! H, H, after H. [*The* HORSE *moves.*] You're moving, you're going to speak. Speak, horse! Dictate the letter after H. [*The* HORSE *strikes with its hoof.* ORPHÉE *counts.*] A, B, C, D, E, is it E?. [*The* HORSE *nods its head.*]

EURYDICE. Of course.

ORPHÉE. [*Furious.*] Sh! [*The* HORSE *taps,*] A, B, C, D, E, F, G, H, I, J, K, L—L. A, B, C, D, E, F, G, H, I, J, K, L—L. [*To* EURYDICE.] You're not to laugh. L, L, can it be L? H, E, L, L, hell? I can't have counted right. Horse! Is it really the letter L? If it is, tap once, and twice if it isn't. [*The* HORSE *taps once.*]

EURYDICE. You needn't insist.

ORPHÉE. Look here, I ask you as a favor to keep quiet. Nothing disturbs this horse so much as incredulous people. Go to your room, or keep quiet.

EURYDICE. I won't open my mouth again.

ORPHÉE. So much the better. [*To the* HORSE.] Hell, hell . . . and after hell? H, E, L, L, hell. I'm listening. Speak. Speak to me, horse. Horse! Come along, don't be afraid. After the letter L? [*The* HORSE *taps* ORPHÉE *counts.*] A, B, C, D, E, F, G, H, I, J, K, L, M, N, O—O. The letter O, my dear! H, E, L, L, O, hello. It was hello! Is that all? Is it just hello? [*The* HORSE *nods its head.*] Just think of that. You see, Eurydice! I might have believed you with your wrong mind, I might have been weak enough to yield and be convinced. . . . Just "Hello," that's amazing!

EURYDICE. Why?

ORPHÉE. What do you mean, why?

EURYDICE. Why amazing? This hello doesn't mean anything.

ORPHÉE. This horse dictated to me last week one of the most moving sentences in the world. . . .

EURYDICE. Oh!

ORPHÉE. . . . dictated one of the most moving sentences in the world. I'll work it out and I shall transfigure poetry. I am immortalizing my horse, and you're surprised to hear him greet me. That "hello" is a masterpiece of tact. And I who thought. . . . [*He puts his arms round the* HORSE's *neck.*]

EURYDICE. Listen, Orphée, my love; don't scold me. Be just! Since that famous sentence you've obtained one word and one word only, and this word isn't really poetic.

ORPHÉE. Do we know what is poetic and what is not poetic?

EURYDICE. Aglaonice used to do table-turning and her table always answered with that word.

ORPHÉE. That's it! Drag that person into our business, as a last straw. I've told you already, I don't want to hear any more of her—a woman who nearly led you astray, a woman who drin! takes tigers out for exercise, turns the heads of our wives, and prevents girls from marrying.

EURYDICE. But that is the cult of the moon.

ORPHÉE. Good! I can leave it to you to defend her. Return to the Bacchantes since their customs give you pleasure.

EURYDICE. I'm just teasing. You know very well that it's only you I love, and you had but to give a sign to make me leave that circle.

ORPHÉE. What a circle too! I shall never forget the tone in which Aglaonice said to me: "Take her, since she accepts. Stupid women adore artists, but—he who laughs last, laughs longest."

EURYDICE. Ugh! That made my blood run cold.

ORPHÉE. If ever I see her again! [*He strikes the inkwell on the table.*]

EURYDICE. Orphée, my poet. . . . Look how irritable you are ever since this horse business of yours. Before, you would laugh, kiss, and fondle me, you had a splendid situation, fame and fortune were yours. You would write poems which were snatched from hand to hand, and which all

Thrace knew by heart. You would sing the praises of the sun, you were its high priest. But the horse has put an end to all that. Now we live in the country, you have given up your position and you refuse to write. Your life is passed in petting the horse, in questioning the horse, in hoping that the horse will answer you. That's not being serious.

ORPHÉE. Not serious? My life, like game, was beginning to get high, and, on the turn, was beginning to stink of success and death. The sun and the moon are all the same to me. There remains night. But not the night of others! My night. This horse plunges into my night and reappears like a diver. He brings back sentences. Don't you feel that the least of these sentences is more remarkable than all the poems? I would give my complete works for one of those little sentences in which I listen to myself as you listen to the sea in a shell. Not serious? But what can you want, my dear? I am discovering a new world, I am living again, I am stalking the unknown.

EURYDICE. You are going to quote me again the famous sentence?

ORPHÉE. [*Gravely.*] Yes. [*He goes toward the* HORSE *and recites.*] "Orphée hunts Eurydice's lost life."

EURYDICE. That sentence doesn't mean anything.

ORPHÉE. It is indeed a question of meaning. Listen carefully to this sentence, listen to the mystery of it. Eurydice alone might be anybody and so might Orphée, but it is a Eurydice whose lost life Orphée would hunt! "Orphée hunts—" that exciting "hunts"—"Orphée hunts Eurydice's—" mark the possessive? and the close: "Eurydice's lost life." You ought to be pleased I am speaking about you.

EURYDICE. It's not you who are speaking of me. It's the horse. [*Pointing.*]

ORPHÉE. Neither he, nor I, nor anyone else. What do we know? Who is speaking? We are knocking against each other in the dark; we are up to our necks in the supernatural. We are playing hide-and-seek with the gods. We know nothing, absolutely nothing. "Orphée hunts Eurydice's lost life"—that's not a sentence—it is a poem, a poem of vision, a flower deep-rooted in death.

EURYDICE. And do you hope to convince the world? to make everyone admit that poetry consists in writing a sentence? to make a success with your horse's sentence?

ORPHÉE. It's not a question of success, nor of the horse, nor of convincing the world. Besides, I no longer stand alone.

EURYDICE. Don't talk to me about your public. Four or five heartless young hooligans, who think you're an anarchist, and a dozen fools who are trying to attract attention.

ORPHÉE. I shall have a better following. I hope one day to charm even the beasts of the field.

EURYDICE. If you despise success, why send this sentence to the Thracian competition? Why attach such importance to winning the prize?

ORPHÉE. We must throw a bombshell and make a sensation. We must have a storm to clear the air. We are suffocating, we can no longer breathe.

EURYDICE. We were so peaceful.

ORPHÉE. Too peaceful.

EURYDICE. You used to love me.

ORPHÉE. I do love you.

EURYDICE. You love the horse. I take second place.

ORPHÉE. Don't be stupid. There's no connection. [*He kisses* EURYDICE *absent-mindedly and goes to the* HORSE.] That's so, isn't it, old boy? Isn't it, my dear old brother, eh? Does he love his friend? Piece of sugar? Then kiss me. No, better than that. There . . . there . . . isn't he just fine! There! [*He takes some sugar out of his pocket and gives it to the* HORSE.] That's right.

EURYDICE. I don't count any more. If I were dead you wouldn't notice it.

ORPHÉE. Without noticing it, we *were* dead.

EURYDICE. Come near me.

ORPHÉE. Sorry, I must be going out. I'm going into the town so as to have everything in order for the competition. Tomorrow's the last day. I haven't a minute to lose.

EURYDICE. [*Bursting out.*] Orphée! my Orphee! . . .

ORPHÉE. You see this empty pedestal. Only a bust worthy of me shall be put there.

EURYDICE. They will throw stones at you.

ORPHÉE. I shall make my bust with them.

EURYDICE. Beware of the Bacchantes.

ORPHÉE. I'm not aware of their existence.

EURYDICE. They do exist, and they are liked. I know their ways. Aglaonice hates you. She is going to take part in the competition.

ORPHÉE. Oh! that woman! that woman!

EURYDICE. Be just . . . she has ability.

ORPHÉE. What?

EURYDICE. Of a fearful kind, of course. But, from a certain angle and on a certain plane, she has ability. She creates fine images.

ORPHÉE. Listen to that. *From a certain angle . . . on a certain plane. . . .* Did you learn that way of speaking from the Bacchantes? Then, on a certain plane her images please you. From a certain angle you approve of my mortal enemies. . . . And yet you insist that you love me. Very well then, by that angle and by that plane I declare that I have had enough of it; that I am persecuted, and this horse is the only one who understands me. [*He strikes his fist on the table.*]

EURYDICE. You needn't break everything.

ORPHÉE. Break everything! That's the limit! Madam breaks a window-pane a day, and now it's I who break every-

thing.

EURYDICE. To begin with. . . .

ORPHÉE. [*Walking up and down.*] I know what you're going to say. You're going to say that you haven't broken a pane today.

EURYDICE. But. . . .

ORPHÉE. Very well, go on and break, break it, break the window-pane.

EURYDICE. How can you get into such a state!

ORPHÉE. See how sly. . . . You're not breaking a window-pane because I am going out.

EURYDICE. [*Sharply.*] What do you mean to insinuate?

ORPHÉE. Do you think I am blind? You break a window-pane every day so that the glazier will come up.

EURYDICE. Very well then, I do. I break a window-pane so that the glazier will come up. He's a good fellow, and he listens to me. He admires you.

ORPHÉE. Too nice.

EURYDICE. And when you are questioning the horse and leave me all alone, I break a pane. You're not jealous, I suppose?

ORPHÉE. Jealous, I? Jealous of a boy-glazier? Why not of Aglaonice too! Upon my word! Look here, since you refuse to break a pane, I will break one. That'll soothe me. [*He breaks a pane.*] Glazier! Glazier! Glazier! [*Is heard.*] Hi! glazier! He's coming up. Jealous?

Scene 2

HEURTEBISE *appears on the balcony. The sun beats on his window-panes. He enters, bends a knee, and crosses his hands over his heart.*

HEURTEBISE. Good day, Ladies and Gentlemen.

ORPHÉE. Good day, my friend. it was I, *I* who broke this pane. Put it in. I'm

going. [*To* EURYDICE.] My dear, you
will superintend the work. [*To the*
HORSE.] Does he love his poet? [*He
embraces him.*] Till this evening. [*He
goes out.*]

Scene 3

EURYDICE. You see. I'm not inventing
anything.

HEURTEBISE. It's unheard of.

EURYDICE. You understand me.

HEURTEBISE. Poor lady.

EURYDICE. Since that horse followed
him in the street, and he brought it
home with him, since it has lived
here, and they talk together. . . .

HEURTEBISE. The horse has spoken to
him again?

EURYDICE. It said "hello" to him.

HEURTEBISE. It knows how to take him.

EURYDICE. In short, for a month now,
our life has been a torture.

HEURTEBISE. Surely you can't be jealous
of a horse!

EURYDICE. I would rather know he had
a mistress.

HEURTEBISE. Do you mean that? . . .

EURYDICE. Without you and your
friendship, I should have gone mad
by now.

HEURTEBISE. Poor Eurydice.

EURYDICE. [*Looking at herself in the mirror
and smiling.*] Just think, I have a faint
ray of hope. He has realized I break
a window-pane every day, and, instead of saying I break a piece of
glass to bring me luck, I told him I
break it so that you come up to see
me.

HEURTEBISE. I should have thought. . . .

EURYDICE. But listen. He made a scene,
and he broke the pane. I believe he's
still jealous.

HEURTEBISE. How you love him. . . .

EURYDICE. The more he ill-treats me
the more I love him. I already had

an idea that he might be jealous of
Aglaonice.

HEURTEBISE. Of Aglaonice?

EURYDICE. He detests everything to do
with my old circle. That is why I fear
we may be committing a terrible indiscretion. Speak softly. I'm always
afraid the horse may be listening to
me. [*They tiptoe up to the niche.*]

HEURTEBISE. He's asleep. [*They return
downstage.*]

EURYDICE. Have you seen Aglaonice?

HEURTEBISE. Yes.

EURYDICE. Orphée would kill you if that
came to his ears.

HEURTEBISE. It won't.

EURYDICE. [*Pulling him still farther from
the* HORSE, *towards her room.*] Have you
. . . got it?

HEURTEBISE. I have.

EURYDICE. In what form?

HEURTEBISE. A piece of sugar.

EURYDICE. What attitude did she take?

HEURTEBISE. A very simple one. She
said: "A bargain! Here is the poison,
bring me back the letter."

EURYDICE. That letter seems to cause
her a lot of trouble.

HEURTEBISE. She even added: "So that
the poor dear doesn't compromise
herself, here is an envelope with my
address in my own handwriting. She
will just have to put the letter in, stick
the envelope down, and there'll be
no trace of our communication.

EURYDICE. Orphée is unjust. She can be
very nice. Was she alone?

HEURTEBISE. With a lady friend. It
wasn't the sort of place for you.

EURYDICE. Of course not, but I don't
think Aglaonice is such a bad girl.

HEURTEBISE. Beware of good girls and
fine fellows. Here's your piece of
sugar.

EURYDICE. Thank you. . . . [*She takes the
sugar with fear and approaches the*
HORSE.] I'm afraid.

HEURTEBISE. Do you draw back?

EURYDICE. No, I don't, but I'm afraid. I
confess that when it comes to the
point, in cold blood, my courage fails

me. [*She returns in front of the writing-table.*] Heurtebise?

HEURTEBISE. What?

EURYDICE. My dear Heurtebise, I suppose you wouldn't like to? . . .

HEURTEBISE. Oh! Ho! You are asking me to do something very serious.

EURYDICE. You told me you would do anything to render me a service.

HEURTEBISE. I repeat that, but. . . .

EURYDICE. Oh! my dear, if it troubles you in the slightest . . . let us speak no more of it.

HEURTEBISE. Pass me the sugar.

EURYDICE. Thank you. You're a good fellow.

HEURTEBISE. Only, will he take it from my hand?

EURYDICE. Still, try.

HEURTEBISE. [*Near the* HORSE.] I confess I don't feel very firm on my feet.

EURYDICE. Be a man! [*She crosses left and stops near the door of her room.*]

HEURTEBISE. Well, here goes. [*In a weak voice.*] Horse . . . horse. . . .

EURYDICE. [*Looking out of the window.*] Heavens! Orphée! He's coming back. He's crossing the garden. Quick, quick, look as though you're working. [HEURTEBIS *throws the lump of sugar on to the set table and pushes it up against the wall between the window and the door of the bedroom.*] Get up on this chair. [HEURTEBISE *gets up on the chair in the framework of the French window and pretends he is taking measurements.* EURYDICE *drops into the chair at the writing-table.*]

Scene 4

ORPHÉE. [*Coming in.*] I've forgotten my birth-certificate. Where did I put it?

EURYDICE. On top of the bookcase, on the left. Shall I look for it?

ORPHÉE. Sit still. I can find it myself. [*He passes in front of the* HORSE *and*

caresses it, takes the chair on which HEUR-TEBISE *is standing, and carries it away.* HEURTEBISE *remains in the same pose, suspended in the air.* EURYDICE *stifles a cry.* ORPHÉE, *without noticing anything, gets up on the chair in front of the book-case and says.*] Here it is. [*Takes the birth-certificate, gets down from the chair, carries it back to its place beneath the feet of* HEURTEBISE, *and goes out.*]

Scene 5

EURYDICE. Heutebise! Will you explain this miracle?

HEURTEBISE. What miracle?

EURYDICE. You're not going to tell me you haven't noticed anything, and that it is natural to remain suspended in mid-air, instead of falling, when a chair is taken from under you?

HEURTEBISE. Suspended in mid-air?

EURYDICE. You needn't make out you are surprised, because I saw you. You stayed in mid-air. You stayed there two feet above the floor, with only emptiness round you.

HEURTEBISE. You really do surprise me.

EURYDICE. You remained a good minute between heaven and earth.

HEURTEBISE. Impossible.

EURYDICE. Exactly. That's why you owe me an explanation.

HEURTEBISE. You mean to say that I stayed without a support between the ceiling and the floor?

EURYDICE. Don't tell a lie, Heurtebise! I saw you, I saw you with my own eyes. I had the greatest difficulty in stifling a cry. In this mad-house, you were my last refuge, you were the only person who didn't frighten me, in your presence I regained my balance. It's all very well living with a horse that talks, but a friend who floats in the air becomes of necessity an object of suspicion. Don't come near me. At the moment even your glistening back gives me gooseflesh. Explain yourself, Heurtebise! I am listening.

HEURTEBISE. I have no need to defend myself. Either I am dreaming or you have dreamt.

EURYDICE. Yes, such things do happen in dreams, but neither of us was asleep.

HEURTEBISE. You must have been the dupe of the mirage between my window-panes and yours. Things do lie at times. At the fair I saw a naked woman walking along the ceiling.

EURYDICE. This was nothing to do with a machine. It was beautiful and outrageous. For the space of a second I saw you as outrageous as an accident and as beautiful as a rainbow. You were the cry of a man who falls from a window, and you were the silence of the stars. You frighten me. I'm too frank not to tell you. If you do not wish to answer me, you needn't, but our relationship can never be the same. I thought you were simple, but you are complex. I thought you were of my race, but you are of the race of the horse.

HEURTEBISE. Eurydice, don't torture me. . . . Your voice is that of a sleep-talker. It's you who are frightening me.

EURYDICE. Don't you use Orphée's method. Don't turn the tables on me. Don't try to make me believe I'm mad.

HEURTEBISE. Eurydice, I swear that. . . .

EURYDICE. You needn't, Heurtebise. I have lost my confidence in you.

HEURTEBISE. What's to be done?

EURYDICE. One moment. [She goes to the bookcase, gets up on the chair, pulls out a book, opens it, takes a letter from it, and returns the book to its place.] Give me Aglaonice's envelope. [He gives it.] Thank you. [She puts the letter in the envelope and licks the edge.] Oh!

HEURTEBISE. Cut your tongue?

EURYDICE. No—curious taste. Take the envelope to Aglaonice. Goodbye.

HEURTEBISE. The window-pane hasn't been put in.

EURYDICE. I'll do without it. Go along.

HEURTEBISE. You want me to leave you?

EURYDICE. I want to be alone.

HEURTEBISE. You are unkind.

EURYDICE. I don't like tradesmen who get suspended.

HEURTEBISE. That cruel play on words isn't worthy of you.

EURYDICE. It isn't a play on words.

HEURTEBISE. [Picking up his bag.] You'll be sorry you have hurt me. [Silence.] Am I discharged?

EURYDICE. All mystery is my enemy. I have decided to fight it.

HEURTEBISE. I am going. I want to please you by my obedience. Goodbye, madam.

EURYDICE. Goodbye. [They cross. EURYDICE goes toward her room. HEURTEBISE opens the door and goes out. The door remains open. His back is seen gleaming immobile in the sun. Suddenly EURYDICE stops and her expression changes. She staggers, puts her hand to her heart, and begins to cry.] Heurtebise! Heurtebise! quick, quick. . . .

HEURTEBISE. [Entering.] What is it?

EURYDICE. Help! . . .

HEURTEBISE. How pale you are! You're like ice.

EURYDICE. I'm going paralyzed. My inside's burning and my heart's thumping.

HEURTEBISE. The envelope!

EURYDICE. The envelope?

HEURTEBISE. [Shouting.] Aglaonice's envelope. You licked it. You said it had a curious taste.

EURYDICE. Ah! that wretched woman! Run quickly. Bring back Orphée. I am dying. I want to see Orphée again. Orphée! Orphée!

HEURTEBISE. I can't leave you alone. There must be something that can be done—take an antidote.

EURYDICE. I know the poison of the Bacchantes. It paralyzes. Nothing will save me. Run quickly. Fetch Orphée.

I want to see him again. I want him to forgive me. I love him, Heurtebise. I am in pain. If you delay it'll be too late. I implore you, Heurtebise, Heurtebise, you are good to me, you pity me. Ah! They are sticking knives between my ribs. Quck, quick, run, fly! Take the short cut. If he's on the way back, you'll meet him. I am going to lie down in my room and wait for you. Help me. [HEURTEBISE *helps her to her room.*] Quick, quick, quick. [*She disappears. At the moment* HEURTEBISE *is going to open the door she comes out of her room.*] Heurtebise, listen, if you do know things . . . well . . . things like a moment ago . . . which allow lightning movement from one place to another. . . . You mustn't bear me ill will, I was irritable and silly. . . . I really like you, Heurtebise . . . try everything. Ah! [*She goes back to her room.*]

HEURTEBISE. I will bring him back, I promise you.

The stage remains empty a moment. The light changes. Rolling and syncopation of drums which accompanies the whole of the following scene—damped.

Scene 6

DEATH *comes on the stage through the mirror, followed by her two assistants,* AZRAEL *and* RAPHAEL. *She is wearing an evening dress and cloak. Her assistants wear surgeon's uniforms. Their eyes are just visible. The rest of the face is covered by a linen mask. Rubber gloves. They are carrying two very elegant large black bags.* DEATH *walks quickly and stops in the middle of the stage.*

DEATH. Quickly!

RAPHAEL. Where does madam want us to put the bags?

DEATH. On the ground, anywhere. Azrael will explain. Azrael, my cloak.

[*He takes off the cloak.*]

RAPHAEL. It's because I'm afraid of making mistakes that I do silly things.

DEATH. You can't pick up Azrael's job in two days. Azrael has been in my service for several centuries now. He was like you at first. My tunic. [AZRAEL *takes the white tunic out of one of the bags and helps* DEATH *to put it over her dress.*]

AZRAEL. [*To* RAPHAEL.] Take the metal boxes and put them on the table. No, first of all, the cloths. Cover the table with them.

DEATH. [*Going to the wash-basin.*] Azrael will tell you that I insist on having everything clean and shipshape.

RAPHAEL. Yes, madam. I hope madam will forgive me . . . but my attention was distracted by this horse.

DEATH. [*Washing her hands.*] Do you like him?

RAPHAEL. Oh! Yes, madam. Very much.

DEATH. What a child! I believe you'd like to have him for yourself. That's very easy. Azrael, the spirit. [*To* RAPHAEL.] You'll find a piece of sugar on the other table.

RAPHAEL. Yes, madam, it is there.

DEATH. Give it to him. If he refuses, I'll give it to him myself. Azrael, my rubber gloves. Thank you. [*She puts on the right-hand glove.*]

RAPHAEL. Madam, the horse won't take the sugar.

DEATH. [*Taking the sugar.*] Eat, horse; I wish it. [*The* HORSE *eats it, withdraws, and disappears. A black curtain closes the niche.*] There you are. [*To* RAPHAEL.] He's yours.

RAPHAEL. Madam is too kind.

DEATH. [*Putting on the left-hand glove.*] Only a week ago you thought I was a skeleton with a winding-sheet and a scythe. You imagined me as a bugbear and a scarecrow.

RAPHAEL. Oh! Madam. . . .[*During these remarks* AZRAEL *is hiding the mirror with a cloth.*]

DEATH. [*Going to take a chair left by* HEUR-

TEBISE *in the French window.*] Oh! yes, you did. Everybody believes that. But, my dear child, if I were as people wish me to be, they would see me, whereas I must enter their homes unseen. [*She puts the chair near the footlights in the middle.*] Azrael, try the contact.

AZRAEL. It's working, madam. [*Deep noise of an electric machine.*]

DEATH. [*Taking a handkerchief from out of her tunic.*] Good! Raphael, would you be so kind as to bind my eyes with this handkerchief? [*While* RAPHAEL *is binding her eyes. . . .*] We have a wave-length of seven and a range of seven to twelve. Set everything at four. If I amplify, go up to five. Don't exceed five on any account. Pull tight. Tie a double knot. Thank you. Are you at your posts? [AZRAEL *and* RAPHAEL *stand behind the table, side by side, their hands inside the metal boxes.*] I'm beginning. [*She comes near the chair. Slow movement of the hands as of a masseuse and hypnotist round the invisible head.*]

RAPHAEL. [*Very softly.*] Azrael. . . .

AZRAEL. [*Very softly.*] Sh!

DEATH. You may talk. It doesn't disturb me.

RAPHAEL. Azrael, where is Eurydice?

DEATH. I was expecting that. You see, Azrael, they all ask the same question. Explain it to him.

AZRAEL. Death, to reach living things, has to pass through an element which deforms and displaces them. Our apparatus allows her to reach them where she sees them, thus saving calculations and a considerable loss of time.

RAPHAEL. It's like fishing with a gun.

DEATH. [*Laughing.*] Yes. [*Gravely.*] Azrael, prepare the bobbin for me.

AZRAEL. Yes, madam. Does Madam know where Heurtebise is?

DEATH. He's bringing Orphée back from town.

RAPHAEL. If they are hurrying shall we have time to finish?

DEATH. That is a question for Azrael.

He changes our speeds. An hour for me is only a minute for them.

AZRAEL. The hand is passing five. Does madam want the bobbin?

DEATH. Disconnect it and give it to me. [AZRAEL *disappears into* EURYDICE'S *room and comes on the stage again with the bobbin.* DEATH *counts the steps between her chair and the room. Then she stops, facing the door.* AZRAEL *gives her the bobbin which is a sort of automatic measure on which a white thread from the room will coil*]

AZRAEL. Raphael, the chronometer.

RAPHAEL. I've forgotten it!

AZRAEL. Now we are in a fix.

DEATH. Don't get alarmed. It's quite easy. [*She speaks softly to* AZRAEL.]

AZRAEL. Ladies and Gentlemen, I am instructed by Death to ask the audience if there's a spectator who would be so kind as to lend her a watch? [*To a gentleman in the first row, who raises his hand*] Thank you, Sir. Raphael, will you take the gentleman's watch? [*Business*]

DEATH. All right?

AZRAEL. Go! [*Rolling of drums. The wire comes from the room and enters the box held by* DEATH. AZRAEL *and* RAPHAEL, *backstage, turn their backs.* AZRAEL *counts with one hand in the air like a referee.* RAPHAEL *goes through movements like naval signals.*] Whoa! [*Rolling of drums stops.* RAPHAEL *freezes. The wire tightens.* DEATH *rushes into the bedroom. She comes out without the bandage over her eyes, with a dove which flaps its wings attached to the thread. The machine is no longer heard.*]

DEATH. Phew! Quick, quick, Raphael, the scissors. [*She runs to the balcony.*] Come here; cut this. [*He cuts the thread and the dove flies away.*] Now clear the things up. Azrael, show him how. It's very simple. Let him do it, he's got to learn. [AZRAEL *and* RAPHAEL *pack up the metal boxes, tunic, etc.* DEATH *leans against the table on the right. She looks into space as if worn out. She slowly passes her right arm and hand*

across her brow, like a sleepwalker who is
reawakening, as if recalling herself from
the hypnotic state.]

AZRAEL. Everything is in order, madam.

DEATH. And now, close the bags and
lock them. I'm ready. My cloak.
[AZRAEL *puts her cloak over her shoulders, while* RAPHAEL *is closing the bags.*]
Have we forgotten anything?

AZRAEL. No, madam.

DEATH. Then, let's be going.

GENTLEMAN IN THE AUDIENCE. Ssss!

AZRAEL. Ah! Of course.

DEATH. What is it?

AZRAEL. The watch. Raphael, take the
watch back to the gentleman and
thank him. [*Business.*]

DEATH. Raphael, hurry up, hurry up.

RAPHAEL. I'm coming, madam. [DEATH
*walks quickly and comes to a standstill
with outstretched arms in front of the
mirror. Then, she penetrates it. Her assistants follow her. They go through the
same movements. She has forgotten her
rubber gloves, which are well in evidence
on the left-hand table.*]

Scene 7

Directly after DEATH's *last remark,* OR-
PHÉE's *voice is heard in the garden.*

VOICE OF ORPHÉE. You don't know her.
You don't know what she's capable
of. This is one of her theatricals to
get me back home. [*The door opens
and they enter.* HEURTEBISE *rushes to the
room, looks in, recoils and kneels on the
threshold.*]

ORPHÉE. Where is she? Eurydice! . . .
She's sulking. Here, I shall go off my
head! The horse! Where's the horse?
[*He opens the niche.*] Gone!—I'm lost.
Some one has opened the door for
him. Some one must have scared
him; Eurydice must have done this.
She shall pay for it! [*He makes a
dash. . . .*]

HEURTEBISE. Stop!

ORPHÉE. Would you dare prevent me
from going to my wife?

HEURTEBISE. Look.

ORPHÉE. Where?

HEURTEBISE. Look through my panes.

ORPHÉE. [*Looking.*] She is sitting. She's
asleep.

HEURTEBISE. She is dead.

ORPHÉE. What?

HEURTEBISE. Dead. We've got here too
late.

ORPHÉE. It can't be. [*He knocks on the
panes.*] Eurydice! My darling! Answer
me!

HEURTEBISE. It's no good.

ORPHÉE. You! Let me go in. [*He pushes
HEURTEBISE aside.*] Where is she? [*In
the wings.*] I saw her a moment ago,
sitting near the bed. The room's
empty. [*He re-enters.*] Eurydice!

HEURTEBISE. You only thought you saw
her. Eurydice is living in the abode
of Death.

ORPHÉE. Ah! The horse is of little con-
sequence! I want to see Eurydice
again. I want her to forgive me for
having neglected and misunderstood
her. Help me. Save me. What can we
do? We're losing precious time.

HEURTEBISE. Those kind words save
you, Orphée. . . .

ORPHÉE. [*Weeping, collapsed on the table.*]
Dead, Eurydice is dead. [*He gets up.*]
Well, then . . . I'll snatch her away
from death! To seek her, I'll brave
the Underworld, if necessary.

HEURTEBISE. Orphée . . . listen to me.
Calm yourself. Are you going to listen to me? . . .

ORPHÉE. Yes . . . I'll be calm. Let's consider things. Let's find a plan. . . .

HEURTEBISE. I know a way.

ORPHÉE. You!

HEURTEBISE. But you must obey me and
not lose a minute.

ORPHÉE. Yes. [*All* ORPHÉE's *remarks are
made in a feverish docility. The scene
moves with extreme rapidity.*]

HEURTEBISE. Death came into your
house to carry off Eurydice.

ORPHÉE. Yes. . . .

HEURTEBISE. She's forgotten her rubber gloves. [*Silence. He goes to the table, hesitates, and picks up the gloves at arm's length, as one touches a sacred object.*]

ORPHÉE. [*In terror.*] Ah!

HEURTEBISE. You'll put them on.

ORPHÉE. Yes.

HEURTEBISE. Put them on. [*He passes them to him.* ORPHÉE *puts them on.*] You must go and see Death under the pretense of returning them, and thanks to them you'll be able to get to her.

ORPHÉE. Right. . . .

HEURTEBISE. Death is going to look for her gloves. If you take them to her, she'll give you a reward. She's miserly, she prefers receiving to giving, and as she never returns what anyone lets her take, your procedure will astonish her not a little. I don't suppose you'll get much, but still you'll get something.

ORPHÉE. Good.

HEURTEBISE. [*Leading him in front of the mirror.*] That's your way.

ORPHÉE. That mirror?

HEURTEBISE. I'm entrusting you with the secret of secrets. Mirrors are the doors through which Death comes and goes. Don't tell anyone. You only have to watch yourself all your life in a mirror, and you'll see Death at work like bees in a glass hive. Goodbye. Good luck!

ORPHÉE. But a mirror—that's hard.

HEURTEBISE. [*With hand raised.*] With those gloves you'll pass through mirrors as through water.

ORPHÉE. Where did you learn all these dreadful things?

HEURTEBISE. [*His hand drops.*] You know, mirrors are connected in a way with glazing. That's our trade.

ORPHÉE. And once I'm past this . . . door. . . .

HEURTEBISE. Breathe slowly and regularly. Don't be afraid; just walk straight ahead. Turn to the right, then to the left, then to the right, then go straight along. There, how can I explain it? . . . There's no more direction . . . you go round; it's a little difficult at first.

ORPHÉE. And then?

HEURTEBISE. Then? No one in the world can tell you. Death begins.

ORPHÉE. I'm not afraid of her.

HEURTEBISE. Farewell. I'll wait for you to come back.

ORPHÉE. But I might be a long time.

HEURTEBISE. A long time . . . for you. For us you'll scarcely do more than go in and come out.

ORPHÉE. I can't see how this mirror can be soft. Anyhow, I'll try.

HEURTEBISE. Yes, try. [ORPHÉE *begins to move.*] First your hands! [ORPHÉE, *with arms outstretched and the red gloves on his hands, sinks into the mirror.*]

ORPHÉE. Eurydice! . . . [*He disappears.*]

Scene 8(a)

HEURTEBISE, *alone, kneels in front of the* HORSE's *niche. A knock.*

HEURTEBISE. What is it?

POSTMAN'S VOICE. Postman. I've a letter for you.

HEURTEBISE. Master's not here.

POSTMAN'S VOICE. And madam?

HEURTEBISE. Not here either. Slip the letter under the door. [*A letter comes under the door.*]

POSTMAN'S VOICE. Have they gone out?

HEURTEBISE. No . . . they're asleep.

The curtain for the Interval falls slowly and rises immediately.

Scene 8(b)

HEURTEBISE *is discovered kneeling in front of the* HORSE's *niche. A knock.*

HEURTEBISE. What is it?

POSTMAN'S VOICE. Postman. I've a letter for you.

HEURTEBISE. Master's not here.

POSTMAN'S VOICE. And madam?

HEURTEBISE. Not here either. Slip the letter under the door. [*A letter comes under the door.*]

POSTMAN'S VOICE. Have they gone out?

HEURTEBISE. No . . . they're asleep.

Scene 9

ORPHÉE. [*Comes out of the mirror.*] What, still here?

HEURTEBISE. Now tell me quickly. . . .

ORPHÉE. My dear fellow, you're an angel.

HEURTEBISE. Not at all.

ORPHÉE. Oh! yes, an angel, a real angel. You have saved me.

HEURTEBISE. And Eurydice?

ORPHÉE. A surprise. Just look.

HEURTEBISE. Where?

ORPHÉE. At the mirror. One, two, three. [EURYDICE *comes out of the mirror.*]

HEURTEBISE. It is she!

EURYDICE. Yes, it is I. I, the happiest of wives; I, the first woman with a husband bold enough to recover her from the dead.

ORPHÉE. "Orphée hunts Eurydice's lost life." And to think we refused to believe this sentence had a meaning.

EURYDICE. Sh! my darling. Remember your promise. We weren't going to speak of the horse any more.

ORPHÉE. Where was my head?

EURYDICE. And you know, Heurtebise, he found the way all by himself. He didn't hesitate one second. He had the ingenious idea of putting on Death's gloves.

HEURTEBISE. Hm! I think I shall have to take up the gloves for myself.

ORPHÉE. [*Very quickly.*] Anyway, the chief thing was to succeed. [*He makes as if to turn to* EURYDICE.]

EURYDICE. Careful!

ORPHÉE. Oh! [*He freezes.*]

HEURTEBISE. What's the matter?

ORPHÉE. A detail, a mere detail. At first it appears terrifying, but with a little care it'll be all right.

EURYDICE. It'll become a matter of habit.

HEURTEBISE. But what's it all about?

ORPHÉE. A pact. I'm allowed to have Eurydice again, but I may not look at her. If I look at her, she'll disappear.

HEURTEBISE. How dreadful!

EURYDICE. How clever to discourage my husband!

ORPHÉE. [*Making* HEURTEBISE *pass in front of him.*] That's all right, I'm not discouraged. What is happening to him, happened to us. Think, after we'd accepted that clause—and we had to, whatever the cost—we went through all your apprehensions. Well, I repeat, it can be done. It isn't easy by any means, but it can be done. I maintain it isn't so hard as to become blind.

EURYDICE. Or as to lose a leg.

ORPHÉE. Besides . . . we had no choice.

EURYDICE. There are even advantages. Orphée won't see my wrinkles.

HEURTEBISE. Bravo! I have nothing more to do but to wish you good luck.

ORPHÉE. Are you going to leave us?

HEURTEBISE. I fear my presence may be embarrassing. You must have so many things to say to each other.

ORPHÉE. We'll say them after lunch. The table is laid. I'm very hungry. You are too much a part of our adventure not to stay to lunch with us.

HEURTEBISE. I'm afraid the presence of a third may vex your wife.

EURYDICE. No, Heurtebise. [*Weighing the words.*] The journey I've made transforms the face of the world. I have learned a lot. I'm ashamed of myself. From now on I shall be a new wife to Orphée, a honeymoon wife.

ORPHÉE. Eurydice! Your promise. We weren't going to speak any more of the moon.

EURYDICE. It's my turn to have no memory. Let's have lunch! Heurtebise on my right. Come and sit down. Orphée opposite me.

HEURTEBISE. Not opposite!

ORPHÉE. Heavens! I did right in keeping Heurtebise. I shall sit on your left with my back turned to you. I shall eat from my lap. [EURYDICE serves them.]

HEURTEBISE. I'm anxious to hear the story of your journey.

ORPHÉE. Lord, I shall find it difficult to relate. It seems as if I'm recovering from an operation. I have a vague memory of it, like that of one of my poems which I recite to keep me awake, and of foul beasts falling asleep. Then a black hole. Then speaking with an invisible lady. She thanked me for the gloves. A sort of surgeon came to take them, and he told me to go, that Eurydice would follow me, and that I wasn't to look at her on any account. I am thirsty. [He takes his glass and turns round.]

EURYDICE and HEURTEBISE. [Together.] Careful!

EURYDICE. I had a rare fright! Without turning round, my dear, feel how my heart is beating.

ORPHÉE. How silly it is. Supposing I bound my eyes!

HEURTEBISE. I don't advise you to do that. You don't know the exact rules. If you cheat, all is lost.

ORPHÉE. You would hardly credit how difficult it is to do such an idiotic thing, and the mental strain it involves.

EURYDICE. What do you expect, my poor dear, when you are always mooning. . . .

ORPHÉE. The moon again! You might as well call me a lunatic.

EURYDICE. Orphée!

ORPHÉE. I leave the moon to your late companions. [Silence.]

HEURTEBISE. Mr. Orphée!

ORPHÉE. I am a sun-worshipper.

EURYDICE. No longer, my love.

ORPHÉE. Perhaps not. But I forbid mention of the moon in my house. [Silence.]

EURYDICE. If only you knew how little importance attaches to this talk of sun and moon.

ORPHÉE. Madam is above these things.

EURYDICE. If only I could speak. . . .

ORPHÉE. It seems to me that for a person who can't speak, you speak quite a lot! A lot too much! [EURYDICE weeps. Silence.]

HEURTEBISE. You're making your wife cry.

ORPHÉE. [Threatening.] You! [He turns round.]

EURYDICE. Ah!

HEURTEBISE. Take care!

ORPHÉE. It's her fault. She would make the dead turn.

EURYDICE. It would have been better to remain dead. [Silence.]

ORPHÉE. The moon! If I were to let her talk, where would we get to? I ask you. We'd go back to the reign of the horse.

HEURTEBISE. You're exaggerating. . . .

ORPHÉE. I am exaggerating?

HEURTEBISE. Yes.

ORPHÉE. And even if I admit that I'm exaggerating. . . . [He turns round.]

EURYDICE. Look out!

HEURTEBISE. [To EURYDICE.] Calm yourself. Don't cry. The difficulty is making you nervous. Orphée, try and make an effort yourself. You'll bring about trouble in the end.

ORPHÉE. And even if I admit that I'm exaggerating, who began it?

EURYDICE. Not me.

ORPHÉE. Not you! Not you! [He turns round.]

EURYDICE and HEURTEBISE. Heigh!

HEURTEBISE. You're dangerous, my dear fellow.

ORPHÉE. You're right. The best thing I can do is to leave the table, and rid you of my presence, since I'm dangerous. [*He rises.* EURYDICE *and* HEURTEBISE *hold him back by his coat.*]

EURYDICE. My dear. . . .

HEURTEBISE. Orphée. . . .

ORPHÉE. No, no. Let me go.

HEURTEBISE. Be reasonable.

ORPHÉE. I shall be what it pleases me to be.

EURYDICE. Don't go. [*She pulls him, he loses his balance, and looks at her. He utters a cry.* EURYDICE, *petrified, rises. Her face expresses terror. The light lowers.* EURYDICE *sinks slowly into the mirror and disappears. The light rises again.*]

HEURTEBISE. It was to be.

ORPHÉE. [*Pale and limp, with an expression of false grace.*] Phew! That's better.

HEURTEBISE. What!

ORPHÉE. [*Same expression.*] We can breathe now.

HEURTEBISE. He's mad.

ORPHÉE. [*Hiding his embarrassment more and more in anger.*] You have to be firm with women, and show them you don't depend on them. You mustn't let them lead you by the nose.

HEURTEBISE. That's going a bit strong, isn't it? Would you have me believe you looked at Eurydice on purpose?

ORPHÉE. Am I an absent-minded man?

HEURTEBISE. You don't lack boldness! You looked inadvertently. You lost your balance, and you turned your head inadvertently; I saw you.

ORPHÉE. I lost my balance on purpose. I turned my head deliberately, and I forbid anyone to contradict me. [*Silence.*]

HEURTEBISE. Very well then, if you did turn your head deliberately, I don't congratulate you.

ORPHÉE. I can do without your congratulations. *I* congratulate myself for having turned my head deliberately toward my wife. That's better than trying to turn the heads of other people's wives.

HEURTEBISE. Is that meant for me?

ORPHÉE. If the cap fits. . . .

HEURTEBISE. That's very unkind. I've never allowed myself to make love to your wife. She would soon have sent me about my business. Your wife was a model wife. You had to lose her the first time to realize that, and you have just lost her a second time, lost her shamefully and tragically, and lost yourself. You have just killed a dead woman, and committed out of sheer wantonness an irreparable act. For she has died, died, died again. Never more will she come back.

ORPHÉE. Oh! come on!

HEURTEBISE. What do you mean, "Oh! come on!"?

ORPHÉE. When have you seen a woman get up from table scolding and not come back?

HEURTEBISE. I leave you five minutes to realize your misfórtune.

ORPHÉE *throws his napkin on the floor, rises, adjusts the table, goes to look at the mirror, touches it, goes to the door, and picks up the letter. Opens the letter.*

ORPHÉE. What's this?

HEURTEBISE. Some bad news?

ORPHÉE. I can't read it; the letter is written backward.

HEURTEBISE. That's a way of disguishing the handwriting. Read it in the mirror.

ORPHÉE. [*In front of the mirror, reads.*] "Sir, excuse my preserving my incognito. Aglaonice has discovered that the initial letters of your sentence: 'Orphée Hunts Eurydice's Lost Life,' togther form a word which is offensive to the jury of the competition." [ORPHÉE *says to himself.*] O, H, E, L, L. O Hell! [ORPHÉE *continues to read.*] "She has convinced the jury that you are a hoaxer. She has stirred up against you half of the women of the town. In short, an enormous troop of mad women under her orders is coming toward your house. The Bacchantes lead the way and demand your death. Escape and hide yourself. Do not lose a minute. From one who wishes you well."

HEURTEBISE. There can't be a word of truth in it.

Drums are heard approaching from a distance, beating a furious rhythm.

ORPHÉE. Listen. . . .

HEURTEBISE. Drums.

ORPHÉE. *Their* drums. Eurydice saw aright. Heurtebise, the horse has befooled me.

HEURTEBISE. A man isn't hacked to pieces for a couple of words.

ORPHÉE. The words are a pretext which hides a deep and religious hatred. Aglaonice was biding her time. I am lost.

HEURTEBISE. The drums are coming nearer.

ORPHÉE. How was it I didn't see this letter? How long ago was it slipped under the door?

HEURTEBISE. Orphée, I'm to blame. The letter was slipped in during your visit to the dead. Your wife's return engrossed me, and I forgot to tell you. Fly!

ORPHÉE. Too late. [*The* HORSE's *spell is ended.* ORPHÉE *is transfigured.*]

HEURTEBISE. Hide in the grove. I'll say you're traveling. . . .

ORPHÉE. It's useless, Heurtebise. Things happen as they must.

HEURTEBISE. I shall save you by force!

ORPHÉE. I refuse.

HEURTEBISE. This is madness!

ORPHÉE. The mirror is hard. It read the letter for me. I know what I can still do.

HEURTEBISE. What are you going to do?

ORPHÉE. Rejoin Eurydice.

HEURTEBISE. Not this time.

ORPHÉE. Why not?

HEURTEBISE. Even if you did manage it, there's be more scenes between you.

ORPHÉE. [*In ecstasy.*] Not there, where she beckons me to join her.

HEURTEBISE. Your face is drawn. You're suffering. I won't let you take your life.

ORPHÉE. Oh! those drums, those drums! They are coming nearer, Heurtebise, they are rumbling and thundering, they'll soon be here.

HEURTEBISE. You have already done the impossible.

ORPHÉE. I have held by the impossible.

HEURTEBISE. You have withstood other plots.

ORPHÉE. Not at the cost of bloodshed, yet.

HEURTEBISE. You frighten me . . . [HEURTEBISE's *face expresses a supernatural joy.*]

ORPHÉE. What are the thoughts of the marble from which a sculptor shapes a masterpiece? It thinks: I am being struck, ruined, insulted, and broken, I am lost. This marble is stupid. Life is shaping me, Heurtebise. It is making a masterpiece. I must bear its blows without understanding them. I must stand firm. I must be still and accept the inevitable. I must help and bear my part, till the work is ended.

HEURTEBISE. Stones! [*Some stones break the window and fall into the room.*]

ORPHÉE. Glass. That's good luck! Luck! I shall have the bust I wished for. [*A stone breaks the mirror.*]

HEURTEBISE. The mirror!

ORPHÉE. Not the mirror! [*He rushes on to the balcony.*]

HEURTEBISE. They'll hack you to pieces. [*Clamoring and drums.*]

ORPHÉE. [*Back to audience, leans over the balcony.*] Ladies! [*Roar of drums.*] Ladies! [*Roar of drums.*] Ladies! [*Roar of drums.*]

He rushes to the right—invisible part of the balcony. The drums drown his voice. Darkness. HEURTEBISE *falls on his knees and hides his face. Suddenly something flies through the window and falls into the room. It is* ORPHÉE's *head. It rolls to the right, and stops on the forestage.* HEURTEBISE *utters a weak cry. The drums are getting farther away.*

Scene 10

ORPHÉE'S HEAD. [*Speaking in the voice of someone greatly hurt.*] Where am I?

How dark it is . . . how heavy my head is. And my body, my body hurts me so much. I must have fallen from the balcony. I must have fallen from a great height, a great height, from a great height on to my head. And my head? . . . as a matter of fact . . . yes, I'm speaking about my head . . . where is my head? Eurydice! Heurebise! Help me! Where are you? Light the lamp. Eurydice! I can't see my body. I can't find my head. I've lost my head, and my body; and I can't understand how. There's an emptiness, all about me there is an emptiness. Explain it to me. Wake me. Help! Help! Eurydice! [*Like a lament.*] Eurydice . . . Eurydice . . . Eurydice . . . Eurydice . . . Eurydice. . . .

EURYDICE *comes through the mirror. She remains on the spot.*

EURYDICE. My darling?

ORPHÉE'S HEAD. Eurydice . . . is it you?

EURYDICE. It is.

ORPHÉE'S HEAD. Where is my body? Where did I put my body?

EURYDICE. Quiet. Don't upset yourself. Give me your hand.

ORPHÉE'S HEAD. Where is my head?

EURYDICE. [*Taking the invisible body by the hand.*] I have your hand in mine. Walk. Don't be afraid. Let yourself go. . . .

ORPHÉE'S HEAD. Where is my body?

EURYDICE. Near me. Against me. You can't see me now, and I may take you away.

ORPHÉE'S HEAD. And my head, Eurydice . . . my head . . . where did I put my head?

EURYDICE. No more of that, my love, let your head be. . . .

EURYDICE *and the invisible body of* ORPHÉE *sink into the mirror.*

Scene 11

A knock on the door. Silence. Knock. Silence.

VOICE OF THE COMMISSIONER OF POLICE. Open, in the name of the law.

HEURTEBISE. Who is it?

VOICE OF THE COMMISSIONER OF POLICE. The police. Open or I'll break in the door.

HEURTEBISE. I'll open it. [HEURTEBISE *rushes to* ORPHÉE'S *head, picks it up, hesitates, puts it on the pedestal, and opens the door. The leaf of the door hides the pedestal. It is now that the actor who plays* ORPHÉE *substitutes his own head for that of the mask.*]

COMMISSIONER OF POLICE. Why didn't you reply to my first summons?

HEURTEBISE. Your Worship. . . .

COMMISSIONER OF POLICE. Commissioner of Police.

HEURTEBISE. Sir, I'm a friend of the family . . . I was still suffering from the shock, as you may well imagine. . . .

COMMISSIONER OF POLICE. Shock? What shock?

HEURTEBISE. I must tell you. I was alone with Orphée at the moment of the drama.

COMMISSIONER OF POLICE. What drama?

HEURTEBISE. The murder of Orphée by the Bacchantes.

COMMISSIONER OF POLICE. [*Turning to the* SCRIVENER.] I was expecting this version. And . . . the wife of the victim . . . where is she? I should like to confront her with you.

HEURTEBISE. She's not here.

COMMISSIONER OF POLICE. Better and better.

HEURTEBISE. She had even abandoned the conjugal domicile.

COMMISSIONER OF POLICE. Do you hear that! [*To the* SCRIVENER.] Sit down at that table, please [*He points to the right-hand table.*] and take notes.

The SCRIVENER *installs himself. Papers and pens. He turns his back to the mirror.* HEURTEBISE *is standing near the mirror. To be more at ease the* SCRIVENER *pulls the table back so that this table renders access to the door impossible.*

HEURTEBISE. I have. . . .

SCRIVENER. Silence.

COMMISSIONER OF POLICE. Let's proceed in order. Don't speak unless I question you. Where's the body?

HEURTEBISE. What body?

COMMISSIONER OF POLICE. When there's a murder, there's a body. I am asking you—where is the body?

HEURTEBISE. But, sir, there isn't a body. It has been torn, decapitated, and carried away by those mad women!

COMMISSIONER OF POLICE. Primo, I am not asking you to make a detrimental judgment on women who perform priestly rites. Secundo, your version is contradicted by five-hundred eyewitnesses.

HEURTEBISE. Do you mean that I. . . .

COMMISSIONER OF POLICE. Silence!

HEURTEBISE. I. . . .

COMMISSIONER OF POLICE. Silence! [*Pompous delivery.*] You just listen to me, my lad. Today is the day of the eclipse. This eclipse of the sun has brought about a tremendous change of popular feeling in Orphée's favor. Mourning's being worn. Triumphal celebrations are being prepared, and the authorities claim his mortal remains. Now, the Bacchantes saw Orphée appear on his balcony, covered with blood and calling for help. They were astonished, as they had come there under his window with the sole purpose of fêting him. They would have flown to his aid, if he hadn't, as they say—and five hundred mouths testify to it—if he hadn't, as I was saying, fallen dead before their eyes. To sum up. These ladies made a long procession. They arrive with cries of "Out with Orphée!" Suddenly Orphée covered with blood rushes out and calls for help. These ladies make ready to mount the steps. Too late! Orphée falls, and the whole troop—don't forget they are women . . . women who make a brave noise, but who are frightened at the sight of blood—the whole troop, I say, turns tail. Eclipse! The town saw in this eclipse the anger of the sun, because one of its late priests had been derided. The authorities came to meet the women, and the women, through the medium of Aglaonice, retailed the strange crime of which they had just been witnesses. The whole town wanted to rush to the scene of the tragedy. Severe measures were taken to suppress the disorder and I was given charge, I, *I*, the head of the Police force, I, who am conducting your examination—and I won't allow anyone to treat me like a country policeman, keep that well in mind.

HEURTEBISE. But, I'm not. . . .

SCRIVENER. Silence. You're not being questioned.

COMMISSIONER OF POLICE. Let's proceed in order. [*To the* SCRIVENER.] Where did I get to?

SCRIVENER. The bust. I beg to remind you of the bust. . . .

COMMISSIONER OF POLICE. Ah! yes. [*To* HEURTEBISE.] Are you a relative?

HEURTEBISE. A friend of the family.

COMMISSIONER OF POLICE. A bust of Orphée is required for the celebrations. Do you know of one?

HEURTEBISE *goes to the door and closes it. The head on the pedestal is discovered. The* COMMISSIONER OF POLICE *and* SCRIVENER *turn round.*

COMMISSIONER OF POLICE. It isn't a likeness.

HEURTEBISE. It's a very fine work.

COMMISSIONER OF POLICE. Who by?

HEURTEBISE. I don't know.

COMMISSIONER OF POLICE. Is the bust not signed?

HEURTEBISE. No.

COMMISSIONER OF POLICE. [*To the* SCRIVENER.] Write down: "Alleged bust of Orphée."

HEURTEBISE. No, no. It is Orphée, of that we're sure. There's doubt only about the authorship.

COMMISSIONER OF POLICE. Then put: "Head of Orphée by X." [*To* HEURTEBISE.] Your name?

HEURTEBISE. Pardon?

SCRIVENER. You were asked for your full name.

COMMISSIONER OF POLICE. For, as regards your profession, I'm not to be deceived. I have eyes. [*He goes to* HEURTEBISE *and fingers the panes.*] You are a glazier, my fine fellow!

HEURTEBISE. [*Smiling.*] Yes, I am a glazier, I confess.

COMMISSIONER OF POLICE. Confess, confess, it's the only defense which carries any weight.

SCRIVENER. Excuse me, Sir, supposing we ask him for his papers.

COMMISSIONER OF POLICE. Quite right. [*He sits down.*] Your papers.

HEURTEBISE. I . . . I haven't any.

COMMISSIONER OF POLICE. What?

SCRIVENER. Ho! ho!

COMMISSIONER OF POLICE. Going about without your papers? Where do you live?

HEURTEBISE. I live . . . that is to say— er—I used to live. . . .

COMMISSIONER OF POLICE. I'm not asking you where you used to live. I'm asking where you're living now.

HEURTEBISE. Now? . . . at the moment I am . . . without an address.

COMMISSIONER OF POLICE. No papers, no fixed abode. Exactly. Vagrancy! a vagrant! Your case is clear, my friend. Your age?

HEURTEBISE. I am. . . . [*He hesitates.*]

COMMISSIONER OF POLICE. [*He questions with his back turned, looking up to the ceiling, moving his feet, like an examiner.*] I suppose, at least, you have some age. . . .

ORPHEE'S HEAD. I'm eighteen.

SCRIVENER. [*Writing.*] Seventeen.

ORPHÉE'S HEAD. Eighteen.

COMMISSIONER OF POLICE. Born at. . . .

SCRIVENER. Half a minute, Sir. I'm erasing the figure.

EURYDICE *comes half-way through the mirror.*

EURYDICE. Heurtebise . . . Heurtebise. I know who you are. Come in, we were waiting for you. You alone were missing. [HEURTEBISE *hesitates.*]

ORPHÉE'S HEAD. Hurry up, Heurtebise. Follow my wife. I'll answer for you. I'll invent something, anything.

HEURTEBISE *plunges into the mirror.*

Scene 12

SCRIVENER. Sir, at your service.

COMMISSIONER OF POLICE. Born at. . . .

ORPHÉE'S HEAD. Maisons-Laffitte.

COMMISSIONER OF POLICE. Maisons what?

ORPHÉE'S HEAD. Maisons-Laffitte, two F's, two T's.

COMMISSIONER OF POLICE. As you can tell me your place of birth, perhaps you'll no longer refuse to tell me your name. You're called. . . .

ORPHÉE'S HEAD. Jean.

COMMISSIONER OF POLICE. Jean what?

ORPHÉE'S HEAD. Jean Cocteau.

COMMISSIONER OF POLICE. Coc. . . .

ORPHÉE'S HEAD. C, O, C, T, E, A, U. Cocteau.

COMMISSIONER OF POLICE. There's a name to go to bed with. Is it true you sleep out of doors? If you don't consent now to tell us where you live. . . .

ORPHÉE'S HEAD. Rue d'Anjou. Number 10.

COMMISSIONER OF POLICE. You're becoming reasonable.

SCRIVENER. Your signature. . . .

COMMISSIONER OF POLICE. Get a pen ready. [*To* HEURTEBISE.] Come here. Come here, I won't eat you. [*Turns round.*] Great! . . .

SCRIVENER. What is it?

COMMISSIONER OF POLICE. Great Heavens! The accused has disappeared.

SCRIVENER. Miraculous!

COMMISSIONER OF POLICE. Miraculous . . . miraculous . . . it's not miraculous at all. [*He strides up and down the stage.*] I don't believe in miracles. An eclipse is an eclipse. A table's a table.

An accused man's an accused man. Let's proceed in order. This door. . . .

SCRIVENER. Impossible, Sir. To go out by this door, he would have to knock over my chair.

COMMISSIONER OF POLICE. The window, then.

SCRIVENER. For the window, he would have to pass in front of us. Besides, the accused was answering. He answered right up to the last minute.

COMMISSIONER OF POLICE. Well?

SCRIVENER. Well, I don't understand at all.

COMMISSIONER OF POLICE. There must be a secret exit of which the assassin—for this flight gives us proof of the crime—of which the assassin, as I was saying, knew the existence. Sound the wall. [SCRIVENER *taps. Investigations.*]

SCRIVENER. The wall sounds solid. . . .

COMMISSIONER OF POLICE. Right. This young dog may leave us and hide in this unmannerly fashion, but we won't give him the satisfaction of seeking him under his very nose. [*At the top of his voice.*] I have men about the house. He can't take two steps outside without being caught, and if he persists, we'll surround him till hunger drives him out. Come on.

SCRIVENER. What an extraordinary affair!

COMMISSIONER OF POLICE. There's nothing extraordinary at all. You're always seeing something extraordinary somewhere.

They go out. While they are going out and the door hides the bust, the actor substitutes the mask for his own head. The stage remains empty.

COMMISSIONER OF POLICE. [*Returning.*] We're forgetting the bust.

SCRIVENER. We mustn't return empty-handed.

COMMISSIONER OF POLICE. Take it. [*The* SCRIVENER *takes the head. Exeunt.*]

Scene 13

The scene changes to Heaven. Through the mirror come EURYDICE *and* ORPHÉE, *led by* HEURTEBISE. *They look at their home as if they were seeing it for the first time. They sit down at table;* EURYDICE *beckons* HEURTEBISE *to her right. They smile and breathe calmness.*

EURYDICE. You were wanting some wine, I think, my dear.

ORPHÉE. One moment. First of all, the prayer.

He rises, also EURYDICE *and* HEURTEBISE. *He recites.*

ORPHÉE. O God, we thank thee for assigning us our house and home as the only paradise, and for having opened to us thy paradise. We thank thee for having sent Heurtebise to us, and we are guilty of not recognizing him as our Guardian Angel. We thank thee for having saved Eurydice, because, through love, she killed the devil in the shape of a horse, and in so doing she died. We thank thee for having saved me because I adored poetry, and thou art poetry. Amen.

They sit again.

HEURTEBISE. May I serve you?

ORPHÉE. [*Respectfully.*] Let Eurydice. . . .

EURYDICE *pours out for him to drink.*

HEURTEBISE. Perhaps we can have lunch at last.

Red Magic

Michel de Ghelderode

Michel de Ghelderode was born on April 3, 1898, in Brussels. Although he spoke and wrote in French, he was of Flemish extraction, and this heritage had a strong influence in his life and work. His father was an archivist and civil servant who wished his son to follow in this secure profession; upon the completion of his high school education in Brussels, Ghelderode did take a government position as an archivist, which he held until he turned to full-time writing. His mother maintained a profound belief in mysticism and the supernatural, and the sensitive boy grew up surrounded by these influences. He began to write poetry as early as age sixteen, and continued throughout his life to produce poetry, novels, and plays at a prodigious rate despite relatively little recognition. He loved the theater, especially marionettes, and thus his urge to write was channeled toward the theater from the beginning. His first major play was *The Death of Doctor Faust,* which was published in 1926.

In 1926, having attracted some attention as a writer, Ghelderode was commissioned by the Flemish Popular Theatre to write plays. The period from 1927 to 1930, therefore, saw a tremendous outpouring of plays, the most notable of which are *Christopher Columbus* (1929), *Escurial* (1929), *Barabbas* (1929), and *Pantagleize* (1930). When the Flemish Popular Theatre's leading actor, Renaat Verheyen, died in 1930, Ghelderode retired from public life almost completely, and continued to write in semi-isolation. His precarious health (he suffered from asthma), his solitary work habits, and his macabre writing style gave rise to reports that he was an eccentric recluse; in fact he was simply a very private person. After the beginning of World War II, he and his wife lived in virtual anonymity in Brussels, and he wrote only one play after 1937, *Marie the Miserable* (1952). He died on April 1, 1962.

Between 1930 and 1937, Ghelderode wrote most of the plays for which he was to gain his principal acclaim. Steeped in the history of Flanders, fascinated by medieval thought and mysticism, and strongly influenced by the paintings of Pieter Breughel and Hieronymus Bosch, Ghelderode created a number of bizarre plays that portray a unique world of Ghelderode's own creation. Ostensibly set in medieval Flanders (sometimes openly labeled "Breughelland"), these plays portray a world of incredible evil, of misshapen, scrofulous dwarfs, hunchbacks and degenerates, of scabrous, indecent and shocking language and activity that reveal the human soul in all of its least attractive aspects. In addition to *Red Magic,* these plays include *Chronicles of Hell* (1929), *The Blind Men* (1933), *Lord Halewyn* (1934), and *Hop, Signor!* (1935). (These dates are those of composition; during this period,

Ghelderode's plays were frequently not produced until much later.) When Jean-Louis Barrault produced *Chronicles of Hell* in Paris in 1949, Ghelderode's work suddenly began to reach an altogether new audience. Hitherto virtually unknown outside Belgium, Ghelderode's works, especially those of the 1930s, were produced throughout Europe, and during his last years Ghelderode began to enjoy a measure of fame if not great financial remuneration. It is upon Ghelderode's "Breughelland" plays that his fame now chiefly rests.

Red Magic was written in 1931 and first produced in Brussels on April 30, 1934. Ghelderode has described it as an "extreme farce," which is perhaps as good a way as any to describe so unusual a play. Beneath the undoubted humor of the play's wildly improbable plot, however, lies the mind-twisting perception of man at his most evil; if expressionism is the conceptualization of a dream, then *Red Magic* is a nightmare from which Hieronymus awakens screaming at the end of the play, still not understanding that his punishment is real. Hieronymus is the traditional comic miser of which Molière's Harpagon is the most famous embodiment, but Hieronymus is so unremitting in his miserliness that redeeming laughter chokes in the throat; one comes to feel that he deserves the fiendishly evil treatment he receives, and one laughs with the consciousness that one's own evil nature is being exposed by the delight he feels in Hieronymus's discomfort. Sybilla and Armador are completely without scruple or redeeming virtue of any sort; they are a couple of animals fiercely in heat and remorselessly devoted to robbery and murder, yet one laughs delightedly at their thoroughly immoral accomplishments. The farting, gluttonous monk is a disgrace to humanity as well as to his church; Ghelderode's plays are full of such ecclesiastical vermin even though Ghelderode was himself a devout Catholic. In short, Ghelderode went beyond the symbolists in "expressing the inexpressible," dredging up the foulest, blackest corners of the human psyche and finding wildly irreverent humor in them.

Critics have found the roots of Ghelderode's unusual drama in a great many places. Ghelderode admired the Elizabethan playwrights greatly, and Ben Jonson's characters created through the theory of humours do bear important resemblances to Ghelderode's; quite aside from any question of an excess of fluids in the body, both writers saw that a person may become so obsessed with one aspect of life as to warp his entire character. In many ways, Ghelderode's work is a throwback to romanticism, for so committed a romanticist as Victor Hugo insisted that it was the business of romantic drama to portray the "grotesque" in life—without, presumably, having anything in mind quite so grotesque as Ghelderode created. It was realism that delighted in laying bare the baser qualities of human nature, and Ghelderode's stage directions do call for a perverse kind of realism in many details, but realism can be described as having had only a peripheral effect on him. The distorted dreamworld of expressionism is a potent influence on Ghelderode's theater, and he once listed Strindberg as one of the playwrights whom he most admired, but he also listed Maeterlinck, whose perception of the spirit world beyond reality is clearly related to Ghelderode's, if nowhere near so macabre. Pirandello's questioning of reality and denial of the dependability of reason are also reflected in Ghelderode's thinking—so much so, that one of Ghelderode's early plays is a parody of *Six Characters in Search of an Author*. Finally, however, Ghelderode's theatrical world is uniquely his own—far more than the sum of its influences. More than most playwrights, Ghelderode created his own world, peopled it with his own characters, endowed his plays with his unique atmosphere, and, despite the horrifying perversity of the world he had created, found the common human element that proclaimed that some of that world lies buried within everyone. Ghelderode's theatrical style is perfectly attuned to expressing the sub-conscious truths that most people would prefer to keep buried.

Ghelderode's plays have aptly been called "theater of the grotesque," and Ghelderode's extraordinary visual and aural senses contribute to the grotesque quality of the total theatrical experience. His detailed set descriptions envision a rich chiaroscuro of light and shadow borrowed from the Flemish Renaissance painters he loved so well. The effect is of dark walls and dark corners, musky with age but rich in texture. Within this setting, Ghelderode calls for actors as angular, distorted, and misshapen as the people in a Brueghel painting—an extraordinary challenge in costuming and makeup unless some truly unusual actors are available. In some plays he specifically calls for masks; in others he has written primarily for marionettes; *Red Magic* contains neither of these, but the stiff, angular, artificial quality of both remains inherent in the characters. Ghelderode prescribed lavish use of music before and during his plays as well, adding to their total impact and mood.

The evil and the revolting details in *Red Magic* are by no means gratuitous. Ghelderode portrays a degenerate world in order to force man to look inside himself and to understand better his own drives and motivations. Ghelderode's methods resemble those of the expressionists and symbolists in reaching an au-dience's consciousness through appeal to the emotions and the subconscious rather than through logic or reason, but the result is still thematically rich and aesthetically sound. The animal force, the greed, and the sensuality that lurk beneath the surface of man's consciousness often need to be brought out into the open for rational examination, and Ghelderode certainly brings them out fully. Far from defending or condoning what he portrays, Ghelderode is masterful at creating an atmosphere of depravity and disgust that makes more than plain Ghelderode's attitude toward human frailty. It is this mood and atmosphere that constitute the most successful aspect of *Red Magic* and of Ghelderode's other plays of this genre.

Hieronymus cannot be said to be as brilliantly insightful a character as Harpag-non, for he is too single-minded and fanatical. On the other hand, almost in the French neoclassic manner of developing characters that are deep even if narrow, Hieronymus is so vivid a picture of the evil warping that can result from unbridled pursuit of money that he is an extraordinary creation in his own right. By the same token, Sybilla, Armador, Romulus, and the Monk are unidimensionally evil, but so thoroughly and evocatively evil that they serve the play magnificently. Ghelderode's use of language is poetically effective in the original as well, with archaic words and outdated grammatical structures in just measure enough to contribute effectively to the play's total impact. The plot, though structured in a fairly routine manner, is sufficiently macabre in its details to further the overall need and atmosphere of the play also. In short, *Red Magic* is as extraordinary a piece of "poetry of the theater" as may be found anywhere. Ghelderode's approach to the theater is so uniquely his own that no later playwrights may be said to be following in his pattern, but his contribution to twentieth-century playwriting is significant and is likely to endure.

Red Magic
(Magie Rouge)

Translated by George Hauger

Characters
Hieronymus
Sybilla
The Cavalier Armador
Romulus
The Monk
The Magistrate
Men at Arms
The Crowd

SCENE. *Flanders, in days of old.*

Act 1

SCENE. *A chamber in the olden style. Door and window, left. Low door, right. Still farther to the right, a staircase leading to the upper floor. Table. Chairs. Great metal-bound chest. It is the end of the night.* HIERONYMUS *enters, a candle in his hand.*

HIERONYMUS. The constellations fill the sky. Who owns all these stars? I swear they burn away in sheer waste. And the moon is missing. It has been stolen. When it comes back, it will have had a piece taken out of it. What a huge night, full of shadows. . . . Shadows, they are not worth much. . . . And a few will o' the wisps—for my house stands on an old burial ground that no one wanted. . . . [*He laughs.*] I own this ground and all that its depths contain. Bones of vanished men. Who has their souls? God or the devil? They are not worth much, souls. . . . [*Tapping with his heel.*] There are treasures in here—copper, silver, jewels, relics. But it would mean digging— not with my hands, with a spade. Must I buy a spade? . . . And there are owls. Who pays them for mounting guard? . . . These owls who see in the dark? . . . I can't see in the dark. I have to have a candle, whose light is poor but quite enough for what I want to see. [*He has slowly made his way around the room.*] Emptiness, everywhere! All the emptiness that this room contains is mine, too. Why can't I pick it up and store it? . . . The silence that reigns in here is mine also. What can I do with it? . . . [*He puts down the candle.*] What emotions this nocturnal round inspires in me! . . . It is only at night that each thing takes on its full value. I am double at night. Rather than lose myself in incoherent and immediately forgotten dreams, I sleep on my feet. I act, I think, I look, and make use of my time. I steal time, so that I shall have lived more waking hours than those people who sink themselves in useless sleep. [*Sitting on the table, he picks up a jug and goes through the*

190

motions of filling a glass.] This jug is empty. Fill the glass. [*He drinks.*] I am hungry. This morsel will do me. [*He pretends to take something from a dish and to put it in his mouth.*] I have had a drink. I have certainly drunk. My thirst is quenched. Good. I chew. I swallow. My hunger is appeased. Well, Hieronymus? Do you maintain there was nothing in your glass, nothing on this dish? Come! Since you are no longer hungry or thirsty. . . . [*He sits at the table and faces the audience. The candle lights him up clearly.*] Shine on me, little flame, and let me profit from your warm light. Creep into the corners and gild my room, so that I am in the center of a golden cube. I shall extinguish you at the very instant of the cock's unpleasant crowing—the cock who doesn't lay, but whose voice does for me as a clock. [*He opens an account book.*] This book of yellow parchment contains the inventory of my possessions. I must go through it again. Hieronymus, healthy in mind and body, owns, by virtue of the just laws, a gabled house, with its garden, well, lawn, trees, the birds that live in the trees, and the air and the wind that circulate around and within the said property. There is the watchdog, that costs little to maintain since he feeds himself by gnawing his chain. I own a wife and her clothing, and, furthermore, utensils and furniture. All of this, counting the wife and the dog, is worth a thousand royal florins. . . . I was forgetting that I own a ghost which is domiciled here and which I bought with the house. It doesn't eat or wear anything out, yet it makes itself useful, for its presence keeps away people with evil designs. What would a ghost be worth? . . . The price of a night watchman. [*Lowering his voice.*] And I own a bronze chest with cunning locks that contains four columns of ten florin pieces bearing the image of the emperor, and four

of the same with the image of the empress, all arranged in battle order. . . . [*He muses.*] These golden columns don't produce anything—nothing except the enchantment of my senses, for as well as looking at the gold, I touch it, I listen to it, I sniff it and I lick it. But there is no interest. Should I entrust it to a banker or a notary? Rather fling it straight away into a bottomless pit! [*He muses.*] Still, gold has magic properties. Listen, Hieronymus. You have male florins bearing the head of the emperor, and female florins with a woman's head. There is a sovereign law in the universe that requires that all that is male and all that is female attract each other, unite and reproduce. It is the Creator's will! [*He stands.*] Tonight I shall mingle the male and female coins. My chest will be a bower of love. Afterward, I shall find young ones, newly born golden florins that will grow up like their parents. I shall marry them. [*He goes and opens his chest. He kneels and, making a great noise, mixes the coins together.*] Make love! Join together your golden bodies, your golden desires! Let gold bring forth gold! Imperial heads, let your haughty lips touch, open, and grow moist! Link together, tongues of gold! I shall not make a hole in the chest to spy on your mysterious work of procreation and childbirth. Conceive! Female coins, become so great that you almost burst! It is blessed, it is just, that your grand race should perpetuate itself, for yours is the domination of the world! [*A drawn-out moan from a woman or an animal is heard from above.* HIERONYMUS *stands up and shuts the chest savagely.*] I heard. Someone moaned. Is it the gold already? Is it the gold enjoying sensual delight? . . . For it was like a sensual cry. [*He listens.*] No. It is the ghost dreaming in the wall. He is dreaming of the past when he had flesh and bones.

And who knows that he isn't gnawed by ancient rheumatics in his vaporous substance? [*He comes back and sits at the table.*] What a fine piece of work I have just done! [*Disturbed.*] But is this good Catholic work? Is there not perhaps witchcraft behind it? I don't want to forgo my salvation. No, the devil shall not have my soul. I am the owner of my soul, and such I shall remain! [*Troubled.*] That is something I had forgotten in the inventory. [*He writes.*] Item, one immortal soul, ornamented with divers virtues. No, I am not deluding myself. I am chaste, abstemious, diligent, without anger, without vanity, without envy. Six deadly sins that I have nothing to do with. The seventh? . . . I am thrifty. [*Pleased with himself.*] Thrifty! . . . They call me a miser? Because I am the opposite of a prodigal? If I were a miser, would you find me joyful and given to laughter, as I am by nature? . . . Above all, would I be fat? Would I have this fine paunch? Have you ever seen a corpulent miser? Pah! Never! Neither in paintings, nor in religious books, nor in the farces of the rhetoricians, nor on the universal stage! All misers are thin, haggard, angry, unpleasant, and miserable. So, I write, "with virtues"! The proof that I have strong virtues is that the devil has never troubled me. He doesn't bother himself about the righteous. And, God knows, the devil is busy in this parish! Last year they burned three witches on the same fire . . . even though it didn't smell very nice. . . . The devil? [*A shape glides rapidly down the stairs, passes in front of the table, blows out the candle and disappears noisily through the door. In the darkness,* HIERONYMUS *howls with fright.*] Help! Who put it out? . . . Who is there? [*He bumps against the furniture.*] Is it you, devil? Answer me! It is dark. I am going to have my immortal soul stolen. Stop, thief! Sybilla! Sybilla,

wife, are you asleep? [*He relights the candle.*] I am trembling. My hair is damp. Hasn't anything been taken? . . . It was a spirit. [*He goes to the door.*] It has closed the door behind it. It was a well-brought-up spirit. [*He thinks.*] It was only the ghost. He gave me a bad turn. Where is he going at this hour? It is still night. [*A cock crows.*] No, dawn. The ghost is punctual. He put my candle out because he knew that dawn was breaking. A good ghost, who practices economy. [*He blows out the candle.*] If I paid you wages, I would give you a raise.

The night has gone. SYBILLA, *wearing a long white nightgown and looking like a sleepwalker, comes downstairs.*

SYBILLA. You called me, Master?

HIERONYMUS. No. Yes. . . . My voice accidentally called you. Dawn is here. The shutters must be opened so that it can settle itself in the room. [SYBILLA *opens the shutters. Pale light.*] Wife, I have been awake all night. There are things to do which are only possible at night, which are only clear in darkness. Have you slept well?

SYBILLA. Badly! . . . How can you sleep in a house where no clock ticks? I have only one sheet. And I dreamed of the ghost. . . .

HIERONYMUS. Was it you who moaned?

SYBILLA. Perhaps I did moan. But do they who do not sleep hear the cries and groans of those who do sleep? I dreamed that the ghost was lying on me and suffocating me. I could feel his elbows, his knees, and his quick breathing. He weighed heavy and moved on me like a living creature.

HIERONYMUS. [*Amused.*] Ho, ho. . . . The spirit was cold. He must have been aware of his strange behavior. Didn't he make off like a thief? . . . He must have stolen your heat from you. All the same, I can't be on the lookout and go after him with an arquebus. Apart from my wasting match and powder, he would make a fool of me and have his revenge.

SYBILLA. Yes, they say the vengeance of ghosts is terrible, since they have nothing to fear from ordinary justice. [*Pause.*] This specter doesn't frighten me. He often visits me, and as I am alone every night, his presence is company for me. [*Apathetic.*] I am going to light the fire.

HIERONYMUS. Don't light the fire. Go back to bed until the sun is up. It is spring.

SYBILLA. I'm hungry.

HIERONYMUS. It's unnecessary for you to eat, since you are going to sleep. [*He takes a picture down from the wall.*] Look at this! Hunger is often suggested by the imagination. Feed your imagination. This is a fine Dutch picture, showing fruits, fish, crested flagons, flowers. Look! Eat with your gaze! Drink with your eyes!

SYBILLA. It's very fine; but I shall still grow thin from it.

HIERONYMUS. I don't like fat women. Your leanness pleases me. [*Someone knocks at the door.*] Who's that? . . . Off with you, in those clothes! If the visitor who is knocking at the door gazed on you, so transparent, so delicate, he would fall in love with you and carry you off.

SYBILLA, *resigned, but with a hypocritical smile, goes back upstairs. The knocking at the door is heard again, then a raucous voice sings.*

VOICE. I-i-i-i-ite . . . mis . . . sa . . . est!

HIERONYMUS. [*Hanging up the picture, and hiding his book.*] It's the matutinal frock, the dawn monk. He's said mass, the pig, and is quit of duties from the morning onward. Still, it doesn't cost much to make oneself agreeable. [*He opens the door.*]

THE MONK. [*Coming in.*] Good morning, my son. You have grown fatter since yesterday.

HIERONYMUS. I shall have the doorway made bigger—for you, spherical monk, not for me. Do you still guzzle as much?

THE MONK. I fast every day that God sends, and in making myself thinner, I make myself fatter. It's a mystery. After my death, people will say it was a miracle. Yes, Master Hieronymus, like you I pretend to eat and drink, and Providence maintains my monkish flesh. [*He slaps his belly.*] Listen how hollow it sounds in my kitchen. . . . [*He fumbles in his robe, brings out a bag, gropes in it, and produces a black pudding and a bottle.*] But, having had to undergo exhausting temptations during the night—all of which I overcame—I am today allowing myself some consolation. [*He eats the black pudding in a couple of bites and drains the bottle.*]

HIERONYMUS. [*Dazed.*] Oh . . . oh. . . . Black pudding! Wine! . . . Oh, Father! I am hungry, thirsty. . . . Oh! . . . I've got gnawing pains. . . . I'm shaky on my pins. . . .

THE MONK. [*Finishing his meal.*] My son, think of the thousands of creatures who are hungry and thirsty, and whose lot one must alleviate in Christian fashion. Give them alms, in the name of Christ. Let the rich begin! That's why I came to see you. . . .

HIERONYMUS. [*Annoyed.*] Willingly. How many times will it be returned to me? Seventy-seven times? Give me your blessing Father.

THE MONK. [*Blessing.*] In nomine Pater. . . .

HIERONYMUS. [*Going through the motions of giving coins.*] For the poor, please. . . . A gesture for a gesture. . . . And this charity is costing me as much as the blessing is costing you.

THE MONK. [*Pretending to take the imaginary money.*] Thanks all the same. . . . [*He laughs coarsely.*]

HIERONYMUS. You laugh at my charity?

THE MONK. [*Hilarious.*] Not at all. . . . I had an evil thought, in view of your pious antics. It has just escaped from me.

HIERONYMUS. [*Holding his nose.*] You

stinking creature . . . pah! You pollute the air I breathe.

THE MONK. I give you it, this incense: I give it to you. Breathe it deeply, before it fades away. It's a reward for your snout. Good-by, my son. [*He goes, laughing.*]

HIERONYMUS. [*Furious.*] I'll talk to you in the same language. [*He turns his bottom to the door—and thinks better of it.*] No, I'll keep these unhealthy fumes for myself. [*Shaking his fist.*] Tramp! [*Calming down.*] No, I shan't say that: I'll only think it. One mustn't annoy the monks. They are a rich and powerful caste. You will inherit from me, holy man. How much for heaven? [*He closes the door and comes back into the room.* SYBILLA *comes down the stairs. She wears a black mantle with a hood.*] You are not asleep? Where are you going so early?

SYBILLA. To mass.

HIERONYMUS. Very good. Since you are fasting, you must take advantage of it by taking Communion. It's free. Pray for me, so that I may increase my indulgences, and if they distribute bread at the table of the poor, sneak in with them—but don't say a word to anyone. I have a horror of scandalmongering. Come let me kiss you.

SYBILLA. [*Draws near.* HIERONYMUS *kisses her from a distance, without touching her lips. His wife hides her face and weeps, or pretends to weep.*]

SYBILLA. Is that all I get? A sham! What did I marry for? Other women know caresses and love.

HIERONYMUS. [*Indignantly.*] Are you reproaching me for my purity? Yes, women are always either being amorous or making passionate grimaces. Why? No, you don't need a man's caresses and love. No, no! You pretend to have desire and tenderness in order the better to enslave us and make us subservient to your will. Incontinence is heavily paid for: it is ruinous. [*Haughtily.*] Haven't I given you a child?

SYBILLA. Yes, a child born of neither your flesh nor mine. A parody of a child that doesn't grow, doesn't cry, doesn't eat a crumb.

HIERONYMUS. That is ideal. Look to him, milkless mother. I love you— prudently. I swear it. I detest these erotic fools who dissipate their nights and their strength on women. [*Uneasy.*] You are faithful to me, aren't you?

SYBILLA. What gallant would make eyes at me, dressed as I am, without colors, without jewels, and with only the odor of my own wretchedness for perfume?

HIERONYMUS. Complaining like this, when I am leaving the greater part of my possessions to you? You still have your virginity. You have a treasure in that.

SYBILLA. The spiders stand guard over it.

HIERONYMUS. You are rich! Ask the theologians. Rich! I shall not rob you of it.

SYBILLA. [*In a low voice.*] What grief to be rich with that, and how I envy the whores! [*She goes out.*]

HIERONYMUS. [*Sneering.*] Trollop! Her thin lips have keen edges. Beware, Hieronymus! No, the son of the he-goat and the she-goat who will satisfy her is not yet born. . . . [*Fondly.*] Sweet child! . . . The monk approves my behaving this way with her. Indeed, it's very hard; and sometimes lustful ideas blaze up in my brain. No, not for anything in the world will I touch this priceless, irreplaceable virginity that so few women can boast of possessing. I should be lost utterly. As for going to seek out the whores that she called on in her low voice, as for haunting shady streets, woe to him who succumbs! A crown drops from your wallet at each spasm. And it infects your blood. I shall ask those sanctimonious knaves the monks how they manage, for they are no less lustful than they are

chaste. They must know how to protect their souls and their pence, while
still enjoying what the instinctive
dogs crave. [*He yawns.*] It would be a
good thing to have a sleep, however
short. [*He settles in his chair.*] In this
convenient solitude. . . . [*He falls
asleep. After a moment, the door opens
quietly. The beggar* ROMULUS *comes in.
He is bearded and filthy, but he is
haughty, like his name. On tiptoe, he
walks around the chair. He strokes the
chest.* HIERONYMUS *is dreaming.*] Item
. . . I own a house . . . with a
ghost. . . . [*Suppressed laughter from*
ROMULUS.] A bronze chest . . . in
which gold pieces are breeding
young. . . . A wife and her virginity
. . . and the spiders that watch over
it. . . . [ROMULUS *tries hard not to burst
out laughing.*] I own . . . a stomach
. . . and a gullet . . . that I must . . .
attend to. . . . [*Long sigh.*]

ROMULUS *takes half a loaf, a roast pigeon,
a bit of candle, and a stone flagon from
his beggar's sack.*

ROMULUS. Your health, dear and noble
Hieronymus!

HIERONYMUS. [*Waking up startled.*] A
dream? . . . Food? . . . Light? . . .
And a flagon for thirst? . . . Wonders
of sleep! . . . [*He catches sight of*
ROMULUS.] It's you, my beloved beggar, my affectionate rascal! [*He
stands.*] You are graciousness itself!
My benefactor! Beggars are the only
wellborn people I know. Thank you,
Romulus. [*He eats gluttonously, and
drinks from the neck of the bottle.*] You
are not plying your trade at the cathedral porch?

ROMULUS. Working every day wears me
out. I came to talk to you.

HIERONYMUS. This feast, is it the left-
overs?

ROMULUS. I accept food, but I only
keep money. I eat according to my
fancy at the inn.

HIERONYMUS. Is charity doing well?

ROMULUS. Well enough. The parishioners who come out after the

sermon have heard such terrifying
revelations of the torments of hell
that they make haste to throw alms
for the forgiveness of their villainy.
Fear is the lever of all charity. And
then, I am skilled in my art! So much
so, that if I put it into practice before
you, you yourself. . . .

HIERONYMUS. Do no such thing! Yes,
yes, you are clever. I have a high
opinion of you. You are a better man
because you have become rich.

ROMULUS. Less rich than you are today.

HIERONYMUS. Today? What about tomorrow?

ROMULUS. Tomorrow? If I wanted to, I
should be richer than you, richer
than the guilds, richer than the
whole town.

HIERONYMUS. [*Laughing.*] You need pur-
ging, Romulus. The effluvia of
springtime are stirring in your mind.
The sap is rising.

ROMULUS. If that were the case, I would
be staggering from port to starboard
like a drunken sailor. But I am
standing upright in front of you, and
I have only come here to speak to
you with well-considered words.
However, we must stop all the hidden ears that there are in the walls.

HIERONYMUS. You are bewildering me,
my friend. What are you saying?
Joseph, Mary, Jesus, I am turning
pale. I am fainting! [*He clutches the
chair.*]

ROMULUS. [*Giving him his flask.*] Drink
this brandy.

HIERONYMUS. [*Emptying it with one
draught.*] That warms the cockles of
your heart.

ROMULUS. In future you can be warm
like this always, if you want.

HIERONYMUS. I do want.

ROMULUS. [*Ambiguously.*] You remember
that at various times I have talked to
you about an amazing character? Yes,
and you have never stopped thinking
about him. . . . Well? . . . Where do
the powerful people in this world get
their wealth? From their labor? No!

Do you ever work, Hieronymus? Wealth may have fabulous or despicable origins, but they are always obscure. And no one would risk shining his lantern into this forbidding darkness. I tell you wealth is made by graft, piracy, confiscation, disinheritance, murder, war, speculation in merchandise. . . . Is that everything? No. There is another way.

HIERONYMUS. A diabolical way? Oh, the devil. . . .

ROMULUS. Don't be afraid. The devil only appears to fools. What do you make of those rare forces in the universe which are only taken and used by certain creatures in whom God has set the flame of genius? . . . There are very few of these creatures; but they do exist. Happy is he who meets them and gains their friendship. . . .

HIERONYMUS. Get to the point!

ROMULUS. The person I have talked to you about belongs to this category of sublime outcasts. He is immortal . . . unhappily. Hunted from one country to another, he found shelter under my protection, and since I am protected by the monks, whom I serve as parish spy, he is protected by the Church itself. He is staying in the loft where I hang out, but he is pining in this refuge which, in his view, is a prison. He wants to get to Muscovy, where he is awaited at the Court. To do this he must repair his fortune as quickly as possible. Let us help him, in silence. We shall have our part of it.

HIERONYMUS. What about the risks? . . . And what is this business going to cost?

ROMULUS. What risks? Give him a cellar to use as his laboratory. He has his apparatus with him. He will also need to have. . . . [Worried.] Tell me, is your wife discreet . . . obedient?

HIERONYMUS. You can take my word for that.

ROMULUS. Then all is well. . . . And in three days [He knocks on the chest.] the sides of this chest will burst open.

HIERONYMUS. [Excited.] You are lying! . . . What a wonderful lie!

ROMULUS. Don't hide your happiness. . . . I'll go and fetch the person. . . . Get the cellar ready. . . . Take care, here is your wife.

SYBILLA comes in from the street.

HIERONYMUS. Sybilla, look me in the face. I am in a turmoil. I am not happy.

SYBILLA. There is something like a glint of gold in your eyes.

HIERONYMUS. Be quiet! . . . Come here! . . . [With authority.] In future you will not speak. You will be dumb. Do you understand? [SYBILLA nods.] She is dumb. I shall go down into the cellar, Romulus. You explain to Sybilla what she must know and what she mustn't know, then get to work Romulus, inestimable Romulus!

He goes out to the right. ROMULUS and SYBILLA gaze at each other. Their teeth begin to show. They laugh.

SYBILLA. Is he coming?

ROMULUS. You know, because your spine is shuddering.

SYBILLA. And Hieronymus?

ROMULUS. That's a fine thing to be bothering about! . . . You are dumb. What does it matter to you as long as you have your burning lips and mouth? . . . I'm off. You are beautiful, Sybilla . . . ugly and beautiful, according to the time of the day. [He caresses her. He takes a dried fish from his sack and gives it to SYBILLA; then he goes. SYBILLA eats the fish greedily.]

SYBILLA. Oh, let him come! . . . I shall eat him like this fish.

HIERONYMUS reappears at the right.

HIERONYMUS. Your mouth! It was moving! Were you eating? No? Then were you learning to be dumb, to chew up your words? You must not only be dumb, but deaf and blind. . . . You will have the reward of your obedience. You will have all that a woman desires, velvet, crystal, a parrot, a lute. . . . Ssh! I shan't promise you any more, since you are deaf and can't hear me. . . . Yes, beloved wife . . . you shall have love. . . . Ssh! . . . Busy yourself like a good housewife. . . . Where is your child? . . . Take care of him, so that he doesn't fall ill. [SYBILLA *goes.*] What a fine thing, oho! . . . What is happening to me? If it's a dream, it's stupendous, and I'm a dream better off. If it's real . . . then I shall be liberal. I shall live like a gentleman. I shall visit courtesans. The good time will have come, the end of hardship, fasting, calculation. [*Sunlight strikes the windows. The room is lit up.*] And if I damage my salvation, the monks. . . . Oh, sun, why do you caress me all of a sudden? Is this a portent? . . . Ssh! . . . Where is the ghost? . . . I shall speak so that no one can hear me. [*He moves his lips. His face wears an expression of great joy.*] There! I have said nothing. I heard myself saying nothing. What more should I add?

ROMULUS *comes in from the street. He carries a black box, and is followed by the cold and haughty* CAVALIER ARMADOR.

ROMULUS. Come into the house of that upright man Hieronymus. he will not be ungenerous to you with either help or hospitality. [*He puts down the box.*]

HIERONYMUS. [*Bowing.*] My lord! May due thanks be rendered to you! You do me honor. I am a good man . . . without a great deal in the way of possessions. I have only this house— which is yours, which you will make use of—without wearing it unduly.

THE CAVALIER ARMADOR. [*Haughtily.*] I appreciate your compliment. We shall know little of each other. In three days I shall be gone. You must never recall what I did nor how I did it. What has Romulus told you?

HIERONYMUS. The essence of the matter, which I have difficulty in believing even now I see you here.

ARMADOR. [*Raising his voice.*] You believe me?

HIERONYMUS. No!

ARMADOR. You don't believe me?

HIERONYMUS. Yes!

ARMADOR. You doubt me, so you will believe even better of me. [*Pause.*] I am the Cavalier Armador. [HIERONYMUS *bows.*] Having told you my name, I have no more to tell you about who I am, where I come from, what I am doing. Look at my profile. Have you ever seen similar ones on ancient coins, surrounded by ostentatious inscriptions? I tell you there is a circular inscription around my head, wherein is set down my destiny; but it is not given to you to be able to read it. [*To* ROMULUS.] Beggar, tell him I accept his help. He will be paid for it according to the value of what I make—to the value of . . . [*Catching sight of the bronze chest.*] the contents of this chest.

HIERONYMUS. [*Scared.*] You can penetrate this bronze with your eyes?

ARMADOR. I can see through this bronze as I can see through your forehead bone, you thick man. [*To* ROMULUS.] Carry my things into the cellar. [*He takes hold of the miser's wrist.*] If you betray me, you will die, die a horrible death, for I not only wield happiness with these hands, I work misery too. It is my tragic privilege to command the two elements that actuate the universe, Good and Evil. [ROMULUS *disappears with the black box.*] I have touched you. You are in my power. One last thing. I must have a servant, a pure creature, not an impure one. Someone draws near. A woman. I shall take her for servant. You have lost all right to her.

HIERONYMUS. My lord? . . .

ARMADOR. Do not question me! You will not leave this room and you will not try to find out what I am doing. Romulus will keep watch outside. Be content with the gold I shall give you without deigning to count it.

HIERONYMUS. How much . . . more or

less?

ARMADOR. How do I know? I expect to make a thousand florins. I don't need more than a hundred to get abroad. The rest. . . . [SYBILLA, *holding her child, comes closer.*] Is this your wife? Yes, it's your wife. [SYBILLA *stands fixedly.*] Come here! You shall be my servant. You shall live with me in the cellar, and you shall carry out all my wishes.

SYBILLA *makes a sign of acquiescence.* ROMULUS *returns.*

ROMULUS. All is ready, Cavalier.

HIERONYMUS. My lord . . . all of this . . . is it all really real?

ARMADOR. [*With irony.*] No, it is only a trick.

HIERONYMUS. I don't believe you. It is true. I swear it.

ARMADOR. You reassure me! [*To* SYBILLA.] Servant, put down this dusty infant. Light a gentle fire in the cellar. You, Romulus, watch the chimney and see if the birds round about don't die. [ROMULUS *goes out.*] Hieronymus, fetch me holy water and six measures of best Burgundy.

HIERONYMUS. At once. . . . Do I have to pay for the wine?

ARMADOR. Here! [*He rubs his sleeve and makes a coin appear. He gives it to the miser.*]

HIERONYMUS. [*Astounded.*] You can already make money from your sleeve?

ARMADOR. I can do all sorts of other wonderful things.

HIERONYMUS, *hypnotized, goes out backward. Pause.* ARMADOR *and* SYBILLA *gaze at each other for a long time, then passionately rush into each other's arms.*

ARMADOR. My virgin!

SYBILLA. My ghost!

They hug each other savagely. The MONK *has pushed open the door, and he gazes on, concupiscently.*

Act 2

SCENE. *The same.*

HIERONYMUS. They have been down below, under my feet, since yesterday. A whole day. . . . [*He gets down on his hands and knees and presses his ear to the floor.*] Nothing. . . . What are they up to, if they are doing nothing? I heard voices in the night, as though litanies were being recited. Then there was a great uproar. There were devils frolicking about in the cellar. They were gnashing their teeth, fighting, gasping. It was hideous. There must have been flames. And what if my house had been set on fire? . . . [*He gets up.*] I have been irresponsible. Who is this stranger, and what is he? Is he a Christian? Do I know what this alchemist is doing, what despicable materials he is contriving with, what witchcraft he perpetuates? . . . And why does he want to get to Muscovy? [*He gazes at the door leading to the cellar.*] I have not dared to sleep. A thought has been nibbling with its sharp teeth at my poor brain: is it possible to make gold? . . . People have been hunting this chimera for centuries now. . . . What a frightful hope! . . . Why hasn't he come to show me what he has made yet? [*He walks about.*] During the night I got it into my head that he was a man of evil intention, who was putting on this cabalistic act in order to get himself into my house—and afterward, under the cover of darkness, to come out of his hiding place and kill me . . . rob me! Kill me, let that pass. But rob me! . . . [*He takes fright.*] I have been killed! I have been robbed! Help! [*He rushes toward his chest.*] Not yet! . . . I shan't be killed until pres-

ently, or during tonight. Don't go to
sleep! Be on the lookout! [*Determinedly.*] Shall I denounce him to the
magistrate? No. Not that. . . . They
would arrest me for complicity. He is
a criminal, perhaps a conspirator. Alchemists are hired poisoners. What
can he have done to have to flee to
Muscovy? . . . Hey! . . . Hold your
tongue. . . . If Justice enters here, it
will take all and leave nothing but the
walls. It will even take the walls! The
predator! Justice is an octopus, a
filthy ghoul! . . . [*He sits.*] How heavily the hours hang on me! . . . And
my wife doesn't come. I no longer
have a wife. It's he, the unknown
man, who gives her orders. What is
he commanding her to do? He for-
bids her to disclose what she sees,
what she must do. All the pomp and
circumstance of this witchcraft! The
ceremonial! And I shall never know
anything of it. Perhaps she will know
the great secret, so that I may use it
in my turn? . . . She won't say anything. And who knows that this
stranger will not make her die mysteriously, so that the things that have
been revealed die with her? I am
afraid. My house is haunted. It is
wrapped in too many mists. Even the
ghost has disappeared, accustomed
as he was to breathe the miasmas of
the beyond. He must be perished
with fright. Where is he hiding? Is he
watching over the sorcerer? . . .
Hallo! . . . The ghost will have overheard the secret of the gold. He, too,
he will know. He is robbing me! . . .
He, too, will die of an unknown evil.
[*Vexed.*] Why didn't I make a hole in
the floor? . . . It is certain that I am
being hoaxed. I am at their mercy. It
is stupid. [*He gets up and looks at the
baby, which is lying on a chair.*] I am not
alone. This bit of humanity was listening to me. [*He takes hold of it.*]
Sleep, little one! Take no notice of
what is happening. Men have unhealthy dreams. They dream of

being more powerful than nature,
than its Creator. They want to make
light out of darkness. When you
grow up—if you grow up—you will
be rich; but never wonder where the
riches came from. Enjoy them stupidly! . . . From time to time say to
yourself that your father was tor-
tured and that he did away with his
tranquility for the happiness of his
kin! . . . [*He puts the baby down.*] Sleep,
or I shall destroy you! . . . [*To himself.*] Do not whine, Hieronymus. Be
like your son, insensible and without
complaint. What is taking place had
to be. It is solemn. It is grotesque. It
is poignant. [*He rubs away a tear.*] I
am no doubt very happy . . . and I
feel very miserable. [*He goes to the
window and opens it.*] Romulu-u-u-us!
Here!

VOICE OF ROMULUS. [*In the street.*] No, I
am not coming in. . . . My mission is
to keep watch. . . . The smoke has
changed color seven times now. . . .
Seven is the number. . . . The great
work must be accomplished!

HIERONYMUS. [*Drawing back.*] You think
so? Tell me! . . . Don't tell me! . . .
You would say that you don't think
so, and then you would persuade me
that the other didn't know how to
make gold. And you would be drunk
every day. If you don't think so, I do!

VOICE OF ROMULUS. This adventure has
upset your understanding. If I didn't
believe it, would I have spent my
whole day keeping watch on the
crowd, the smoke, the passers-by, the
cats on the tiles, when begging is
more profitable to me? You don't
deserve what is happening to you,
Hieronymus.

HIERONYMUS. I deserve it a hundred
times over, by my insomnia and my
gripes. . . . That's enough talking. . . . There are echoes in this
neighborhood. . . . Romulus, I have a
presentiment of the best and the
worst.

VOICE OF ROMULUS. [*Laughing.*] That is

because the best and the worst are going to happen. What do you know better and worse than gold? . . . I am going back to my watch. . . . Close the window. Here is the monk, coming at the trot. . . . Look out for this rascal! [*His footsteps are heard going away.*]

HIERONYMUS. [*Closing the window.*] The rascal! . . . He has smelled it! He has nosed out the gold from the distance, the rogue! What is he coming here for? To stink up my room? [*Distressed.*] Or has he some revelation of what is being manufactured below? They have visions, these monks who pretend to be advised by the angels. . . . They haven't only those. . . . Tribunals, torture chambers, the stake. . . . They open at will the portals of heaven or the gates of hell. . . . But later? [*Joyfully.*] I shall buy them all! . . . And the bishops . . . and even the Pope. . . . With my gold I shall buy the Trinity! [*He rubs his hands.*] Come in, scorpion!

There is a knock on the door.

VOICE OF THE MONK. It is the suffering Church that is passing by! . . . "Knock, and it shall be opened unto you," said Our Lord—who knew what he was talking about.

The door opens. THE MONK *comes in, laughing.*

THE MONK. Good day, Master Hieronymus. How's your health?

HIERONYMUS. [*Bittersweet.*] Like that of the suffering Church in person. . . . Good day, Father! . . . My health? . . . Ha! . . . I am radiant. I shall die a centenarian!

THE MONK. [*Sententiously.*] Reckless man! Death comes like a thief.

HIERONYMUS. Drive the thief away!

THE MONK. Take heart! He is not coming in. . . . But do you know that he will not come in tomorrow? There is sudden death. There is Lucifer, who sometimes strangles those whose virtues exasperate him. There is the wickedness of neighbors coveting

property. There are epidemics. And all the plagues. Finally, there is our ecclesiastical Justice, that sees to the rooting out of thorns from the human meadow. And all mean death.

HIERONYMUS. [*Quaking.*] Why are you delivering this speech to me . . . to me, precisely?

THE MONK. Stupid! . . . It's the little salutary sermon that I whisper to all the parishioners. . . . [*He fixes his gaze on him.*] Master Hieronymus, you seem anxious.

HIERONYMUS. No, no, no! . . . I am cheerful, well, tranquil. . . . Or if I appear anxious, it is old age, it is cares showing through.

THE MONK. Some remorse? Your hands are twitching.

HIERONYMUS. [*Rambling.*] Yes. . . . The result of a bad night. . . . Because of the owls. . . . It was cold.

THE MONK. You have lit a fire against the cold? At this time of year?

HIERONYMUS. [*Stammering.*] That is it . . . yes . . . yes.

THE MONK. [*Taking his hand.*] My son, do you not want to make confession?

HIERONYMUS. Me? . . . What have I done? . . . Oh, no, Father. I have nothing to confess to you.

THE MONK. And if, in fatherly fashion, I help you to confess nothing? [*He gazes into his eyes.*] We monks receive from God the faculty of reading souls like reading books.

HIERONYMUS. [*Regaining himself.*] It's a lie! . . . There is nothing written in my soul. All is written in the folio here. It is my inventory. [*He hesitates.*] What I confess to you, Father, is that I am troubled. . . . My heart is veiled. . . .

THE MONK. I knew it. There are very heavy secrets that one cannot entrust to men. Confessors are not men: they are sepulchers. I am listening my son. . . . Afterward, you will no longer need to light a fire, for you will be deluged with rays of divine love. . . . Yes! . . . This night I had a very clear vision that you were in danger. Come, I am listening.

HIERONYMUS. [*Very quietly.*] In the name of the Father . . . and of the Son . . . *Mea culpa* . . . [*Fiercely.*] Come back presently—when it is darker. . . . [*He jokes.*] I have a story to tell you—no, a comical nightmare. I like you a great deal. Presently! . . . You will find something to your profit in it. Yes, your monastery will reap its benefit.

THE MONK. As your soul will reap its. . . . Till presently! . . . It is as it ought to be. . . . In the evening words have other sounds than they have in the morning. That is why confessionals are always dark . . . [*He yawns.*] so that truth can shine forth. . . . And the darkness symbolizes the mystery in which we enshroud the confessions of the living. . . . I bless you! . . . [*He obliges, laughing derisively.*]

HIERONYMUS. [*Holding his nose.*] Thank you! . . . Go! . . . He has made a stink! . . . He has farted his benediction! . . . No, your bottom is no censer!

THE MONK. [*Delighted.*] Alas, my contemptible body is carrion. All my attentions are addressed to the soul. . . .

He goes.

HIERONYMUS. [*Angered.*] The barefaced . . . He knows. . . . I am betrayed. . . . He wants me to confess. . . . How could he know? . . . I am going to call Romulus. . . . No. This beggar is the monks' friend. . . . The monks know all. They did not want the Cavalier to make gold in their monastery. They sent him to me, and they are keeping watch on him, and keeping watch on me at the same time. . . . This is a good place here. . . . These monks are abominable rogues. . . . Why should I have scruples with respect to them? . . . [*He is out of breath.*] Watch out for traps! . . . Once the gold is made, are they not going to rush in, run straight to the cellar

door, bawling, "Evil! Evil!" and deliver me up alive to the inquisitors, who will seize the gold—both the gold and my carcass, which they will meekly burn with mansuetude, not without absolving and regaling their accomplice Romulus? . . . I am sold, delivered up, lost, burned, damned. . . . And robbed, above all, robbed! . . . Enough of this deception! . . . I shall unmask them! . . . I shall kick this pale cavalier and his trickery tools out of doors! I am master in my house! Where is my sword? . . . I shall break the doors open! . . . [*He takes a sword down from the wall.*] Like this! . . . [*He makes passes like a swordsman.*] Ah! . . . Oh! . . . [*The cellar door has opened.* ARMADOR, *hands behind his back and smiling, contemplates the scene.*] I cleave him! . . . I cut him in twain! . . . Back . . . bleed . . . die . . . no quarter . . . charlatan . . . suborner . . . sacrilegious . . . accursed . . . sneak . . . robber! . . . This is justice. . . . I slice you, coward! . . . What? You are immortal? You defy death? . . . I stab you, interstab you, and counterstab you! . . . Ah! . . . Oh! . . . And I fling your remains like old refuse into the gutter. . . . Ha! . . . He is dead. . . . There he lies. . . . It serves him right! . . . [*He is bathed in perspiration and wants to sit down.* ARMADOR *comes forward nonchalantly.* HIERONYMUS *gives a cry of fright and lets his sword fall. He retreats, seeks to hide himself, and stammers.*] Ah, sire! . . . I was doing my exercise. . . . I belong to the Old Order of Saint Michael. . . . How are you, may I ask?

ARMADOR. [*Icily.*] He is dead. . . . There he lies. . . . [*He advances toward* HIERONYMUS.] Fool! . . . Vulgar creature! [*He spits at* HIERONYMUS.] At the very moment that I bring you a prodigious message, you are in imagination killing me—me, your benefactor! . . . If you had a less opaque skull, I would prove to you that the Cavalier Armador is invulnerable. He could not die, were he pierced by seven swords. I, just as you see me, have been hanged, shot, drowned, felled, even fastened to a gibbet, and buried. . . . It is supernatural, unbelievable, isn't it? . . So many things under the planets that watch over us remain unexplained. I am neither alive nor dead; but one sees on our globe beings with human appearances who do not belong to humanity. They are dangerous and good-natured—it all depends—and they possess the terrifying power of meting out death to those who give offense to them.

HIERONYMUS. [*On his knees.*] Sire! . . . Pardon! . . . I was wandering in my mind. . . . I admire you. . . . You are noble. . . . You are generous. . . . I am only an earthworm. . . . Let me make amends for my effrontery. [*He stands.*] So, you cannot die? Why, you are the richest of men, since you possess immortality! . . . Yes, I have heard that certain beings change their shapes ceaselessly across the centuries. It is extraordinary! You possess immortality? . . . Share this possession, sire! . . . I am so afraid of death. . . . Sell me the recipe.

ARMADOR. What would you do with it? Is it not enough that I give you gold?

HIERONYMUS. [*Bewildered.*] Gold? . . . He gives me gold? . . . Where is it, this gold? Show me!

ARMADOR. [*Bringing his hands from behind his back and displaying a coin.*] Here!

HIERONYMUS. [*Jumping about.*] Noel! Noel! [*He seizes the coin.*] I want to touch it. . . . You have made this, sire?

ARMADOR. [*Disdainfully.*] It is the first proof. Yes, the gold is made. It is cooling in its earthen mold. This piece is for you.

HIERONYMUS. [*Lyrical.*] Oh, joy! . . . He has made gold for me! . . . He is a god! [*He tosses the coin.*] It is real, it has weight, it rings! [*He kisses it.*] I

love it. It is a sacred host. [*He takes* ARMADOR's *hands.*] Lord Armador, I am your slave. . . . I would not be more affected if Christ were to give me His holy cross! . . . There now, do I not blaspheme in your honor? . . . [*He draws back.*] What? There is gold on your hands! The wise man has hands of gold! . . . Give me your hands! Cut them off! No. Keep them to work with again, these sweet hands, these sublime hands, these hands of fire. . . . Let them work hard. . . . My chest is huge. . . . I have empty rooms. . . . What does it matter to you, my friend, my brother, you whom I love most in this life? [*He puts the coin in his pocket.*] Are you sure that this coin will pass, that no one will guess its origin?

ARMADOR. [*Annoyed.*] Are you saying that I am a counterfeiter? [*He raises his fist, but changes his mind.*] Go, run to the inn. With that coin you will buy some Burgundy wine.

HIERONYMUS. You had some yesterday. Have you drunk it already?

ARMADOR. Obey! . . . What does it matter to you, since nothing is costing you anything, not even the gold without which nothing can be bought. I need this wine to finish my work.

HIERONYMUS. Wine for your work?

ARMADOR. You do not need to understand. Get the wine . . . and hide the excitement that is making your snout blaze.

HIERONYMUS *goes out. Left alone,* ARMADOR *goes to the chest, takes some keys from his pocket, and tries them in the lock. The lid opens.* SYBILLA *comes in. She is disheveled and she staggers. She is visibly happy. Her eyes have violet rings round them. She has patches of gold on her cheeks, her arms, her throat.*

SYBILLA. Armador, leave the chest. It is not time yet.

ARMADOR. I was trying the skeleton key. . . . [*He clasps her in his arms.*] Soon we shall have finished playing this comedy. Tonight we shall run away.

SYBILLA. Yes, I shall follow you along the roads, across the plains, over the seas, as far as hell, which will burn less than your skin, the skin of a young devil. . . . Come. . . . I need more loving.

ARMADOR. Aren't you weary? I have spent a whole day tenderly tearing you with my teeth and my claws. . . . Ah, if only I could forge myself a priapus of bronze that would finally satisfy you!

SYBILLA. I am broken as though I had been put on the wheel; but, my executioner, I am still hungry. . . . I am happy, happy! . . . My life has begun with you. I was a thin white corpse that you quickened with your heat. You were the voluptuous ghost that came to enchant my nights as a lonely wife. . . . As a virgin, I wept. As a bitch, I rejoice. . . . I am well revenged. . . . I am overflowing with love and hatred, and the two are good for me. . . . Armador, my wizard, what did you do to bewitch me? . . . You are handsome. . . . That is your secret. . . . You are passionate. . . . That is all your guile.

ARMADOR. Oh, that night were come . . . far away . . . very far away . . .

SYBILLA. Where?

ARMADOR. Near the Western sea, in the town of bells, where we were both of us born; where, lad and girl, we played on the quays; where the sails of the ships swelled up. . . . Do you remember? . . . With the gold we take with us we shall open a tavern where the men from Osterland will come, and the English, and the Genoese, and the Levantines. There will be dicing there, and we shall secretly sell virgins. It is a rich town, another Venice, where all the vessels from the open sea make land. And the shores of the Zwijn endlessly echo with the throaty rattle of the orgy. Later, we shall have houses, fields, servants. No, I am not an adventurer, and if I followed the armies, if I lived the inflammed life of the Flemish mercenaries, it was because I was without love and without home, the saddest of orphans. Now I have found you again. You have the odor of birth. Your flesh is salt, like the sand of my country. You have become beautiful in my hands, more precious than gold. And what does the ruin of this baleful old man matter to me, when a look from you makes me like a child, and makes me oblivious of my crimes? . . . [*He takes her in a long embrace.*] Do not tell me that you love me. . . . You are dumb. . . . [*He frees himself.*] I hear someone running. Stand absolutely still.

SYBILLA *arranges herself in ghostly fashion, her eyes closed.* HIERONYMUS *enters, out of breath. He is laden with flasks.*

HIERONYMUS. There are six . . . dating from the time of the blue comet . . . the best of the purple wines . . . that makes you drunk . . . that would make Bacchus lightheaded. . . . Ho! the coin was a good one. They said to me, "By Saint Matthew, you can see well enough where the bags of crowns lie!" [*He puts the bottles on the table; then he looks at his wife.*] Sybilla? . . . You? . . . You are like a wax candle. . . . Is she dead? . . . In a trance? . . . Hey, Cavalier, what have you done with her? . . . Are you a vampire? . . . She is a statue in snow. . . . Have you killed her? . . . [ARMADOR *gives signs of impatience.*] I beg your pardon. . . . All is very well. . . . You were allowed. . . . All is well because the gold is good. . . . I do not reproach you for anything.

ARMADOR. I am taking these three flasks for my work. Keep the others for yourself. Drink them. You may do that, now that you are rich. [*He goes back to the cellar, armed with his bottles.*]

HIERONYMUS. [*Walking around* SYBILLA, *examining her from all sides.*] Tell me, wife, what have you seen? . . . What did he do? . . . The secret? . . . The gold? . . . Did you help him? . . . The

formulas? . . . The rites! . . . Speak!
. . . I call on you to speak! . . . Look,
he is robbing me. . . . He will keep
the greater part. . . . How many coins
has he made? . . . Make an estimate!
. . . A hundred? . . . More? . . . Will
you speak, good-wife? [SYBILLA *indicates that she will not.*] No? . . . No? . . .
[*He raises his fist.*] She will not speak.
. . . True. . . . She is dumb. . . . Now
is my chance. . . . Sybilla, I cancel my
order. . . . I am going to strike you.
. . . I strike you. . . . [SYBILLA *looks at
him with a hard expression.*] As well
beat an ass. . . . Capable woman! . . .
Be dumb! . . . Your silence is a wise
economy. . . . Forget how to use
words. . . . In that way you will never
betray me. . . . *"Cherchez la femme,"*
they say in legal jargon. With me,
they will seek her in vain. As for your
secret, I shall not ask you. . . . I make
you a gift of it. . . . You will end up
by whispering it in your dreams,
without knowing it. . . . You speak
quite loudly at night. . . . I often
eavesdrop on you, with my ear to the
wall. . . . You laugh. . . . You pant.
. . . You ramble. . . . You groan. . . .
It is comical! [*He looks at her closely. In
a shaky voice.*] All the same, I would
like to know . . . What did he order
you to do? . . . What have you done
in that cellar, since yesterday, with
this man who has such strange
power? . . . [*Pause.*] I am not jealous
. . . hee, hee, hee . . . not jealous . . .
not a cuckold . . . hee, hee, hee . . .
[*Hissing.*] But he has touched you. It
is written on your body. See how
shrewd I am! . . . There . . . and
there . . . on your face, your neck,
your wrists. . . . [*He sniffs at her.*]
Perhaps he ordered you to strip
yourself naked, as on a witches' sab-
bath? . . , Yes? . . . Answer! . . . Hold
your tongue! . . . What does it matter
when the gold is here? . . . I see
traces of it on your flesh. . . . Doubtless there is some on your breasts . . .
on your stomach . . . on your thighs.

Take off your dress! No! . . . That is
unnecessary. . . . He will explain to
me. . . . You could be all gold, and it
would still leave me unexcited. But
take care, with your mask of dumb-
ness, with your green eyes! . . . Be
without a memory! [*Footsteps are
heard.*] He is coming back. . . . His
steps seem heavy. . . . What burden is
he carrying?

ARMADOR *appears, holding a leather bag
which he swings around. Sound of money.*

ARMADOR. Listen to these chimes!

HIERONYMUS. [*Rejoicing.*] Heavenly music! . . . More! . . . [*He holds out his
hands.*] Give it to me! . . . It is the
fountainhead of life. . . . Redemp-
tion. . . . [*He tears the bag from
ARMADOR's hands.*] Give it to me! . . . I
am rich! [*Catching sight of SYBILLA.*]
Go! . . . You must not know what I
possess. [SYBILLA *goes out, like a phan-
tom.*] Cavalier! . . . *Te Deum!* . . . How
many coins? . . . Is it an installment?
. . . Not enough, no, no, not enough.

ARMADOR. [*Arms folded.*] Glutton! Not
enough? When I make you the
richest citizen in the town? Count it!

HIERONYMUS. I haven't got my spec-
tacles. I shall count it tonight. . . .
One only counts well at night. [*He
opens his chest and throws the bag in.*] It
is not too much, sire. And do not
think yourself a Maecenas. . . . I have
given you shelter. . . . I have risked
my skin and my salvation, defied the
law and the devil. . . . You have
burned my wood. . . . She is ill from
it, poor woman. . . . [*Fiercely.*] What
have you done with her? Why are
there these patches of gold on her
skin? . . . Such a beautiful woman!
. . . She will die of a mysterious ill-
ness. . . . Tell me, do you think you
have paid me for all this?

ARMADOR. [*Amused.*] I have only drawn
blood from your wife.

HIERONYMUS. [*Amazed.*] Blood! . . . That
costs nothing. . . . Why?

ARMADOR. Because the blood of virgins
contains an essential principle, with-

out which you cannot make gold. The people, with their common sense, often say that gold is made from blood. . . .Yes, your royal florins have your wife's blood in their alloy.

HIERONYMUS [*moaning.*] *Miserere!* She has no more blood! . . . Her lovely blood!

ARMADOR. The moon makes blood again in women. Besides, I made your virgin drink wine all the time.

HIERONYMUS. I had the presentiment that he was a vampire! . . . You have drunk the blood. . . . She is going to die. . . . Pay me! . . . If not, I shall denounce you. . . . And they will drive a stake into your grave and it will pierce your heart.

ARMADOR. [*Shrugs his shoulders.*] It that all? . . . I am going back to my laboratory. Just now I am going to make gold for my own use.

HIERONYMUS. Not with my wife's blood! . . . I forbid you! . . . How many coins? . . . How many?

ARMADOR. As many as there is blood for. . . . Anger yourself, my good man, howl, yell. . . . What do your threats matter to me? Am I not immortal?

HIERONYMUS. [*Furiously.*] True. [*Servilely.*] Carry on, sire . . . but leave her alive . . . in appearance, at least. . . . Otherwise there will be the burial and the service, and expense, expense! . . . And set aside for me a little of this gold which is costing me the blood of a beloved creature.

ARMADOR. Yes, if you give me a drink. . . . This is a memorable day, Hieronymus. You are rich, are you not? Give me a drink.

HIERONYMUS. This wine would improve by keeping. . . . Yes, let us drink. . . . I have had so much excitement. [*He opens a flask and offers it to* ARMADOR *who drinks from its neck.*] Not all of it! Is this the way you alchemists drink? . . . Cavalier, I drain this flask in your honor! [*He takes the flask from* ARMA-

DOR's *hands, and drinks in turn.*]

ARMADOR. [*Drinking.*] Make merry! . . . And disguise your pleasure. Woe betide him who shows his joy. . . . Drink! . . . Here you can wear a beatific smile. . . . Get soaked, Hieronymus! What? I am making you rich, and you seem dismayed? . . . Do you find the wine bitter?

HIERONYMUS. [*Taking the flask again.*] Not at all! . . . It is a wine that makes you drunk. . . . I am getting fuddled. . . . I am tipsy. . . . Stop! . . . Cavalier, how dear you are to me! [*He hugs him.*] I am touched. . . . You get soaked, too! [*He offers the flask.*] I am standing treat. Almost all of my desires are fulfilled. . . . All . . . save one. . . .

ARMADOR. [*Still drinking, and pretending to get confused.*] What a good wine. . . . It is like a wave of sunlight in my guts. What are you saying? What wish can you still give utterance to? You are rich.

HIERONYMUS. I would like to be richer than rich. . . . To be rich among the rich. . . . Has this wine got hold of you? . . . Listen. I am not happy. I shall be when, in my turn, I can make gold, like you.

ARMADOR. [*In a thick voice.*] Really? . . . Is that all? Ask your wife. She knows the procedure. She knows all. . . . I'm thirsty. . . . [*He drinks.*] Except the formula. I have it on me.

HIERONYMUS. If you are thirsty, drink. . . . What grapes! . . . Oh! . . . Oh! . . . Is this formula in Arabic, in Hebrew, or in honest Latin? . . . I do not speak any of these tongues.

ARMADOR. [*As though in a daze.*] Beast! . . . Look! . . . [*He takes a square of parchment from his pocket, and holds it out.*] Any apothecary will decipher that for you. [HIERONYMUS *reads the formula and pockets it.*] Give me the parchment back. I will give you the furnace and the retorts that are below.

HIERONYMUS *draws back.*

HIERONYMUS. [*Sharply.*] But . . . I have given it back to you. . . . Thank you for the retorts. I shall not do anything with them, since you haven't given me the formula.

ARMADOR. [*Drinking.*] You want too much, my friend! . . . My eyes are growing dim. . . . Go and get some more flasks. . . . [*He sits holding his forehead.*]

HIERONYMUS. Why are you holding your forehead? Are you ill? . . . My friend?

ARMADOR. [*Stammering.*] Tired . . . worn out . . . flee . . . all the time . . . to Muscovy this time . . . my enemies. . . . If I could sleep . . . Ah! . . . This immortality . . . what a burden!

HIERONYMUS. Do you want me to relieve you of it . . . out of kindness? . . . If I had immortality! . . . I am getting impatient. . . . What is the good of possessing so much gold, if I must leave it?

ARMADOR. [*Talking to himself.*] I would never have the strength to throw off the black stone, heavier than a millstone, that I wear on my chest. . . . I shall not die . . . as long as I cannot find that strength. . . . Fabulous stone . . . accursed . . . fatal . . . [*He lays his head on the table.*]

HIERONYMUS. Black stone . . . on his chest? . . . [*He wipes his forehead.*] Now I know. . . . Immortality . . . black stone. . . . Are you asleep, my friend? . . . Rest. . . . He hasn't the strength? . . . I have. . . . [*He drinks.*] I draw it from the wine. . . . What a formidable deed I am going to accomplish. . . . Accursed stone . . . fabulous . . . fatal. . . . My friend, there are beads of sweat on your brow. . . . You are hot, aren't you? . . . Let me see to you. . . . I will open your shirt. . . . [ARMADOR *has fallen asleep.* HIERONYMUS *undoes* ARMADOR'S *collar.*] This silver chain is in your way. . . . I shall take it off. . . . And here is the black stone! . . . [*He weighs the chain and the stone in his hand.*] It can't be worth much. But immortality . . . ho, ho! [*He fastens the stone around his neck and does up* ARMADOR'S *shirt.*] The daring one gets from wine! Was it I who just did something? No, it was someone else. . . . I have done nothing. Tomorrow I shall hardly remember it any more. . . . [*He drinks.*] Cavalier . . . you are no longer anything at all . . . not anything! . . . [*He laughs with joy.*] I am everything. All that you were! . . . It only needed a little drink. . . . You are despicable! . . . If I were to pull your nose, eh? . . . You have been robbed, yes, robbed as though you had been waylaid in a forest. . . . Long live Hieronymus!

ARMADOR. [*Suddenly standing up.*] Long live Hieronymus!

HIERONYMUS. [*Falling seated on his chest with fright.*] You are no longer drunk?

ARMADOR. It has gone. . . . What have I told you during this brief drunkenness?

HIERONYMUS. I shall try to remember. . . . [*There is a knock at the door.*] Hide! It is the monk. He was against the shutter.

ARMADOR. I am going. The beggar's share is still to be minted, and the gold for my journey. [*He takes* HIERONYMUS' *hand.*] I shall say good-by at dawn. Make good use of your fortune. And give all the gold you find scattered on the flags of the cellar to the poor, in my name. [*He goes out to the right.*]

HIERONYMUS. So be it! [*He puts his fingers to his nose in the direction of the door through which* ARMADOR *has gone, lights the candle, for night has gradually come during the last conversation, and runs to open the door.*] Father! . . . You, at last!

THE MONK *enters.*

THE MONK. Wine? Who treated you? Wine at Hieronymus'?

HIERONYMUS. [*Caught by surprise.*] Yes. . . . It was for the two of us. . . . Since you didn't come, I drank alone. . . . I am rich, you understand!

THE MONK. You must have drunk to

dare to confess that to me.

HIERONYMUS. I haven't drunk . . . not enough. . . . I was poor. . . . But I have suddenly come into a legacy. . . . [*Insistent.*] I am very rich!

THE MONK. How talkative you are, my son. Why these confidences? Does your wine have such a violent effect? Let me taste it.

HIERONYMUS. I am not raving. Do you hear me, monk? . . . I am incalculably rich. . . . [*Suddenly.*] Would you like some gold?

THE MONK. [*Without surprise.*] Gold? No. My order, which is a very humble one, does not accept gold. . . . If you were to give me a little wine, rather?

HIERONYMUS. [*Nervously.*] You shall have gold and wine. [*He gives him the second flask of wine.*] And if I were to make my will, eh?

THE MONK. He is going to die! I shall run and get the holyoils! Do not forget the poor monks, my son. What a blow! Let me drink this wine to recover myself. [*He drinks from the neck of the flask.*] Exquisite! This venerable wine is a revelation of a Capuchin who only gets *aqua pumpa* in his monastery. [*He drinks.*]

HIERONYMUS. A real monk! A dirty dog! I swear you are in my will. . . . No. . . . I shall write a provision for you at once.

THE MONK. The notary will authenticate it before the magistrates. . . . Do it, for the love of God! . . . But no money in gold. . . . Ciboria, shrines, reliquaries, they are all right. . . . Wait! Leave us this house and its orchard. Nothing else. This suspect house that no one will ever buy, this haunted house built on a cemetery. We shall sanctify this gruesome land where criminals are buried, and Jews, Mohammedans, and suicides. As for your gold, my son . . . make use of it . . . enjoy it.

HIERONYMUS. Mum's the word! . . . The house is yours—which does not mean that I am going to give up the ghost immediately, eh? I believe that I shall live to be very old, longer than the customary span of years. [*He sits at the table and takes up his pen.*] And in return?

THE MONK. Twenty masses a year for eternity.

HIERONYMUS. With music, of course? . . . Is eternity long?

THE MONK. Fairly. . . . And you will have the certainty of being [*He sings.*] *in paradisum!*

HIERONYMUS. Agreed, by God! . . . I shall write it down. . . . I, Master Hieronymus, quite clear-sighted, solemnly give to the Capuchins my house and the orchard, on condition that they hoist me up to paradise. And I sign it, Hieronymus, landowner.

THE MONK. [*Taking the paper.*] In the name of the order, thank you! [*He laughs coarsely.*]

HIERONYMUS. [*Standing up and holding his nose.*] Pig! . . . He makes the place stink! . . . Is that your thanks?

THE MONK. I cannot contain my pleasure. It is the same with all my sentiments. . . . You were talking about this legacy. Is it an important one?

HIERONYMUS. [*Uneasy.*] I haven't valued it. [*He goes to the chest, opens it, and takes out a bag of gold.*] Is this good gold, my monk? [*He jingles the bag.*]

THE MONK. Authentic, if I believe my ears on the matter. . . . There's a good hundred florins. . . . What good works you are going to do! [*He opens the bag and looks at a coin.*] It was in this gold that they cast the Biblical calf that Moses destroyed. Let us drink to your fortune!

HIERONYMUS *closes the chest and takes hold of the flask.*

HIERONYMUS. I drink. [*He drinks.*] What an unction! I am hazy with it. . . . This wine is expensive. . . . You seemed to say that I could sin . . . more or less. Is drinking wine a sin?

THE MONK. Such a little one. I never

drink anything else. But drinking wine and not giving some to him who is thirsting is a great sin.

HIERONYMUS. [*Giving him the flask.*] Take it. . . . My body is swelling up. I'm afloat. . . . Ah! I haven't drunk as much as this in thirty years! [*He staggers.*] Monk . . . I would like to know . . . if the clergy . . . ever trouble themselves . . . to find out . . . the origins . . . of the fortunes . . . of pious benefactors?

THE MONK. Such mean cares are far from us. [*Sententiously.*] Fortune comes to them from Providence. It is the reward of virtue and labor.

HIERONYMUS. Bravo! . . . That's exactly it. . . . I was thinking of confessing. . . . It is unnecessary. . . . One has these scruples. . . .

THE MONK. Oh, guileless heart! Bah! If the Evil One were to lodge here in person, I would belt him outside with blows from the holy scapular. . . .

HIERONYMUS. [*Drunk.*] Long live the monks! . . . I want to embrace you. . . . You have a lovely puss. . . .

THE MONK. Let us embrace in Jesus Christ, dear Hieronymus. [*They embrace.* HIERONYMUS *falls down.*]

HIERONYMUS. I'm giving way. . . . The room is going round. . . . The floor is sinking. . . . Monk, you are rising to the ceiling. . . . Who is lighting these candles?

THE MONK. Enjoy a foretaste of heaven. . . . You are experiencing grace. . . . It will leave you. . . . Have a drink, my son. [*He forcibly introduces the flask into* HIERONYMUS' *mouth and pours it.* HIERONYMUS *collapses, face down.*] I thought he was made of sterner stuff. A capital wine, indeed! [*He runs to the door leading to the street.*] Romulus! [*He runs to the cellar door.*] Armador! Sybilla! [*The three characters appear simultaneously to left and right.* SYBILLA *is disheveled and half-naked.* ROMULUS *carries a lantern.*] Praised be the Lord Bacchus! The masterwork begins!

ROMULUS. I'll open the chest. . . . Come. . . . [*The four of them, clearly lit up by the lantern, lean over the yawning chest.*] I'll take back the bag of gold florins, real florins, that I loaned for the make-believe.

ARMADOR. [*Holding out a similar bag.*] And replace it with this, which contains well-minted discs, but of gilded metal. [*This is done.*]

THE MONK. Now. . . . We find in this chest eighty unquestionable gold florins, the fortune of Master Hieronymus. Let our eight hands carry them to their destiny.

SYBILLA. In this bag. Until we can share them out according to our deserts. [*The gold is thrown into the bag.*]

ARMADOR. And as all in this universe is nothing more than seeming, let us generously make good the loss by scattering eighty florins bearing the image of the ape—the grand master of doubtful coinage. [*He empties another bag into the chest.*]

ROMULUS. This is called the transmutation of metals. I have spoken!

The chest is closed again. HIERONYMUS, *who has heard the noise of the metal, raises himself. The four accomplices scatter into dark corners.*

HIERONYMUS. [*Falling again.*] I am in a cave. . . . They are unloading gold. . . . My throat . . . wants to drink . . . water from a river . . . that carries gold nuggets.

THE MONK. [*Hastening to him.*] Here is the river, my son. [*He forces him to drink. Hiccuping from the drunken man.*]

ROMULUS. And now? . . . It is dead of night. You, Armador and Sybilla, must wait till dawn to flee. The gates of the town are shut. The wagons that go to Bruges leave at five o'clock. . . . I shall watch the drunk from the back of the room. Take your amusement in the cellar. Have you still some wine? Go with them, monk. You have done well. You deserve some relaxation.

THE MONK. [*Reddening.*] Lovely Sybilla, I

want to poke my brush in your flue.
[*He tries to hug her.* SYBILLA *laughs.*]

ARMADOR. Come along, monk! Joyful
offices are celebrated in this crypt.
You will lose your salvation there.

THE MONK. I lost that when I was still a
novice. [*He goes out to the right.*]

SYBILLA. [*Embracing* ARMADOR *and dragging him away.*] Come, my ghost! Let
us make love until dawn, and let us
pretend we have all the abandon-
ments, for dissembled thoughts are
turning in the air like flies. I shall
follow them on the wing, for I too
am a fly.

They go out to the right. ROMULUS *goes to
station himself at the back of the room.
Laughter and talking dies away below.
Pause. A haggard* HIERONYMUS *rises on
his elbows.*

HIERONYMUS. Thirst! . . . Monk! . . . He
has gone, the rogue . . . with my will.
. . . I have robbed you, jackal! . . . It
serves you right. . . . I am immortal!
[*He tries to get up, but falls back. He
groans.*] Rich . . . rich . . . and more,
a magician. . . . Sleep . . . no . . . not
sleep when one is rich. . . . They
might come. . . . [*Hiccuping, he drags
himself toward his chest.*] I want you,
my gold. . . . [*He opens his chest and
half plunges in.*] I want to lie with you
. . . my gold. . . . [*With difficulty, he
hoists himself up and disappears into his
chest. His voice can be heard.*] How
good it is . . . good . . . good. . . .

*The chest closes on the miser. In the semi-
darkness* ROMULUS *abandons himself to
his noiseless, irrepressible laughter.*

Act 3

SCENE. *The same. It is night. The candle is
shining. Nothing is seen, except an atten-
tive shadow near the staircase. Twelve
strikes in the distance, then there are
tremendous snores that suddenly stop as*

the lid of the chest opens. HIERONYMUS'
head emerges.

HIERONYMUS. Where am I? In gold. . . .
What a grand sleep! . . . The night is
bewitched. . . . Golden walls. . . .
Golden darkness. . . . Golden silence.
. . . I too am gold, and am shaped
like a disc with my face in the center.
. . . No, I dreamed. . . . I breathed
golden dust, golden vapor. Gold
came in through my mouth, my
nostrils, my eyes. My saliva was
yellow. . . . I bought the globe and all
that covers it, oceans, mountains, em-
pires, peoples, and ruins. And the
seasons, storms, and creation. . . .
That was a miscalculation, for I shall
lose on it when the end of the world
comes. . . . Ho! I shall buy the Vale
of Josaphat. . . . Between whiles,
there shone sovereign faces modeled
on the coins, and their engraved lips
deferentially spoke words of gold to
me. I replied to them unsatisfac-
torily: my mouth was sour. . . . I was
forgetting. . . . I bought Calvary . . .
Jerusalem . . . Mecca and Rome. . . .
I possess the Mohammedan paradise
and the keys to the Christian heaven.
. . . [*Halfway out of the chest.*] I should
have had a bed that wasn't so hard.
My forehead is ringing like a bell.
The monk made me drunk on my
own wine; but he drank the greater
part of it. I shall buy all the vineyards. I alone shall drink wine. . . .
Later, I gazed on wonder-struck
crowds. I juggled with crowns. . . .
Pardon. . . . With a sling, I flung
them to the zenith. And the crew of
humans leaped up with greedy
hands. What a lot of gold! The sea
does not contain more shells. Too
much gold! I shall plunge the sur-
plus in a river. Or I shall make
statues from it . . . mine . . . all in
gold . . . huge . . . on a golden ele-
phant trampling on the illustrious
mighty. [*He hoists himself out of his
chest.*] What brown, or black, or gray
thoughts there are on my poor head!

It has all happened to me so suddenly! And what an overwhelming role I must play in future. Yesterday I was the timid Hieronymus with his little economies. Tonight I find myself flung outside time and law. [*He feels himself.*] It's me. . . . And I am all alone with myself. . . . First they will say I am mad, then they will say I am a genius. Every man will be my enemy and my friend at the same time. And I shall remain alone, among the thousands of idolaters who are full of hatred. [*He searches around him.*] No one? They leave me, in spite of my treasure. Capuchin! Ungrateful wretch! He has run off with his will. He has gone to collect his monastic brethren together. . . . Frame the lying paper! This old house will have crumbled and all the monks will have been eaten by worms, when old Hieronymus is still laughing, and he will be the last to laugh! . . . Hasn't the gentleman of the cloth taken anything? In his panic, he has even forgotten to empty the bottle. I shall do it. [*He drinks.*] The peculiar thirst you get from drinking! My blood must have changed its complexion. Is it I, so temperate, who am bending my elbow? What a transformation in my substance! Here I am, hungry and thirsty, wanting to do things, to speak out loud. We shall see! I shall have fireworks set off. I shall give feasts. I shall illuminate my house. I shall command the bagpipe to sound, and the Theban trumpets. . . . I shall laugh contagious laughter that will win over the whole country. And the people will shout, "Down with misers! . . . Long live Hieronymus the philanthropist! He who scatters money!" [*He drinks.*] In your great honor, Hieronymus! I am very pleased with you! . . . Long life, Hieronymus! [*He laughs.*] What a good joke I'm playing on death! . . . What? [*He listens.*] What quiet! It is as still as a spider's web. . . . [*He shivers.*] What

is there to be afraid of? The spite of the Almighty, who is angry at my power? God the Father, I shall fling up a great golden cathedral for you. And you demons, I shall make you a present of some volcanoes for your lewd ceremonies. . . . Yes, I shall give you the bowels of the earth as a present, caverns, passages, underground lakes. Am I liberal enough? [*He throws the bottle away.*] This wine is playing havoc with my throat. . . . I am thirsty. . . . It is as though there were wings beating in my temples. I am heavy and light at the same time. My left hand is frozen. My right hand is on fire. My flesh is alive! [*He shuts his chest and sits on it.*] Strange moments! [*He rocks himself.*] I am watched, even though there is no one. . . . Who? . . . Through the walls, the ceiling. . . . There are eyes. [*Politely.*] I am doing nothing odd. . . . Watchers, you are wasting your time. [*He catches sight of the child.*] It is you who are looking at me? You are not asleep? True, you were born with your eyes open. You haven't got eyelids. [ROMULUS, *at the back of the room, has covered himself with a sheet.*] Stop spying! Your eyes are red. What do I see in them? [*He gets up and comes closer to the child.*] I can guess. You reveal your mean little soul to me. Coveter! You see yellow. You see gold. You assess your inheritance. You have the eyes of a bad son. Parricide! No, my vicious little fellow, you will never inherit, for that would mean my dying, and that is impossible. [*He takes a knife from the drawer in the table.*] So I shall spare you your life . . . the life of a pauper that yours would be. I shall put an end to you. . . . Will you submit, like a dutiful child? [*He thrusts the knife into the child's chest.*] What a bitter taste there is, seasoning my mouth. . . . He is not bleeding? . . . What an economical child, keeping his blood for himself. [*He goes back to the table.*] No more wine? And I want to take it in great swigs! I shall go to the taverns. . . . I am able to do that. . . . What will people say? "Hieronymus is drinking! . . . Hieronymus is drunk!" Yes, boorish citizens! . . . I am standing drinks! . . . Yes, I have dared to leave my hunble dwelling. [*He hesitates.*] Your duty, chest, is to stay firmly put, and not to allow your jaws to gape on any pretext—even if you are sleepy. As for the Cavalier, as for my wife, they have gold as I have. . . . So they will not rob me. . . . If I were certain that they were asleep. [*He glues his ear to the floor and listens.*] Nothing! . . . Yes . . . a buzzing . . . voices . . . whispering. . . . Formulas. . . . Eh? . . . Someone is laughing. . . . A fine crystal laugh. [*A woman's hysterical laughter is heard.*] Is my wife laughing? Is it necessary to laugh to breed gold? [*He listens.*] She is speaking faster . . . faster. She is choking. [*A moan is heard.*] Is she moaning? . . . Is it with pain? . . . Is it with pleasure? . . . The two are so alike. . . . What is being done to her? What do they do to women to draw these long animal moans from them? . . . Are they standing up? Are they lying on the ground? . . . And if they are together, aren't they one on top of the other? And moving? . . . How? . . . What do they call what they are doing . . . if they are lying . . . moving . . . and moaning? [*He gets up, crimson.*] I do not know, I do not want to know. This woman was not moaning. [*Moan.*] I maintain that she was not moaning! [*Another moan.*] I do not love this woman. She has contributed to my enrichment. I despise her. Have I not given her up, body and soul, to the stranger? That shows what little value I set on her. . . . Enjoy yourself, lecherous woman! Be melodious like an alley cat. . . . There are other women. . . . Troops of them. . . . I can buy entire harems. . . . Your head will bristle with count-

less horns. A porcupine will not have as many quills. I shall work away at fat women, very fat, with the most meat possible, for my money. They will moan better than you. The whole town will hear them bellowing in their climaxes. And the town will exclaim, "Listen, Hieronymus is copulating! . . . Hurrah! . . . The fine fellow!" . . . I am sweating. [*He is panting.*] This very night. . . . I have deserved it. . . . My loins are filled with live coals. My organ swells up hugely like a club that I shall use to threaten the whores. Who is armed like me? I want to exercise myself at once—with a sow, if necessary! Give me the most bestial kind of love! Give me the sins of unchastity . . . the worst . . . those that common people cannot afford. [*At last he sees the ghost, and draws back.*] I beg your pardon, ghost. You were there? . . . Listen. . . . Do not reproach me. You would be ill advised to read a lecture to me at present. I am in a trance. You too have committed sins. I do not ask you which. . . . Stay here. Watch over my treasure. You won't get any gold, because you wouldn't know what to do with it. But I shall redeem your purgatory. . . . Ah! . . . for me, it will be the first time that I have made my way to the shady side streets. I am sinning in good faith. It is the call of nature. . . . One word more, ghost. Watch the Cavalier . . . and my wife. Spy on them. Make a list of their most precise gestures. You can go through walls. . . . I shall have great satisfaction listening to you recounting the abominable sights. . . . Don't let yourself get excited. You, with your unreal person, couldn't go to the gay ladies. . . . You understand? . . . I speak to you as a friend. . . . I am going. [*He opens the chest and takes out a coin.*] With this golden florin I shall have ten well-tried whores. . . . Ho! . . . The monk will die with envy. [*He puts on his hat, throws a cloak over his shoulders, and goes to the door.*] Ghost! . . . a little discretion . . . [*He bows politely.*] I beg your pardon. I have a fever. [*He goes out and shuts the door. As soon as he is alone,* ROMULUS *bursts into great laughter, and still covered in his sheet, runs to the cellar door.*]

ROMULUS. Hello! . . . Hey there, below! . . . Here!

Noises of voices and footsteps.

THE MONK [*Appearing, flushed and staggering.*] By the devil's buttocks! You are disturbing our ceremonies. . . . By God! She was lifting her petticoat up. . . .

ROMULUS. Hieronymus has come in heat. He is on his way to the trollops. . . . This is not in our plan. . . . The magistrate isn't due till dawn.

THE MONK. Armador and his servant girl mustn't have time to get away. . . . Risky! . . . Really risky! . . . Listen, Romulus. I'm afraid those two have an inkling. They were slipping knowing glances to each other. Look out for mischief.

ROMULUS. Right! . . . I shall go and warn the magistrate.

THE MONK. Not yet. Armador would understand. . . . And what about me? . . . Alone with them? . . . I would be bled like a stuck pig. . . . Be quiet. They are coming up. Let us divide it up first.

ARMADOR. [*Appearing.*] What? He has taken wing? Everything is working out. I like that very much. Let us cut it short, friends.

SYBILLA *appears. She is mistrustful.*

THE MONK. [*To* SYBILLA.] Sybilla, with your body of a succubus! . . . White frog! . . . I throb under my robe!

SYBILLA. You will take it off for me, father monk. . . . [*To* ARMADOR.] Look here! . . . Hieronymus has killed my child! [*She draws him toward the front of the stage; then, in a low voice.*] The monk let it out to me in his lustful delirium. There is a traitor with a Roman name. In exchange, I

have promised him my body.

ROMULUS. [*Uneasy.*] Where is the real gold? If the miser were to come back . . .

SYBILLA. [*To* ARMADOR.] We are all delivered up to Justice.

THE MONK. Divide it up? . . . I will give my share for Sybilla's crupper.

ARMADOR. [*Coming back.*] You can see very clearly in this room, even though there is only one candle. . . . Let us divide it up! . . . Come here, comrades. [*He takes the bag from his cloak.*] You see, I am already fitted out for the journey. [ROMULUS *and* THE MONK *draw near to the light.*] We are among honest folk. . . . Here are eighty florins, taken from the chest. Twenty for Romulus, honest Romulus. [*He gives them.*] Ten for the father—no more since he has the will. [*He gives them.*] Fifty for me and the wench, who have well deserved them. And take heed that ill-gotten gains always thrive. [*He pockets his gold and laughs, showing his teeth.*] Now, let us forget one another! I do not want to watch the downfall of the old fellow whose ruin we have accomplished. The Flemish roads will be pleasant under my feet. I shall never again in this life see either you, bearded beggar, or you, scarlet monk. To the one his fleas, to the other his holy deeds! . . . Each knowing what he must do on earth. . . . Good-by!

ROMULUS. [*Animatedly.*] Already? Dawn is still far away, and the miser is in the hands of the women. In the name of brotherhood, let us stay. . . . Wait! . . . I am going to put my gold in a safe place, and I shall come back with more wine. [*He goes toward the left.*]

ARMADOR. [*Following him step by step.*] Go, comrade! And beware of scoundrels. A stab is soon given. [*He draws his dagger and stabs* ROMULUS *between the shoulders.*] One hardly notices it.

ROMULUS. [*Staggering.*] They're killing

me! . . . It is cold! [*He collapses to his knees.*]

ARMADOR. [*Laughing.*] They're killing you? . . . Where are the assailants, so that I can go and inform the magistrate? . . . Eh, Romulus?

The beggar remains on his knees for a moment, rattling in his throat, then he slumps to the floor. SYBILLA *laughs brutally.*

THE MONK. [*Frightened.*] Cavalier . . . so good a spy!

ARMADOR. [*Wiping his dagger.*] Here he is a real ghost!

THE MONK. It serves him right. . . . Sybilla, you remember the terms? [*He hugs her.*] Little girl . . . I shall eat you up.

SYBILLA. Come along, since I promised you. You are not angry, Armador?

ARMADOR. Go along! It is your reward, Capuchin. I must busy myself with the ghost and bury it.

SYBILLA. [*To* THE MONK.] Quick, then, in my room! [*She runs up the stairs.*]

THE MONK. [*Following her, panting.*] Oh, delight! . . . Quick, yes. . . . Very quick! . . . I can't contain myself any longer.

They disappear upstairs.

ARMADOR. [*Dragging* ROMULUS' *corpse to the chest.*] I bear no malice, you understand. You shall have a decent burial. And a shroud. All the Christian things you don't deserve. [*He opens the chest and rams in the beggar's body, which is still wrapped in its sheet.*] I was forgetting. . . . [*He takes the dead man's purse.*] Your fine gold wouldn't be accepted as currency in hell. [*He closes the chest.*] Rot among the false gold, false man! [*He goes toward the staircase, listens, and goes up one or two stairs.*] A last piece of work waits for me up there, at the price of ten royal florins! [*He disappears upstairs.*]

Pause. The street door opens with a crash. HIERONYMUS *enters, bent double, out of breath, and without hat or cloak.*

HIERONYMUS. [*In a hoarse voice.*] Help! . . . There are wasps tormenting me.

Sticky insects are running over me. All the terrors of the fields made up an escort for me. There were vipers, wolves, brown owls. Drive all these evil beasts away! . . . I am afraid! . . . I am unclean! . . . I have seen the green flesh of monsters with stinking breath and decaying nails, in vermin among the mushrooms and the nettles. I was the prey of slobbering gargoyles. I was beaten to a jelly. What did I do to these ribald creatures and their females? What witches' lair did I wander into? Help! . . . Drive off the furies and the shrews! . . . I paid, and the old sweats in the taverns threw the stools in my path and swore horribly in German and Spanish! And the butchers wanted to pull down my breeches and cut my organ off! I did nothing, said nothing! And the beggars were none the less frenzied. . . . With blows from their crutches. . . . On me, noble Hieronymus! . . . And their bawling! . . . Oh! Oh! . . . They kicked me into the filth of the gutter. And mangy dogs suddenly appeared in blind alleys. They bit me. And attic windows opened. And bald and toothless creatures emptied their chamber pots on my skull. People shouted, "Run him to earth! Arrest him!" Why? They are on their way here. I ran, but the dogs caught me up. The dogs stopped at the door. All the host of beggary is going to collect and lay siege. They want my gold. Help! . . . I would rather let them kill me on my chest. . . . [*Fiercely.*] Yes indeed! . . . I make game of them. . . . I have a magic breastplate. . . . What have I to fear? I am indestructible! [*Distracted.*] Why do they do ill to rich people? Why this anger at an honest citizen who seeks his distraction in the stews? A filthy performance! It seems as though I have buboes, pustules, abscesses, growing on me. There is a spiky plant growing in my belly, a hideous plant that is slowly devouring my organs, my liver, my entrails, my heart. . . . Away with these filthy women! . . . I shall be chaste! . . . I shall have myself castrated, cut off close! And I shall have my revenge. I shall have all these brigands massacred by people in my pay. I want to abolish physical love in this kingdom. Do you hear me, monk? . . . Where are you? . . . Are you listening, you stinking creature? . . . I shall pay you. You shall preach calm to the beggars, if they dare to come. Take my sword. Monks know how to slash about. . . . And you, Sybilla, come here! Go and inform the men of the law. . . . Armador, my good friend, hasten with your magic! Let it rain down saltpeter and pitch on this evil crew! I shall proclaim who I have become. I shall promulgate my power. The insolent shall do penance, with a rope around their necks. . . . Are you coming, monk? . . . Cavalier! . . . Wife! . . . And you, ghost? . . . Coward! He sleeps when his master is in danger. [*A muffled cry, then the noise of a struggle are heard from above.*] He is coming. He was spying. Come here, I command you! [*He takes down the sword.*] You shall strike fear into them. And if they maintain that I was with women, you shall bear witness against the liars. You shall swear that I have not left my room. [*He dances with rage.*] Are you coming?

Two shadows, covered by dark cloaks, hurry down the stairs. HIERONYMUS *draws back.*

ARMADOR. [*Disguising his voice.*] Hieronymus, open the door!

SYBILLA. [*Disguising her voice.*] So that we can run at your enemies.

HIERONYMUS, *trembling, opens the door. The pair rush outside and laugh without restraint. They disappear, but they can be heard laughing in the distance.*

HIERONYMUS. Thank you! . . . Why are they laughing? . . . They are laughing at my enemies. . . . They are going to slaughter my enemies! [*He laughs.*] Ha! . . . Ha! . . . Ha! . . . [*And shuts the door.*] There were two of them! Who is the second? . . . No. . . . There is only one ghost in this house. I am being robbed. I am being taken in. Arrest the ghosts! It is a conspiracy. The demons are taking a hand in it! And you, my gold! . . . What a horrible night! [*He brandishes his sword.*] I have had enough of it. I say there is enough gold. I say we must finish with it. Cavalier, I discharge you! Leave your den, or I shall tell the provost! [*He listens. Silence.*] Nothing? It is disturbing! [*He sits down.*] I am the prey of misfortune. Misfortune entered this house with that stranger. No, Hieronymus, one does not meddle in the forbidden arts with impunity. [*He whimpers.*] Riches are costing you a very high price. [*He stands up.*] I was wrong to take fright. The street is still dead. They will not come. The butchers have lost track of me. But the bawds will recognize me. The whole town will know from their accursed tongues that I had gold. [*Determinedly.*] I shall go. I shall take my fortune and leave the town. [*Faltering.*] I ought to take my house. . . . There are too many bricks. I shall go tomorrow. I shall put myself under the protection of the monks. They will hear my confession. [*Inspired.*] I want to become a monk. At once! . . . Come here, fat Father, come and hear my confession!

VOICE OF THE MONK. [*Upstairs.*] My confession!

HIERONYMUS. I hear an echo. Is it the ghost moaning at the door? . . . He has been thrashed! . . . No. It came from above. Hello! [*At the staircase.*] Come down! . . . Sybilla, wife, where are you!

VOICE OF THE MONK. Sybilla! . . . Her body!

HIERONYMUS. [*Furious.*] Again? . . . Are they in the roof? . . . You have got her body? . . . They will never finish. . . . Stop your loathsome games. . . . Enough abomination!

THE MONK *appears above. His face is swollen. He clings to the handrail. He snorts.*

THE MONK. My confession!

HIERONYMUS. [*Joyfully.*] The monk! What next! Exactly, my confession . . .

THE MONK. [*Coming down painfully.*] Damned! . . . Damned!

HIERONYMUS. Damned? Me? You don't know a thing about it. . . . I repent.

THE MONK. On her. . . . Killed . . . the demon!

HIERONYMUS. It was him! . . . I knew it! . . . Satan! . . . You say he was on her? You killed him? [*He lights up the* MONK, *who has got to the bottom of the stairs.*] Who are you? . . . The monk? . . . But you are loathsome! . . . He is drunk . . . dead drunk! . . . Ha, ha! What a masquerade! . . . A fine state you are in!

THE MONK. [*With a gasp.*] Lust!

HIERONYMUS. True! . . . It is despicable. Never again! . . . Father, I am going to become a monk!

THE MONK. [*Collapsing.*] Hell! . . .

HIERONYMUS. [*Moving away from him and laughing coarsely.*] Bravo! . . . You have guzzled my wine! . . . He is being punished. He is snoring. Stink at your pleasure. I shall go and tell your superior. You will be taken back to your monastery processionally— accompanied by the gibes of the populace. Ho, ho, ho! Let him stink! No, I don't want to become a monk. Repulsive crew! [*He gives him several kicks.*] You will be damned. You will die in your fat and your filth. [*He holds his nose.*] Pah! . . . Air! [*He rushes to the window and opens it. It is dawn. Pale light.*] The night is over. What a release! [*He blows out the candle.*] Everything is growing clear. I am coming out of the darkness. I am going to be alone, as I was before. No nightmares. I shall sleep. And at

night I shall peacefully make gold. I want to forget. Hieronymus, you must not drink so much any more. It gives me delusions. It makes you have bitter dreams, like the one I had. You dream that you go after women, that the populace becomes indignant. Drive these phantasms away! [*He laughs.*] I am saved . . . delivered . . . [*Suddenly a windowpane flies in. A clamor grows in the street.* HIERONYMOUS *howls.*] They are coming! I am being attacked! I am being plundered! [*He seizes his sword.*] Have mercy! I am innocent!

VOICE OF THE CROWD. Boo! . . . Boo! . . . Hieronymus! . . . Boo! . . . Boo!

Yelling. Blows on the door. Shattering of windows.

HIERONYMUS. What are they shouting? My gold! . . . I am being robbed. Be calm. I shall give you gold. Come here, you monks! Protect your benefactor!

The door is burst in. The shouts die down, but the crowd continues to snarl. The MAGISTRATE *appears. He is dressed in black and is followed by* MEN AT ARMS.

THE MAGISTRATE. Surrender yourself, Hieronymus. Give up your sword.

HIERONYMUS. [*Giving up his sword.*] Thank you. . . . Good day, sire. It is good of you to demand that the rabble disperse. Thank you.

THE MAGISTRATE. Have you been with the women tonight . . . and did you pay them with this coin! [*He shows a coin.*]

HIERONYMUS. Never. . . . Ask the ghost . . . the monk . . .

THE MAGISTRATE. Open the chest!

HIERONYMUS. [*Opening the chest.*] Is it necessary? [*He draws back.*] The ghost is inside! . . . Look! . . . He wanted to rob me. He is caught in the trap. [*He jumps for joy.*] What a good trick!

The MEN AT ARMS *take out* ROMULUS' *enshrouded body and lay it down.*

THE MAGISTRATE. Is this gold yours? [*He takes hold of a handful of coins.*]

HIERONYMUS. Mine alone. . . . Do not

touch it. . . . By what right? . . .

THE MAGISTRATE. This monk, who has killed him?

HIERONYMUS. The monk? He is drunk. That isn't blood. It's wine.

THE MAGISTRATE. And this doll, stabbed with a knife?

HIERONYMUS. I do not know. . . . Will you speak to me with respect? You had better understand that I am rich.

THE MAGISTRATE. Seize him! [*The* MEN AT ARMS *lay hold of the miser.*] Sorcerer, counterfeiter, felon! . . . He is thrice guilty! [*Going to the door.*] People, I deliver him up to Justice. . . .

THE CROWD. Death! . . . The excecutioner! . . . Long live the law! . . .

Boo! . . . Boo!

HIERONYMUS. [*Arrogantly.*] I do not understand. . . . Say it again. . . . Death? . . . The executioner? [*He frees himself.*] It is better to laugh at it! [*He laughs.*] Ho, ho! . . . You will be well sold! Of all living beings, I am the chief. Bah! I am as great as the emperor! . . . Me die! . . . I shall buy Justice. . . . Ho, ho, ho! . . . Listen to me! . . . I am like God. It is true! You do not know that I am immortal, do you? . . .

He laughs heartily. He is dragged away to the accompaniment of the boos and jeers of the crowd.

Blood Wedding

Federico García Lorca

Federico García Lorca is widely acclaimed as the most important Spanish dramatist since the Golden Age. The theater flourished in Spain throughout the eighteenth and nineteenth centuries, and many playwrights wrote works that achieved a considerable measure of popularity with Spanish-speaking audiences in Europe and the Americas, but only in the twentieth century did there emerge a Spanish poet-playwright whose techniques and insights were truly international in scope. Lorca's career was abruptly ended by a firing squad during the Civil War when presumably his talent was just reaching its full maturity. Nowhere in the history of the theater has there been a more tragic loss through the violence of warfare.

Federico García Lorca was born on June 5, 1898, in the village of Fuentevaqueros, near Granada. His mother, doña Vicenta Lorca, was the second wife of Federico García Rodríguez, and the boy was so deeply attached to his mother that, among other things, he used the name Lorca during most of his adult life rather than García Lorca as Spanish custom would require. The family moved into Granada, where Lorca received much of his education, entering the University of Granada in 1914 at his father's insistence to study law. Already deeply committed to the arts, accomplished as a musician and a painter as well as a poet, Lorca was an indifferent law student; later he was to transfer to the University of Madrid and to complete a law degree in 1923, but by that time he had no intention whatsoever of practicing law. In 1918 he published his first book, a volume of notes and observations resulting from extended travel through several Spanish provinces with a student group, and he was already gaining a reputation, at least among his peers, as a poet. In 1919, he plunged into the exciting literary and artistic whirlpool of Madrid.

Lorca had been fascinated by the theater since childhood, staging puppet plays with his friends and forcing the servants to dress in outlandish costumes, but it was in Madrid in 1920 that his first professionally produced play appeared. It was *The Evildoing of the Butterfly,* and it was a failure. Throughout the 1920s, however, Lorca continued to experiment with playwriting, as well as to publish poetry and to interact with the artistic community in Madrid. His close relationship with Salvador Dalí, whose surrealistic painting was soon to startle the world, had a profound influence on Lorca's development, as did his continued growth in music and painting as well as writing. Fortunately, his family was willing and able to support him through these years. By the time he visited New York in 1929–30, Lorca was already well-known as a poet. His first play of importance, *Mariana Pineda,* had premiered in Barcelona in 1927, and the first drafts of several other plays had been written. Shortly after his return to Spain in 1930, Lorca was named director of La Barraca, a newly formed group consisting chiefly of university students, whose purpose it was to bring touring productions of classical and modern plays to provincial Spanish audiences. Lorca enthusiastically devoted much of the next several years to directing and writing for this group, although his major plays were produced by professional groups in Madrid as well. *The Shoemaker's Prodigious Wife* (1930), *The Love of Don Perlimplin with Belisa in the Garden* (1933), *Yerma* (1934), and *Blood Wedding* (1933) are perhaps best known among them. One other play of major importance, *The House of Bernarda Alba,* was not produced during his lifetime.

In 1936, the complex Spanish political situation erupted into full-scale civil war, with neighbor fighting neighbor throughout the country. Although Lorca took no great interest in politics, he was popularly identified with the liberal avant-garde, and some of his friends urged him to flee the country. Not believing that an artist could be in serious political danger, Lorca remained in his native Granada when Fascist elements began a purge of intellectuals and socialists. On August 18, 1936, he was arrested, and on the morning of August 19 he was summarily shot. His body was buried in an unmarked pit along with scores of others. No satisfactory explanation of this barbarity has ever emerged, although it provoked an international outcry.

In the relatively few years available to him for playwriting, Lorca experimented with a number of different styles. From farce to tragedy, from expressionism to starkest realism, from spare prose to lush and luxuriant poetry, Lorca sought to unite his Spanish heritage with the cross-currents then flowing in European drama. *Blood Wedding* is his most widely admired play and the most interesting combination of styles, a work of maximum sensual impact exploring the innermost depths of human feeling. Yet its story was derived from a newspaper account that might, in the hands of another dramatist, have emerged as a work of the most sordid naturalism. *Blood Wedding* was first performed in Madrid in March, 1933, and represents Lorca at the height of his powers.

First and foremost, *Blood Wedding* is an emotional and sensual immersion that goes beyond the wildest imaginings of the romanticists. The rich imagery of its poetry, the color inherent in its settings and lighting, the music both proposed and implied, and the potent symbolism of its heat and sexuality, all are designed to enfold the spectator utterly in the theatrical experience. One of Lorca's favorite topics was the power of repressed sexual instinct as he observed it in the severe folkways of rural Spain, and nowhere does he express his understanding of this power more potently than in *Blood Wedding*. The classical Spanish confrontation between reason and passion is here given a modern setting equally as powerful as any provided by the antique code of honor of the Golden Age, and one is irresistibly caught up in an emotional experience that probes deeply into the forces that control human behavior. Far from being simply romanticism, however, *Blood Wedding* uses expressionistic techniques that reveal graphically, as though in a dream, the emotional workings of its central characters. This expressionism is blended in some scenes with the spare literality of realism to create a staged equivalent of Dali's surrealism. *Blood Wedding* is a curious combination of styles, but one that achieves a powerful theatrical effect.

Perhaps the most notable of the elements creating this effect is Lorca's language. Lorca was a poet of rare ability and rich lyricism, and this poetic language shines through even in translation to elevate rather ordinary characters and story line toward high tragedy. Such recurring images as those of heat, water, knives, and horses are brilliantly selected to enrich the individual line, to supercharge the sexual atmosphere that pervades the play, and to reflect real objects on the stage. Some of the poetic lyrics, such as those of the lullaby or the wedding morning, would be further enhanced in production by the music that is intended to accompany them. Individual poetic lines arrest the spectator's attention at moments of intense feeling such as the woodcutters scene ("Better dead with the blood drained away than alive with it rotting") or the concluding refrain: "With a knife, / with a tiny knife / that barely fits the hand, / but that slides in clean / through the astonished flesh / and stops at the place / where trembles, enmeshed, / the dark root of a scream." Lorca combines brilliantly his excellent poetic language with what Cocteau termed "poetry of the theatre," so that all the theatrical elements work together in poetic fashion to create a powerful total effect.

Although character development is not a primary focus in *Blood Wedding,* it is more than interesting. Lorca was more interested in portraying the elemental forces that lie beneath human personality than in lacing together the more traditional straws of motivation and response; why these characters do as they do is less important than that they *must* do it. The Bride, for example, does everything in her power to kill the intense passion she feels for Leonardo, even to marrying the Bridegroom when she doesn't really love him in hope of thereby killing her illicit desire, but all is to no avail. Even while running away with Leonardo she knows that her behavior is wrong by every standard in which she believes, and in the last scene she begs for the punishment that she is convinced is rightly hers. Yet despite all this, she runs directly to Leonardo's arms when he offers them. Apparently only the hardness represented by the Mother is sufficient to control such sexual passion, and clearly this passion in the Mother has been misdirected into a depth of hate and vengefulness that causes her almost to deserve the harsh fate that is hers. In the world that Lorca has created, the strict code of one woman for one man results in twisted, embittered, and tragically wasted lives. Each of the major characters reflects in his own way this sharp struggle, but the very fact that most of them are without proper names is evidence of the morality play breadth that Lorca expected them to project.

Structurally, Lorca borrows much from the expressionists in forming his play. The series of relatively short scenes is highly reminiscent of the work of the Germans of a decade earlier, and such scenes as that of the woodcutters move altogether into a dreamlike world that expresses the emotional turmoil of the Bride and Leonardo in objectified terms. The staccato speech patterns of the prose portions of the dialogue strongly suggest expressionist counterparts. Above all, *Blood Wedding* resembles the work of the expressionists in attempting to portray the inmost feelings of its principal characters, cutting past scientifically observable data such as the realists might have emphasized to the deeper truths underneath. Along the way, Lorca successfully creates a sense of inevitable fate moving the tragedy toward its conclusion, so that the outcome seems both profound and inescapable. What Synge achieved in *Riders to the Sea,* with the sea as an implacable force claiming its victims, is equated by Lorca to the Spanish code of honor—or, in more modern terms, to the Victorian moral standards of the Spanish people.

The comparison between Lorca and Synge has often been made, for in addition to the brooding sense of fate that hangs over the plays there are plot and thematic similarities as well. Just as Maurya is, despite the young priest's promises, left with no sons living, so the Mother is similarly bereft of all male issue. Poignant enough for any mother, this bereavement takes on added significance in a society in which the male is viewed as the master because he is the agent of fecundity, the means by which the continuance of the family name is assured as well as the land made to become fertile and bear fruit. In both plays, it is the man who must go out to fight while the women can only stay behind and grieve; in both, the mother feels some sense of relief at the end since no further tragedy can possibly happen to her—she has lost everything. In both the only mercy available from God is the peace of death. Thematically, both authors found life hard and unyielding in the societies they were portraying, with Lorca's Mother the harsher of the two women since she thirsts so powerfully for revenge. Yet both rise to a kind of dignity in despair, and both suggest that even in so harsh a world mankind will never give up.

Above all, *Blood Wedding* is a sensual feast unexcelled in twentieth-century drama. From the rich color imagery of Lorca's set suggestions to the lyricism of the songs and poetry, from the overpowering sexual passion to the equally strong images of heat, from the knife fixation with its double connotations of death and sex to the horse imagery of sex and vibrant life (and then sometimes of death as well), *Blood Wedding* is an appeal to every corner of the spectator's aesthetic sensitivity and an invitation to give one's self up totally to an emotional experience. Insofar as twentieht-century playwrights have attempted to dig beneath surface realism to the deeper human truths subliminally sensed and approachable only emotionally, Lorca has gone about as far with this ideal as it seems possible to go.

Blood Wedding
(Bodas de sangre)

Translated by James Graham-Luján and Richard L. O'Connell

Characters
The Mother
The Bride
The Mother-in-Law
Leonardo's Wife
The Servant Woman
The Neighbor Woman
Young Girls
Leonardo
The Bridegroom
The Bride's Father
The Moon
Woodcutters
Young Men

Act 1

Scene 1

A room painted yellow.
BRIDEGROOM. [*Entering.*] Mother.
MOTHER. What?
BRIDEGROOM. I'm going.
MOTHER. Where?
BRIDEGROOM. To the vineyard.
He starts to go.
MOTHER. Wait.
BRIDEGROOM. You want something?
MOTHER. Your breakfast, son.
BRIDEGROOM. Forget it. I'll eat grapes.
   Give me the knife.

MOTHER. What for?
BRIDEGROOM. [*Laughing.*] To cut the
   grapes with.
MOTHER. [*Muttering as she looks for the
   knife.*] Knives, knives. Cursed be all
   knives, and the scoundrel who invented them.
BRIDEGROOM. Let's talk about something else.
MOTHER. And guns and pistols and the
   smallest little knife—and even hoes
   and pitchforks.
BRIDEGROOM. All right.
MOTHER. Everything that can slice a
   man's body. A handsome man, full of
   young life, who goes out to the vineyards or to his own olive groves—his
   own because he's inherited them. . . .
BRIDEGROOM. [*Lowering his head.*] Be
   quiet.
MOTHER. . . . and then that man doesn't
   come back. Or if he does come back
   it's only for someone to cover him
   over with a palm leaf or a plate of
   rock salt so he won't bloat. I don't
   know how you dare carry a knife on
   your body—or how I let this serpent
   [*She takes a knife from a kitchen chest.*]
   stay in the chest.
BRIDEGROOM. Have you had your say?
MOTHER. If I lived to be a hundred I'd
   talk of nothing else. First your father; to me he smelled like a
   carnation and I had him for barely
   three years. Then your brother. Oh,

221

is it right—how can it be—that a small thing like a knife or a pistol can finish off a man—a bull of a man? No, I'll never be quiet. The months pass and the hopelessness of it stings in my eyes and even to the roots of my hair.

BRIDEGROOM. [*Forcefully.*] Let's quit this talk!

MOTHER. No. No. Let's not quit this talk. Can anyone bring me your father back? Or your brother? Then there's the jail. What do they mean, jail? They eat there, smoke there, play music there! My dead men choking with weeds, silent, turning to dust. Two men like two beautiful flowers. The killers in jail, carefree, looking at the mountains.

BRIDEGROOM. Do you want me to go kill them?

MOTHER. No . . . If I talk about it it's because. . . . Oh, how can I help talking about it, seeing you go out that door? It's. . . . I don't like you to carry a knife. It's just that . . . that I wish you wouldn't go out to the fields.

BRIDEGROOM. [*Laughing.*] Oh, come now!

MOTHER. I'd like it if you were a woman. Then you wouldn't be going out to the arroyo now and we'd both of us embroider flounces and little woolly dogs.

BRIDEGROOM. [*He puts his arm around his mother and laughs.*] Mother, what if I should take you with me to the vineyards?

MOTHER. What would an old lady do in the vineyards? Were you going to put me down under the young vines?

BRIDEGROOM. [*Lifting her in his arms.*] Old lady, old lady—you little old, little old lady!

MOTHER. Your father, he used to take me. That's the way with men of good stock; good blood. Your grandfather left a son on every corner. That's what I like. Men, men; wheat, wheat.

BRIDEGROOM. And I, Mother?

MOTHER. You, what?

BRIDEGROOM. Do I need to tell you again?

MOTHER. [*Seriously.*] Oh!

BRIDEGROOM. Do you think it's bad?

MOTHER. No.

BRIDEGROOM. Well, then?

MOTHER. I don't really know. Like this, suddenly, it always surprises me. I know the girl is good. Isn't she? Well behaved. Hard working. Kneads her bread, sews her skirts, but even so when I say her name I feel as though someone had hit me on the forehead with a rock.

BRIDEGROOM. Foolishness.

MOTHER. More than foolishness. I'll be left alone. Now only you are left me—I hate to see you go.

BRIDEGROOM. But you'll come with us.

MOTHER. No. I can't leave your father and brother here alone. I have to go to them every morning and if I go away it's possible one of the Félix family, one of the killers, might die—and they'd bury him next to ours. And that'll never happen! Oh, no! That'll never happen! Because I'd dig them out with my nails and, all by myself, crush them against the wall.

BRIDEGROOM. [*Sternly.*] There you go again.

MOTHER. Forgive me.

Pause.

How long have you known her?

BRIDEGROOM. Three years. I've been able to buy the vineyard.

MOTHER. Three years. She used to have another sweetheart, didn't she?

BRIDEGROOM. I don't know. I don't think so. Girls have to look at what they'll marry.

MOTHER. Yes. I looked at nobody. I looked at your father, and when they killed him I looked at the wall in front of me. One woman with one man, and that's all.

BRIDEGROOM. You know my girl's good.

MOTHER. I don't doubt it. All the same, I'm sorry not to have known what her mother was like.

BRIDEGROOM. What difference does it make now?

MOTHER. [*Looking at him.*] Son.

BRIDEGROOM. What is it?

MOTHER. That's true! You're right! When do you want me to ask for her?

BRIDEGROOM. [*Happily.*] Does Sunday seem all right to you?

MOTHER. [*Seriously.*] I'll take her the bronze earrings, they're very old— and you buy her . . .

BRIDEGROOM. You know more about *that* . . .

MOTHER. . . . you buy her some open-work stockings—and for you, two suits—three! I have no one but you now!

BRIDEGROOM. I'm going. Tomorrow I'll go see her.

MOTHER. Yes, yes—and see if you can make me happy with six grand-children—or as many as you want, since your father didn't live to give them to me.

BRIDEGROOM. The first-born for you!

MOTHER. Yes, but have some girls. I want to embroider and make lace, and be at peace.

BRIDEGROOM. I'm sure you'll love my wife.

MOTHER. I'll love her. [*She starts to kiss him but changes her mind.*] Go on. You're too big now for kisses. Give them to your wife. [*Pause. To herself.*] When she is your wife.

BRIDEGROOM. I'm going.

MOTHER. And that land around the little mill—work it over. You've not taken good care of it.

BRIDEGROOM. You're right. I will.

MOTHER. God keep you. [*The* SON *goes out. The* MOTHER *remains seated—her back to the door. A* NEIGHBOR WOMAN *with a 'kerchief on her head appears in the door.*] Come in.

NEIGHBOR. How are you?

MOTHER. Just as you see me.

NEIGHBOR. I came down to the store and stopped in to see you. We live so far away!

MOTHER. It's twenty years since I've been up to the top of the street.

NEIGHBOR. You're looking well.

MOTHER. You think so?

NEIGHBOR. Things happen. Two days ago they brought in my neighbor's son with both arms sliced off by the machine.

She sits down.

MOTHER. Rafael?

NEIGHBOR. Yes. And there you have him. Many times I've thought your son and mine are better off where they are—sleeping, resting—not running the risk of being left helpless.

MOTHER. Hush. That's all just something thought up—but no consolation.

NEIGHBOR. [*Sighing.*] Ay!

MOTHER. [*Sighing.*] Ay!

Pause.

NEIGHBOR. [*Sadly.*] Where's your son?

MOTHER. He went out.

NEIGHBOR. He finally bought the vineyard!

MOTHER. He was lucky.

NEIGHBOR. Now he'll get married.

MOTHER. [*As though reminded of something, she draws her chair near the* NEIGHBOR.] Listen.

NEIGHBOR. [*In a confidential manner.*] Yes. What is it?

MOTHER. You know my son's sweetheart?

NEIGHBOR. A good girl!

MOTHER. Yes, but. . . .

NEIGHBOR. But who knows her really well? There's nobody. She lives out there alone with her father—so far away—fifteen miles from the nearest house. But she's a good girl. Used to being alone.

MOTHER. And her mother?

NEIGHBOR. Her mother I *did* know. Beautiful. Her face glowed like a saint's—but *I* never liked her. She didn't love her husband.

MOTHER. [*Sternly.*] Well, what a lot of things certain people know!

NEIGHBOR. I'm sorry. I didn't mean to

offend—but it's true. Now, whether she was decent or not nobody said. That wasn't discussed. She was haughty.

MOTHER. There you go again!

NEIGHBOR. You asked me.

MOTHER. I wish no one knew anything about them—either the live one or the dead one—that they were like two thistles no one even names but cuts off at the right moment.

NEIGHBOR. You're right. Your son is worth a lot.

MOTHER. Yes—a lot. That's why I look after him. They told me the girl had a sweetheart some time ago.

NEIGHBOR. She was about fifteen. He's been married two years now—to a cousin of hers, as a matter of fact. But nobody remembers about their engagement.

MOTHER. How do you remember it?

NEIGHBOR. Oh, what questions you ask!

MOTHER. We like to know all about the things that hurt us. Who was the boy?

NEIGHBOR. Leonardo.

MOTHER. What Leonardo?

NEIGHBOR. Leonardo Félix.

MOTHER. Félix!

NEIGHBOR. Yes, but—how is Leonardo to blame for anything? He was eight years old when those things happened.

MOTHER. That's true. But I hear that name—Félix—and it's all the same. [*Muttering.*] Félix, a slimy mouthful. [*She spits.*] It makes me spit—spit so I won't kill!

NEIGHBOR. Control yourself. What good will it do?

MOTHER. No good. But you see how it is.

NEIGHBOR. Don't get in the way of your son's happiness. Don't say anything to him. You're old. So am I. It's time for you and me to keep quiet.

MOTHER. I'll say nothing to him.

NEIGHBOR. [*Kissing her.*] Nothing.

MOTHER. [*Calmly.*] Such things! . . .

NEIGHBOR. I'm going. My men will soon be coming in from the fields.

MOTHER. Have you ever known such a hot sun?

NEIGHBOR. The children carrying water out to the reapers are black with it. Goodbye, woman.

MOTHER. Goodbye.

The MOTHER *starts toward the door at the left. Halfway there she stops and slowly crosses herself.*

Scene 2

A room painted rose with copperware and wreaths of common flowers. In the center of the room is a table with a tablecloth. It is morning.

Leonardo's MOTHER-IN-LAW *sits in one corner holding a child in her arms and rocking it. His* WIFE *is in the other corner mending stockings.*

MOTHER-IN-LAW.
Lullaby, my baby
once there was a big horse
who didn't like water.
The water was black there
under the branches.
When it reached the bridge
it stopped and it sang.
Who can say, my baby,
what the stream holds
with its long tail
in its green parlor?

WIFE. [*Softly.*]
Carnation, sleep and dream,
the horse won't drink from the
stream.

MOTHER-IN-LAW.
My rose, asleep now lie,
the horse is starting to cry.
His poor hooves were bleeding,
his long mane was frozen,
and deep in his eyes
stuck a silvery dagger.
Down he went to the river,
Oh, down he went down!
And his blood was running,
Oh, more than the water.

WIFE.
Carnation, sleep and dream,
the horse won't drink from the
stream.

MOTHER-IN-LAW.
My rose, asleep now lie,
the horse is starting to cry.
WIFE.
He never did touch
the dank river shore
though his muzzle was warm
and with silvery flies.
So, to the hard mountains
he could only whinny
just when the dead stream
covered his throat.
Ay-y-y, for the big horse
who didn't like water!
Ay-y-y, for the snow-wound
big horse of the dawn!
MOTHER-IN-LAW.
Don't come in! Stop him
and close up the window
with branches of dreams
and a dream of branches.
WIFE.
My baby is sleeping.
MOTHER-IN-LAW.
My baby is quiet.
WIFE.
Look, horse, my baby
has him a pillow.
MOTHER-IN-LAW.
His cradle is metal.
WIFE. His quilt a fine fabric.
MOTHER-IN-LAW.
Lullaby, my baby.
WIFE.
Ay-y-y, for the big horse
who didn't like water!
MOTHER-IN-LAW.
Don't come near, don't come in!
Go away to the mountains
and through the grey valleys,
that's where your mare is.
WIFE. [*Looking at the baby.*]
My baby is sleeping.
MOTHER-IN-LAW.
My baby is resting.
WIFE. [*Softly.*]
Carnation, sleep and dream,
The horse won't drink from the
    stream.
MOTHER-IN-LAW. [*Getting up, very softly.*]
My rose, asleep now lie

for the horse is starting to cry.
She carries the child out. LEONARDO *enters.*
LEONARDO. Where's the baby?
WIFE. He's sleeping.
LEONARDO. Yesterday he wasn't well. He
cried during the night.
WIFE. Today he's like a dahlia. And
you? Were you at the blacksmith's?
LEONARDO. I've just come from there.
Would you believe it? For more than
two months he's been putting new
shoes on the horse and they're always
coming off. As far as I can see he
pulls them off on the stones.
WIFE. Couldn't it just be that you use
him so much?
LEONARDO. No. I almost never use him.
WIFE. Yesterday the neighbors told me
they'd seen you on the far side of the
plains.
LEONARDO. Who said that?
WIFE. The women who gather capers. It
certainly surprised me. Was it you?
LEONARDO. No. What would I be doing
there, in that wasteland?
WIFE. That's what I said. But the horse
was streaming sweat.
LEONARDO. Did you see him?
WIFE. No. Mother did.
LEONARDO. Is she with the baby?
WIFE. Yes. Do you want some
lemonade?
LEONARDO. With good cold water.
WIFE. And then you didn't come to eat!
LEONARDO. I was with the wheat
weighers. They always hold me up.
WIFE. [*Very tenderly, while she makes the
lemonade.*] Did they pay you a good
price?
LEONARDO. Fair.
WIFE. I need a new dress and the baby a
bonnet with ribbons.
LEONARDO. [*Getting up.*] I'm going to
take a look at him.
WIFE. Be careful. He's alseep.
MOTHER-IN-LAW. [*Coming in.*] Well!
Who's been racing the horse that
way? He's down there, worn out, his
eyes popping from their sockets as
though he'd come from the ends of
the earth.

LEONARDO. [*Acidly.*] I have.

MOTHER-IN-LAW. Oh, excuse me! He's your horse.

WIFE. [*Timidly.*] He was at the wheat buyers.

MOTHER-IN-LAW. He can burst for all of me!

She sits down. Pause.

WIFE. Your drink. Is it cold?

LEONARDO. Yes.

WIFE. Did you hear they're going to ask for my cousin?

LEONARDO. When?

WIFE. Tomorrow. The wedding will be within a month. I hope they're going to invite us.

LEONARDO. [*Gravely.*] I don't know.

MOTHER-IN-LAW. His mother, I think, wasn't very happy about the match.

LEONARDO. Well, she may be right. She's a girl to be careful with.

WIFE. I don't like to have you thinking bad things about a good girl.

MOTHER-IN-LAW. [*Meaningfully.*] If he does, it's because he knows her. Didn't you know he courted her for three years?

LEONARDO. But I left her. [*To his* WIFE.] Are you going to cry now? Quit that! [*He brusquely pulls her hands away from her face.*] Let's go see the baby.

They go in with their arms around each other. A GIRL *appears. She is happy. She enters running.*

GIRL. Señora.

MOTHER-IN-LAW. What is it?

GIRL. The groom came to the store and he's bought the best of everything they had.

MOTHER-IN-LAW. Was he alone?

GIRL. No. With his mother. Stern, tall. [*She imitates her.*] And such extravagance!

MOTHER-IN-LAW. They have money.

GIRL. And they bought some open-work stockings! Oh, such stockings! A woman's dream of stockings! Look: a swallow here, [*She points to her ankle.*] a ship here, [*She points to her calf.*] and here, [*She points to her thigh.*] a rose!

MOTHER-IN-LAW. Child!

GIRL. A rose with the seeds and the stem! Oh! All in silk.

MOTHER-IN-LAW. Two rich families are being brought together.

LEONARDO *and his* WIFE *appear.*

GIRL. I came to tell you what they're buying.

LEONARDO. [*Loudly.*] We don't care.

WIFE. Leave her alone.

MOTHER-IN-LAW. Leonardo, it's not that important.

GIRL. Please excuse me.

She leaves, weeping.

MOTHER-IN-LAW. Why do you always have to make trouble with people?

LEONARDO. I didn't ask for your opinion.

He sits down.

MOTHER-IN-LAW. Very well.

Pause.

WIFE. [*To* LEONARDO.] What's the matter with you? What idea've you got boiling there inside your head? Don't leave me like this, not knowing anything.

LEONARDO. Stop that.

WIFE. No. I want you to look at me and tell me.

LEONARDO. Let me alone.

He rises.

WIFE. Where are you going, love?

LEONARDO. [*Sharply.*] Can't you shut up?

MOTHER-IN-LAW. [*Energetically, to her daughter.*] Be quiet! [*Leonardo goes out.*] The baby!

She goes into the bedroom and comes out again with the baby in her arms. The WIFE *has remained standing, unmoving.*

MOTHER-IN-LAW.
His poor hooves were bleeding,
his long mane was frozen,
and deep in his eyes
stuck a silvery dagger.
Down he went to the river,
Oh, down he went down!
And his blood was running,
Oh, more than the water.

WIFE. [*Turning slowly, as though dreaming.*]
Carnation, sleep and dream,

the horse is drinking from the
    stream.
MOTHER-IN-LAW.
    My rose, asleep now lie
    the horse is starting to cry.
WIFE.
    Lullaby, my baby.
MOTHER-IN-LAW.
    Ay-y-y, for the big horse
    who didn't like water!
WIFE. [*Dramatically.*]
    Don't come near, don't come in!
    Go away to the mountains!
    Ay-y-y, for the snow-wound,
    big horse of the dawn!
MOTHER-IN-LAW. [*Weeping.*]
    My baby is sleeping. . . .
WIFE. [*Weeping, as she slowly moves closer.*]
    My baby is resting. . . .
MOTHER-IN-LAW.
    Carnation, sleep and dream,
    the horse won't drink from the
      stream.
WIFE. [*Weeping, and leaning on the table.*]
    My rose, asleep now lie,
    the horse is starting to cry.

Scene 3

Interior of the cave where the BRIDE *lives.*[1]
*At the back is a cross of large rose colored
flowers. The round doors have lace curtains with rose colored ties. Around the
walls, which are of a white and hard
material, are round fans, blue jars, and
little mirrors.*
SERVANT. Come right in. . . . [*She is very
affable, full of humble hypocrisy. The*
BRIDEGROOM *and his* MOTHER *enter.
The* MOTHER *is dressed in black satin and
wears a lace mantilla; the* BRIDEGROOM
*in black corduroy with a great golden
chain.*] Won't you sit down? They'll be
right here.
She leaves. The MOTHER *and* SON *are left
sitting motionless as statues. Long pause.*
MOTHER. Did you wear the watch?
BRIDEGROOM. Yes.
He takes it out and looks at it.
MOTHER. We have to be back on time.
    How far away these people live!

BRIDEGROOM. But this is good land.
MOTHER. Good; but much too lone-
    some. A four hour trip and not one
    house, not one tree.
BIRDEGROOM. This is the wasteland.
MOTHER. Your father would have cov-
    ered it with trees.
BRIDEGROOM. Without water?
MOTHER. He would have found some.
    In the three years we were married
    he planted ten cherry trees, [*Remem-
    bering.*] those three walnut trees by
    the mill, a whole vineyard and a
    plant called Jupiter which had scarlet
    flowers—but it dried up.
Pause.
BRIDEGROOM. [*Referring to the* BRIDE.]
    She must be dressing.
The BRIDE'S FATHER *enters. He is very old,
with shining white hair. His head is
bowed. The* MOTHER *and the* BRIDE-
GROOM *rise. They shake hands in silence.*
FATHER. Was it a long trip?
MOTHER. Four hours.
They sit down.
FATHER. You must have come the long-
    est way.
MOTHER. I'm too old to come along the
    cliffs by the river.
BRIDEGROOM. She gets dizzy.
Pause.
FATHER. A good hemp harvest.
BRIDEGROOM. A really good one.
FATHER. When I was young this land
    didn't even grow hemp. We've had to
    punish it, even weep over it, to make
    it give us anything useful.
MOTHER. But now it does. Don't com-
    plain. I'm not here to ask you for
    anything.
FATHER. [*Smiling.*] You're richer than I.
    Your vineyards are worth a fortune.
    Each young vine a silver coin. But—
    do you know?—what bothers me is
    that our lands are separated. I like to
    have everything together. One thorn
    I have in my heart, and that's the
    little orchard there, stuck in between
    my fields—and they won't sell it to
    me for all the gold in the world.
BRIDEGROOM. That's the way it always is.

FATHER. If we could just take twenty teams of oxen and move your vineyards over here, and put them down on that hillside, how happy I'd be!

MOTHER. But why?

FATHER. What's mine is hers and what's yours is his. That's why. Just to see it all together. How beautiful it is to bring things together!

BRIDEGROOM. And it would be less work.

MOTHER. When I die, you could sell ours and buy here, right alongside.

FATHER. Sell, sell? Bah! Buy, my friend, buy everything. If I had had sons I would have bought all this mountainside right up to the part with the stream. It's not good land, but strong arms can make it good, and since no people pass by, they don't steal your fruit and you can sleep in peace.

Pause.

MOTHER. You know what I'm here for.

FATHER. Yes.

MOTHER. And?

FATHER. It seems all right to me. They have talked it over.

MOTHER. My son has money and knows how to manage it.

FATHER. My daughter too.

MOTHER. My son is handsome. He's never known a woman. His good name cleaner than a sheet spread out in the sun.

FATHER. No need to tell you about my daughter. At three, when the morning star shines, she prepares the bread. She never talks: soft as wool, she embroiders all kinds of fancy work and she can cut a strong cord with her teeth.

MOTHER. God bless her house.

FATHER. May God bless it.

The SERVANT appecrs with two trays. One with drinks and the other with sweets.

MOTHER. [*To the* SON.] When would you like the wedding?

BRIDEGROOM. Next Thursday.

FATHER. The day on which she'll be exactly twenty-two years old.

MOTHER. Twenty-two! My oldest son would be that age if he were alive. Warm and manly as he was, he'd be living now if men hadn't invented knives.

FATHER. One mustn't think about that.

MOTHER. Every minute. Always a hand on your breast.

FATHER. Thursday, then? Is that right?

BRIDEGROOM. That's right.

FATHER. You and I and the bridal couple will go in a carriage to the church which is very far from here; the wedding party on the carts and horses they'll bring with them.

MOTHER. Agreed.

The SERVANT passes through.

FATHER. Tell her she may come in now. [*To the* MOTHER.] I shall be much pleased if you like her.

The BRIDE appears. Her hands fall in a modest pose and her head is bowed.

MOTHER. Come here. Are you happy?

BRIDE. Yes, señora.

FATHER. You shouldn't be so solemn. After all, she's going to be your mother.

BRIDE. I'm happy. I've said "yes" because I wanted to.

MOTHER. Naturally. [*She takes her by the chin.*] Look at me.

FATHER. She resembles my wife in every way.

MOTHER. Yes? What a beautiful glance! Do you know what it is to be married, child?

BRIDE. [*Seriously.*] I do.

MOTHER. A man, some children and a wall two yards thick for everything else.

BRIDEGROOM. Is anything else needed?

MOTHER. No. Just that you all live— that's it! Live long!

BRIDE. I'll know how to keep my word.

MOTHER. Here are some gifts for you.

BRIDE. Thank you.

FATHER. Shall we have something?

MOTHER. Nothing for me. [*To the* SON.] But you?

BRIDEGROOM. Yes, thank you.

He takes one sweet, the BRIDE another.

FATHER. [*To the* BRIDEGROOM.] Wine?

MOTHER. He doesn't touch it.

FATHER. All the better.

Pause. All are standing.

BRIDEGROOM. [*To the* BRIDE.] I'll come tomorrow.

BRIDE. What time?

BRIDEGROOM. Five.

BRIDE. I'll be waiting for you.

BRIDEGROOM. When I leave your side I feel a great emptiness, and something like a knot in my throat.

BRIDE. When you are my husband you won't have it any more.

BRIDEGROOM. That's what I tell myself.

MOTHER. Come. The sun doesn't wait. [*To the* FATHER.] Are we agreed on everything?

FATHER. Agreed.

MOTHER. [*To the* SERVANT.] Goodbye, woman.

SERVANT. God go with you!

The MOTHER *kisses the* BRIDE *and they begin to leave in silence.*

MOTHER [*At the door.*] Goodbye, Daughter.

The BRIDE *answers with her hand.*

FATHER. I'll go out with you.

They leave.

SERVANT. I'm bursting to see the presents.

BRIDE. [*Sharply.*] Stop that!

SERVANT. Oh, child, show them to me.

BRIDE. I don't want to.

SERVANT. At least the stockings. They say they're all open work. Please!

BRIDE. I said no.

SERVANT. Well, my Lord. All right then. It looks as if you didn't want to get married.

BRIDE. [*Biting her hand in anger.*] Ay-y-y!

SERVANT. Child, child! What's the matter with you? Are you sorry to give up your queen's life? Don't think of bitter things. Have you any reason to? None. Let's look at the presents.

She takes the box.

BRIDE. [*Holding her by the wrists.*] Let go.

SERVANT. Ay-y-y, girl!

BRIDE. Let go, I said.

SERVANT. You're stronger than a man.

BRIDE. Haven't I done a man's work? I wish I were.

SERVANT. Don't talk like that.

BRIDE. Quiet, I said. Let's talk about something else.

The light is fading from the stage. Long pause.

SERVANT. Did you hear a horse last night?

BRIDE. What time?

SERVANT. Three.

BRIDE. It might have been a stray horse—from the herd.

SERVANT. No. It carried a rider.

BRIDE. How do you know?

SERVANT. Because I saw him. He was standing by your window. It shocked me greatly.

BRIDE. Maybe it was my fiancé. Sometimes he comes by at that time.

SERVANT. No.

BRIDE. You saw him?

SERVANT. Yes.

BRIDE. Who was it?

SERVANT. It was Leonardo.

BRIDE. [*Strongly.*] Liar! You liar! Why should he come here?

SERVANT. He came.

BRIDE. Shut up! Shut your cursed mouth.

The sound of a horse is heard.

SERVANT. [*At the window.*] Look. Lean out. Was it Leonardo?

BRIDE. It was!

Act 2

Scene 1

The entrance hall of the BRIDE's *house. A large door in the back. It is night. The* BRIDE *enters wearing ruffled white petticoats full of laces and embroidered bands, and a sleeveless white bodice. The* SERVANT *is dressed the same way.*

SERVANT. I'll finish combing your hair out here.

BRIDE. It's too warm to stay in there.

SERVANT. In this country it doesn't even cool off at dawn.

The BRIDE *sits on a low chair and looks into a little hand mirror. The* SERVANT *combs her hair.*

BRIDE. My mother came from a place with lots of trees—from a fertile country.

SERVANT. And she was so happy!

BRIDE. But she wasted away here.

SERVANT. Fate.

BRIDE. As we're all wasting away here. The very walls give off heat. Ay-y-y! Don't pull so hard.

SERVANT. I'm only trying to fix this wave better. I want it to fall over your forehead. [*The* BRIDE *looks at herself in the mirror.*] How beautiful you are! Ay-y-y!

She kisses her passsionately.

BRIDE. [*Seriously.*] Keep right on combing.

SERVANT. [*Combing.*] Oh, lucky you— going to put your arms around a man; and kiss him; and feel his weight.

BRIDE. Hush.

SERVANT. And the best part will be when you'll wake up and you'll feel him at your side and when he caresses your shoulders with his breath, like a little nightingale's feather.

BRIDE. [*Sternly.*] Will you be quiet.

SERVANT. But, child! What *is* a wedding? A wedding is just that and nothing more. Is it the sweets—or the bouquets of flowers? No. It's a shining bed and a man and a woman.

BRIDE. But you shouldn't talk about it.

SERVANT. Oh, *that's* something else again. But fun enough too.

BRIDE. Or bitter enough.

SERVANT. I'm going to put the orange blossoms on from here to here, so the wreath will shine out on top of your hair.

She tries on the sprigs of orange blossom.

BRIDE. [*Looking at herself in the mirror.*] Give it to me.

She takes the wreath, looks at it and lets her head fall in discouragement.

SERVANT. Now what's the matter?

BRIDE. Leave me alone.

SERVANT. This is no time for you to start feeling sad. [*Encouragingly.*] Give me the wreath. [*The* BRIDE *takes the wreath and hurls it away.*] Child! You're just asking God to punish you, throwing the wreath on the floor like that. Raise your head! Don't you want to get married? Say it. You can still withdraw.

The BRIDE *rises.*

BRIDE. Storm clouds. A chill wind that cuts through my heart. Who hasn't felt it?

SERVANT. You love your sweetheart, don't you?

BRIDE. I love him.

SERVANT. Yes, yes. I'm sure you do.

BRIDE. But this is a very serious step.

SERVANT. You've got to take it.

BRIDE. I've already given my word.

SERVANT. I'll put on the wreath.

BRIDE. [*She sits down.*] Hurry. They should be arriving by now.

SERVANT. They've already been at least two hours on the way.

BRIDE. How far is it from here to the church?

SERVANT. Five leagues by the stream, but twice that by the road.

The BRIDE *rises and the* SERVANT *grows excited as she looks at her.*

SERVANT.
 Awake, O Bride, awaken,
 On your wedding morning waken!
 The world's rivers may all
 Bear along your bridal Crown!

BRIDE. [*Smiling.*] Come now.

SERVANT. [*Enthusiastically kissing her and dancing around her.*]
 Awake,
 with the fresh bouquet
 of flowering laurel.
 Awake,
 by the trunk and branch
 of the laurels!

The banging of the front door latch is heard.

BRIDE. Open the door! That must be the first guests.

She leaves. The SERVANT *opens the door.*

SERVANT. [*In astonishment.*] You!

LEONARDO. Yes, me. Good morning.

SERVANT. The first one!

LEONARDO. Wasn't I invited?

SERVANT. Yes.

LEONARDO. That's why I'm here.

SERVANT. Where's your wife?

LEONARDO. I came on my horse. She's coming by the road.

SERVANT. Didn't you meet anyone?

LEONARDO. I *passed* them on my horse.

SERVANT. You're going to kill that horse with so much racing.

LEONARDO. When he dies, he's dead!

Pause.

SERVANT. Sit down. Nobody's up yet.

LEONARDO. Where's the bride?

SERVANT. I'm just on my way to dress her.

LEONARDO. The bride! She ought to be happy!

SERVANT. [*Changing the subject.*] How's the baby?

LEONARDO. What baby?

SERVANT. Your son.

LEONARDO. [*Remembering, as though in a dream.*] Ah!

SERVANT. Are they bringing him?

LEONARDO. No.

Pause. Voices sing distantly.

VOICES.
Awake, O Bride, awaken,
On your wedding morning waken!

LEONARDO.
Awake, O Bride, awaken,
On your wedding morning waken!

SERVANT. It's the guests. They're still quite a way off.

LEONARDO. The bride's going to wear a big wreath, isn't she? But it ought not to be so large. One a little smaller would look better on her. Has the groom already brought her the orange blossom that must be worn on the breast?

BRIDE. [*Appearing, still in petticoats and wearing the wreath.*] He brought it.

SERVANT. [*Sternly.*] Don't come out like that.

BRIDE. What does it matter? [*Seriously.*] Why do you ask if they brought the orange blossom? Do you have something in mind?

LEONARDO. Nothing. What would I have in mind? [*Drawing near her.*] You, you know me; you know I don't. Tell me so. What have I ever meant to you? Open your memory, refresh it. But two oxen and an ugly little hut are almost nothing. That's the thorn.

BRIDE. What have you come here to do?

LEONARDO. To see your wedding.

BRIDE. Just as I saw yours!

LEONARDO. Tied up by you, done with your two hands. Oh, they can kill me but they can't spit on me. But even money, which shines so much, spits sometimes.

BRIDE. Liar!

LEONARDO. I don't want to talk. I'm hot-blooded and I don't want to shout so all these hills will hear me.

BRIDE. My shouts would be louder.

SERVANT. You'll have to stop talking like this. [*To the* BRIDE.] You don't have to talk about what's past.

The SERVANT *looks around uneasily at the doors.*

BRIDE. She's right. I shouldn't even talk to you. But it offends me to the soul that you come here to watch me, and spy on my wedding, and ask about the orange blossom with something on your mind. Go and wait for your wife at the door.

LEONARDO. But, can't you and I even talk?

SERVANT. [*With rage.*] No! No, you can't talk.

LEONARDO. Ever since I got married I've been thinking night and day about whose fault it was, and every time I think about it, out comes a new fault to eat up the old one; but always there's a fault left!

BRIDE. A man with a horse knows a lot of things and can do a lot to ride roughshod over a girl stuck out in the desert. But I have my pride. And that's why I'm getting married. I'll lock myself in with my husband and

then I'll have to love him above
everyone else.

LEONARDO. Pride won't help you a bit.
He draws near to her.

BRIDE. Don't come near me!

LEONARDO. To burn with desire and
keep quiet about it is the greatest
punishment we can bring on ourselves. What good was pride to me—
and not seeing you, and letting you
lie awake night after night? No good!
It only served to bring the fire down
on me! You think that time heals and
walls hide things, but it isn't true, it
isn't true! When things get that deep
inside you there isn't anybody can
change them.

BRIDE. [*Trembling.*] I can't listen to you.
I can't listen to your voice. It's as
though I'd drunk a bottle of anise
and fallen asleep wrapped in a quilt
of roses. It pulls me along and I
know I'm drowning—but I go on
down.

SERVANT. [*Seizing* LEONARDO *by the
lapels.*] You've got to go right now!

LEONARDO. This is the last time I'll ever
talk to her. Don't you be afraid of
anything.

BRIDE. And I know I'm crazy and I
know my breast rots with longing;
but here I am—calmed by hearing
him, by just seeing him move his
arms.

LEONARDO. I'd never be at peace if I
didn't tell you these things. I got
married. Now you get married!

Voices are heard singing, nearer.

VOICES.
Awake, O Bride, awaken,
On your wedding morning waken!

BRIDE.
Awake, O Bride, awaken,

She goes out, running toward her room.

SERVANT. The people are here now. [*To*
LEONARDO.] Don't you come near her
again.

LEONARDO. Don't worry.

He goes out to the left. Day begins to break.

FIRST GIRL. [*Entering.*]
Awake, O Bride, awaken,

the morning you're to marry;
sing round and dance round;
balconies a wreath must carry.

VOICES.
Bride, awaken!

SERVANT. [*Creating enthusiasm.*]
Awake,
with the green bouquet
of love in flower.
Awake,
by the trunk and the branch
of the laurels!

SECOND GIRL. [*Entering.*]
Awake,
with her long hair,
snowy sleeping gown,
patent leather boots with silver—
her forehead jasmines crown.

SERVANT.
Oh, shepherdess,
the moon begins to shine!

FIRST GIRL.
Oh, gallant,
leave your hat beneath the vine!

FIRST YOUNG MAN. [*Entering, holding his
hat on high.*]
Bride, awaken,
for over the fields
the wedding draws nigh
with trays heaped with dahlias
and cakes piled high.

VOICES.
Bride, awaken!

SECOND GIRL.
The bride
has set her white wreath in place
and the groom
ties it on with a golden lace.

SERVANT.
By the orange tree,
sleepless the bride will be.

THIRD GIRL. [*Entering.*]
By the citron vine,
gifts from the groom will shine.

Three GUESTS *come in.*

FIRST YOUTH.
Dove, awaken!
In the dawn
shadowy bells are shaken.

GUEST.
The bride, the white bride

today a maiden,
tomorrow a wife.

FIRST GIRL.
 Dark one, come down
 trailing the train of your silken gown.

GUEST.
 Little dark one, come down,
 cold morning wears a dewy crown.

FIRST GUEST.
 Awaken, wife, awake,
 orange blossoms the breezes shake.

SERVANT.
 A tree I would embroider her
 with garnet sashes wound,
 And on each sash a cupid,
 with "Long Live" all around.

VOICES.
 Bride, awaken.

FIRST YOUTH.
 The morning you're to marry!

GUEST.
 The morning you're to marry
 how elegant you'll seem;
 worthy, mountain flower,
 of a captain's dream.

FATHER. [*Entering.*]
 A captain's wife
 the groom will marry.
 He comes with his oxen the treasure
  to carry!

THIRD GIRL.
 The groom
 is like a flower of gold.
 When he walks,
 blossoms at his feet unfold.

SERVANT.
 Oh, my lucky girl!

SECOND YOUTH.
 Bride, awaken.

SERVANT.
 Oh, my elegant girl!

FIRST GIRL.
 Through the windows
 hear the wedding shout.

SECOND GIRL.
 Let the bride come out.

FIRST GIRL.
 Come out, come out!

SERVANT.
 Let the bells
 ring and ring out clear!

FIRST YOUTH.
 For here she comes!
 For now she's near!

SERVANT.
 Like a bull, the wedding
 is arising here!

The BRIDE *appears. She wears a black dress in the style of 1900,*[2] *with a bustle and large train covered with pleated gauzes and heavy laces. Upon her hair, brushed in a wave over her forehead, she wears an orange blossom wreath. Guitars sound. The* GIRLS *kiss the* BRIDE.

THIRD GIRL. What scent did you put on your hair?

BRIDE. [*Laughing.*] None at all.

SECOND GIRL. [*Looking at her dress.*] This cloth is what you can't get.

FIRST YOUTH. Here's the groom!

BRIDEGROOM. Salud!

FIRST GIRL. [*Putting a flower behind his ear.*]
 The groom
 is like a flower of gold.

SECOND GIRL.
 Quiet breezes
 from his eyes unfold.

The GROOM *goes to the* BRIDE.

BRIDE. Why did you put on those shoes?

BRIDEGROOM. They're gayer than the black ones.

LEONARD'S WIFE. [*Entering and kissing the* BRIDE.] Salud!

They all speak excitedly.

LEONARDO. [*Entering as one who performs a duty.*]
 The morning you're to marry
 We give you a wreath to wear.

LEONARDO'S WIFE.
 So the fields may be made happy
 with the dew dropped from your
  hair!

MOTHER [*To the* FATHER.] Are those people here, too?

FATHER. They're part of the family. Today is a day of forgiveness!

MOTHER. I'll put up with it, but I don't forgive.

BRIDEGROOM. With your wreath, it's a joy to look at you!

BRIDE. Let's go to the church quickly.

BRIDEGROOM. Are you in a hurry?

BRIDE. Yes. I want to be your wife right now so that I can be with you alone, not hearing any voice but yours.

BRIDEGROOM. That's what I want!

BRIDE. And not seeing any eyes but yours. And for you to hug me so hard, that even though my dead mother should call me, I wouldn't be able to draw away from you.

BRIDEGROOM. My arms are strong. I'll hug you for forty years without stopping.

BRIDE. [*Taking his arm, dramatically.*] Forever!

FATHER. Quick now! Round up the teams and carts! The sun's already out.

MOTHER. And go along carefully! Let's hope nothing goes wrong.

The great door in the background opens.

SERVANT. [*Weeping.*]
As you set out from your house,
oh maiden white,
remember you leave shining
with a star's light.

FIRST GIRL.
Clean of body, clean of clothes
from her home to church she goes.

They start leaving.

SECOND GIRL.
Now you leave your home
for the church!

SERVANT.
The wind sets flowers
on the sands.

THIRD GIRL.
Ah, the white maid!

SERVANT.
Dark winds are the lace
of her mantilla.

They leave. Guitars, castanets and tambourines are heard. LEONARDO *and his* WIFE *are left alone.*

WIFE. Let's go.

LEONARDO. Where?

WIFE. To the church. But not on your horse. You're coming with me.

LEONARDO. In the cart?

WIFE. Is there anything else?

LEONARD. I'm not the kind of man to ride in a cart.

WIFE. Nor I the wife to go to a wedding without her husband. I can't stand any more of this!

LEONARDO. Neither can I.

WIFE. And why do you look at me that way? With a thorn in each eye.

LEONARDO. Let's go!

WIFE. I don't know what's happening. But I think, and I don't want to think. One thing I do know. I'm already cast off by you. But I have a son. And another coming. And so it goes. My mother's fate was the same. Well, I'm not moving from here.

Voices outside.

VOICES.
As you set out from your home
and to the church go
remember you leave shining
with a star's glow.

WIFE. [*Weeping.*]
Remember you leave shining
with a star's glow!
I left my house like that too. They could have stuffed the whole countryside in my mouth. I was that trusting.

LEONARDO. [*Rising.*] Let's go!

WIFE. But you with me!

LEONARDO. Yes. [*Pause.*] Start moving!

They leave.

VOICES.
As you set out from your home
and to the church go,
remember you leave shining
with a star's glow.

Scene 2

The exterior of the BRIDE's *Cave Home, in white gray and cold blue tones. Large cactus trees. Shadowy and silver tones. Panoramas of light tan tablelands, everything hard like a landscape in popular ceramics.*

SERVANT. [*Arranging glasses and trays on a table.*]
A-turning,
the wheel was a-turning

and the water was flowing,
for the wedding night comes.
May the branches part
And the moon be arrayed
at her white balcony rail.
In a loud voice.
Set out the tablecloths!
In a pathetic voice.
 A-singing,
bride and groom were singing
and the water was flowing
for their wedding night comes.
Oh, rime-frost, flash!—
and almonds bitter
fill with honey!
In a loud voice.
Get the wine ready!
In a poetic tone.
 Elegant girl,
most elegant in the world,
see the way the water is flowing,
for your wedding night comes.
Hold your skirts close in
under the bridegroom's wing
and never leave your house,
for the Bridegroom is a dove
with his breast a firebrand
and the fields wait for the whisper
of spurting blood.
 A-turning
the wheel was a-turning
and the water was flowing
and your wedding night comes.
Oh, water, sparkle!

MOTHER. [*Entering.*] At last!

FATHER. Are we the first ones?

SERVANT. No. Leonardo and his wife arrived a while ago. They drove like demons. His wife got here dead with fright. They made the trip as though they'd come on horseback.

FATHER. That one's looking for trouble. He's not of good blood.

MOTHER. What blood would you expect him to have? His whole family's blood. It comes down from his great grandfather, who started in killing, and it goes on down through the whole evil breed of knife wielding and false smiling men.

FATHER. Let's leave it at that!

SERVANT. But how can she leave it at that?

MOTHER. It hurts me to the tips of my veins. On the forehead of all of them I see only the hand with which they killed what was mine. Can you really see me? Don't I seem mad to you? Well, it's the madness of not having shrieked out all my breast needs to. Always in my breast there's a shriek standing tiptoe that I have to bear down and hold in under my shawls. But the dead are carried off and one has to keep still. And then, people find fault.

She removes her shawl.

FATHER. Today's not the day for you to be remembering these things.

MOTHER. When the talk turns on it, I have to speak. And more so today. Because today I'm left alone in my house.

FATHER. But with the expectation of having someone with you.

MOTHER. That's my hope: grand-children.

They sit down.

FATHER. I want them to have a lot of them. This land needs hands that aren't hired. There's a battle to be waged against weeds, the thistles, the big rocks that come from one doesn't know where. And those hands have to be the owner's, who chastises and dominates, who makes the seeds grow. Lots of sons are needed.

MOTHER. And some daughters! Men are like the wind! They're forced to handle weapons. Girls never go out into the street.

FATHER. [*Happily.*] I think they'll have both.

MOTHER. My son will cover her well. He's of good seed. His father could have had many sons with me.

FATHER. What I'd like is to have all this happen in a day. So that right away they'd have two or three boys.

MOTHER. But it's not like that. It takes a long time. That's why it's so terrible to see one's own blood spilled out on the ground. A fountain that spurts for a minute, but costs us years. When I got to my son, he lay fallen in the middle of the street. I wet my hands with his blood and licked them with my tongue—because it was my blood. You don't know what that's like. In a glass and topaze shrine I'd put the earth moistened by his blood.

FATHER. Now you must hope. My daughter is wide-hipped and your son is strong.

MOTHER. That's why I'm hoping.

They rise.

FATHER. Get the wheat trays ready!

SERVANT. They're all ready.

LEONARD'S WIFE. [*Entering.*] May it be for the best!

MOTHER. Thank you.

LEONARDO. Is there going to be a celebration?

FATHER. A small one. People can't stay long.

SERVANT. Here they are!

Guests begin entering in gay groups. The BRIDE *and* GROOM *come in arm-in-arm.* LEONARDO *leaves.*

BRIDEGROOM. There's never been a wedding with so many people!

BRIDE. [*Sullen.*] Never.

FATHER. It was brilliant.

MOTHER. Whole branches of families came.

BRIDEGROOM. People who never went out of the house.

MOTHER. Your father sowed well, and now you're reaping it.

BRIDEGROOM. There were cousins of mine whom I no longer knew.

MOTHER. All the people from the seacoast.

BRIDEGROOM. [*Happily.*] They were frightened of the horses.

They talk.

MOTHER. [*To the* BRIDE.] What are you thinking about?

BRIDE. I'm not thinking about anything.

MOTHER. Your blessings weigh heavily.

Guitars are heard.

BRIDE. Like lead.

MOTHER. [*Stern.*] But they shouldn't

weigh so. Happy as a dove you ought to be.

BRIDE. Are you staying here tonight?

MOTHER. No. My house is empty.

BRIDE. You ought to stay!

FATHER. [*To the* MOTHER.] Look at the dance they're forming. Dances of the far away seashore.

LEONARDO *enters and sits down. His* WIFE *stands rigidly behind him.*

MOTHER. They're my husband's cousins. Stiff as stones at dancing.

FATHER. It makes me happy to watch them. What a change for this house!

He leaves.

BRIDEGROOM. [*To the* BRIDE.] Did you like the orange blossom?

BRIDE. [*Looking at him fixedly.*] Yes.

BRIDEGROOM. It's all of wax. It will last forever. I'd like you to have had them all over your dress.

BRIDE. No need of that.

LEONARDO *goes off to the right.*

FIRST GIRL. Let's go and take out our pins.

BRIDE. [*To the* GROOM.] I'll be right back.

LEONARDO'S WIFE. I hope you'll be happy with my cousin!

BRIDEGROOM. I'm sure I will.

LEONARDO'S WIFE. The two of you here; never going out; building a home. I wish I could live far away like this, too!

BRIDEGROOM. Why don't you buy land? The mountainside is cheap and children grow up better.

LEONARDO'S WIFE. We don't have any money. And at the rate we're going! . . .

BRIDEGROOM. Your husband is a good worker.

LEONARDO'S WIFE. Yes, but he likes to fly around too much; from one thing to another. He's not a patient man.

SERVANT. Aren't you having anything? I'm going to wrap up some wine cakes for your mother. She likes them so much.

BRIDEGROOM. Put up three dozen for her.

LEONARDO'S WIFE. No, no! A half-dozen's enough for her!

BRIDEGROOM. But today's a day!

LEONARDO'S WIFE. [*To the* SERVANT.] Where's Leonardo?

BRIDEGROOM. He must be with the guests.

LEONARDO'S WIFE. I'm going to go see. *She leaves.*

SERVANT. [*Looking off at the dance.*] That's beautiful there.

BRIDEGROOM. Aren't you dancing?

SERVANT. No one will ask me.

TWO GIRLS *pass across the back of the stage; during this whole scene the background should be an animated crossing of figures.*

BRIDEGROOM. [*Happily.*] They just don't know anything. Lively old girls like you dance better than the young ones.

SERVANT. Well! Are you tossing me a compliment, boy? What a family yours is! Men among men! As a little girl I saw your grandfather's wedding. What a figure! It seemed as if a mountain were getting married.

BRIDEGROOM. I'm not as tall.

SERVANT. But there's the same twinkle in your eye. Where's the girl?

BRIDEGROOM. Taking off her wreath.

SERVANT. Ah! Look. For midnight, since you won't be sleeping, I have prepared ham for you, and some large glasses of old wine. On the lower shelf of the cupboard. In case you need it.

BRIDEGROOM. [*Smiling.*] I won't be eating at midnight.

SERVANT. [*Slyly.*] If not you, maybe the bride. *She leaves.*

FIRST YOUTH. [*Entering.*] You've got to come have a drink with us!

BRIDEGROOM. I'm waiting for the bride.

SECOND YOUTH. You'll have her at dawn!

FIRST YOUTH. That's when it's best!

SECOND YOUTH. Just for a minute.

BRIDEGROOM. Let's go.

They leave. Great excitement is heard. The BRIDE *enters. From the opposite side* TWO GIRLS *come running to meet her.*

FIRST GIRL. To whom did you give the first pin; me or this one?

BRIDE. I don't remember.

FIRST GIRL. To me, you gave it to me here.

SECOND GIRL. To me, in front of the altar.

BRIDE. [*Uneasily, with a great inner struggle.*] I don't know anything about it.

FIRST GIRL. It's just that I wish you'd. . . .

BRIDE. [*Interrupting.*] Nor do I care. I have a lot to think about.

SECOND GIRL. Your pardon.

LEONARDO *crosses at the rear of the stage.*

BRIDE. [*She sees* LEONARDO.] And this is an upsetting time.

FIRST GIRL. We wouldn't know anything about that!

BRIDE. You'll know about it when your time comes. This step is a very hard one to take.

FIRST GIRL. Has she offended you?

BRIDE. No. You must pardon me.

SECOND GIRL. What for? But *both* the pins are good for getting married, aren't they?

BRIDE. Both of them.

FIRST GIRL. Maybe now one will get married before the other.

BRIDE. Are you so eager?

SECOND GIRL. [*Shyly.*] Yes.

BRIDE. Why?

FIRST GIRL. Well . . .

She embraces the SECOND GIRL. *Both go running off. The* GROOM *comes in very slowly and embraces the* BRIDE *from behind.*

BRIDE. [*In sudden fright.*] Let go of me!

BRIDEGROOM. Are you frightened of me?

BRIDE. Ay-y-y! It's you!

BRIDEGROOM. Who else would it be? [*Pause.*] Your father or me.

BRIDE. That's true!

BRIDEGROOM. Of course, your father would have hugged you more gently.

BRIDE. [*Darkly.*] Of course!

BRIDEGROOM. [*Embracing her strongly and a little bit brusquely.*] Because he's old.

BRIDE. [*Curtly.*] Let me go!

BRIDEGROOM. Why?

He lets her go.

BRIDE. Well . . . the people. They can see us.

The SERVANT *crosses at the back of the stage again without looking at the* BRIDE *and* BRIDEGROOM.

BRIDEGROOM. What of it? It's consecrated now.

BRIDE. Yes, but let me be. . . . Later.

BRIDEGROOM. What's the matter with you? You look frightened!

BRIDE. I'm all right. Don't go.

LEONARDO'S WIFE *enters.*

LEONARDO'S WIFE. I don't mean to intrude. . . .

BRIDEGROOM. What is it?

LEONARDO'S WIFE. Did my husband come through here?

BRIDEGROOM. No.

LEONARDO'S WIFE. Because I can't find him, and his horse isn't in the stable either.

BRIDEGROOM. [*Happily.*] He must be out racing it.

The WIFE *leaves, troubled. The* SERVANT *enters.*

SERVANT. Aren't you two proud and happy with so many good wishes?

BRIDEGROOM. I wish it were over with. The bride is a little tired.

SERVANT. That's no way to act, child.

BRIDE. It's as though I'd been struck on the head.

SERVANT. A bride from these mountains must be strong. [*To the* GROOM.] You're the only one who can cure her, because she's yours.

She goes running off.

BRIDEGROOM. [*Embracing the* BRIDE.] Let's go dance a little.

He kisses her.

BRIDE. [*Worried.*] No. I'd like to stretch out on my bed a little.

BRIDEGROOM. I'll keep you company.

BRIDE. Never! With all these people here? What would they say? Let me be quiet for a moment.

BRIDEGROOM. Whatever you say! But don't be like that tonight!

BRIDE. [*At the door.*] I'll be better

tonight.

BRIDEGROOM. That's what I want.

The MOTHER *appears.*

MOTHER. Son.

BRIDEGROOM. Where've you been?

MOTHER. Out there—in all that noise. Are you happy?

BRIDEGROOM. Yes.

MOTHER. Where's your wife?

BRIDEGROOM. Resting a little. It's a bad day for brides!

MOTHER. A bad day? The only good one. To me it was like coming into my own. [*The* SERVANT *enters and goes toward the* BRIDE'S *room.*] Like the breaking of new ground; the planting of new trees.

BRIDEGROOM. Are you going to leave?

MOTHER. Yes. I ought to be at home.

BRIDEGROOM. Alone.

MOTHER. Not alone. For my head is full of things: of men, and fights.

BRIDEGROOM. But now the fights are no longer fights.

The SERVANT *enters quickly; she disappears at the rear of the stage, running.*

MOTHER. While you live, you have to fight.

BRIDEGROOM. I'll always obey you!

MOTHER. Try to be loving with your wife, and if you see she's acting foolish or touchy, caress her in a way that will hurt her a little: a strong hug, a bite and then a soft kiss. Not so she'll be angry, but just so she'll feel you're the man, the boss, the one who gives orders. I learned that from your father. And since you don't have him, I have to be the one to tell you about these strong defenses.

BRIDEGROOM. I'll always do as you say.

FATHER. [*Entering.*] Where's my daughter?

BRIDEGROOM. She's inside.

The FATHER *goes to look for her.*

FIRST GIRL. Get the bride and groom! We're going to dance a round!

FIRST YOUTH. [*To the* BRIDEGROOM.] You're going to lead it.

FATHER. [*Entering.*] She's not there.

BRIDEGROOM. No?

FATHER. She must have gone up to the railing.

BRIDEGROOM. I'll go see!

He leaves. A hubbub of excitement and guitars is heard.

FIRST GIRL. They've started it already!

She leaves.

BRIDEGROOM. [*Entering.*] She isn't there.

MOTHER. [*Uneasily.*] Isn't she?

FATHER. But where could she have gone?

SERVANT. [*Entering.*] But where's the girl, where is she?

MOTHER. [*Seriously.*] That we don't know.

The BRIDEGROOM *leaves. Three guests enter.*

FATHER. [*Dramatically.*] But, isn't she in the dance?

SERVANT. She's not in the dance.

FATHER. [*With a start.*] There are a lot of people. Go look!

SERVANT. I've already looked.

FATHER. [*Tragically.*] Then where is she?

BRIDEGROOM. [*Entering.*] Nowhere. Not anywhere.

MOTHER. [*To the* FATHER.] What does this mean? Where is your daughter?

LEONARDO'S WIFE *enters.*

LEONARDO'S WIFE. They've run away! They've run away! She and Leonardo. On the horse. With their arms around each other, they rode off like a shooting star!

FATHER. That's not true! Not my daughter!

MOTHER. Yes, your daughter! Spawn of a wicked mother, and he, he too. But now she's my son's wife!

BRIDEGROOM. [*Entering.*] Let's go after them! Who has a horse?

MOTHER. Who has a horse? Right away! Who has a horse? I'll give him all I have—my eyes, my tongue even. . . .

VOICE. Here's one.

MOTHER. [*To the* SON.] Go! After them! [*He leaves with two young men.*] No. Don't go. Those people kill quickly and well . . . but yes, run, and I'll follow!

FATHER. It couldn't be my daughter.

Perhaps she's thrown herself in the well.

MOTHER. Decent women throw themselves in water; not that one! But now she's my son's wife. Two groups. There are two groups here.

They all enter.

My family and yours. Everyone set out from here. Shake the dust from your heels! We'll go help my son.

The people separate into two groups.

For he has his family: his cousins from the sea, and all who came from inland. Out of here! On all roads. The hour of blood has come again. Two groups! You with yours and I with mine. After them! After them!

Act 3

Scene 1

A forest. It is nighttime. Great moist tree trunks. A dark atmosphere. Two violins are heard. Three WOODCUTTERS *enter.*

FIRST WOODCUTTER. And have they found them?

SECOND WOODCUTTER. No. But they're looking for them everywhere.

THIRD WOODCUTTER. They'll find them.

SECOND WOODCUTTER. Sh-h-h!

THIRD WOODCUTTER. What!

SECOND WOODCUTTER. They seem to be coming closer on all the roads at once.

FIRST WOODCUTTER. When the moon comes out they'll see them.

SECOND WOODCUTTER. They ought to let them go.

FIRST WOODCUTTER. The world is wide. Everybody can live in it.

THIRD WOODCUTTER. But they'll kill them.

SECOND WOODCUTTER. You have to follow your passion. They did right to run away.

FIRST WOODCUTTER. They were deceiv-

ing themselves but at the last blood
was stronger.

THIRD WOODCUTTER. Blood!

FIRST WOODCUTTER. You have to follow
the path of your blood.

SECOND WOODCUTTER. But blood that
sees the light of day is drunk up by
the earth.

FIRST WOODCUTTER. What of it? Better
dead with the blood drained away
than alive with it rotting.

THIRD WOODCUTTER. Hush!

FIRST WOODCUTTER. What? Do you hear
something?

THIRD WOODCUTTER. I hear the crickets,
the frogs, the night's ambush.

FIRST WOODCUTTER. But not the horse.

THIRD WOODCUTTER. No.

FIRST WOODCUTTER. By now he must be
loving her.

SECOND WOODCUTTER. Her body for
him; his body for her.

THIRD WOODCUTTER. They'll find them
and they'll kill them.

FIRST WOODCUTTER. But by then they'll
have mingled their bloods. They'll be
like two empty jars, like two dry ar-
royos.

SECOND WOODCUTTER. There are many
clouds and it would be easy for the
moon not to come out.

THIRD WOODCUTTER. The bridegroom
will find them with or without the
moon. I saw him set out. Like a
raging star. His face the color of
ashes. He looked the fate of all his
clan.

FIRST WOODCUTTER. His clan of dead
men lying in the middle of the street.

SECOND WOODCUTTER. There you have
it!

THIRD WOODCUTTER. You think they'll
be able to break through the circle?

SECOND WOODCUTTER. It's hard to.
There are knives and guns for ten
leagues 'round.

THIRD WOODCUTTER. He's riding a good
horse.

SECOND WOODCUTTER. But he's carrying
a woman.

FIRST WOODCUTTER. We're close by now.

SECOND WOODCUTTER. A tree with forty
branches. We'll soon cut it down.

THIRD WOODCUTTER. The moon's coming out now. Let's hurry.

From the left shines a brightness.

FIRST WOODCUTTER.
O rising moon!
Moon among the great leaves.

SECOND WOODCUTTER.
Cover the blood with jasmines!

FIRST WOODCUTTER.
O lonely moon!
Moon among the great leaves.

SECOND WOODCUTTER.
Silver on the bride's face.

THIRD WOODCUTTER.
O evil moon!
Leave for their love a branch in
shadow.

FIRST WOODCUTTER.
O sorrowing moon!
Leave for their love a branch in
shadow.

They go out. The MOON *appears through the
shining brightness at the left. The* MOON
*is a young woodcutter with a white face.
The stage takes on an intense blue radi-
ance.*

MOON.
Round swan in the river
and a cathedral's eye,
false dawn on the leaves,
they'll not escape; these things am I!
Who is hiding? And who sobs
in the thornbrakes of the valley?
The moon sets a knife
abandoned in the air
which being a leaden threat
yearns to be blood's pain.
Let me in! I come freezing
down to walls and windows!
Open roofs, open breasts
where I may warm myself!
I'm cold! My ashes
of somnolent metals
seek the fire's crest
on mountains and streets.
But the snow carries me
upon its mottled back
and pools soak me
in their water, hard and cold.

But this night there will be
red blood for my cheeks,
and for the reeds that cluster
at the wide feet of the wind.
Let there be neither shadow nor
    bower,
and then they can't get away!
O let me enter a breast
where I may get warm!
A heart for me!
Warm! That will spurt
over the mountains of my chest;
let me come in, oh let me!
To the branches.
I want no shadows. My rays
must get in everywhere,
even among the dark trunks I want
the whisper of gleaming lights,
so that this night there will be
sweet blood for my cheeks,
and for the reeds that cluster
at the wide feet of the wind.
Who is hiding? Out, I say!
No! They will not get away!
I will light up the horse
with a fever bright as diamonds.

*He disappears among the trunks, and the
stage goes back to its dark lighting. An*
OLD WOMAN *comes out completely covered by thin green cloth. She is barefooted.
Her face can barely be seen among the
folds. This character does not appear in
the cast.*

BEGGAR WOMAN.
That moon's going away, just when
    they're near.
They won't get past here. The river's
    whisper
and the whispering tree trunks will
    muffle
the torn flight of their shrieks.
It has to be here, and soon. I'm worn
    out.
The coffins are ready, and white
    sheets
wait on the floor of the bedroom
for heavy bodies with torn throats.
Let not one bird awake, let the
    breeze,
gathering their moans in her skirt,
fly with them over black tree tops

or bury them in soft mud.
Impatiently.
Oh, that moon! That moon!
The MOON *appears. The intense blue light
returns.*
MOON. They're coming. One band
through the ravine and the other
along the river. I'm going to light up
the boulders. What do you need?
BEGGAR WOMAN. Nothing.
MOON. The wind blows hard now, with
a double edge.
BEGGAR WOMAN. Light up the waistcoat
and open the buttons; the knives will
know the path after that.
MOON.
But let them be a long time a-dying.
    So the blood
will slide its delicate hissing between
    my fingers.
Look how my ashen valleys already
    are waking
in longing for this fountain of
    shuddering gushes!
BEGGAR WOMAN. Let's not let them get
past the arroyo. Silence!
MOON. There they come!
He goes. The stage is left dark.
BEGGAR WOMAN. Quick! Lots of light!
Do you hear me? They can't get
away!
The BRIDEGROOM *and the* FIRST YOUTH
enter. The BEGGAR WOMAN *sits down
and covers herself with her cloak.*
BRIDEGROOM. This way.
FIRST YOUTH. You won't find them.
BRIDEGROOM. [*Angrily.*] Yes, I'll find
them.
FIRST YOUTH. I think they've taken an-
other path.
BRIDEGROOM. No. Just a moment ago I
felt the galloping.
FIRST YOUTH. It could have been an-
other horse.
BRIDEGROOM. [*Intensely.*] Listen to me.
There's only one horse in the whole
world, and this one's it. Can't you
understand that? If you're going to
follow me, follow me without talking.
FIRST YOUTH. It's only that I want
to. . . .

BRIDEGROOM. Be quiet. I'm sure of meeting them there. Do you see this arm? Well, it's not my arm. It's my brother's arm, and my father's, and that of all the dead ones in my family. And it has so much strength that it can pull this tree up by the roots, if it wants to. And let's move on, because here I feel the clenched teeth of all my people in me so that I can't breathe easily.

BEGGAR WOMAN. [*Whining.*] Ay-y-y!

FIRST YOUTH. Did you hear that?

BRIDEGROOM. You go that way and then circle back.

FIRST YOUTH. This is a hunt.

BRIDEGROOM. A hunt. The greatest hunt there is.

The YOUTH *goes off. The* BRIDEGROOM *goes rapidly to the left and stumbles over the* BEGGAR WOMAN, *Death.*

BEGGAR WOMAN. Ay-y-y!

BRIDEGROOM. What do you want?

BEGGAR WOMAN. I'm cold.

BRIDEGROOM. Which way are you going?

BEGGAR WOMAN. [*Always whining like a beggar.*] Over there, far away. . . .

BRIDEGROOM. Where are you from?

BEGGAR WOMAN. Over there . . . very far away.

BRIDEGROOM. Have you seen a man and a woman running away on a horse?

BEGGAR WOMAN. [*Awakening.*] Wait a minute. . . . [*She looks at him.*] Handsome young man. [*She rises.*] But you'd be much handsomer sleeping.

BRIDEGROOM. Tell me; answer me. Did you see them?

BEGGAR WOMAN. Wait a minute. . . . What broad shoulders! How would you like to be laid out on them and not have to walk on the soles of your feet which are so small?

BRIDEGROOM. [*Shaking her.*] I asked you if you saw them! Have they passed through here?

BEGGAR WOMAN. [*Energetically.*] No. They haven't passed; but they're coming from the hill. Don't you hear them?

BRIDEGROOM. No.

BEGGAR WOMAN. Do you know the road?

BRIDEGROOM. I'll go, whatever it's like!

BEGGAR WOMAN. I'll go along with you. I know this country.

BRIDEGROOM. [*Impatiently.*] Well, let's go! Which way?

BEGGAR WOMAN. [*Dramatically.*] This way!

They go rapidly out. Two violins, which represent the forest, are heard distantly. The WOODCUTTERS *return. They have their axes on their shoulders. They move slowly among the tree trunks.*

FIRST WOODCUTTER.
O rising death!
Death among the great leaves.

SECOND WOODCUTTER.
Don't open the gush of blood!

FIRST WOODCUTTER.
O lonely death!
Death among the dried leaves.

THIRD WOODCUTTER.
Don't lay flowers over the wedding!

SECOND WOODCUTTER.
O sad death!
Leave for their love a green branch.

FIRST WOODCUTTER.
O evil death!
Leave for their love a branch of green!

[*They go out while they are talking.*
LEONARDO *and the* BRIDE *appear.*]

LEONARDO.
Hush!

BRIDE.
From here I'll go on alone.
You go now! I want you to turn back.

LEONARDO.
Hush, I said!

BRIDE.
With your teeth, with your hands, any way you can,
take from my clean throat
the metal of this chain,
and let me live forgotten
back there in my house in the ground.
And if you don't want to kill me
as you would kill a tiny snake,

set in my hands, a bride's hands,
the barrel of your shotgun.
Oh, what lamenting, what fire,
sweeps upward through my head!
What glass splinters are stuck in my
    tongue!

LEONARDO.
We've taken the step now; hush!
because they're close behind us,
and I must take you with me.

BRIDE.
Then it must be by force!

LEONARDO.
By force? Who was it first
went down the stairway?

BRIDE.
I went down it.

LEONARDO.
And who was it put
a new bridle on the horse?

BRIDE.
I myself did it. It's true.

LEONARDO.
And whose were the hands
strapped spurs to my boots?

BRIDE.
The same hands, these that are
    yours,
but which when they see you would
    like
to break the blue branches
and sunder the purl of your veins.
I love you! I love you! But leave me!
For if I were able to kill you
I'd wrap you 'round in a shroud
with the edges bordered in violets.
Oh, what lamenting, what fire,
sweeps upward through my head!

LEONARDO.
What glass splinters are stuck in my
    tongue!
Because I tried to forget you
and put a wall of stone
between your house and mine.
It's true. You remember?
And when I saw you in the distance
I threw sand in my eyes.
But I was riding a horse
and the horse went straight to your
    door.
And the silver pins of your wedding

turned my red blood black.
And in me our dream was choking
my flesh with its poisoned weeds.
Oh, it isn't my fault—
the fault is the earth's—
and this fragrance that you exhale
from your breasts and your braids.

BRIDE.
Oh, how untrue! I want
from you neither bed nor food,
yet there's not a minute each day
that I don't want to be with you,
because you drag me, and I come,
then you tell me to go back
and I follow you,
like chaff blown on the breeze.
I have left a good, honest man,
and all his people,
with the wedding feast half over
and wearing my bridal wreath.
But you are the one will be punished
and that I don't want to happen.
Leave me alone now! You run away!
There is no one who will defend you.

LEONARDO.
The birds of early morning
are calling among the trees.
The night is dying
on the stone's ridge.
Let's go to a hidden corner
where I may love you forever,
for to me the people don't matter,
nor the venom they throw on us.

He embraces her strongly.

BRIDE.
And I'll sleep at your feet,
to watch over your dreams.
Naked, looking over the fields,
as though I were a bitch.
Because that's what I am! Oh, I look
    at you
and your beauty sears me.

LEONARDO.
Fire is stirred by fire.
The same tiny flame
will kill two wheat heads together.
Let's go!

BRIDE.
Where are you taking me?

LEONARDO.
Where they cannot come,

these men who surround us.
Where I can look at you!

BRIDE. [*Sarcastically.*]

Carry me with you from fair to fair,
a shame to clean women,
so that people will see me
with my wedding sheets
on the breeze like banners.

LEONARDO.

I, too, would want to leave you
if I thought as men should.
But wherever you go, I go.
You're the same. Take a step. Try.
Nails of moonlight have fused
my waist and your chains.

*This whole scene is violent, full of great
sensuality.*

BRIDE.

Listen!

LEONARDO.

They're coming.

BRIDE.

Run!

It's fitting that I should die here,
with water over my feet,
with thorns upon my head.
And fitting the leaves should mourn
me,
a woman lost and virgin.

LEONARDO.

Be quiet. Now they're appearing.

BRIDE.

Go now!

LEONARDO.

Quiet. Don't let them hear us.

The BRIDE hesitates.

BRIDE.

Both of us!

LEONARDO. [*Embracing her.*]

Any way you want!
If they separate us, it will be
because I am dead.

BRIDE.

And I dead too.

*They go out in each other's arms. The MOON
appears very slowly. The stage takes on a
strong blue light. The two violins are
heard. Suddenly two long, ear-splitting
shrieks are heard, and the music of the
two violins is cut short. At the second
shriek the BEGGAR WOMAN appears and*
stands with her back to the audience. She
opens her cape and stands in the center of
the stage like a great bird with immense
wings. The MOON halts. The curtain
comes down in absolute silence.

Scene 2

The Final Scene

*A white dwelling with arches and thick
walls. To the right and left, are white
stairs. At the back, a great arch and a
wall of the same color. The floor also
should be shining white. This simple
dwelling should have the monumental
feeling of a church. There should not be a
single gray nor any shadow, not even
what is necessary for perspective.*

TWO GIRLS *dressed in dark blue are wind-
ing a red skein.*

FIRST GIRL.

Wool, red wool,
what would you make?

SECOND GIRL.

Oh, jasmine for dresses,
fine wool like glass.
At four o'clock born,
at ten o'clock dead.
A thread from this wool yarn,
a chain 'round your feet
a knot that will tighten
the bitter white wreath.

LITTLE GIRL. [*Singing.*]

Were you at the wedding?

FIRST GIRL.

No.

LITTLE GIRL.

Well, neither was I!
What could have happened
'midst the shoots of the vineyards?
What could have happened
'neath the branch of the olive?
What really happened
that no one came back?
Were you at the wedding?

SECOND GIRL.

We told you once, no.

LITTLE GIRL. [*Leaving.*]

Well, neither was I!

SECOND GIRL.
  Wool, red wool,
  what would you sing?
FIRST GIRL.
  Their wounds turning waxen,
  balm-myrtle for pain.
  Asleep in the morning,
  and watching at night.
LITTLE GIRL. [*In the doorway.*]
  And then, the thread stumbled
  on the flinty stones,
  but mountains, blue mountains,
  are letting it pass.
  Running, running, running,
  and finally to come
  to stick in a knife blade,
  to take back the bread.
She goes out.
SECOND GIRL.
  Wool, red wool,
  what would you tell?
FIRST GIRL.
  The lover is silent,
  crimson the groom,
  at the still shoreline
  I saw them laid out.
She stops and looks at the skein.
LITTLE GIRL. [*Appearing in the doorway.*]
  Running, running, running,
  the thread runs to here.
  All covered with clay
  I feel them draw near.
  Bodies stretched stiffly
  in ivory sheets!
The WIFE *and* MOTHER-IN-LAW *of*
  LEONARDO *appear. They are anguished.*
FIRST GIRL. Are they coming yet?
MOTHER-IN-LAW. [*Harshly.*] We don't
  know.
SECOND GIRL. What can you tell us
  about the wedding?
FIRST GIRL. Yes, tell me.
MOTHER-IN-LAW. [*Curtly.*] Nothing.
LEONARDO'S WIFE. I want to go back and
  find out all about it.
MOTHER-IN-LAW. [*Sternly.*]
  You, back to your house.
  Brave and alone in your house.
  To grow old and to weep.
  But behind closed doors.
  Never again. Neither dead nor alive.

  We'll nail up our windows
  and let rains and nights
  fall on the bitter weeds.
LEONARDO'S WIFE. What could have hap-
  pened?
MOTHER-IN-LAW.
  It doesn't matter what.
  Put a veil over your face.
  Your children are yours,
  that's all. On the bed
  put a cross of ashes
  where his pillow was.
They go out.
BEGGAR WOMAN. [*At the door.*] A crust of
  bread, little girls.
LITTLE GIRL. Go away.
The GIRLS *huddle close together.*
BEGGAR WOMAN. Why?
LITTLE GIRL. Because you whine; go
  away!
FIRST GIRL. Child!
BEGGAR WOMAN.
  I might have asked for your eyes! A
    cloud
  of birds is following me. Will you
    have one?
LITTLE GIRL. I want to get away from
  here!
SECOND GIRL. [*To the* BEGGAR WOMAN.]
  Don't mind her!
FIRST GIRL. Did you come by the road
  through the arroyo?
BEGGAR WOMAN. I came that way!
FIRST GIRL. [*Timidly.*] Can I ask you
  something?
BEGGAR WOMAN.
  I saw them: they'll be here soon; two
    torrents
  still at last, among the great boulders,
  two men at the horse's feet.
  Two dead men in the night's
    splendor.
With pleasure.
  Dead, yes, dead.
GIRL GIRL. Hush, old woman, hush!
BEGGAR WOMAN.
  Crushed flowers for eyes, and their
    teeth
  two fistfuls of hard-frozen snow.
  Both of them fell, and the Bride
    returns

with bloodstains on her skirt and
hair.
And they come covered with two
sheets
carried on the shoulders of two tall
boys.
That's how it was; nothing more.
What was fitting.
Over the golden flower, dirty sand.

She goes. The GIRLS *bow their heads and
start going out rhythmically.*

FIRST GIRL.
Dirty sand.
SECOND GIRL.
Over the golden flower.
LITTLE GIRL. They're bringing the dead
from the arroyo.
Dark the one,
dark the other.
What shadowy nightingale flies and
weeps
over the golden flower!

She goes. The stage is left empty. The
MOTHER *and a* NEIGHBOR WOMAN *appear. The* NEIGHBOR *is weeping.*

MOTHER. Hush.
NEIGHBOR. I can't.
MOTHER. Hush, I said. [*At the door.*] Is
there nobody here? [*She puts her
hands to her forehead.*] My son ought to
answer me. But now my son is an
armful of shrivelled flowers. My son
is a fading voice beyond the mountains now. [*With rage, to the*
NEIGHBOR.] Will you shut up? I want
no wailing in this house. Your tears
are only tears from your eyes, but
when I'm alone mine will come—
from the soles of my feet, from my
roots—burning more than blood.
NEIGHBOR. You come to my house;
don't you stay here.
MOTHER. I want to be here. Here. In
peace. They're all dead now: and at
midnight I'll sleep, sleep without terror of guns or knives. Other mothers
will go to their windows, lashed by
rain, to watch for their sons' faces.
But not I. And of my dreams I'll
make a cold ivory dove that will carry
camellias of white frost to the grave-

yard. But no; not graveyard, not
graveyard: the couch of earth, the
bed that shelters them and rocks
them in the sky. [*A woman dressed in
black enters, goes toward the right, and
there kneels. To the* NEIGHBOR.]
Take your hands from your face. We
have terrible days ahead. I want to
see no one. The earth and I. My
grief and I. And these four walls. Ay-
y-y! Ay-y-y!

She sits down, overcome.

NEIGHBOR. Take pity on yourself!
MOTHER. [*Pushing back her hair.*] I must
be calm. [*She sits down.*] Because the
neighbor women will come and I
don't want them to see me so poor.
So poor! A woman without even one
son to hold to her lips.

The BRIDE *appears. She is without her
wreath and wears a black shawl.*

NEIGHBOR. [*With rage, seeing the* BRIDE.]
Where are you going?
BRIDE. I'm going here.
MOTHER. [*To the* NEIGHBOR.] Who is it?
NEIGHBOR. Don't you recognize her?
MOTHER. That's why I asked who it was.
Because I don't want to recognize
her, so I won't sink my teeth in her
throat. You snake! [*She moves
wrathfully on the* BRIDE, *then stops. To
the* NEIGHBOR.] Look at her! There
she is, and she's crying, while I stand
here calmly and don't tear her eyes
out. I don't understand myself. Can
it be I didn't love my son? But,
where's his good name? Where is it
now? Where is it?

She beats the BRIDE *who drops to the floor.*

NEIGHBOR. For God's sake!

She tries to separate them.

BRIDE. [*To the* NEIGHBOR.] Let her; I
came here so she'd kill me and they'd
take me away with them. [*To the*
MOTHER.] But not with her hands;
with grappling hooks, with a sickle—
and with force—until they break on
my bones. Let her! I want her to
know I'm clean, that I may be crazy,
but that they can bury me without a
single man ever having seen himself

in the whiteness of my breasts.

MOTHER. Shut up, shut up; what do I
care about that?

BRIDE. Because I ran away with the
other one; I ran away! [*With anguish.*]
You would have gone, too. I was a
woman burning with desire, full of
sores inside and out, and your son
was a little bit of water from which I
hoped for children, land, health; but
the other one was a dark river,
choked with brush, that brought near
me the undertone of its rushes and
its whispered song. And I went along
with your son who was like a little
boy of cold water—and the other
sent against me hundreds of birds
who got in my way and left white
frost on my wounds, my wounds of a
poor withered woman, of a girl caressed by fire. I didn't want to;
remember that! I didn't want to.
Your son was my destiny and I have
not betrayed him, but the other one's
arm dragged me along like the pull
of the sea, like the head toss of a
mule, and he would have dragged
me always, always, always—even if I
were an old woman and all your son's
sons held me by the hair!

A NEIGHBOR *enters.*

MOTHER. She is not to blame; nor am I!
[*Sarcastically.*] Who is, then? It's a delicate, lazy, sleepless woman who
throws away an orange blossom
wreath and goes looking for a piece
of bed warmed by another woman!

BRIDE. Be still! Be still! Take your revenge on me; here I am! See how
soft my throat is; it would be less
work for you than cutting a dahlia in
your garden. But never that! Clean,
clean as a new-born little girl. And
strong enough to prove it to you.
Light the fire. Let's stick our hands
in; you, for your son, I, for my body.
You'll draw yours out first.

Another NEIGHBOR *enters.*

MOTHER. But what does your good
name matter to me? What does your
death matter to me? What does any-

thing about anything matter to me?
Blessed be the wheat stalks, because
my sons are under them; blessed be
the rain, because it wets the face of
the dead. Blessed be God, who
stretches us out together to rest.

Another NEIGHBOR *enters.*

BRIDE. Let me weep with you.

MOTHER. Weep. But at the door.

The GIRL *enters. The* BRIDE *stays at the
door. The* MOTHER *is at the center of the
stage.*

LEONARDO'S WIFE. [*Entering and going to
the left.*]
He was a beautiful horseman,
now he's a heap of snow.
He rode to fairs and mountains
and women's arms.
Now, the night's dark moss
crowns his forehead.

MOTHER.
A sunflower to your mother,
a mirror of the earth.
Let them put on your breast
the cross of bitter rosebay;
and over you a sheet
of shining silk;
between your quiet hands
let water form its lament.

WIFE.
Ay-y-y, four gallant boys
come with tired shoulders!

BRIDE.
Ay-y-y, four gallant boys
carry death on high!

MOTHER.
Neighbors.

LITTLE GIRL. [*At the door.*]
They're bringing them now.

MOTHER.
It's the same thing.
Always the cross, the cross.

WOMEN.
Sweet nails,
cross adored,
sweet name
of Christ our Lord.

BRIDE. May the cross protect both the
quick and the dead.

MOTHER.
Neighbors: with a knife,

with a little knife,
on their appointed day, between two
    and three,
these two men killed each other for
    love.
With a knife,
with a tiny knife
that barely fits the hand,
but that slides in clean
through the astonished flesh
and stops at the place
where trembles, enmeshed,
the dark root of a scream.
BRIDE.
    And this is a knife,
    a tiny knife
    that barely fits the hand;
    fish without scales, without river,
    so that on their appointed day,
        between two and three,

with this knife,
two men are left stiff,
with their lips turning yellow.
MOTHER.
    And it barely fits the hand
    but it slides in clean
    through the astonished flesh
    and stops there, at the place
    where trembles enmeshed
    the dark root of a scream.
The NEIGHBORS, *kneeling on the floor, sob.*

1. Interior of the cave where the BRIDE lives. It is not uncommon for the homes of even well-to-do Spanish families to be built, cavelike, into a hillside.

2. She wears a black dress in the style of 1900. At which time, black was the traditional color for a Spanish wedding dress.

Ondine

Jean Giraudoux

Hippolyte Jean Giraudoux was born in Bellac, a small village in Limousin, on October 29, 1882. Although he lived in several nearby towns during a happy childhood and a well-adjusted youth, he later was to think of Bellac as an idyllic home, and many of his novels and plays were either literally or figuratively set there. Achieving marked academic distinction throughout his early schooling, Giraudoux was eventually admitted to the Ecole Normale Supérieure in Paris, a distinguished institution preparing its graduates for university teaching and for high governmental positions. During his four years there, Giraudoux made many contacts that were later useful to him, but became dissatisfied with his own work in German literature and never completed his degree. He spent several years in a variety of positions and in traveling, including a year teaching French at Harvard University, but in 1910 he entered the French Foreign Ministry, where, with time out for military service during World War I (during which he was awarded the Legion of Honor), he was to enjoy a notable career.

Concomitantly with his diplomatic career, Giraudoux devoted much time to writing. He published several novels and was firmly established as a literary figure of some note when, at the unusually advanced age of forty-five, he first turned his hand to playwriting. His novel *Siegfried et le Limousin* had been successful in 1922, and Louis Jouvet, the distinguished director and actor, encouraged Giraudoux to adapt this work for the stage. *Siegfried* opened in Paris on May 3, 1928, and France suddenly found itself with its most successful serious playwright in many decades; for the remaining years of his life, Giraudoux devoted his primary creative energy to the theater. Notable among his successful plays were *Amphytryon 38* (1929), *La Guerre de Troie n'aura pas lieu* (translated as *Tiger at the Gates*, 1935), *Electra* (1937), and *The Madwoman of Chaillot* (produced posthumously in 1945). Giraudoux's previously happy marriage to Suzanne Boland (there was one son, Jean-Pierre) disintegrated into bickering, recriminations, and virtual separation during this time, and the onset of yet another war between France and Germany also colored Giraudoux's mood. His extraordinary blend of optimism and sardonic cynicism emerges in most of his plays as brilliant linguistic wit and elegant style in the face of human life in which genuine happiness is impossible. Giraudoux attempted to continue diplomatic work within the Vichy government during the war, as well as devoting himself to writing, but declining health forced his withdrawal from most activities. He died in Paris on January 31, 1944.

Giraudoux continued his productive collaboration with Louis Jouvet throughout his theatrical career, with Jouvet producing most of his plays and frequently playing the leading roles. This regular access to a producing unit of high caliber and professional excellence was of incalculable importance in shaping Giraudoux's approach to the theater, and Giraudoux was always quick to acknowledge his debt to Jouvet. Whereas theatrical practice of earlier centuries had routinely associated playwrights directly with production companies, Giraudoux was somewhat unusual in the twentieth century for this association, and its effects are evident in the theatrical skill that quickly became apparent in his work despite his lack of earlier training. Giraudoux usually created his plays as adaptations from novels or other works, and he soon became adept at judging what would work for an audience. *Ondine,* which opened at the Théâtre de l'Athénée in Paris on April 27, 1939, under the direction of Louis Jouvet and starring Jouvet in the role of Hans, illustrates very effectively all of these traits in Giraudoux's work. *Ondine* was adapted from a story by the German writer Frédéric de La Motte-Fouqué (1777–1843) which Giraudoux had first encountered during his studies of German literature at the Ecole Normale Supérieure. Despite the impending disaster on the war front, Giraudoux's adaptation is a romantic affirmation of goodness and purity, though, sadly, such goodness was never meant for ordinary mankind. That it exists at all, even in a sea nymph, gives the play a sweet poignance and optimism that are startling enough in any age and truly remarkable as Europe approached Armageddon.

What characterizes *Ondine* more than its philosophy is its style, a style uniquely Giraudoux's own and based chiefly on his impressionistic use of language. One writer has suggested that Giraudoux uses words the way Monet uses paint, an observation that fixes Giraudoux's style as accurately as any. Playful, elegant, and valuable for their sound as well as for their sense, Giraudoux's words need to be spoken aloud by especially skilled actors to achieve anything like their full effect. Often the substance of a scene lies more in its sound than in its denotation, for Giraudoux seeks to evoke the spirit world more than corporal reality, to link the mundane to the transcendent, to "express the inexpressible" just as surely as any Symbolist of forty years before him. Where the Symbolists were never completely successful in finding theatrical techniques that would support this gossamer superstructure, Giraudoux delighted audiences throughout Europe and the rest of the world, and has continued to do so in numberless revivals.

Giraudoux's language-based style permeates every aspect of his play. The wonder of innocence and of nature that Ondine must evoke is accomplished in the first instance by utter honesty, a truthfulness that cannot survive in the world of mankind. Ondine captivates Hans from their first encounter by an enchanting blend of truthful innocence and sexuality, and Hans is frankly seduced by this beautiful escapee from the spiritual world. Giraudoux frequently portrayed the innocence of the young girl as the saving hope of mankind, but in Ondine he went a step further by making the young girl literally an emissary from a better world. Aghast that the purity of love is not maintained by humans as it is by dogfish, Ondine is early established as one who cannot function effectively in the imperfect world of mankind. Hans, an ordinary mortal, attains a tragic glimpse of the beauty of the infinite, but he has realized by the end of the play that he cannot function in Ondine's world either. "I accuse this woman of adoring me beyond human endurance," Hans tells the judges. Ondine represents absolute love, and Hans, like other humans, cannot function in the realm of absolutes. Thus the play, though not attempting tragedy in the usual sense, is surely tragic in its essential rhythm, as man dies in a quest for the unattainable.

Although *Ondine* is traditionally structured in many respects, Giraudoux employs some unusual and interesting devices in the second act. Having established a theatrical world that vibrates easily between the spiritual and the corporeal, Giraudoux then employs the Illusionist, who is the King of the Ondines in disguise, to compress time in an openly theatricalized way, thus both facilitating the quick movement of the story and calling attention to the contrasts between theater and life that Pirandello was so interestingly exploring in Italy. Yet life-as-theater is seen to have an ennui about it which, although entertaining to the court functionaries privileged to watch it, is finally contrasted with the inherent vitality of the spirit world. Giraudoux's frankly theatrical way of structuring these concepts in Act 2 works in perfect harmony with the style already established to create a fuller and richer theatrical event than would otherwise be possible.

As the title character and a truly enchanting spirit, Ondine is clearly the center of the play, but her very purity has the effect of making her less than a complex character. Hans, by contrast, is an ordinary mortal, strong and handsome but in no other way distinguishable from any other man. Neither bright nor insightful, hopelessly destroyed by his brief glimpse of the immortal, Hans must carry the complexity of the play in contrast to Ondine's charming simplicity. Bertha, too, with even fewer clues provided by the playwright, needs to be a human being of complexity and contrast, for she is not just the "other woman," but in fact is the good wife whom Hans would orinarily have married and who probably would have been good for him. Characterization too in Giraudoux's plays tends to be as airy and insubstantial as the language, and a heavy burden falls on the actors to render such characters theatrically viable. Giraudoux's characters must simultaneously transcend reality and be anchored in it.

It was after World War II before *Ondine* became widely known outside France. Maurice Valency's adaptation was completed in 1951 and opened in New York on February 18, 1954, with Audrey Hepburn and Mel Ferrer in the leading roles; the production was a work of extraordinary beauty. Valency's version of Giraudoux's play has come in for a good deal of criticism because of the extensive changes that he introduced. In the original, for example, Queen Yseult is the understanding member of the court who, in place of the King, befriends Ondine and advises her to give up Hans. Many lines are cut, transposed, or changed, and the explicit sexuality of the original is considerably softened in the adaptation. Valency's theatrical judgment regarding a Broadway audience may be accurate, it has been argued, but the reader should be exposed to Giraudoux pure and uncut. Other English translations of the play adhere more faithfully line by line to the original, but the all-important tone and spirit and style of Giraudoux is largely lost. Whatever may be said of his structural changes, Valency has captured in his translation a remarkably faithful rendering of Giraudoux's gossamer language, and in this respect as in all others having to do with this extraordinary play, stylish language transcends all other considerations. The spirit of Giraudoux is alive and thriving in this version of *Ondine*.

Ondine

English Version by Maurice Valency

Characters
(In order of appearance)

Auguste
Eugenie
Ritter Hans
Ondine
The Ondines
The Old One
The Lord Chamberlain
The Superintendent of the Theatre
The Trainer of Seals
Bertha
Bertram
Violante
Angelique
Venus
Matho
Salammbo
A Lord
A Lady
The Illusionist (The Old One)
The King
A Servant
The First Fisherman
The Second Fisherman (The Old One)
The First Judge
The Second Judge
The Executioner
The Kitchen Maid

ACT ONE: *A Fisherman's Cottage*
ACT TWO: *A Hall in the King's Palace*
ACT THREE: *The Courtyard in the Castle of the Wittenstein*
TIME: *The Middle Ages*

Act 1

A fisherman's hut near a lake in the forest. The living room has a fireplace, a door that leads into the kitchen, and a door that leads into the forest. The windows are shuttered. There is a table near the fireplace, with a bench next to it and a heavy wooden chair next to the fire, which is blazing. It is night. A storm is raging.

Two old people, AUGUSTE *and* EUGENIE, *are in the room.* EUGENIE *is setting the table.* AUGUSTE *is at the window. He has opened the shutters and is peering out into the storm.*

AUGUSTE. What can she be doing out there at this hour?

EUGENIE. Don't worry about her. She can see in the dark.

AUGUSTE. In this storm!

EUGENIE. She's quite safe. The rain doesn't wet her.

AUGUSTE. She's singing. Is it she that's singing? You think that's her voice?

EUGENIE. Whose else? There is no other house within twenty leagues.

AUGUSTE. Now it comes from the top of the waterfall and now from the middle of the lake.

EUGENIE. Because now she's on top of the waterfall and now in the middle of the lake.

AUGUSTE. It's all so simple, isn't it? But did you, by any chance ever amuse yourself by diving down the water-falls in the nude when you were her age?

EUGENIE. Yes. Once. They fished me out by the feet. Every girl tries just once to do what Ondine does fifty times a day. I jumped into the whirlpool once, and I tried to catch the water-fall once in a bowl, and once I tried to walk on the water. It seems very long ago.

AUGUSTE. You've spoiled her, Eugenie. A girl of sixteen has no business running around in the forest in the dark in a storm. A well-brought-up girl does not insist on doing her sewing on the brink of a waterfall. She doesn't insist on saying her prayers under water. Where would we be today if you had been brought up like that?

EUGENIE. She's very helpful with the housework.

AUGUSTE. That brings up another question.

EUGENIE. Doesn't she wash the dishes? Doesn't she clean your boots?

AUGUSTE. I don't know. Does she?

EUGENIE. It's not clean, this dish?

AUGUSTE. That's not the point. Have you ever, in all her life, seen her cleaning or washing anything?

EUGENIE. What difference does it make whether or not I've seen her? She gets it done.

AUGUSTE. Yes. But explain this—three dishes or twelve, one shoe or eight, it takes her exactly the same time to do them. She takes them out; she's hardly gone a minute, and she's back. The dishcloth is dry. The shoe polish hasn't been used. But everything is clean, everything sparkles. And that affair of the golden plates on her birthday—did you ever get to the bottom of that? And her hands. Why are they never soiled, like anyone else's?

EUGENIE. Because she's not like anyone else. She's never been like anyone else.

AUGUSTE. Today she lifted the gate of the trout pond. All the trout are gone. All but the one I brought home for supper. Are you going to broil it? [*The windows spring open suddenly.*] Who did that?

EUGENIE. The wind, Auguste.

AUGUSTE. I hope she doesn't start that performance again with the lightning, and those horrible heads that peer in the window out of the storm. The old man with the crown—oh!

EUGENIE. I love the woman with the pearls. Well, bar the window if you're afraid. [AUGUSTE *crosses to close the windows. There is a flash of lightning. The head of an old man with a crown and a streaming beard appears in the window frame.*]

THE HEAD. No use, Auguste. No lock so strong, no bar so stout will serve to keep the old one out!

He vanishes, laughing in a clap of thunder.

AUGUSTE. I'll show you if it's too late, Ondine. [*He closes the window. It immediately bursts open. There appears, in another lightning flash, a charming naiad's head with a necklace of pearls.*]

THE NAIAD. Good evening, Eugenie! [*It vanishes.*]

EUGENIE. Ondine, you're annoying your father. It's time to come in.

AUGUSTE. Ondine, I'm going to count up to three. If you're not inside when I finish, I'll bolt the door. And you can sleep out. [*There is a roar of thunder.*]

EUGENIE. You're not serious?

AUGUSTE. You'll see if I'm serious. Ondine, one! [*A roar of thunder.*]

EUGENIE. Stop it, Auguste. It's deafening.

AUGUSTE. Am I doing it?

EUGENIE. Well, then, hurry. We all know you can count up to three.

AUGUSTE. Ondine, two! [*Thunder.* EUGENIE *covers her ears.*]

EUGENIE. Really, Auguste, I don't see the use—

AUGUSTE. Ondine, three!

EUGENIE. [*Waiting for the thunder.*] Well,

well, finish, Auguste, finish— [*There is no thunder.*]

AUGUSTE. I've finished. [*He bolts the door.*] There. I'd like to see anyone come in now. [*The door springs open. They turn in terror. A knight in full armor stands on the threshold. He holds his helmet under his arm.*]

RITTER HANS. [*Clicking his heels.*] Ritter Hans von Wittenstein zu Wittenstein.

AUGUSTE. [*Bows.*] My name is Auguste. I am a fisherman.

RITTER HANS. I took the liberty of putting my horse in your shed. The horse, as we know, is the most important part of the knight-errant. And the most sensitive.

AUGUSTE. I'll go and rub him down at once, my lord.

HANS. Thanks very much. I've already done it. I make it an invariable rule, away from home, to rub down my horse myself. In these parts, you rub horses down Swabian fashion, against the grain—the coat soon loses its luster. May I sit down?

AUGUSTE. The house is yours, my lord.

HANS. [*Sets down his helmet and puts by his sword.*] What a storm! The water has been running down my neck steadily since noon. Of course it doesn't stay. it runs out again through the blood gutters. But once it gets in, the damage is done. [*He sits down ponderously.*] That's what we fear most, we knights-errant, the rain. The water. And, of course, a flea. Once a flea gets in here—

AUGUSTE. Would you care to remove your armor, my lord?

HANS. My dear Auguste, have you ever watched a lobster shed his carapace? Then you know it's not the affair of a moment. I will rest first. You said your name was Auguste, I believe?

AUGUSTE. And my wife, Eugenie.

HANS. [*Bows to* EUGENIE.] Ah. Auguste and Eugenie. Charming names.

EUGENIE. Excuse them, my lord. They are not names for knights-errant.

HANS. Dear Eugenie, when a knight-errant has spent a month in the forest, searching in vain for Osmond and Pharamond, you cannot imagine his joy when he comes suddenly at dinner time upon Auguste and Eugenie.

EUGENIE. Thank you, my lord. It's ill-mannered, I know, to annoy a guest with questions, but perhaps you will forgive this one: are you hungry?

HANS. I am hungry. I am extremely hungry. It will give me great pleasure to share your meal.

EUGENIE. We have already supped, my lord. But there is a trout. Would you honor us by eating it?

HANS. With the greatest pleasure.

EUGENIE. Would you like it broiled or fried?

HANS. Poached, if you please. [AUGUSTE *and* EUGENIE *make a gesture of fear.*]

EUGENIE. Poached? I really do them best *sautée, meunière,* with a little white butter. It's very good.

HANS. Since you ask my preference—

AUGUSTE. *Gratinée,* perhaps with fresh cream? Eugenie's specialty.

HANS. When we say poached—that's when the fish is thrown into the boiling water alive?

EUGENIE. Yes. Alive.

HANS. So that the fish retains all its tenderness because the heat takes it by surprise?

AUGUSTE. Surprise is the word, my lord.

HANS. Then that's it. I'll have it poached.

EUGENIE. [*Walks slowly to the kitchen. She turns at the door.*] Broiled, they're very nice, with a slice of lemon—

HANS. Poached, if you please. [EUGENIE *goes into the kitchen.* HANS *makes himself comfortable in the chair by the fireside.*] I'm happy to see, Auguste, that knights-errant are not unwelcome in these parts? . . .

AUGUSTE. Much more welcome than armies, my lord. When the winter is over, the robins come; when the wars are over, the knights. A knight-errant is a sign of peace.

HANS. I love war.

AUGUSTE. Each to his taste, my lord.

HANS. Don't misunderstand me. [*Expansively.*] If I love war, it's because by nature, I'm a friendly person. I love company. Now in a war, you always have someone to talk to. If your comrades don't feel like chatting, there's always the enemy—you can always get yourself a prisoner. He shows you his wife's picture. You tell him about your sister. That's what I call living. But a knight-errant! . . . Would you believe it, in all the time I've spent riding about this enchanted forest, I haven't so much as heard a human voice.

AUGUSTE. But isn't it true that knights-errant can understand the language of animals?

HANS. Ah, yes, that's true enough—they speak to us, the animals. And we understand them very well. But it's not quite what you think, the language of animals. For us every animal is a symbol, naturally, and its message is written indelibly on our souls. But that's it, you see, the animals write—they don't speak.

AUGUSTE. They don't speak?

HANS. They speak without speaking. What they say is important, of course. The stag speaks to us of nobility. The unicorn, of chastity. The lion, of courage. It's stimulating—but you don't call that a conversation.

AUGUSTE. But the birds? . . .

HANS. To tell you the truth, Auguste, I'm a little disappointed in the birds. They chatter incessantly. But they're not good listeners. They're always preaching.

AUGUSTE. That surprises me. Especially with the lark. I should have thought the lark would love to confide in one.

HANS. The knight's headgear does not permit him to converse with larks.

AUGUSTE. But what sent you, if I may ask, into the black forest?

HANS. What do you suppose? A woman.

AUGUSTE. I ask no more questions, my lord.

HANS. Please, Auguste! It's thirty days since I've said a word about her to a living soul. No, no, ask me questions. Ask me anything. Ask me her name.

AUGUSTE. My lord—I wouldn't dare.

HANS. Ask me. Ask me.

AUGUSTE. What is her name, my lord?

HANS. Bertha. Bertha! Tell me fisherman, have you ever heard such a beautiful name? Bertha!

AUGUSTE. It's beautiful, my lord.

HANS. There are those who are called Angelique, Diane, Violante. Anybody can be called Angelique, Diane, Violante. But she alone deserves a name so solemn, vibrating, passionate: Bertha! [EUGENIE *comes in with a loaf of bread.*] And now, Eugenie, you will ask me is she beautiful?

EUGENIE. Is she beautiful?

AUGUSTE. We are speaking of Bertha, the Princess Bertha, Eugenie.

EUGENIE. Ah, yes, of course. And is she beautiful?

HANS. Eugenie, it is I who am entrusted with the purchase of horses for the king. You understand, then, my eye is sharp. No blemish, however slight, ever escapes me. The Angelique in question is not bad, but she had a ridge in her left thumbnail. Violante has a fleck of gold in her eye. Bertha is flawless.

AUGUSTE. That must be a lovely thing to see, a fleck of gold in a woman's eye.

EUGENIE. Stick to your fishing, Auguste.

HANS. A fleck of gold? Don't deceive yourself, my dear fellow. That might amuse you, a thing like that, for a day, two days at the most—

AUGUSTE. What is it like, exactly?

HANS. Well, it sparkles.

AUGUSTE. Like a grain of mica?

EUGENIE. Come, Auguste—you're getting on our nerves with your gold and your mica. Let the knight speak.

HANS. Yes, my dear Auguste, why this sudden partiality for Violante? Violante, when she joins with us in the hunt, crowns a white mare. And it's a pretty sight, a red-headed girl on a white mare, there's no denying it. And Violante, when she brings the queen the three-branched candlestick, always bears it high in both hands, like the celebrant approaching the altar. But Violante, when the old Duke takes her hand and tells her a spicy story, never laughs. She cries.

AUGUSTE. Violante cries?

HANS. I know. You are going to ask me what happens to these flecks of gold when they are drowned in tears—

EUGENIE. He's surely thinking of it, my lord. Once he gets his mind on anything! . . .

HANS. Yes, he will think of it till the day when he sees Bertha. For you shall certainly come to our wedding, both of you. You are invited. The condition Bertha made to our marriage was that I should come back alive after spending a month in the forest. And if I do come back, it will be thanks to you, my friends. And so, you shall see your Violante, fisherman, with her little red mouth and her pink ears and her little straight nose, you shall see what effect she makes next to my great dark angel! And now, fetch me my poached trout, Eugenie, or it will be overdone.

The door opens slowly. ONDINE *appears on the threshold. She stands there motionless for a moment.*

AUGUSTE. Ondine!

ONDINE. How beautiful he is!

AUGUSTE. What did she say?

ONDINE. I said, how beautiful he is!

AUGUSTE. It is our daughter, my lord. She has no manners.

ONDINE. It's thrilling to know that men are so beautiful. My heart is racing.

AUGUSTE. Will you keep still?

ONDINE. I'm trembling from head to foot.

AUGUSTE. She's only sixteen, my lord.

ONDINE. I knew there must be some reason for being a girl. The reason is

that men are so beautiful.

AUGUSTE. You are embarrassing our guest, Ondine.

ONDINE. I'm not embarrassing him. He likes me. What's your name?

AUGUSTE. That's not the way to speak to a knight, my child.

ONDINE. [*Coming closer.*] Look at his ear. Father. It's a perfect little shell. Do you expect me to treat it like a stranger? To whom do you belong, little shell? What is his name.

HANS. His name is Hans.

ONDINE. I should have guessed it. When people are happy and they open their mouths, they say Hans.

HANS. Hans von Wittenstein.

ONDINE. When there is sun in the morning, and the cloud of sadness lifts from your soul, when you sigh, you say Hans.

HANS. Hans von Wittenstein zu Wittenstein.

ONDINE. How lovely when a name makes its own echo! Why have you come, Hans? To take me away?

AUGUSTE. That will do, Ondine. Go to your room now.

ONDINE. Very well, take me. Take me with you.

EUGENIE *comes in with the trout on a platter.*

EUGENIE. Here is your trout, my lord.

ONDINE. His trout!

HANS. It looks magnificent.

ONDINE. You dared to poach a trout, Mother?

EUGENIE. Be quiet. In any case, it's done.

ONDINE. Oh, my poor darling trout! You who loved the cold water! What have they done to you?

AUGUSTE. You're not going to make a scene before our guest, Ondine?

ONDINE. They caught you—and they quenched your life in boiling water!

HANS. It was I, my girl, who asked them to.

ONDINE. You? I should have known. When one looks closely at your face, it all becomes clear. You're not very bright, are you? No. You are stupid.

EUGENIE. She doesn't know what she's saying, my lord.

ONDINE. That's chivalry! That's courage! You run about looking for giants who don't exist, and when you come upon a little joyous creature springing in the clear water, you boil it alive.

HANS. And I eat it. And I find it delicious.

ONDINE. You shall see how delicious it is! [*She snatches up the dish and throws it out of the window.*] Now eat it! [*She runs to the door.*]

AUGUSTE. Ondine!

EUGENIE. Where are you going, child?

ONDINE. There is someone out there who knows about men. So far I have refused to listen to him. Now that's over. I shall listen.

AUGUSTE. Ondine!

ONDINE. In a moment, I shall know. I shall know what they are, what they do, what they become. And so much the worse for you!

AUGUSTE. You're not going out. [*She springs aside.*]

ONDINE. I already know that they lie, that their beauty is ugliness, that their courage is cowardice. And I already know that I hate them.

HANS. And they already know that they love you.

ONDINE. [*Stops at the door, without turning.*] What did he say?

HANS. Nothing.

ONDINE. Say it once more, just to see.

HANS. They already know that they love you.

ONDINE. I hate them! [*She runs out into the darkness.*]

HANS. My compliments. You've brought her up well.

AUGUSTE. God knows I scold her often enough.

HANS. You should beat her.

EUGENIE. Beat her? Try and catch her.

HANS. You should send her to bed without supper.

AUGUSTE. What good would that do? She's never hungry.

HANS. I'm starved.

AUGUSTE. That was the last of the trout, my lord. But we have smoked a ham. Eugenie will go down and cut you some slices.

HANS. Then she permits you to kill her poor darling pigs?

AUGUSTE. She has no interest in pigs.

HANS. That's a mercy. [EUGENIE *goes out for the ham.*]

AUGUSTE. You are annoyed with the girl, my lord.

HANS. I'm annoyed because I'm vain just as she said. When she said I was handsome, though I know I'm not handsome, I was pleased. And when she said I was a coward, though I know I'm no coward, I was hurt. I'm annoyed with myself.

AUGUSTE. You're very kind to take it so well.

HANS. Oh, I don't take it well at all. I'm furious.

EUGENIE *comes in.*

EUGENIE. Where is the ham, Auguste? I can't find it.

AUGUSTE. The ham? Why, the ham is hanging in the cellar. Excuse me, my lord, I'll go and get it. [*He goes out with* EUGENIE. HANS *turns to the fire and warms his hands.* ONDINE *comes in noiselessly and stands just behind him. He doesn't hear her till she speaks.*]

ONDINE. My name is Ondine.

HANS. [*Without turning.*] It's a pretty name.

ONDINE. Hans and Ondine. There are no more beautiful names in the world, are there?

HANS. Yes. Ondine and Hans.

ONDINE. On no. Hans first. He is the man. He commands. Ondine is the girl. She is always one step behind. She keeps quiet.

HANS. She keeps quiet? Now how the devil does she manage that?

ONDINE. Hans is always one step ahead. In the processions—before the king—before all the world, he goes first. He is the first to age. He is the first to die. It's terrible! But Ondine follows at once. She kills herself.

HANS. What are you talking about?

ONDINE. There is the little moment of agony to live through. The moment that comes after the death of Hans. But it is short.

HANS. At your age, luckily, it doesn't mean much to talk about death.

ONDINE. At my age? Is that what you think? Very well, try—[*She pulls his dagger from its sheath.*] Here, kill yourself. You'll see if I am not dead the next moment.

HANS. [*Takes the dagger from her hand.*] I never felt less like killing myself.

ONDINE. Say you don't love me. You'll see if I don't die.

HANS. Fifteen minutes ago, you didn't even know I existed. And now you want to kill yourself on my account. I thought we had quarreled on account of the trout.

ONDINE. Oh, I can't be bothered with the trout. They're not very clever, the trout. If they don't like to be caught, all they have to do is keep away from men. It's different with me. I want to be caught.

HANS. In spite of your mysterious friend outside?

ONDINE. I learned nothing from him that I didn't already know.

HANS. Naturally not. You asked the questions. You gave the answers.

ONDINE. Don't joke. He's very near. And he's very dangerous.

HANS. Who?

ONDINE. The Old One.

HANS. The Old One?

ONDINE. The King of the Sea. I'm afraid, Hans.

HANS. [*Smiles.*] You're afraid of what?

ONDINE. I'm afraid you will deceive me. That's what he said. He also said you were not handsome. But you are!

HANS. Do you know that you're beautiful?

ONDINE. No, I don't know it yet. I would prefer to be beautiful. But I can be beautiful only if I love you.

HANS. You're a little liar. You were just as beautiful a moment ago when you hated me. Is that all he told you?

ONDINE. He said that if ever I kissed you, I would be lost. That was silly of him. I hadn't even thought of it till then.

HANS. And now you are thinking of it?

ONDINE. Very much.

HANS. Well, there is no harm in thinking.

ONDINE. On, no. It's good to think about it. Of course, in the end I shall do it. But first we shall wait a long time, as long as possible. We shall wait an hour. Then in after years we shall have this hour always to remember. The hour before you kissed me.

HANS. My little Ondine—

ONDINE. The hour before you said you loved me. Hans, I can't wait an hour. There isn't time. Tell me now.

HANS. You think that's something one says—just like that?

ONDINE. No? Well, then speak, command. What must I do? What is the appropriate posture? Do I sit in your lap, is that it?

HANS. In my lap in full armor?

ONDINE. Oh. Take it off quickly.

HANS. Do you know what you're saying? It takes me fifteen minutes to unbolt the shoulder-plates alone.

ONDINE. I have a way of removing armor. [*The armor falls to the floor.*]

HANS. Well!

ONDINE. Sit down. [*He sits. She springs into his lap.*]

HANS. You're mad, Ondine!

ONDINE. Yes. That's what he said.

HANS. And my arms—do you think they open to the first comer?

ONDINE. I have a way of opening arms—[HANS *opens his arms, with an expression of surprise.*] And of closing them. [*He closes them. A woman's voice is heard outside the window.*]

THE VOICE. Ondine!

ONDINE. [*Turns furiously to the window.*] No! Go away. Nobody called you.

THE VOICE. Ondine! Be careful!

ONDINE. Do I meddle in your affairs? Did you consult me about your husband?

THE VOICE. Ondine!

ONDINE. A fine handsome husband you found yourself, wasn't it? A seal with nostrils like rabbit holes and no nose. He gave you a string of pearls and you were his. And not even matched pearls.

HANS. To whom are you speaking, Ondine?

ONDINE. Oh, one of the neighbors.

HANS. But I saw no other house in the forest. Do you have neighbors?

ONDINE. Thousands. And all jealous.

A SECOND VOICE. Ondine! Be careful!

ONDINE. Oh, you're a fine one to speak! You were careful, weren't you? A narwhal dazzled you with his jet of water, and you gave yourself to him without a word.

THE SECOND VOICE. Ondine!

HANS. Their voices are charming.

ONDINE. My name is charming, not their voices. Kiss me, Hans. Kiss me.

A MAN'S VOICE. Ondine!

ONDINE. It's too late, Old One. Let me alone.

HANS. Is that the friend?

ONDINE. I'm sitting in his lap. He loves me.

THE MAN'S VOICE. Ondine!

ONDINE. It's too late, I say. It's finished. I'm already his mistress. Yes, his mistress. You don't understand? That's another word they have for wife. [*There is a noise at the kitchen door.*]

HANS. [*Pushing* ONDINE *gently from his lap.*] That's your father, Ondine.

ONDINE. Oh. I didn't think I had taught you that?

HANS. What?

ONDINE. My way of opening arms.

AUGUSTE *and* EUGENIE *come in.*

EUGENIE. Your supper is almost ready, my lord.

AUGUSTE. I can't imagine who put the ham in the attic.

ONDINE. I did. So I could be alone with Hans.

AUGUSTE. Ondine! Have you no shame?

ONDINE. I've not wasted my time. He's going to marry me.

AUGUSTE. You might help your mother with the table instead of talking nonsense.

ONDINE. You're right. Give me the silver, Mother. From now on, it's I who will serve Hans.

AUGUSTE. I brought up a bottle of wine, my lord. If you permit, we shall drink a glass with you. The glasses, Ondine.

ONDINE. You will have to teach me everything, my lord Hans. From morning to night, I shall be your handmaid. In the morning, I shall wake you. . . .

HANS. You won't find that easy. I sleep very soundly.

ONDINE. [*Sits down next to him and looks at him closely.*] Tell me, what does one do to awaken you?

EUGENIE *comes out with a platter.*

EUGENIE. The glasses, Ondine.

ONDINE. Oh Mother, you set the table. Hans is teaching me how to awaken him. Let's see, Hans. Make believe you're asleep.

HANS. With this wonderful odor of cooking? Out of the question.

ONDINE. Wake up, little Hans. It's dawn. Take this kiss in your darkness and this in your day. . . .

HANS. [*Accepting a slice of ham.*] Thank you.

AUGUSTE. Pay no attention to the child, my lord. She doesn't know what she's saying.

ONDINE. I love you.

EUGENIE. She's young. She becomes attached. It's nothing.

ONDINE. I love you, Hans.

HANS. [*Eating.*] This is what I call ham!

AUGUSTE. It's smoked with juniper.

HANS. Marvelous.

ONDINE. It was a mistake to awaken you, Hans. We should never awaken the man we love. In his sleep, he's ours completely. But the moment he opens his eyes, he escapes. Sleep again, little Hans—

HANS. [*Accepting another slice.*] Yes, thank you. Simply wonderful.

ONDINE. You don't want to be loved, you want to be stuffed.

HANS. Everything in its place, my dear.

EUGENIE. Ah, you'd make a fine wife, you would!

ONDINE. I?

AUGUSTE. Silence, Ondine. I want to say a word. [*He lifts his glass.*]

ONDINE. I shall certainly make a fine wife. You think you're a wife because you know how to cook a ham? That's not being a wife.

HANS. No? What else is it?

ONDINE. It's to be everything your husband is and everything he loves. It's to be the humblest part of him and the noblest. I shall be the shoes of your feet, my husband. I shall be the breath of your lungs. I shall be the hilt of your sword and the pommel of your saddle. I shall be your tears, your laughter and your dreams. What you are eating there, it's I.

HANS. It's seasoned to perfection.

ONDINE. Eat me, Hans. Eat me all. [AUGUSTE *clears his throat.*]

EUGENIE. Your father wishes to speak, Ondine. Quiet.

AUGUSTE. [*Lifting his glass again.*] Quiet! My lord, since you are doing us the honor of spending the night under our humble roof—

ONDINE. A hundred nights. A thousand nights—

AUGUSTE. Permit me to drink to the lady of your heart—

ONDINE. How nice of you, Father!

AUGUSTE. She who is even now trembling for your safety—

ONDINE. She's not trembling now. He's safe enough.

AUGUSTE. She whom you rightly call the most beautiful of women, although for my part, I am a little partial to Violante on account of—

EUGENIE. Yes, yes, we know. Go on.

AUGUSTE. I drink, then, to the most beautiful and noblest of women, to

your dark angel, to your betrothed, the Princess Bertha.

ONDINE. [*Rising to her feet.*] What name did you say?

AUGUSTE. The name the knight told me.

ONDINE. Since when am I called Bertha?

EUGENIE. We were not speaking of you, dear.

AUGUSTE. The knight is going to marry the Princess Bertha, Ondine, as soon as he returns to court. Isn't that so, my lord?

ONDINE. It's not so at all!

HANS. My little Ondine—

ONDINE. Ah, he's emerging from the ham at last, that one. Well, speak, since your mouth is no longer full— is there a Bertha? Yes or no?

HANS. Let me explain—

ONDINE. Is there a Bertha? Yes or no?

HANS. Yes. There is a Bertha. No. There was a Bertha.

ONDINE. So it's true, what he told me about men! They're all deceivers. They draw you to them with a thousand tricks, they seat you in their laps, they pass their hands all over your body and kiss you till you can't breathe—and all the time they are thinking of a dark angel called Bertha!

HANS. I did nothing like that to you, Ondine!

ONDINE. You did. Don't you dare deny it. And you hurt me, too. [*She bites her arm.*] Look at that, Father. See how he bit me? Let him deny it, if he dares!

HANS. You don't believe this nonsense, I hope?

ONDINE. I shall be the humblest part of you and the noblest, he said. I am your bare feet. I am the wine you drink. I am the bread you eat. Those were his words, Mother! And the things one has to do for him! One has to spend the whole morning waking him up. One has to kill oneself the moment he dies. Yes! And all the time, in their secret hearts, they are nursing the thought of a dark angel called Bertha!

HANS. Ondine, on my word—

ONDINE. I despise you! I detest you!

HANS. Nevertheless, you might listen to me—

ONDINE. I can see her from here, the dark angel, with her little shadowy mustache and her plucked eyebrows.

HANS. Now, Ondine, really! . . .

ONDINE. Don't come near me! Or I'll throw myself into the lake. [*She opens the door. It is raining heavily.*] So her name is Bertha!

HANS. I think there is no longer any Bertha, Ondine.

ONDINE. Leave this house at once, or I shall never enter it again! [*She turns suddenly.*] What did you say?

HANS. I said, I think there is no longer any Bertha, Ondine.

ONDINE. You lie! Farewell. [*She runs out into the rain.*]

HANS. Ondine! [*He runs to the door.*]

AUGUSTE. My lord, my lord—you'll get drenched! [*To* EUGENIE.] There's a pretty kettle of fish.

EUGENIE. Yes, there's a pretty kettle of fish.

AUGUSTE. I might as well tell him everything now.

EUGENIE. Yes, you might as well tell him everything now. [HANS *turns.*]

HANS. She's not your daughter, is she?

EUGENIE. No, my lord.

AUGUSTE. We had a daughter. She was stolen from the cradle.

HANS. Who left Ondine with you?

AUGUSTE. We found her at the edge of the lake the day our daughter disappeared.

HANS. These things happen only in fairy tales.

AUGUSTE. Yes, my lord. But it happened to us.

HANS. Then it is you who must be asked for her hand?

AUGUSTE. She calls us her parents, my lord.

HANS. Then, my friends, I have the honor of asking you for the hand of your daughter.

AUGUSTE. My lord, are you in your right mind?

HANS. Do you think that little wine of yours would turn my head?

AUGUSTE. The wine? Oh, never. It's a little Moselle, very modest, very reliable.

HANS. I assure you, I have never been more sober in my life. I ask you for the hand of Ondine with nothing in mind but the hand of Ondine. I want to hold this hand in mine. I want it to lead me to church, to war, and when the time comes, to death.

AUGUSTE. But, my lord, you already have a hand for that. This would be a hand too many.

HANS. A hand? Whose hand?

AUGUSTE. The lady Bertha.

HANS. Bertha? Do you know Bertha? I know her. I know her, that is, now that I know Ondine—

AUGUSTE. But is not a knight, above all, required to be loyal?

HANS. To his quest, yes. And I shall be loyal, above all, to my quest. Because, you know, up to now, we knights have been fools, all of us. We've been exploited; they take us for imbeciles. When we kill a monster, we're expected to vanish gracefully. When we find a treasure, we give it away. Well, that's finished. From now on I shall try to profit a little by my exploits. I have found a treasure and I shall keep it. Whether or not I knew it, my quest was Ondine, and I have found Ondine, and I shall marry Ondine. And nobody else in this world.

EUGENIE. You are making a mistake, my lord.

HANS. Eugenie—there was once a knight and his quest was to find something wonderful. And one night in a forest on the edge of a lake, he found a girl called Ondine. In her hands, tin turned to gold and water to jewels. The rain did not wet her. Her eyes were full of joy and her manner was royal. And not only was she the most wonderful creature he had ever seen, but he knew also that she would bring him all the delight and tenderness and goodness he would ever know in this world. Whereupon he bowed to her and went off to marry a girl called Bertha. Tell me, Eugenie, what sort of knight was this?

AUGUSTE. You don't put the question properly, my lord.

HANS. I ask you what sort of knight this would be. You don't dare to answer, but you know as well as I do. He would be a sort of idiot, would he not?

EUGENIE. But, my lord, since you have given your word to another—

HANS. He would be an idiot!

EUGENIE. Speak, Auguste.

HANS. Yes, speak. If there is any reason why I should not have Ondine, tell it to me now.

AUGUSTE. My lord, you are asking us for the hand of Ondine. It's a great honor for us—but she's not ours to give.

HANS. You must have some idea who her parents may be?

AUGUSTE. With Ondine it's not a question of parents. If we had not adopted Ondine, she would have grown up just the same. Ondine is strange. You saw her tonight in the storm. You understand, my lord, it's not that she's in the storm. She is the storm. She's a beautiful child, my lord, there's no denying it. But there is more than beauty in Ondine. There is power.

HANS. It's because she's young.

EUGENIE. It's true, she's young—

AUGUSTE. When I first married you, my poor Eugenie, you too were young. But your youth had no effect on the lake. You were beautiful. But the lake remained what it had always been, selfish and rude. And the floods were brutal and senseless as always, and the storm was a beast of prey. But

since Ondine came to us, everything has changed. The water has become gentle.

HANS. It's because you're old.

AUGUSTE. It's true I'm no longer young. But a lake that counts into your net each day exactly the same twelve fish, a lake that never enters your boat, not even if it happens to have a hole in the bottom—I think you will agree that is a remarkably courteous lake.

HANS. Well, suppose it is. What do you suggest? That I apply to the lake for permission to marry?

AUGUSTE. I wouldn't joke about the lake. The lake has ears.

HANS. And what's it to me if the lake has ears? I have no designs on the lake.

AUGUSTE. We are speaking of Ondine, my lord. Ondine belongs to the lake. Ondine is the lake, my lord.

HANS. Then I shall gladly take the lake to my bosom, and with it all the water in the world. The rivers shall be my brothers, the sea my mother, and the ocean itself my father-in-law. I love the water.

AUGUSTE. Beware of the water, my lord!

HANS. But why, Auguste? Why?

AUGUSTE. That's all I know, my lord.

HANS. Give me Ondine, Auguste.

AUGUSTE. Give you Ondine! And who am I to give you Ondine? Where is she now, Ondine? Oh, I remember, naturally, having seen her once, the little Ondine. I remember her voice, her laughter, I remember she threw your trout out of the window, a twelve-inch trout, the only one I had left. But we shall never see her again, she will never again come to us except in tender little lightnings, in little storms; she will never again tell us she loves us except with the waves lapping at our feet, or the rain on our cheeks, or perhaps, suddenly one day with a great salt-water fish in my pike-weir. That wouldn't surprise me a bit.

EUGENIE. Auguste, you're tired. It's

time you came to bed.

AUGUSTE. Do you remember the morning we found her, Eugenie?

EUGENIE. Permit us to retire, my lord.

AUGUSTE. There wasn't a mark on the sand, not a footprint—nothing—to show how the child got there. Only the wind and the sun and the lake staring at us fixedly with its eye—

EUGENIE. I will show you to your room.

HANS. Thank you. I shall sit here by the fire a little longer, if I may.

EUGENIC. Come, Auguste. Tomorrow we shall speak of Ondine.

AUGUSTE. If there is an Ondine. [*He shakes his head.*]

EUGENIE. Good night, my lord.

HANS. Good night. Good night. [AUGUSTE *and* EUGENIE *go out.* HANS *sits down by the fire and closes his eyes for a moment. The wall of the hut slowly becomes transparent, and through it appear the lake and the forest. In the half-light there rises the figure of an* ONDINE, *blonde and nude.*]

THE ONDINE. Take me, handsome knight.

HANS. [*Looking up with a start.*] What?

THE ONDINE. Kiss me.

HANS. I beg pardon?

THE ONDINE. Take me. Kiss me.

HANS. What are you talking about?

THE ONDINE. Am I too bold, handsome knight? Do I frighten you?

HANS. Not in the least.

THE ONDINE. Would you rather I were clothed? Shall I put on a dress?

HANS. A dress? What for?

THE ONDINE. Come to me. Take me. I am yours. [*She vanishes. Another* ONDINE *appears. She is dark and clothed.*]

THE SECOND ONDINE. Don't look at me, handsome knight.

HANS. Why not?

THE SECOND ONDINE. Don't come near me. I'm not that sort. If you touch me, I'll scream.

HANS. Don't worry.

THE SECOND ONDINE. If you touch my hair, if you touch my breasts, if you kiss my lips, I swear, I'll kill myself. I will not take off my dress!

HANS. As you please.

THE SECOND ONDINE. Don't come out, handsome knight. Don't come near me. I am not for you, handsome knight. [*She vanishes.* HANS *shrugs his shoulders. The* TWO ONDINES *appear together at opposite sides of the room.*]

FIRST ONDINE. Take me.

SECOND ONDINE. Don't touch me.

FIRST ONDINE. I am yours.

SECOND ONDINE. Keep your distance.

FIRST ONDINE. I want you.

SECOND ONDINE. You frighten me.

ONDINE. [*Appears suddenly.*] Oh how silly you look, both of you! [*The* TWO ONDINES *vanish.*]

HANS. [*Takes* ONDINE *in his arms.*] Little Ondine! What is this nonsense? Who are those women?

ONDINE. My friends. They don't want me to love you. They say anyone can have you for the asking. But they're wrong.

HANS. They're very nice, your friends. Are those the prettiest?

ONDINE. The cleverest. Kiss me, Hans.

FIRST ONDINE. [*Reappears.*] Kiss me, Hans—

ONDINE. Look at that fool! Oh, how silly a woman looks when she offers herself! Go away! Don't you know when you've lost? Hans—

SECOND ONDINE. [*Appears again next to the first.*] Hans—

ONDINE. Go away, I say! Hans—

A THIRD ONDINE. [*Appears next to the others.*] Hans—

ONDINE. It's not fair! No!

HANS. Let them speak, Ondine.

ONDINE. No. It's the Song of the Three Sisters. I'm afraid.

HANS. Afraid? Of them?

ONDINE. Cover your ears, Hans.

HANS. But I love music.

THE FIRST ONDINE. [*Sings.*]
Hans Wittenstein zu Wittenstein,
Without you life is but a fever.
Alles was ist mein ist dein,
Love me always, leave me never.

HANS. Bravo! That's charming.

ONDINE. In what way is that charming?

HANS. It's simple. It's direct. It's charming. The song of the sirens must have been about like that.

ONDINE. It was exactly like that. They copied it. They're going to sing again. Don't listen.

THE THREE ONDINES. [*Sing.*]
Heed no more the west wind's
    urging,
Slack your sail and rest your oar.
Drift upon the current surging
Powerfully toward our shore.

HANS. The tune is not bad.

ONDINE. Don't listen, Hans.

THE THREE ONDINES. [*Sing.*]
Sorrow once for all forsaking,
Take our laughter for your sighs.
These are yours but for the taking,
Tender breasts and wanton thighs.

ONDINE. If you think it's pleasant to hear others singing the things one feels and can't express. . . .

THE THREE ONDINES. [*Sing*]
Come and take your fill of pleasure
Taste delight and drink it deep.
We shall give you beyond measure
Joy and rest and love and sleep.

HANS. That's wonderful! Sing it again' Sing it again!

ONDINE. Don't you understand? They don't mean a word of it. They're just trying to take you away from me.

THE FIRST ONDINE. You've lost, Ondine, you've lost!

HANS. What have you lost?

ONDINE. Your song means nothing to him!

FIRST ONDINE. He holds you in his arms, Ondine, but he looks at me!

SECOND ONDINE. He speaks your name, Ondine, but he thinks of me!

THIRD ONDINE. He kisses your lips, Ondine, but he smiles at me!

THE THREE ONDINES. He deceives you! He deceives you! He deceives you!

HANS. What are they talking about?

ONDINE. He may look at you and smile at you and think of you as much as he pleases. He loves me. And I shall marry him.

THE FIRST ONDINE. Then you agree? You make the pact?

HANS. What pact?

ONDINE. Yes. I agree. I make the pact. [*The words are taken up mysteriously. They echo and re-echo from every quarter.*]

THE FIRST ONDINE. I am to tell them?

ONDINE. Yes. Tell them. Tell them all. Those who sit and those who swim, those who float in the sunlight and those who crawl in darkness on the ocean floor.

HANS. What the devil are you saying?

ONDINE. Tell them I said yes. [*The word "yes" is taken up by a thousand whispering voices.*]

THE FIRST ONDINE. And the Old One? Shall we tell him also?

ONDINE. Tell him I hate him! Tell him he lies!

THE FIRST ONDINE. Yes?

ONDINE. Yes! Yes! Yes! [*Again the sound is taken up. The mysterious voices whisper through the darkness until the air is filled with echoes. There is a climax of sound, then silence.* THE ONDINES *vanish. The walls of the hut regain their solidity.*]

HANS. What a fuss! What a racket!

ONDINE. Naturally. It's the family. [HANS *sits in the armchair.* ONDINE *sits at his feet.*] You're caught, my little Hans?

HANS. Body and soul.

ONDINE. You don't wish to struggle a little more? Just a little more?

HANS. I'm too happy to struggle.

ONDINE. So it takes twenty minutes to catch a man. It takes longer to catch a bass.

HANS. Don't flatter yourself. It took thirty years to catch me. All my life. Ever since I was a child, I've felt something drawing me toward this forest and this lake. It was you?

ONDINE. Yes. And now after thirty years, would it be too much if you told me at last that you love me?

HANS. I love you.

ONDINE. You say it easily. You've said it before.

HANS. I've said something like it that

meant something else.

ONDINE. You've said it often?

HANS. I've said it to every woman I didn't love. And now at last I know what it means.

ONDINE. Why didn't you love them? Were they ugly?

HANS. No. They were beautiful. But they no longer exist.

ONDINE. Oh, Hans, I meant to give you everything in the world, and I begin by taking everything away. Some day you will hate me for it.

HANS. Never, Ondine.

ONDINE. Shall I ever see them, these women you don't love?

HANS. Of course.

ONDINE. Where?

HANS. Everywhere. In their castles. In their gardens. At the court.

ONDINE. At the court? I?

HANS. Of course. We leave in the morning.

ONDINE. Oh, Hans, am I to leave my lake so soon?

HANS. I want to show the world the most perfect thing it possesses. Did you know you were the most perfect thing the world possessed?

ONDINE. I suspected it. But will the world have eyes to see it?

HANS. When the world sees you, it will know. It's really very nice, Ondine, the world.

ONDINE. Tell me, Hans. In this world of yours, do lovers live together always?

HANS. Together? Of course.

ONDINE. No. You don't understand. When a man and a woman love each other are they ever separate?

HANS. Separate? Of course.

ONDINE. No, you still don't understand. Take the dogfish, for instance. Not that I'm especially fond of dogfish, mind you. But, once the dogfish couples with its mate, he never leaves her, never as long as he lives, did you know that? Through storm and calm they swim together, thousands and thousands of miles, side by side, two fingers apart, as if an invisible link held them together. They are no longer two. They become one.

HANS. Well?

ONDINE. Do lovers live like that in your world?

HANS. It would be a little difficult for lovers to live like that in our world, Ondine. In our world, each has his own life, his own room, his own friends—

ONDINE. What a horrible word that is, each.

HANS. Each has his work—his play—

ONDINE. But the dogfish too have their work and their play. They have to hunt, you know, in order to live. And sometimes they come upon a school of herrings which scatter before them in a thousand flashes, and they have a thousand reasons to lose each other, to swerve one to the right, the other to the left. But they never do. As long as they live, not even a sardine can come between them.

HANS. In our world, Ondine, a whale can come between a husband and wife twenty times a day, no matter how much they love each other.

ONDINE. I was afraid of that.

HANS. The man looks to his affairs; the woman to hers. They swim in different currents.

ONDINE. But the dogfish have to swim through different currents also. There are cold currents and warm currents. And sometimes the one likes the cold and the other the warm. And sometimes they swim into currents so powerful that they can divide a fleet, and yet they cannot divide these fish by the breadth of a nail.

HANS. That merely proves that men and fish are not the same.

ONDINE. And you and I, we are the same?

HANS. Oh yes, Ondine.

ONDINE. And you swear that you will never leave me, not even for a moment?

HANS. Yes, Ondine.

ONDINE. Because now that I love you, two steps away from you my loneliness begins.

HANS. I will never leave you, Ondine.

ONDINE. Hans, listen to me seriously. I know someone who can join us forever, someone very powerful. And if I ask him, he will solder us together with a band of flesh so that nothing but death can separate us. Would you like me to call him?

HANS. No, Ondine.

ONDINE. But, Hans, the more I think of it, the more I see there is no other way to keep lovers together in your world.

HANS. And your dogfish? Do they need to be soldered like that?

ONDINE. It's true. But they don't live among men. Let me call him. You'll see. It's a very practical arrangement.

HANS. No. Let's try this way first. Later, we'll see.

ONDINE. I know what you're thinking. Of course, she's right, you're thinking, the little Ondine, and naturally I shall be with her always, but once in a while, for just a little moment perhaps I shall go and take a turn by myself, I shall go and visit my friend.

HANS. Or my horse.

ONDINE. Or your horse. When this angel falls asleep, you're thinking, this angel whom I shall never leave not even for a moment, then, at last, I shal have a chance to go and spend a good half hour with my horse.

HANS. As a matter of fact, I had better go and have a look at him now, don't you think? We're leaving at dawn, you know, and I ought to see if he's bedded properly. Besides I always tell him everything.

ONDINE. Ah yes. Well, tonight you shall tell him nothing.

HANS. But why, Ondine?

ONDINE. Because tonight you're going to sleep, my little Hans. [*And with a gesture, she throws sleep into his eyes.*] Good night, my love. [*He falls asleep.*]

THE FIRST ONDINE. [*Her voice seems very far away.*] Good-bye, Ondine.

ONDINE. Look after my lake!

THE SECOND ONDINE. Good-bye, Ondine.

ONDINE. Take care of my stream!

THE KING OF THE SEA. Ondine!

ONDINE. Farewell, Old One.

THE KING OF THE SEA. Don't leave us, Ondine.

ONDINE. I have left you, Old One.

THE KING OF THE SEA. The world of men is not your world, Ondine. It will bring you sorrow.

ONDINE. It will bring me joy.

THE KING OF THE SEA. The man will deceive you. He will abandon you.

ONDINE. Never! Never!

THE KING OF THE SEA. And when he deceives you? When he abandons you? You will remember our pact?

ONDINE. I shall remember our pact.

THE KING OF THE SEA. [*His voice recedes.*] Remember, Ondine.

THE ONDINES. [*Their voices are like the murmur of water.*] Remember, Ondine.

HANS. [*Turning in his sleep.*] Remember, Ondine—

ONDINE. Oh dear, from this time on, how much I shall have to remember!

Act 2

The hall of honor of the king's palace. It is a large vaulted loggia of Gothic design. The roof is supported by columns. The upstage side opens on the palace gardens, in which may be seen three jets of water playing in marble basins in the sunshine. To the left is a dais with the king's throne, and above the throne a mural depicting one of the labors of Hercules. There are arched doorways.

The LORD CHAMBERLAIN and the SUPERINTENDENT OF THE ROYAL THEATRES are engaged in a conference. To one side stand respectfully the TRAINER OF THE SEALS and the ILLUSIONIST.

THE CHAMBERLAIN. My dear Superintendent, this is a matter that will require all your skill, and all your inventiveness. The Knight of Wittenstein has at last been persuaded to present his bride at court. His Majesty has asked me to provide an amusing interlude with which to grace the occasion. But the reception is to take place immediately.

THE SUPERINTENDENT. The time is short, my Lord Chamberlain.

THE CHAMBERLAIN. It couldn't be shorter. Well? As Superintendent of the Royal Theatres, what do you propose?

THE SUPERINTENDENT. *Salammbo.*

At this word MATHO *and* SALAMMBO *appear and begin at once to sing.*

THE CHAMBERLAIN. [*Striking the floor with his staff for silence.*] But you played *Salammbo* only last night for the Margrave's birthday. Besides, *Salammbo* is sad.

THE SUPERINTENDENT. It's sad. But it's ready. [*He signs to his actors who burst at once into their duet.*]

THE CHAMBERLAIN. [*Stops them again.*] I don't see why it is any more ready than *Orpheus*, which has only one character. Or the *Interlude of Adam and Eve*, which requires no costumes.

THE SUPERINTENDENT. Excellency, my success in the theatre is based solely on the discovery that each particular stage has its likes and dislikes which it is useless to combat.

THE CHAMBERLAIN. Time presses, my good man.

THE SUPERINTENDENT. Each theatre, Excellency, is built for one play and one play only. The whole secret of management is to discover what play that is. It's not easy, especially when the play is not yet written. And so, a thousand disasters—until that happy day when the play for which it was intended comes to its proper theatre and gives it its life, its soul, and, if I may say so, its sex.

THE CHAMBERLAIN. Superintendent—

THE SUPERINTENDENT. For years I managed a theatre which bumbled along miserably with the classics until suddenly one night it found its joy in a bawdy farce with sailors. It was a female theatre. I knew another which tolerated only *Othello*. It was male. Last year I was forced to close the Royal Ballet. Impossible to determine its sex.

THE CHAMBERLAIN. And you believe the Royal Auditorium—

THE SUPERINTENDENT. Exists only for *Salammbo*, yes, your Excellency. At the word *Salammbo*, the tightness of throat with which the royal chorus is normally afflicted suddenly relaxes, and the hall resounds with voices full of resonance and joy. [MATHO *and* SALAMMBO *begin singing, at first softly, crescendo to the end of the speech.*] I tell you, my Lord Chamberlain, sometimes when I play a German opera, I notice one of my singers, brimming with happiness, making magnificent gestures, sending out full-throated tones which fill the audience with such joy and comfort that it breaks into spontaneous applause—Why? Because among his fellow-actors, who are merely grinding out their parts by rote, this actor in the general confusion is blissfully singing his role in *Salammbo*.

THE CHAMBERLAIN. [*Silencing the singers.*] No. It would hardly do to entertain a newly married couple with a tragedy of unhappy love. *Salammbo* is out of the question. [*The* SUPERINTENDENT *waves his singers away. They go reluctantly. The* CHAMBERLAIN *turns to the* TRAINER OF SEALS.] Who are you?

THE TRAINER. I am the Trainer of Seals, your Excellency.

THE CHAMBERLAIN. What do they do, your seals?

THE TRAINER. They don't sing *Salammbo*.

THE CHAMBERLAIN. That's a pity. A chorus of seals singing *Salammbo* would constitute a very appropriate entertainment. Besides, I am told that your head seal has a beard that makes him look like his Majesty's father-in-law. Is that true?

THE TRAINER. I could shave him, Excellency.

THE CHAMBERLAIN. By a regrettable coincidence, his Majesty's father-in-law shaved his beard only yesterday. We had best avoid even the shadow of a scandal. And who are you?

THE ILLUSIONIST. I am an illusionist, Excellency.

THE CHAMBERLAIN. Where is your apparatus?

THE ILLUSIONIST. I am an illusionist without apparatus.

THE CHAMBERLAIN. Now what do you take us for? You don't produce claps of thunder and lightning without apparatus.

THE ILLUSIONIST. Yes. [*There is a clap of thunder and lightning.*]

THE CHAMBERLAIN. [*Cowering with fear.*] Nonsense. You can't produce sudden clouds of smoke which leave the stage covered with flowers without apparatus? [*There is a sudden cloud of smoke, and flowers fall from the ceiling.*]

THE ILLUSIONIST. Yes.

THE CHAMBERLAIN. What stubbornness! You don't suddenly produce before the eyes of the Lord Chamberlain—

BERTRAM. [*Comes in.*] Your Excellency—

THE CHAMBERLAIN. Just a moment.— Venus completely nude—without apparatus.

THE ILLUSIONIST. Yes.

BERTRAM. Excellency— [*A nude* VENUS *appears.* BERTRAM *bows.*] Madame. [VENUS *disappears.*]

THE CHAMBERLAIN. I've always wondered who these Venuses are that magicians produce out of thin air? Relatives?

THE ILLUSIONIST. Or Venus herself. It depends on the magician.

BERTRAM. Excellency, his Majesty is unavoidably detained by the African envoy. The reception is postponed for an hour.

THE CHAMBERLAIN. Excellent. That gives us time to think of something. [*To the* SUPERINTENDENT.] Have you thought of something?

THE SUPERINTENDENT. Yes, Excellency.

THE CHAMBERLAIN. Ah. Splendid. What?

THE SUPERINTENDENT. *Salammbo.* [*The two singers appear, only to be waved off peremptorily by the* CHAMBERLAIN.]

THE CHAMBERLAIN. [*To the* ILLUSIONIST.] And how do you propose to amuse his Majesty?

THE ILLUSIONIST. If your Excellency permits, I shall do what the occasion inspires.

THE CHAMBERLAIN. That's asking a great deal. After all, we have never seen your work.

THE ILLUSIONIST. I shall be happy, while we are waiting, to offer a little private entertainment by way of demonstration.

THE CHAMBERLAIN. Ah. Very good.

THE ILLUSIONIST. What would your Excellency like to see?

THE CHAMBERLAIN. I should very much like to see—

THE ILLUSIONIST. Splendid. I shall bring them together at once.

THE CHAMBERLAIN. You are also a mind-reader?

THE ILLUSIONIST. Yes, Excellency, I can, if you wish, bring together before your eyes a man and a woman who have been carefully avoiding each other for the past three months.

THE CHAMBERLAIN. Here? Now?

THE ILLUSIONIST. Here and now. If you will be so good as to conceal yourselves—

THE CHAMBERLAIN. But it's impossible, my dear fellow. Consider that the gentleman in question is at this very moment in the royal apartments supervising the last details of his wife's costume. A tornado could not draw him from her. The injured lady, on the other hand, is locked up in her room. She has sworn she will under no circumstances appear. These two cannot possibly meet.

THE ILLUSIONIST. Yes. But suppose that a dog were to steal the bride's glove and run out into the garden with it? And suppose that the lady's pet bullfinch should fly out of its cage and come to perch on the edge of the fountain?

THE CHAMBERLAIN. That will get you nowhere. It is the halberdier's high duty to divert all dogs from the royal apartments. And as for the bird—the king has just loosed a falcon in the garden. It is hovering over the bullfinch's cage.

THE ILLUSIONIST. Yes. But suppose that the halberdier slips on a banana peel? And suppose a gazelle distracts the falcon's attention?

THE CHAMBERLAIN. Bananas and gazelles are unknown in these parts.

THE ILLUSIONIST. Yes. But the African envoy peeled a banana while waiting for his morning audience. And among the gifts sent by his government, there was a gazelle which is at this moment feeding in the garden.

THE CHAMBERLAIN. Quite resourceful, you magicians.

THE ILLUSIONIST. Yes. Take your places. In a moment you shall see the Princess Bertha and the Knight of Wittenstein come together in this hall.

VIOLANTE *and* ANGELIQUE *come in from the garden. They hear the last words.*

VIOLANTE. Really?

ANGELIQUE. Really?

THE CHAMBERLAIN. [*Beckoning to the ladies to join him behind a column.*] Sh! Come here.

BERTRAM. But, Excellency, why are we doing this evil thing?

THE CHAMBERLAIN. Sooner or later it would have to happen. That's life.

BERTRAM. Then why not let life take its course?

THE CHAMBERLAIN. My dear Bertram, you are young and you are a poet. When you have reached my age, you will understand that life is a very

poorly constructed play. As a rule, the curtain goes up in the wrong places, the climaxes don't come off, the denouement is interminably postponed, so that those who should die at once of a broken heart die instead of a kidney ailment at an advanced age. If this excellent illusionist can make us see a life unfold for once with the concision and logic that a good play requires— [*To the* ILLUSIONIST.] Can you?

THE ILLUSIONIST. Perhaps.

THE CHAMBERLAIN. Just one little scene, then. Just one little scene.

BERTRAM. But, Excellency, the poor girl—

THE CHAMBERLAIN. The girl has caused a knight to be false to his word. She deserves to suffer.

BERTRAM. But why should we? . . .

THE CHAMBERLAIN. Don't excite yourself, my boy. Six months from now, in the normal course of events, Hans and Bertha would meet. Six months after that, they would kiss. A year after that, beyond a shadow of doubt, they would—it's inevitable. And if we spare ourselves these delays, and bring their hands together at once; and, ten minutes later, their lips, and five minutes after that, whatever else is necessary—will we be changing their story, really, in any way? We shall just be giving it a little pace, a little tempo— Magician!— What's that noise?

THE TRAINER. The halberdier. He slipped on a banana peel.

THE CHAMBERLAIN. Splendid.

BERTRAM. Excellency, I beg of you, let's carry this no further. It's a mischievous thing. Left to themselves, perhaps these two would never meet again. [*There is a scream from the garden.*] What's that scream?

THE SUPERINTENDENT. The gazelle. The falcon struck it.

THE CHAMBERLAIN. Perfect. You think you can bring off the whole thing at this pace, magician?

THE ILLUSIONIST. Perhaps. [*The bird appears, perched on the fountain.*]

THE SUPERINTENDENT. The bird!

THE TRAINER. [*Looking out into the garden.*] The dog!

VIOLANTE. The knight! [HANS *is seen running after the dog in the garden.*]

THE SUPERINTENDENT. The lady!

BERTHA *runs in and catches the bird.*

HANS. Ah! There you are, you rascal! At last I've caught you!

BERTHA. Ah! There you are, you rascal! At last I've found you. [*Each goes off without seeing the other. The spectators poke their heads out of their hiding places. They hiss.*]

BERTRAM. [*Sighs with relief.*] Thank heaven!

THE CHAMBERLAIN. What's this, magician? Are you making fun of us?

THE ILLUSIONIST. Sorry, sir. A fault in direction.

THE CHAMBERLAIN. Are they going to meet or are they not?

THE ILLUSIONIST. They are going to meet. And this time there will be no mistake about it. I'll knock their heads together. [*The spectators hide once more.*] Now!

The dog runs across the garden, glove in mouth, with HANS *in pursuit. The bird flies in and settles on the fountain.* BERTHA *runs in from the right and catches it.*

BERTHA. Again! What a bad bird you are!

HANS. Again! What an obstinate beast! [*He enters the room with the glove in his hand, just as* BERTHA *runs up with the bird. They collide.* HANS *takes her hands to keep her from falling. They recognize each other.*] Oh! I beg your pardon, Bertha.

BERTHA. Oh! I'm sorry, Hans.

HANS. Did I hurt you?

BERTHA. Not a bit.

HANS. I'm a clumsy brute, Bertha.

BERTHA. Yes. You are. [*There is a moment of embarrassed silence. Then each tuns and walks off slowly.* BERTHA *stops.*] Pleasant honeymoon?

HANS. Marvelous.

BERTHA. A blonde, I believe?

HANS. Blonde, like the sun.

BERTHA. Sunlit nights! I prefer the darkness.

HANS. Each to his taste.

BERTHA. It was dark that night under the oak tree. My poor Hans! You must have suffered!

HANS. Bertha!

BERTHA. I didn't suffer. I loved it.

HANS. Bertha, my wife is coming in at any moment.

BERTHA. I was happy that night in your arms. I thought it was for always.

HANS. And so it could have been, had you not insisted on sending me into the forest on a wild-goose chase. Why didn't you keep me with you, if you wanted me?

BERTHA. One takes off a ring sometimes to show to one's friends. Even an engagement ring.

HANS. I'm sorry. The ring didn't understand.

BERTHA. No. And so it rolled, as rings do, under the nearest bed.

HANS. I beg your pardon!

BERTHA. Forgive me. I shouldn't have mentioned a bed. Among peasants, you sleep in the straw, I believe? You pick it out of your hair the morning after. Is it fun?

HANS. One day you will see.

BERTHA. No, I don't think so. Black hair and straw don't go well together. That's for blondes.

HANS. You may be right. Although in love, these details don't seem to matter. But, of course, you've never had that experience.

BERTHA. You think?

HANS. When you're in love, you don't think of yourself so much. You think of the other. You will see one day. But when it happens to you, don't let your lover go.

BERTHA. No?

HANS. Don't send him into senseless danger and loneliness and boredom.

BERTHA. One would say you had a bad

time in the black forest.

HANS. You are haughty. But when you meet the man you love, take my advice—pocket your pride, throw your arms around his neck and tell him, before all the world, that you love him.

BERTHA. [*She throws her arms around his neck.*] I love you. [*She kisses him, then tries to run off. But he holds her by the hands.*]

HANS. Bertha!

BERTHA. Let me go, Hans.

HANS. What game are you playing with me now, Bertha?

BERTHA. Be careful, Hans. I have a bird in my hand.

HANS. I love another woman, Bertha.

BERTHA. The bird!

HANS. You should have done that before, Bertha.

BERTHA. Hans, don't squeeze my hand so. You're going to kill it.

HANS. Let the bird go, Bertha.

BERTHA. No. Its little heart is beating with fear. And just now I need this little heart next to mine.

HANS. What is it you want of me, Bertha?

BERTHA. Hans— Oh! [*Opening her hand and showing the bird.*] There. You've killed it.

HANS. Oh, Bertha! [*Taking the bird.*] Forgive me, Bertha. Forgive me. [BERTHA *looks at him a long moment. He is completely contrite.*]

BERTHA. Give it to me. I'll take the poor little thing away. [*She takes it from him.*]

HANS. Forgive me.

BERTHA. I want nothing of you now, Hans. But once, I wanted something for you, and that was my mistake. I wanted glory—for the man I loved. The man I had chosen when I was a little girl, and whom I led one night under the oak tree on which long ago I had carved his name. I thought it was a woman's glory to lead her lover not only to his table and his bed, but to whatever in the world is hardest to find and most difficult to conquer. I was wrong.

HANS. No, Bertha. No, Bertha.

BERTHA. I am dark. I thought that in the darkness of the forest this man would see my face in every shadow. I am dark, I trusted my love to the darkness. How could I have known that in these shadows, he would come one night upon a head of gold?

HANS. How could anyone have known it?

BERTHA. That was my error. I have confessed it. And that's the end of it. I shall carve no more initials in the bark of trees. A man alone in a dream of glory—that's already foolish. But a woman alone in a dream of glory is completely ridiculous. So much the worse for me.

HANS. Forgive me, Bertha?

BERTHA. Farewell, Hans.

She goes out, right. He goes out, left. The spectators appear, crying "Bravo!"

THE ILLUSIONIST. There it is, your Excellency. The scene that would have taken place, without my assistance, next winter. I have brought it about, as you see, here and now. It has happened.

BERTRAM. It is amply sufficient. We can stop here, can we not?

THE CHAMBERLAIN. No. No. No. No. I'm dying to see the next. The next, Magician, the next!

THE ILLUSIONIST. The next scene?

VIOLANTE. The next!

ANGELIQUE. The next!

THE ILLUSIONIST. At your service, ladies. Which one?

VIOLANTE. The one in which Hans unlaces the helmet of the knight he has killed and it is the Lady Bertha? . . .

THE ILLUSIONIST. That scene is in another play, Mademoiselle.

THE SUPERINTENDENT. The scene in which the knight in the nick of time saves Bertha from the dragon? . . .

THE TRAINER. The scene in which the knight, while twirling a ball on his nose—

THE ILLUSIONIST. Please!

THE CHAMBERLAIN. The scene in which Bertha and Hans first speak of Ondine.

THE ILLUSIONIST. Very well, Excellency. That takes place next spring.

THE CHAMBERLAIN. So much the better. I love the spring. [*He goes behind his column. The lights dim.* BERTHA *and* HANS *come in slowly from opposite directions.*]

HANS. [*Calls.*] Bertha.

BERTHA. [*Calls.*] Hans. [*They catch sight of each other.*] I was looking for you, Hans.

HANS. I was looking for you, Bertha.

The CHAMBERLAIN *comes out suddenly.*

THE CHAMBERLAIN. Magician! What does this mean? What have you done to me?

THE ILLUSIONIST. It is one of the inconveniences of my system. You have grown an eight months' beard. You see, it is now next spring.

THE CHAMBERLAIN. Ah—

He disappears. The scene continues.

BERTHA. Hans, must there be this awful cloud between us? Can't we be friends?

HANS. I wish we could be, Bertha. But—

BERTHA. I know. We can't be friends without Ondine. But it's your fault, Hans. You haven't let me see her since that awful day of the king's reception. And that's eight months ago, and quite forgotten. Send her to me this evening, Hans. I am illuminating a manuscript of the *Aeneid* for the king. Ondine can draw in the initials, and I shall teach her the secret of the gold leaf.

HANS. Thanks, Bertha. But I doubt very much—

BERTHA. Ondine doesn't letter?

HANS. Ondine doesn't write.

BERTHA. How lucky she is! When you write, it takes away half the pleasure of reading. She has a charming voice. I'm sure she reads aloud beautifully?

HANS. Ondine doesn't read.

BERTHA. How I envy her! How wonderful among all these pedants to be able to give oneself up to the luxury of not reading. But she dances, I know—

HANS. Never.

BERTHA. You're joking, Hans! You don't mean to say that she neither reads, nor writes, nor dances?

HANS. Yes. And she doesn't recite. And she doesn't play the rote. Nor the harp, nor the lute. And she won't go hunting. She can't bear to see things killed.

BERTHA. But what then does she do, in heaven's name?

HANS. Oh, she swims. Occasionally.

BERTHA. That's nice. Though it's not by swimming that a girl advances her husband's interests at court. And yet, let's be just, Hans. After all, these accomplishments mean nothing. A pretty woman has the right to be ignorant of everything, provided she knows when to keep still.

HANS. It is this point precisely, Bertha, that worries me the most. Ondine does not know when to keep still. Quite the contrary. She says whatever comes into her head—and the things that come into the girl's head! Bertha, you know, the jousting season opens this week. And the thought of the phrases which will issue from Ondine as she watches these tournaments in which every step and pass-at-arms has its appropriate term—it makes me shudder.

BERTHA. She can learn.

HANS. I spent the morning trying to teach her the rudiments. Each time I give her a new term, she thanks me with a kiss. Now in the first position of the horseman alone there are thirty-three points to identify—

BERTHA. Thirty-six.

HANS. God, that's true! What am I thinking of? I tell you, I'm losing my wits, Bertha!

BERTHA. Send her to me, Hans. I'll see

that she learns what she needs to know.

HANS. Thanks. But, what she needs to know above all is the special signs and prerogatives of the Wittenstein. And those are a family secret.

BERTHA. You forget, Hans. I was almost one of the Wittenstein. Ask me a question.

HANS. If you can answer this, I shall owe you a forfeit. What device does a Wittenstein bear on his shield when he enters the lists?

BERTHA. On a field azure, a squirrel passant, gules.

HANS. Does he bear this device into combat?

BERTHA. Never. At the moment he lowers his visor, his squire hands him a shield on which are emblazoned three lions rampant or, on a field sable. That is his device of war.

HANS. Bertha! You're incredible! And how does a Wittenstein approach the barrier?

BERTHA. Lance squared, charger collected, slow trot.

HANS. Ah, Bertha, what a lucky man the knight will be who marries you! [*He kisses her hand. She snatches it away. They go off in opposite directions.*]

THE CHAMBERLAIN. [*No beard.*] Bravo! Bravo! Bravo! And how right he is! The Princess Bertha knows everything. She does everything. She is the ideal woman, beyond a doubt. You have us on pins and needles, Magician. The third scene! Quickly!

VIOLANTE. The scene in which Bertha sees Ondine dancing in the moonlight with her fairies.

THE ILLUSIONIST. You appear to be still a little confused, Mademoiselle.

THE CHAMBERLAIN. The first quarrel of Hans and Ondine.

BERTRAM. Couldn't we let that, at least, take care of itself?

THE CHAMBERLAIN. No, no. We'd never get to see it. Magician—

BERTRAM. But Excellency! His Majesty will be here in a moment.

THE CHAMBERLAIN. By heaven, that's true. I will just have time to give this young lady the customary words of advice before the reception begins. You're not planning to do anything more till I get back, Magician?

THE ILLUSIONIST. Just one tiny scene, perhaps.

THE CHAMBERLAIN. In connection with what?

THE ILLUSIONIST. In connection with nothing at all. Just a trifle to please an old fisherman whom I love. But your Excellency needn't leave.

THE CHAMBERLAIN. Oh no, I must. It is the Lord Chamberlain's duty to instruct all those who are presented at court. And in this particular case—

THE ILLUSIONIST. If your Excellency wishes, I can save you the trouble of going. Take your place and you shall see yourself speaking to her.

THE CHAMBERLAIN. You can't do it!

THE ILLUSIONIST. Nothing simpler.

THE CHAMBERLAIN. [*He backs away in astonishment until he is lost from sight.*] What an extraordinary illusion!

THE ILLUSIONIST. Yes. But first, the Lady Violante. [VIOLANTE *steps forward.* AUGUST *walks in from the garden. He looks in bewilderment at* THE ILLUSIONIST.] The fleck of gold, Auguste.

AUGUSTE. [*He sees* VIOLANTE.] Are you the Lady Violante?

VIOLANTE. Yes. What do you wish?

AUGUSTE. [*Looking into her eyes.*] I was right! It's marvelous!

THE VOICE OF EUGENIE. Auguste! Stick to your fishing! [AUGUSTE *makes a gesture of resignation, bows and goes.*]

THE ILLUSIONIST. Thank you, my lady. Here you come, your Excellency. [VIOLANTE *goes behind the column. The* CHAMBERLAIN *comes in leading* ONDINE *by the hand.*]

THE CHAMBERLAIN. Absolutely out of the question, dear lady!

ONDINE. But it would make me so happy—

THE CHAMBERLAIN. I regret deeply. To change the court reception, third class, into a water festival is entirely out of the question. The Minister of Finance would never hear of such a thing. Every time we turn the water into the pool, it costs us a fortune.

ONDINE. But this will cost you nothing.

THE CHAMBERLAIN. Please don't insist. There is absolutely no precedent for a court reception in the water.

ONDINE. But I am so much more at ease in the water.

THE CHAMBERLAIN. I am not.

ONDINE. You would be. You especially. Your palm is damp. In the water, it wouldn't show.

THE CHAMBERLAIN. I beg your pardon. My palm is not damp.

ONDINE. Oh, it is. Touch it and you will see.

THE CHAMBERLAIN. Madame, do you feel strong enough to listen for a moment to a word of advice which will help you to avoid a great deal of trouble in the future?

ONDINE. Oh yes.

THE CHAMBERLAIN. To listen without interrupting?

ONDINE. Oh, I shouldn't dream of interrupting.

THE CHAMBERLAIN. Splendid. Now, in the first place—the court is a sacred precinct—

ONDINE. Excuse me just one moment. [*She goes to the place where* BERTRAM *is hidden and fetches him out.*] What is your name? You?

BERTRAM. Bertram.

ONDINE. You are the poet, are you not?

BERTRAM. So they say.

ONDINE. You are not beautiful.

BERTRAM. They say that too. But usually they whisper it.

ONDINE. Writing doesn't improve the appearance?

BERTRAM. Oh yes. I used to be much uglier. [ONDINE *laughs and goes back to* THE CHAMBERLAIN. BERTRAM *stands by.*]

ONDINE. Excuse me.

THE CHAMBERLAIN. [*Controlling himself.*] As I was saying. The court is a sacred precinct in which it is necessary for a man at all times to control—his face and his tongue. Here, when a man is afraid, he seems brave. When he lies, he seems frank. It is quite appropriate also, if by chance one is telling the truth, to appear to be lying. It inspires confidence.

ONDINE. I see.

THE CHAMBERLAIN. Let us take the example that you in your innocence bring up. It is true, my palm perspires. Ever since I was a child it has caused me infinite embarrassment. But damp as my hand is, my arm is long. It reaches to the throne. To displease me is to put oneself in jeopardy—and it does not please me to hear any mention of my physical shortcomings, to be precise, of my sole physical shortcoming. And now, lovely Ondine, tell me, as a sophisticated court lady, how is my hand, damp or dry?

ONDINE. Damp. Like your feet.

THE CHAMBERLAIN. What?

ONDINE. Just a moment. Do you mind?

THE CHAMBERLAIN. I mind very much! [ONDINE *crosses once more to the poet, who comes this time to meet her.*]

ONDINE. What was the first poem you ever wrote?

BERTRAM. The most beautiful.

ONDINE. The most beautiful of your poems?

BERTRAM. The most beautiful of all poems. It so far surpassed the others as you, Ondine, surpass all women.

ONDINE. Tell it to me quickly.

BERTRAM. I don't remember it. It came to me in a dream. When I awoke, it was gone.

ONDINE. You should have written it down sooner.

BERTRAM. I did. Even a little too soon. I was still dreaming when I wrote it. [ONDINE *smiles and leaves him. She joins* THE CHAMBERLAIN *who is fuming.*]

ONDINE. Yes, your Excellency?

THE CHAMBERLAIN. [*With a prodigious effort.*] My lady, let us admit that the

Lord Chamberlain's palm is damp, and let's admit that he admits it. But tell me this—would you tell his Majesty that his hand was damp?

ONDINE. Oh no!

THE CHAMBERLAIN. Ah, bravo! And why not?

ONDINE. Because it's not.

THE CHAMBERLAIN. But I put you a case where it is! Look here, my girl, suppose his Majesty should question you about the wart on his nose. And his Majesty, believe me, has a wart on his nose. And for heaven's sake don't make me shout. It is death to mention it. No one ever has. Now— suppose he asked you what his wart resembled?

ONDINE. Is it usual for a monarch who meets a lady for the first time to ask her what his wart resembles?

THE CHAMBERLAIN. My dear girl, I am putting you a hypothetical case. In the event that you had a wart on your nose—

ONDINE. I shall never have a wart on my nose.

THE CHAMBERLAIN. The girl is impossible!

ONDINE. Warts come from touching frogs. Did you know that?

THE CHAMBERLAIN. No.

BERTRAM. [*Coming forward.*] Madame, the Lord Chamberlain is merely trying to tell you that it is inconsiderate to remind people of their ugliness.

ONDINE. It is inconsiderate of them to be ugly. Why should they be ugly?

THE CHAMBERLAIN. Courtesy is an investment, my dear girl. When you grow old, in your turn, people will tell you, out of courtesy, that you look distinguished. When you grow ugly, they will say that you look interesting. And all this in return for a tiny payment on your part now.

ONDINE. I don't need to make it. I shall never grow old.

THE CHAMBERLAIN. What a child you are!

ONDINE. Yes. Excuse me a moment. [*She*

goes to BERTRAM.]

THE CHAMBERLAIN. [*Exasperated.*] Ondine!

ONDINE. I like you, Bertram.

BERTRAM. I'm delighted. But the Chamberlain is annoyed.

ONDINE. Oh dear. [*She goes back to* THE CHAMBERLAIN.] I'm sorry.

THE CHAMBERLAIN. [*A bit stiffly.*] There is just time now for me to instruct you on the question that his Majesty asks of every debutante at court. It has to do with the sixth labor of Hercules. Hercules, as you know, is his Majesty's name—he is Hercules the Sixth. Now listen carefully.

ONDINE. [*Taking a little step toward* BERTRAM.] If I could just—

THE CHAMBERLAIN. Madame, his Majesty is almost here. When he asks you about the sixth labor of Hercules— [*A flourish of trumpets at some little distance.*] Too late.

HANS *enters angrily.*

HANS. Excellency—

ONDINE. Don't interrupt, Hans. His Excellency is speaking.

HANS. What does this mean, Excellency? Have you put me below the Margrave of Salm?

THE CHAMBERLAIN. Yes, Knight.

HANS. I am entitled to the third rank below the king and the silver fork.

THE CHAMBERLAIN. You were. And even to the first, and even to the golden fork, if a certain project had materialized as we expected. But your present marriage assigns you to the fourteenth place and the pewter spoon.

HANS. The fourteenth place!

ONDINE. What difference does it make, Hans? I've been to the kitchen. I'm sure there's enough for all. [BERTRAM *laughs.*]

HANS. And why are you laughing, Bertram?

BERTRAM. I am laughing because my heart is gay.

ONDINE. You don't wish to stop him from laughing, Hans?

HANS. He's laughing at you.

ONDINE. He's laughing at me because he likes me.

BERTRAM. That's very true, Madame.

HANS. My wife must provoke no laughter of any description.

THE CHAMBERLAIN. Gentlemen! Gentlemen!

ONDINE. He won't laugh if you don't like it. He has no desire to displease me. Have you, Bertram?

BERTRAM. My only wish is to please you, madame.

ONDINE. Don't be angry with my husband, Bertram. It's flattering that he should be so scrupulous on my account. Don't you think so?

BERTRAM. We all envy him the privilege.

HANS. [*Belligerently.*] Thanks very much.

ONDINE. Don't show your nervousness, Hans. Be like me. I'm trembling. But an earthquake could not shake this smile from my lips.

Meanwhile people have streamed in from all sides. THE ILLUSIONIST *comes up to* ONDINE.

THE ILLUSIONIST. Ondine—

ONDINE. What are you doing here?

THE ILLUSIONIST. I am furnishing the entertainment. Pardon the intrusion.

ONDINE. Yes. On one condition. Go away.

THE ILLUSIONIST. If you like. But in a little while, you will call me back, Ondine. [*He walks off. There is another flourish of trumpets near at hand. The* CHAMBERLAIN *takes his place at the door. He strikes the floor with his staff three times.*]

THE CHAMBERLAIN. His Majesty, the King!

The KING *enters, bowing.*

THE KING. Hail, Knight von Wittenstein.

HANS. Your Majesty. [*The* KING *mounts his throne.*]

THE CHAMBERLAIN. [*Advancing with* ONDINE.] Your Majesty, with your gracious permission, may I present the Lady von Wittenstein zu Wittenstein.

THE KING. Madame.

ONDINE. My name is Ondine. [BERTHA *takes her place on the lower step of the dais.* ONDINE *looks at no one else.*]

THE CHAMBERLAIN. [*Whispers.*] Your curtsey, madame. [ONDINE *curtseys, with her eyes still on* BERTHA.]

THE KING. We receive you with pleasure, dear child, in this gallery which is called the Hall of Hercules. I love Hercules. Of all my many names, his is by far my favorite, and of course the one by which I am known. The resemblance between Hercules and myself has been noticed by everyone, ever since I was a little child, and I must confess that at work or at play I have tried to emulate him in everything. And speaking of work—you know, I presume, how many labors Hercules brought to a successful conclusion?

THE CHAMBERLAIN. [*Whispers.*] Twelve.

ONDINE. [*Without taking her eyes from* BERTHA's *face.*] Twelve.

THE KING. Twelve. Exactly. The Lord Chamberlain prompts a little loudly, but your voice is delightful. It will be a little more difficult for him to whisper in your ear the complete description of the sixth labor, but he won't have to. If you lift your eyes, you will see it depicted on the wall. Look. Who is this woman who is trying to seduce Hercules, with a smile on her lips and a lie in her heart? Her name, my dear?

ONDINE. Bertha.

THE KING. I beg pardon?

ONDINE. [*Taking a step toward* BERTHA.] You shall never have him, Bertha!

BERTHA. What?

ONDINE. He will never be yours, Bertha. Never!

THE KING. Is the girl quite well?

THE CHAMBERLAIN. Madame, His Majesty is addressing you.

ONDINE. If you say a word to him, if you dare to touch him, I'll kill you!

HANS. Ondine!

BERTHA. The girl is mad!

ONDINE. Majesty, I'm frightened! I beg

you, save us!

THE KING. Save you from what, my child?

HANS. Your Majesty, she's not used to the court.

ONDINE. You, be quiet. You don't see what's happening? Oh, King, isn't it a pity? You have a husband for whose sake you'd give up anything in the world. He's strong—he's brave—he's handsome—

HANS. Ondine, for heaven's sake!

ONDINE. I know what I'm saying. You're stupid, but you're handsome. It's no secret—all the women know it. And they say, what a lucky thing it is for us that being so handsome, he's so stupid! Because he's so handsome, how sweet it will be to take him in our arms. And how easy—since he's so stupid. Because he's so handsome, he will give us such joy as our husbands can never give us. And this, without the slightest danger to ourselves—since he's so stupid.

BERTRAM. Bravo!

ONDINE. I am right, am I not, Bertram?

HANS. Ondine, please! And you—what do you mean by saying, Bravo?

BERTRAM. When I say Bravo, Knight, I mean Bravo.

THE KING. That's quite enough, Count Bertram.

THE CHAMBERLAIN. [*Intervening suavely.*] Your Majesty, I had hoped to offer by way of interlude, a little diversion—

BERTHA. His Majesty is sufficiently diverted. His adopted daughter has been insulted before all the court by a peasant!

HANS. Majesty, permit us to take our leave. I have an adorable wife, but she is not like other women. She is very innocent, and she says whatever comes into her head. I humbly beg your forgiveness.

ONDINE. You see, King? You see what's happening?

THE KING. Bertha is the soul of sweetness. She wants only to be your

friend—

ONDINE. You're entirely mistaken!

HANS. Ondine!

ONDINE. You think it's sweet to kill a bird?

THE KING. Bird? What bird? Why should Bertha kill a bird?

ONDINE. To trouble Hans. To bring him to his knees. To make him beg her pardon.

BERTHA. The bird was in my hand, Majesty. He pressed my hand so hard that the bird was killed.

ONDINE. He did not. A woman's hand, no matter how soft, becomes a shell of iron when it protects a living thing. If the bird were in my hand, Your Majesty, Hercules himself could press with all his strength and never hurt it. But Bertha knows men. These knights whom dragons cannot frighten grow faint at the death of a bird. The bird was alive in her hand. She killed it.

HANS. It was I who pressed her hand.

ONDINE. It was she who killed it.

THE KING. Ondine, my dear, I want you to be Bertha's friend.

ONDINE. If you wish. On condition she stops shouting.

HANS. But she hasn't said a word, Ondine.

THE KING. She really hasn't.

ONDINE. Are you deaf? Don't you hear? She says that a week of this foolishness will cost me my husband, and a month will cost me my life, that all she needs to do is to wait and I shall vanish. That's what your soul of sweetness is saying. Oh Hans, take me in your arms, here, now, before her eyes, or we are lost forever!

HANS. You forget where you are, Ondine.

ONDINE. The bird is alive, Hans. I wouldn't let it die.

BERTHA. She is out of her mind. The bird is dead.

ONDINE. Go and see if you don't believe me. You killed it. I brought it to life. Which of us is out of her mind?

THE KING. You brought the bird back to life, you say?

ONDINE. Yes, King. Now do you see what a hypocrite she is?

HE KING. Bertha is no hypocrite, Ondine.

ONDINE. She is. She calculates her every word. She flatters you constantly.

THE KING. Nonsense, my dear.

ONDINE. Has she ever dared to speak to you about—

THE KING. About my descent from Hercules on the sinister side? Do you think that makes me blush?

ONDINE. No. About the wart on your nose.

THE KING. [Rises.] What? [General consternation. VIOLANTE faints and is carried out.] Leave us, all of you.

THE CHAMBERLAIN. Clear the room! Clear the room! [All leave, with the exception of the KING and ONDINE.]

THE KING. Ondine!

ONDINE. [Desperately.] If you ask me what it resembles, it resembles a flower, a mountain. It resembles a cathedral. Hercules had two in exactly the same place, one alongside of the other. They were called the Pillars of Hercules.

THE KING. Ondine!

ONDINE. He got them by touching the Hydra. He had to touch the Hydra, naturally, in order to strangle it. It was his fifth labor.

THE KING. [Sitting down again.] My little Ondine, I like you very much. It's a rare pleasure to hear a voice like yours at court, even when this voice insists on discussing my wart—which, incidentally, I do inherit from Hercules, precisely as you say. But, for your own sake—tell me the truth.

ONDINE. Yes. Yes, I shall tell you the truth.

THE KING. Who are you?

ONDINE. I belong to the water. I am an Ondine.

THE KING. How old are you?

ONDINE. Sixteen. But I was born many ages ago. And I shall never die.

THE KING. What are you doing here? Does our world attract you?

ONDINE. From the water it seems so beautiful.

THE KING. And from the land?

ONDINE. There are ways to have water before one's eyes always.

THE KING. It is in order to make the world seem beautiful that you are weeping?

ONDINE. No. It's because they wish to take Hans away from me.

THE KING. And suppose they do? Would that be so great a misfortune?

ONDINE. Oh yes. If he deceives me, he will die.

THE KING. Don't worry, my dear. Men have been known to survive under those conditions.

ONDINE. Not this one.

THE KING. And what makes you think that Hans will deceive you?

ONDINE. I don't know. But they knew it the moment they saw him. Isn't it strange? The lake had never known deceit, not even the sound of the word. Then one day there appeared on its banks a handsome man with a loyal face and an honest voice, and that very moment the word deceit thrilled through the depths.

THE KING. Poor Ondine!

ONDINE. It's because your world is inverted in ours. All the things that I trust in Hans—his straight look, his clear words—to the water they seem crooked and cunning. He said he would love me always—and the water said, he deceives you!

THE KING. The water speaks?

ONDINE. Everything in the universe speaks, even the fish. Each time I left the cottage that night, they spat the word at me. He is beautiful, I said. Yes, said the bass, he will deceive you. He is strong, I said. Yes, said the perch, he will deceive you. Are you fond of perch, by any chance?

THE KING. I have no particular feeling about them.

ONDINE. Spiteful little things! But I was

proud of him. I decided to take the risk. I made the pact.

THE KING. The pact? What pact?

ONDINE. The king, my uncle, said to me, you agree that he shall die if he deceives you? What could I answer?

THE KING. But he hasn't deceived you—yet.

ONDINE. But he is a man. He will. And then he will die.

THE KING. A king's memory is short. Your uncle will forget.

ONDINE. No.

THE KING. But, after all, what power has your uncle over him? What danger is he in?

ONDINE. Whatever is wave or water is angry with him. If he goes near a well, the level rises. When it rains, the water drenches him to the skin. Wherever he goes, the water reaches after him.

THE KING. Will you take my advice, little Ondine?

ONDINE. Yes.

THE KING. Go away, my dear.

ONDINE. With Hans?

THE KING. Dive into the first river you come to, and vanish forever.

ONDINE. But he's so clumsy in the water.

THE KING. You have had three months of happiness with Hans. In our world, that is a lifetime. Go while there is time.

ONDINE. Without Hans?

THE KING. He's not for you. His soul is small.

ONDINE. I have no soul.

THE KING. Because you don't need one. You are a soul. But human souls are tiny. There is no man whose soul is great enough for you.

ONDINE. I wouldn't love him if there were. I have already seen men with great souls—they are completely wrapped up in them. No, the only men whom one can love are those who are just like other men, whose thoughts are the thoughts of other men, who are distinguished from other men only by being themselves and nothing more.

THE KING. You are describing Hans.

ONDONE. Yes. That is Hans.

THE KING. But don't you see, my dear, that Hans loves what is great in you only because he sees it small? You are the sunlight; he loves a blonde. You are grace itself; he loves a madcap. You are adventure; he loves an adventure. One day he will see his mistake—and at that moment, you will lose him.

ONDINE. He will never see it. If it were Bertram, he would see it. Not Hans.

THE KING. If you wish to save him, leave him.

ONDINE. But I cannot save him by leaving him. If I leave him, they will say he deceived me, and Hans will die. No, it's here that I must save him. Here.

THE KING. And how will you do that, my little Ondine?

ONDINE. I have the remedy. It came to me while I was quarreling with Bertha. Did you notice—each time I came between Hans and Bertha, I succeeded only in bringing them more closely together. The instant I said something against Bertha, he sprang to her defense. Very well, from now on I shall do exactly the opposite. I shall tell him twenty times a day how beautiful Bertha is, how right she is. Then she will be wrong. I shall manage so that they are always alone. Then they will no longer feel the slightest desire for each other. In that way, with Bertha always there, I shall have Hans completely to myself. Oh, how well I understand men! Don't I? [*The* KING *rises and kisses her.*] Oh, Your Majesty! What are you doing?

THE KING. The king thanks you, my child.

ONDINE. Thanks me? For what?

THE KING. For a lesson in true love.

ONDINE. My idea is good?

THE KING. Stupendous.

Enter the CHAMBERLAIN.

THE CHAMBERLAIN. Forgive me, Your Majesty. The court is in complete consternation. What is your will? Shall I tell them all to withdraw?

THE KING. By no means.

THE CHAMBERLAIN. The reception is to continue?

THE KING. Of course.

THE CHAMBERLAIN. And the interlude? You wish to see it?

THE KING. At once.

ONDINE. How wonderful! Now I shall be able to ask Bertha's pardon before everyone. [*The* CHAMBERLAIN *goes to the door and waves his staff. The* COURT *comes in from all sides.* BERTHA *takes her place, haughtily.*]

THE KING. Princess Bertha, Ondine has something to say to you.

ONDINE. I ask your pardon, Bertha.

THE KING. Very nice, my child.

ONDINE. Yes. But she might answer me.

HANS. What?

ONDINE. I have asked her pardon, though I don't want it. She might at least answer me.

THE KING. Bertha, Ondine has acknowledged her error, whatever it was. I should like you to be friends.

BERTHA. Very well, Your Majesty. I pardon her.

ONDINE. Thank you, Bertha.

BERTHA. On condition that she admits publicly that I did not kill the bird.

ONDINE. I admit it publicly. She did not kill the bird. The bird is alive—you can hear it singing. But she tried to kill it.

BERTHA. You see, Your Majesty?

HANS. One doesn't speak like that to the royal princess, Ondine!

ONDINE. The royal princess? Would you like to know who she is, this royal princess? Shall I show you? Shall I?

HANS. Silence, Ondine.

ONDINE. I happen to know the father of this royal princess. He is not a king. He is a fisherman—

BERTHA. Hans!

HANS. Ondine. You've said enough. [*He takes* ONDINE *by the wrist.*] Come.

ONDINE. [*Resisting.*] Not yet, Hans!

HANS. Come, I say!

ONDINE. Old One! Old One! Help me!

The ILLUSIONIST *appears. He is followed by the* CHAMBERLAIN.

THE ILLUSIONIST. Your Majesty, the interlude.

THE KING. [*As they seat themselves.*] Yes, Ondine, you have gone too far. Everyone knows there was a golden crown on Bertha's pillow when she was found.

ONDINE. The crown was mine! [*The lights go out, and come up immediately on a little set on the garden level. It depicts the fisherman's cottage on the edge of the lake. Two* ONDINES *are dancing in the waterfall. An* ONDINE *comes in with a child in its arms. The others join her as she puts the child into a basket which she covers with rich silks.*]

THE ONDINE. [*Sings.*]
Wrap the child in silk and lace
So the princess of the sea
May be nurtured in her place
By Auguste and Eugenie.

At this moment the burly tenor dressed as MATHO *and the robust soprano dressed as* SALAMMBO *advance to either side of the set and begin singing loudly. The* ONDINES *stop in astonishment.*

MATHO. [*Sings.*] I am a soldier, that is all.

SALAMMBO. [*Sings.*] And I the niece of Hannibal. [*The* ILLUSIONIST *steps forward.*]

THE ILLUSIONIST. Who are these people, Excellency? They have nothing to do with my show.

MATHO. [*Sings.*] I am a common mercenary.

SALAMMBO. I stand at the other pole.

MATHO. But I love this sacred person.

SALAMMBO. I adore this humble soul.

THE ILLUSIONIST. Where did they come from? What are they singing?

THE CHAMBERLAIN. *Salammbo.*

THE ILLUSIONIST. But they're spoiling the illusion. Tell them to stop.

THE CHAMBERLAIN. Impossible. Once they begin, nothing can stop them.

SALAMMBO. [*Sings.*] Take me, take me, and Carthage too.

THE ILLUSIONIST. Enough! [*He makes a gesture. The two singers continue singing and posturing, but without a sound. The ONDINES resume.*]

FIRST ONDINE. [*Sings.*]
Set the little creature down,
Whom we stole from Eugenie,
And beside her set the crown
Of the princess of the sea.

SECOND ONDINE. [*Sings.*]
Weep not, we shall not forsake you,
Helpless, human little thing,
Soon a knight will come and take you
To the palace of the king.

THIRD ONDINE. [*Sings.*]
But lest it ever be forgotten
Who she is and whence begotten,
On her skin I draw the sign
Of her father's hook and line.

The ONDINES turn toward BERTHA and sing together.

THE ONDINES.
Bertha, Bertha, if you dare,
Show the world your shoulder bare!

The lights go on suddenly; the fisherman's cottage and the ONDINES vanish. Hubbub. BERTHA is on her feet.

ONDINE. Well, Bertha?

BERTHA. It's a lie!

ONDINE. Is it? [*She tears the dress from BERTHA's shoulders. The sign is there.*] You see! [*BERTHA kneels before the KING.*]

MATHO. } [*Suddenly audible, they walk
SALAMMBO. } off together, singing.*]
All is love beneath the stars,
Is love, is love, is love!

BERTHA. It's a lie! [*She kneels before the KING.*] It's a lie, Your Majesty. [*The KING glances at her shoulder on which the mark is visible.*]

THE KING. Is this true, Ondine?

ONDINE. Yes, King.

BERTHA. [*Desperately.*] Hans! [*HANS makes a protecting gesture.*]

ONDINE. Old One! Where are they? [*The ILLUSIONIST lifts a hand. AUGUSTE and EUGENIE appear. They see BERTHA.*] Oh, my darlings!

THE KING. Bertha, it is your father. Have you no word to say to him, to your mother! [*BERTHA is silent.*] As you *please.* . . . [*AUGUSTE and EUGENIE go. The KING walks off. The court follows slowly.*] But—[*He stops.*]—until you have asked their pardon, I forbid you to show your face at court. [*He goes off, followed by the court. BERTHA is left sobbing bitterly.*]

ONDINE. Forgive me, Bertha. [*There is no answer.*] You will see. The king will call you back in a moment. And they will all love you more than before. [*BERTHA says nothing.*] Ask her to come and stay with us, Hans.

HANS. Bertha. Come with us. [*BERTHA turns silently.*]

ONDINE. Oh, how difficult it is to live among you, where what has happened can never again not have happened! How terrible to live where a word can never be unspoken and a gesture can never be unmade! But I will undo it all. You will see.

HANS. Come with us, Bertha. My castle is large. You shall live with us always, in the wing that looks out on the lake.

ONDINE. A lake? Your castle has a lake, Hans?

HANS. It has a lake. The other side faces the Rhine.

ONDINE. The Rhine?

The CHAMBERLAIN comes in.

THE CHAMBERLAIN. The king wishes to know whether the pardon has been asked.

ONDINE. It has been asked. From the heart.

THE CHAMBERLAIN. In that case, Princess—

ONDINE. Oh Hans, haven't you a castle in the plains, in the mountains far from the water?

THE CHAMBERLAIN. Princess Bertha, the king desires your presence. He forgives you.

ONDINE. You see?

HANS. Tell him we have asked you to come with us.

ONDINE. He already knows that.
[BERTHA *and the* CHAMBERLAIN *go out.* HANS *and* ONDINE *cross in the direction of the garden.*]

HANS. [*As they pass the fountain.*] And why all this fear of the water? What is it that threatens you from the water?

ONDINE. Me? Nothing.

HANS. If I sit down at the edge of a brook, you drag me away. If I walk near a pond, you come between us. What is it you fear?

ONDINE. Nothing, Hans.

HANS. Yes, Ondine, my castle is surrounded by water. And in the mornings, I shall bathe under my waterfall, and at noon I shall fish in my lake, and in the evening I shall swim in the Rhine. You don't frighten me with these tales about the water. What's water? Can it see? Can it hear? [*As he passes, the jets of water rise high and threatening over their basins. The* ILLUSIONIST *appears.*]

ONDINE. Yes, Hans. [*They go. The* CHAMBERLAIN *comes out from behind his column, and a moment later, the* SUPERINTENDENT, *the* TRAINER, BERTRAM *and the* TWO LADIES *come out of hiding.*]

THE CHAMBERLAIN. Wonderful! Wonderful! [*To the* ILLUSIONIST.] Very nice indeed.

THE SUPERINTENDENT. Wonderful!

VIOLANTE. But is all this really going to happen?

THE ILLUSIONIST. My dear, it has happened.

THE CHAMBERLAIN. And what happens next, Magician?

THE COURT. Yes. What next?

THE CHAMBERLAIN. Does he decide to marry Bertha?

THE COURT. Does he?

THE CHAMBERLAIN. Does he deceive Ondine?

THE COURT. Does he?

THE ILLUSIONIST. Naturally.

THE CHAMBERLAIN. When can we see that?

THE ILLUSIONIST. At once, if you like.

THE CHAMBERLAIN. Splendid. Let's see

it. [*He goes behind his column.*] Go on.

BERTRAM. No, Excellency. No.

THE CHAMBERLAIN. Yes, yes. Go on. Go on. But what's this? What's happened? [*He comes out.*] I'm bald?

THE ILLUSIONIST. Five years have passed.

THE CHAMBERLAIN. My teeth are gone? I'm stuttering?

THE ILLUSIONIST. Shall I continue?

THE CHAMBERLAIN. No. No, for heavens sake! An intermission! An intermission!

Act 3

The courtyard of the castle of the Wittenstein. The yard is surrounded on three sides by the walls of the castle. Arched doorways lead into it. At one side there is a platform with a well.

It is the morning of the marriage of BERTHA *and* HANS. *There is a sound of church bells from the chapel.* HANS, *splendidly dressed, is sitting on the platform steps with his head in his hands. A* SERVANT ENTERS.

THE SERVANT. My lord, the choir has filed into the chancel.

HANS. What did you say?

THE SERVANT. I refer to the choir which will sing at your wedding.

HANS. Do you have to use this pompous tone? Can't you talk like a human being?

BERTHA *comes in. She too is dressed for a wedding.*

THE SERVANT. Long life to the bride! To the Lady Bertha!

HANS. Oh. Go away!

BERTHA. But, Hans, why are you angry on the day of our wedding?

HANS. What? You too?

BERTHA. I had hoped that your face would be radiant with joy.

HANS. Stop it, stop it! Stop it!

BERTHA. Hans, really!

HANS. I'm lost, Bertha! I'm lost!

BERTHA. Hans, you frighten me. You're so strange today.

HANS. There is a tradition in our family, Bertha. Whenever misfortune threatens, the servants feel it before anyone else, and they begin to speak all at once in solemn language. On the day of misfortune, the kitchen maids are filled with grandeur. The swineherds see what they never saw before. They speak of the curve of the stream; the shape of the flower fills them with awe; they exclaim with wonder at the honeycomb. They speak of nature, of the soul of man. They become poets. That day, misfortune strikes.

BERTHA. But the man wasn't speaking in poetry, Hans. There were no rhymes.

HANS. When I hear him speak in rhymes, I shall know that death is at hand.

BERTHA. Oh Hans, that's superstitious!

HANS. You think?

BERTHA. This is not the day of your death, Hans. It is the day of your wedding.

HANS. [*He calls.*] Walter! [*The* SERVANT *enters.*] Where is the swineherd?

THE SERVANT. Under a spreading oak—

HANS. Hold your tongue.

THE SERVANT. On a grassy bank he lies—

HANS. Go fetch him. Quickly. [*The* SERVANT *goes out.* BERTHA *takes* HANS *in her arms.*]

BERTHA. Oh Hans, my dear, I love you.

HANS. [*Absently.*] You're good to me, Bertha.

BERTHA. You are holding me in your arms, Hans, but you are not thinking of me. What are you thinking?

HANS. I was weak, Bertha. I should have made her confess. I should have made her suffer as she made me suffer.

BERTHA. Can't you put her out of your mind, Hans? Not even today?

HANS. Today less than any other. Oh, Bertha, you should have married a man full of joy and pride. And look at me! Oh, Bertha, how she lied to me, that woman!

BERTHA. She never lied to you, Hans. She was no woman. You married a creature of another world. You married an Ondine. You must forget her.

HANS. If she would only let me forget her! But that cry that awakened me the morning she left—"I have deceived you with Bertram!" Has it stopped echoing for even a moment? Does one hear anything else from the river, from the lake? Does the waterfall ever stop dinning it in my ears? Day and night, in the castle, in the city, from the fountains, from the wells—it's deafening! But why does she insist on proclaiming to the world that she deceived me with Bertram? [*An echo comes from the well.*]

THE ECHO. Deceived you with Bertram. [*Another echo whispers from the right.*] With Bertram. [*From the left.*] With Bertram.

HANS. You hear? You hear?

BERTHA. Let's be just, Hans. You had already deceived her with me. And of course she knew it. It was only in revenge that she deceived you with Bertram.

THE ECHOES. [*Whisper back.*] Deceived you with Bertram. With Bertram.

HANS. Where is she now, Bertha? What is she doing? In the six months since she left, every huntsman, every fisherman in the region has been trying to find her. You would say she had vanished. And yet she's not far off. This morning at dawn they found a wreath of starfish and sea urchins on the chapel door. She put it there, of course. You know that.

BERTHA. Oh, my darling, who would have thought that you of all men would have seen anything in a girl like Ondine? When I sent you into the forest, I thought, this man will surely come back. He will look carefully, right and left, but he will never find an enchanted lake, nor the cave of a dragon, he will never glimpse among the trees at twilight the white forehead of a unicorn. He has nothing to do in that world. He will follow the human path. He will not lose his way.

HANS. I lost it.

BERTHA. Yes, but you found it again. It was in the fifth year of your marriage, that night in the winter when you told me it was me you had always loved, and I ran away from you, and you followed my tracks in the snow. They were deep and wide. They spoke plainly of my distress. They were not the tracks of a spirit. They were human tracks, and you found them, and once more you found your way. You carried me back in your arms that night.

HANS. Yes. Like Bertram when he carried away Ondine. [*The* SERVANT *enters.*] Where is the swineherd?

THE SERVANT. In the shadow of an oak, by the banks of a stream—

HANS. Well?

THE SERVANT. I called him, but he did not answer. He is gazing at the sky. He is looking at the clouds.

HANS. Never mind. Fetch me the kitchen maid.

THE SERVANT. There is a fisherman to see you, my lord.

HANS. Get me the kitchen maid at once, do you hear, no matter what she's gazing at.

THE SERVANT. Yes, my lord. The fisherman. [*The* SERVANT *goes. The* FISHERMAN *comes in.*]

FIRST FISHERMAN. My lord! My lord!

HANS. Say it twice more and it's poetry.

FIRST FISHERMAN. We have her! She's caught.

HANS. Ondine?

FIRST FISHERMAN. Yes. Yes. An Ondine!

BERTHA. Are you sure?

HANS. Where did you catch her?

FIRST FISHERMAN. In the Rhine. In my net.

HANS. You're sure it's she?

FIRST FISHERMAN. Positive. Her hair was over her face, but her voice was marvelous, her skin like velvet. She's wonderfully formed, the little monster.

The SECOND FISHERMAN *appears.*

SECOND FISHERMAN. Prepare yourself. The judges are coming.

BERTHA. Judges?

HANS. What judges?

SECOND FISHERMAN. The Imperial and Episcopal judges who have jurisdiction over the supernatural.

BERTHA. So soon?

SECOND FISHERMAN. They were already holding assizes below in the city.

FIRST FISHERMAN. They came from Bingen, you see, to hang a werewolf. Now they will try the Ondine.

BERTHA. But why must they try her here?

FIRST FISHERMAN. Because an Ondine must be tried on a rock.

SECOND FISHERMAN. And besides, you are the complainant.

HANS. That's true.

BERTHA. Don't they know what day this is? Couldn't they try her another time?

SECOND FISHERMAN. My lady, the trial must be now.

HANS. They're right, Bertha. The trial must be now.

BERTHA. Hans—don't see her again. I beg you.

HANS. I shall never see her again. You heard what he said—he caught an Ondine in the Rhine. What I shall see won't even know me.

BERTHA. Don't look at her, Hans.

THE SERVANT. [*Comes in.*] The judges my lord.

HANS. Just a few minutes more, Bertha, and we shall be at peace.

THE FISHERMEN. The Judges.

The JUDGES *come in, puffing a little. They are followed by an* ANCIENT CLERK *with a great book.*

FIRST JUDGE. Marvelous! The exact altitude. Just above the realm of the water. Just below the realm of the

air. It couldn't be better. [*He bows to*
BERTHA.] My lady. Our felicitations.
SECOND JUDGE. Our compliments, my
lord.
BERTHA. I shall be within call, Hans, if
you want me.
BERTHA *goes out.*
HANS. You come in the nick of time,
gentlemen. But how did you know
there was work for you here?
FIRST JUDGE. Our work gives us a degree of insight unknown to our
colleagues in the civil and criminal
law.
SECOND JUDGE. It is also more difficult.
[*The* SERVANTS *arrange the court. The*
CLERK *sits down, opens his register and
sharpens his quill.*]
FIRST JUDGE. To determine the line that
divides two vineyards is easy. But to
fix the proper boundaries between
humanity and the spirits, *hoc opus,
hic*—excuse me—*hic labor est.*
SECOND JUDGE. But in the case at hand,
our task appears to be easy.
FIRST JUDGE. It is the first time we have
tried an Ondine who does not deny
being an Ondine.
SECOND JUDGE. All the more reason to
be careful.
FIRST JUDGE. Quite right, my dear colleague.
SECOND JUDGE. You have no idea of the
subterfuges these creatures use to
elude our investigations. The salamanders pretend to be Ondines. The
Ondines pretend to be salamanders.
[*He sits down.*]
FIRST JUDGE. Excuse me.
SECOND JUDGE. You remember, my dear
colleague, that affair at Kreiznach,
when we tried the pretended Dor-
othea, the alderman's cook? She gave
us every eason to believe she was a
salamander. But we didn't jump to
conclusions. We put her to the torch
to make sure. She burnt to a crisp.
FIRST JUDGE. [*Smiles reminiscently.*] She
was no more salamander than I am.
[*He sits down.*]
SECOND JUDGE. She was an Ondine.

FIRST JUDGE. We had a similar case last
week, the matter of a certain
Gertrude, a blonde barmaid of
Tübingen. It was clearly established
that in her presence the beer glasses
filled by themselves and, what is even
more miraculous, without heads of
foam. You would have been certain
she was an Ondine. We threw her
into the water with her hands tied—
SECOND JUDGE. She immediately
drowned.
FIRST JUDGE. [*He shrugs.*] A salamander.
HANS. Did you bring Ondine with you?
FIRST JUDGE. We have her in custody.
But before we examine her, Knight,
it would be extremely valuable for us
to ascertain the exact nature of your
complaint.
HANS. My complaint? My complaint is
the complaint of all mankind. Is it so
much after all that God has granted
us, these few yards of air between
hell and heaven? Is it so attractive,
after all, this bit of life we have, with
these hands that get dirty, these teeth
that fall out, this hair that turns gray?
Why must these creatures trespass on
our little world? Gentlemen, on the
morning of my marriage, I claim the
right to be left in peace in a world
that is free of these intrusions, these
threats, these seductions, alone with
myself, with my bride, alone at last.
FIRST JUDGE. That is a great deal to ask,
Knight.
SECOND JUDGE. Yes. It may seem surprising that these creatures should
derive all their satisfaction from staring at us while we wash our feet, kiss
our wives, or beat our children. But
that is the undeniable fact. Around
each human gesture, the meanest,
the noblest, a host of grotesque pres-
ences with tails and horns is
constantly dancing its round. What's
to be done? We must resign ourselves.
HANS. Has there never been an age
when they did not infest us?
SECOND JUDGE. An age? To my knowl-

edge, Knight, there has never been a moment.

FIRST JUDGE. Yes, once there was a moment. One only. It was late August, near Augsburg, in the harvest season when the peasants were dancing. I had stretched out under an apple tree. I looked up into the sky. And suddenly I felt that the whole world was free of these shadows that beset it. Above my head I saw a lark soaring in the heavens—without its usual twin, the raven. Our Swabia spread to the Alps, green and blue, without my seeing over it the Swabia of the air, peopled with blue angels, nor below it the Swabia of hell, teeming with green devils. On the road there trotted a horseman with a lance, unattended by the horseman with the scythe. By the river, in the sun, the mill wheel turned slowly, without dragging in its orbit that enormous shadowy wheel that grinds the souls of the damned. For that instant, the whole world was singlehearted, at work, at play, at peace—and yet I tasted for the first time a certain loneliness, the loneliness of humanity. But the next moment, the horseman was joined by Death, the clouds bristled as always with lances and brooms, and the customary fish-headed devils had joined the dancing couples. There they were, all back at their posts again just as before. Bring in the accused.

ONDINE *is led in by the* EXECUTIONER. *She is nude, but draped around her body is the net in which she was caught. She is made to stand on a little elevation opposite the* JUDGES. *A number of people come in to witness the trial.*

SECOND JUDGE. [*Peering at her.*] Her hands are not webbed, apparently. She is wearing a ring.

HANS. Remove it.

ONDINE. No! [*The* EXECUTIONER *removes it by force and hands it to* HANS.]

HANS. It is my wedding ring. I shall need it presently.

FIRST JUDGE. Knight—

HANS. The necklace too. The locket has my picture in it.

ONDINE. No! [*The* EXECUTIONER *takes it off.*]

FIRST JUDGE. Knight, with all respect, I must ask you not to interfere with the conduct of this trial. Your anger is doubtless justified, but we must avoid even the semblance of confusion. We will proceed with the identification.

HANS. It is she.

FIRST JUDGE. Beyond a doubt. But we must follow the indicated procedure. Where is the fisherman who caught her? Summon the fisherman to the bar. [*The* FIRST FISHERMAN *takes the stand.*]

FIRST FISHERMAN. It's the first time I ever caught one, your honor. This is my lucky day!

FIRST JUDGE. Congratulations. Now— what was she doing when you caught her?

FIRST FISHERMAN. I knew that some day I'd catch one. I have known it every morning for the last thirty years. How often have I said—today I'm going to catch one. But this morning, I was certain.

FIRST JUDGE. I asked you what she was doing.

FIRST FISHERMAN. And, mind you, I caught her alive. The one they caught at Regensburg, they bashed its head in with an oar. But I was careful. I just knocked her head against the side of the boat a few times to stun her. Then I dragged her in.

HANS. You ox. You hurt her head.

FIRST JUDGE. Answer my questions. Was she swimming when you caught her?

FIRST FISHERMAN. She was swimming. She was showing her breasts, her buttocks. She can stay under a full fifteen minutes. I timed her.

FIRST JUDGE. Was she singing?

FIRST FISHERMAN. She was making a little sound, like a moan. If it was a dog, you'd call it a yelp, a bark. I remember what she was barking. She was barking: I deceived you with Bertram.

FIRST JUDGE. You're talking nonsense. Since when can you understand a bark?

FIRST FISHERMAN. As a rule, I don't. To me a bark is a bark, as a rule. But this one I understood. And what it said was—

FIRST JUDGE. She had an odor of sulphur when you pulled her out?

FIRST FISHERMAN. She had an odor of algae, of pine.

SECOND JUDGE. That's not the same thing. Did she have an odor of algae or an odor of pine?

FIRST FISHERMAN. She had an odor of algae, of pine.

FIRST JUDGE. Never mind, my dear colleague.

FIRST FISHERMAN. She had an odor that said plainly: I deceived you with Bertram.

FIRST JUDGE. Since when do odors speak?

FIRST FISHERMAN. Odors don't speak. But this one said—

FIRST JUDGE. She struggled, I presume?

FIRST FISHERMAN. No. Not at all. You might say, she let herself be caught. But when I had her in the boat, she shuddered. It was a sort of movement of the shoulders that said, as clear as clear can be: I deceived you with—

HANS. Have you quite finished, you idiot?

FIRST JUDGE. You must excuse the man, Knight. These simple souls are always imagining things. That is the origin of folklore.

FIRST FISHERMAN. I swear by all that's holy that that's one of them. I'm sorry about the tail. She didn't have it when I caught her. There's a double reward for catching them alive?

FIRST JUDGE. You may collect it after the trial. Very well, Fisherman. That's all.

FIRST FISHERMAN. And what about my net? Can I have my net back?

FIRST JUDGE. Your net is in evidence. It will be returned to you in due course.

SECOND JUDGE. Out you go.

The FISHERMAN *goes out, grumbling.*

FIRST JUDGE. Proceed with the examination. [*The* SECOND JUDGE *extends a very long telescope and focuses it on* ONDINE.]

HANS. What are you doing?

SECOND JUDGE. I am going to examine the body of this girl—

HANS. No one is going to examine her body!

FIRST JUDGE. Calm your fears, Knight. My colleague is an experienced anatomist. It was he who personally established the physical integrity of the Electress Josepha in connection with the annulment of her marriage, and she commented especially on his tact.

HANS. I tell you, this is Ondine. That's enough.

SECOND JUDGE. Knight, I understand that it is painful for you to have me oculate in public the body of someone who was once your wife. But I can, without touching her, study through the glass those parts which differentiate her species from the human race.

HANS. Never mind the glass. You can look at her from where you are.

SECOND JUDGE. To identify with the naked eye and from a distance the very subtle variations that distinguish an Ondine from a human being seems to me an extremely impractical operation. She could at least take off the net and walk a little. She could show us her legs?

HANS. She will do nothing of the sort.

FIRST JUDGE. It would perhaps be in better taste not to insist, my dear colleague. In any case, the evidence is sufficient. Is there anyone present who denies that this is an Ondine?

SECOND FISHERMAN. [*Without moving.*] I deny it.

FIRST JUDGE. Who said that? Remove that man.

THE SERVANT. Don't kill her, your honor. She was good to us.

SECOND JUDGE. [*Shrugs his shoulders.*] She was a good Ondine, that's all.

THE SERVANT. She loved us.

SECOND JUDGE. There are affectionate varieties even among turtles.

FIRST JUDGE. Since we hear no objection, we declare that the supernatural character of the accused has been established beyond a reasonable doubt. We proceed to the second part of the trial. Knight, do you accuse this creature, by reason of her illegal intrusion into our world, of having caused disorder and confusion in your domain?

HANS. I? Certainly not.

FIRST JUDGE. But you do accuse her of being a sorceress?

HANS. Ondine, a sorceress?

FIRST JUDGE. We are merely trying to define her crime, Knight.

SECOND FISHERMAN. [*Stepping forward.*] Ondine, a sorceress?

FIRST JUDGE. Who is this man?

SECOND FISHERMAN. I am a witness.

ONDINE. He's lying!

FIRST JUDGE. Ah. In that case, you may speak.

SECOND FISHERMAN. This Ondine is no longer an Ondine. She has renounced her race and betrayed its interests. She has become a woman.

FIRST JUDGE. A sorceress.

SECOND FISHERMAN. This woman could call upon the earth and the heavens to do her bidding. The Rhine is her servant. But she gave up her power in favor of such human specialties as hay fever, headaches and cooking. Is that true, Knight, or is it false?

FIRST JUDGE. You accuse her, if I understand correctly, of having taken on a favorable appearance in order to ferret out the secrets of the human race?

HANS. Rubbish!

SECOND FISHERMAN. The human race has no secrets, your honor. It has only afflictions.

FIRST JUDGE. It also has treasures. Doubtless she stole your gold, Knight, your jewels?

HANS. She?

SECOND FISHERMAN. All the gold and the jewels of the world meant nothing to Ondine. Of the treasures of humanity, she preferred only the humblest—the stove, the kettle, the spoon. The elements loved Ondine, but she did not return their affection. She loved the fire because it was good for making omelettes, and the water because it made soup, and the wind because it dried the wash. Write this into your record, Judge—this Ondine was the most human being that ever lived. She was human by choice.

SECOND JUDGE. We are informed that the accused was in the habit of locking herself up for hours each day in order to practice her magic arts. What do you say to that?

SECOND FISHERMAN. It's true. And what was the result of her magic, you?

THE SERVANT. A meringue, your honor.

SECOND JUDGE. A meringue? What sort of meringue?

THE SERVANT. She worked for two months to discover the secret of a good meringue.

SECOND JUDGE. That is one of the deepest of human secrets. Did she succeed?

FIRST JUDGE. Fisherman, we thank you. We shall take account of these facts in considering our judgment. If these creatures envy us our pastry, our bric-a-brac, our ointments for eczema, it is hardly to be wondered at. It is only natural that they should recognize the pre-eminence of the human condition.

SECOND JUDGE. There's nothing in the world like a good meringue. You say she discovered the secret?

THE SERVANT. Her crust was pure magic, your honor.

SECOND JUDGE. [*To the* FIRST JUDGE.] You don't suppose that with a few turns on the rack we might perhaps induce her to—?

FIRST JUDGE. No, my dear colleague, no. [*He clears his throat.*] We come now to the heart of the matter. At last, Knight, I understand the full import of your complaint. Ondine, you are accused of having cheated this knight of the joys of marriage. In place of the loving companion to which every man is entitled, you foisted upon this knight a wearisome existence with a woman who cared for nothing but her kitchen. In this way—and this is the greatest of the crimes against the human spirit—you have robbed him of love. Naturally. An Ondine is incapable of love.

HANS. Ondine incapable of love?

FIRST JUDGE. Really, Knight, it is becoming a trifle difficult to follow you. Of what, precisely, do you accuse this woman?

HANS. I accuse this woman of adoring me beyond human endurance. I accuse her of thinking only of me, of dreaming only of me, of living only for me.

FIRST JUDGE. That is not a crime, exactly.

HANS. I was this woman's god, do you understand?

FIRST JUDGE. Now, now—

HANS. You don't believe me? Very well. Answer me, Ondine. Who was your god?

ONDINE. You.

HANS. You hear? She pushes love as far as blasphemy.

FIRST JUDGE. Oh, come, there's no need to complicate the issue. These creatures are not Christians. They cannot blaspheme. All she means is that she had a proper wifely reverence for you.

HANS. Who were your saints, Ondine?

ONDINE. You.

HANS. Who were your angels? Whose face did you see in the holy pictures in your Book of Hours?

ONDINE. Yours.

HANS. You see?

FIRST JUDGE. But where is all this leading us, Knight? We are here to try an Ondine, not to judge the nature of love.

HANS. Nevertheless, that is what you are required to judge. It is Love I am accusing. I accuse the highest love of being the foulest and the truest love of being the most false. This woman who lived only for me deceived me with Bertram.

FIRST JUDGE. You are heaping confusion on confusion, Knight. If what this woman says is true, she could not possibly have deceived you with anyone.

HANS. Answer, Ondine. Did you or did you not deceive me with Bertram?

ONDINE. With Bertram.

HANS. Swear it, then. Swear it before these judges.

ONDINE. [*Rises to her feet.*] I swear it before these judges.

FIRST JUDGE. If she deceived you, we shall see soon enough. My dear colleague, put the three canonical questions. The first?

SECOND JUDGE. Ondine, when you see this man running, what do you do?

ONDINE. I lose my breath.

FIRST JUDGE. Hm.

SECOND JUDGE. And when he snores in his sleep—excuse me, Knight—what do you hear?

ONDINE. I hear the sound of singing.

FIRST JUDGE. So far her answers are correct. The third question, if you please.

SECOND JUDGE. When he tells an amusing story for the twentieth time in your presence, how does it seem to you?

ONDINE. Twenty times funnier than before.

FIRST JUDGE. And nevertheless you deceived him with Bertram?

ONDINE. I deceived him with Bertram.

SECOND FISHERMAN. You needn't shout, Ondine. I heard you.

ONDINE. [*Whispers.*] I deceived him with

Bertram.

HANS. There you have it.

FIRST JUDGE. Do you realize, young woman, what the punishment for adultery is? Do you realize that this is a crime that is never confessed, because the confession doubles the injury?

ONDINE. All the same—

SECOND FISHERMAN. You deceived him with Bertram?

ONDINE. Yes.

SECOND FISHERMAN. Answer me, now, Ondine. And see that you answer me truly. Where is Bertram now?

ONDINE. In Burgundy, where he is waiting for me to join him.

SECOND FISHERMAN. Where was it that you deceived your husband with Bertram?

ONDINE. In a forest.

SECOND FISHERMAN. In the morning? At noon?

ONDINE. At noon.

SECOND FISHERMAN. Was it cold? Was it warm?

ONDINE. It was icy. Bertram said: Our love will keep us warm. One doesn't forget such words.

SECOND FISHERMAN. Very good. And now, if you please, summon Bertram to the bar.

FIRST JUDGE. Bertram has been gone these six months, Fisherman. He is beyond the power of the law.

SECOND FISHERMAN. Its power seems limited. Here he is.

BERTRAM *comes in.*

HANS. Bertram!

FIRST JUDGE. Just a moment, Knight. You are the Count Bertram?

BERTRAM. Yes.

FIRST JUDGE. This woman says she deceived her husband with you.

BERTRAM. What?

FIRST JUDGE. Is it true?

BERTRAM. If she says it, it is true.

FIRST JUDGE. Where did it happen?

BERTRAM. In her room. In this castle.

FIRST JUDGE. In the morning? At night?

BERTRAM. At midnight.

FIRST JUDGE. Was it cold? Was it warm?

BERTRAM. The logs were blazing on the hearth. Ondine said: How hot it is, the way to hell! One doesn't forget such words.

SECOND FISHERMAN. Perfect. And now everything is clear.

ONDINE. And why is it so clear? Why should we remember these trifles? When people really love each other do you think they know whether it is warm or cold or noon or midnight?

SECOND FISHERMAN. Count Bertram, take this woman in your arms and kiss her lips.

BERTRAM. I take my orders only from her.

SECOND FISHERMAN. Ask him to kiss you, Ondine.

ONDINE. Before all these people? Never.

SECOND JUDGE. And yet you expect us to believe that you gave yourself to him?

ONDINE. Kiss me, Bertram.

BERTRAM. You really wish it?

ONDINE. Yes. I wish you to kiss me. Just for a moment. Just to prove that we can. And if I should shudder a little when you take me in your arms, Bertram, it's only because it's cold.

SECOND JUDGE. We are waiting, Ondine.

ONDINE. Couldn't I have something to cover myself with, at least?

SECOND JUDGE. No. As you are.

ONDINE. Very well. So much the better. I love to feel Bertram's hands on my body when he kisses me. Come, Bertram. But if I should scream a little, Bertram, when you take me in your arms, it's only because I'm frightened here before these people. Besides, I may not scream.

SECOND JUDGE. Make up your mind, Ondine.

ONDINE. Or if I should faint. But if I faint, Bertram, you may do whatever you please with me, whatever you please.

FIRST JUDGE. Well, Ondine?

ONDINE. Well, Bertram?

BERTRAM. Ondine! [*He takes her in his arms and kisses her.*]

ONDINE. Hans! Hans!

SECOND FISHERMAN. There's your proof, gentlemen. [*The* JUDGES *put on their hats.*]

ONDINE. But you don't understand. If I say Hans when I kiss Bertram, it is only to deceive him the better. If I loved Bertram with no thought of Hans, would that be deceit? No, but every moment that I love Bertram, I think of Hans and I deceive him. With Bertram.

SECOND FISHERMAN. We understand. The trial is over. You may go, Count Bertram.

BERTRAM. Must I go, Ondine?

ONDINE. Farewell, Bertram.

BERTRAM. Farewell.

BERTRAM *goes.*

FIRST JUDGE. The court will now deliver its judgment.

SECOND JUDGE. Oyez! Oyez!

FIRST JUDGE. It is the judgment of this court that this Ondine has transgressed the boundaries of nature. However the evidence indicates that in so doing she brought with her nothing but kindness and love.

SECOND JUDGE. And even a little too much kindness and love.

FIRST JUDGE. Why she wished to make us believe that she deceived you with Bertram when in fact she did not, is a question beyond the scope of our inquiry. As she has done no great harm, it is our judgment that she shall be spared the humiliation of a public execution. She shall have her throat cut without witnesses this day directly after sunset. Until that time, we place her in the custody of the public executioner. [*Church bells begin to ring again.*] What's that?

SECOND JUDGE. Wedding bells, my dear colleague. The Knight is about to be married.

FIRST JUDGE. Ah, of course. The nuptial procession is forming in front of the chapel. Knight, permit us to join you

in the hour of your happiness. [*The* KITCHEN MAID *walks up to* HANS.]

HANS. Who is this?

FIRST JUDGE. Who?

HANS. This woman who walks toward me like a creature from the other world?

SECOND JUDGE. We don't know her.

FIRST JUDGE. She seems to be of this world.

THE SERVANT. It's the kitchen maid, my lord. You asked me to fetch her.

HANS. How beautiful she is!

FIRST JUDGE. Beautiful?

HANS. How very beautiful!

SECOND JUDGE. We shall not contradict you. Will you precede us?

HANS. No, no. I have to hear first what she says. She alone knows the end of this story. Speak! Speak! We are listening.

SECOND JUDGE. Is he out of his mind?

FIRST JUDGE. He has every reason.

HANS. Speak! Speak!

THE KITCHEN MAID.
My face is plain, my nature sour,
But, oh, my soul is like a flower.

HANS. That rhymes?

FIRST JUDGE. Rhymes? Not at all.

THE KITCHEN MAID.
Had I been free to choose my lot,
My hands had never touched a pot.

HANS. You're going to tell me these verses don't rhyme?

SECOND JUDGE. Verses?

FIRST JUDGE. What verses?

THE KITCHEN MAID.
My clothes are poor, my face is plain,
And yet of high rank is my pain;
There is as much salt in my tears
As in those shed by emperors.
And when the butler vents his spleen,
It hurts as if I were a queen.
Oh, when we two come to your city,
And, kneeling, ask for grace and pity,
Both bearing on our brows the same
Affronts and thorns and marks of

shame,
Will you know us one from the
    other,
My Lord, my savior and my
    brother?

HANS. That's a poem, is it not? Would
you call that a poem?

FIRST JUDGE. A poem? All I heard was a
scullion complaining that she had
been falsely accused of stealing a
spoon.

SECOND JUDGE. She said her corns have
been aching since November.

HANS. Is that a scythe she bears in her
hand?

FIRST JUDGE. A scythe? No, that's a spin-
dle.

SECOND JUDGE. It's a broom.

HANS. I thank you, kitchen maid. When
next you come, I shall be ready.
Come, gentlemen. [The KITCHEN
MAID *goes out. The* SERVANT *crosses the
stage solemnly. He turns.*]

THE SERVANT. Your bride is in the
chapel, my lord. The priest is waiting.

HANS. Go and say that I am coming.
[*The wedding bells begin to toll as for a
funeral. They all go out, except the* EX-
ECUTIONER, *the* SECOND FISHERMAN
and ONDINE.]

THE EXECUTIONER. [*Taking hold of* ON-
DINE.] Now then, Mistress—

SECOND FISHERMAN. One moment. Executioner. [*With a gesture of his hand,
he turns the* EXECUTIONER *into an au-
tomaton and waves him off the stage.*]
The end is near, Ondine.

ONDINE. Don't kill him, Old One.

SECOND FISHERMAN. You haven't forgotten our pact?

ONDINE. Don't judge men by our standards, Old One. Men don't deceive
their wives unless they love them.
When they love them most, they deceive them. It's a form of fidelity,
their deceit.

SECOND FISHERMAN. Ah, Ondine, what a
woman you are!

ONDINE. It's only because he wished to
honor me that he deceived me. It was

to show the world how pure I was,
how true. I really don't see how else
he could have done it.

SECOND FISHERMAN. You have always
suffered from a lack of imagination.

ONDINE. When a man comes home in
the evening with his eyes full of gratitude and his arms full of flowers, and
he kisses our hands and calls us his
savior and his angel—we all know
what that means. It's scarcely an hour
since he has deceived us. And is
there anything more beautiful in
marriage?

SECOND FISHERMAN. He has made you
suffer, my little Ondine.

ONDINE. Yes. I have suffered. But remember we are speaking of humans.
Among humans you are not unhappy when you suffer. On the
contrary. To seek out in a world full
of joy the one thing that is certain to
give you pain, and to hug that to
your bosom with all your strength—
that's the greatest human happiness.
People think you're strange if you
don't do it. Save him, Old One.

SECOND FISHERMAN. He is going to die,
Ondine.

ONDINE. Old One!

SECOND FISHERMAN. What does it matter
to you, Ondine? You have only a few
minutes left of human memory. Your
sisters will call you three times, and
you will forget everything.

ONDINE. Save him! Save him!

SECOND FISHERMAN. If you wish, I will
let him die at the same moment that
you forget him. That seems humane.

ONDINE. He is so young. So strong.

SECOND FISHERMAN. You have strained
his heart, Ondine.

ONDINE. I? How could I?

SECOND FISHERMAN. Since you show
such interest in dogfish, perhaps you
remember a couple who broke their
hearts one day while swimming together peacefully in a calm sea. They
had crossed the entire width of the
ocean side by side in winter, through
a tempest, without the slightest diffi-

culty. And then one day in a blue gulf, they swam against a little wave. All the steel of the sea was in that ripple of water, and the effort was too much for them. For a week their eyes grew pale, their lips drooped. But there was nothing wrong with them, they said . . . but they were dying. And so it is with men, Ondine. What breaks the woodsman's heart, or the knight's, is not the great oak, nor the battle with the dragon: It is a slender reed, it is a child who loves him.—He has only a few minutes left to live.

ONDINE. But he has everything to live for now. His life is in order.

SECOND FISHERMAN. His brain is full of the music of those who are dying. When the kitchen maid held forth just now on the price of eggs and cheese, you saw, it was all sheer poetry in his ears.

ONDINE. He has Bertha—

SECOND FISHERMAN. She is waiting for him in vain in the chapel. He is in the stable with his horse. His horse is speaking to him. Dear master, good-bye till we meet in the sky, his horse is saying. Today his horse has become a poet.

ONDINE. I can hear them singing in the chapel. He is being married.

SECOND FISHERMAN. What does this marriage mean to him now? The whole thing has slipped away from him like a ring too wide for the finger. He is wandering about by himself. He is talking to himself; he doesn't know what he's saying. It's a way men have of escaping when they come up suddenly against a reality. They become what is called mad. All at once they are logical. They don't compromise. They don't marry the woman they don't love. They reason simply and clearly like the plants and the water. Like us.

ONDINE. Listen to him. He is cursing me. [HANS *is heard speaking offstage.*]

SECOND FISHERMAN. He loves you. He's

mad. He's here. [*He goes.* HANS *comes in slowly and stands behind* ONDINE *for a moment.*]

HANS. My name is Hans.

ONDINE. It's a beautiful name.

HANS. Ondine and Hans. The most beautiful names in the world, are they not?

ONDINE. Yes. Hans and Ondine.

HANS. Oh, no. Ondine first. That's the title. Ondine. It will be called *Ondine,* this story in which I appear from time to time. And I don't play a very brilliant part in it, do I, because, as you said, once, I'm not very bright; I'm just the man in the story. I loved Ondine because she wanted me; I deceived her because I had to. I didn't count for much. I was born to live between the stable and the kennels—such was my fate, and I might have been happy there. But I strayed from the appointed path, and I was caught between nature and destiny. I was trapped.

ONDINE. Forgive me, Hans.

HANS. But why do you make this error, all of you? Was I the man for love? Lovers are of a different stamp— little threadbare professors full of fury, stockbrokers with heavy glasses; such men have the time and capacity for enjoyment and suffering. But you never choose such men, never. Instead you fall with all your weight on some poor general called Antony, or some poor knight called Hans, ordinary men of action for whom love is a torment and a poison. And then it's all up with them. Between the wars and the chase and the tourneys and the hospital, did I ever have a spare moment in my life? But you had to add also the poison in my veins, the flame in my eyes, the gall in my mouth! And then, oh God, how they shook me between them and bruised me, and flayed me between hell and heaven! It wasn't very just of you, Ondine.

ONDINE. Farewell, Hans.

HANS. And then, you see? One day they leave you. The day when suddenly everything becomes clear, the day you realize that you would die if they left you—that day they leave you. The day when you find them again, and with them, everything that gives life its meaning, that day, they look you in the eye with a limpid glance, and they say farewell.

ONDINE. I am going to forget everything, Hans.

HANS. And a real farewell, a farewell forever! Not like those lovers who part on the threshold of death, but are destined to meet again in another world, to jostle each other eternally in the same heaven. These part only in order never to part again—you don't call that a parting. But Ondine and I will never meet again. We part for eternity, we go to different worlds. We must do this properly, Ondine. It is the first real farewell that has ever been said in this world.

ONDINE. Live, Hans. You too will forget.

HANS. Live! It's easy to say. If at least I could work up a little interest in living—but I'm too tired to make the effort. Since you left me, Ondine, all the things my body once did by itself, it does now only by special order. The grass doesn't look green to my eyes unless I order them to see it green. And it's not very gay, you know, when the grass is black. It's an exhausting piece of management I've undertaken. I have to supervise five senses, two hundred bones, a thousand muscles. A single moment of inattention, and I forget to breathe. He died, they will say, because it was a nuisance to breathe . . . [He shakes his head.] He died of love. Why did you let the fisherman catch you, Ondine? What did you wish to tell me?

ONDINE. That an Ondine will mourn for you always.

HANS. No. No one will mourn for me. I am the last of my house. I shall leave no trace behind me. There will be only an Ondine, and she will have forgotten.

ONDINE. No, Hans. I have taken my precautions. You used to laugh at me because I always made the same movements in your house. You said I counted my steps. It was true. It was because I knew the day would come when I would have to go back. I was training myself. And now, in the depths of the Rhine or the ocean, without knowing why, I shall go on forever making the movement that I made when I lived with you. When I plunge to the bottom, I shall be going to the cellar—when I spring to the surface, I shall be going to the attic. I shall pass through doors in the water. I shall open windows. In this way I shall live a little with you always. Among the wild Ondines there will be one who will forever be your wife. Oh! What is it?

HANS. I forgot for a moment.

ONDINE. Forgot what?

HANS. To breathe. Go on, Ondine, go on.

ONDINE. Before I left, I took some of the things in our room. I threw them into the river. They seem strange to me in the water, these bits of wood and metal that speak to me of you; they float about aimlessly out of their element. It's because I'm not used to it yet: tomorrow they will seem as firm and stable as the currents in which they float. I shall not know what they mean, exactly, but I shall live among them, and it will be strange if I don't use them sometimes. I shall drink from your cup. I shall look into your mirror. Sometimes perhaps your clock will strike. Timeless, I shall not understand this sound but I shall hear it. And so, in my way, though death and the infinite come between us, I shall be true to you always.

HANS. Thank you, Ondine. And I—

THE FIRST VOICE. Ondine!

HANS. They are calling you, Ondine.

ONDINE. They will call me three times. I shall remember until the last. Hans, let us not waste these moments! Ask me something quickly. What is it, Hans? What is it? You're pale.

HANS. I too am being called, Ondine.

ONDINE. Speak! Question me!

HANS. What did you say, Ondine, when you came out of the storm, the first time I saw you?

ONDINE. I said: How beautiful he is!

HANDS. And when you saw me eating the trout?

ONDINE. I said: How stupid he is!

HANS. And when I said: It does no harm to think?

ONDINE. I said: In after years we shall have this hour to remember. The hour before you kissed me.

HANS. I can't wait now, Ondine. Kiss me now.

THE SECOND VOICE. Ondine!

ONDINE. It's all whirling about in my head! Speak, Hans, speak!

HANS. I can't speak and kiss you at the same time.

ONDINE. I'll be quiet. [*He kisses her. The* KITCHEN MAID *comes in with her broom.*]

HANS. Look! Look! There she is!

ONDINE. Who?

HANS. Her face is plain, her nature sour. But oh, her soul is like a flower!

[*He falls.*]

ONDINE. Help! Help!

HANS. Ondine—

THE THIRD VOICE. Ondine! [HANS *dies.* ONDINE *looks about in surprise.*]

ONDINE. How did I get here? How strange! It's solid. It's empty. It's the earth?

The SECOND FISHERMAN *appears.*

SECOND FISHERMAN. It is the earth, Ondine. It's no place for you.

ONDINE. No—[*The* ONDINEs *are heard singing in the distance.*]

SECOND FISHERMAN. Come, little one, let us leave it.

ONDINE. Oh yes. Let us leave it. [*She takes a few steps, then stops before the body of* HANS *which is lying on the platform steps.*] Wait. Why is this handsome young man lying here? Who is he?

SECOND FISHERMAN. His name is Hans.

ONDINE. What a beautiful name! But why doesn't he move? Is there something wrong with him!

SECOND FISHERMAN. He is dead.

FIRST ONDINE. Come, Ondine.

ONDINE. Oh, I like him so much! Can you bring him back to life, Old One?

SECOND FISHERMAN. Impossible.

ONDINE. What a pity! How I should have loved him!

Thieves' Carnival

Jean Anouilh

Jean Anouilh is the only European playwright of major importance whose productive career in playwriting may be said to extend both before and after World War II. Although several other writers represented in these volumes lived beyond 1945, none wrote plays during the postwar period at all comparable with those they had written before or during the war. On the other hand, no European playwright who achieved prominence after the war had written a play of much significance before it. Jean Anouilh is the one exception, a writer whose plays of the 1930s brought him to significant recognition in France and to the beginning of an international reputation, and whose postwar plays were to be among his finest. Anouilh's postwar career is beyond the scope of this volume, but his early work contains the seeds of his later success, and several of his early plays are excellent theatrical works by any standards. Furthermore, in a curious way, most of the major currents of the twentieth-century French theater flowed together in Jean Anouilh's work, though it remained for the postwar generation to bring these elements into new focus in what has become known as the "Theatre of the Absurd." Anouilh thus becomes both an ending and a beginning point, a suitable representative of both the fading echoes of *fin de siecle* optimism and the despair of mid-twentieth-century nihilism.

Jean Anouilh was born on June 23, 1910, in the village of Cérisole, near Bordeaux. His father was a tailor, and Anouilh was later to insist that he had learned pride of workmanship and scrupulous attention to detail from his father's dedicated craftsmanship. His mother was a violinist and an occasional member of a theater orchestra in a casino in Bordeaux; the young Anouilh evidently spent many hours watching from the wings the productions of light operettas and other entertainment with which she was involved. The recurrence in Anouilh's plays of bittersweet, disillusioned musicians, often from casino orchestras, can surely be associated with this theatrical upbringing. The family moved to Paris when Jean was young; following the disruption of World War I, he was educated at the École Colbert and at the Collège Chaptal. He studied law at the University of Paris for a time, but limited financial resources forced him to withdraw and to take a job in an advertising agency. Anouilh was well acquainted with poverty throughout his childhood and youth, and the plight of those with and without money is another recurrent theme in his later work. With characteristic elan, Anouilh was later to insist that writing advertising slogans was excellent training for writing theatrical dialogue.

In 1931, Anouilh obtained a position as secretary to Louis Jouvet, the actor and director whose influence was so important in Giraudoux's career. In the same year, Anouilh married the actress Monelle Valentin, and their apartment was furnished with the properties from Jouvet's production of *Siegfried;* when Giraudoux's play was revived in Jouvet's repertory, the young couple found their apartment bare and their infant daughter without her accustomed dresser drawer/crib. Despite these new responsibilities and his continued poverty, Anouilh determined to devote his career to writing for the theater; only in 1935, when he sold the rights to one of his early plays for motion picture adaptation, did he finally achieve the financial security that was to grow into opulent success. From an early age, Anouilh had been writing romantic plays in imitation of Edmond Rostand, but it was Giraudoux's example that finally suggested to him a style of theater compatible with his own inclinations and viable with the Parisian public. Anouilh succeeded in combining the financial success of the popular theater with a measure of the philosophical content of the avant-garde.

It is not appropriate here to trace Anouilh's career in the postwar period. His plays covered a wide gamut of themes and theatrical styles from the lightest comedy to the most austere tragedy, while his conservative political views and reclusive life-style isolated him from the more glamorous and publicity-seeking theatrical endeav-ors. Most would agree that his finest plays date from during and after World War II, including *Antigone* (1944), *L'Invitation au Château* (1947; translated as *Ring 'Round the Moon*), and *Becket* (1959). In his plays of the 1930s, however, which Anouilh divided (for publication) into "black" plays and "pink," or "rosy" plays, may be found many of the themes that infused his later work as well. The "black" plays of the 1930s were effectively realistic in style and pessimistic and gloomy in content; none is now regarded among his best. The "pink" plays, although often containing charac-teristic Anouilh piquancy, are light, fantastic theatrical games lying somewhere between farce and fantasy; none is rosier than *Thieves' Carnival.*

Thieves' Carnival was written in 1932, when Anouilh was only twenty-two years old. As Anouilh struggled to get his plays produced, it was 1938 before *Thieves' Carnival* first appeared on a stage; it opened at the Théâtre des Arts in Paris on September 17, 1938, under the direction of André Barsacq. The play is a delightful fusion of sense and nonsense, of music, dance and story line, of an unworldly innocence reminiscent of Giraudoux with a despair and absurdity that looks back-ward to Alfred Jarry and forward to the postwar absurdists. In later years, when asked about the origin of his theatrical practice, Anouilh was to remark, "It seems to me that everything is in *Le Bal de Voleurs.* My characters, my themes." The play is not only a delightful piece of theater in its own right, it is also a microcosm of much that Anouilh was to create later in his career.

Although literary "influences" can easily be overemphasized, one can see es-pecially clearly in Anouilh the confluence of the theatrical ideas of Pirandello, Cocteau, Giraudoux, and Feydeau. The profound theatricalism of Pirandello, the playing with the differences between illusion and reality, the delight in masks behind masks behind masks that infuse *Six Characters in Search of an Author,* are also to be found in a lighter mode in *Thieves' Carnival.* Anouilh has acknowledged his indebtedness to Cocteau's concept of "poetry of the theater," and certainly in *Thieves' Carnival* can be found a complex interweaving of music and dance, light and sound, seriousness and frivolity, all as light as a meringue and yet all unified like a theatrical poem, with each part making its contribution to a beautifully conceived whole. Yet most obviously of all, one can see in Anouilh's work a curious blend of Giraudoux and Feydeau, of linguistic agility and romantic idealism with madcap farce and the solid theatrical structure of the box office success.

Anouilh's interesting use of music and dance epitomize much of the success of *Thieves' Carnival.* The lone clarinetist who serves as mock chorus, and who provides a musical signature for each character as well as mood underscoring in each scene, is a marvelous theatrical stroke. This conceit is then cleverly reversed near the end of the play when, having ignored the clarinetist throughout the play, Lady Hurf suddenly turns on him and drives him from the stage in irritation—only to be reversed once again when the clarinetist returns as a bearded character and reverts to clarinet playing in the final dance. Such playing with theatrical convention and technique provides exactly the right blend of zany nonsense with lighthearted shifting of identity. In the same vein, dance is used throughout the play in ways which, although by no means realistic, yet grow with some kind of fantasy logic out of the procedings: the policemen and the three thieves engage in an elaborate "ballet" in the "Three Musketeers Maneuver"; everyone dances out on the way to the Carnival of Thieves, with the Dupont-Duforts bringing up the rear with their own especially wicked dance step; the policemen carry off the Dupont-Duforts in the last act in a great sweep of balletic movement that underscores the ridiculousness of all the proceedings. As the play ends, the entire cast dances in and out of the drawing room doors, exchanging beards as they go, thus reinforcing both the gay, musical fun of the performance and the shifting identity themes that have pervaded the play.

Without in any way reducing the farcial fun which makes *Thieves' Carnival* such a delight in the theater, Anouilh also introduces telling, though hardly overbearing, thematic content. Lady Hurf, bored and lonely despite her wealth (or perhaps because of it), amuses herself by deliberately creating the myth that Peterbono is the Duke of Miraflores. Eva, just as bored but even sadder because she is younger, finds that she cares only for external appearances, not for whatever human reality may lie underneath. She goads Hector into a frantic search for the appearance that first appealed to her, only to conclude at the play's end that even that appearance is no longer amusing to her. Gustave and Juliette, separated throughout the play by the need to play their respective societal roles in a way that is less farcical and closer to reality than anything else in the play, are finally united by a transparent ruse, but it is immediately apparent to Juliette that the reality is of no importance at all so long as Gustave can be persuaded to accede to the illusion. But even illusion and reality, false and true identities, are but masks for a somewhat more metaphysical questioning of how life should be lived in the face of chameleon reality. "You will always find yourself pursued by desires with changing beards," the worldly wise Lady Hurf points out, "and never have the courage to tell one of them: stay as you are—I love you." And in her concluding, and summary, comment in the play she adds, "It's only for those who have played it with all the zest of youth that the comedy is a success, and only then because they were playing their youth, a thing which succeeds always." It would be naive to pretend that these ideas are stunningly new, but Anouilh serves them up with just the right blend of cheekiness and nonchalance to allow them to make their point while reinforcing the overall pleasure and lightness of the play.

Clearly Anouilh owes a debt to Giraudoux in the style and language that appear in his play; Anouilh was still surrounded by the furniture of *Siegfried* when he wrote it. On the other hand, the differences between Anouilh and Giradudoux in this respect are perhaps more important than the similarities. Giraudoux makes greater use of extensive debate, whereas Anouilh skips lightly and with linguistic facility over the points he wishes to make. Giraudoux senses another world, a spirit world, somewhere next to the real one, and invokes it in most of his plays; Anouilh senses only nothingness beyond the absurdity of the real world. Giraudoux, therefore, creates a sense of beauty, wonder, and narrowly missed opportunity, whereas Anouilh focuses on the innocence and dedication of youth and love as the only antidote to meaninglessness. It is no accident that the innocence of a child both begins and ends Act 2 of *Thieves' Carnival*, although Anouilh is hardly the first thinker to suggest that the kingdom of God must be received "as a little child." Giraudoux tends to depend upon the romanticism of elaborate scenery, costumes, and lush spectacle to create the total environment of his plays, whereas Anouilh inclines toward stripping theatrical trappings to their simplest forms: one musician for a whole orchestra, one beard for a whole identity. The language of Anouilh is clever, facile, and poetically effective, while that of Giraudoux is lush, verdant, and metaphorical—poetic in an altogether different way.

Anouilh went on, later in his career, to write plays in a number of different styles, and to move further and further from the early influences that shaped his creativity. At their kernel, however, most of these later works carry the themes, the characters, and the essence that can be found in *Thieves' Carnival*, just as Anouilh has pointed out. The play is an amazing accomplishment for a writer only twenty-two years of age. The "zest of youth" that Anouilh praised in his characters has served him admirably in creating *Thieves' Carnival*, as theatrically delightful a play as any he wrote.

Thieves' Carnival
(Le Bal des Voleurs)

Translated by Lucienne Hill

Characters

Peterbono ⎫
Hector ⎬ thieves
Gustave ⎭
Lord Edgard
Lady Hurf
Eva ⎫
Juliette ⎬ her nieces
Dupont-Dufort Senior
Dupont-Dufort Junior
The Town Crier
The Policemen
The Nursemaid
The Little Girl
The Musician
A Servant

Act 1

*The public gardens of a watering place
which saw its heyday in the 1880's. In the
middle, a bandstand. The orchestra is
represented by a single* MUSICIAN, *who at
the rise of the curtain is executing a solo
of superlative virtuosity on the clarinet. A
woman deck-chair attendant goes to and
fro. The summer visitors stroll up and
down to the rhythm of the music. In the
foreground* EVA *and* HECTOR *are locked
in a dramatic screen embrace. The music
stops. So does the kiss, from which* HEC-
TOR *emerges, reeling a little. Applause*

for the MUSICIAN.

HECTOR. [*Covered in confusion.*] I say,
steady. They're applauding us!

EVA. [*Bursts out laughing.*] Of course not,
it's the orchestra. I must say you
appeal to me enormously.

HECTOR. [*Instinctively fingering his hair
and mustache.*] What do you like about
me specially?

EVA. Everything. [*She blows him a kiss.*]
We mustn't stay here, it's too risky. I'll
see you tonight at eight in the Phoenix Bar. And if you should meet me
with my aunt, whatever you do, pretend you don't know me.

HECTOR. [*Yearningly.*] Your little hand,
once more.

EVA. Careful. My aunt's old friend Lord
Edgard is over there by the bandstand reading his paper. He'll see us.
[*She holds out her hand, but turns away
to watch* LORD EDGARD.]

HECTOR. [*Passionately.*] I want to inhale
the perfume of your hand!

*He bends over her hand, and surreptitiously
draws a jeweler's eyeglass from his pocket
to take a closer look at* EVA's *rings.* EVA
*withdraws her hand, unaware of the ma-
neuver.*

EVA. Till tonight. [*She goes.*]

HECTOR. [*Weak at the knees.*] My beloved. . . . [*He follows her out of sight,
then comes downstage again, putting
away his eyeglass, and mutters with icy
self-possession.*] A good two hundred
thousand. And not a flaw in the lot.

300

At this point the TOWN CRIER *enters with his drum and the crowd gathers around to listen.*

TOWN CRIER. Townsmen of Vichy! The Municipality, anxious to preserve the well-being and security of the invalids and bathers, issues a warning for their information and protection! Numerous complaints from visitors have been lodged at the Town Hall and at the main police station, Market Street. A dangerous pack of picklepockets—[*He has a little trouble with this word, at which the clarinet plays a little accompaniment. The* TOWN CRIER *swings around on him, furious.*]—a dangerous pack of pockpickets—[*Again the clarinet renders the word in music.*]—is at this very hour within our gates. The local police are on the watch. Members of the force, in plain clothes and in uniform, are ready to protect our visitors. . . . [*Indeed, even as he speaks* POLICEMEN *are threading their several ways gracefully through the crowd.*] Visitors are nevertheless requested to exercise the greatest possible caution, particularly on the public highway, in public parks, and in all other places of public amusement. A reward is offered by the Tourist Association to anyone supplying information leading to the apprehension of the felons! Tell your friends!

A roll of drums. During the proclamation HECTOR *has relieved the* TOWN CRIER *of his enormous copper watch and bulging purse. The crowd scatters, and the drum and the harangue are heard again farther off.* HECTOR *takes a seat, and the chair woman approaches.*

CHAIR WOMAN. Will you take a ticket, sir, please?

HECTOR. [*Largely.*] Since it's customary. . . .

CHAIR WOMAN. That'll be five francs, please.

While HECTOR *feels for the money, the woman steals his wallet, then the huge watch and the purse he has just taken*

from the TOWN CRIER.

HECTOR. [*Seizing the hand on its next trip into his pocket.*] Hey! What do you think you're up to? [*The woman struggles to free herself and loses her wig.*] Have you gone crazy? [*He lifts his own wig and mustache a trifle.*] It's me!

The chair attendant readjusts her wig. It is PETERBONO.

PETERBONO. Sorry, old chap. It's me, too. Had a good day?

HECTOR. The purse and a watch, and a cigarette lighter.

PETERBONO. [*Examining them.*] I know that watch. It's the town crier's and it's made of copper. I put it back into his pocket, the poor devil, that and the purse, which you'll find if you check up contains just fifteen cents and the receipt for a registered parcel. As for the lighter, we've already got nine hundred and three, out of which only a couple work. I've known you to do better, my lad!

HECTOR. I've a date tonight with a girl who'll be mine before you can say mischief, and who wears over two hundred thousand francs' worth of diamonds on her middle finger.

PETERBONO. We'll look into it. Have you noticed that little thing over there? The necklace?

HECTOR. [*Examining the girl through the field glasses he wears around his neck.*] Phew! The stones are enormous!

PETERBONO. No wishful thinking. They're smaller to the naked eye. Still, off we go. Small-change Maneuver. I get offensive and you interfere. [*They cross to the girl with a terrible affectation of indifference.*] Ticket? Ticket? [*The girl gives him a coin;* PETERBONO *begins to yell.*] I've got no change! I tell you I've got no change! No change, do you hear? No change at all, I keep on telling you!

HECTOR. What's this? No change, eh? Excuse me, mademoiselle, allow me to put this insolent baggage in her place!

There follows a tussle under cover of which

HECTOR *invvestigates the clasp of the girl's necklace.*

THE GIRL. [*Violently freeing herself.*] No, you don't!

HECTOR. [*Taken aback.*] What do you mean, no, you don't!

PETERBONO. No, you don't what?

THE GIRL. [*Lifting her wig; it is* GUSTAVE.] It's me.

HECTOR. [*Falling into a chair.*] Charming!

PETERBONO. [*Exploding.*] That's what comes of not working to plan! I can't rely on anybody! Running errands, that's all you're fit for! Errand boys! If it weren't for your poor old mothers, who put you in my charge to learn the business, you'd be out on your ear, the pair of you. Do you hear me? Out on your ear! And without your week's pay in lieu of notice, make no mistake! And complain to the union if you dare! I'll tell them a thing or two, the dance you've led me, both of you! [*To* GUSTAVE.] You! You haven't done a stroke today, naturally!

GUSTAVE. Yes, I have. I've done two. First, there's this magnificent wallet.

PETERBONO. Let's have a look. [*He examines it, then searches himself anxiously.*] Where did you get this? Who from?

GUSTAVE. I got it in the Boulevbard Ravachol off an old gentleman with a long white beard. . . .

PETERBONO. [*Terrible in his anger.*] Check trousers, olive-green jacket, and deerstalker cap; am I right, pigeonbrain?

GUSTAVE. [*Quaking.*] Yes, sir. Did you see me?

PETERBONO. [*Sinks into a chair, flattened by this latest blow.*] That was me, idiot, that was me! At this rate we'll be lucky if we cover our expenses!

GUSTAVE. But I've got something else, Mr. Peterbono, sir.

PETERBONO. [*Profoundly discouraged.*] If it's something else you stole from me, you can imagine my curiosity.

GUSTAVE. It isn't a thing, it's a girl. And she looks rich.

HECTOR. [*Jumping up.*] Good God! Don't say it's the same girl. A redhead? About twenty-five? Name of Eva?

GUSTAVE. No. Dark hair, about twenty. name of Juliette.

HECTOR. Oh, that's all right.

PETERBONO. What did you get?

GUSTAVE. Nothing yet. But I helped her fish a kid out of the Thermes Fountain. We sat in the sun to dry and we got talking. She told me she liked me.

PETERBONO. Any jewels?

GUSTAVE. One very fine pearl.

PETERBONO. Good. We must look into that. Hector, can you spare a moment this afternoon, other engagements permitting?

GUSTAVE. No! I'd like to handle this myself.

PETERBONO. What's this? What's this? Handle it yourself, would you? Well, whatever next?

GUSTAVE. It was me she took a fancy to.

PETERBONO. All the more reason. Hector will swallow her in one.

GUSTAVE. No, I tell you! Not this one!

PETERBONO. [*Severely.*] Gustave, listen to me. Your mother put you in my care, and I took you into the firm as assistant decoy. You're young and you're ambitious. That's fine. I was ambitious myself when I was your age. But just a minute! In our profession, as in all professions, you have to work your way up from the bottom. Hector here is the finest professional seducer I know this side of Monte Carlo. There's a chap who hits the bull's-eye three times out of four, and take it from me, that's a pretty handsome average. You don't mean to tell me that you, a mere apprentice, expect to turn out better work than that?

GUSTAVE. To hell with it! I'll get her for myself.

PETERBONO. [*Tight-lipped.*] If you wish to do a job on the side in your spare time, there's nothing to stop you.

You'll owe me just the sixty-five per-cent on what you make, that's all.

HECTOR. [*Who has been watching a* NURSE-MAID *during this altercation.*] Peter?

PETERBONO. Hector?

HECTOR. That nursemaid over there. See the gold chain?

PETERBONO. [*Contemptuously.*] Pooh! It's probably wire.

HECTOR. Listen, it's ten to seven. We've ten minutes to go before supper.

PETERBONO. Very well, if you're set on it. We'll give her the Three Mus-keteers Maneuver.

HECTOR. Three Musketeers Maneuver?

PETERBONO. It's the classic routine for nursemaids. Number one gets off with her, number two plays ten little pigs with the baby, and number three starts whistling bugle calls without a break to make her senses reel.

They go. Enter LADY HURF *and* JULIETTE.

JULIETTE. The little boy was barely five years old. He was only in up to his waist, but he was frightened and he kept falling over. He would have drowned, I'm sure.

LADY HURF. How dreadful! Have you noticed all these little chimney-pot hats everywhere? How absurd they look!

JULIETTE. Fortunately this young man came to the rescue. He was wonder-ful and very sweet.

LADY HURF. All children are sweet at five. But at twelve they begin to get silly. That's why I never wanted any.

JULIETTE. I was talking about the young man, Aunt.

LADY HURF. Oh yes, of course. There's another of those grotesque little hats. The young man was very sweet—yes, go on.

JULIETTE. That's all.

LADY HURF. We must invite him to din-ner.

JULIETTE. He's gone. I'd never seen him before.

LADY HURF. Good. One always knows far too many people. Besides, I can't stand stories about drowning. Your

poor uncle swam like a lump of lead. He drowned himself seven times; I could have hit him. Ah, there's Edgard. Edgard, have you seen Eva?

LORD EDGARD. [*Appearing from behind his paper.*] How are you, my dear?

LADY HUFF. I asked if you'd seen Eva.

LORD EDGARD. Eva? No, I haven't. That's very odd. Now what can I have done with her? Perhaps she's at the Baths.

LADY HURF. At seven o'clock at night? Don't be silly.

JULIETTE. Shall we try the Phoenix Bar? She often goes there.

LADY HURF. Edgard, don't stir from this spot for any reason whatsoever.

LORD EDGARD. Very good, my dear.

LADY HURF. [*Going.*] But of course if you see her, run after her.

LORD EDGARD. Very good, my dear.

LADY HURF. Or better still, don't; you'd only lose her—just come and tell us which way she went.

LORD EDGARD. Very good, my dear.

LADY HURF. On second thought, no. You'd never manage to find us. Send one attendant after her, another at-tendant to let us know, and put a third in your place to tell us where you've gone so we can pick you up on the way home if we should hap-pen to be passing.

LORD EDGARD. Very good, my dear.

He retires, stunned, behind his paper. Exit LADY HURF *with* JULIETTE. *Enter the* DUPONT-DUFORTS, *father and son, ac-companied by the little jig on the clarinet, which is their signature tune.*

D.D. SENIOR. Let's follow. We'll meet them casually on the promenade, and try to tempt them to a cocktail. Didier, I don't know what's come over you. You, a hard-working, con-scientious lad, brimful of initiative, and look at you. You're not paying an atom of attention to young Juliette.

D.D. JUNIOR. She snubs me.

D.D. SENIOR. What does that matter? To begin with, you aren't just anybody. You are Dupont-Dufort Junior. Her aunt thinks a great deal of you. She's prepared to make any investment on your recommendation.

D.D. JUNIOR. That ought to be enough for us.

D.D. SENIOR. Son, in matters of money there's no such thing as enough. I'd far and away prefer you to pull off this marriage. Nothing short of that will put our bank fairly and squarely on its feet again. So let me see a bit of charm, a little fascination.

D.D. JUNIOR. Yes, Dad.

D.D. SENIOR. We couldn't wish for more propitious circumstances. They're bored to tears, and there's nobody here in the least presentable. So let's make ourselves agreeable, superlatively agreeable.

D.D. JUNIOR. Yes, Dad.

Exeunt the DUPONT-DUFORTS. LORD EDGARD, *who has heard every word, looks over his* Times *to watch them go.* PETERBONO, HECTOR, *and* GUSTAVE *come in dressed as soldiers as the* MUSICIAN *begins his second number. The* POLICEMEN *enter at the same time from the other side. They all perform a flirtatious little ballet around the* NURSEMAID, *the maneuvers of the* POLICEMEN *seriously impeding those of the three thieves. The* NURSEMAID *finally goes; the* POLICEMEN, *twirling their white batons behind their backs, make gallant attempts to hinder her departure. During the ballet* LADY HURF *returns alone and goes to sit beside* LORD EDGARD. *The music stops at the exit of the* POLICEMEN *and the* NURSEMAID.

PETERBONO. [*Thwarted.*] Lads, that's the first time I've ever known the Three Musketeers Maneuver to miscarry.

LADY HURF. [*To* LORD EDGARD.]. Well, Edgard, my dear, and what have you done with yourself today?

LORD EDGARD. [*Surprised and embarrassed as always at* LADY HURF's *customary abruptness.*]. I—er—I read *The Times.*

LADY HURF. [*Sternly.*] The same as yesterday?

LORD EDGARD. [*Ingenuously.*] Not the same copy as yesterday.

HECTOR. [*Who has been watching the scene, gives a whistle of admiration.*] See those pearls?

PETERBONO. Four million!

HECTOR. How about it? What's it to be? Russian princes?

PETERBONO. No. She knows her onions by the look of her. Ruined Spanish noblemen.

GUSTAVE. That's bright of you. Whenever you masquerade as Spaniards you're rigged out like a couple of rats.

PETERBONO. Quiet, shaver! You're speaking of a trade you know nothing about.

GUSTAVE. Well, anyway, if you think I'm dressing up as your ecclesiastical secretary like the last time, it's no go. I'm not wearing a cassock in this heat.

PETERBONO. Gustave, you're trying my patience! Come along, home! Hector and I will be Spanish grandees, and you'll put on that cassock, heat or no heat.

The unwilling GUSTAVE *is borne away, to the accompaniment of a little jig on the clarinet.*

LADY HURF. [*Who has been deep in thought.*] Edgard, the situation is grave. . . .

LORD EDGARD. I know. According to *The Times,* the Empire. . . .

LADY HURF. No, no. Here.

LORD EDGARD. [*Looking around him anxiously.*] Here?

LADY HURF. Listen to me. We have two tender creatures in our care. Intrigues are fermenting—marriages are brewing. Personally, I can't keep track of them—it gives me the vertigo. Who is to uncover them, Edgard; who is to supervise them?

LORD EDGARD. Who?

LADY HURF. Juliette is a scatterbrain. Eva is a scatterbrain. As for me, I haven't a notion what's going on and the mere idea of it bores me to extinction. Besides, I've no more common sense than those two senseless girls. That leaves you in the midst of these three scatterbrains.

LORD EDGARD. That leaves me.

LADY HURF. Which is another way of saying nobody. I am perplexed, excessively perplexed. Anything may happen in this watering place. Intrigues spring up under one's very feet like so much jungle vegetation. Should we do better to leave Vichy, I wonder? Ought we perhaps to bury ourselves in some rustic backwater? Edgard, for heaven's sake, say something! You are the guardian of these two young things, aren't you?

LORD EDGARD. We might ask Dupont-Dufort his advice. He seems to be a man of character.

LADY HURF. A deal too much character. What a ninny you are. He's the last man from whom we want advice. The Dupont-Duforts are after our money.

LORD EDGARD. But they're rich.

LADY HURF. Exactly. That's what worries me. They're after a lot of money. An investment or a marriage settlement. Our two little ones with their millions are exceptionally tempting morsels.

LORD EDGARD. Could we not telegraph to England?

LADY HURF. What for?

LORD EDGARD. Scotland Yard might send us a detective.

LADY HURF. That would be a great help, I must say! They're crooked as corkscrews, the lot of them!

LORD EDGARD. The problem, then, is in effect insoluble.

LADY HURF. Edgard, you simply must bestir yourself. Our fate, the girls' and mine, is in your hands.

LORD EDGARD. [*Looks at his hands, very worried.*] I don't know that I am very well equipped.

LADY HURF. [*Sternly.*] Edgard, do you call yourself a man? And a gentleman?

LORD EDGARD. Yes.

LADY HURF. Then make a decision!

LORD EDGARD. [*Firmly.*] Very well! I shall nevertheless summon a detective from Scotland Yard, with a special proviso that I want him honest.

LADY HURF. Over my dead body! If he's honest, he'll philander with the kitchenmaids and he won't wash. It will be insufferable. And yet I don't know why I should be telling you all this. What do I want with absolute security? I'm as bored as a piece of old carpet!

LORD EDGARD. Oh, my dear! . . .

LADY HURF. That's all I am, a piece of old carpet.

LORD EDGARD. You, who were once so beautiful.

LADY HURF. Yes, in the nineteen hundreds. Oh, I could scream with rage! I want to enjoy my last few years—I want to laugh a little. Sixty years I've spent deluded into thinking life a serious business. That's sixty years too long. I am in the mood, Edgard, for a gigantic piece of folly.

LORD EDGARD. Nothing dangerous, I hope?

LADY HURF. I don't know. I'll see what occurs to me. [*She leans toward him.*] I think I should like to massacre the Dupont-Duforts.

In they come, accompanied by their particular little tune, with EVA *and* JULIETTE.

D.D. SENIOR. How are you today, milady?

D.D. JUNIOR. Milady.

D.D. SENIOR. Ah, dear Lord Edgard.

LORD EDGARD. [*Drawing him aside.*] Take the greatest possible care.

D.D. SENIOR. But why, milord?

LORD EDGARD. Hush! I can't tell you. But take care. Leave Vichy.

D.D. JUNIOR. We ran into these ladies on the promenade.

EVA. Vichy's an impossible place. Nothing to do, nowhere to go, and all the men are hideous.

D.D. JUNIOR. Oh, how true! Quite, quite hideous, all of them!

D.D. SENIOR. All of them! [*Aside to his son.*] Excellent thing for us.

EVA. I have an engagement tonight, Aunt. I shall be late for dinner—if I'm back at all.

D.D. SENIOR. [*Aside to his son.*] With you?

D.D. JUNIOR. No.

JULIETTE. Eva, I haven't told you. I rescued a little boy who fell into the Thermes Fountain, and I met an enchanting young man, who helped me to save him.

LADY HURF. Juliette talks of nothing else.

The DUPONT-DUFORTS *look at each other anxiously.*

D.D. SENIOR. Wasn't that you?

D.D. JUNIOR. No.

JULIETTE. We sat in the sun till we were dry, and chatted. You've no idea how pleasant he was! He's slight, with dark hair, and—he's not the same as yours by any chance?

EVA. No. Mine's tall, with red hair.

JULIETTE. Thank goodness!

D.D. SENIOR. [*Whispers.*] Son, you have absolutely *got* to sparkle. [*Raising his voice.*] Didier, dear boy, have you been to the swimming pool with these ladies yet? You must give them a demonstration of your impeccable crawl. You could have rescued the toddler with the greatest of ease.

JULIETTE. Oh, the crawl would have been quite useless. The Thermes Fountain is only eighteen inches deep.

Toward the end of this scene, PETERBONO, *as a very noble—all too noble—old Spanish gentleman,* HECTOR *as a grandee, an equally spectacular achievement, and* GUSTAVE, *their ecclesiastical secretary, come in and slowly approach the others.*

PETERBONO. Careful. This is big game. Stay close, and take no risks.

HECTOR. Your monocle.

PETERBONO. The big act: Noblesse Oblige. Wait for the word "go." Gustave, two paces behind.

The clarinet strikes up a march, heroic and ultra-Spanish. Suddenly LADY HURF, *who has been watching this curious trio, runs to them and throws her arms around*

PETERBONO'S *neck.*

LADY HURF. Why, if it isn't that dear, dear Duke of Miraflores!

Music stops.

PETERBONO. [*Surprised and uneasy.*] Huh?

LADY HURF. Don't say you've forgotten! Biarritz, 1902. The luncheon parties at Pampeluna! The bullfights! Lady Hurf.

PETERBONO. Ah! . . . Lady Hurf. Bullfights. Lunch. Dear friend. [*To the other two.*] I must have made up like one of her acquaintances.

LADY HURF. I am so, so happy! I was disintegrating with boredom. But where is the Duchess?

PETERBONO. Dead.

Tremolo from the orchestra.

LADY HURF. Oh, heavens! And your cousin, the Count?

PETERBONO. Dead.

Tremolo from the orchestra.

LADY HURF. Oh, heavens! And your friend, the Admiral?

PETERBONO. Also dead. [*The orchestra begins a funeral march.* PETERBONO *turns to his friends.*] Saved!

LADY HURF. My poor friend. So many funerals.

PETERBONO. Alas! However, may I present my son, Don Hector? And my ecclesiastical secretary, Dom Petrus?

LADY HURF. Lord Edgard, whom you knew years ago. It was he whom you beat each morning at golf, and who was always losing his golf balls.

PETERBONO. Ha, golf—yes. Dear friend.

LORD EDGARD. [*Panic-stricken, to* LADY HURF.] But, my dear—

LADY HURF. [*Sternly.*] What's the matter? Do you mean to say you don't remember the Duke?

LORD EDGARD. This is insane. Come now, think back—

LADY HURF. Your memory is abominable. Don't say another word or I shall lose my temper. My nieces, Eva and Juliette, who worry me so dreadfully because they're both very marriageable and their dowries are exceptionally tempting to fortune hunters.

The DUPONT-DUFORTS *look at each other.*

D.D. SENIOR. Dignity, lad, dignity.

D.D. JUNIOR. She can't mean us.

PETERBONO *and* HECTOR *indulge in violent nudging.*

LADY HURF. I am so delighted to have met you again. Vichy is such a dull hole. Tell me, do you remember the Ridottos on the Riviera?

PETERBONO. I should think I do!

D.D. JUNIOR. [*To his father.*] We're forgotten.

D.D. SENIOR. Let's introduce ourselves. Dupont-Dufort Senior.

D.D. JUNIOR. Junior.

During the introductions EVA *stares hard at* HECTOR, *who simulates an enormous interest in the conversation.* GUSTAVE *has all but disappeared into his brief case and rummages feverishly among his papers to avoid* JULIETTE's *gaze, which is fixed on him in puzzled interest.*

LADY HURF. You must be as bored as I am. It's an undreamed-of stroke of fortune, our meeting, don't you think?

PETERBONO. [*Nudging* HECTOR.] Yes. Undreamed of—absolutely undreamed of.

In their glee, they go much too far, but no one seems to notice.

LADY HURF. Your son is most charming. Don't you think so, eva?

EVA. Yes.

PETERBONO. He was the most dashing officer in the entire Spanish army—before the revolution.

LADY HURF. Alas! You suffered a great deal?

PETERBONO. A great deal.

LADY HURF. Where are you staying? Not at a hotel?

PETERBONO. [*Vaguely.*] Yes.

LADY HURF. It's out of the question, Edgard! The Duke is staying at a hotel!

LORD EDGARD. But, my dearest, I assure you—

LADY HURF. Be quiet! Dear Duke, you

cannot, you simply cannot stay at a hotel. Will you do us the honor of accepting our humble hospitality? Our villa is enormous, and we shall put the west wing entirely at your disposal.

PETERBONO. Certainly, certainly, certainly, certainly—

Stupendous nudging between PETERBONO *and* HECTOR. *The* DUPONT-DUFORTS *exchange crestfallen glances.*

LADY HURF. You may, needless to say, bring your entourage. [*She looks inquiringly at* GUSTAVE.] Is he looking for something?

PETERBONO. A document, yes. Dom Petrus!

GUSTAVE. [*Emerging from the brief case.*] Your Grace? [*He has put on some dark glasses.*]

LADY HURF. Has he got bad eyes?

PETERBONO. Oh, very bad. His condition requires a certain amount of care. I couldn't burden you with his presence. Dom Petrus, we shall accept Lady Hurf's generous offer of hospitality. Call at the hotel, will you, and have our luggage sent on. And stay there until further notice. You will collect the mail and come to us each morning for instructions.

GUSTAVE. [*Furious.*] But, your Grace. . . .

PETERBONO. Enough!

GUSTAVE. Your Grace—

PETERBONO. Off with you!

HECTOR *gives* GUSTAVE *a push, and he wanders reluctantly away.*

LADY HURF. [*Moved.*] Just as he used to be! That same commanding tone—the vocal magic of the Miraflores! Your cousin had it too.

PETERBONO. Alas!

LADY HURF. How did he die?

PETERBONO. Er, how he died?

LADY HURF. I was so fond of him.

PETERBONO. You want me to relate the circumstances of his passing?

LADY HURF. Yes.

PETERBONO. [*Turns to* HECTOR *in his panic.*] Well, he died. . . .

HECTOR *mimes a motor accident, but this* PETERBONO *cannot grasp.*

PETERBONO. He died insane.

LADY HURF. Ah, poor fellow! He always was eccentric. But your wife, the dear Duchess?

PETERBONO. Dead.

LADY HURF. Yes, I know. But how?

HECTOR *touches his heart several times.* PETERBONO *is slow to take the suggestion, but since he has no imagination whatever himself, he gives way.*

PETERBONO. Of love.

LADY HURF. [*In confusion.*] Oh, I beg your pardon! And your friend, the Admiral?

PETERBONO. Ah, now, the Admiral. . . . [*He looks at* HECTOR, *who indicates that he has run out of ideas. He again misinterprets the pantomine.*] Drowned. But please excuse me, you are reopening wounds which time has not yet healed.

LADY HURF. Oh, forgive me, dear friend, forgive me! [*To the others.*] What breeding! What grandeur in adversity! Don't you think so, Edgard?

LORD EDGARD. My dear, I still insist that—

LADY HURF. Do stop insisting. Can't you see the Duke is suffering?

D.D. SENIOR [*To his son.*] Let us join in the conversation.

D.D. JUNIOR. What an appalling avalanche of misfortunes!

D.D. SENIOR. Falling on such venerable heads!

No one listens.

LADY HURF. [*In a peal of laughter.*] How beautiful Biarritz was in those days. Do you remember the balls?

PETERBONO. Ah, the balls. . . .

LADY HURF. And Lina Veri?

PETERBONO. Lina Veri. I can't quite recall. . . .

LADY HURF. Come, come. Why, you were intimate! [*To the others.*] He's aged so much.

PETERBONO. Oh, Lina Veri. Of course. The darling of Italian society.

LADY HURF. No, no, no. She was a dancer.

PETERBONO. Oh yes, but her mother was the darling of Italian society.

LADY HURF. [*To the others.*] He's wandering a little. He's very tired. My dear Duke, I would like to show you your apartments right away. The villa is close by, at the end of the avenue.

GUSTAVE *comes running in, this time as his own charming self, but magnificently dressed.*

GUSTAVE. Good morning, Father!

PETERBONO. [*Off balance.*] Stinker! Allow me to present my second son, Don Pedro, whom I'd forgotten to mention.

LADY HURF. Gracious, you have another son? By whom?

PETERBONO. [*Panicking again.*] Ah, that's a long story—[*He looks at* HECTOR, *who signs to him to go carefully.*] But that one also opens wounds as yet unhealed by time.

LADY HURF. Come along, Edgard.

LORD EDGARD. But, my dear—

LADY HURF. And keep quiet!

They go, HECTOR *paying elaborate attentions to* EVA, *who has continued to stare at him.*

JULIETTE. [*To* GUSTAVE.] Now, will you kindly tell me what is going on?

GUSTAVE. Ssh! I'll explain later.

They go too. The DUPONT-DUFORTS *are left alone.*

D.D. JUNIOR. Father, they've forgotten us—!

D.D. SENIOR. All the same, we'll follow. And, Didier, twice the affability. Let's hope these young men are already attached or better still that they aren't interested in women!

They go.

Act 2

A drawing room in LADY HURF's *house. It is evening, after dinner, and* JULIETTE *and*

GUSTAVE *are sitting side by side; a little romantic air is heard in the distance.*

JULIETTE. It's nice here. No one is disturbing us tonight.

GUSTAVE. Yes, it is nice.

JULIETTE. For three days now you've been sad. Are you homesick for Spain?

GUSTAVE. Oh no.

JULIETTE. I'm sorry now I wouldn't work at my Spanish at school. We might have spoken it together. It would have been fun.

GUSTAVE. I only speak a few words myself.

JULIETTE. Do you? That's funny.

GUSTAVE. Yes, it is rather.

A silence.

JULIETTE. It must be amusing to be a prince.

GUSTAVE. Oh, one gets used to it, you know.

A silence.

JULIETTE. Don Pedro, what's the matter? We were much friendlier three days ago.

GUSTAVE. Nothing's the matter.

A pause. LORD EDGARD *crosses the room, laden with papers.*

LORD EGARD. [*Muttering.*] Though I should die in the endeavor, I'll set my mind at rest. [*He drops his papers. They jump up to help him, but he bars their path.*] Don't touch them! Don't touch them! [*He picks up the papers himself and goes out muttering.*] This momentous discovery, if discovery there be, must be surrounded with the greatest possible precautions.

GUSTAVE. What is he looking for? He's done nothing but ferret about among those old papers since we came here.

JULIETTE. I don't know. He's a little mad. Only he's painstaking as well, you see, so sometimes the results are quite prodigious.

A LITTLE GIRL *comes in.*

JULIETTE. Oh, here's my little friend.

LITTLE GIRL. Mademoiselle Juliette, I've picked some daisies for you.

JULIETTE. Thank you, darling.

LITTLE GIRL. They haven't very many petals. Daddy says they aren't the ones that lovers use.

JULIETTE. Never mind.

LITTLE GIRL. Shall I get some others?

JULIETTE. No. Yes. You're very sweet. [*She kisses her.*] Run away now.

The LITTLE GIRL *goes.* JULIETTE *turns to* GUSTAVE, *shamefaced.*

JULIETTE. Do you think it's silly of me?

GUSTAVE. No.

JULIETTE. You said you loved me, Don Pedro, yet for three days now you haven't even looked at me.

GUSTAVE. I do love you, Juliette.

JULIETTE. Then why—?

GUSTAVE. I can't tell you.

JULIETTE. My father wasn't titled, I know, but my aunt is a Lady, and my grandfather was an Honorable.

GUSTAVE. How funny you are. It isn't that.

JULIETTE. Do you think the Duke of Miraflores would consent to my marrying you?

GUSTAVE. [*Smiling.*] I'm sure he would.

JULIETTE. Why do you look so sad then, if you love me and everyone approves?

GUSTAVE. I can't tell you.

JULIETTE. But you do feel, don't you, that our lives might meet and join one day?

GUSTAVE. I would be lying if I told you I felt that.

JULIETTE. [*Turning away.*] That's unkind of you.

GUSTAVE. Careful. Here's your cousin.

JULIETTE. Come into the garden. It's getting dark. I want you to tell me everything.

The music fades as they go. EVA *comes in, followed by* HECTOR, *in a totally different make-up from the one he wore in Act 1.*

HECTOR. There, you see, they've left us the place to ourselves.

EVA. But I don't in the least need a place to myself—that's the pity of it—I could adapt myself quite easily to a great crowd around us.

HECTOR. How cruel you are!

EVA. I don't like you. I'm cruel to those I dislike. It's in my nature. But, on the other hand, when someone appeals to me, there's hardly anything I wouldn't do for him.

HECTOR. [*In despair.*] Why, why can I not manage to appeal to you a second time?

EVA. You know perfectly well why. You're not the same now.

HECTOR. What abominable absent-mindedness! This disguise, I tell you, is the fancy of an aristocrat wearied to death of his own personality, a pastime which affords him an escape from his oppressive self. And for this accursed fancy, must I lose my love?

EVA. I remember with delight a young man who spoke to me in the park. Find him for me. I might still think him lovable.

HECTOR. This is ridiculous! Won't you even tell me if I'm getting warm? At least tell me, did I have a beard when I first appealed to you?

EVA. But it wouldn't amuse me if I were to tell you.

HECTOR. [*Who has turned away to change his make-up, turns back again wearing a completely new face.*] It wasn't like this, I suppose?

EVA. [*In a burst of laughter.*] No, oh no!

HECTOR. Yet you remember my voice, my eyes?

EVA. Yes, but it isn't enough.

HECTOR. I'm the same height as I was. I'm tall, well built—I assure you I am, very well built.

EVA. I only judge by faces.

HECTOR. This is horrible! Horrible! I'll never find the face that pleased you, ever! It wasn't as a woman, by any chance?

EVA. What do you take me for?

HECTOR. Or, as a Chinaman?

EVA. You're evidently out of your mind. I'll wait till you're in it again. [*She goes to sit farther off; he starts to follow her and she turns on him.*] No, no, no! For heaven's sake, will you stop following

me around and changing your beard every five minutes! You're making my head spin.

HECTOR. [*Stricken.*] And to think that idiot Peterbono keeps on swearing it was as a test pilot!

LORD EDGARD *crosses the room laden with papers.*

LORD EDGARD. This is unthinkable! I must find this letter, from which the truth will spring in such a curious fashion. [*He sees* HECTOR *in his latest make-up, drops his papers, and leaps on him.*] At last! The detective from Scotland Yard.

HECTOR. No sir. [*He makes to go.*]

LORD EDGARD. Excellent! The perfect answer. I specially stipulated secrecy. But don't be afraid. I am Lord Edgard in person. You may disclose your identity.

HECTOR. I tell you I'm not the man you're expecting. [*He goes.*]

LORD EDGARD. [*Following him.*] I see! I see! Perfect! You're keeping word for word to my instructions! I stressed the need for caution!

LADY HURF *enters, holding a magazine.*

LADY HURF. My little Eva is bored, isn't she?

EVA *smiles and says nothing. Unseen by* LADY HURF, HECTOR *comes back in another make-up, which he silently shows* EVA. *She shakes her head and he retires, heavy-hearted.* LADY HURF *puts down her magazine with a sigh.*

LADY HURF. My little Eva is as bored as she can be.

EVA. [*With a smile.*] Yes, Aunt.

LADY HURF. So am I, darling, very bored.

EVA. Only I'm twenty-five, so you see, it's rather sad.

LADY HURF. You'll see how much sadder it can be when you are sixty. For you there's always love. As you may guess, it's several years now since I officially renounced it.

EVA. Oh, love!

LADY HURF. *What* a deep sigh! Since you've been a widow, surely you've had lovers?

EVA. I never had a single one who loved me.

LADY HURF. You want the moon. If your lovers bore you, marry one of them. That will give the others an added fascination.

EVA. Marry? Whom?

LADY HURF. Needless to say these Dupont-Duforts exasperate us both. What about the Spaniards?

EVA. Prince Hector chases after me changing his mustache in the hope of rediscovering the one that first appealed to me.

LADY HURF. Truly appealed to you?

EVA. [*Smiling.*] I don't remember.

LADY HURF. They're curious individuals.

EVA. Why?

LADY HURF. Oh, I don't know. I tell you, I'm an old carcass who doesn't know what to do with herself. I've had everything a woman could reasonably, or even unreasonably, wish for. Money, power, lovers. Now that I'm old, I feel as alone inside my skin as I did as a little girl and they made me face the wall when I'd been naughty. And here's the rub; I know that between that little girl and this old woman, there has been, under the charivari and the noise, nothing but an even greater loneliness.

EVA. I've always thought of you as happy.

LADY HURF. You don't see much, do you? I am playing a part. Only, like everything else I do, I play it well, that's all. Yours now, you play badly, little girl. [*She strokes her hair.*] Child, child, you will always find yourself pursued by desires with changing beards and never have the courage to tell one of them: stay as you are—I love you. Don't think yourself a martyr now. All women are the same. My little Juliette, though, will come through because she is romantic. Her simplicity will save her. It's a favor only granted to few.

EVA. There are some who can love.

LADY HURF. Yes. There are some who love a man. Who kill him with loving, who kill themselves for him, but they are seldom heiresses to millions. [*She strokes her hair again, with a rueful smile.*] Ah, you'll finish up like me, an old woman covered in diamonds who plays at intrigues in an effort to forget that she has never lived. And yet, I'd like to laugh a little. Here am I, playing with fire, and the fire won't even burn my fingers.

EVA. What do you mean, Aunt?

LADY HURF. Shush—here come our marionettes.

PETERBONO *and* HECTOR *appear in the doorway, preceded by the* MUSICIAN *and followed almost at once by the* DUPONT-DUFORTS. *They all rush toward the ladies, but it is the thieves who get there first to kiss their hands.*

LADY HURF. [*Jumps to her feet and utters a sudden cry.*] Ah! I have an idea!

PETERBONO. [*Frightened, to* HECTOR.] She scares the life out of me. Every time she screams like that, I think my beard's loose.

LADY HURF. Where is Juliette?

EVA. In the garden, with Prince Pedro. They're inseparable.

PETERBONO. Ah, the dear children!

LADY HURF. [*Calling.*] Juliette!

JULIETTE. [*Coming in with* GUSTAVE.] Did you want me, Aunt Emily?

LADY HURF. [*Drawing her aside.*] Your eyes are red, child. Now mind, you mustn't be unhappy, or I cut the strings and the puppets will fall down.

JULIETTE. What do you mean, Aunt?

LADY HURF. If I appear to be talking through my hat, it's precisely so you won't understand me. Come along, both of you. [*She takes them by the waist and leads them into the garden.*] I have an idea to brighten up this evening; I want you to tell me what you think of it.

They go. The DUPONT-DUFORTS *look at each other.*

D.D. SENIOR. After them, my boy. And a

hundred times more charm. Remember, it's our future that's at stake.

D.D. JUNIOR. Yes, Dad.

Left alone, the three thieves can unbend.

HECTOR. [*Offering* PETERBONO *a box of cigars.*] Would you care for a cigar?

PETERBONO. [*Helping himself.*] I'm savoring them. They're remarkably good.

HECTOR. [*Pouring out.*] A little brandy?

PETERBONO. Thank you.

They drink.

HECTOR. Another cigar, perhaps?

PETERBONO. [*Grabbing a fistful without more ado.*] You're too kind. No, no, really, you embarrass me. [*He feels a slight remorse and takes the box.*] But may I in return press you to a cigar?

HECTOR. [*Pulling them out of his pockets in handfuls.*] Thank you so much. I'm all right just now.

There is a moment of beatitude and exquisite refinement. They spread themselves blissfully on the sofa. Suddenly HECTOR *indicates* GUSTAVE, *sitting sad and somber in his corner.*

PETERBONO. [*Rises and goes to him.*] What's wrong, laddie? Why so sad? Here you are with a wonderful room, lovely food, and a pretty little thing to flirt with, you're playing at princes, and for all that you can manage to be gloomy?

GUSTAVE. I don't want to stay here.

The other two give a start.

PETERBONO. Huh? You want to leave?

GUSTAVE. Yes.

PETERBONO. Leave here?

GUSTAVE. Yes—leave here.

PETERBONO. Hector, the boy's lost his reason.

HECTOR. What do you want to leave for?

GUSTAVE. I'm in love with Juliette.

HECTOR. Well then?

GUSTAVE. Really in love.

HECTOR. Well then?

PETERBONO. Why not? You've never been better off. She takes you for a prince, and rich at that. Go in and win, lad, she's as good as yours.

GUSTAVE. I don't want to take her for a day and then be forced to leave her.

PETERBONO. You'll have to leave her one day.

GUSTAVE. And—I'm ashamed of this game I have to play with her. I'd rather go away, now, and never see her again.

HECTOR. He's out of his mind.

PETERBONO. Completely.

GUSTAVE. Look, what are we here for?

PETERBONO. What are we here for? We're working, lad. It's the height of our season.

GUSTAVE. We're here to do a job. Let's do it, then, and go.

PETERBONO. And the preliminaries? Have you spared a single thought for the preliminaries?

GUSTAVE. They've gone on long enough, your damn preliminaries!

PETERBONO. I ask you, Hector, isn't it painful? Having to listen to an apprentice teaching us our trade!

HECTOR. Of course we'll do a job—that's what we came for—but have you even the first idea what that job's going to be?

GUSTAVE. Strip the drawing room?

PETERBONO. With carpetbags, eh? Like raggle-taggle gypsies! The lowness, Hector, the abysmal lowness of this youngster's mind! Understand, boy, that we haven't yet decided on the job we're going to do. And if our behavior strikes you, a novice, as peculiar, tell yourself it's because we're in the process of investigating the possibilities of this—establishment.

GUSTAVE. You're lingering on here for the brandy and cigars, and because Hector still hopes he'll get Eva to remember him. But in actual fact you haven't the smallest inkling what you want to do. I may be an apprentice, but I'll tell you something—that's no way to work.

PETERBONO. [*Running to* HECTOR.] Hector, hold me back!

HECTOR. [*Still blissfully smoking.*] Gustave, don't be difficult. Try to understand.

PETERBONO. Hector, hold me back!

HECTOR. You see, we're wavering. . . .

PETERBONO. Hold me back, Hector! Hold me back!

HECTOR. [*Takes his arm to please him.*] All right, I've got you.

PETERBONO. [*Deflated.*] Just as well.

HECTOR. [*To* GUSTAVE.] We're wavering between several possible courses of action. . . .

GUSTAVE. Which?

HECTOR. Shall we confide in him, Pete? Is it safe to risk the indiscretion of a youth?

PETERBONO. [*Shrugs.*] Oh, confide in him, do. Since we're answerable to him now.

HECTOR. Right. Tell him your idea first, Pete.

PETERBONO. After you, Hector, after you.

HECTOR. [*Embarrassed.*] Aaaaaaah . . . well. . . .

GUSTAVE. You haven't thought of a thing!

HECTOR. [*In righteous rage.*] We haven't thought of a thing?!!! We're wavering between the trick of the bad check given in exchange for real jewels on a Saturday, which gives us the weekend to make our getaway, or the trick of the good check received in exchange for fake jewels under the same conditions. We've also considered giving Lady Hurf some orchids sprayed with ether (taking good care not to smell them ourselves) so as to relieve her of the pearls as soon as she nods off.

PETERBONO. [*Equally incensed.*] Or we might provoke the Dupont-Duforts to a duel! We wound them and then in the commotion we make off with the silver!

GUSTAVE. What if you're the ones to get wounded?

PETERBONO. Impossible!

GUSTAVE. Why?

PETERBONO. [*Yelling.*] I don't know. But it's impossible!

HECTOR. Or, again, we could make out we'd been robbed and demand a colossal sum for hush money!

PETERBONO. Pretend we found a pearl in the oysters at dinner, for instance, and swap it for a pearl of Lady Hurf's, or something.

GUSTAVE. There's no "r" in the month.

PETERBONO. I said, for instance!

GUSTAVE. In other words, you just don't know. Well, I'm going to do the job tonight, and then I'm off.

PETERBONO. Tonight? And why not right away?

GUSTAVE. Yes, why not right away? I want to go away. I want to leave here as soon as possible.

PETERBONO. He'll be the ruin of us! Gustave, think of your poor old mother, who put you in my care!

GUSTAVE. No!

PETERBONO. I'll put my curse on you! Naturally you don't care a rap if I put my curse on you?

GUSTAVE. No.

PETERBONO. [*Bellowing.*] Hector! Hold me back! [*He seizes* GUSTAVE.] Just another two weeks. We'll do the job all right, but it's nice here, and it isn't so often we're in a nice place. . . .

GUSTAVE. No. I'm too unhappy. [*He goes.*]

HECTOR. [*Leaps after him.*] After him! We've got to stop him before he starts a scandal.

PETERBONO. [*Calling after him.*] I've got an idea! Suppose we pretended not to know him?

HECTOR *shrugs his shoulders and goes out, refusing even to consider such a solution. Enter* LORD EDGARD, *preceded by the* MUSICIAN *playing a succession of tremolos as if he had intimations of a sudden blow of destiny.* LORD EDGARD *is rummaging in his ever-present pile of papers. All of a sudden he utters a loud cry and falls in a dead faint among his scattered letters. The* MUSICIAN *runs for help, emitting isolated notes from his instrument.* JULIETTE *comes in.*

JULIETTE. Uncle, Uncle, what's the matter? [*She props him up against a sofa and feels his hands.*] Ice cold! What's this? [*She picks up a letter, reads it, and hurriedly thrusts it into her pocket! Running out.*] Aunt Emily! Aunt Emily! Come quickly!

The clarinet in great confusion multiplies the tragic tremolos. Everyone comes rushing in shouting at once.

ALL.
Stroke!
At his age!
No, he's only fainted.
Stand back—give him air.
Get a doctor!
He's coming around.
He's all right now.
A sudden shock.
Perhaps he found what he was looking for.

The music stops. An enormous silence.

PETERBONO. [*Breathes to* HECTOR *in the silence.*] The chance of a lifetime.

HECTOR. Yes. But what do we do about it?

PETERBONO. Well, nothing, obviously, but it's still the chance of a lifetime.

LORD EDGARD. [*Sitting up slowly, says in a toneless voice.*] My friends, I have a ghastly piece of news for you. The Duke of Miraflores died in Biarritz in 1904.

Everyone looks at PETERBONO *who is very ill at ease. An impish little jig on the clarinet.*

PETERBONO. Nonsense!

HECTOR. [*Aside.*] Talk about the chance of a lifetime!

PETERBONO. This is a fine time to be funny! Ease over to the window.

LADY HURF. Edgard, are you out of your mind?

LORD EDGARD. No, I tell you. I've found the notification. I knew I'd find it eventually. Ever since the day. . . . [*He searches himself.*] Where is it? This is too much! Where is it? I had it a moment ago! Oh, my goodness! It's gone again.

D.D. SENIOR. Everything is coming to light!

D.D. JUNIOR. We are saved! [*To* PETERBONO, *who is imperceptibly edging toward the window.*] Aren't you staying to make sure your host is all right?

PETERBONO. Yes, oh yes!

LADY HURF. Edgard, that's a ridiculous joke to play on the dear Duke.

LORD EDGARD. But, my dear, I guarantee—

LADY HURF. Come along, dear Duke, and show him you aren't dead.

PETERBONO. [*Uneasy.*] No, no, I'm not dead.

LORD EDGARD. Yet I found the notification. . . .

LADY HURF. [*Pinching him.*] Edgard, you're making a mistake, I'm sure. You must apologize.

LORD EDGARD. [*Rubbing his arm.*] Ouch! Why yes, now that you mention it, I think I must have been confusing him with the Duke of Orléans.

LADY HURF. Of course. Shall we call the incident closed?

PETERBONO. [*In great relief.*] Completely closed.

LADY HURF. Let's go outside, shall we? I've ordered coffee on the terrace. I want to tell you about my idea.

D.D. SENIOR. [*In step with her.*] I think it's a wonderful idea.

LADY HURF. [*Exasperated.*] Wait a minute, my dear man, I haven't told you yet. Listen. They're holding a Thieves' Carnival tonight at the Casino. We're all going to dress up as thieves and go to it.

D.D. SENIOR *and* JUNIOR. [*Immediately burst out laughing.*] He! He! He! How terribly, terribly amusing!

D.D. SENIOR. [*To his son as they go out.*] Play up to her, son.

PETERBONO. [*Furious, as he goes out with* HECTOR.] I call that in very poor taste, don't you?

JULIETTE *is alone. She stands motionless a moment. The music is heard some way away, playing a romantic theme.*
JULIETTE *takes out the fatal letter and reads it.*

JULIETTE. "We regret to announce the

sad death of His Serene Highness the Duke of Miraflores y Grandes, Marquis of Priola, Count of Zeste and Galba. The funeral will take place. . . ." [*She stands in thought a moment.*] If his father isn't the Duke of Miraflores—then who can he be? Why has he taken the car out of the garage? Why is he hiding from me?

LITTLE GIRL. [*Entering.*] Mademoiselle Juliette, I found some. Look, daisies with lots of petals.

JULIETTE. Haven't you gone to bed yet?

LITTLE GIRL. I was picking daisies for you.

JULIETTE. Thank you, you're an angel. [*She kisses her.*] His father may be an adventurer, but, you see, he loves me. He does love me, doesn't he?

LITTLE GIRL. Yes, of course he does.

JULIETTE. We don't care, do we, if he's an adventurer, or worse? If you were me, you'd love him, wouldn't you, just the same? Only why does that hard look come into his eyes whenever I ask him about himself? If he has designs on me, and he'd be wise to have because I'm very rich, he should be very pleasant to me all the time—whereas—do you think he prefers Eva? That would be terrible—

LITTLE GIRL. I don't know.

JULIETTE. No, of course you don't. Come along, I'll take you home. Are you afraid of the dark?

LITTLE GIRL. No.

JULIETTE. That's a good girl. Nor am I. There's nothing to be afraid of, you know. Thieves won't hurt you.

They go.

Act 3

The same set. The room is dark; a figure is seen moving about with a flashlight. It is GUSTAVE, *dressed in dark clothes and wearing a cap. He is silently examining* the objects in the drawing room. Suddenly he hears a noise and switches off the flashlight; a low whistle; two dark figures spring up, two flashlights light up and focus on* GUSTAVE.

GUSTAVE. Who's that?

FIRST FIGURE. Tonight's the night.

GUSTAVE. Peterbono?

FIRST FIGURE. No. We're the new ones.

SECOND FIGURE. The new bandits.

GUSTAVE. For God's sake, what's going on? [*He draws a revolver.*] Hands up!

D.D. SENIOR. [*It is no other.*] Ha-ha-ha! That's good! Where did you get the gun? It's magnificent!

GUSTAVE. Stay where you are or I fire!

D.D. SENIOR. Come quietly! The game's up.

GUSTAVE. Stay where you are, damn you! [*He fires.*]

D.D. SENIOR. [*Blissfully unaware of his danger.*] Oh, well done! Bravo!

GUSTAVE. What do you mean, bravo? [*He fires again.*]

D.D. JUNIOR. It's a wonderful imitation! Where on earth did you buy those caps?

GUSTAVE. For the last time, stay where you are! [*He fires again and shatters a vase, which falls with a terrible clatter.*]

D.D. SENIOR. Didier, why do you have to be so clumsy!

D.D. JUNIOR. [*Protesting in the dark.*] But, Dad, I didn't do it!

D.D. SENIOR. Well, it can't have been I, can it? I'm in the middle of the room.

D.D. JUNIOR. But, Dad, so am I!

D.D. SENIOR. [*Suddenly anxious.*] Well then, who broke the vase?

LORD EDGARD. [*Enters and switches on the light; he is dressed up as a policeman.*] Now, now, what is all this noise? How do you like my helmet?

D.D. SENIOR. [*Who has got himself up, along with his son, in a terrifying apache disguise.*] Superb, my lord, superb! [*Exit* LORD EDGARD. D.D. SENIOR *goes to* GUSTAVE.] My word, I don't think much of your costume. It doesn't come off—it's much too simple. It's the little touches that mean so much. For instance, look, this little scar here.

D.D. JUNIOR. And the black eye patch.

GUSTAVE. What are you doing dressed up like that?

D.D. SENIOR. We're going to the Casino.

D.D. JUNIOR. To the Thieves' Carnival. And so are you.

GUSTAVE. Oh? Oh yes, of course. So am I.

D.D. SENIOR. Only if I were you, I'd touch up your makeup, my boy. It's a shade too simple. You don't look a bit like a thief.

GUSTAVE. You're quite right. I'll see to it at once. [*He turns at the door.*] Tell me, is everybody going to the Thieves' Carnival?

D.D. SENIOR. Of course—everybody.

GUSTAVE. That's fine. See you later. [*He goes.*]

D.D. SENIOR. Not an ounce of imagination in him, that boy.

D.D. JUNIOR. If the other two have rigged themselves up as absurdly as that, which they probably have, we're well on the way. The girls will have eyes for nobody but us!

D.D. SENIOR. Have you seen the latest batch of telegrams?

D.D. JUNIOR. Yes.

D.D. SENIOR. If we don't leave this house with a fat settlement, it's the colonies for us, I can tell you. Make yourself irresistible, there's a good boy.

D.D. JUNIOR. I'm doing my best, Dad.

D.D. SENIOR. I know you are. You're an honest, conscientious lad, but you mustn't slacken for one moment. The success of this evening's entertainment means a great deal to us. What's more, there's something shady about our rivals which is bound to give rise to a scandal one of these days. It was quite obviously Lady Hurf who made the old duffer keep quiet this afternoon when he insisted the Duke of Miraflores died in 1904. Keep your eyes open, and be ready for any emergency.

D.D. JUNIOR. We have got to get rid of these adventurers. It's a matter of life and death.

D.D. SENIOR. We'll let them dig their own graves, while we'll be more and more agreeable. Ssh! Here comes Lady Hurf.

Enter LADY HURF *and* EVA *as thieves in petticoats. The* DUPONT-DUFORTS *cough desperately to attract attention.*

LADY HURF. [*Seeing them.*] Oh, breathtaking! Aren't they. Eva? Breath-taking! Who would have thought they had it in them! What do you think of our guests, Eva?

EVA. What a spectacular effect! How in the world did you manage it?

D.D. SENIOR. [*Simpering.*] We're delighted. . . .

D.D. JUNIOR. . . . that we delight you.

LADY HURF. They always look as though they're waiting for a tip.

EVA. Which, in a way, they are.

LADY HURF. The Duke and his sons are being very slow.

EVA. I called out to them as I went by. They can't manage to dress up as thieves, they said.

LADY HURF. [*As she goes.*] Go up and fetch them, gentlemen, if you would be so good, and give them a few wrinkles.

D.D. SENIOR. Certainly! Certainly! [*Aside to his son.*] Let us be pleasant.

D.D. JUNIOR. Very, very pleasant. [*They bow themselves out.*]

JULIETTE *crosses furtively.*

EVA. Why, you're not dressed!

JULIETTE. I'm going up now.

EVA. You'll make us late.

JULIETTE. Go on ahead. I'll take the two-seater.

EVA. [*Unexpectedly.*] Are you in love with this boy?

JULIETTE. Why do you ask me?

EVA. Yes indeed, why does one ask people if they're in love, when one can tell at a glance, always?

JULIETTE. Can you tell?

EVA. Yes.

JULIETTE. Well, you're wrong. I'm not

in love with anyone.

She turns to go when EVA *calls her back.*

EVA. Juliette! Why do you look upon me as your enemy?

JULIETTE. You are my enemy.

EVA. No, I love you very much. Sit down.

JULIETTE. [*Turning on her.*] You're in love with him, too—that's it, isn't it? You're going to take him away from me, and you want to warn me first so that I won't be hurt too much? Why, you've even agreed on that between you, probably. You have, haven't you? haven't you? For heaven's sake, say something! Why do you smile like that?

EVA. How lucky you are to be in love as much as that.

JULIETTE. You're prettier than I am; you can get any man you want.

EVA. Oh, if I could only bring myself to want one.

JULIETTE. Don't you want him, then?

EVA. No, little silly.

JULIETTE. Have you never spoken to him when I wasn't looking?

EVA. Had I ever wanted to, I should have found it very difficult. He only has to come near me by accident and you can't take your eyes off us.

JULIETTE. I'm wary. I love him, you see.

EVA. Lucky you.

JULIETTE. You swear you've never set out to attract him?

EVA. I swear.

JULIETTE. Even the day you danced with him twice running?

EVA. The orchestra had struck up a second tango.

JULIETTE. Even the day you went out on the river while the Dupont-Duforts tried to teach me roulette?

EVA. Even then. He looked so sad that I suggested he should row straight back, but we couldn't find you anywhere.

JULIETTE. That day I'm not so sure. He had a strange look in his eyes that evening.

EVA. Because he'd asked me if I thought you cared for him, and I said you were an unpredictable little girl and there was no knowing what went on inside your heart.

JULIETTE. Was that truly why? [*A little pause.*] All the same, I do think you might have told him something else.

EVA. Are you satisfied now?

JULIETTE. Did you never try to attract him, not even at the beginning, not even the very first day?

EVA. Not even the first day.

JULIETTE. Yes, then, I'm satisfied.

EVA. Why will you never trust me? I feel like an old woman beside you sometimes.

JULIETTE. You're so much better-looking than I am, so much more poised, more feminine.

EVA. Do you think so?

JULIETTE. It surprises me, you know, in spite of what you say. You must admit that he's a good deal more attractive than Hector, and you don't mind *his* attentions.

EVA. Do you think I couldn't have denied myself a mere flirtation when I could see you were so much in love?

JULIETTE. That's grand of you.

EVA. Oh no. I wish I could have wanted him so much that I'd have sacrificed you without giving you a moment's thought.

JULIETTE. When you chew your pearls, I know there's something wrong.

EVA. Yes, there's something wrong.

JULIETTE. Yet you look so lovely tonight. You'll have all the men around you at the ball.

EVA. All of them.

JULIETTE. I'm not joking.

EVA. Nor am I. I'll have them all. And yet it's very sad.

JULIETTE. Aren't you happy?

EVA. No.

JULIETTE. Yet it's so easy. You only need to let yourself go. Why, hardly a moment goes by that one isn't unhappy, yet I think that must be what it means, to be happy.

EVA. You've always thought me cleverer,

stronger, more beautiful than you because the men flocked around me. And yet you see, there's only one who is alive, in this house—you're the only one perhaps in Vichy, perhaps in the whole world.

JULIETTE. [*Smiling, lost in her dream.*] Yes, I am alive.

EVA. And untouched, and eager to believe. . . .

JULIETTE. To believe everything.

EVA. You've never had, as I have, a man without love in your bed. You haven't even a jewel at your throat, not a ring on your finger. You're wearing nothing but this simple linen dress, and you're twenty years old, and you are in love. [JULIETTE *sits motionless yielding to the unseen with a faint smile.* EVA *looks sharply at her.*] Juliette, why aren't you in thieves' dress like the rest of us?

JULIETTE. [*Bursting with sudden joy.*] Oh, I'm too happy! I haven't the courage to stay beside you who are sad. When I'm a little less happy, I'll think of you, I swear I will! [*She kisses her and runs off.*] Ssh!

EVA. All this mystery! What are you trying to say?

Enter LADY HURF *with the* DUPONT-DUFORTS.

LADY HURF. We will make a truly magnificent entrance.

D.D. SENIOR. The Spanish gentlemen are ready.

LADY HURF. Do they look all right?

D.D. SENIOR. That's a matter of taste.

D.D. JUNIOR. Anyway, here they come.

Enter PETERBONO *and* HECTOR. *They have contrived to disguise themselves as absolutely ludicrous comic-opera bandits. They are greeted with shrieks of laughter.*

HECTOR. What are they laughing at?

PETERBONO. What do they *think* thieves look like? Don't they ever go to the theatre?

LADY HURF. But, my dear Duke, what are you supposed to be?

PETERBONO. A thief.

HECTOR. [*To* EVA.] It wasn't like this, I

suppose?

EVA. Heavens, no!

PETERBONO. [*To* LADY HURF.] Don't you like us?

LADY HURF. Enormously!

PETERBONO. Admit there's something wrong.

LADY HURF. My dear friend, one really can't expect a Spanish grandee to make much of a showing as a common thief.

PETERBONO. Well said, eh, Hector?

Enormous nudgings.

LADY HURF. Come along, all of you. The car's waiting. Where is Lord Edgard? Still glued to the mirror, I suppose. Edgard!

He appears, still in his own suit, and wearing his police helmet, but he has shaved off his mustache.

LORD EDGARD. Do you think I did well to shave off my mustache?

LADY HURF. [*Without looking at him.*] I don't know! Come along! To the carnival!

The music immediately strikes up a lively quadrille, which the thieves dance with the ladies, without the DUPONT-DUFORTS *getting a sporting chance. Then follows a piece of extremely vulgar jive, and the* DUPONT-DUFORTS *making the best of a bad job, finish up by dancing together with tremendous spirit. All the characters dance their way out.*

D.D. SENIOR. [*Bringing up the rear with his son.*] Things are getting better and better and better.

D.D. JUNIOR. Let's be as witty as the very devil!

D.D. SENIOR. And, remember, Didier, twice as nice.

The room remains empty for an instant. A SERVANT *comes in to close the windows and turn out the lights. Another moment of silence, and* GUSTAVE *appears and listens. The car is heard driving off. He goes around the room, examining its contents one by one. All of a sudden he flattens himself against the wall.*

JULIETTE *enters, dressed for a journey.*

JULIETTE. Here I am.

GUSTAVE. What are you doing here? Why didn't you go with the others?

JULIETTE. I've come to find you.

GUSTAVE. Get out of here, will you?

JULIETTE. Why are you so harsh with me?

GUSTAVE. Go on, get out!

JULIETTE. I'll go, of course, if you don't want me, only I thought you would want me. What's the matter?

GUSTAVE. I've got a headache. I want to stay here.

JULIETTE. Why this yarn, to me?

GUSTAVE. It isn't a yarn. Get out, will you. Go on, quick march!

JULIETTE. But—you've never spoken to me like this!

GUSTAVE. There's a first time for everything.

JULIETTE. What have I done?

GUSTAVE. Nothing in particular. It's too difficult to explain, and anyway you wouldn't understand.

JULIETTE. But, Señor Pedro. . . .

GUSTAVE. There isn't any Señor Pedro, for a start. My name is Gustave. And, secondly, will you please go away?

JULIETTE. And there was I thinking that you loved me—

GUSTAVE. We all make mistakes, don't we?

JULIETTE. But you used to tell me so.

GUSTAVE. I was lying.

JULIETTE. Oh no! I don't believe it!

GUSTAVE. [*Going to her purposefully.*] Listen, my little pet, I'm telling you to get out of here, double quick.

JULIETTE. Why?

GUSTAVE. You'll see why later on. In the meantime go up to your room and weep over your lost illusions. [*He takes her arm to lead her to the door.*] What are you dressed up in this coat for? What kind of a costume is that meant to be?

JULIETTE. Traveling costume.

GUSTAVE. Traveling costume? You're mad.

JULIETTE. Please don't be angry. I came to find you so we could go away. You told me once we'd go away together.

GUSTAVE. I was joking. Anyway, how do you know I mean to go away?

JULIETTE. I know.

GUSTAVE. You look as though you know a lot of things. Come along with me.

JULIETTE. We might meet one of the servants in the passage. [*He looks at her.*] We'd better not move from here. We'll be quite safe in this room.

GUSTAVE. The Dupont-Duforts must be waiting for you. Go and dress up as a pickpocket like the rest of them.

JULIETTE. Don't pickpockets ever wear traveling clothes?

GUSTAVE. You're not going to travel. You're going to a carnival.

JULIETTE. Once they've stolen, thieves go away as a rule. Why won't you let me come with you, since you're going away?

GUSTAVE. [*Seizes her.*] You know too much, my girl!

JULIETTE. Oh, please, don't hurt me!

GUSTAVE. Don't be afraid. Just a precaution.

He ties her to a chair and searches in her handbag.

JULIETTE. Oh, don't rob my bag. There's nothing in it. Anyway, I give it to you.

GUSTAVE. Thank you. All I want is a handkerchief.

JULIETTE. What for?

GUSTAVE. To gag you with. [*He finds her handkerchief, which is microscopic.*] I ask you, what's the point of a handkerchief that size? Never mind, mine's clean.

JULIETTE. I'm not going to scream—I swear I won't scream—Señor Pedro! Gustave—Gusta——

He gags her.

GUSTAVE. There. If you think this a Thieves' Carnival, my lass, you'll have to think again. I'm a real thief, I am. So is Hector, and so is the Duke of Miraflores. Except that those two, they're imbeciles as well. You've built yourself a castle in the air, that's all, and your aunt, who's got bats in her belfry, has built herself a dozen. But let me tell you I came to do a job, and I intend to do it. [*She struggles.*] All right. All right. It's no good trying to soften me. I'm used to girls. [*He begins to fill his sacks with the most unlikely objects in the room. After a while he looks at her with misgiving.*] It's not too tight, is it? [*She shakes her head.*] That's a good girl. You see, old girl, I did a bit of billing and cooing, I know, but to be frank I didn't mean a word of it. I had to do it for the job. [*She struggles again.*] Does that upset you? Yes, I know, It isn't very pretty. But then in every trade there's always a little bit like that which isn't very pretty. Apart from that, I'm an honest sort of chap in my own way. I follow my trade, simply, without frills and fancies. Not like Hector and Peterbono. Peterbono has to be the Duke of Miraflores. One must be honest in one's own particular line. Life's not worth living otherwise. [*He takes a furtive look at her.*] You sure it's not too tight? [*He gives her a smile.*] It worries me a bit, playing a trick like that on you, because you know, I lied just now. I am fond of you really. [*He goes back to his work.*] After all, when God invented thieves he had to deprive them of a thing or two, so he took away from them the esteem of honest folk. When you come to think of it, it's not so terrible. It could have been much worse. [*He shrugs and laughs, without daring to meet her eyes.*] In a little while, you'll see, we'll have forgotten all about it. [*He goes on collecting objects. She struggles again, and he looks at her.*] If there's anything you care for specially, you must tell me. I'll leave it for you as a souvenir. I mean, I'd *like* to give you a little present. [*She looks at him and he stops in embarrassment.*] Please, don't look at me like that! You're breaking my heart! Can't you see I've got to do this? So just let me get quietly on with my job. [*She moves.*] Are you uncomfortable? You're not choking,

are you? Look, Juliette, if you swear not to call out, I'll take the gag off. Do you swear? [*She nods.*] All right, then, I trust you. [*He removes the handkerchief.*] What are you going to say to me, now that you know I'm a real thief? [*He sits down, resigned.*]

JULIETTE. [*The moment she is ungagged.*] This is absurd! Absolutely absurd. Untie me at once!

GUSTAVE. *Oh,* no! I'm a good sort, but business is business.

JULIETTE. At least listen to me!

GUSTAVE. What do you want to say?

JULIETTE. You don't imagine I came to find you, wearing my traveling coat, merely in order to sit here like a nincompoop bound and gagged in a chair? Of course I know you're a thief. If you weren't a real thief, I wouldn't have thought you were planning to leave in the middle of the night, would I, seeing you're a guest of my aunt's?

GUSTAVE. What are you talking about?

JULIETTE. I've been telling you over and over again for the last hour. I love you. I saw you take a car out of the garage, I guessed you really were a thief, and that tonight was the night. Since I supposed you'd go the minute the job was done, I dressed and got ready to go with you. You don't intend to stay, do you?

GUSTAVE. That's no question to ask a thief.

JULIETTE. Well then, take me with you.

GUSTAVE. But I'm a thief.

JULIETTE. [*Crying out in exasperation.*] I tell you I know you're a thief! There's no need to go on and on about it. I wonder you don't draw attention to yourself. Come along, untie my hands.

GUSTAVE. But, Juliette——

JULIETTE. Untie my hands. They're terribly painful.

GUSTAVE. Do you swear not to run away and raise the alarm?

JULIETTE. Yes, yes, I swear. Oh, how stupid you are!

GUSTAVE. I trust you of course, but I just don't understand.

He unties her. She immediately powders her face and then gets up with determination.

JULIETTE. We've wasted at least a quarter of an hour. Make haste. It wouldn't do to get caught now. Have you enough? [*She indicates the sacks with her foot.*]

GUSTAVE. What are you doing?

JULIETTE. Really, I shall begin to wonder if you're all there soon. Yes, or no, do I appeal to you?

GUSTAVE. Oh yes, but——

JULIETTE. Good. That's the main thing. Now, listen to me, Gustave, if you like me, I love you and I want to be your wife—oh, don't worry, if you're afraid of awkward questions at the License Bureau, we won't get properly married. There. Now then—— [*She picks up one of the sacks.*] Is this all we're taking with us?

GUSTAVE. [*Snatching the sack from her.*] Juliette, no! You don't know what you're doing! You mustn't come with me. What would become of you?

JULIETTE. I'd help you. I'd keep a lookout, and I'd whistle when I saw someone coming. I can whistle beautifully. Listen——[*She gives an earsplitting whistle.*]

GUSTAVE. [*Terrified.*] Ssssh! For heaven's sake!

They listen for a moment.

JULIETTE. [*Humbly.*] I'm sorry. What a fool I am. Take me away. I'll whistle very quietly, I promise you, and then only when it's absolutely necessary.

GUSTAVE. Juliette, this is only a whim. You're playing with me. It's unkind of you.

JULIETTE. Oh no, you mustn't think that! Never think that! I love you.

GUSTAVE. But do you know the dangers of this kind of life?

JULIETTE. Yes. Kiss me.

GUSTAVE. Juliette, it's good-by to your tranquillity.

JULIETTE. It was on the way to killing me, my tranquillity. Kiss me.

GUSTAVE. But you're happy here, Juliette. You don't know what it means to be on the run, to be afraid. You're used to luxury.

JULIETTE. Why, we're rich! Look at this! If it worries you, we won't steal as long as the police are out looking for me.

GUSTAVE. Thieves aren't wealthy folk. You get precious little for what you sell.

JULIETTE. Well, we'll be poor then. Kiss me.

They join in a long kiss.

JULIETTE. [*Radiantly.*] I am so happy. Now, hurry. [*She stops.*] Why, you haven't taken the little Fragonards. You're mad, my darling; they're the most valuable things in the house. [*She runs to take them down.*] And the little enamels. [*She rummages in the sack.*] Leave the candlesticks. They're imitation bronze. You see how useful I am to you. I shall be such a help, you'll see. Kiss me.

GUSTAVE. [*Taking her in his arms again.*] My little robber girl.

They go.

Act 4

In the conservatory an hour later. The clarinet, which has begun by playing the carnival theme, takes it up again in a nostalgic manner. The characters wander in in single file, heads hanging, and sit down, vexed and dejected.

LADY HURF. It's positively absurd.

HECTOR. I do think they might have let us in.

LADY HURF. Too absurd. Fancy writing the title of the carnival in microscopic lettering. Economy is an absolute obsession with the French.

LORD EDGARD. We were turned away in the most humiliating fashion.

EVA. What do you expect, Uncle? I can

quite see that our attire alarmed them.

LADY HURF. A Carnival of Leaves! The idiocy of it! A Carnival of Leaves!

D.D. SENIOR. What puzzles me is how you could confuse a Carnival of Leaves with a Carnival of Thieves.

LADY HURF. You should have consulted the notices yourself then, my good friend, if your eyesight is so sharp.

D.D. SENIOR. But, damn it. . . .

D.D. JUNIOR. Don't be rash, Dad.

LADY HURF. To begin with, it's thanks to your disguises that our party was shown the door.

PETERBONO. I should definitely have got in, for one. It's a funny thing. They really thought I was going as a palm tree.

LADY HURF. Of course, but for them we should all have been admitted. What abominable taste! Look at them, will you? They might be a couple of pantomime buccaneers.

D.D. SENIOR. I should have thought for a Carnival of Thieves. . . .

LADY HURF. Leaves! Leaves! Leaves! Are you going to spend the rest of the evening calling it a Carnival of Thieves?

D.D. JUNIOR. Keep calm, Father. [*To* LADY HURF.] We are dreadfully sorry.

D.D. SENIOR. [*Abjectly.*] We'll never do it again.

LADY HURF. A fine time to say so!

LORD EDGARD. Couldn't we perhaps spend the evening as we are, among ourselves, so as not to waste our efforts altogether?

LADY HURF. Edgard, what an insane idea. Let us go up and change. We'll play yet one more stupefying game of bridge.

She sighs and the guests sigh with her.

LORD EDGARD. If I'd known we were going to play bridge, I would have preferred to keep my mustache.

LADY HURF. [*Distractedly.*] So would I! [*To* PETERBONO, *on her way out.*] My dear Duke, can you forgive me for this wasted evening?

PETERBONO. [*Nudging* HECTOR.] No evening is ever really wasted.

LADY HURF. Another time I'll be more careful when I read the posters, and more discriminating in my choice of company.

She goes out with EVA *and* LORD EDGARD.

PETERBONO. Ring. Pearls.

HECTOR. Pocketbook.

PETERBONO. Perfect.

The DUPONT-DUFORTs *find themselves alone.*

D.D. SENIOR. Things are going badly.

D.D. JUNIOR. Very badly.

D.D. SENIOR. These gay dogs are here on the same errand we are, that's quite obvious, but everything is going their way and nothing is coming ours.

D.D. JUNIOR. [*Looking in a mirror.*] Yet we achieved a really lovely make-up.

D.D. SENIOR. Not for a Carnival of Leaves.

D.D. JUNIOR. Fancy organizing a Carnival of Leaves!

D.D. SENIOR. Fancy, what's more, reading "Carnival of Thieves" when it's down in black and white on all the posters "Carnival of Leaves." The old goose!

D.D. JUNIOR [*Catching sight of the drawing room through the open window.*] Dad!

D.D. SENIOR. What is it?

D.D. JUNIOR. Look at the wall!

D.D. SENIOR. What about the wall?

D.D. JUNIOR. The Fragonards!

D.D. SENIOR. If you think at a time like this I feel like going into ecstasies over a lot of paintings I . . .

D.D. JUNIOR. Dad, the Fragonards aren't on the wall. [*He rushes into the room.*]

D.D. SENIOR. Well?

D.D. JUNIOR. [*From the room.*] Nor are the enamels! The bronze candlesticks are missing! And the snuffboxes! All the drawers are open! [*Rushing out again.*] Dad, there's been a burglary!

D.D. SENIOR. Let's go. They'll think we did it.

D.D. JUNIOR. Don't be ridiculous! We were at the carnival with everybody else! Dad! There's been a robbery here!

D.D. SENIOR. [*Who has looked to make sure.*] You're absolutely right. There's been a robbery. But what are you so pleased about? That won't set our affairs to rights.

D.D. JUNIOR. Don't you understand? There's been a robbery while we were at the Casino. Don't you see suspicion can only fall on the one person who made himself conspicuous by his absence? Now then, who, I ask you, made himself conspicuous by his absence?

D.D. SENIOR. Young Pedro?

D.D. JUNIOR. Of course! Young Pedro.

D.D. SENIOR. In that case, surely the others would be his accomplices.

D.D. JUNIOR. They are his accomplices. They came with us to allay suspicion, that's quite clear. But now you may be sure they're gone, or will have before very long.

D.D. SENIOR. Didier, you're magnificent! You do my old heart good. Kiss me, Son! At last they are unmasked. They're done for, laddie, and our affairs have never looked so promising.

D.D. JUNIOR. We must clinch matters. There's to be no escape and no denial. We must telephone the police at once. [*He picks up the receiver.*] Give me the police please. And hurry!

D.D. SENIOR. [*Trundling around the drawing room and bellowing.*] The Fragonards! The enamels! The candlesticks! The snuffboxes! Two drawers burst open! Magnificent!

D.D. JUNIOR. Hello? Is that the police station? This is the Villa des Boyards. A serious robbery has just taken place. Yes, the thieves are still on the premises. You'll catch them redhanded if you hurry. Hurry!

D.D. SENIOR. [*Coming back radiant.*] Come to your father, laddie!

They embrace.

D.D. JUNIOR. Let's call the company and confront the rascals! Hey there! Come quickly, everybody!

D.D. SENIOR. Hey there! Hey!

LORD EDGARD. [*Entering; he, and likewise the others when they come down, have all changed back into their usual clothes.*] What's the matter?

D.D. JUNIOR. There's been a burglary!

LORD EDGARD. That's no surprise to anybody in these troubled times. Where?

D.D. JUNIOR. Here!

LORD EDGARD. Here!

D.D. SENIOR. [*Breathless with excitement.*] Here! Here in this very room!

LORD EDGARD. In the drawing room? What did they take?

D.D. SENIOR. [*Like a street hawker.*] Fragonards! Enamels! Snuffboxes! Candlesticks! Drawers! Come in and see! Come and see!

LORD EDGARD *goes into the room, comes back, and staggers into an armchair.*

LORD EDGARD. Terrible! Terrible! I had an idea this would happen.

D.D. SENIOR *and* JUNIOR. So did we!

LORD EDGARD. Do you know who did it?

D.D. SENIOR. We have an idea!

LORD EDGARD. So have I!

Enter EVA.

LORD EDGARD. My child, we've just been burgled!

EVA. What?

D.D. SENIOR. [*Off again.*] The Fragonards! The enamels! The candlesticks! The snuffboxes!

EVA. I'm glad about the candlesticks; they were appalling. But it's a shame about the Fragonards.

HECTOR *enters triumphantly in new make-up.*

HECTOR. Eva, this time I've got it!

EVA. No.

LORD EDGARD. [*Leaping on him.*]. At last! The detective! My dear fellow, you're in the nick of time. A serious robbery has just been committed. We suspect some impostors whom we are entertaining at the moment, owing to a curious fancy of my cousin's. Kindly arrest them at once, my dear fellow.

EVA. What's come over you, Uncle?

That's Prince Hector. Hector, do take off that beard.

HECTOR. [*Modestly, as he reveals himself.*] Yes, sir, it's me.

LORD EDGARD. [*In a sudden rage.*] How much longer do you intend to make a fool of me, young man?

HECTOR. [*Backing imperceptibly toward the door.*] But, your Lordship, I'm not making a fool of you, really.

LORD EDGARD. I can take a joke, in doubtful taste though it is with a man of my years, but don't repeat it a dozen times a day!

HECTOR. [*Nearing the door.*] But I'm not making a fool. . . .

He bumps into the DUPONT-DUFORTS, *who have cut off his retreat.*

D.D. JUNIOR. Oh no.

D.D. SENIOR. Of course you're not making a fool of him. Don't go. Everything will be all right.

HECTOR. Look here, what's going on? Am I under suspicion?

EVA. Gentlemen, will you please leave his Highness alone?

HECTOR. I should think so. Why, it's absurd, isn't it, Eva?

LADY HURF. [*Entering with* PETERBONO.] What is all this shouting? I've never heard such a commotion!

PETERBONO. We simply can't hear ourselves speak!

LORD EDGARD. It's terrible! There's been a dreadful robbery! I had my suspicions all along. I told you he died in 1904! I told you they were all impostors!

D.D. SENIOR. [*At the same time.*] The Fragonards! The enamels! The snuffboxes! The candlesticks! The drawers!

LADY HURF. One at a time, please! I don't know what you're talking about. First of all, I must sit down. I'm worn out.

During the ejaculations of the others and the silence which follows, HECTOR *is desperately indicating to* PETERBONO *that they must be off.* PETERBONO *thinks his cuff links are undone, his tie crooked, or that*

something is hanging down. He brushes himself, looks in the mirror, still fails to understand, and finally shrugs his shoulders and gives up.

LADY HURF. Now. Tell me all about it.

PETERBONO. [*Engagingly.*] Splendid idea. Tell us all about it.

LORD EDGARD. [*Before they stop him.*] Didn't I tell you he died in—

D.D. SENIOR. [*At the same time.*] Everything! Everything! The Fragonards! The. . . .

They look at each other and stop dead.

EVA. There's been a burglary.

LADY HURF. A burglary?

EVA. Yes. While we were out the enamels were stolen, and the Fragonards, and, believe it or not, the candlesticks.

LADY HURF. Oh, good. They were imitation.

LORD EDGARD. I told you so! I told you so!

LADY HURF. One of the servants, I expect. Are they all here?

EVA. I don't know.

D.D. SENIOR. We must inform the police.

LADY HURF. No.

D.D. SENIOR. What do you mean, no?

LADY HURF. No, I tell you. I will not have policemen in my house.

D.D. JUNIOR. But we've already telephoned, your Ladyship.

LADY HURF. My good sirs, have you completely forgotten your manners? I beg you to remember that this is my house. You appear to have abandoned every vestige of constraint these last few days.

D.D. JUNIOR. But we—

D.D. SENIOR. You see, we—

LADY HURF. Eva, call them back at once and tell them not to come.

D.D. SENIOR. Too late. They're bound to be on the way.

All this time PETERBONO *and* HECTOR *have been quietly edging toward the door. When* LADY HURF *tells* EVA *to call off the police, they stop, still hopeful. At these last words, they make a frenzied dash for it.*

D.D. SENIOR. Look! They're getting

away!

D.D. JUNIOR. This is too much! We'll save you, whether you like it or not! Hands up!

D.D. SENIOR. Hands up!

They cover the thieves with their revolvers.

LADY HURF. Gentlemen, I am mistress in this house! I order you to put away those firearms!

D.D. JUNIOR. No!

D.D. SENIOR. No. You'll thank us for it later on.

LADY HURF. Eva, I'm going to have hysterics! Call the servants! Emile! Here, quickly! Joseph! Help!

Enter POLICEMEN *during her cries.*

POLICEMAN. Here we are! Horace, you take the fat one!

They have seen these two horrible bandits pointing their guns at the gentry. Without a moment's indecision, they hurl themselves on the DUPONT-DUFORTS.

POLICEMAN. Aha, me beauties! We've got you!

D.D. SENIOR *and* JUNIOR. [*Backing away.*] But—but—We didn't do anything! No, no, not us! Not us! Quite the reverse! We're the ones who telephoned! This is preposterous! It's them!

They collide as they retreat, try to escape the other way and collide again in the course of a droll little ballet which culminates in their capture.

POLICEMEN. [*Hoisting them onto their shoulders with the showmanship of circus acrobats.*] Upsy-daisy! [*To* HECTOR.] If you'd like to give us a hand, sir, by taking the trouble to open the door, sir, it'd be much appreciated.

The POLICEMEN *carry off the* DUPONT-DUFORTS *despite their agonizing protestations.*

LORD EDGARD. [*Wildly.*] But, my dear. . . .

LADY HURF. [*Sternly.*] Edgard! Be quiet.

D.D. SENIOR. [*Yelling in vain as he is borne away.*] For God's sake, say something! Tell them! Tell them!

D.D. JUNIOR. [*As he whirls past her.*] Mademoiselle Eva!

They have gone, ushered out by their own little melody.

LADY HURF. [*Calmly.*] There! That's a relief. Three whole weeks those people have been here, and I hadn't a notion how to get rid of them.

LORD EDGARD. [*Overcome by so many emotions, falls semiconscious into an armchair.*] When I think I came here to cure my liver trouble!

LADY HURF. Eva dear, run up and get your uncle his smelling salts.

EVA *goes.* LADY HURF *looks at* PETERBONO, *who ever since the arrest of the* DUPONT-DUFORTS *has been choking in the grip of irrepressible hysteria.*

LADY HURF. My dear man, save your laughter. I know perfectly well you are the real thief. [*He stops dead. She feels in his pocket.*] Give me back my pearls. You haven't been very clever.

PETERBONO. What do you mean?

LADY HURF. Have you a lot of luggage? How long will it take you to pack?

PETERBONO. [*Piteously.*] Not long.

LADY HURF. Then I advise you to make the greatest possible haste upstairs.

PETERBONO. Yes.

Enter HECTOR.

HECTOR. [*Superbly.*] There. The rascals are in good hands, your Ladyship. [PETERBONO *coughs.*] Father dear, aren't you feeling well?

LADY HURF. No, he's not feeling at all well. I think you had both better go up to your rooms.

HECTOR. Really, Father? Where's the trouble exactly?

LORD EDGARD. [*Himself once more.*] I told you the Duke of Miraflores died in 1904!

LADY HURF. I knew it long ago, my dear.

HECTOR. [*Still not understanding* PETERBONO's *desperate dumb show, says waggishly.*] Ha-ha-ha! Still the same old joke, eh?

LADY HURF. The Duke died in my arms, or near enough. So that I knew quite well whom we were dealing with. Only you see, my poor old Edgard, I was so very, very bored.

HECTOR. [*Finally going to* PETERBONO.] What's the matter, for heaven's sake?

PETERBONO. Idiot! I've been trying to tell you for the last half hour. The game's up, but she's letting us go free.

HECTOR. Huh? Don't be silly, they've arrested the others.

LADY HURF. [*Going to them with a smile.*] You don't, I'm sure, want to await the visit of the inspector of police, gentlemen.

HECTOR. This is unthinkable! What are we accused of? We were with you the whole evening!

PETERBONO. Don't be canny. Come on.

HECTOR. My dear Father, I don't know what you're talking about. Madame, we are here as your guests, and this robbery is no reason to treat us, the Miraflores y Grandes, in this cavalier fashion.

PETERBONO. [*Unable to suppress a giggle, despite the tragic situation.*] Miraflores y Grandes! Oh, my Lord! You're off your head, old chap. Come on.

LADY HURF. Go along, sir, do, as everyone advises you.

HECTOR. I will not tolerate this attitude. [*To* PETERBONO.] Play up, will you?

EVA. [*Coming back.*] Here are the salts.

HECTOR. I will not tolerate this attitude. Because if you consider our presence undesirable, I laugh to scorn—do you hear, to scorn—your utterly unfounded and insulting allegations. There's someone here, I know, who will think my presence far from undesirable. Eva, Eva, my darling, I've found my face at last! [*He turns away and rapidly re-creates the appearance he had in the first scene.*]

PETERBONO. Hector, stop playing around. The police are on their way.

HECTOR. [*Making up.*] Let me alone. We're saved, I tell you!

LADY HURF. [*Sits down, dispirited.*] Edgard, if this headstrong child falls in love with him again, the situation is absolutely hopeless.

LORD EDGARD. I have not the faintest idea what is going on. What is he doing? Is this another joke? He goes very much too far, that boy.

HECTOR. [*Turning around triumphantly.*] Eva, beloved! It was like this, wasn't it?

A silence. EVA *looks at him. The others hold their breath.*

EVA. [*Calmly breaking the tension.*] Yes, that's how you were. Only I must have looked at you too hastily, I think, because now you don't appeal to me at all.

LADY HURF. [*Leaping up.*] Heaven be praised! Now, off with you! Quickly, off with you!

HECTOR. But, Eva, listen! Eva, I can't believe . . .

PETERBONO. [*In a whisper.*] Hurry, idiot, hurry! She's taken back the necklace, but I've still got the ring.

They go with great dignity. A gay little tune signals their departure.

LADY HURF. [*Watching them go with a tender smile.*] Poor old fellow. I let him keep the ring. They stayed here a full two weeks after all, because of me. We haven't any right to make them waste their time. I imagine it's a trade that doesn't bring in all that much.

LORD EDGARD. What I don't fathom is where the boy comes in. [*The two women look at him in sudden anguish.*] The boy, the young one, who was so pleasant, you remember?

EVA. Juliette! Where's Juliette?

LADY HURF. Juliette! She didn't come to the carnival. Isn't she upstairs? Perhaps in the morning room? Or in the garden?

EVA. I'll run and see. Oh, it's inconceivable.

LORD EDGARD. What is inconceivable? I don't understand, quite. [LADY HURF *drops onto the sofa and plays nervously with her pearls.*] Why do you look so tragic? It's all over now, isn't it?

LADY HURF. No, stupid, it is not all over. This boy has carried off Juliette along with the pictures in the drawing room. How many times did I tell you to bestir yourself and take precautions if we didn't want disaster?

EVA. [*Coming back.*] She's not upstairs. The servants are combing the grounds.

LADY HURF. It's horrible!

LORD EDGARD. Juliette, our little Juliette. Is it possible? Can she have been stolen?

EVA. Yes.

LORD EDGARD. But she's a big girl now. She could have defended herself. Or called for help. The house is overrun with staff.

LADY HURF. Can't you understand? She's in his power! He's bewitched her. He'll make her steal for him, or walk the streets!

LORD EDGARD. The streets. [*It dawns on him.*] The streets!

He staggers under the blow. The clarinet plays an air heavy with tragedy. The three of them lapse into pensive and painful silence. The clarinet resumes its tragic theme with an overtone of mockery, and then leads into the romance which is indeed altogether fitting at this moment, for GUSTAVE *enters on tiptoe, laden with so many things that he cannot see where he is going. He is carrying* JULIETTE, *who is asleep, and his various sacks. He crosses the drawing room, unseen by anybody; suddenly he bumps into an armchair. He drops his sacks with a clatter and startles the others, who see him and cry out.*

LADY HURF. He's killed her!

A tremolo from the clarinet. GUSTAVE, *terrified, starts to put* JULIETTE *down on the sofa, but at the cries she wakens and clings to him.*

JULIETTE. No, no, no! Why did you bring me back? No, he's not to go! If he goes I'm going with him!

LADY HURF. Juliette!

LORD EDGARD. My child.

JULIETTE. [*Screaming through a flood of tears.*] Yes, you despise him, I know, but I love him. Don't try to tell me anything—I want to go with him be-cause I love him. Don't say a word, I'd only hate you for it. Gustave, Gustave, why did you bring me back? [*He struggles and tries to run away but she clutches him.*] No. Stay here, or let me come with you. Why did you bring me back? Was I too stupid for you? Too naïve? Is it because I fell asleep beside you in the car that you don't want me? It's true one doesn't as a rule doze off on the night of one's elopement, but I was tired, my darling. I'm not used to staying up so late. [*She hides her head in his arms.*]

LORD EDGARD. What is she saying?

LADY HURF. [*Moved.*] Do be quiet! It's very lovely what she is saying.

JULIETTE. [*Turning to them like a little fury, without letting go of* GUSTAVE.] No, no, I'm not ashamed! I'm not ashamed! You can say anything you like, I'll never be ashamed! I love him. I want him for my lover, since you will never let him be my husband. Look. I'm going to kiss him now in front of you.

She throws her arms around his neck. He holds back for a second; then as he sees her tousled hair and her radiant tear-stained face, he too forgets the others.

GUSTAVE. I love you, Juliette.

JULIETTE. You see, we're kissing here, in front of them.

They kiss.

LORD EDGARD. [*Adjusting his pince-nez.*] Why, they're kissing.

LADY HURF. That's right. They're kissing. What about it? Did you never do as much? [*She contemplates them, entranced.*] How enchanting they are!

LORD EDGARD. Aren't they? Do you remember, Emily?

LADY HURF. They make a delightful couple, don't they?

LORD EDGARD. [*Lost in his memories.*] Delightful. Do you remember? The Crystal Palace?

LADY HURF. She's nearly as tall as he is. He is adorable. Look at the breeding in that profile. The exquisite shyness and yet the strength of it. He will make a fairy-tale husband for our terrible, gentle little Juliette. [*She stops.*] Edgard, what are you talking me into? He's a thief!

LORD EDGARD. [*Smiling.*] Ah yes, a thief.

LADY HURF. Well then, it's out of the question. He must go at once.

The clarinet stops from shock.

LORD EDGARD. [*Crestfallen.*] But—but they love each other.

LADY HURF. I know they love each other. But it's the only thing to do. Absolutely the only thing. She simply cannot marry a boy who has neither a father nor a mother.

LORD EDGARD. Ah! [*He thinks furiously for a moment, then cries suddenly.*] Wait a minute! Wait a minute!

GUSTAVE *and* JULIETTE, *startled by his cry, come out of their embrace.* LORD EDGARD *runs out like one demented.*

LADY HURF. Where do you suppose he's going?

JULIETTE. I'll never leave him, never, never, never.

GUSTAVE. [*Holding her to him, says by way of explanation.*] We love each other.

The clarinet plays a little supplication.

LADY HURF. I gather so. But there it is. You're nothing but a nobody, if not worse. I'm afraid you'll have to go.

Another entreaty from the clarinet.

JULIETTE. If he goes I go with him.

LADY HURF. This time we will be here to stop you. [*The clarinet's plea becomes heart-rending.* LADY HURF *turns furiously on the* MUSICIAN.] As for you, my good sir, you're beginning to get on my nerves! Go away! [*The clarinet attempts a musical protest.*] Get out of here this instant!

She drives him out. Pathetically the MUSICIAN *goes, expressing his despair on his instrument.* LORD EDGARD *returns like a meteor, carrying ribbons, medals, and a photograph. He marches threateningly over to* GUSTAVE.

LORD EDGARD. You are twenty years old, are you not?

GUSTAVE. Yes.

LORD EDGARD. Right. [*He looks at the photograph, looks at it a second time, backs, screwing up his eyes in the manner of a painter scrutinizing a picture.*] Hold your head up. Fine. Open your shirt. Fine. Now for the mark behind the ear. [*He turns back his ear.*] Fine. [*He shows him the medal.*] Do you recognize this medal?

GUSTAVE. No.

LORD EDGARD. [*Throwing it away.*] Never mind. You are my son! My son who was stolen from me at a tender age. [*He falls into his arms.*]

LADY HURF. Edgard, have you taken leave of your senses?

GUSTAVE. [*Furiously.*] Let me go, sir. I don't know what you're talking about. [*To* JULIETTE.] What's the matter with him?

LORD EDGARD. [*To* LADY HURF.] Do you deny that a son was stolen from me at a tender age? [*To* GUSTAVE.] Do you deny that you are uncertain of your paternal origins? Yes, yes, you are my son, my own son, my beloved son! [*He falls on his neck again.*]

JULIETTE. Isn't that lucky! Gustave, isn't that lucky!

GUSTAVE. [*Freeing himself roughly.*] No, it won't work.

LORD EDGARD. What won't work?

GUSTAVE. I'm quite sure I'm not your son.

LORD EDGARD. So I shall have waited twenty years for Heaven to give me back my child, and now when Heaven at last sees fit to give him back to me, it is this very child who refuses to acknowledge his own father!

GUSTAVE. No. It's all a scheme because you can see your little girl is in love with me, but I'm sorry, I can't accept.

LADY HURF. That's very honorable of him.

LORD EDGARD. This is horrible! Horrible! My son denies me! [*He prances with rage.*]

GUSTAVE. No, I can't accept. It's nice of you to do it, very nice of you. But I can't. I'm not one of your kind.

LADY HURF. It is really unfortunate that this boy should be the only one among us to suffer from class consciousness.

LORD EDGARD. I am abominably humiliated. Such contempt from my own son! I shall crumple up with sorrow. [*He does in fact crumple up with sorrow on the nearest sofa.*] Here I am, crumpled up. How much longer do I have to stay crumpled?

LADY HURF. Couldn't you see your way to accepting? You're making your father very unhappy.

GUSTAVE. How can I! I haven't any reason—

JULIETTE. Oh, but you have! Come into the garden as you did before. I'm going to explain all your reasons to you. Do come, please. Come, anyway. You haven't anything to lose, after all, by coming into the garden. [*She drags him out.*]

LADY HURF. [*As soon as they're gone.*] Edgard, it's not true! You never had a son stolen from you at a tender age!

LORD EDGARD. No, it isn't true. It's a picture I cut out of a magazine.

LADY HURF. So you've acted like an imbecile for over fifty years and yet you had it in you to think of that all by yourself.

EVA. How happy they are going to be.

LADY HURF. [*Dreamily.*] Yes.

EVA. And I shall continue to play the young and charming widow who is always such a great success.

LADY HURF. My poor Eva, faith is a gift, alas, and there's no learning it. It's over, our fine escapade. Here we are alone again, like bobbing corks. It's only for those who have played it with all the zest of youth that the comedy is a success, and only then because they were playing their youth, a thing which succeeds always. They were not even conscious of the comedy.

Enter a bearded gentleman.

BEARDED GENTLEMAN. I am from Scotland Yard.

LORD EDGARD. [*Lets out a roar, leaps onto him, and pulls his beard.*] Oh no, it won't work this time!

DETECTIVE. Stop it! You're hurting me!

LORD EDGARD. [*Greatly astonished.*] What! Do you mean it's your own?

DETECTIVE. Of course it's my own!

LORD EDGARD. Then you really are the detective I sent for?

DETECTIVE. I've just said so, haven't I?

LORD EDGARD. Well, we don't need you any more. The entertainment is over.

DETECTIVE. [*Blithely.*] In that case. . . .

He pulls his clarinet out of his pocket—for it is none other than the MUSICIAN—*and strikes up a quickstep which does duty as a finale. The characters come in through all the doors, dancing and exchanging beards.*